Microsoft®

Microsoft® Office Communications Server 2007 Resource Kit

Jeremy Buch, Rui Maximo, and Jochen Kunert

with Byron Spurlock, Hao Yan, James O'Neill, John Clarkson, Kintan Brahmbhatt, Mitch Tulloch, Rick Kingslan, Stephanie Lindsey, and the Microsoft Office Communications Server Team

PUBLISHED BY
Microsoft Press
A Division of Microsoft Corporation
One Microsoft Way
Redmond, Washington 98052-6399

Library of Congress Control Number: 2007941087

Printed and bound in the United States of America.

1 2 3 4 5 6 7 8 9 QWT 3 2 1 0 9 8

Distributed in Canada by H.B. Fenn and Company Ltd.

A CIP catalogue record for this book is available from the British Library.

Microsoft Press books are available through booksellers and distributors worldwide. For further information about international editions, contact your local Microsoft Corporation office or contact Microsoft Press International directly at fax (425) 936-7329. Visit our Web site at www.microsoft.com/mspress. Send comments to rkinput@microsoft.com.

Acquisitions Editor: Martin DelRe
Developmental Editor: Jenny Moss Benson
Project Editor: Laura Sackerman
Editorial Production: Custom Editorial Production, Inc.
Technical Reviewer: Rick Kingslan; Technical Review services provided by Content Master, a member of CM Group, Ltd.
Cover: Tom Draper Design; Illustration by Todd Daman

Body Part No. X14-38408

Foreword

During my 17 years at Microsoft, I have seen computers and software become an increasingly important part of communication. E-mail, instant messaging, presence, Web conferencing, and VoIP telephony are completely transforming the way that we communicate. By combining these modes of communication, Microsoft Office Communications Server provides enterprise users with easy and flexible ways to communicate with colleagues and contacts. This is a major shift from device-centric communication to people-centric communication. This software-powered transformation is so fundamental that we are redefining the traditional communication models, deployment models, and programmability. This is the new world of Microsoft Unified Communications.

Communication is critical to every business. Before you make the leap to any unified communications solution, you will want to know all the facts about making the transition. Most unified communications solutions involve migration from and interoperating with existing PBXs, as well as network infrastructure, such as routers, firewalls, and load balancers. If you want to understand how all the components work together, determine how to use and secure the solution, and ensure performance, this book is for you.

The Microsoft Office Communications Server 2007 Resource Kit is the most in-depth technical reference to date on Office Communications Server. The authors and contributors are key engineers and consultants who built, tested, and deployed the product. They provide their unique perspective and deep knowledge of how Office Communications Server works and explain ways to better plan, deploy, and troubleshoot your own unified communications infrastructure. In addition, there are scenario-based walkthroughs that take you through the experience of planning and deploying Office Communications Server, with insights and tips from consultants who are currently leading Office Communications Server deployments in major enterprises around the world.

I have known the authors and contributors for many years. We built and learned about this product together. As the designers and implementers of key features in Office Communications Server, both Jeremy and Rui educated Microsoft IT and Support teams, many enterprise customers, and fellow engineers about the inner workings of the product. As a member of the Technical Adoption Program team, Jochen leveraged his many years of industry experience migrating PBX infrastructures to software VoIP systems to help numerous customers understand and successfully roll out their Office Communications Server systems. This book passes on the expertise and experiences of these key people to you.

Jeremy, Rui, Jochen, and the contributing authors have done a fantastic job providing the key information about the inner workings of Office Communications Server in a clear, concise style that will appeal to any architect or IT-professional. As an engineer, I especially appreciate the tools and detailed diagnostic resources that can be used by developers and administrators alike to understand, monitor, and troubleshoot their Office Communications Server system.

Leading the Microsoft Unified Communications effort from the beginning has been an amazing experience for me. I hope that implementing these ground-breaking products in your unified communications strategy is an empowering experience for you as well.

Gurdeep Singh Pall
Corporate Vice President, Office Communications Group, Microsoft Corporation

Table of Contents

Part II Key Usage Scenarios

Part VI Technical Reference

Acknowledgments

The authors of *Microsoft Office Communications Server 2007 Resource Kit* would like to collectively thank numerous members of the Office Communications Server product team and other key experts, both inside and outside of Microsoft, for helping us make this Resource Kit the comprehensive and accurate resource our customers need. These experts have contributed their time and effort to this project in several important ways including: by contributing sidebars that bring the product to life by describing real world implementations or providing in-depth information on how certain features work; by peer-reviewing each author's chapters to help ensure the information being presented is technically accurate; and by providing many other valuable insights, lots of advice, and tons of general encouragement and support.

We would particularly like to express our thanks to the following individuals, listed in alphabetical order by their first names:

Alan Shen, Ali Rohani, Amey Parandekar, Anjali Verma, Antenehe Temteme, Cezar Ungureanasu, Chandler Bootchk, Christophe Leroux, CJ Vermette, Conal Walsh, Deepak Rao, Dhigha Sekeran, Duncan Blake, Francois Doremieux, Indranil Dutta, James Undery, Jason Epperly, Jeff Reed, Jens Trier Rasmussen, Joel Schaeffer, John Lamb, Kiran Kulkarni, Les Viger, Linda Wells, Mahendra Sekaran, Mihir Vaidya, Nirav Kamdar, Paul Tidwell, Rick Varvel, Robert L. Cameron, Rudi Petersen, Sankaran Narayanan, Sean Olson, Shaun Cox, Shawn Mahan, Steve Whitney, Steve Wood, Thomas Laciano, Vadim Eydelman, Venky Venkateshaiah, Vijay Kishen Hampapur Parthasarathy, Vlad Eminovici, Xuan Chen, Yong Zhao

If we've forgotten to include anyone in the above list, please forgive us!

Special thanks to:

- James O'Neil for his efforts developing the more than one hundred Windows PowerShell functions that are included on the companion CD. These functions demonstrate how an Office Communications Server environment can be administered using PowerShell commands.
- Michael Hefner, Rick Kingslan, and Rui Maximo for their long hours and hard work testing the PowerShell functions.
- Salman Khalid and Sasa Juratovic for their work developing prototypes for some of the PowerShell functions.
- Rick Kingslan who, in addition to being a contributing author for this title, was also our technical reviewer. Rick spent numerous long hours testing procedures and identifying errors so we could ensure this book is an accurate and comprehensive resource for our customers.

- Robert Heuer of Linda Werner & Associates Inc., who assisted us greatly by getting several of our chapters into shape for publication.
- Tim Toyoshima, cross-team project sponsor and ever resourceful champion of providing customers with the product information they need, and Patricia Anderson, early project leader, both of the Office Communications Server User Assistance (UA) team. They helped ensure that the Resource Kit complements the UA documentation set.
- Jerry Smith, who was one of the first to have the vision of a book that would fill a critical need for 300-400 level content for Office Communications Server. Thanks from all of us, Jerry, for being the champion for the book by starting it off and enabling the rest of the authors and contributors to share their knowledge about Office Communications Server.
- Susan S. Bradley, our Project Manager, whose tireless energy and attention to detail helped ensure this project reached a successful conclusion. Susan was the leader for this project and she found timely and effective solutions to the logistical challenges that came up, ensuring that we all made it to the finish line as a team. Susan's patience, humor, and willingness to track the schedule were an invaluable aid to the team, and her efforts made everyone's contribution stronger and better.
- Mitch Tulloch, our Technical Project Lead, who helped organize the author team and coordinate our efforts to ensure a consistent level and approach and helped us avoid the kind of duplication of content and effort that can easily happen with a multi-author project such as this one.

We'd also like to especially thank our outstanding editorial team at Microsoft Learning, including Martin DelRe, who helped us plan this project and get it going; Jenny Moss Benson, our Development Editor; and Laura Sackerman, our Project Editor. Thanks also to Custom Editorial Productions who handled the production aspects of this book and to Roger LeBlanc, our copy editor, who showed careful attention to detail throughout this project.

-The Author Team

Personal Acknowledgments from Individual Authors

Jeremy Buch Thanks be to God for the love He shows us all and for the gifts He gives us each to share on His behalf. I am especially thankful for the love and compassion shown to me in the midst of this effort by my family (Teresa, Joanna, and Stephen); the support from my mother and extended family; the Hart and the Simons families for making time for us and for excusing my delays or absences; Rui Maximo and Jochen Kunert for agreeing to do this and for following up with such great results out of their personal time; Stephanie Lindsey, Robert Heuer, John Clarkson, and Byron Spurlock for their effort providing chapter content I originally intended to; Mitch Tulloch for his guidance, efficiency, and intelligent feedback; Thomas Laciano for his extra time, support, and personal attention to detail; my employer Microsoft

(Gurdeep Singh Pall, Shaun Pierce, Srikanth Shoroff, Bimal Mehta, and Leon Rosenshein) for allowing me time; the people at Microsoft I have been working with; and finally all of the folks who have been acknowledged elsewhere for their help and guidance. This resource is for the community–the product team at Microsoft, support staff, consultants, and customers–but it was created by these same folks and I am so thankful to be able to include so many voices and points of view. Finally, thanks to the people in the product UA team and the Microsoft Learning staff who have helped with this effort and helped me to move things forward that didn't seem possible given my time constraints.

Rui Maximo The effort to produce this book was not possible without the participation of a large number of contributors including members of the UCG product team, the UA team led by Tim Toyoshima, and the Microsoft and MVP specialists in LCS and OCS. I'm thankful for the opportunity to have been one of the primary authors on this project. Thank you, Susan and Mitch, for project managing. Keeping everyone on task is no small feat! I also want to thank my co-authors (you're listed on the front cover) and my reviewers (John Lamb, Nirav Kamdar, Steve Whitney, Tom Laciano, Paul Tidwell, Robert Heuer, and Mitch Tulloch) for providing your feedback. I also owe my wonderful wife and kids a large debt of quality time for many, many weeknights and weekends as they patiently waited for me to finish my chapters. Anne, you're the best wife I've ever had: beautiful, smart...and French! Marie, keep up the hard work. As long as you continue being a self starter, you'll always succeed in life. Mathew, stay curious about life and you'll find the answers yourself through smart thinking and hard work. Chloe, keep striving for what you want and you'll get it. I have no doubt. I love you kids.

Jochen Kunert This was the first book that I had the chance to participate in as an author and I would like to encourage everyone to get the same experience. I always wanted to get a look "behind the scenes" to see how much work is actually involved in creating a book. Now I know it and I wouldn't have been able to get my part accomplished without the help of amazingly knowledgeable people such as Rick Varvel, Jens Trier Rasmussen, and John Lamb, who spent nights with me pulling the content together. I also want to thank numerous people for helping me to enrich and review the content of my chapters. Poor Mitch, who had to correct my drafts into proper English! Thanks also to Susan for her amazing efforts to encourage each one of us to stick to the schedule. And finally, I have to apologize to my wife, Aniko, for several evenings, when she had to bring our son, Quentin, to bed while I was writing.

Byron Spurlock I would like to thank Nicholas (5) and Jada (2) for going to bed early and letting Daddy help with writing this book. Also I would like to thank my wife Maggie Spurlock for encouragement and my mom Mary Spurlock for giving me inspiration.

Hao Yan Thanks to Ming Chia Lee for her understanding and support during the long nights I spent on my chapter.

James O'Neill My thanks to all the people who've worked with me on this book for their help and inspiration. In addition I'd like to thank Robin and Eileen for showing faith in me when no one else would. And my wife, Jackie, for reasons so numerous and so varied, I'd need a volume bigger than this to cover them properly.

John Clarkson Thanks to Betsy for sticking by me.

Kintan Brahmbhatt I would like to thank Rui Maximo for his encouragement, patience, and guidance; Steve Wood and Mihir Vaidya for the hard work on monitoring; and Linda Wells and Antenehe Temteme for persistent efforts on developing backup and restore guidelines.

Mitch Tulloch Thanks to everyone I worked with on this project including, especially, Susan, Laura, the author team, and various experts inside Microsoft. I really enjoyed working on this project with all of you, though at times it was–to say it politely–challenging! Thanks also to Bill Gates and Steve Ballmer for building the greatest company in the world: Microsoft. Your company motto, "Your Potential. Our Passion." says it all. Your passion has developed software that changed the world, and working with you on various projects over the last eight years has helped me realize my potential in ways I couldn't have imagined.

Rick Kingslan To my wife and partner Sue: thank you for giving me the time and dealing with the frustration of me helping to produce a great book and for taking care of the girls through my many absences. To my daughters Kristin and Amanda: Dad loves and misses you. To my son Mark: keep safe, keep your head down. Semper Fi! To my colleagues at Microsoft: thanks for letting me work for the greatest company on the planet. Lastly, to my good friends at the "Diver's Bar" in Aufkirchen, Bavaria, Germany: Gutan tag! http://www.indoor-tauchen.de.

Stephanie Lindsey I'd like to thank Dhigha Sekaran, Sankaran Narayanan, Vadim Eydelman, Shaun Cox, and Sean Olson for their expertise and help in writing these book chapters. I'd also like to thank Tim Toyoshima and Patricia Anderson for giving me an opportunity to contribute to this book.

Introduction

Welcome to the *Microsoft Office Communications Server 2007 Resource Kit*!

The *Microsoft Office Communications Server 2007 Resource Kit* is a comprehensive technical resource for planning, deploying, maintaining, and troubleshooting Microsoft Office Communications Server 2007. While the target audience for this Resource Kit is experienced IT professionals who work in medium- and large-sized organizations, anyone who wants to learn how to deploy, configure, support, troubleshoot, and develop for Office Communications Server 2007 will find this Resource Kit invaluable.

Within this Resource Kit, you'll find in-depth information and task-based guidance on managing all aspects of Office Communications Server 2007 including Instant Messaging, Web Conferencing with audio and video support, Remote Call Control, and Enterprise Voice. You'll be exposed to troubleshooting techniques and diagnostic tools to help you be successful in deploying and monitoring Office Communications Server. You'll also find numerous sidebars contributed by members of the Unified Communications product team and Microsoft consultants that provide deep insight into how Office Communications Server 2007 works, best practices for managing the platform, and invaluable troubleshooting tips. Finally, the Companion CD includes additional tools, worksheets, documentation, and over 100 sample Windows PowerShell functions that you can use and customize to help you automate various aspects of managing Office Communications Server 2007 in enterprise environments.

What's New in Office Communications Server 2007

Office Communications Server 2007 is the successor to Microsoft's real-time communications server, Live Communications Server 2005 with SP1. To existing support for IM, presence, federation, and public IM connectivity, Communications Server 2007 adds the following capabilities.

- **Enterprise voice** As Microsoft's software-powered VoIP solution, Office Communications Server 2007 provides a flexible, economical, full-featured alternative to hardware-based VoIP offerings. Enterprise Voice can be deployed in various scenarios, ranging from greenfield deployments to full integration with existing PBX installations.
- **On-premise Web conferencing** Office Communications Server 2007 offers an alternative to Microsoft's existing online conferencing service, Office Live Meeting. Like Live Meeting, Office Communications Server 2007 on-premise Web conferencing supports slide presentations, whiteboarding, application sharing, and other familiar real-time collaboration features. A single Live Meeting console serves as client for both on-premise and online conferencing. On-premise Web conferencing also supports inviting partners, consultants, and other outside users who lack enterprise credentials to participate in conferences.

- **Multiparty IM** Office Communications Server 2007 makes it possible to add new participants to an existing IM conversation and to escalate a conversation on the fly to an on-premise, audio/video Web conference.
- **Enhanced presence** Office Communications Server 2007 enables users to optionally expose more detailed contact information to selected watchers and to assign various groups of watchers permissions to view different sets of presence information.
- **Improved federation support** Office Communications Server 2007 makes federation at once easier to manage and more secure.

The above features dramatically raise the bar for unified communications solutions in the enterprise. At the same time, they represent new vulnerabilities that Office Communications Server 2007 addresses in a variety of ways.

Overview of the Book

The six parts of this book cover the following topics:

- **Part I: Overview and Architecture** Provides an overview of the features of Office Communications Server 2007; describes the usages for the different server roles; and considers the infrastructure and security required for an Office Communications Server deployment.
- **Part II: Key Usage Scenarios** Describes in-depth the scenarios that the real-time communications features in Office Communications Server 2007 enables and the technical details behind them.
- **Part III: Planning and Deployment** Provides guidance on how to plan an Office Communications Server deployment through an example.
- **Part IV: Operations** Describes how to administer, back up, and restore Office Communications Servers and maintain the health of Office Communications Servers by monitoring performance and events using Office Communications Server 2007 Management Console, MOM Pack for Microsoft Operations Manager 2005, and SQL Reporting.
- **Part V: Technical Troubleshooting and Diagnostics** Provides in-depth information on diagnostics tools available in Office Communications Server 2007, including tips for troubleshooting the most common problems.
- **Part VI: Technical Reference** Describes the internals of Office Communications Server 2007, including the architecture and components that make up the server and the fundamentals of the SIP protocol, routing, enhanced presence, and security in the product.

The book also includes a glossary for reference as well as several appendixes on various topics, all of which are on the Companion CD.

Document Conventions

The following conventions are used in this book to highlight special features or usage:

Reader Aids

The following reader aids are used throughout this book to point out useful details:

Reader Aid	Meaning
Note	Underscores the importance of a specific concept or highlights a special case that might not apply to every situation.
Important	Calls attention to essential information that should not be disregarded.
Caution	Warns you that failure to take or avoid a specified action can cause serious problems for users, systems, data integrity, and so on.
On the CD	Calls attention to a related script, tool, template, or job aid on the Companion CD that helps you perform a task described in the text.

Sidebars

The following sidebars are used throughout this book to provide added insight, tips, and advice concerning different Office Communications Server features:

Sidebar	Meaning
Direct from the Source	Contributed by experts at Microsoft to provide "from-the-source" insight into how Office Communications Server 2007 works, best practices for managing Office Communications Server clients, and troubleshooting tips.
Real World	Contributed by experts to share best practices and lessons learned when deploying and supporting Office Communications Server 2007.

Command-line Examples

The following style conventions are used in documenting command-line examples throughout this book:

Style	Meaning
Bold font	Used to indicate user input (characters that you type exactly as shown).
Italic font	Used to indicate variables for which you need to supply a specific value (for example *file_name* can refer to any valid file name).
`Monospace font`	Used for code samples and command-line output.
%SystemRoot%	Used for environment variables.

Companion CD

The Companion CD is a valuable addition to this book and includes the following:

- **Appendixes and Glossary** Four appendixes covering such topics as managing Office Communications Server using Windows PowerShell, worksheets to help you perform backup and restore, performance monitor counters, and availability/activity levels for Office Communicator, plus a glossary of important terms.
- **Scripts, Tools, and Additional Readings** Over 100 sample Windows PowerShell functions for administering different aspects of Office Communications Server 2007, which can be used either as-is or customized to meet your administrative needs. Appendix A of this book (also on the CD) provides an overview of these PowerShell functions and includes examples of how to use them. Also included on the companion CD are additional tools, worksheets, and documentation that supplement the text. All of these resources are organized by chapter and the sample administration scripts are also packaged as a single .zip file for easy access.
- **eBook** An electronic version of the entire *Microsoft Office Communications Server 2007 Resource Kit* is also included on the CD.

Full documentation of the contents and structure of the companion CD can be found in the Readme.txt file on the CD.

Resource Kit Support Policy

Every effort has been made to ensure the accuracy of this book and the companion CD content. Microsoft Press provides corrections to this book through the Web at the following location:

http://www.microsoft.com/learning/support/search.asp

If you have comments, questions, or ideas regarding the book or Companion CD content, or if you have questions that are not answered by querying the Knowledge Base, please send them to Microsoft Press by using either of the following methods:

E-mail: *rkinput@microsoft.com*

Postal Mail:
Microsoft Press
Attn: *Microsoft Office Communications Server 2007 Resource Kit,* Editor
One Microsoft Way
Redmond, WA 98052-6399

Please note that product support is not offered through the preceding mail addresses. For product support information, please visit the Microsoft Product Support website at the following address:

http://support.microsoft.com

Part I
Overview and Architecture

In this part:

Microsoft Office Communications Server 2007 is an enterprise grade real-time communications solution that offers instant messaging, Web conferencing, audio/video and Voice over Internet Protocol (VoIP) services within the context of the user's presence. It leverages an organization's investment in Microsoft products by integrating with Active Directory, Microsoft SQL Server 2005, Microsoft Windows Server 2003, a public key infrastructure (PKI), the Microsoft Management Console (MMC), the Domain Name Service (DNS), Microsoft Internet Security and Acceleration (ISA) Server 2005, Microsoft Office SharePoint Server and the 2007 Microsoft Office system. It also requires use of hardware load balancers and media gateways from third-party partners.

Deploying Office Communications Server 2007 can be complex. It's important, therefore, to have a clear understanding of what purpose the different server roles offered by Office Communications Server 2007 perform to make sure administrators deploy the right topology that will meet their organization's needs.

Part I introduces key aspects of Office Communications Server 2007. Chapter 1 provides an overview of the functionality that Office Communications Server 2007 offers. Chapter 2 introduces the various server roles included in Office Communications Server 2007 to create a deployment. Chapter 3 covers supporting technologies necessary to deploy Office Communications Server within your environment.

Chapter 1

Overview of Office Communications Server 2007

In this chapter:

Microsoft Office Communications Server 2007 is an enterprise server product that combines corporate instant messaging (IM), presence, federation, conferencing, and telephony (Voice over IP, or VoIP) in a fully integrated unified communications solution. It can integrate with existing Private Branch eXchange (PBX) infrastructure to leverage the investment in communications already made by organizations.

Office Communications Server 2007 is available in two editions, Standard Edition and Enterprise Edition. The Standard Edition Server is a single-server configuration, whereas the Enterprise Edition pool is a multiserver configuration that provides the same functionality as the Standard Edition Server with higher scalability and reliability. An Enterprise pool splits the different Office Communications Server roles onto separate physical servers. These server roles are as follows:

- Front-end server (also runs the IM Conferencing Server)
- Back-end server (running SQL Server)
- Web Components Server
- Web Conferencing Server
- A/V Conferencing Server

There are two possible configurations for the Enterprise pool: the consolidated configuration and the expanded configuration. The Enterprise pool expanded configuration provides the highest scalability option. It also has the highest deployment cost because it requires the largest number of physical servers.

To enable Office Communications Server 2007 telephony, a Mediation Server, which is an Office Communications Server role, might be required to function as an intermediate between Office Communications Servers and the media gateway. If the enterprise is integrating Office Communications Server with an existing PBX infrastructure, the media gateway should be connected to the PBX. (See Figure 1-1.)

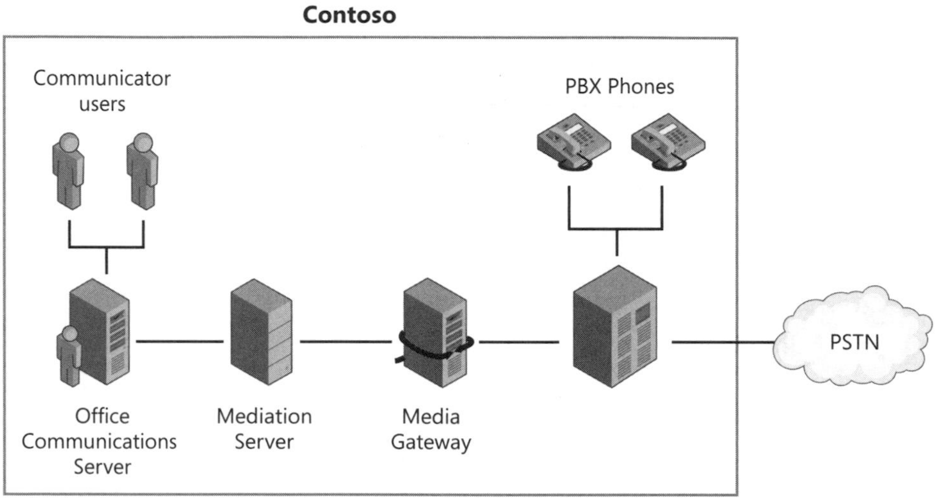

Contoso

Communicator users

PBX Phones

PSTN

Office Communications Server

Mediation Server

Media Gateway

Figure 1-1 Office Communications Server telephony

Organizations can also enable remote access for their users and federation with other organizations that have deployed Office Communications Server 2007. To configure Office Communications Server for remote access and federation, a deployment must include the following server roles in the perimeter network:

- **Access Edge Server** This server role is required to allow IM only across the firewall. If allowing audio/video and Web conferencing across the firewall, the Access Edge Server is also required in addition to the other Edge Server roles.
- **Web Conferencing Edge Server** This server role is required to allow Web Conferencing across the firewall.
- **A/V Edge Server** This server role is required for audio and video to work across the firewall.

The Evolution of Office Communications Server 2007

Office Communications Server 2007 is the next iteration of a Microsoft product line that began with Live Communications Server 2003, 2005, and Service Pack 1 (SP1).

Live Communications Server 2003 introduced the availability of presence information that is updated automatically instead of requiring users to constantly update their status manually. This presence information was updated based on a variety of information, including user activity on the computer and calendar information from Microsoft Office Outlook. Live Communications Server 2003 also introduced corporate IM as a real-time means of communication. Presence and IM were incorporated into all of Microsoft's Office Suite, making them readily available to information workers.

Live Communications Server 2005 SP1 expanded on the functionality offered by Live Communications Server 2003. Remote access, federation, and public IM connectivity (PIC) became available. Integration with PBXs allowed Office Communicator 2005 to control the user's PBX phone. This functionality is referred to as Remote Call Control (RCC). Phone activity was integrated into the user's presence so that it was possible to tell whether the user was on the phone.

This present version, Office Communications Server 2007, introduces a large set of new features since the last release, Live Communications Server 2005 SP1, where Instant Messaging was the only mode of communication supported. In particular, Office Communications Server 2007 introduces support for the following additional modes of communication, also referred to as modalities:

- **IM Conferencing** Two or more users can participate in the same Instant Messaging session.
- **Web Conferencing** Two or more users can collaborate on the same document or application in real time or on a whiteboard.
- **Audio/Video Conferencing** Two or more users can share a video session along with audio or just an audio conference.
- **Enterprise Voice** Users can call phone numbers of other internal users or external users over the Public Switched Telephone Network (PSTN).

These new features and additional capabilities of Office Communications Server 2007 are discussed further in their corresponding sections found later in this chapter.

In addition to the new capabilities just listed, the presence model introduced in Live Communications Server 2003 has also been substantially overhauled in Office Communications Server 2007 to provide a more granular permission model for users to control the level of access that is visible to contacts. This enhanced presence model is discussed in the next section.

Finally, accompanying this lineup of Unified Communications (UC) products is the availability of the UC software developer kit (SDK). The SDKs available for customizing the platform are described in the "Customizing the Platform" section near the end of this chapter.

Understanding the Enhanced Presence Model

Although everyone is accustomed to contacting a person by sending an e-mail message, starting an IM session, or calling a phone number, there's no knowing whether the person is available and can be reached immediately. If the IM request, e-mail message, or call goes unanswered, the user retries at a later time until she can reach the intended recipient. This trial-and-error process can be avoided if the user can determine the availability of the person she is trying to contact.

Live Communications Server 2003 introduced the capability of providing presence information of users to other users allowed to subscribe to it. From the user's presence, contacts could easily establish a communication session by using the most appropriate modality of the user's choice. This simplified the user's communication experience. Office Communications Server 2007 overhauled this presence model to provide a richer presence model with multiple permission levels of presence that contacts can be added to. This is a more granular permission model than the binary permission model (allow or block) available in Live Communications Server 2003 and 2005.

Office Communications Server 2007's presence feature provides the following access levels:

- **Personal** Contacts with this level of permission have the most access to the user's presence information, including the ability to interrupt the user even when the user's presence is set to Do Not Disturb. Phone numbers the user chooses to publish will be visible only to contacts in the Personal access level.
- **Team** This access group is meant for team members. Contacts in this access level have the next highest access to the user's presence information after contacts in the Personal access level. Contacts in this access level can also interrupt the user if the user's presence is set to Do Not Disturb. Phone numbers the user chooses to publish will be visible only to contacts in the Team access level.
- **Company** This access group is the default level for employees in the user's organization. With this level, contacts are able to view the user's availability but are not able to interrupt the user when the user has set his or her presence level to Do Not Disturb.
- **Public** This access level is targeted for contacts outside of the user's organization, such as federated partners and public IM connectivity (PIC) users. Contacts in this access category have the least visibility into the user's presence information after contacts in the Blocked access category level.
- **Blocked** Contacts in this list cannot see the user's presence information at all. To the contact, the user always appears as Offline. The contact cannot initiate any communications directly with the user.

Figure 1-2 shows how Office Communicator can display the distribution of the contact list based on access level.

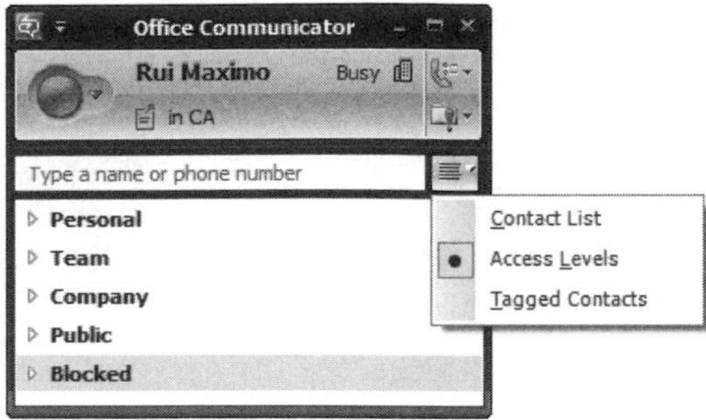

Figure 1-2 Presence permission model

To better understand what information is published and therefore visible to contacts in each access level, Table 1-1 details the information available to contacts in each access level.

Table 1-1 Presence Information Available to Contacts for Each Access Level

Publications	Block	Public	Company	Team	Personal
Offline Presence	X				
Presence		X	X	X	X
Display Name	X	X	X	X	X
E-mail Address	X	X	X	X	X
Title		X	X	X	X
Work Phone[a]			X	X	X
Mobile Phone[a]				X	X
Home Phone[a]					X
Other Phone[a]					X
Company		X	X	X	X
Office			X	X	X
Work Address			X	X	X
SharePoint Site			X	X	X
Meeting Location				X	
Meeting Subject				X	
Free Busy			X	X	X

Table 1-1 Presence Information Available to Contacts for Each Access Level

Publications	Block	Public	Company	Team	Personal
Working Hours			X	X	X
Endpoint Location				X	X
Notes (out-of-office note)			X	X	X
Notes (Personal)			X	X	X
Last Active				X	X
DND[b]				X	X

a. Home, work, mobile, and other phone numbers are published only if the user publishes them in the Options settings.

b. DND–Do Not Disturb. Only contacts in the Personal and Team access levels can interrupt the user. The user is shown as Busy to these contacts. Contacts in the other access levels will not be able to interrupt the user.

Instead of calling a phone number and reaching a voicemail service, the user can check the presence availability of the contact before even attempting to make the call. Presence provides a higher degree of connectivity between users, and it can encourage more efficient collaboration.

Overview of IM Conferencing Capabilities

Because IM support has been available since the first release of this product line, it might be interesting to compare the IM feature set available in each subsequent release, ending with Office Communications Server 2007. Table 1-2 provides an overview of the features available in each release.

Table 1-2 Overview of IM Conferencing Capabilities in Each Release of the Platform

Features	Live Communications Server 2003	Live Communications Server 2005 SP1	Office Communications Server 2007
IM (peer-to-peer)	X	X	X
IM Conferencing			X
IM remote users		X	X
IM federated partners		X	X
IM public cloud connectivity		X	X

Table 1-2 Overview of IM Conferencing Capabilities in Each Release of the Platform

Features	Live Communications Server 2003	Live Communications Server 2005 SP1	Office Communications Server 2007
File transfer between internal users	X	X	X
Add audio/video to IM session			X
Add Web conferencing to IM session			X
Add VoIP to IM session			X
Make participant a leader			X
Microsoft Windows client available	X	X	X
Web client available		X	X
Mobile client available		X	X

Overview of Web Conferencing Capabilities

Office Communications Server 2007 introduces the capability for users, including remote users, to create and join real-time Web conferences that are hosted on internal corporate servers. Users can invite external users from other organizations to participate in the Web conferences they've created. This is similar to the Live Meeting functionality that is now available as a hosted service from Microsoft. Because Office Communications Server 2007 is an on-premise hosted solution, an organization can comply with regulatory and legal requirements for meeting content archiving and retention policies.

Web conferencing supports a rich set of Web-based meeting features:

- **PowerPoint support** Users can upload and present slide decks created with Microsoft Office PowerPoint, including animations.
- **Application and desktop sharing** Users can share applications among multiple participants and give other participants control of the desktop or application.
- **Whiteboard** Users can view a shared whiteboard space for drawing, brainstorming, and capturing ideas.
- **Polling** Users have the ability to create questions for and answers to poll participants.
- **Q&A** Users can ask and answer questions during a meeting.
- **Chat** Users can use Instant Messaging within the context of a meeting.
- **Shared notes** Users can edit and share meeting notes with other participants.

Overview of Audio/Video Conferencing Capabilities

Office Communications Server 2007 also supports multiparty audio/video (A/V) conferencing. Like the Web Conferencing feature, A/V conferencing can be extended to external users. This includes users working remotely and federated users or anonymous participants.

While on the call, users can perform the following actions:

- Transfer to another person
- Transfer to another device
- Place the call on hold
- Invite additional participants
- Incorporate IM into the conference call
- Incorporate video into the conference call
- Set and change a conversation subject
- Mark a call as having high importance
- Take notes by using Microsoft OneNote
- Mute speaker
- Mute microphone

A lot of these features are also available when using other modes of real-time communications offered in Office Communications Server 2007.

Overview of Enterprise Voice Capabilities

Office Communications Server 2007 offers a competitive VoIP solution to the market. Although its feature set does not rival the feature set provided by most PBX vendors' solutions, Office Communications Server 2007 provides the necessary features to enable the core telephony scenarios most used by users. With the availability of the user's presence information, Office Communications Server 2007 provides novel features that integrate telephony with presence.

Enterprise Voice can be integrated to leverage an organization's PBX that is compatible with Office Communications Server 2007. This integration allows calls to be forked to both Office Communications Server clients (Office Communicator, Office Communicator Mobile Edition) and PBX phones. Alternatively, if Enterprise Voice is not an option for an organization, RCC can be enabled with Office Communications Server to allow Office Communicator to control users' desktop PBX phones.

Table 1-3 provides a breakdown of the features available to contrast each configuration.

Table 1-3 Matrix of Functional Voice Scenario Configurations

Features	RCC	Enterprise Voice with PBX integration	Enterprise Voice
PBX phone	X	X	
Communicator controlling PBX phone	X		
Communicator as a softphone		X	X
Internal call routing through PBX	X	X	
Internal call routing through IP network		X	X
External call routing through PBX	X	X	
External call routing through IP network			X
Least-Cost Routing		X	X
PBX voicemail	X	X	
Exchange UM voicemail			X
Caller ID	X	X	X
Call forwarding	X	X	X
Find me/Follow me	X	X	X
Auto-Attendant	X	X	X
Conference Auto-Attendant	X	X	
Boss/Admin	X	X	
E-911	X	X[a]	
Common area (conference/lobby) phones	X	X	
Automatic Call Distribution (ACD)	X	X	
Music on Hold	X	X	

a. Requires third-party integration

Overview of Office Communications Server Clients

Microsoft offers a number of different clients that enable users to sign in to Office Communications Server 2007. There are a number of new clients available for Office Communications Server 2007 that are not available in previous releases.

Clients for Live Communications Server 2003 include the following:

- Windows Messenger 5.1

Clients for Live Communications Server 2005 SP1 include the following:

- Office Communicator 2005
- Office Communicator Mobile 2005
- Communicator Web Access (2005 release), which is available as a Web download

Clients for Office Communications Server 2007 are as follows:

- Office Communicator 2007, a Windows client that runs on the latest service packs of Windows Vista, Windows XP, and Windows 2000.
- Communicator Web Access (2007 release), a Web-based AJAX client that runs on multiple browsers, including Internet Explorer, FireFox, and Safari. This client is available on the same CD as Office Communications Server 2007.
- Office Communicator Mobile, a client for Windows Mobile devices.
- Office Communicator Phone Edition, a hardphone available in various form factors offered by Microsoft's hardware partners.
- Roundtable 2007, a 360-degree conference device.

Each of these clients provides a consistent user experience across clients, making it easy for users familiar with one client to use another Microsoft client without retraining themselves on how the next client functions.

Although it is not comprehensive, Table 1-4 illustrates the features supported by the different Microsoft clients.

Table 1-4 Feature Support by Client

Feature	Communicator	Communicator Web Access (CWA)	Communicator Mobile	Communicator Phone Edition
Zero-download		X		
Web-based		X		
Windows	X			

Table 1-4 **Feature Support by Client**

Feature	Communicator	Communicator Web Access (CWA)	Communicator Mobile	Communicator Phone Edition
Windows Mobile			X	
Hardware phone				X
Non-Windows compatible		X		
Rich presence	X	X	X	X
IM	X	X	X	
IM Conferencing	X	X	X	
Web Conferencing	X			
Audio/Video conferencing	X		X	X
VoIP calls	X		X	X
RCC	X			
Federation	X	X	X	X
Public IM Connectivity	X	X	X	X
Call forwarding rules	X	X	X	X
Notification alerts	X	X	X	X
Toast call deflection	X	X		
File transfer	X			
Outlook calendar integration	X			
Windows-based application programming interface (API)	X			
Web-based AJAX API		X		
Windows Mobile–based API			X	X

Customizing the Platform

Although this book doesn't target the development platform that Office Communications Server offers, it's worth pointing out what SDKs are available to developers who want to customize the UC experience or build applications on the UC platform.

Microsoft Unified Communications AJAX SDK

The Microsoft Unified Communications AJAX SDK includes documentation and sample applications of the AJAX Service API for cross-platform Unified Communications application development. Use of these APIs is best targeted for Web-based applications. Because it is based on XML, no knowledge of the Session Initiation Protocol (SIP) is necessary.

Microsoft Unified Communications Managed API SDK

The Software Development Kit for the Microsoft Unified Communications Managed API version 1.0 (UCMA v1.0) includes documentation of the API, sample applications that use the API, and a redistributable package. UCMA v1.0 is an endpoint API that provides the flexibility and scalability required by advanced developers to build and integrate server applications (for example, alert broadcasting, persistent chat, instant messaging response bots, and so on) into an existing Microsoft Office Communications Server 2007 infrastructure. A working knowledge of the SIP protocol is required to use these APIs.

Microsoft Unified Communications Client API SDK

Microsoft Unified Communications Client SDK provides a powerful and flexible API for building client applications, similar to Office Communicator, for Office Communications Server 2007. The SDK allows application developers to integrate Office Communications Server 2007 enhanced VoIP, Video, Instant Messaging, Conferencing, Telephony, Contact Management, and Presence into their applications. This API offers developers full control over the user interface of their client application. An understanding of the SIP protocol is valuable.

Microsoft Office Communicator 2007 SDK

The Microsoft Office Communicator 2007 SDK enables quick integration of Office Communicator 2007 in Windows and Web applications. You can use this SDK to show presence on Web pages and embed communication entry points to Office Communicator 2007 in line-of-business applications. Unlike the Microsoft Unified Communications Client API SDK, use of these APIs will launch Office Communicator UI. No knowledge of SIP is necessary.

Microsoft Office Communications Server 2007 SDK

The Microsoft Office Communications Server 2007 Software Development Kit (SDK) includes documentation, Microsoft SIP Processing Language (MSSPL), WMI APIs, and sample applications to develop against the Office Communications Server 2007. Extensive knowledge of SIP is required to use these APIs. Plug-ins for Microsoft Office Communications Server that can monitor, archive, and have an affect on the routing of messages through the server are possible. MSSPL supports .NET applications. Examples of applications that can be created are as follows:

- Content filters (remove or modify specific words/phrases or types of data)
- Custom archiving of messages to specific stores or in specific formats
- "Ethical Wall" applications that block specific people from communication (most often because of regulatory requirements)
- Data mining, where the contents of the message exchange are used to provide enhanced information to the participants

Summary

Office Communications Server 2007 is a major upgrade that builds on the design of the previous release, Live Communications Server 2005 SP1. It is no longer limited to being an enterprise Instant Messaging product. It provides the full set of real-time means of communication: IM, Web Conferencing, Audio/Video, and VoIP. This makes Office Communications Server 2007 an even more compelling server product for organizations looking for ways to improve the collaboration efficiency of their information workers.

Additional Resources

- Office Communications Server 2007 product home page, found at *http://technet.microsoft.com/en-us/office/bb267356.aspx*
- Office Communications Server 2007 system requirements, found at *http://www.microsoft.com/technet/prodtechnol/office/communicationsserver/evaluate/sysreqs/default.mspx*
- Office Communications Server 2007 Release Notes, found at *http://www.microsoft.com/downloads/details.aspx?familyid=011d0448-3a8b-47e1-a469-32bedf9d21bd&displaylang=en*
- Office Communications Server 2007 Technical Library, found at *http://technet.microsoft.com/en-us/library/bb676082.aspx*

- Office Communications Server 2007 Documentation, found at *http://technet.microsoft.com/en-us/library/bb676082.aspx*
- Office Communications Server 2007 free evaluation download, found at *http://technet.microsoft.com/en-us/evalcenter/bb684921.aspx*
- Unified Communications Group Team Blog, found on Microsoft TechNet at *http://blogs.technet.com/uc/*

On the Companion CD

There is no companion CD content for this chapter.

Chapter 2

Server Roles

In this chapter:

Microsoft Office Communications Server 2007 includes a number of specialized server roles. These server roles perform specific tasks that enable various usage scenarios. The configuration of these server roles in relation to each other defines a deployment topology. This chapter focuses on explaining the different server roles so that you can decide when to use them to fit your particular deployment needs. Most of these logical server roles can be collocated on the same physical servers–meaning different server roles on the same physical server–although restrictions do apply, because not all collocation scenarios are supported.

Note Supported co-location configurations of server roles is covered toward the end of this chapter.

Standard Edition Server

The basic building block of Office Communications Server 2007 is the home server. A *home server* refers to a Standard Edition Server role with users enabled for Session Initiation Protocol (SIP) Communications assigned to it. The Standard Edition Server is both a SIP registrar and a SIP proxy, as defined in RFC 3261, in a single physical server. (More on the SIP standard is covered in Chapter 19, "Microsoft Office Communications Server 2007 Internals.") Users enabled for SIP Communications are homed on a Standard Edition Server. When installing a

Standard Edition role, the Microsoft SQL Server Desktop Engine (MSDE) database is automatically installed. This database stores data for all users enabled for Live Communications homed on the Standard Edition Server.

The data that is stored for each user includes the following:

- Contact information (contact lists)
- Permissions (Allow/Block lists)
- Endpoints (devices that the user is currently registered on)
- Subscription information (pending subscriptions)
- Office Communications Server user settings published in Active Directory

Contact information refers to the list of contacts and groups created by the user and how these contacts are organized within these groups, as shown in Figure 2-1.

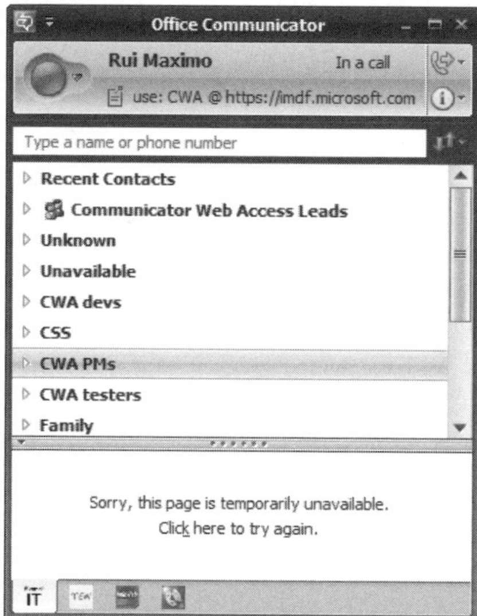

Figure 2-1 Contact list

Permissions refer to whether contacts are allowed or blocked from viewing the presence state of users. Office Communications Server 2007 advanced the permissions model from Live Communications Server 2005 SP1 from a simple binary option (that is, block or allow) to an extensible permission model referred to as *enhanced presence*. Enhanced presence breaks down the presence document into a hierarchical XML set of containers and elements. Viewing permissions can currently be specified at five different levels of access in Office Communicator 2007 and Communicator Web Access (2007 release). The user can specify the permission level a contact is allowed to have. The permission level dictates how much of the user's presence the contact is allowed to view. The different permission levels are Personal, Team, Company, Public, and Blocked, as shown in Figure 2-2.

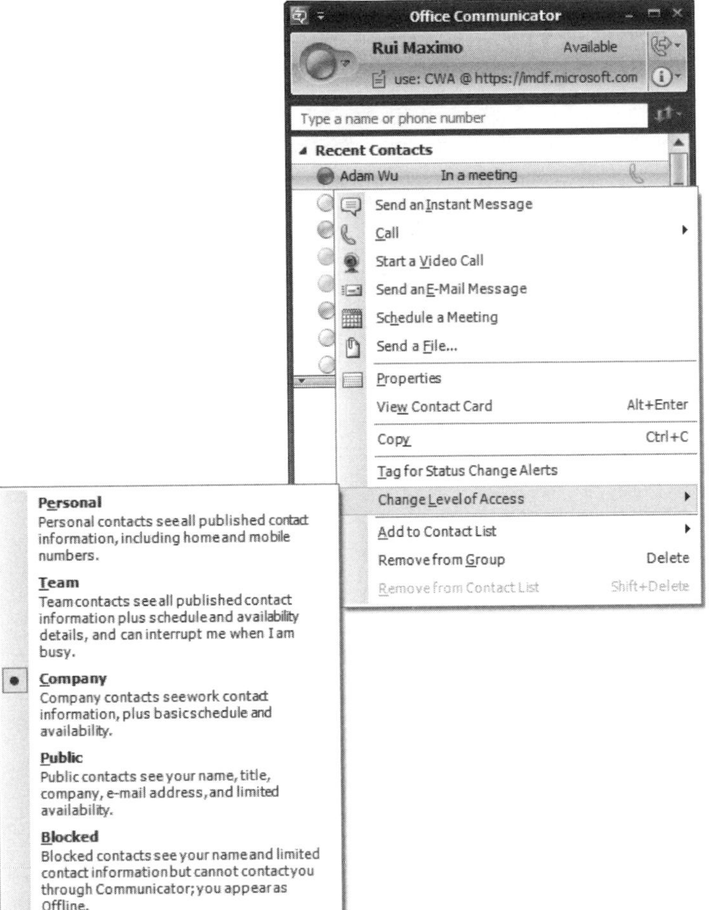

Figure 2-2 Permission levels

Enhanced presence endpoints refer to each of the clients from which the same user is signed in to Office Communications Server. It is not uncommon for users to be signed in from multiple devices. Users might be simultaneously signed in to Office Communications Server from Office Communicator on their desktop computers, from their laptops, from their smart phones running Office Communicator Mobile, or from Communicator Web Access running on Web browsers. The server tracks each of these endpoints to determine the most accurate presence state of the user. When an incoming invitation is sent to the user, Office Communications Server forks the invitation by sending the invitation to all of the user's endpoints. The user responds from one of her devices. The server stops forking incoming messages from that contact, and it routes all subsequent messages for this session to the device from which the user accepted the original invite. After the session is terminated, any new messages from the same contact or any other contact are again forked to all endpoints to which the user is signed in.

Direct from the Source: What Is Forking and How Does It Conceptually Work?

When a phone call "forks," all of your devices begin to ring at the same time. It is similar to what happens at your house: the phones in the kitchen, the living room, and the bedroom all ring when someone dials your home phone number. When you answer in the living room, for example, the phones in the bedroom and kitchen stop ringing. The experience with Office Communicator is the same except the locations are not necessarily in the same building or even the same city. Instead you might be signed in at your office downtown, your home in the suburbs, and your laptop in an airport in Arizona. Whenever you receive a phone call, Office Communicator begins to ring in all of those locations so that you can answer wherever you happen to be at the moment. If you answer on your laptop, the phones at your office and at home stop ringing. Unlike your home phone, your conversation is private and cannot be overheard by picking up one of your far-flung extensions.

When an instant message forks, the message is sent to each place where you are signed in. If you reply to the message by using your laptop, each additional message you receive from the other person will go only to your laptop. The conversion continues this way until you close the conversation window, turn off the computer, or there is a long lull in the conversation.

–Paul Tidwell
Software Development Engineer, Microsoft Corporation

Subscription information contains the list of contacts a user is a subscriber to. Do not confuse this with the list of contacts who have subscribed to the user's presence information. (These contacts are known as *watchers*.) This subscription information tracks all the contacts the user wants to get presence updates. Examples of presence updates include getting notifications when the contact signs in to Office Communications Server, changes their presence state (such as changing it to being in a call), and so on.

Figures 2-3 and 2-4 show the Office Communications Server user settings stored in Active Directory. User information and global Office Communications Server settings stored in Active Directory are synchronized to the database during Office Communications Server replication. This replication process is performed by a component of the Office Communications Server service called the *user replicator* (UR). The UR only reads information from Active Directory and never writes back to it. The logic of the UR process is to contact the closest Active Directory global catalog (GC). If this GC is unavailable, the Standard Edition Server cannot start; or if it is already running, it will fail to synchronize any updates.

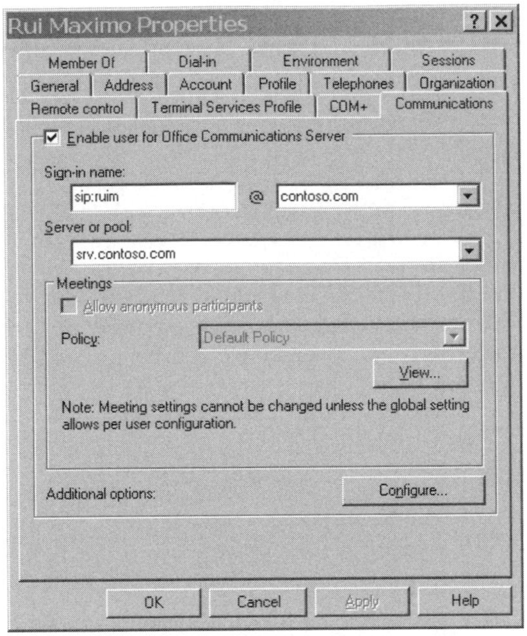

Figure 2-3 User settings

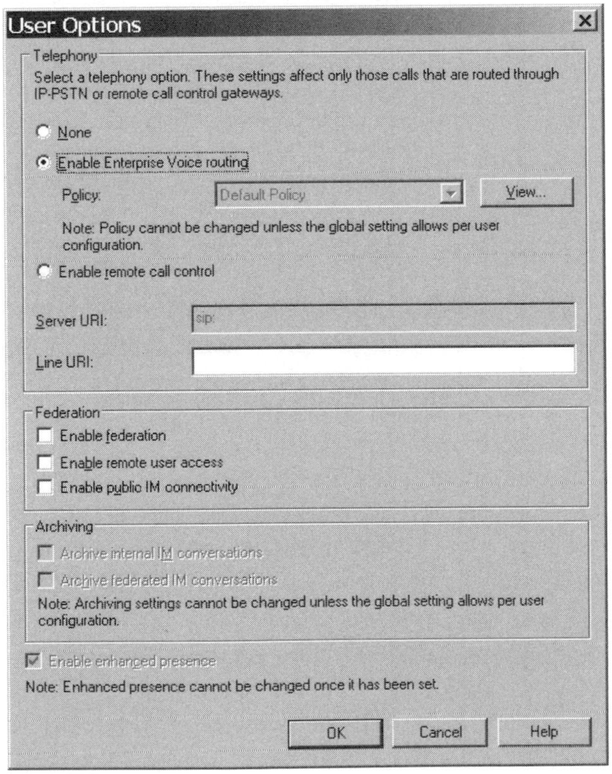

Figure 2-4 Advanced user settings

As a single-server solution, this becomes a single point of failure. Because a Standard Edition Server maintains user information, it is important to periodically back up the database so that, in the event of a server failure, this data can be restored. Because of its scale characteristics and ease of deployment as a standalone server, the Standard Edition Server targets small- to medium-sized businesses or branch offices within large organizations.

Table 2-1 lists the system requirements for Office Communications Server 2007, Standard Edition.

Note To get the most up-to-date information about Office Communications Server 2007 Standard Edition, refer to *http://www.microsoft.com/downloads/details.aspx?FamilyID=1068beb2-4370-4c66-a3dc-55bdd032b857&displaylang=en* or *http://www.microsoft.com/technet/prodtechnol/office/communicationsserver/evaluate/sysreqs/ocs-ee.mspx#EIB*.

Table 2-1 Hardware and Software Requirements for Standard Edition Servers

Component	Requirement
Computer and processor	PC with 2.0-GHz or faster processor (two or more processors recommended)
Memory	256 MB of RAM (2 GB or more recommended)
Hard disk	Dual Ultra2 Small Computer System Interface (SCSI) hard drives with 36 GB of available hard disk space recommended
Operating system (with latest service pack)	Windows Server 2003 Standard Edition, Windows Server 2003 R2 Standard Edition, Windows Server 2003 Enterprise Edition, Windows Server 2003 R2 Enterprise Edition, Windows Server 2003 Datacenter Edition (supports 32-bit versions of Windows Server 2003), or Windows Server 2003 R2 Datacenter Edition
Other	Active Directory directory service for Windows Server 2003 or Windows 2000 with Service Pack 3 required

Enterprise Edition Pool

The Enterprise Edition is the same building block as the Standard Edition Server. In fact, it performs the same functionality as the Standard Edition Server. The primary difference is that it improves the scalability and availability of a Standard Edition Server by separating the logical operations that a Standard Edition Server performs into individual servers. An Enterprise Edition deployment is referred to as an *Enterprise pool* because such a deployment involves multiple physical servers. An Enterprise pool decouples the database from the back-end server running SQL Server and the SIP proxy and registrar service from the front-end servers. The front-end servers no longer maintain persistent data because that data is stored in the SQL back-end server. This is an advantage, because in the event of a system failure, a new front-end server can be quickly brought up to replace it. The front-end servers can further be expanded into specialized server roles by separating the multipoint control units (MCUs) and Web Components onto separate physical servers.

This results in the following two Enterprise pool models:

- **Enterprise pool, consolidated configuration** In this configuration, shown in Figure 2-5, all front-end servers are configured identically with the same set of server roles used uniformly across all front-end servers in the Enterprise pool. The front-end servers, in addition to running the Instant Messaging (IM) Conferencing Server, can run any of the following additional server roles:
  - Web Conferencing Server
  - A/V Conferencing Server
  - Telephony Conferencing Server
  - Web Components Server
  - Communicator Web Access Server

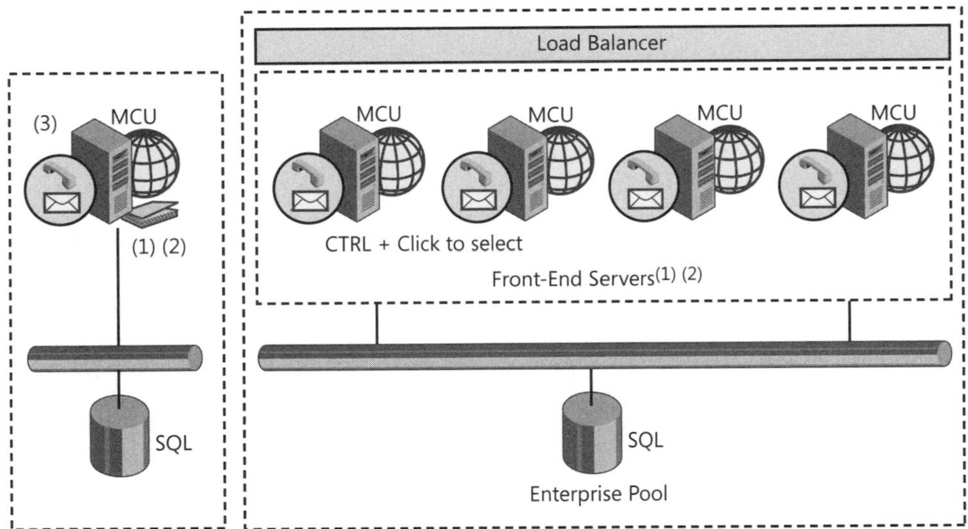
Load Balancer
(3)
MCU
(1) (2)
SQL
MCU
MCU
MCU
MCU
CTRL + Click to select
Front-End Servers(1) (2)
SQL
Enterprise Pool
(1) All front-end servers are configured with the same set of Conferencing Servers (MCUs). These server roles must be configured uniformly to all front-ends.
(2) All IIS service must be configured in locked down mode.
(3) Hardware load balancer not required.

Figure 2-5 Consolidated configuration

- **Enterprise pool, expanded configuration** In this configuration, shown in Figure 2-6, each server member of the Enterprise pool runs a single server role per physical server, dedicating a server role for each physical server. This arrangement allows this configuration to scale beyond the consolidated configuration because of the specialization of having a server for each role.

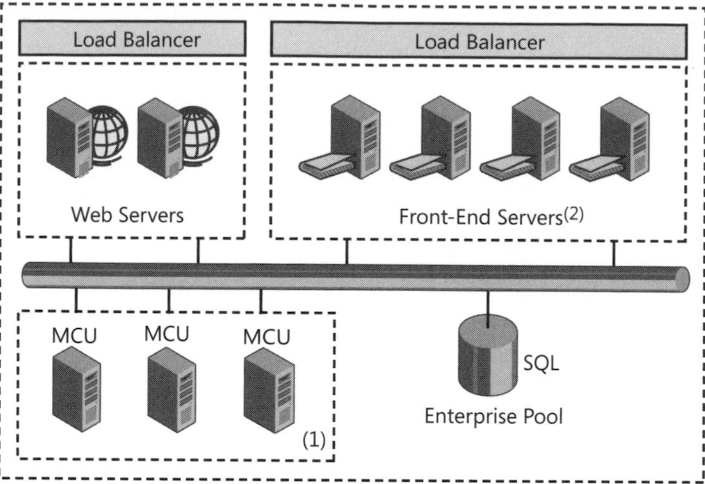

(1) Conferencing Servers must be individually addressable
(2) IIS must not be installed on the front-end servers

Figure 2-6 Expanded configuration

An Enterprise Edition pool deployment requires a hardware load balancer (HLB) to load balance client connections to the front-end servers and Web servers in the expanded configuration case. The HLB's virtual IP (VIP) must be manually published in DNS. Clients connect to this VIP when signing in to the Enterprise pool. The HLB is configured to load balance incoming client connections among the available front-end servers. In both configurations, an Enterprise pool can scale up to four front-end servers.

For high availability on the back end, because the back-end server is a SQL Server, an Enterprise Edition pool deployment can be clustered by taking advantage of Microsoft Clustering Service (MSCS). MSCS is a feature of the Enterprise Edition and Datacenter Edition of Windows Server 2003 and Windows Server 2003 R2. Microsoft officially supports *only* active-passive SQL clustering for Office Communications Server 2007 Enterprise pool deployments. Active-passive SQL clustering means one SQL node is active while the other SQL node is passive. The front-end servers in the pool are connected to the active node. The passive node takes over when the active node fails. The passive node must be an exact replica of the active node in the system configuration.

Office Communications Server 2007 does not support active-active SQL clustering. It does support running the back-end SQL Server on a 64-bit server. The back-end server cannot be collocated on a same physical server with a front-end server. Because only the back-end server stores persistent information about each user homed on the pool, the front-end servers maintain transient information—such as logged-on state and control information for an IM, Web, or A/V conference—only for the duration of a user's session.

All servers belonging to an Enterprise pool must be running on a Windows Server 2003 SP1 or Windows Server 2003 R2 computer joined to an Active Directory domain. Thus a scenario in which half of the front-end servers are deployed in domain A and half in domain B, while the back-end servers are deployed in domain C, is not supported by Microsoft. Also, all servers in an Enterprise pool should be within geographic proximity with 1-GB connectivity between front-end servers and back-end servers.

Table 2-2 lists the system requirements for Office Communications Server 2007 Enterprise Edition.

> **Note** To get the most up-to-date information about system requirements, refer to *http://www.microsoft.com/technet/prodtechnol/office/communicationsserver/evaluate/sysreqs/ocs-ee.mspx*.

Table 2-2 Hardware and Software Requirements for Front-End Servers

Component	Requirement
Computer and processor	Dual processor, dual core with 3.0-GHz or faster processor
Memory	4 GB or more of RAM recommended
Cache	1 MB L2 per core recommended
Hard disk	2 SCSI hard drives with 18 GB of available hard disk space recommended
Network	1-GBit network interface card (NIC) recommended
Operating system	Windows Server 2003 Standard Edition, Windows Server 2003 R2 Standard Edition, Windows Server 2003 Enterprise Edition, Windows Server 2003 R2 Enterprise Edition, Windows Server 2003 Datacenter Edition (supports 32-bit versions of Windows Server 2003), or Windows Server 2003 R2 Datacenter Edition
Other	Active Directory directory service for Windows Server 2003 or Windows 2000 with Service Pack 3 required

Director Role

When you are deploying a single Standard Edition Server or Enterprise pool, your topology remains simple. However, as the number of Standard Edition Servers and Enterprise pools grows within your organization, the complexity of your infrastructure increases. Deploying multiple Standard Edition Servers and Enterprise pools might be necessary to handle a large number of users, users within your organization who are geographically dispersed, or both. In such situations, it is best to deploy a Director or array of Directors. The Director server role directs client traffic to the correct home server. Before explaining why it is important to deploy this role, some background information is necessary.

When users sign in to Office Communications Server, Office Communicator performs a DNS SRV query. The client contacts the IP address returned from the DNS query and attempts to sign in to this server. If this server is the user's home server, the server signs in the user.

This will always be the case if your organization has only a single home server or pool. However, if you have deployed multiple Standard Edition Servers and Enterprise pools within your organization, which Standard Edition Servers and Enterprise pools do you advertise for this SRV record in DNS? Maybe you publish the fully qualified domain name (FQDN) of all your Standard Edition Servers and Enterprise pools. In that case, the DNS SRV query might or might not return the user's home server when Office Communicator queries DNS. If the DNS query returns the FQDN of a server that is not the user's home server, this server must redirect the client to the user's home server. This makes the initial sign-in traffic nondeterministic because clients signing in are not guaranteed to reach the user's home server in the first hop.

This nondeterministic configuration has several effects. First, each home server and pool must account for the performance load created from redirecting client requests attempting to sign in users not homed on that server or pool. In the worst-case scenario, every home server and pool must handle the load of redirecting sign-in traffic for all users in your organization. Second, if the DNS query returned directs the client to a server that is unavailable, the sign-in experience will be affected because the client must wait for the network timeout to expire before attempting to connect to another server.

To avoid home servers from having to redirect client traffic to the correct home server, you can elect to advertise a single Standard Edition Server or Enterprise pool in DNS for this SRV record. This server can be solely in charge of directing Communicator clients to their user's correct home server when signing in. This, in effect, specializes the role of a Standard Edition Server or Enterprise pool to that of a Director redirecting client traffic to the correct home server. Therefore, the server role name, Director, was designated. Although the Director can serve as a home server by assigning users to it, it is not recommended to assign users to the Director.

It is recommended to deploy a Director role when your organization hosts multiple Standard Edition Servers and Enterprise pools. The Director role forces the sign-in traffic into a deterministic path. Instead of publishing the FQDN of the Standard Edition Servers and Enterprise pools in DNS, the DNS SRV publishes the FQDN of the Director or bank of Directors. When Communicator attempts to sign in the user, its DNS SRV query returns the FQDN of the Director. The Director knows how to locate the user's home server and redirects the client to that server. The Director's role is to redirect internal clients to the correct Standard Edition Server or Enterprise pool where the user is homed on, as shown in Figure 2-7. This configuration allows Standard Edition Servers and Enterprise pools to handle SIP traffic only for their users.

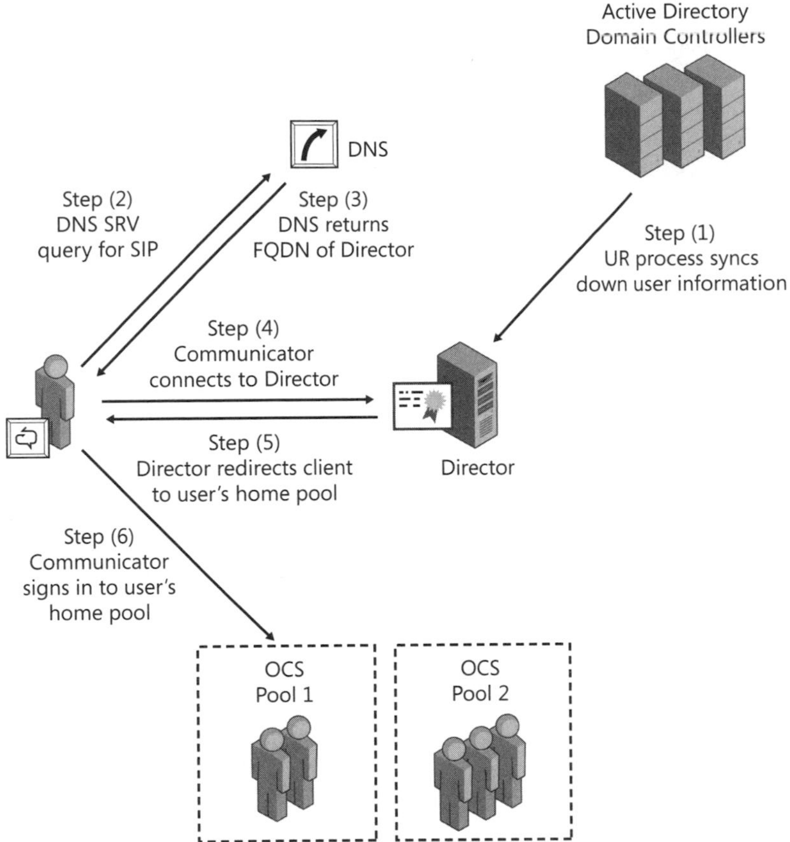

Figure 2-7 Director routing internal traffic

In addition to helping route traffic for internal deployments, a Director plays an important role for external topologies. When configuring Federation, Public IM Connectivity, or Remote Access, deploying a Director as the Access Edge Server's next hop is strongly recommended. By using a Director or bank of Directors, the only IP address and port number that needs to be opened on the internal firewall is access to the Director on port 5061 for SIP traffic. By restricting the Access Edge Server to reach only the Director, you can limit access to your internal network if the Access Edge Server is ever compromised. None of the internal Standard Edition Servers and Enterprise pools are directly accessible by the Access Edge Server.

The Director provides the following benefits:

- Authenticates remote users. The Director prevents unauthorized users from entering the internal network.
- Proxy remote user connections to the correct Standard Edition Server or Enterprise pool. This is necessary because remote user connections cannot be redirected.

- Denial of Service (DoS) mitigation: Verify the intended recipient of a message is a valid user. This protects internal servers from processing invalid messages from a public IM connectivity or federated partner.

The Director is responsible for authenticating the user and routing the client connection to the correct Standard Edition Server or Enterprise pool. The Standard Edition Server or Enterprise pool responds to the client request by routing SIP traffic through the Director. From a security perspective, the Director serves as an additional security checkpoint. For outgoing connections to the Access Edge Server, the Standard Edition Servers and Enterprise pools route traffic destined for external users (that is, Federated contacts, public IM connectivity contacts, and remote users) to the Director. The Director then proxies the connection to the Access Edge Server. This is shown in Figure 2-8.

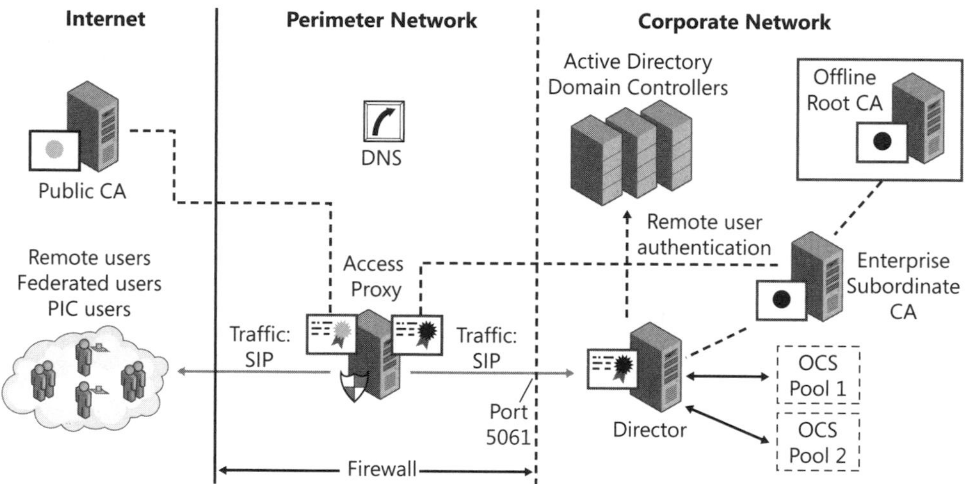

Figure 2-8 Director routing external traffic

Conferencing Servers

Conferencing Servers, also known as MCUs (Multipoint Conferencing Units), are associated with a Standard Edition Server or Enterprise pool. They are software-based and collocated on a Standard Edition Server and front-end servers of an Enterprise pool in a consolidated configuration. They are installed on separate physical servers in the case of the Enterprise pool in an expanded configuration. The IM Conferencing Server and the Telephony Conferencing Server are the only exceptions. These server roles are always installed on the front-end servers, even in the Enterprise pool in the expanded configuration case.

Each of these server roles communicates directly with clients participating in a conferencing session via their own protocol, which is optimized for the media they support. These server roles also synchronize the state of the conference with a process called the *focus* that runs on the front-end server or Standard Edition Server. The protocol used to control the state of the conference session is called Centralized Conference Control Protocol (CCCP), also referred to as C3P. The focus sends state updates to the Conferencing Server using C3P, which the Conferencing Server listens for over an HTTPS channel.

Office Communications Server 2007 provides the following MCUs:

- IM Conferencing Server
- Web Conferencing Server
- A/V Conferencing Server
- Telephony Conferencing Server

Each of these Conferencing Servers is described in more detail in the following sections. They share the same hardware and software requirements, which are detailed in Table 2-3.

> **Note** To get the most up-to-date information about Conferencing Servers, refer to *http://www.microsoft.com/technet/prodtechnol/office/communicationsserver/evaluate/sysreqs/ocs-ee.mspx#EMD*.

Table 2-3 Hardware and Software Requirements for Conferencing Servers

Component	Requirement
Computer and processor	Dual processor, dual core with 3.0-GHz or faster processor
Memory	4 GB or more of RAM recommended
Cache	1 MB L2 per core recommended
Hard disk	2 SCSI hard drives with 18 GB of available hard disk space recommended
Network	1-GBit NIC recommended
Operating system	Windows Server 2003 Standard Edition, Windows Server 2003 R2 Standard Edition, or higher
Other	Active Directory directory service for Windows Server 2003 or Windows 2000 with Service Pack 3 required

IM Conferencing Server

The IM Conferencing Server is automatically installed on every Standard Edition Server and every front-end server member of an Enterprise pool in both configurations (consolidated and expanded). It cannot be installed separately on a separate physical server. This service enables users to escalate a two-party IM session into a multiparty IM conference.

Escalating from a two-party IM session to a multiparty IM conference involves more than just adding new participants. New state information is involved in an IM conference, and this information must be synchronized across all the parties in an IM conference, such as tracking the roster (that is, a list of participants), determining which participants are conference leaders, displaying the participants' network of origin, as well as exposing a set of actions participants can perform (for example, mute, eject, promote, and so on).

The management of the conference session is controlled by the focus and is enforced by the IM Conferencing Server. The focus and the IM Conferencing Server communicate via the C3P protocol. Only port 5061 is required by the IM Conferencing Server.

If you use internal firewalls to compartmentalize your network, the IM Conferencing Server needs to have the same set of ports opened as the Standard Edition Server and Enterprise pool front-end server.

Web Conferencing Server

The Web Conferencing Server is responsible for multiplexing the Web conferencing data feed (for example, documents, application sharing, whiteboarding, and so on) from the leader to all participants in the session. Persistent Shared Object Model (PSOM) is the protocol used by the Web Conferencing Server to share documents and application content in real time to provide that collaborative experience. PSOM uses the port number 8057.

The Web Conferencing Server is collocated with the Standard Edition Server and every front-end server in an Enterprise pool in a consolidated configuration. It can also be installed on its separate physical server for higher scalability. Installing a Web Conferencing Server on its own physical server is supported only in an Enterprise pool in an expanded configuration.

Just like the IM Conferencing Server, the Web Conferencing Server hosts only Web conferences for organizers that are homed on the Standard Edition Server or Enterprise pool the Web Conferencing Server is a part of. Users homed on other Standard Edition Servers and Enterprise pools can join as participants to the Web conference, but they cannot schedule a meeting on a Web Conferencing Server that is not part of their home server. More details are covered in Chapter 5, "Conferencing Scenario."

A/V Conferencing Server

Similar to the IM Conferencing Server and the Web Conferencing Server, the A/V Conferencing Server is an MCU for audio and video media. In the case of audio, the A/V Conferencing Server mixes the audio feeds from every participant before returning the mixed audio back to each participant. This is computationally intensive. Therefore, it is recommended that you allocate a high-end server for this purpose.

The A/V Conferencing Server uses the Real Time Audio (RTAudio) codecs for audio and Real Time Video (RTVideo) codecs for video. Both of these protocols are designed to optimize performance in high-latency, low-bandwidth networks such as the Internet. Two-way communications are peer-to-peer. Therefore, for voice calls (which make up the large majority of audio communications), the A/V Conferencing Server is not involved.

Telephony Conferencing Server

The Telephony Conferencing Server provides the functionality of joining and controlling an audio conference hosted on a Public Switched Telephone Network (PSTN) bridge from a service provider such as AT&T, Verizon, BT, Intercall, Premier, or another company. When users use the Microsoft Conferencing add-in for Microsoft Office Outlook to schedule a Live Meeting with audio or a conference call (as shown in Figure 2-9), at the time of the conference your desktop phone will be automatically set up to join the audio bridge hosted by your organization's carrier. The organizer will be able to control the audio from Communicator and perform activities such as muting everyone except the presenter, muting themselves, removing participants, and so on.

Figure 2-9 Conferencing add-in for Microsoft Office Outlook

The Telephony Conferencing Server is installed automatically as part of the Standard Edition Server and also on the front-end server in an Enterprise pool. It cannot be installed separately as its own service running on a separate physical server.

Archiving and CDR Server

If your organization has a policy that requires the content of every communication to be logged for compliance purposes, you should deploy the Archiving and CDR (call detail records) Server. If you need to track only call detail records (for example, *when* a conversation occurred between users without archiving the conversation itself), you also should deploy the Archiving and CDR Server. This server role enables archiving of all messages at the server level. You can enable only archiving or only call detail records (if you don't want to archive the actual body of the IM conversation, but you do want to collect statistical usage data). Because all IM conversations travel through the user's home server, it is possible to enforce archiving at the server level without requiring any cooperation from the client. This architecture offers the most control to the administrator.

The Archiving and CDR Server must be installed on a Windows Server 2003 or Windows Server 2003 R2 computer with SQL Server 2000 SP3a (or higher) or SQL Server 2005 SP1 (or higher) installed. The Archiving and CDR Server cannot be collocated on the same physical server with any other Office Communications Server role. See Table 2-4 for the hardware and software requirements for this role.

Table 2-4 Hardware and Software Requirements for Archiving and CDR Servers

Component	Requirement
Computer and processor	Dual processor, dual core with 2.6-GHz or faster processor
Memory	4 GB or more of RAM recommended if only CDR is enabled 16 GB or more of RAM recommended if CDR and Archiving are enabled
Cache	2 MB L2 per core recommended
Hard disk	Drive 1 (2 × 18 GB) for operating system and Page File Drive 2 for database log file, and drive 3 for database file: (4 × 36GB, 15K RPM, RAID 0+1) if only CDR is enabled Drive 2 (6 × 72GB, 15K RPM, RAID 0+1) if CDR and Archiving are enabled
Network	1-GBit NIC recommended
Operating system	Windows Server 2003 Standard Edition, Windows Server 2003 R2 Standard Edition, or higher
Other	Active Directory directory service for Windows Server 2003 or Windows 2000 with Service Pack 3 required

Edge Servers

Office Communications Server 2007 defines three Edge Server roles. These server roles are referred to as "Edge Servers" because they are deployed in the network perimeter of an organization's network. These server roles enable an organization to expose Office Communications functionality across the corporate network boundary to remote employees, federated partners, and public IM connectivity users. Office Communications Server 2007 exposes the following edge server roles:

- Access Edge Server
- Web Conferencing Edge Server
- A/V Edge Server

These server roles are explained in more detail in the following sections. Hardware and software requirements for Edge Servers are shown in Table 2-5.

Note To get the most up-to-date information about Edge Servers, refer to *http://www.microsoft.com/technet/prodtechnol/office/communicationsserver/evaluate/sysreqs/ocs-ee.mspx#EMD*.

Table 2-5 Hardware and Software Requirements for Edge Servers

Component	Requirement
Computer and processor	Dual processor, dual core with 3.0-GHz or faster processor
Memory	4 GB or more of RAM recommended
Cache	1 MB L2 per core recommended
Hard disk	2 SCSI hard drives with 18 GB of available hard disk space recommended
Network	2 1-GBit NICs: one NIC for the external edge, and the second NIC for the internal edge
Operating system	Windows Server 2003 Standard Edition, Windows Server 2003 R2 Standard Edition, or higher
Other	Active Directory directory service for Windows Server 2003 or Windows 2000 with Service Pack 3 required

Access Edge Server

If you've deployed Live Communications Server 2005 SP1 and enabled remote user access, federation, or public IM connectivity, you're already familiar with this server role. In Live Communications Server 2005 SP1, this server role was called *Access Proxy*. It has been renamed to offer a consistent naming convention with the two new additions, the Web Conferencing Edge Server and the A/V Edge Server. Despite the name change, the Access Edge Server role serves the same function as Access Proxy.

The Access Edge Server must be deployed if you want to enable Federation, public IM connectivity, or remote user access. Because most organizations do not have Active Directory access from their network perimeter for security reasons, the Access Edge Server is deployed on a computer running Windows Server 2003 or Windows Server 2003 R2 in a workgroup environment. Therefore, it cannot authenticate users. Users are authenticated by the Director.

The Access Edge Server cannot be collocated on the same physical server with any other network perimeter service, such as Microsoft Internet Security and Acceleration (ISA) Server; however, it can be collocated on the same physical server with the Web Conferencing Edge Server and the A/V Edge Server. Scaling requirements for your organization might demand that you install these Edge Server roles on separate physical servers.

The Access Edge Server must be configured with two IP addresses. One IP address should be visible to the Internet, and the second IP address should be visible to the enterprise network.

The recommended configuration (for performance and ease of securing the server) is to install two network interface cards (NICs) and connect the Internet to one and the enterprise network to the other. If the Access Edge Server is protected by firewalls on both sides of the network perimeter, the internal firewall must be configured to open port 5061. This is necessary so that the Access Edge Server can connect to the Director in the corporate network, and vice versa. If you are configuring Federation or public IM connectivity, you must open port 5061 on the external firewall to allow connectivity from the Internet to the Access Edge Server. If remote user access is configured, you have the option to configure whichever port number you prefer because you control the clients connecting to your Access Edge Server, because these are internal users. The recommendation is to open port 5061 or 443. A best practice is to open port 443 because this allows your users to connect back to your Access Edge Server from another organization's network, because this port number is usually opened. This is particularly important for professionals, such as consultants, who work at customer sites.

To provide high availability, a bank of Access Edge Servers can be deployed. An HLB must be configured on both sides of the Access Edge Servers, as shown in Figure 2-10.

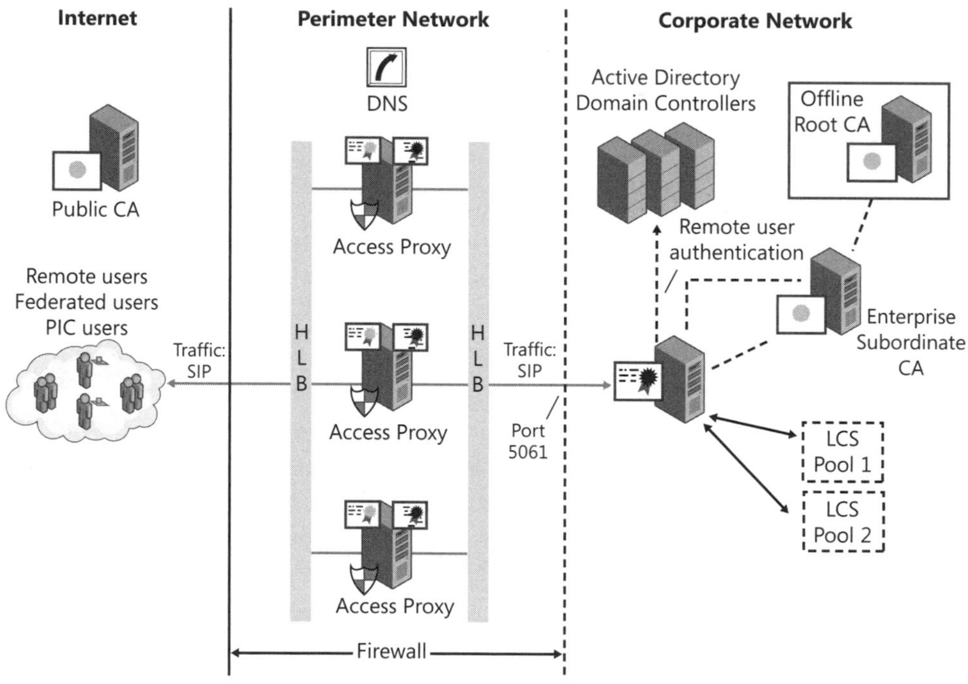

Figure 2-10 Bank of Access Edge Servers

Web Conferencing Edge Server

Similar to the Access Edge Server, the Web Conferencing Edge Server proxies Web conferencing media across the firewall to and from the Internet and the corporate network. Where the Access Edge Server proxies SIP traffic, the Web Conferencing Edge Server proxies PSOM traffic from a Web conferencing session. Similar to the Access Edge Server, the Web Conferencing Edge Server must be configured with two NICs: one network card connected to the Internet, and the other network card connected to the internal network. The network security administrator needs to open port 443 on the external NIC to allow users to connect from the Internet and open port 8057 on the internal NIC for Web Conferencing Servers to connect to it. This is because the Web Conferencing Edge Server never establishes a connection to the Web Conferencing Server directly. Only the Web Conferencing Server connects to the Web Conferencing Edge Server. This design has the advantage of reducing the number of vectors into the corporate network.

The Web Conferencing Edge Server role cannot be collocated with any other server role except the Access Edge Server and the A/V Edge Server.

To provide high availability, a bank of Web Conferencing Edge Servers can be deployed. An HLB must be configured on both sides of the Web Conferencing Edge Servers.

The Access Edge Server role and Web Conferencing Edge Server role can also be combined on the same physical servers in a bank. This configuration provides high availability while consolidating the number of Edge Servers required. This architecture is shown in Figure 2-11.

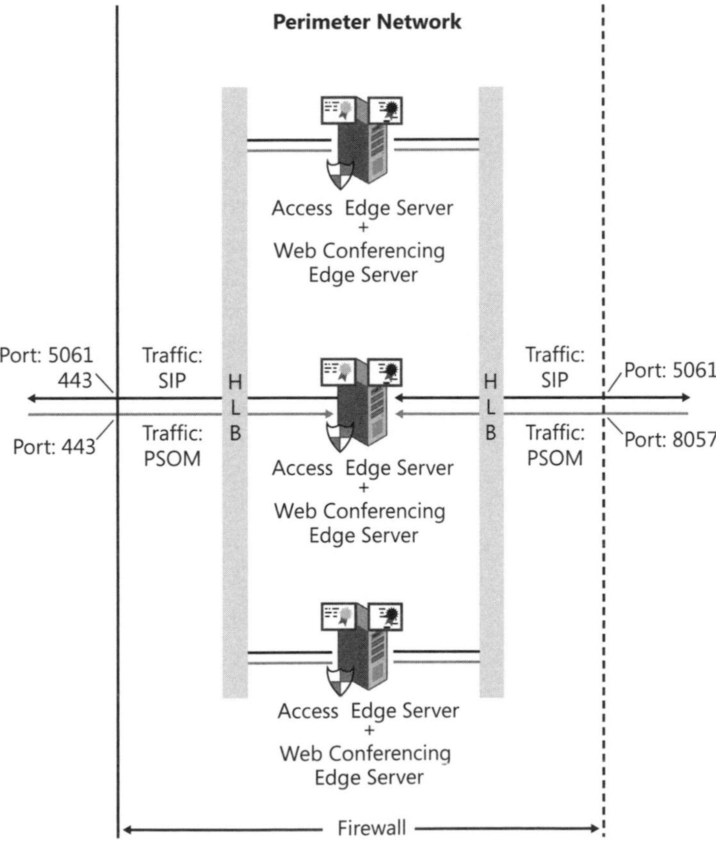

Figure 2-11 Bank of (Access + Web Conferencing) Edge Servers

A/V Edge Server

The A/V Edge Server enables audio and video traffic to traverse the corporate perimeter network. The A/V Edge Server serves as a meeting point for bridging users connecting from the Internet to an A/V Conferencing Server associated with the user's home server. Users connect to the A/V Edge Server, and the A/V Conferencing Server connects to the A/V Edge Server. The A/V Edge Server relays the Real-Time Protocol (RTP) traffic between the users and A/V Conferencing Server. Similar to the other Edge Server roles, the A/V Edge Server must be configured with two NICs: one network card connected directly to the Internet, and the other network card connected to the internal network. The A/V Edge Server uses the Information and Content Exchange (ICE) protocol to enable clients to traverse firewalls that might lie in between the end-user's client and the A/V Edge Server.

For A/V to work properly, the following ports need to be opened on the firewall adjacent to the external edge of the A/V Edge Server. Because User Datagram Protocol (UDP) is preferred for RTP traffic, Communicator will attempt to first connect to UDP port 3478. If Communicator fails to connect to UDP port 3478, it attempts to connect to the A/V Edge Server on TCP port 443. If successful, the A/V Edge Server negotiates with the client a port in the range 50,000 through 59,999 for the media stream.

Following is the set of ports to open on the A/V Edge Server external NIC:

1. STUN over UDP port 3478
2. RTP over UDP port range 50,000–59,999
3. STUN over TCP port 443
4. RTP over TCP port range 50,000–59,000

Here is the set of ports to open on the A/V Edge Server internal NIC:

1. STUN over TCP port 443
2. SIP port 5062
3. STUN over UDP port 3478

These sets of ports are shown in Figure 2-12.

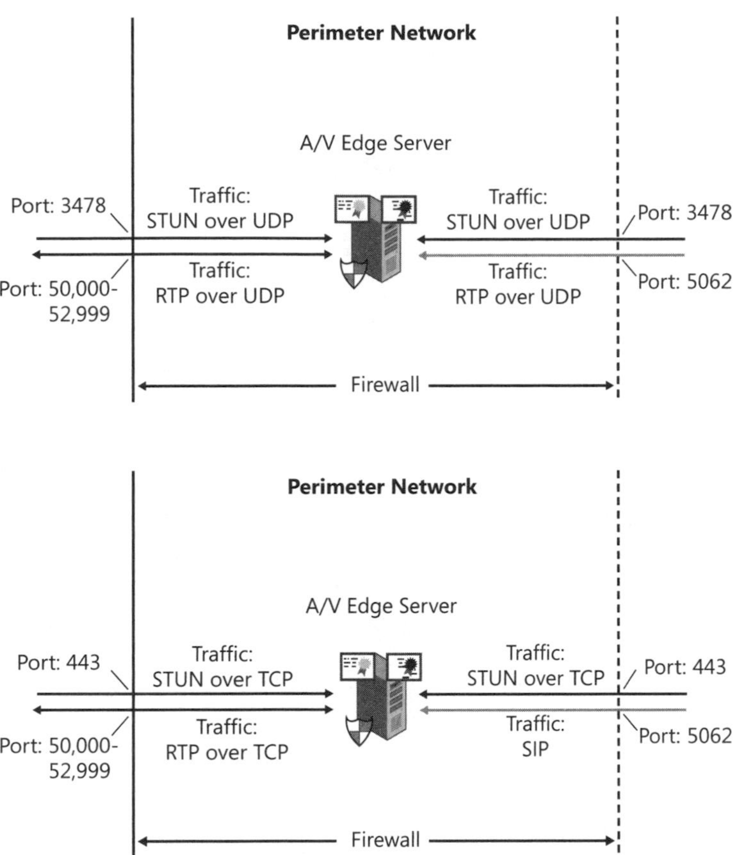

Figure 2-12 A/V Edge Server ports

To provide high availability, a bank of A/V Edge Servers can be deployed. An HLB must be configured on both sides of the A/V Edge Servers.

Communicator Web Access

Communicator Web Access for Office Communications Server 2007 is a Web service that allows users to sign in to Office Communications Server without needing to install Microsoft Office Communicator. This server role makes it possible to connect to Office Communications Server with simply a Web browser. This browser-based, zero-download client for Office Communications Server 2007 makes it possible for users using non-Windows systems, users using locked-down Windows systems, and home users without Office Communicator installed to have a similar experience as users using Office Communicator. Communicator Web Access browser experience has a striking fidelity to Office Communicator. Users will feel comfortable with the familiar UI. Table 2-6 lists the platform and browser matrix that is supported by Communicator Web Access.

Table 2-6 Platform/Browser Support

Platform	Browser
Windows	Internet Explorer
	Firefox
Mac OS X	Safari
	Firefox
Solaris	Firefox

This server role is located in the Other Servers section of the Setup menu. Communicator Web Access (CWA) provides its own management console (MMC), which is why CWA servers cannot be managed from the same MMC as servers running Office Communications Server. This server role must be installed on a computer joined to your Active Directory forest, because it needs Active Directory connectivity to authenticate and authorize user access. CWA can be deployed for internal usage (that is, for users within the organization's network) or for external usage (that is, for users outside the organization's network).

When a user connects to CWA, the Web service authenticates the user. CWA supports forms-based authentication, or integrated Windows authentication (IWA), or custom authentication. Integrated Windows authentication refers to the native authentication protocols Kerberos and NTLM that are supported by Active Directory. Custom authentication allows administrators to use a third-party authentication system to enable single sign-on or two-factor authentication for a more robust authentication solution. Integrated Windows authentication is supported only for internal usage, whereas forms-based or custom authentication must be used for external usage. Custom authentication can be used for both internal and external users. After the user is properly authenticated, CWA determines the user's home server and registers the user. Note that the user is not authenticated by the user's home server again. Because the user's home server trusts the CWA server, no further user authentication is performed by the home server. At this point, CWA proxies all traffic to and from the user's home server, as shown in Figure 2-13.

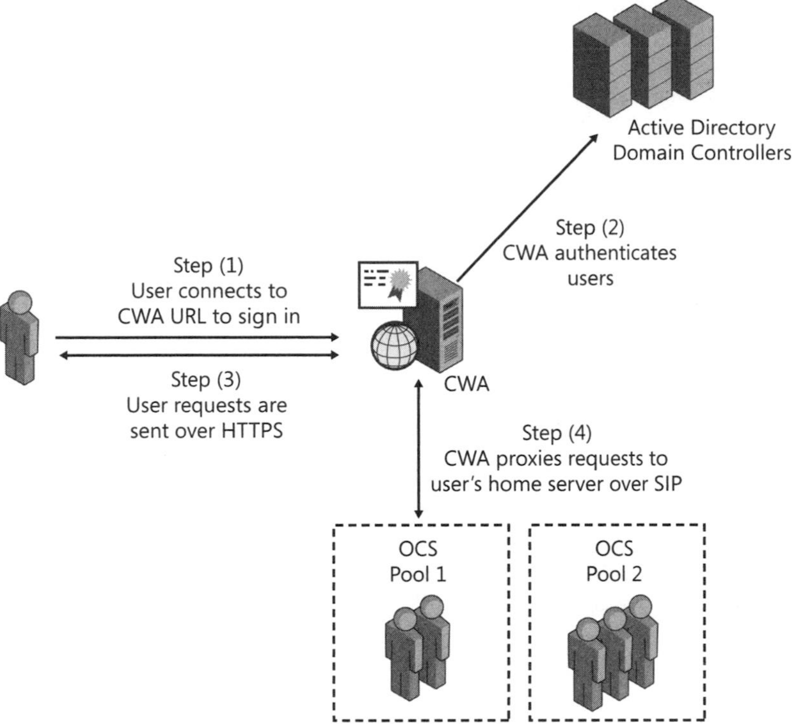

Figure 2-13 Internal deployment of CWA

Communicator Web Access can be installed on a separate computer, or it can be installed on the same computer running a Standard Edition Server or front-end server or a standalone Web Components server. When Communicator Web Access is collocated on the same physical computer as another supported server role, be aware that the overall performance of your server will be diminished.

CWA performs a similar role as the Director, except it always proxies client connections instead of redirecting them for internal users. This makes CWA a prime candidate to be deployed on the same physical server as a Director for smaller deployments. This is what most customers have done to avoid the cost and management of yet another physical server. If you have deployed Office Communicator to all your users, the usage of CWA is likely to be light enough that a Director could easily handle it, because Office Communicator will be their primary client.

When making Communicator Web Access accessible from outside your organization's firewall, you should take precautions to protect your CWA server. To properly secure your CWA server, it is strongly recommended that you use a reverse proxy such as Microsoft Internet Security and Acceleration (ISA) Server 2006 behind the firewalls in your network perimeter. When configuring CWA for external access, you should use port 443. This topology is illustrated in Figure 2-14.

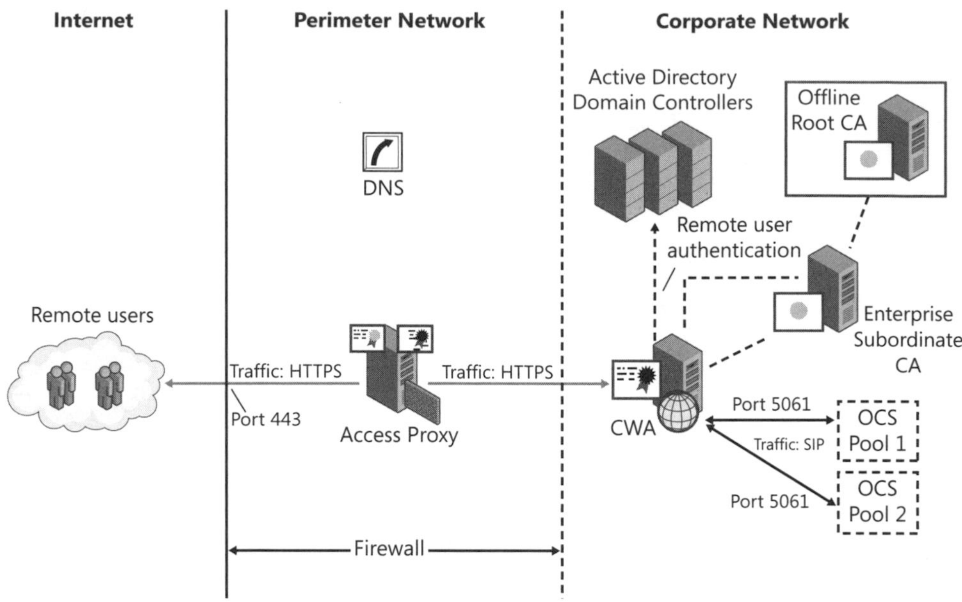

Figure 2-14 External deployment of CWA

In addition to providing a Web-based, zero-download client for Office Communications Server 2007, CWA provides a server-scale set of application programming interfaces (APIs)—called UC AJAX APIs—for developers who want to build server-side mashups and custom IM and presence clients. UC AJAX APIs consist of 27 simple APIs that eliminate the need for deep SIP expertise to build custom clients.

Table 2-7 lists the system requirements for Communicator Web Access, including the various browsers that are supported.

> **Note** To get the most up-to-date information about Communicator Web Access, refer to *http://www.microsoft.com/technet/prodtechnol/office/communicationsserver/evaluate/sysreqs/cwa.mspx.*

Table 2-7 Hardware and Software Requirements for CWA

Component	Requirement
Computer and processor	Dual Intel Xeon 3.06-GHz, 1-MB cache, 533-MHz FSB (front-side bus)
Memory	2-GB DDR (double data rate), 266-MHz RAM
Hard disk	18 GB of available hard disk space
Network adapter	100-Mb or higher network adapter
Operating system	Microsoft Windows Server 2003 Service Pack 1 (SP1)

Table 2-7 Hardware and Software Requirements for CWA

Component	Requirement
Supported browsers	Internet Explorer 6.0 (SP1 recommended), Firefox 1.0, Safari 1.2.4, Netscape 7.2
Other	Office Communications Server 2007, .NET Framework 2.0, ASP.NET 2.0, Public Key Certificates for Transport Layer Security (TLS), and HTTPS

Web Components Server

The Web Components Server is an ASP.NET Web service running on Internet Information Services (IIS). This virtual directory is used to perform distribution list (DL) expansions and join users to a Web conference when they click on the URL given in the meeting request. This server role is automatically installed on the Standard Edition Server and front-end servers of an Enterprise pool in a consolidated configuration. In an Enterprise pool, expanded configuration, the Web Components Server is installed on a separate physical server. This server role is well suited to be collocated with the Communicator Web Access server role in the Enterprise pool, expanded configuration, because both server roles are Web services and require IIS. See Table 2-8 for the hardware and software requirements for this role.

Table 2-8 Hardware and Software Requirements for Web Components Servers

Component	Requirement
Computer and processor	Dual processor, dual core with 2.6 GHz or faster processor
Memory	2 GB or more of RAM recommended
Cache	1-MB L2 per core recommended
Hard disk	2 SCSI hard drives with 18 GB of available hard disk space recommended
Network	1-GBit NIC recommended
Operating system	Windows Server 2003 Standard Edition, Windows Server 2003 R2 Standard Edition, or higher
Other	Active Directory directory service for Windows Server 2003 or Windows 2000 with Service Pack 3 required

Mediation Server

The Mediation Server is a server role necessary to bridge the PSTN traffic to and from the media gateway to the Office Communications Server network. Because some existing media gateways do not currently support the SIP protocol over TCP and optimized media codecs used by Office Communications Server 2007, the Mediation Server is needed to translate the RTAudio and RTVideo codecs to the G.711 codec commonly used by media gateways. In addition to performing codec translation, the Mediation Server performs reverse number lookups (RNL) to resolve phone numbers from incoming calls arriving from the media gateway to the corresponding SIP URI. After phone numbers are resolved into SIP URIs, the Mediation Server routes the call to the user's home server.

Table 2-9 lists the hardware requirements for the Mediation Server role.

Note To get the most up-to-date information about the Media Server role, refer to *http://www.microsoft.com/technet/prodtechnol/office/communicationsserver/evaluate/sysreqs/ocs-ee.mspx#EBG*.

Table 2-9 Hardware and Software Requirements for Mediation Server

Component	Requirement
Computer and processor	Dual processor, dual core with 3.0-GHz or faster processor for up to 120 concurrent calls
Memory	2 GB or more of RAM recommended
Cache	1-MB L2 per core recommended
Hard disk	1 SCSI hard drive with 36 GB of available hard disk space recommended
Network	2 1-GBit NICs: one NIC connected to the Office Communications Server network, and the second NIC connected to the media gateway
Operating system	Windows Server 2003 Standard Edition, Windows Server 2003 R2 Standard Edition, or higher
Other	Active Directory directory service for Windows Server 2003 or Windows 2000 with Service Pack 3 required

Supported Collocation Server Roles

The list of supported collocation server roles for Office Communication Server 2007 is shown in Table 2-10.

Table 2-10 Supported Collocation Server Roles for Office Communications Server 2007

Server Role	Collocation Support
Standard Edition Server	IM Conferencing Server
	Web Conferencing Server
	A/V Conferencing Server
	Telephony Conferencing Server
	Web Components Server
	Communicator Web Access Server

Table 2-10 Supported Collocation Server Roles for Office Communications Server 2007

Server Role	Collocation Support
Enterprise pool, front-end server	IM Conferencing Server Web Conferencing Server A/V Conferencing Server Telephony Conferencing Server Web Components Server Communicator Web Access Server
Enterprise pool, back-end server	None
Web Conferencing Server	Standard Edition Server Enterprise pool, front-end server
A/V Conferencing Server	Standard Edition Server Enterprise pool, front-end server
IM Conferencing Server	Standard Edition Server Enterprise pool, front-end server
Telephony Conferencing Server	Standard Edition Server Enterprise pool, front-end server
Web Components Server	Standard Edition Server Enterprise pool, front-end server Communicator Web Access Server
Access Edge Server	A/V Edge Server Web Conferencing Edge Server
A/V Edge Server	Access Edge Server Web Conferencing Edge Server
Web Conferencing Edge Server	Access Edge Server + A/V Edge Server
Mediation Server	None
Communicator Web Access Server	Standard Edition Server Enterprise pool, front-end server Web Components Server
Archiving and CDR Server	None

Summary

Office Communications Server 2007 provides the following server roles with specific purposes for building your Enterprise instant messaging and conferencing infrastructure:

- Standard Edition
- Enterprise Edition

    - Consolidated configuration
    - Expanded configuration
- Director
- Conferencing Servers
    - IM Conferencing Server
    - Web Conferencing Server
    - A/V Conferencing Server
- Telephony Conferencing Server
- Edge Servers
    - Access Edge Server
    - Web Conferencing Edge Server
    - A/V Edge Server
- Archiving and CDR Server
- Communicator Web Access
- Web Components Server
- Mediation Server

The Enterprise Edition scales the capacity of the Standard Edition Server to a larger magnitude by splitting the different logical functionality into separate physical servers. The Director is a logical server role and really is a Standard Edition Server. What differentiates the Director from a Standard Edition Server is the lack of users homed on it. It serves to proxy or redirect user connections to the user's home server or home pool.

The Edge Servers are deployed in the network perimeter to enable connectivity outside the organization's private network. The Access Edge Server allows remote users to sign in to their organization's Office Communications Server infrastructure, and communicate using IM. The Access Edge Server is also required to allow internal users to communicate over IM with federated partners and with subscribers to any of the three public IM providers (AOL, MSN, Yahoo). The Web Conferencing Edge Server allows internal users to collaborate with external users. The A/V Edge Server allows internal users to communicate via audio and video with external users.

The Archiving and CDR Server serves the role of performing server-side recording of call details and archiving of all IM communications of employees within the organization's network, as well as outside the network.

Communicator Web Access provides a Communicator client experience from a Web browser for users without Office Communicator installed on their computers.

Additional Resources

- TechNet resources including webcasts, trial software, online course, and virtual labs can be found at *http://technet.microsoft.com/en-us/office/bb267356.aspx*.
- TechNet Technical Library can be found at *http://technet.microsoft.com/en-us/library/bb676082.aspx*.
- The Communications Group Team Blog includes announcements by the Microsoft product team and is found at *http://blogs.technet.com/uc/default.aspx*.

On the Companion CD

There is no Companion CD content for this chapter.

Chapter 3

Infrastructure and Security Considerations

In this chapter:

Microsoft Office Communications Server 2007–similar to previous versions Live Communications Server 2003 and Live Communications Server 2005–leverages other technologies to provide an integrated management experience and capitalize on existing technology investments customers might have already made. The primary technologies that Office Communications Server 2007 relies on are as follows:

- Microsoft Active Directory Domain Services
- Microsoft Windows Server 2003 operating system
- Public key infrastructure (PKI) (Windows Certificate Server and public CAs)
- Domain name services (DNS)
- Microsoft SQL Server
- Hardware load balancers
- Media gateways
- HTTPs Reverse Proxy (ISA Server)

Understanding How Office Communications Server Leverages Active Directory

If your organization uses Active Directory as its primary directory service, you certainly understand the value of Active Directory. It is worthwhile, however, to understand how the integration of Office Communications Server 2007 with Active Directory is beneficial to the organization and the IT administrator. This integration provides the following benefits:

- Global information that will be shared by all servers running Office Communications Server can be stored in Active Directory, instead of replicating the information across servers.
- Server information can be published in Active Directory for easy discovery and asset management. This makes it possible to remotely manage servers running Office Communications Server from any computer joined to the Active Directory forest, using the Administrator's tools that are installed as part of Office Communications Server.
- Users can sign in to Office Communications Server by using their Windows credentials, which provides a single sign-on experience. With single sign-on, users do not have to manage separate credentials.

Office Communications Server stores *global settings*–information that is needed by every server in the forest–in the system container of the root domain of the forest or in the configuration container. The choice is selected by the enterprise administrator during Forest Prep.

If the first option (system container) is chosen, Active Directory replicates information stored in the system container only among the domain controllers (DCs) and global catalogs (GCs) in the root domain. DCs and GCs in child domains will not have the Office Communications Server global settings replicated to them. Every Office Communications Server deployed in the forest must connect to a root domain GC to obtain this information. Because the best practice is to deploy servers running Office Communications Server in a child domain of the forest, servers will fail to activate if firewalls prevent them from accessing the root domain DCs and GCs–or if already activated, they will fail to start. Figure 3-1 shows this root domain GC dependency.

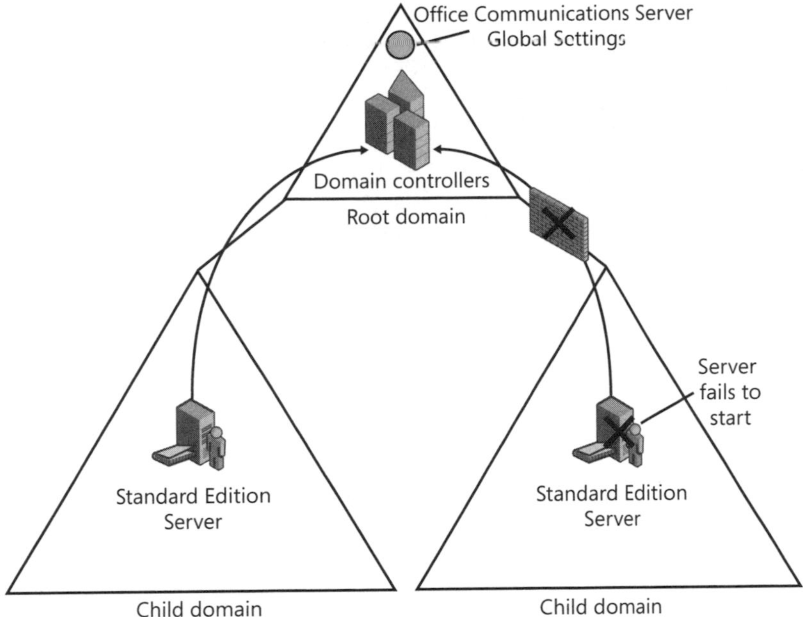

Figure 3-1 Global settings stored in system container—Root domain GC dependency

The problem just described does not exist if you select the second option–using the configuration container to store the global settings. Data defined in the configuration container is replicated across all GCs in the forest. This implies that servers running Office Communications Server can also contact GCs in their domain for the global settings. This is illustrated in Figure 3-2. If network connectivity between child domains and the root domain is slow, it is also recommended that you use the configuration container to store global settings.

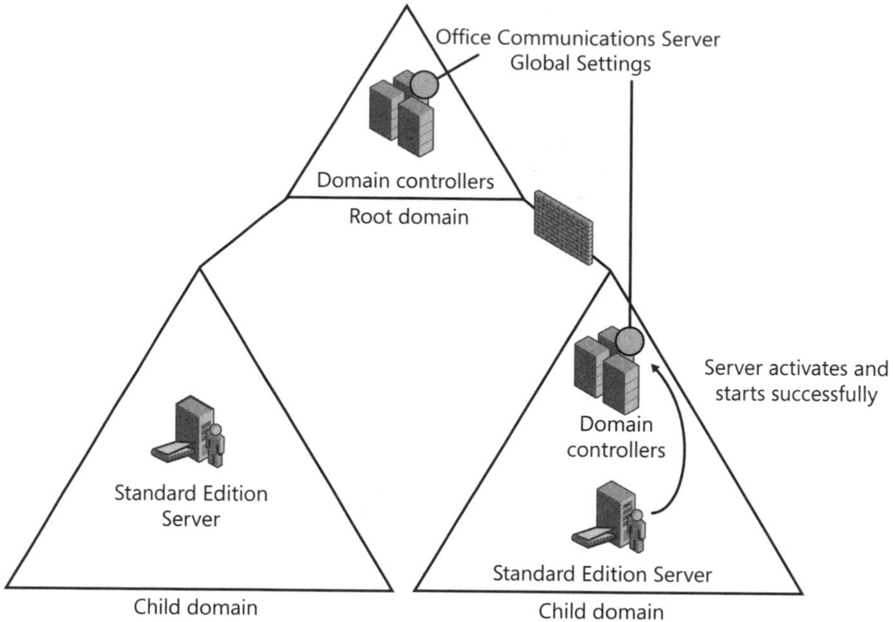

Figure 3-2 Global settings stored in configuration container—Local domain GC dependency

Office Communications Server leverages Active Directory to publish service information. This means every Office Communications Server role is discoverable by querying Active Directory. A visible example of this feature is the automatic population of servers deployed in your Active Directory forest when you open the Office Communications Server Microsoft Management Console (MMC). Office Communications Server publishes this information in Active Directory during activation. This is why activation requires RTCUniversalServerAdmins or RTCUniversalGlobalWriteGroup privileges and membership in the Domain Admins group. The Administrator needs sufficient permissions to write to Active Directory during activation.

During activation, the Setup program creates a service principal name (SPN) and registers this SPN with the service account used to run the service. By default, this service account is a user account called RTCService. The SPN is registered in the *servicePrincipalName* attribute of this object and is of the form *sip/<fqdn>*, as shown in Figure 3-3. For a detailed understanding of how SPNs and service connection points (SCPs) work, see the Microsoft TechNet article at *http://technet2.microsoft.com/WindowsServer/en/library/8127f5ed-4e05-4822-bfa9-402ceede47441033.mspx?mfr=true*.

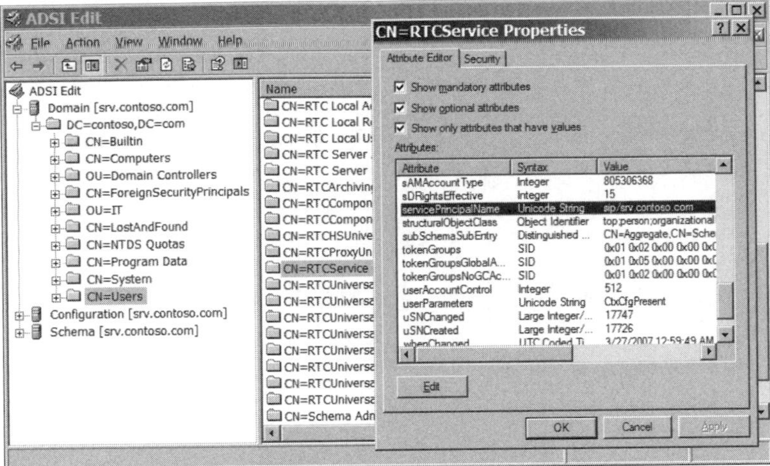

Figure 3-3 Service principal name

Activation publishes server information in three locations in Active Directory. Following Microsoft's best practices for Active Directory, Office Communications Server creates an SCP on the computer object belonging to the physical server where Office Communications Server is installed. By creating an SCP on the computer object, third-party asset management applications can query the types of services running on each machine. This SCP, called RTC Services, appears below the Microsoft node under the computer object. In the example shown in Figure 3-4, we use the MMC snap-in, adsiedit.msc, to view the SCP on the computer object called SRV. Of the most important SCP attributes (*keywords*, *serviceDNSName*, *serviceDNSNameType*, *serviceClassName*, and *serviceBindingInformation*), Office Communications Server 2007 populates only the *keywords* attribute with globally unique identifier (GUID) values to represent the service.

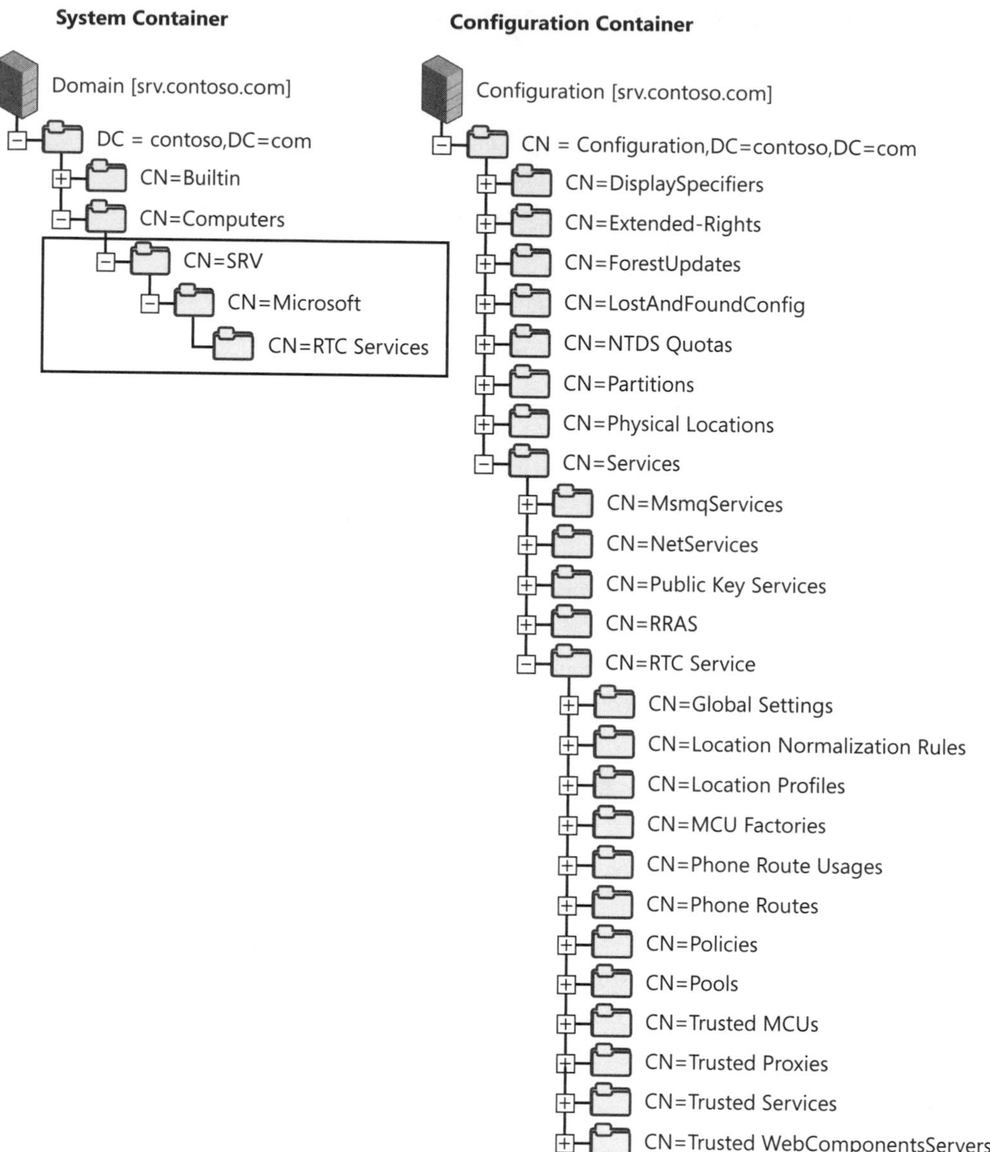

Figure 3-4 Active Directory global settings

Adsiedit.msc is available as a Web download from Microsoft as part of the Windows Support Tools. You must register the dynamic-link library (DLL), adsiedit.dll, first by running the following command from a command prompt window: regsvr32 adsiedit.dll.

When a Standard Edition Server is activated or when an Enterprise pool is created, Office Communications Server creates a new entry under the Pools container of class type *msRTCSIP-Pools* in Active Directory. Each entry represents a logical pool and is of class type *msRTCSIP-Pool*. The *msRTCSIP-Pool* class defines the fully qualified domain name (FQDN) of the pool, as well as the association between front-end servers and the back-end server to a pool.

You can think of a Standard Edition Server as a pool with a single front-end server collocated on the same physical computer as the back-end server. Every time a new Standard Edition Server is installed and activated, a new pool entry is created. This is not the case for front-end servers in an Enterprise pool. When a new front-end server is installed and activated, it is linked to an existing entry previously established when creating the initial Enterprise pool. The common name (CN) of each object created under the msRTCSIP-Pools container is defined by the name of the pool. Each new pool entry contains a subnode called Microsoft. Under the Microsoft subnode, the following subnodes exist: LC Services, LS WebComponents Services, and GUIDs, as shown in Figure 3-5.

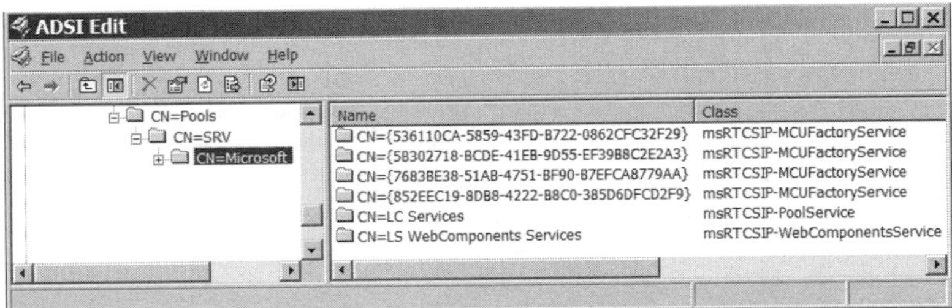

Figure 3-5 Pool representation in Active Directory

The LC Services subnode lists all the front-end servers as distinguished names (DNs) associated with the pool in the multivalued attribute, *msRTCSIP-FrontEndServers*. The LS WebComponents Services subnode lists all the Web Components Servers as DNs associated with the pool in the multivalued attribute, *msRTCSIP-WebComponentsService*. Each unique combination of vendor and type set of Conferencing Servers are represented as a GUID subnode of the *msRTCSIP-MCUFactoryService* type. Each GUID multipoint control unit (MCU) factory links to an entry in the MCU Factories container through the *msRTCSIP-MCUFactoryPath* attribute. The MCU Factory entry lists all the Conferencing Servers of the particular vendor and type associated with the pool. The logical representation of the relationship between pools, MCU factories, and Conferencing Servers is illustrated in Figure 3-6.

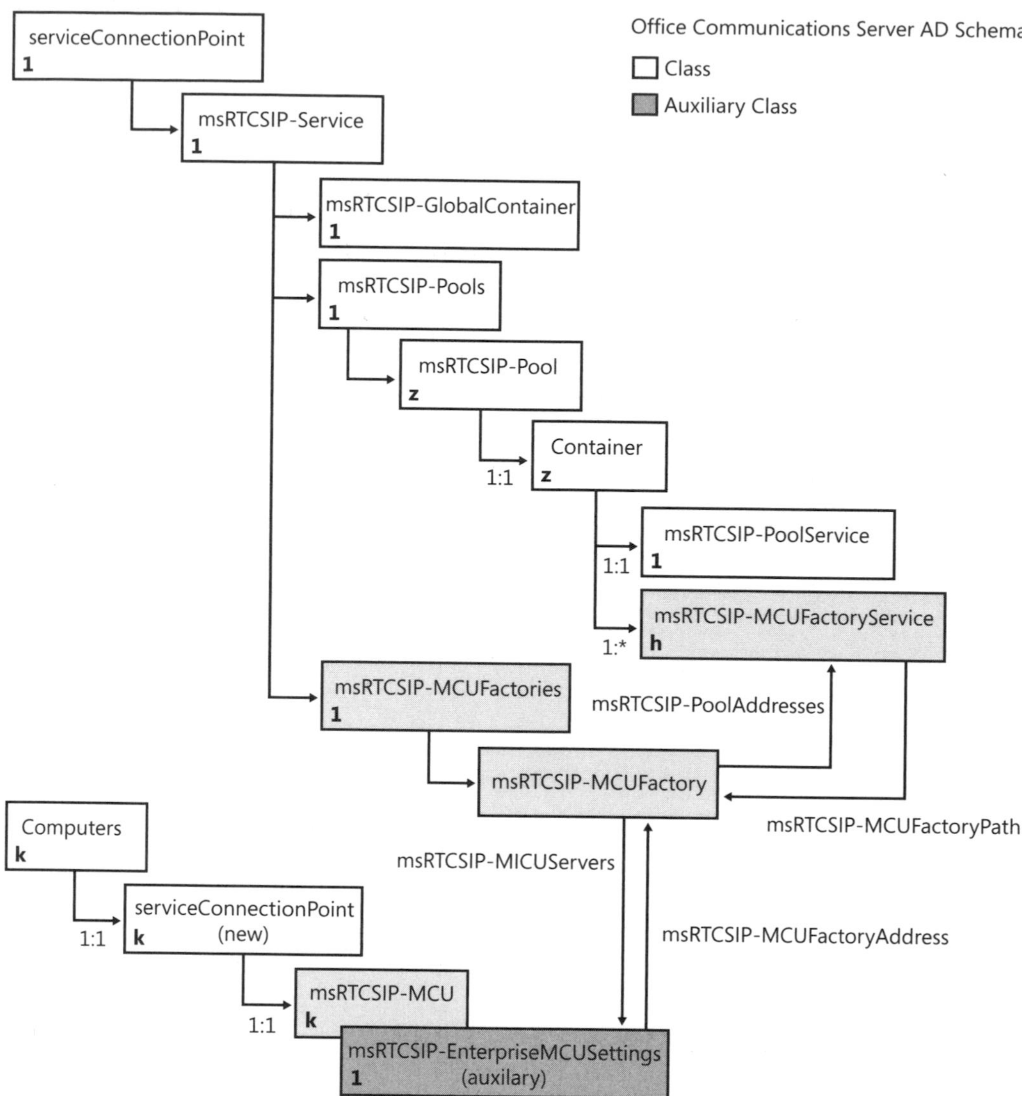

Figure 3-6 Logical representation of Conferencing Servers associated with a pool

The third location where the server information is published in Active Directory is in the trusted server list. The FQDN of every Office Communications Server server role is published. In addition to using server certificates to verify the authenticity of a server that claims to own a specific FQDN, the trusted server list is used to determine whether the server can be trusted. Without an entry containing its FQDN, a server is not trusted by other server roles and therefore cannot establish any communication with these other servers. If you find that users homed on a particular pool are not able to communicate with users homed on other pools, this could be the reason. Check that the pool's FQDN is listed in the trusted server list in Active Directory.

It might seem odd that every server's FQDN is defined again in the trusted server list when it is already available on the computer object. After all, you could determine the set of computers running Office Communications Server by querying all computer objects with the RTC Services SCP. The primary reason that Office Communications Server does not use this approach is security. By default Active Directory allows computer owners to modify the attributes on the corresponding computer object. This permission privilege allows a rogue user to modify the computer object to appear as a server running Office Communications Server. Although this is not necessarily a concern in all organizations, administrators might lock down this privilege, reducing this threat dramatically. By using a trusted server list that only an administrator with RtcUniversalServerAdmin permission can modify, rogue users cannot spoof their computers to appear as trusted servers running Office Communications Server.

Performance of the Office Communications Server 2007 management console is a secondary benefit. In most organizations, the number of computers tends to be at least as large as, if not larger than, the number of users. Querying all the computers in the organization to determine which ones are running Office Communications Server would be time-consuming. Such a query would have a substantial impact on the administrator's experience when loading the Office Communications Server 2007 management console. Searching a smaller list makes it possible for the MMC to load faster.

In previous versions–Live Communications Server 2003, Live Communications Server 2005, and Live Communications Server 2005 SP1–the way the trusted server list is represented in Active Directory is located in the System container under Microsoft/RTC Service/Global Settings as an *msRTCSIP-TrustedServer* class entry. Each trusted server entry is represented as a GUID under the Global Settings container. The GUID is generated during the activation step. To determine which GUID object matches a particular Standard Edition server or Enterprise Edition front-end server, you must look at the properties of the object in ADSIEDIT.MSC. The attribute *msRTCSIP-TrustedServerFQDN* contains the FQDN of the server that you can then recognize.

With the number of new server roles introduced in Office Communications Server 2007, instead of storing all trusted servers under a single container (Global Settings), new containers were defined to separate trusted servers based on role. In Office Communications Server 2007, these trusted server entries are located in the System container under Microsoft/RTC Service or in the Configuration container under Services/RTC Service. The various trusted server roles are defined in the following containers (and highlighted in Figure 3-7):

- Trusted Standard Edition Server and Enterprise pool front-end server entries are located in the RTC Service/Global Settings container. This location is the same as in Live Communications Server 2003 and 2005.
- Trusted Conferencing Server entries are located in the RTC Service/Trusted MCUs container.

- Trusted Web Components Server entries are located in the RTC Service/TrustedWebComponentsServers container.
- Trusted Communicator Web Access Server, Mediation Server entries are located in the RTC Service/Trusted Services container. Third-party SIP servers should create a trusted server entry in this container as well; otherwise, Office Communications Servers will not trust their servers and any MTLS connections will be refused.
- Trusted Proxy Server entries are located in the RTC Service/Trusted Proxies container.

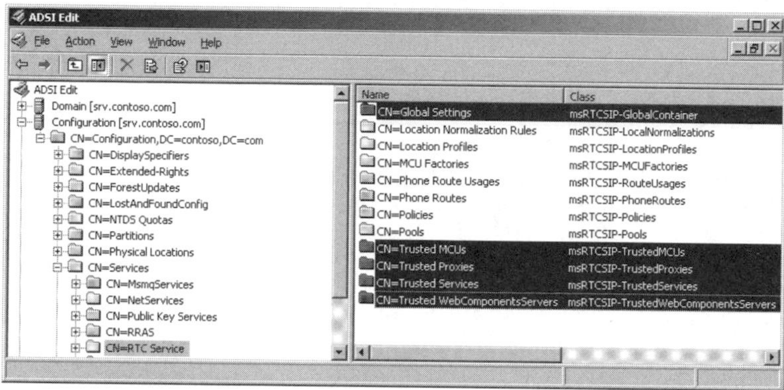

Figure 3-7 Trusted server representation in Active Directory

Note that not all GUIDs under the Global Settings container represent GUIDs of trusted servers. As the name indicates, the Global Settings container contains settings that are global to Office Communications Server.

In addition to storing global settings in Active Directory and publishing Office Communications Server information, all Standard Edition Servers and Enterprise Edition pools create an msRTCSIP-Pools object under the RTC Service/Pools container, as shown in Figure 3-8.

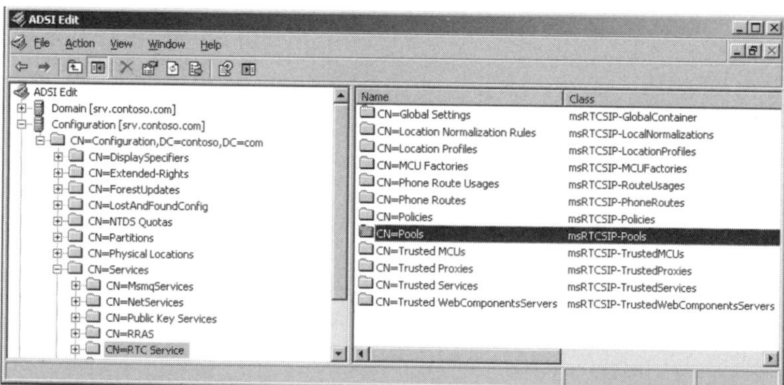

Figure 3-8 Pool settings

Each pool entry is associated with an MCU factory. Every MCU factory is defined in the RTC Service/MCU Factories container, as shown in Figure 3-9. An MCU factory is created when the first instance of a unique media type (defined by the attribute *msRTCSIP-MCUType*) and vendor (defined by the attribute *msRTCSIP MCUVendor*) of a Conferencing Server is activated.

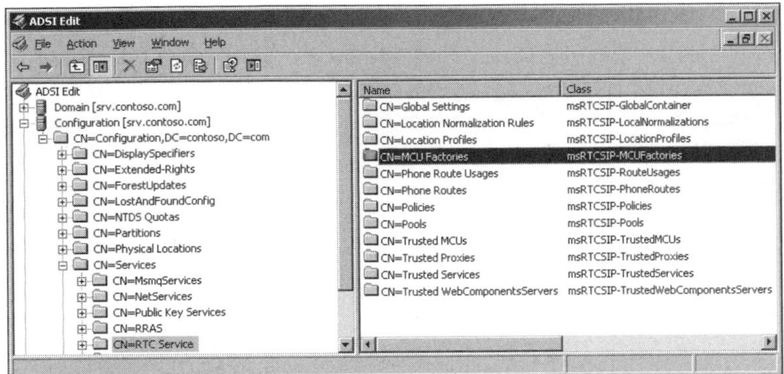

Figure 3-9 MCU factories

The currently available media types are as follows:

- Meeting
- Instant Messaging
- Phone-conf
- Audio-video

Chapter 5, "Conferencing Scenario," covers this area in more detail.

Office Communications Server 2007 defines Voice over Internet Protocol (VoIP) settings used to normalize phone numbers and translate phone numbers to SIP URI where applicable before routing the call to its destination. Figure 3-10 shows the classes used for VoIP. There is additional information on this topic in Chapter 10, "VoIP Scenario."

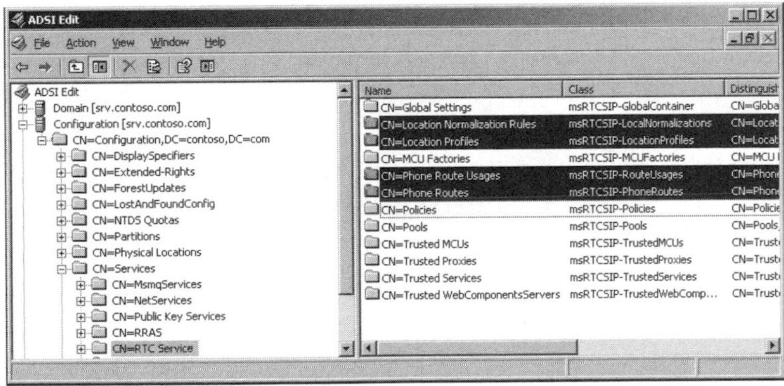

Figure 3-10 Global VoIP settings

The user class that represents a user account in Active Directory is also extended with attributes specific to Office Communications Server. Such attributes define settings that are configurable by an administrator member of the RTCDomainUserAdmins or RTCDomain-ServerAdmins group. Chapter 15, "Administration," covers user settings in greater detail.

Before Office Communications Server can add this information to the Active Directory services, the Active Directory schema must be extended. This is the first step in preparing the Active Directory forest. Office Communications Server 2007 requires the following three steps to prepare an organization's Active Directory forest:

1. **Prep Schema** This step extends the Active Directory schema with new classes and attributes specific to Office Communications Server 2007.
2. **Prep Forest** This step creates the global settings in the system container in the root domain or the configuration container of the forest, which are used by all Office Communications Servers. Universal groups are also created during this step.
3. **Prep Current Domain** This step must be run in every Active Directory domain where Office Communications Server 2007 servers will be deployed or where users will be enabled for Office Communications. This step creates domain-level global security groups in the domain where it is run. These groups are used to manage Office Communications Servers deployed in the domain. Domain Prep gives permissions to the Universal groups created during Forest Prep to properties on user objects in the domain.

These steps are the same in both the Standard Edition and the Enterprise Edition SKUs. It does not matter whether you complete them with the Standard Edition or Enterprise Edition SKU. Setup automatically detects whether any required steps were not run, and it prevents the administrator from activating a Standard Edition Server or Enterprise Edition front-end server until these steps are completed successfully.

Performing the Prep Schema Step

To fully leverage Active Directory, Office Communications Server extends the schema with requirements specific to its needs–similarly to how Microsoft Exchange Server extends the schema. Office Communications Server 2007 extends the schema with 45 new classes and 106 new attributes. A root doman administrator who is a member of the Schema Administrators group must run this step once on a domain controller acting as the schema master in the root domain of the forest. This step is illustrated in Figure 3-11.

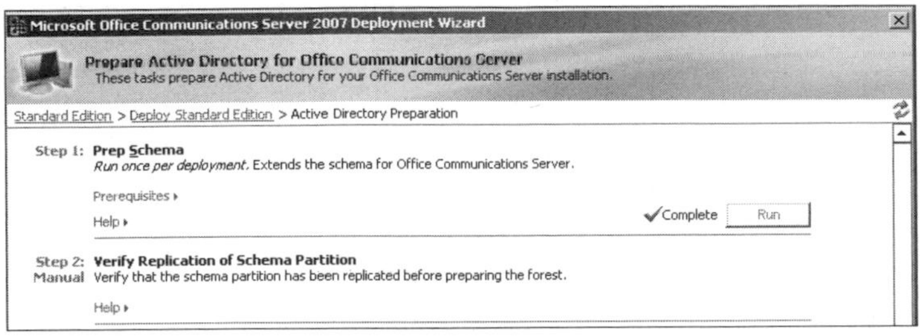

Figure 3-11 Prep schema step

All schema extensions start with a unique namespace that is specific to Office Communications Server. This namespace is called *msRTCSIP-"name"*, where *name* is the name of a class or attribute. RTC, which stands for *Real-time Communications*, was the original name of the product group at Microsoft responsible for building Office Communications Server. SIP stands for *Session Initiation Protocol* (RFC 3261). Office Communications Server 2007 is based on this protocol standard. By using a common namespace for all schema extensions, schema administrators can clearly identify which extensions are specific to Office Communications Server and know not to reuse them for other purposes. Setup provides a convenient way to verify that the schema extension has replicated throughout the forest before moving on to the next step, Prep Forest.

Performing the Prep Forest Step

After you extend the forest's Active Directory schema, you must next perform the Prep Forest step, as shown in Figure 3-12. No objects are created in Active Directory with the Prep Schema step. The Prep Forest step must be run from the forest's root domain and is run only once. Until Prep Schema is completed successfully, the Setup program disables this step in the same way that Setup.exe grays out the Prep Schema step.

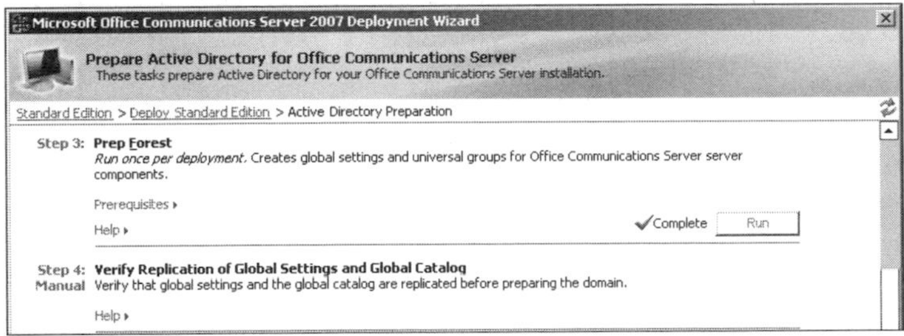

Figure 3-12 Prep Forest step

Running the Prep Forest step creates an instance of the *msRTCSIP-Service* class, called RTC Service. This container is the root where all global settings used by Office Communications Server are stored. Under this container are the following additional containers:

- **Global Settings** This container contains a set of attributes, plus the following three subcontainers.

- GUID of class type *msRTCSIP-Domain*. This object defines the default SIP domain name for which this Active Directory forest is authoritative. By default, the SIP domain name is set to the forest's root domain FQDN. Each SIP domain supported in your organization is represented by a different GUID of this class type. This setting is exposed on the General tab of the Forest properties, as shown here:

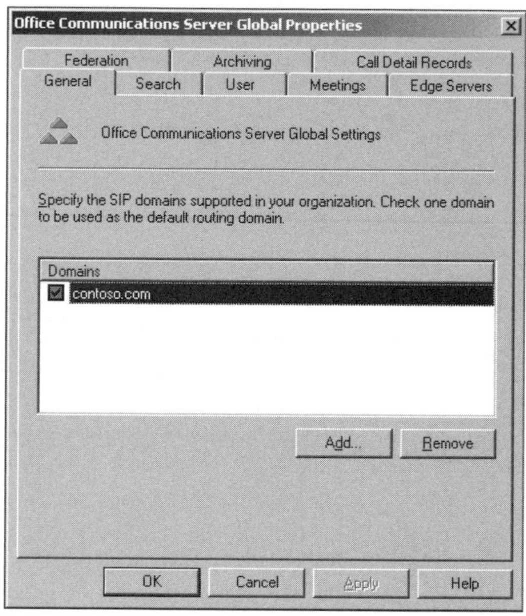

- GUID of class type *msRTCSIP-TrustedServer*. Each GUID represents a Standard Edition Server or an Enterprise pool front-end server that is trusted. This list of trusted servers is displayed in the tree view pane of the Admin Tools.
- GUID of class type *msRTCSIP-EdgeProxy*. Each GUID represents the internal FQDN of an Edge Server deployed in your organization's network perimeter and trusted by your Office Communications Server infrastructure, as shown here:

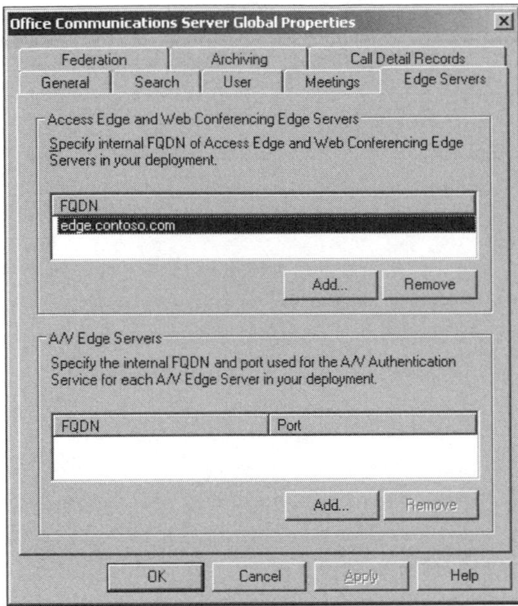

- **Policies** This container lists all global policies defined by the administrator. Users assigned by the administrator to a policy are subject to the restrictions defined in the policy. Office Communications Server 2007 exposes two types of policies: a Meeting type policy and a UC type policy. Each policy type contains a different set of configurable settings.
- **Location Normalization Rules** This container stores the set of rules defined by the administrator for how Office Communication Server clients should normalize phone numbers input by users to conform to the E.164 format. Each rule is composed of a pair of regular expressions (regex): the first regular expression is the match, and the second regular expression is the transform. This topic is covered in more detail in Chapter 10.
- **Location Profiles** This container lists all the locations defined by the administrator. Each location is associated with a set of normalization rules that represent the dialing habits that users for that region are accustomed to. This topic is covered in more detail in Chapter 10.
- **Phone Route Usages** This container stores all usages defined by the administrator. A usage is an arbitrary string that describes a set of routes. A phone route usage is associated with one or more phone routes. This topic is covered in more detail in Chapter 10.
- **Phone Routes** This container contains all the phone routes as defined by the administrator. A phone route is a rule that defines which Mediation Servers should be routed to by phone calls that match a specific number pattern. This topic is covered in more detail in Chapter 10.

> **Note** All the aforementioned settings are directly exposed in the Office Communications Server's Admin Tools. To access them, launch the Office Communications Server 2007 link from the Administrative Tools folder. Right-click the **Forest** node, select **Properties**, and then select either **Global Properties** or **Voice Properties**.

- **Pools** This container stores all Standard Edition Servers and Enterprise pools.
- **MCU Factories** This container stores all instances of MCU factories. An MCU factory is created when the first instance of a specific vendor and type of MCU (such as Conferencing Server) is activated. An MCU factory manages the set of MCUs of a specific type that belongs to a Standard Edition Server or Enterprise pool.
    - The MCU factory is associated with one, and only one, Standard Edition Server or Enterprise pool.
- **Trusted MCUs** This container lists all trusted instances of Conferencing Server. Office Communications Server 2007 creates an entry in this list when a Conferencing Server is activated. Office Communications Server blocks any communications with a Conferencing Server that are not listed in this container. It does this to prevent spoofing attacks (such as another server posing as a Conferencing Server). Office Communications Server validates that the FQDN listed in the Subject Name or Subject Alternate Name field of the certificate presented by Conferencing Server is listed in this container. If the FQDN of the Conferencing Server is not present in this list, the server is not trusted.
- **Trusted Proxies** Similar to the Trusted MCUs container, this container lists all trusted instances of Proxy Server. Instead of storing all server roles in the same container, Office Communications Server 2007 creates separate containers for each server role.
- **Trusted Services** This container is meant to list trusted SIP servers, including third-party SIP servers, Communicator Web Access servers, and Mediation Server servers.
- **Trusted Web Components Servers** This container lists all the trusted servers of the server role type Web Components.

After creating the global objects, Prep Forest creates the universal security groups that administrators need to be members of, Administrator servers, and users of Office Communications Server. These universal security groups are created in the Users organizational unit (OU) and can be found using the Active Directory Users and Computers console. They are summarized in Table 3-1.

Table 3-1 Universal Groups Created by Office Communications Server

Universal Group	Description
RTCUniversalUserAdmins	Members of this universal security group can manage users within the Active Directory forest who are enabled for Office Communications Server. Prep Domain grants this group read/write permissions to RTCPropertySet.
RTCUniversalReadOnlyAdmins	Members of this universal security group have read-only access to server and user settings in Active Directory.
RTCUniversalServerAdmins	Members of this universal security group can manage all aspects of Office Communications Server within the forest, including all server roles and users.
RTCUniversalGlobalReadOnlyGroup	Members of this universal security group have read-only access to Office Communications Server global settings in Active Directory.
RTCUniversalGlobalWriteGroup	Members of this universal security group have write access to Office Communications Server global settings in Active Directory.
RTCUniversalUserReadOnlyGroup	Members of this universal security group have read-only access to Office Communications Server global settings in Active Directory.
RTCUniversalGuestAccessGroup	Members of this universal security group have read-only access to certain Office Communications Server settings in Active Directory.
RTCUniversalServerReadOnlyGroup	Members of this universal security group can read server-related settings in Active Directory.
RTCHSUniversalServices	Members of this universal security group are service accounts used to run the Office Communications Server 2007 Standard Edition servers and Enterprise Edition front-end servers. This group allows servers read/write access to Office Communications Server global settings, as well as to user objects in Active Directory. This group has full access to RTCPropertySet. The name of this group might seem a bit cryptic. The "HS" in the name of the group refers to *Home Server*, which represents a Standard Edition server or an Enterprise pool.
RTCArchivingUniversalServices	Members of this universal security group are service accounts used to run the Office Communications Server 2007 Archiving and CDR Servers. This group provides permission to access the service's database.

Table 3-1 Universal Groups Created by Office Communications Server

Universal Group	Description
RTCProxyUniversalServices	Members of this universal security group are service accounts used to run the Office Communications Server 2007 Proxy Server.
RTCComponentsUniversalServices	Members of this universal security group are service accounts used to run the Office Communications Server 2007 Conferencing Server, Web Components Server, and Mediation Server.

Direct from the Source: Infrastructure Groups

The infrastructure groups that are used by Office Communications Server 2007 to build the other groups are as follows:

- RTCUniversalGlobalWriteGroup
- RTCUniversalUserReadOnlyGroup
- RTCUniversalGuestAccessGroup

Administrators should not modify permissions on these groups or add members directly to them.

–Nirav Kamdar
Senior Development Lead, Office Communications Server

Prep Forest defines two new property sets. With a *property set*, you can group a number of attributes into a set. You can apply security permissions to the property set, instead of to each individual attribute, through a single access control entry (ACE). These property sets are called RTCPropertySet and RTCUserSearchPropertySet and are of class type *controlAccess-Right*. They are defined under the Extended-Rights object in the Configuration container, as shown in Figure 3-13.

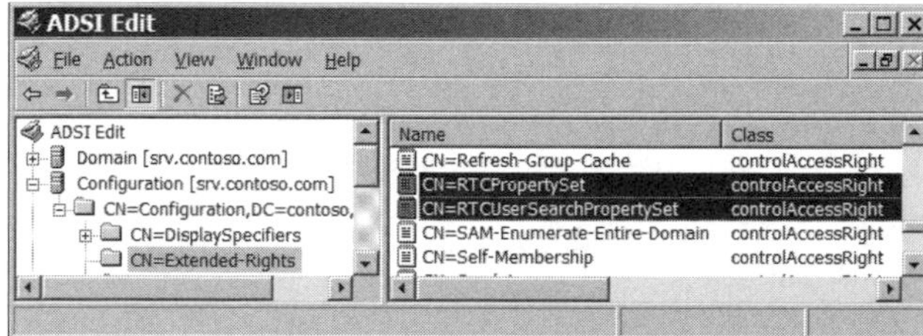

Figure 3-13 Office Communications Server property sets

The property set RTCPropertySet contains all the user attributes extended by Office Communications Server. To configure users for Office Communications Server, administrators must have read/write privileges to this property set. The RTCUniversalServerAdmins security group is given read permissions to this property set, so administrators of this group can view user configuration details but cannot configure users. The RTCUniversalUserAdmins security group is given read/write permissions to the property set, so administrators of this group are able to configure users for Office Communications Server. The RTCHSUniversalServices security group is given read/write permissions to this property set.

The RTCPropertySet property set is composed of the following attributes:

- *msRTCSIP-PrimaryUserAddress*
- *msRTCSIP-PrimaryHomeServer*
- *msRTCSIP-TargetHomeServer*
- *msRTCSIP-OptionFlags*
- *msRTCSIP-UserEnabled*
- *msRTCSIP-ArchivingEnabled*
- *msRTCSIP-FederationEnabled*
- *msRTCSIP-InternetAccessEnabled*
- *msRTCSIP-OriginatorSid*
- *msRTCSIP-Line*
- *msRTCSIP-LineServer*
- *msRTCSIP-UserExtension*

The property set RTCUserSearchPropertySet is used to determine whether a user is authorized to search other users in the organization by using the Find functionality available in Microsoft Office Communicator 2007. By default, domain users are allowed to search each other without restriction, and only the RTCDomainUsersAdmins group has full permissions on this property set.

RTCUserSearchPropertySet is composed of a single attribute: *msRTCSIP-PrimaryUserAddress*.

Performing the Prep Domain Step

After Prep Forest is successfully completed, the Prep Domain step becomes available in the Setup program, as shown in Figure 3-14. Unlike Prep Schema and Prep Forest, Prep Domain remains available to run again in another child domain where Prep Domain has not been run yet.

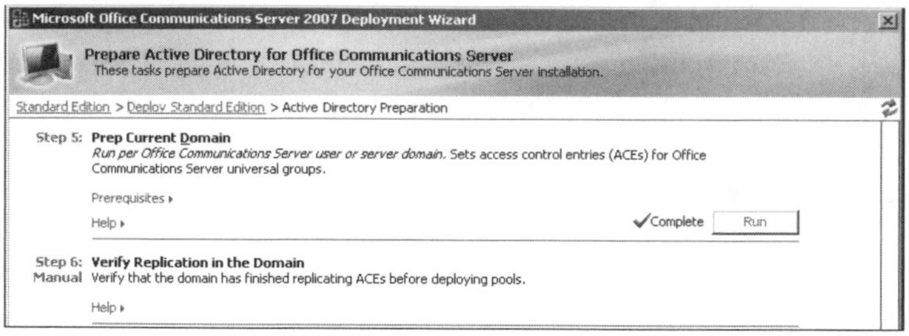

Figure 3-14 Prep Domain step

The general rule for knowing when to run Prep Domain is simple. This step must be run in every Active Directory domain where Office Communications Server will be deployed and in Active Directory domains where users will be hosted on Office Communications Server. It needs to be run only once per domain. If no servers running Office Communications Server will be deployed in the domain, running this step is not necessary. Domain Administrator privileges are required to run Prep Domain.

Prep Domain adds permissions for the universal security groups created in the Prep Forest step to manage its domain users.

Using DNS to Publish Office Communications Server

Office Communications Server uses DNS (Domain Name Services) to publish Enterprise pools and Edge Servers so that they can be discoverable by other home servers and Edge Servers. Standard Edition Servers automatically publish their FQDN as A (Host) records in DNS; however, the FQDN of Enterprise pools need to be published in DNS manually by administrators. Administrators create an A record for the Enterprise pool's FQDN, mapped to the virtual IP (VIP) of the Enterprise pool's hardware load balancer (HLB). To federate with other partners and public IM connectivity (PIC) partners or allow remote users to connect to the internal Office Communication Server infrastructure, the external network interface card (NIC) of Edge Servers deployed in the network perimeter must be published in the public DNS.

Office Communications Server introduces the concept of Session Initiation Protocol (SIP) namespaces or domains to route SIP requests internally and externally by using DNS. This is similar to how e-mail messages are routed.

When installing Office Communications Server 2007, the default SIP domain server becomes authoritative for the Active Directory's forest (that is, root domain) name. For example, if your forest's FQDN is *contoso.com*, Office Communications Server will be authoritative for the SIP domain *@contoso.com*. In the case of a multitree Active Directory forest, Office Communications Server 2007 picks up only the first tree's FQDN as its SIP domain. The other tree's FQDN must be defined manually. However, this default namespace is probably not the namespace you will want to expose externally. In most cases, you will want to make the user's SIP URI identical to the user's e-mail address for simplicity. This is not a requirement, but it keeps the user's corporate identity consistent. If your corporate e-mail namespace does not match your Active Directory root domain FQDN, you must change the default SIP namespace to match your Simple Mail Transfer Protocol (SMTP) namespace. Fortunately, you can modify the list of SIP domains.

You can easily modify the set of authoritative SIP domains through the Administrative Tools MMC. To open global settings, right-click the Forest node and then select Properties. The General tab appears by default. Use the Add and Remove buttons to modify the list of authoritative SIP domains, as shown in Figure 3-15.

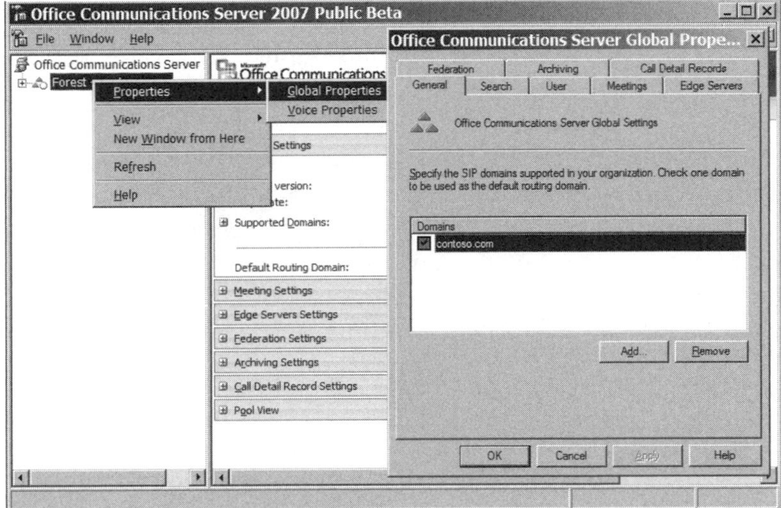

Figure 3-15 Configuring SIP domains for Office Communications Server

> **Direct from the Source: Default Domain**
>
> One of the domains must be marked as the default domain. The default domain is used internally by Office Communications Servers to address each other using Globally Routable User-Agent URIs (GRUUs).
>
> *–Nirav Kamdar*
> *Senior Development Lead, Office Communications Server*

Users in your organization must be enabled for Office Communications Server with a SIP URI that has a domain suffix supported by the Office Communications Servers in your organization.

After the initial configuration, there is little need to add or remove SIP domains; however, sometimes this need does arise. For example, if a company changes its public identity, the old SIP domain must be discontinued and the new SIP domain must be added. If a company with an existing deployment of Office Communications Server is merged with your organization and you want to support only a single SIP domain namespace, the acquired company's SIP domain name must be added to your Domain list until the migration is completed. For these and other reasons, simply adding the new SIP domain to the Domain list and removing the old SIP domain is not sufficient. In addition to this step, you must migrate all users whose SIP URI uses the acquired SIP domain to the existing SIP domain. To remain valid, each user's contacts also need to be updated from the acquired SIP domain to the new corporate SIP domain.

Migrate users from one SIP namespace to another

1. Add the new SIP domain to the Domains list.
2. Update each user's SIP URI to the new SIP domain suffix.
3. Update each user's contact to the new SIP domain suffix.
4. Update all Access Edge Servers' public certificates to include the new SIP domain.

Performing step 1 is easy; however, steps 2 and 3 become more challenging because there are no tools to perform these steps. Fortunately, Office Communications Server 2007 provides Windows Management Instrumentation (WMI) APIs that can be leveraged via scripting (for example, VBScript, PowerShell) to automate these steps.

One approach is to query all users in Active Directory that are enabled for Office Communications Server, determine if any user matches the source SIP domain to change, and change the domain portion of the SIP URI (leaving the username portion intact) to the target SIP domain desired. Because users could have added a contact with a SIP URI that you must change to match the new SIP domain name, this utility needs to "peek" into each user enabled for Office Communications Server, check whether any contact's SIP URI matches the same source SIP domain, and update the domain portion of the contact's SIP URI. Step 4 involves requesting a new server certificate from your preferred public certificate authority (CA) provider. For additional details, see the "Configuring the Subject Alternative Name" section later in this chapter.

Securing Office Communications Server with PKI

Because Office Communications Server 2007 leverages certificates to enforce the strong authentication of servers, it is important for Administrators to understand how Office Communications Server uses certificates. Certificates are digital equivalents to a driver's license or a passport. Their purpose is to authoritatively identify an entity–in this case, a server. Similar to a driver's license and passport, which identify your height, weight, hair and eye color, address, and so on, the digital certificate provides specific properties that identify the server.

Every certificate is tied to a public key. Any information encrypted with this public key can be decrypted only by the holder of the corresponding private key. This is a public and private key pair and is unique. If you have a public key, it's important to know who the holder of the private key is, thus uniquely identifying the certificate owner. To determine whether I hold the private key, you generate a random piece of information that only you know (that is, the secret), encrypt it with the public key, and send it to me. If I am able to send back the plain text (that is, the secret) by decrypting the message you sent, you know that I hold the private key to the certificate.

Knowing that I hold the private key proves only that much: that I hold the private key to the certificate. The certificate could claim that I am Kim Akers, in the same way that a fake driver's license could identify me as Kim Akers. How then do you determine whether the information contained in the certificate can be trusted? Because you cannot trust me to tell the truth, you must find a more reliable source to validate that the information contained in the certificate is legal. In the case of a United States driver's license or passport, this source of authority is the government of the United States. In the case of digital certificates, the federal government is not in the business of issuing certificates to private businesses and citizens. So you must rely on a trusted public certificate authority (CA)—such as VeriSign, eTrust, and others—to issue certificates that other organizations are likely to trust. Certificates for Edge Servers must be requested and issued from public CAs. To reduce costs, certificates for internal Office Communications Servers that interact only with other servers and clients within your organizations can be issued certificates from a private CA trusted within your organization.

Understanding how Office Communications Server uses the different properties of a certificate goes a long way toward helping you avoid pitfalls in configuring your servers. Microsoft TechNet provides a good overview of certificates at *http://www.microsoft.com/technet/security/guidance/cryptographyetc/certs.mspx.*

Configuring the Common Name or Subject Name

The common name (CN) of a certificate, also known as the *subject name* (SN) in the case of an Office Communications Server, identifies the server's FQDN, as defined in Active Directory. In the case of a front-end server member of an Enterprise pool, the CN must match the pool's FQDN. For a Standard Edition Server, the CN should match the computer's FQDN. You can find the CN of a certificate in the Subject field (on the Details tab) when viewing the properties of a certificate, as shown in Figure 3-16.

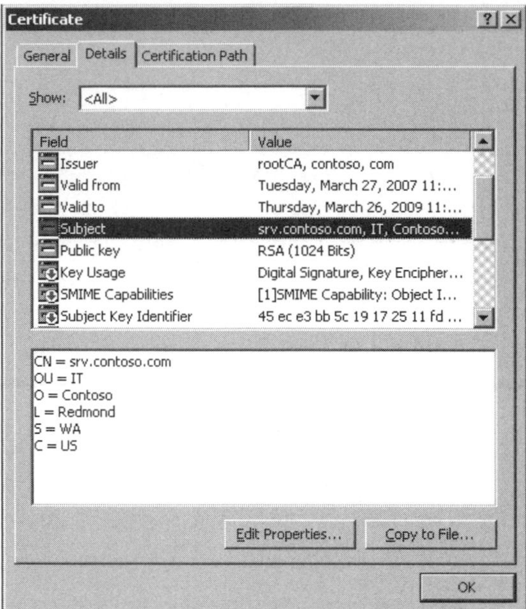

Figure 3-16 Certificate properties: Subject

Although an organization's internal DNS service is considered to be trustworthy, it is possible for a rogue server to do DNS cache poisoning and take over another server's FQDN. To prevent such possible attacks, the CN is used to authoritatively tie Office Communications Server to its FQDN. Office Communications Servers locate other Office Communications Servers through their FQDNs. After resolving the FQDN to an IP address, they validate that the server they reached is not a rogue server by verifying that the CN of the server's certificate lists the right FQDN. This allows any connecting server to authenticate the Office Communications Server. To verify that the server is an authorized Office Communications Server within your organization, the connecting server checks that the server's FQDN is listed in the Trusted Server list in Active Directory.

Configuring the Subject Alternative Name

The Subject Alternative Name (SAN) can be used to expose multiple SIP domains. An organization can have multiple SIP domains that it wants to publish to the public (that is, the Internet). Each SIP domain can represent a different business unit's brand of the organization. For example, the company Contoso, Inc. has three brands: Datum, Fabrikam, and Contoso. It would be confusing for customers, partners, and vendors who are unaware of this brand's parent structure to reach Datum employees with a SIP URI of *user@contoso.com*. It would be more intuitive for those employees to have a SIP URI of *user@datum.com*. Such an organization can expose multiple SIP domains to the Internet

The certificate of an Access Edge Server can certify multiple SIP domains by placing additional SIP domains in the SAN field. If a SAN field is present, the SAN should contain the CN of the certificate (that is, the FQDN of the Access Edge Server or the FQDN of the hardware load balancer in the case of a bank of Access Edge Servers) as the first entry in the SAN to bind the original name into the SAN, followed by the complete list of SIP domains for which your organization is authoritative. The use of SAN allows a single Access Edge Server to be authoritative for multiple SIP domains. Without this approach, you could expose only one SIP domain per Access Edge Server. This limitation would require deploying multiple Access Edge Servers when an organization needs to expose multiple SIP domains, as in the case of Contoso Inc. Figure 3-17 illustrates an example of a certificate with a populated SAN.

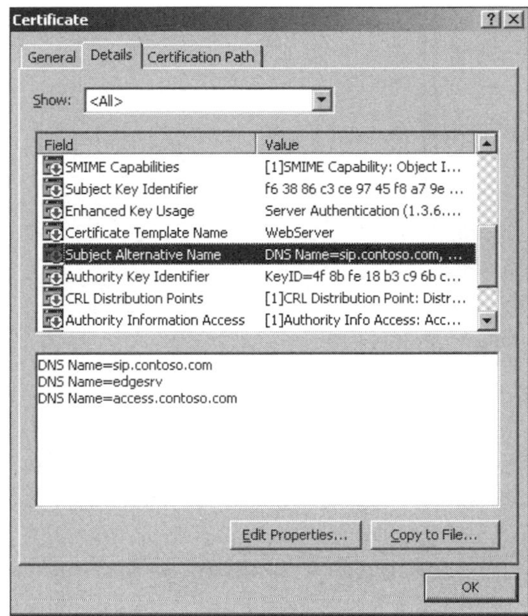

Figure 3-17 Certificate properties: Subject Alternative Name

Using a SAN can also be beneficial for your internal deployment of Office Communications Server, particularly when you do not want to deploy a Director. If the DNS SRV record for Contoso Inc., _sipinternaltls._tcp.contoso.com, points to the A record, *sip.contoso.com*, and if every home server's certificate contains *sip.contoso.com* in the SAN field, then clients configured for automatic configuration will successfully authenticate these home servers. Because the A record, *sip.contoso.com*, matches the server's certificate SAN field, users are able to sign in.

Configuring the CRL Distribution Points

The certificate distribution point (CDP) is a field used to publish the distribution point or points from where you can download certificate revocation lists (CRLs). The CRL is used to verify that the certificate has not been revoked since the time it was issued. You can download CRLs through a variety of methods indicated in the CDP. The most common CDPs are HTTP and LDAP URLs. Edge Servers should be configured to download CRLs. Figure 3-18 illustrates an example of a CDP.

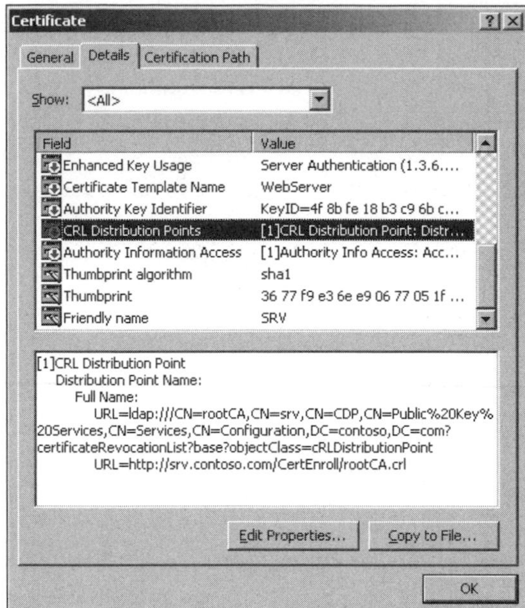

Figure 3-18 Certificate properties: CRL Distribution Points

Configuring for Enhanced Key Usage

The Enhanced Key Usage (EKU) field identifies the intended purpose of the certificate. If no EKU field is present in the certificate, the certificate is valid for all uses; however, the intended purpose of the certificate can be limited based on the EKU listed in the certificate of the CAs part of the certificate path. (Not having an EKU provides no limitations.) The EKU restrictions are inherited from the issuing parent CAs.

The two EKUs that Office Communications Server uses are as follows:

- Server Authentication
- Client Authentication

Figure 3-19 illustrates these two EKUs.

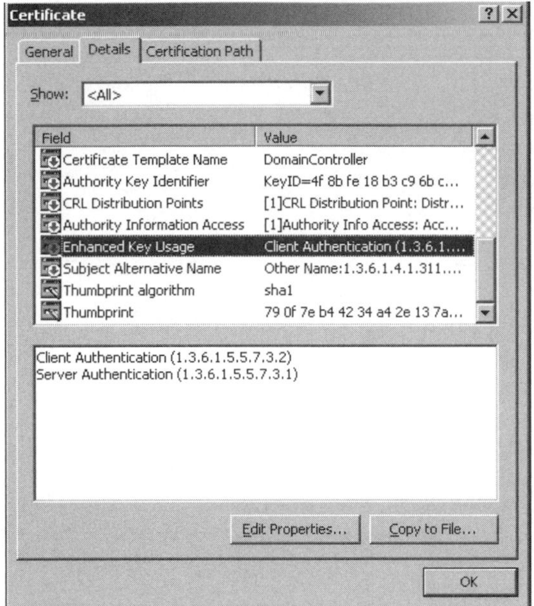

Figure 3-19 Certificate properties: Enhanced Key Usage

Server Authentication

This EKU must be present to grant the certificate the right to act as a server. This EKU is required for the host to be treated as a server when using mutual transport layer security (MTLS).

Client Authentication

This EKU must be present to initiate outbound MTLS connections with the following server types:

- Office Communications Server 2003
- Office Communications Server 2005
- Public IM Connectivity (PIC) to AOL

Office Communications Server 2007 removes the need for servers to have a client EKU when initiating outbound MTLS connections. However, AOL still requires this client EKU to be present in the certificate used by Access Edge Server connecting to AOL through PIC.

Configuring the Certification Path

The certificate must be issued from a CA that your organization trusts. The CA represents the reliable source that can vouch for the trustworthiness of the certificate. To view the certificate chain leading to its root certificate, select the Certification Path tab when viewing the certificate, as illustrated in Figure 3-20. If the root certificate or any of its subordinate certificates are not trusted or have been revoked, the certificate will not be trusted. This is especially useful when validating properties of the issuing CAs to make sure that EKU usage rights of interest have been inherited, as well as granted locally.

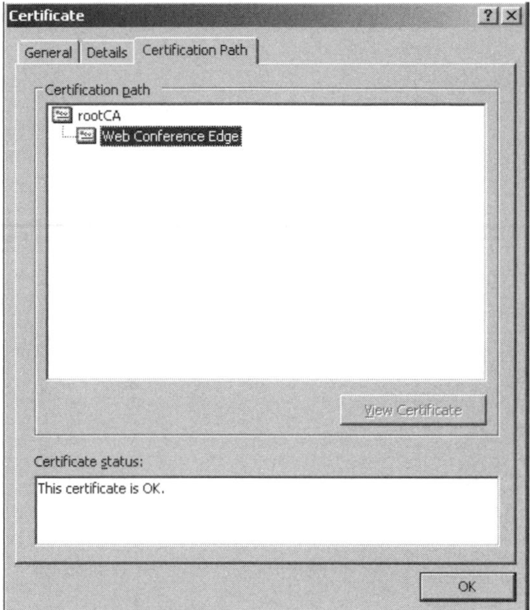

Figure 3-20 Certificate properties: Certification Path

Scaling with SQL Server

Office Communications Server 2007 uses SQL Server to store user and configuration data. The Standard Edition uses SQL Server 2005 Express, which is automatically installed by Office Communications Server Setup. The Enterprise Edition uses SQL Server 2005 SP1, which must be installed separately on the back-end server. The back-end server computer must be installed with Windows Server 2003 and cannot be collocated with the front-end server. Encrypted File Systems (EFS) should not be turned on in the %TEMP% directory; if it is, Setup will fail.

Note An easy way to verify that encryption is not turned on is to start Windows Explorer, type **%temp%** in the Address field, and press the Enter key. Right-click anywhere in the empty space of the folder, and select Properties. Click the Advanced button. Verify that the Encrypt Contents To Secure Data check box is not selected.

For best results, two hard drives with fast access time should be installed on the back-end server. One hard drive is used for the SQL Server database and the other hard drive is used for the log files. A 4-PROC server is the minimum requirement. For larger deployments, an 8-PROC server is recommended. A 1-GB network interface card (NIC) for the back-end server is recommended. Office Communications Server 2007 supports the use of 32-bit and 64-bit servers for the SQL Server back-end server.

You can build redundancy into the back-end server for the Enterprise Edition case. Office Communications Server 2007 supports only single-instance failover, also commonly referred to as *active/passive clustering*. A two-node cluster is configured to fail over to the standby SQL Server if the primary SQL Server fails. SQL backup and restore remains the supported way for interpool disaster recovery.

Building Redundancy with Hardware Load Balancing

A hardware load balancer (HLB) is required for every Enterprise pool. The HLB is an important element of the redundancy story offered by Enterprise Edition. An Enterprise pool contains one or more front-end servers that perform the same function. Therefore, clients can connect to any of the available front-end servers. It is important that the client does not need to know which front-end server it should connect to. By using an HLB, clients connect to a single FQDN and the HLB determines which front-end server should service the request based on availability and workload. After a client's connection is routed by the HLB to a particular front-end server, the HLB must be capable of routing all traffic from that client to the same front-end server for the duration of the user's session.

At the time of writing, Microsoft has tested and supports Office Communications Server 2007 with the following HLBs (see the Additional Resources section at the end of this chapter for the link):

- F5 Big-IP
- Nortel Application Switch (NAS)
- CAI Networks WebMux
- Foundry Networks ServerIron

You must configure a static IP address for the virtual IP address (VIP) of the HLB. The HLB must be configured with the static IP address of each front-end server of the Enterprise pool to load balance. For details on how to configure the specific HLB of your choice, see the Partner Documentation section at *http://office.microsoft.com/en-us/FX011526591033.aspx*.

Finally, you must publish the FQDN of the Enterprise pool in DNS. An A(Host) record must be defined for the pool FQDN, and the IP address to match to this FQDN should be the IP address of the HLB's VIP.

Select Start, select Administrative Tools, and then select DNS. Right-click your domain's node under Forward Lookup Zones and select New Host (A), as shown in Figure 3-21. Enter the Enterprise pool's FQDN in the Name field of the New Host dialog box.

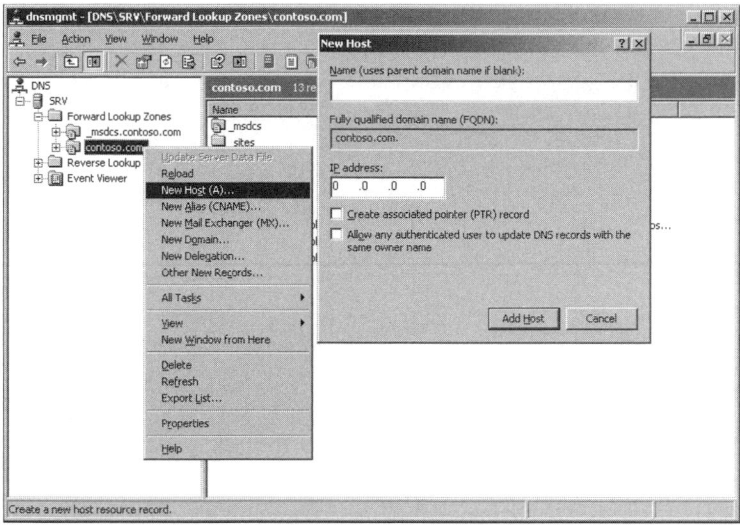

Figure 3-21 Publishing an Enterprise pool in DNS

Verify that you configured the HLB with this IP address, and make sure you can resolve the pool's FQDN. You can easily do this by performing a ping command. Open a Command Prompt window, and type **ping <pool fqdn>**.

The pool's FQDN is automatically defined once you specify the pool name. It is composed of the name specified in the Pool Name field and the domain's name shown in the Domain field in the Create Enterprise Pool Wizard. This is shown in Figure 3-22.

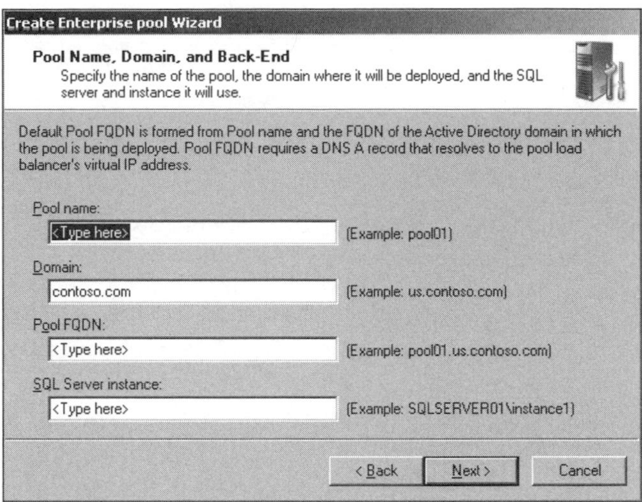

Figure 3-22 Create Enterprise Pool Wizard

The pool name can be any value you select, as long as it does not conflict with the name of an existing pool. The pool name gets populated as the common name (CN) of the pool object and the value of the *msRTCSIP-PoolDisplayName* attribute.

The SQL Server instance is parsed, and the server name portion is stored in the *msRTCSIP-BackEndServer* attribute. By default, if no instance name is supplied, the instances created are called RTC, RTCDYN, and RTCCONFIG. It is recommended not to specify any instance name when creating a new pool. The RTC database contains user and pool information synchronized from Active Directory. The RTCDYN database stores transient information, such as subscriptions, endpoints, and publications. The RTCCONFIG database contains pool-level configuration settings specific to the Enterprise pool.

Bridging VoIP to the PSTN Network by Using a Media Gateway

For voice calls from Office Communications Server 2007 to reach the Public Switched Telephone Network (PSTN), a third-party media gateway is required to bridge the IP network and the PSTN network by translating the signaling and media to the protocols used by each network, as shown in Table 3-2.

Table 3-2 Protocol Translation Performed by Media Gateway

Technology	PSTN Network	IP Network
Signaling protocol	SS7 and others	SIP
Media codecs	G.711	RTAudio
Transport Protocol	T-Carrier/E-Carrier	RTP (Real-Time Protocol)/SRTP (Secure RTP)
Network Type	Circuit switched	Packet-based

Such a media gateway is provided by Microsoft partners. (See the Additional Resources section at the end of this chapter for the link.) The two types of media gateways that Office Communications Server 2007 supports are:

- **Basic media gateways** At the time of writing, Microsoft has tested and supports media gateways from Dialogic, AudioCodes and Quintum.
- **Advanced media gateways** At the time of writing, there are no Microsoft partners that currently offer advanced media gateways.

The third-party basic media gateways cannot translate media from real time (RT) Audio codecs to G.711 codecs or the other way around. Therefore, a Mediation Server role provided by Office Communications Server 2007 is required to translate RT Audio to G.711, and it must be understood by the basic media gateway. If the media gateway does not support MTLS, the Mediation Server translates SIP from MTLS to Transmission Control Protocol (TCP). There must be a one-to-one mapping of Mediation Server to media gateway. You cannot configure a Mediation Server to service multiple media gateways.

The third-party advanced media gateways do not require the assistance of a Mediation Server and are capable of directly translating RT Audio to and from G.711. Essentially, the advanced media gateway incorporates the functionality of the Mediation Server in the media gateway.

Alternatively, if the media gateway runs on Windows Server 2003, it might be possible to colocate the Mediation Server and the basic media gateway on the same server, if supported by the media gateway vendor. Although not an advanced media gateway, this configuration improves overall return on investment (ROI), as it reduces the number of servers required to bridge to the PSTN network.

Publishing Web Interfaces to the Internet by Using HTTPS Reverse Proxy

Office Communications Server 2007 uses a Web service managed by the Web Components Server role to allow users to join a Web conference session, and it uses Office Communicator 2007 to expand distribution groups (DGs) and download the Address Book when connecting externally. Office Communications Server 2007 also offers another server role, called Communicator Web Access, for users to sign in to Office Communications Server by using a browser.

Internal users can connect to both of these server roles directly. For remote users and anonymous users, these server roles must be accessible externally from the Internet. The recommended way to securely expose your Web Components server is through an HTTPS reverse proxy.

Users directly connect to the reverse proxy on a secure connection (HTTPS) by using a published URL. The reverse proxy then proxies the client request over another HTTPS connection to the Web Components or Communicator Web Access server through a private URL. This is shown in Figure 3-23.

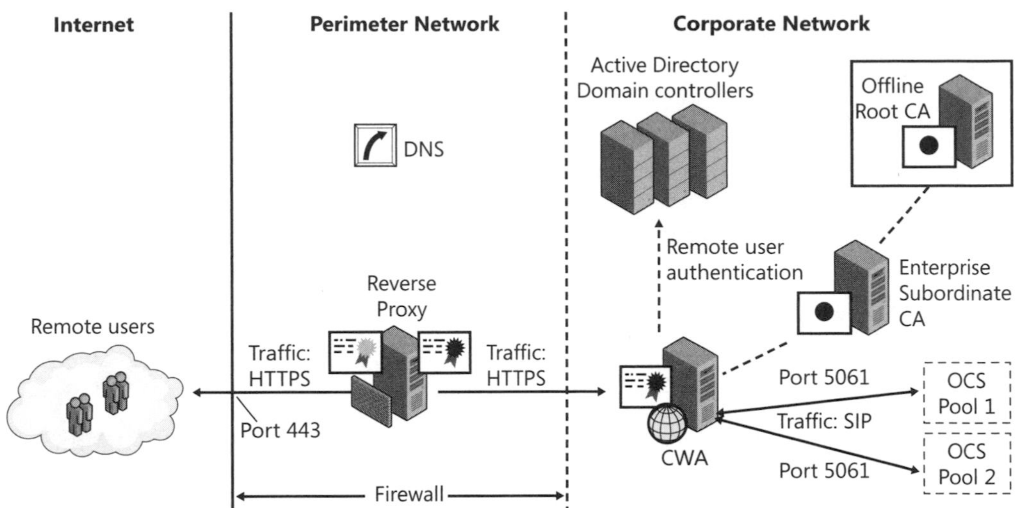

Figure 3-23 HTTPS reverse proxy

The reverse proxy is deployed in the perimeter network, whereas the Web Components and Communicator Web Access servers are deployed on the internal network. Any reverse proxy can be used; however, only ISA Server 2006 has been tested by Microsoft. For more information on how to securely publish Web applications to the Internet by using ISA Server, see the TechNet article at *https://www.microsoft.com/technet/isa/2006/secure_web_publishing.mspx*.

Summary

Office Communications Server 2007 leverages existing technologies to best meet its needs. Technologies such as Active Directory, PKI, DNS Server, SQL Server, ISA Server (as a reverse proxy), hardware load balancers, and media gateways support the deployment of Office Communications Server. It is important that you understand how these technologies are used so that your deployment of Office Communications Server is successful.

Additional Resources

- Microsoft Unified Communications home page at *http://www.microsoft.com/uc/default.mspx*
- Microsoft media gateway partners page at *http://www.microsoft.com/uc/pdgtrials/default.mspx*
- Microsoft load balancer partners page at *http://office.microsoft.com/en-us/communicationsserver/FX011526591033.aspx#5* (note that the list of partners for Live Communications Server 2005 also applies for Office Communications Server 2007)

On the Companion CD

There is no companion CD content for this chapter.

Part II
Key Usage Scenarios

In this part:

Part II of the Resource Kit describes several key features and usage scenarios that are enabled by Office Communications Server, Office Communicator, Communicator Web Access, and other components. These scenarios each have an introduction explaining how they are useful and why they are of technical interest to understand in depth. Each chapter also has an overview of the scenario from a user's perspective and then a detailed technical walk-through of the scenario.

Office Communications Server can be installed in many different ways in order to build server infrastructure to enable secure communications within and across enterprise networks. When Office Communicator connects to and authenticates with the Office Communications Server infrastructure, many useful communications scenarios become available. This infrastructure enables users to send instant messages to others individually or as a group and allows presence information that identifies how and whether to contact each person to be managed and shared. Security infrastructure is in place to help prevent anonymous spam, to prevent sharing more information than is desired, and to be able to prevent connectivity from undesirable external organizations. Chapter 4 will explain the basic login, instant messaging, and presence scenarios and then go into depth about how the technology supports this functionality.

Office Communications Server also introduces conferencing functionality that allows individuals to easily establish large virtual forums. Attendees can be contacted and brought into a conference directly, or a scheduled conference invitation can be sent out. These meetings can be open to anyone, open to any authenticated party, or locked to prevent uninvited participants. Because conferencing can support enterprise users connecting from the enterprise network, enterprise users connecting from the Internet, anonymous users from the Internet, and users from other federated partner networks, setting up remote meetings with a wide variety of contacts can be done easily, securely, and inexpensively compared to service-based, charge-by-the-conference hosting systems. Chapter 5 will provide an overview of conferencing and then go into depth explaining the technology behind conferencing.

Because Office Communications Server supports bridging networks with the Edge Server role, it is possible to configure an enterprise network so that enterprise users connecting from the Internet can authenticate and communicate almost as if they were inside the enterprise. Via the Edge Server role, Office Communications Server enables remote users and trusted partners who are also running Office Communications Server to operate almost as if they were inside the enterprise. Chapter 6 explains what is possible when connecting from outside the enterprise network and provides background on the security technology involved. Chapter 7 and Chapter 8 show how server infrastructure can be configured for the enterprise to enable secure, managed communications with other enterprises as well as public instant messaging providers like AOL, MSN and Yahoo!.

Office Communications Server also introduces telephony capabilities. Office telephony can now be integrated and controlled based on a user's commands or presence information. Chapter 9 explains how Office Communicator can be used to configure and control how phone calls are initiated or incoming calls forwarded and provides background information to help configure the network or troubleshoot to ensure smooth integration. Finally, Chapter 10 introduces the new devices that can be used with Office Communications Server, the way a phone network can be set up without a traditional phone system, and details on the technology used to enable these scenarios.

Chapter 4

Basic IM and Presence Scenarios

In this chapter:

This chapter introduces the basic login process, presence, and instant messaging (IM), and it discusses the services and capabilities that these provide. The chapter walks through a user-level view of actions taken in Microsoft Office Communicator 2007 for each of these three areas, and then explains in depth the same actions with a view of the protocols, algorithms, and systems that make these processes work. This chapter also provides the core background on basic server and client operations in terms of discovery, connectivity and communications over the Session Initiation Protocol (SIP) and as such is useful to refer back to as reference material when exploring other scenarios.

The login process seems simple from the user perspective, because it involves only starting Office Communicator 2007 and typing in a user name and credentials. However, this section provides a more in-depth understanding of how Microsoft Office Communications Server 2007 and Communicator 2007 interact to help provide security and to establish a reliable communications channel. This information is critical for troubleshooting user logins that fail, as well as providing the technical background to troubleshoot most client connectivity, authentication, or discovery issues.

Presence information can be managed and shared, allowing users to know if contacts are available, all available means to reach the contact, and how the contact might best be reached based on the contact's current activity level. This capability is critical for many enterprises, especially distributed or mobile organizations. Being able to receive notification when someone is at his or her desk and finished with a meeting, contact someone without having to initiate a phone conversation in order to get an immediate answer, or locate someone's contact information (including private information, if the contact allows it) all simplify communications in secure and productive ways. This section shows some of the user operations that control requesting presence information from others, publishing presence information, and managing and controlling how presence information is shared.

Instant messaging is a useful tool for getting quick answers from colleagues, reaching someone while in a meeting without distracting others, or receiving and acting on a message while in a meeting (rather than stepping out to take a phone call). This section provides an overview of instant messaging, for an individual and a group, as well as pointers for sending hyperlinks and emoticons. Even though these are relatively simple user scenarios, technical details on how these are accomplished and how content filtering works are provided to help with troubleshooting or configuration.

Understanding the Login Process

Before walking through the login process, it is important to understand why logging in is important at all, given the fact that it seems like such a simple operation. We will then walk through the login process from the user perspective, based on the steps taken and the feedback Communicator 2007 provides. Then we will walk through the technical steps, decisions, and protocols that are going on in the background. Doing so will provide a rich experiential understanding that will aid in troubleshooting login problems, infrastructure problems, and even extending the system programmatically.

Why Talk About the Login Process?

When looking at key usage scenarios for Office Communications Server 2007, simply logging in from Communicator 2007 is a critical step. When this works properly, it seems to be nothing more than a way to get access to interesting scenarios, such as instant messaging and presence. However, when there are problems with the system, logging in might be the key issue. Additionally, understanding the technology details behind the login process can be a key difference between becoming an expert administrator or consultant and simply having experience using Communicator. The simple login process exercises so many key aspects of the technology behind Communicator and the server infrastructure that it is worth understanding in detail.

Overview of the Login Process

This scenario walks through a fictitious user, Jeremy Los, using Communicator 2007 to log in to Office Communication Server 2007. Office Communication Server 2007 must have already been installed on the enterprise network, and Jeremy must have already installed Communicator on his workstation. This overview assumes that he has just finished installation and is logging in for the first time. However, much of what will be shown applies to subsequent logins as well. The overview shows what Jeremy sees during the login process and what steps he takes to complete the login.

Step 1: Signing In to an Account

Jeremy launches Communicator 2007 and clicks the Sign In button. Communicator asks for the Sign-In Address for his Communicator account, and he enters **jeremy@contoso.com**, which is the Session Initiation Protocol (SIP) Uniform Resource Identifier (URI) with which his administrator provisioned him, as shown in Figure 4-1. Most administrators use a URI that matches the user's e-mail address, because it is easy for the user to remember. Jeremy then clicks OK.

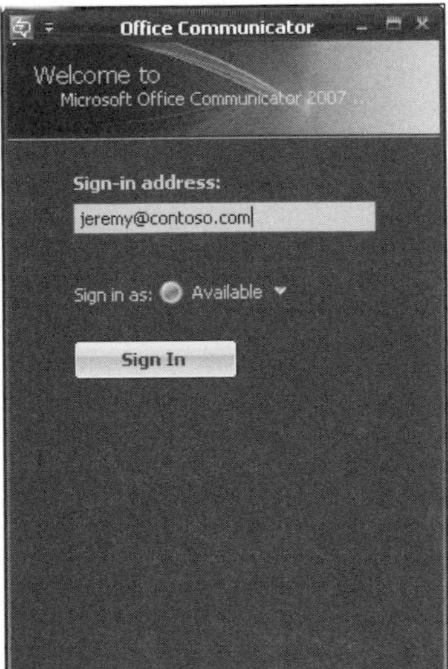

Figure 4-1 Communicator 2007—Sign-In

Step 2: Supplying Account Credentials (If Prompted)

If the user is not currently logged in to the workstation with domain credentials, Communicator prompts him for sign-in information. Jeremy enters his Windows Server operating system account user name and password, and then clicks Sign In, as shown in Figure 4-2. If Jeremy is logged in to his workstation with domain credentials, this step is not necessary.

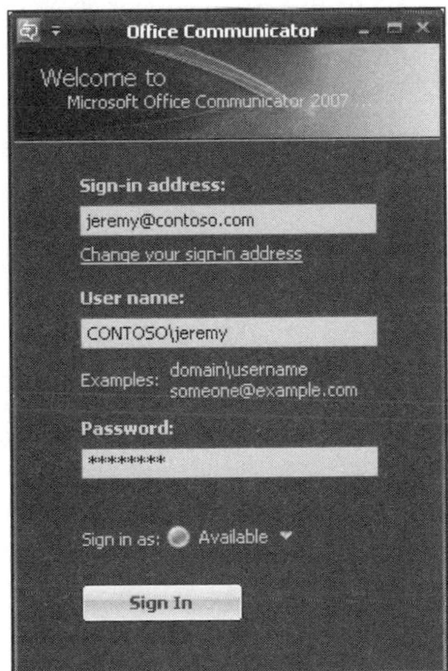

Figure 4-2 Communicator 2007—Credentials

Step 3: The Login Process

After Jeremy enters his credentials, Communicator begins the login process to Office Communications Server, as shown in Figure 4-3.

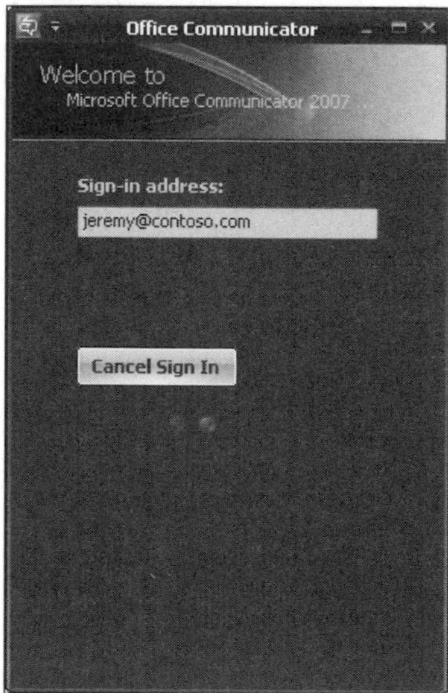

Figure 4-3 Communicator 2007—Login Processing

Step 4: Login Complete

After the login process completes, Communicator shows Jeremy's presence information, call forwarding details (if phone control is set up), and contact list, as shown in Figure 4-4.

Figure 4-4 Communicator 2007—Active

Examining the Technical Details Behind the Login Process

Let's explore what is happening with Communicator 2007 and the Office Communications Server network in technical detail at the network level. We will explore registry settings, logging, Domain Name System (DNS) usage, authentication, connectivity, and the SIP in detail, as they are all involved in the login process. The following diagram provides an overview of the steps involved in the login process, which we will analyze:

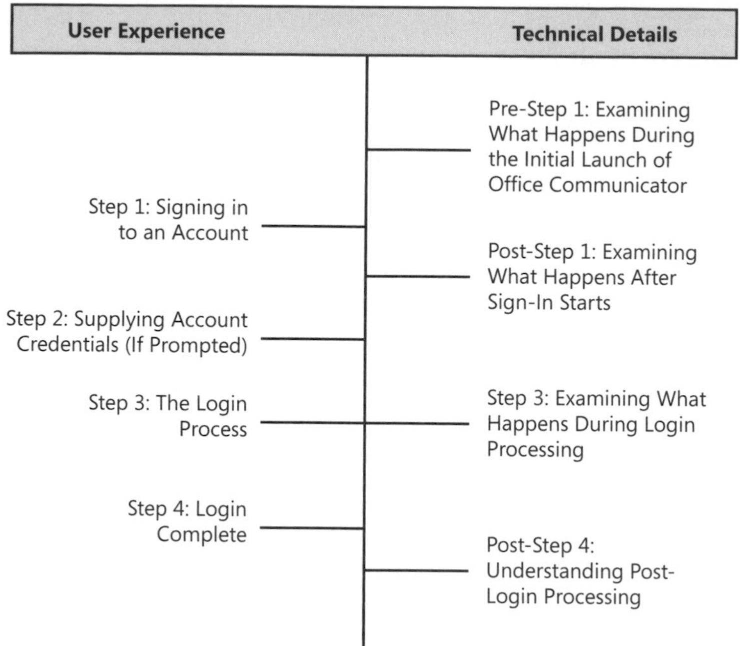

Examining What Happens During the Initial Launch of Communicator 2007 (Pre-Step 1)

When Communicator is first launched, it determines if a log of its actions and activity needs to be written. As of this release, Communicator logging can now be controlled through the General menu when you select Options from the Tools menu. There are two check boxes on the dialog box to control logging and event log messages. All of the protocol messages for the remainder of this section were captured by enabling logging in Communicator and gathering protocol messages from the log.

Note Even if you are a protocol and technical expert, you will likely find only about half of the contents of these log files to be of use, because they contain raw programmer data from the Communicator protocol stack. Because of this, it is best to use a tool to examine the log files, or read through the explanation of client log files provided in Chapter 16, "Diagnostic Tools and Resources." Also important to note is that in Windows Vista, a user must be a member of the Performance Log Users group to enable logging.

Enabling the Communicator Protocol Logs The logging options shown in the Communicator user interface (UI) manage values under the registry key HKEY_CURRENT_USER\Software\Microsoft\Tracing\Uccp\Communicator. The value *EnableFileTracing* can be turned on or off by setting it to 0 or 1, respectively. *MaxFiles* is set to 2 by default, but you can specify that only one file should be created or that many files should exist to maintain more history when the log file is recycled. *MaxFileSize* is set to 0x800000 (~8.3MB) by default. It determines how large the log file can get before it is cleared and starts over. *FileDirectory* determines the directory where log files are stored. It is set to %USERPROFILE%\Tracing by default. For almost all users, the default settings should be fine and no adjustments will need to be made, but it can be valuable to increase the maximum file size when diagnosing problems. Please note that manually changing these registry values requires a restart of Communicator, in order for them to be read and to take effect.

The default settings create the log in *%USERPROFILE%*\tracing\Communicator-uccp-0.uccplog, which is generally in C:\Documents and Settings\<*username*>\tracing\Communicator-uccp-0.uccplog. As previously mentioned, the default settings create two log files with up to 8.3 MB of logs for each. After the first file (mentioned earlier) fills, the second file, Communicator-uccp-1.uccplog, is used. After it fills, the content from it overwrites the first log file, it clears itself, and then it adds new content–until it runs out of space and overwrites the first log file again.

> **Note** Note that enabling the Turn On Logging In Communicator check box also creates an .etl file, which is used only by Product Support Services (PSS) to troubleshoot issues.

Working with Communicator Application Event Logs Even though the detailed log provides a lot of information, if event logs are enabled in Communicator, it also creates entries in the Application Event logs when there are failures, in order to provide diagnostic information. These entries are useful for diagnosing login problems. A few examples of messages are shown next for reference. They clearly explain the problem, point at the data related to the problem, and explain the steps required for solving the problem.

This first error message shown occurred because Communicator was configured with an invalid server name, IConfiguredAnInvalidServerName.contoso.com. The message explains that Communicator could not find a server with that name anywhere, as follows:

```
Communicator was unable to resolve the DNS hostname of the login server
IConfiguredAnInvalidServerName.contoso.com.

Resolution:
If you are using manual configuration for Communicator, please check that the  server name
is typed correctly and in full.  If you are using automatic  configuration, the network
administrator will need to double-check the DNS A  record configuration for
IConfiguredAnInvalidServerName.contoso.com because it could not be resolved.

For more information, see Help and Support Center at
http://go.microsoft.com/fwlink/events.asp.
```

The second event log error occurred because Communicator was configured to connect to an invalid port (9999) on the server, instead of a valid port (5061, for example). The message explains that Communicator was unable to connect and by using a tool such as winerror.exe or lcserror.exe, the error code can be interpreted. Error 10065 is the Windows sockets error code for WSAEHOSTUNREACH, which means the host was unreachable.

```
Communicator failed to connect to server srv.contoso.com (192.168.3.1) on port  9999 due
to error 10065. The server is not listening on the port in question, the service is not
running on this machine, the service is not responsive, or network connectivity doesn't
exist.

Resolution:
Please make sure that your workstation has network connectivity.  If you are using manual
configuration, please double-check the configuration.  The network administrator should
make sure that the service is running on port 9999 on server srv.contoso.com
(192.168.3.1).

For more information, see Help and Support Center at
http://go.microsoft.com/fwlink/events.asp.
```

Note Winerror.exe is part of the Windows Server 2003 Resource Kit Tools, and Lcserror.exe is part of the Office Communications Server 2007 Resource Kit Tools. Both of these can be found at *http://www.microsoft.com/downloads* with a search for either one of the Resource Kit Tools.

Communicator additionally loads up its configuration settings from group policy and the registry, and discovers whether it is set to automatically log in. For this example, it was assumed that it is not set to automatically log in, so it simply waits for the user to prompt login.

Examining What Happens After Sign-In Starts (Post Step 1)

At this point, Communicator must determine which server it should log in to by using the user's URI (jeremy@contoso.com) and any manual settings configured on the client. If manual settings were provided, the server to use is clear, but if the URI was the only thing provided, some discovery is necessary. The way in which Communicator does discovery varies based on configuration, because Communicator can be instructed to allow only Transport Layer Security (TLS) over Transmission Control Protocol (TCP), to allow only strict server names, or both. At any rate, automatic configuration takes over at this point to allow the server to determine where to log in. For additional details, see the "Understanding Client Automatic Configuration and DNS Discovery" section later in this chapter.

After the client discovers the server to connect to, it attempts to connect using TCP or TLS over TCP. This might have its own complications or stumbling points. If the TCP connection comes up and TLS will be used, the server provides a certificate to authenticate itself for the connection, and the client must validate the certificate. Finally, the client might negotiate compression (if using TLS over TCP), and then it will try to initiate a SIP registration. For additional details, see the "Understanding Connectivity Establishment and Optional Compression Negotiation" section later in this chapter.

Next, the client sends a SIP REGISTER message to the server without any credentials. This prompts Office Communications Server to challenge for credentials, and it allows Communicator to discover the authentication protocols that can be used for subsequent logins to this server. Without this step, Communicator does not know which authentication protocols to use, which information can be used for the authentication process (such as Kerberos or NTLM), or which service principal name (SPN) should be used when obtaining a Kerberos ticket. For additional details, see the "Examining the Initial Registration" section later in this chapter.

When it comes to providing credentials, Communicator has two options. Communicator can use the user's current desktop credentials to log in, or it can ask the user for credentials and they can be provided manually through the UI. This second option is what was shown earlier in the "Step 2: Supplying Account Credentials (If Prompted)" section.

> **Note** The credentials manager in Windows can also be used to manage credentials. More information on the credentials manager can be found in the Microsoft TechNet article "Windows XP Resource Kit: Understanding Logon and Authentication" at *http://technet.microsoft.com/en-us/library/bb457114.aspx*, in the "Stored User Names and Passwords" section.

Because of the order in which Communicator tries to satisfy the server's request for credentials, authentication failures can occur during the first part of login processing. This can happen when credentials are not already saved or if the desktop credentials do not match the account that Communicator is trying to use. This can also happen when the SIP URI, account name, or password is typed incorrectly or when credentials and the SIP URI do not match. An example of this is if Jeremy tries to log in with the URI sip:jeremy@contoso.com, but he uses the user account and password for CONTOSO\vadim instead of the account owner's own credentials, CONTOSO\jeremy. For additional details, see the "Examining the Authenticated Registration" section later in the chapter.

Understanding Client Automatic Configuration and DNS Discovery When the client is set to use automatic configuration, it leverages the SIP URI that was provided to discover where it should log in to. Communicator does this using DNS SRV records published for the domain portion of the SIP URI. For example, if sip:jeremy@contoso.com is the URI that is provided, Communicator takes *contoso.com* and tries to discover a SIP server using DNS. Communicator can query for the following SRV records in its search for an appropriate server:

- _sipinternaltls._tcp.contoso.com
- _sipinternal._tcp.contoso.com
- _sip._tls.contoso.com

Failing these, it falls back to host (A) record queries:

- sipinternal.contoso.com
- sipexternal.contoso.com

The first query looks for an internal server in the contoso.com domain that offers ports supporting TLS over TCP for clients. The second query seeks to discover an internal server in the contoso.com domain that offers TCP ports for clients. Finally, the third query looks for an Internet-reachable server for the contoso.com domain that offers ports supporting TLS over TCP for clients. Communicator never looks for an Internet-reachable server that supports TCP, because use of clear-text SIP on the Internet does not make sense from a security standpoint. In other words, Communicator is not aware whether the network that is being used is internal or external. Communicator queries for all DNS SRV records; however, it tries TLS over TCP connections first. TLS over TCP is forced through an Edge Server (no option to allow for unsecured TCP connections).

Finally, if all the DNS SRV records do not exist (not if they fail to be valid; only if they do not exist at all), the client falls back to sipinternal.<*URI domain*> and attempts to resolve that hostname. If the hostname resolves to an IP address, Communicator tries to connect using TLS over TCP, TCP, or both, depending on what the policy allows. If this fails, it will try one last time with sipexternal.<*URI domain*>.

Communicator policies can be put in place to prevent TCP from being used, and this prevents the second query from being issued. Policy can also be specified that requires strict names for the machines discovered. In this case, the only server name allowed is 'sip.' If this limitation is not imposed, any server name of the form <servername>.<URI domain> is allowed. As an example, for sip:jeremy@contoso.com, the host sip.contoso.com is always allowed (strict policy or not). Server77.contoso.com, sipfed.contoso.com, and ap.contoso.com are all also allowed if strict naming policy is not enabled. The following server names are never allowed because they do not tightly fit the domain that the user's URI specified, and therefore, the client does not trust these servers as valid login points: sip.eng.contoso.com, sip.contoso.net, sip.com, sip.contoso.com.cpandl.com, and so on.

This tight validation between the hostname and the URI is done specifically because the only configuration with which the client is provided is the SIP URI. Because of this, the client must be very careful not to allow DNS attacks to allow it to connect to any man-in-the-middle, who could thereby watch Communicator's traffic. By having a tight tie between the URI and the hostnames allowed for login, Communicator has better certainty that the certificate the user is validating actually has authority for the domain to which he is trying to log in.

After the hostname is identified, Communicator also resolves the hostname to an IP address. This usually happens as the result of the DNS SRV request, but until the IP address is resolved, Communicator cannot connect. This can be a problem during login as well.

The latest version of Communicator enables the ability to manually specify *both* an internal and external server to log in against. Communicator always attempts to connect to the internal server if it is available, but it falls back to the external server. Previously, Communicator had only a single manual entry, which created problems for mobile workers. With the ability to specify an internal and external server, it is now easy for administrators to configure and enable laptop configurations that work across internal and external networks. This increased functionality is also important for companies where the domain in the user's URI is not the same as their SIP enterprise server's domain. Because the administrator can configure Communicator (on a laptop, for example) once, the user does not need to remember the internal or external servers and administrators do not have to publish DNS SRV records for all the domains they want to support for remote access users.

New Features of Communicator 2007

Organizations with a large number of domains (such as sales or service companies that own or host large numbers of domains for a variety of users) will be very interested in these new configuration settings in Communicator. This functionality allows these organizations to simply configure Communicator without having to worry about setting up DNS entries and certificate credentials for all the domains they host. Additionally, Communicator now tries to connect to both manually specified servers—the internal server first and *then* the external server—if both can be resolved through DNS.

One great update is that Communicator 2007 handles fall-back during automatic configuration when both the internal and external SRV records are published, the host A records are published, but the internal hosts are not reachable. This allows seamless logins across all DNS publishing schemes instead of requiring separate publishing rules for the internal and external networks. As an aside, Communicator will connect with TLS over TCP if it gets a response for TLS over TCP, but will connect over unsecured TCP if that is the only supported option provided by the SRV records. More about these DNS SRV records and concepts (as they relate to Federation) is covered in Chapter 7, "Federation Scenario."

Understanding Connectivity Establishment and Optional Compression Negotiation

When a TCP or TLS over TCP connection is established with the server, there are some basic things that can go wrong. To start with, the IP address could be unreachable because of firewalls, service outage, or lack of connectivity. It might be possible to create a connection, but traffic on the connection could be filtered, or the connection could be torn down by an intermediary firewall or proxy.

Note To verify network connectivity, you can use ping.exe <*server_FQDN*> to connect to the server and telnet.exe <*server_FQDN*> 5060 or 5061 to see if the server is listening. As an aside, for Windows Vista workstations the telnet.exe is not installed by default. It can, however, be enabled via the Control Panel by enabling the Windows feature named Telnet Client.

If connectivity is not an issue, TLS negotiation might take place. TLS negotiation involves an exchange of credentials from the server and the exchange of a symmetric encryption key that is used to authenticate and encrypt the secure channel. This can fail when Communicator attempts TLS negotiation to an Office Communications Server port that is configured for only "TCP," when the server's certificate does not pass validation, or when the server wants to support only servers on a mutual transport layer security (MTLS) port and closes the connection when Communicator cannot provide a valid server certificate.

> **Note** A technical reference for TLS can be found by searching for the Microsoft TechNet article "TLS/SSL Technical Reference" at *http://technet.microsoft.com*.

If Communicator validates the server certificate, Communicator might request compression on the connection. Communicator enables compression only on encrypted links, and it determines whether to enable compression based on group policy settings (which defaults to enabling compression when there is less than or equal to a 128-Kb link speed). Communicator negotiates compression by using a NEGOTIATE request immediately after TLS is established. This message is only sent hop-to-hop for a given connection. The server can accept or reject this request based on its configuration. By default, the server accepts client compression requests.

Real World: Testing Certificates

How do you validate a certificate? By using the trusted authority and the certificate revocation list!

To view the list of certificates on the computer, use the following commands:

```
certutil -store MY
certutil -store enterprise
```

To export a certificate for analysis (high-level):

1. Export the bad certificate to a *.cer file format, and have the customer send it to you via e-mail.
2. Run **certutil -verify -urlfetch *.cer >c:\cert.txt** from the customer's machine.
3. Check for the subject of the certificate.
4. Check for the validity date.
5. Check the key usage.
6. Check for a valid certificate revocation list (CRL).
7. Check for trust for the Issuer.

Now, if you need the explicit instructions, here they are.

To export a certificate for analysis (detail-level):

1. Load the Certificates MMC snap-in focused on the local computer. This requires Administrator credentials.
2. Click Start, click Run, type **mmc.exe**, and press Enter.
3. Click the File menu, and select Add/Remove Snap-in.
4. Click the Add button.
5. Select Certificates from the list of snap-ins, and click Add.
6. Select User Or Computer Account, and click Next.
7. Select Local Computer, and click Finish.
8. Click Close, and then click OK.
9. Expand Certificates (Local Computer/User).
10. Expand the Personal folder, and select Certificates.
11. Export the certificate.
12. In the list of certificates, select the one you want to export.
13. Right-click and select All Tasks, and then select Export. This will start the Certificate Export Wizard.
14. Click Next.
15. Select No, Do Not Export The Private Key.
16. Click Next.
17. Select DER Encoded Binary X.509 (.cer), and click Next.
18. Enter the location and file name for the file, and click Next.
19. Click Finish.
20. Click OK.

Warning! We do not recommend exporting the private key and sending it to Microsoft. This is a security risk and often not required to resolve the problem.

–Thomas Laciano
Program Manager, RTC Customer Experience

Examining the Initial Registration After connectivity is established, the initial registration from the client is made to ensure that SIP is allowed on this port and to discover what authentication mechanism should be used with the server. A SIP REGISTER message is used for this purpose, and here is an example of that request:

```
REGISTER sip:contoso.com SIP/2.0
Via: SIP/2.0/TLS 192.168.3.100:2060
Max-Forwards: 70
From: <sip:jeremy@contoso.com>;tag=7ad9af1eb1;epid=aa6d968e18
To: <sip:jeremy@contoso.com>
Call-ID: 5d2ad5f9e7a24dacaf1075b97a04df91
CSeq: 1 REGISTER
Contact: <sip:192.168.3.100:2060;transport= tls;ms-opaque=aacb364544>;methods="INVITE,
MESSAGE, INFO, OPTIONS, BYE, CANCEL, NOTIFY, ACK, REFER,
BENOTIFY";proxy=replace;+sip.instance= "<urn:uuid:6BF396BA-A7D6-5247-89FB-C13B52F5840D>"
User-Agent: UCCP/2.0.6093.0 OC/2.0.6093.0 (Microsoft Office Communicator)
Supported: gruu-10, adhoclist, msrtc-event-categories
Supported: ms-forkingms-keep-alive: UAC;hop-hop=yes
Event: registrationContent-Length: 0
```

Note Access to raw protocol logs is available in Communicator with this release simply by selecting a check box in the configuration process. A walkthrough of how to enable logging and a pointer to where the log files show up can be found in the "Examining What Happens During the Initial Launch of Communicator 2007 (Pre-Step 1)" section earlier in this chapter.

The server's expected response is to challenge the request for authentication. In the response shown next, the server is asking for Kerberos or NTLM authentication so that Communicator knows what authentication mechanisms can be used and also knows (for this connection) which server it needs to authenticate against (srv.contoso.com).

```
SIP/2.0 401 Unauthorized
Date: Fri, 04 May 2007 22:48:06 GMT
WWW-Authenticate: NTLM realm="SIP Communications Service",
targetname="srv.contoso.com", version=3
WWW-Authenticate: Kerberos realm="SIP Communications Service",
targetname="sip/srv.contoso.com", version=3
Via: SIP/2.0/TLS 192.168.3.100:2060;ms-received-port=2060;ms-received-cid=2600
From: <sip:jeremy@contoso.com>;tag=7ad9af1eb1;epid=aa6d968e18
To: <sip:jeremy@contoso.com>;tag=A1F542AB99D66616F9252CB6DF50257F
Call-ID: 5d2ad5f9e7a24dacaf1075b97a04df91
CSeq: 1 REGISTER
Content-Length: 0
```

Examining the Authenticated Registration After Communicator has the credentials, it is ready to start authenticating with the server. At this point, Communicator can simply use the credentials it has available to respond to the authentication challenge.

For NTLM, this takes three handshaking steps, because Communicator must submit an anonymous REGISTER again, identify that NTLM is challenged for again, and then specify that it wants to use NTLM in its next REGISTER to prompt the server to generate a true NTLM challenge (instead of just stating that NTLM authentication is required as it did in the previous

401 response). The server then provides an NTLM challenge to which Communicator can respond by utilizing the user's credentials. As an aside, the server does not generate a true NTLM challenge unless the client prompts for one by asking for NTLM because generating challenges is an expensive operation for the server. When the REGISTER message is sent this time, with the NTLM challenge response, the server can verify the user and will actually process the REGISTER request.

For Kerberos, this takes only two handshaking steps because Communicator always submits an anonymous REGISTER, identifies that Kerberos is challenged for, and then provides a Kerberos response in the REGISTER message that is sent next. The server can directly verify this response and process the REGISTER request. Kerberos has one less step because simply knowing the server name is enough for the client to request a Kerberos ticket to validate itself against the server.

> **Note** For more detailed information on Kerberos and NTLM, search for the Microsoft TechNet article "Kerberos Authentication Technical Reference" at *http://technet.microsoft.com* or the Microsoft Developer Network (MSDN) article "NTLM Authentication" at *http://msdn.microsoft.com*.

Figure 4-5 shows the protocol messages exchanged by the client and the server during initial registration. An example using Kerberos authentication is shown in the upper half. The lower half shows the handshaking process when NTLM is used. This diagram also provides an overview to help in interpreting the actual protocol messages that are shown later.

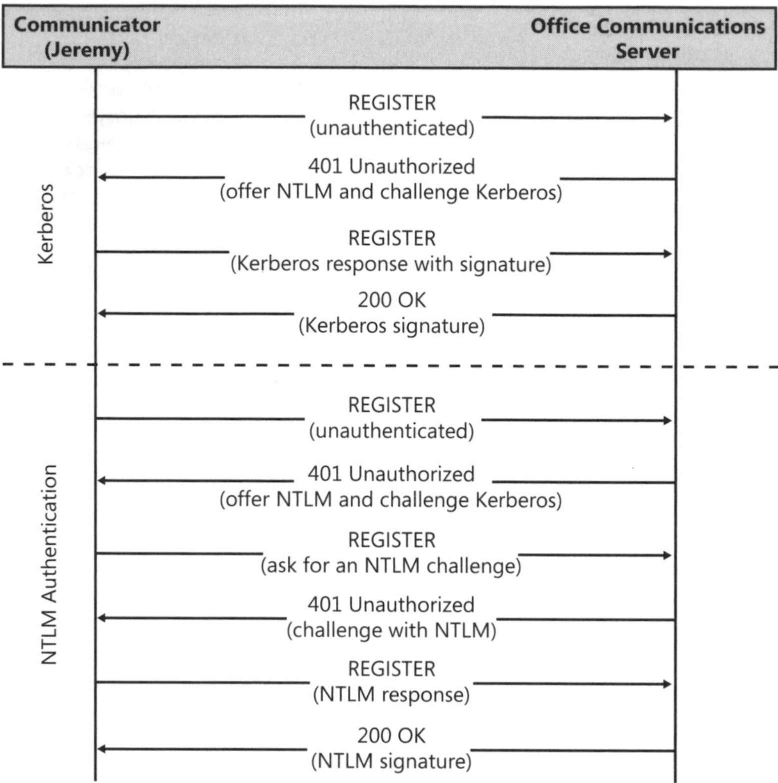

Figure 4-5 Initial registration—Authentication handshaking

In this example, the client provides its REGISTER request with a Kerberos ticket for the server that issued the original challenge, as follows:

```
REGISTER sip:contoso.com SIP/2.0
Via: SIP/2.0/TLS 192.168.3.100:2062
Max-Forwards: 70
From: <sip:jeremy@contoso.com>;tag=59e091cf1e;epid=aa6d968e18
To: <sip:jeremy@contoso.com>Call-ID: 2fd39df030554515a412e3aa2964489f
CSeq: 2 REGISTER
Contact: <sip:192.168.3.100:2062;transport= tls;ms-opaque=4d8a610d50>;methods="INVITE,
MESSAGE, INFO, OPTIONS, BYE, CANCEL, NOTIFY, ACK, REFER,
BENOTIFY";proxy=replace;+sip.instance=
"<urn:uuid:6BF396BA-A7D6-5247-89FB-C13B52F5840D>"
User-Agent: UCCP/2.0.6093.0 OC/2.0.6093.0 (Microsoft Office Communicator)
Authorization: Kerberos qop="auth", realm="SIP Communications Service",
targetname="sip/srv.contoso.com", gssapi-data=
"YIIEmwYJKoZIhvcSAQICAQBuggSKMIIEhqADAgEFoQMCAQ6iBwMFAAAAAACjggOzYYIDrz
CCA6ugAwIBBaENGwtDT05UT1NPLkNPTaIhMB+gAwIBAqEYMBYbA3NpcBsPc3J2LmNvbnRvc28uY2
9to4IDcDCCA2ygAwIBF6EDAgECooIDXgSCA1rI7odT+1XkCmcmUku44wiQe9tfZ5/zWmqYhJJuqS
l3u1qDE465czd3oazEyfIOOrDHzghrQE+CDtRe88oy2iwcVPHK4fl9QhovQy1xGjszfSBjfwR7O3
0zDlgODRb+1Yvw8zN2viDrc/N2s5vaIJtPyt2XZCV48BQYGBa1P8i4BuMvm52R11H2oc2JGtmAnR
qX/25ox9YWh48eGMvE1e3qfVRAkNVjfqDTZ1CfRUzJ6rNMKjuL2bgByyMMR3/VnFGURA0p/tUZxN
```

```
gUuSckeFM2WM8YCJWno2Q2ISZ8TMYVSKeh3WWLSAsxnS71qQmgQ1oXmEfdqAEKXUSmAT+X7NqT2Y
u1VVvUYQnFfE9dHEcPE+5KyTM2gRMhAJXzUqVKKDK0dHbzsHqYGbn0kB5+NU+STKvy0V0PGIMIPN
FXTyHHFdfBpwykYRr6Nayoxdmv06+EJ9I5GFPV7zFlJHaan1TwDTMUvGW4LZla2wkPQDfiuuTsMl
QgaXwD4vEZVPou0vMKiJMGtZawSuxisRTxsiD0n9TJCaBYYiHFntWI1Gk/m+rnMglkOFkgEUybUp
5k9S2lE8zyf1U50+e8rUtGkgIdeJesjBuYXFrYVOYEOL6aR/5Fsm7sAOTjEjtoA/3HyYKm1eHgiv
3GVwMGP8dtSwsIZwT5XQN81VZpkfgihjAcNt9oe/lO2t6z61+Uw/XPFUf43prpqESkWN/7FFyccV
K8IkKnyixXeBSRuNDR/SXq7RSm+UEQH2Yfd+JPl4Q67eX1oynvXtb1c9VB0aT7FoOPBMpgxMG/PR
9VdCsSSVU4u+FC2z0gGb/8EDExxX5fI3q05Ge5msgcS8WfZn1D9KphfpFYl7SHki3ddo4A4Eu28T
lxS2JjC9lOijwUd3hG4ah1DmpIPNfvL51a2GBG9o/aucJceya0ZhOzwwbx6vfyPPwhIH5/nfQ0rA
zsrnj/caCYxA12/IA9j8zXA/4rQoLYv+G9ezv3uMZcGi8t3/UdXhAToFn5g7sTelhRCs7Mw2GjQV
78UbNaIYfD3okEkV6q8oVJAQZrO+HTmzupbBKJSLE52vLDi/xP5zu5vMdiYLC2rK6KVnKRcviQUi
QO7y1wqt01LslJgy/hi1/t54fy6g+oo1LEb+h/RB6kgbkwgbagAwIBF6KBrgSBq0IepRK7up8fT8
PamkrLq/cQBwiMqZcoLGt/MMs2bAlQOVZ6alrnK4m5OX4PeZtF+YhLf65NnDBt4ye7HhenecTLWN
DvH/FHSW1DbvgqnmM8j2KhFQSFrJfuqEYNB159mEfJRp6KE+mYIBASTVR0BqCCoSmsFQiQ3pRr1r
yx4ACRI74BzN6ODtncwEnXWQbuJYxsem0Xmf01SZoiDl2upGIvzcKYpFJ2atKgsw=="
Supported: gruu-10, adhoclist, msrtc-event-categories
Supported: ms-forking
ms-keep-alive: UAC;hop-hop=yes
Event: registration
Content-Length: 0
```

As the message shows, the Kerberos credentials can be a relatively large portion of the protocol message for the initial handshake, but it is a relatively minimal cost for the security provided for this and all future messages. Because subsequent messages will only reference the credentials and pass minimal data to validate the keys embedded in this exchange, this is a fairly minimal one-time, up-front cost.

For clarity and completeness, the authentication headers are shown as snippets for an exchange if NTLM was in use, as follows:

```
REGISTER sip:contoso.com SIP/2.0...
Call-ID: 2fd39df030554515a412e3aa2964489f
CSeq: 2 REGISTER...
Authorization: NTLM qop="auth", realm="SIP Communications Service",
targetname="srv.contoso.com", gssapi-data=""...
```

The server responds by offering a true NTLM challenge that Communicator can respond to by using user credentials. This true challenge is easy to see because it is rather large (380 bytes) and starts with a standard header "TlRMTVN....", as follows:

```
SIP/2.0 401 Unauthorized...
WWW-Authenticate: NTLM opaque="33E7D13B", gssapi-data=
"TlRMTVNTUAACAAAAAAAAADgAAADzgpjiFRIiVZ/HsigAAAAAAAAAAOQA5AA4AAAABQLODgAAAA8C
AA4AUgBFAEQATQBPAE4ARAABABgAUgBFAEQALQBMAEMAUwBEAFIALQAwADEABAA0AHIAZQBkAG0Ab
wBuAGQALgBjAG8AcgBwAC4AbQBpAGMAcgBvAHMAbwBmAHQALgBjAG8AbQADAE4AcgBlAGQALQBsAG
MAcwBkAHIALQAwADEALgByAGUAZABtAG8AbgBkAC4AYwBvAHIAcAAuAG0AaQBjAHIAbwBzAG8AZgB
0AC4AYwBvAG0ABQAkAGMAbwByAHAALgBtAGkAYwByAG8AcwBvAGYAdAAuAGMAbwBtAAAAAAA=",
targetname="srv.contoso.com", realm="SIP Communications Service"...
Call-ID: 2fd39df030554515a412e3aa2964489f
CSeq: 2 REGISTER...
```

Communicator can now use this NTLM challenge to generate an NTLM response, and it packages this in the next REGISTER message that it sends, as follows:

```
REGISTER sip:contoso.com SIP/2.0...
Call-ID: 2fd39df030554515a412e3aa2964489f
CSeq: 3 REGISTER...
Authorization: NTLM qop="auth", opaque="33E7D13B", realm="SIP Communications
Service", targetname="srv.contoso.com", gssapi-data=
"TlRMTVNTUAADAAAAGAAYAHgAAAAYABgAkAAAAA4ADgBIAAAACgAKAFYAAAAYABgAYAAAABAAEACo
AAAAVYKQQgUBKAoAAAAPUgBFAEQATQBPAE4ARABqAGIAdQBjAGgARABFAEwATAAtAFgAUABTAC0AN
AAwADAARYHHoHZkV6SMRG47yl+zcIrUcTec6pSnLajtPCReLpIB6dFgYb0k9fWgnTl9Lg6N+wo5vP
1tIFyxOX6CU6kP3g=="...
```

Either way authentication was received, the server now has an authenticated REGISTER message and must respond to it. The server's response to the REGISTER message can fall into one of the following categories:

- **301 Redirect** In this case, the server tells Communicator what the user's home server is so that the user can directly connect and register most efficiently, as follows:
  - The existing connection will be closed, and the client will go through the connection process to connect to the server to which it was redirected.
  - The entire authentication and registration process will repeat with the new server to get back to this point, where a 200 OK message from the server (accepting the registration) would be expected.
- **200 OK** In this case, the server directly accepts the registration because it is the user's home server, or it is acting as a proxy because a redirect would fail as a result of Communicator not having direct connectivity to the home server. (Access Edge Servers will proxy registrations.)
- **403 Forbidden** In this case, the client is not allowed to log in because the SIP URI exists, but it is owned by a different user than the credentials that were supplied. Therefore, the following causes are possible:
  - The user account is not enabled for Office Communications Server.
  - The user account is disabled, or the password is expired.
  - The credentials are invalid, or there was a typo in the account or password.
  - Communicator is logging in from the Internet, and the user is not enabled for remote access with Office Communications Server.
- **404 Not Found** In this case, the client is not allowed to log in because the user URI that was specified does not exist, even though valid user credentials were provided. (This failure could be because of a typo in the URI.)

- **504 Server Time-Out** In this case, the server handling the request (probably an Access Edge Server) had difficulty routing the message and there is either a configuration problem in the network or a service outage is occurring.

> **Real World: 403 Forbidden**
>
> Another possible cause of a 403 response is that the user is enabled but User Replicator has failed to synchronize changes from the domain to Microsoft SQL Server.
>
> The most common problem caused by a customer is not allowing inheritable permissions on an organizational unit (OU). Beyond that, check the event log.
>
> *–Thomas Laciano*
> *Program Manager, RTC Customer Experience*

If Communicator receives a 504 or 403 error, it reports to the user that a general error has occurred and provides more details in the trace log. The event log should also provide a detailed description of the problem, along with hints to help understand how to resolve the problem. An example of one of the event log messages for when an Access Edge Server was unable to route a message is shown next. This problem can be replicated easily on your own domain if your network has an Access Edge Server installed with Open Federation enabled. Simply try to send a message to a user in a domain that does not exist. (The example is from sending a message to unknownuser@cpandl.com, which is a fictitious domain that does not support SIP.) The nice thing about the log shown next is that it even tells you which server in the network failed. (sipfed.contoso.com identifies itself in the ms-diagnostics field from the 404 response and explains what failed: "Unable to resolve DNS SRV record.")

```
A SIP request made by Communicator failed in an unexpected manner (status
code404). More information is contained in the following technical data:

RequestUri:   sip:unknownuser@cpandl.com
From:         sip:jeremy@contoso.com;tag=a7e16ad66d
To:           sip:unknownuser@cpandl.com;tag=498ED6D80FE772442E7B51A625FB667E
Call-ID:      7ff2d267efa846778d741480d85fd522
Content-type: application/sdp

v=0
o=- 0 0 IN IP4 157.57.6.160
s=session
c=IN IP4 157.57.6.160
t=0 0
m=message 5060 sip null
a=accept-types:text/rtf application/x-ms-ink image/gif multipart/alternative
application/ms-imdn+xml

Response Data:

100  Trying
```

```
 404  Not Found
ms-diagnostics:  1008;reason="Unable to resolve DNS SRV
record";source="sipfed.contoso.com"

Resolution:
If this error continues to occur, please contact your network administrator.
The network administrator can use a tool like winerror.exe from the Windows
Resource Kit or lcserror.exe from the Office Communications Server Resource
Kit in order to interpret any error codes listed above.

For more information, see Help and Support Center at
http://go.microsoft.com/fwlink/events.asp.
```

If Communicator receives a 301 response, the connection process starts again by resolving the hostname it received in the Contact header and attempting to connect and register with this server.

> **Note** Communicator has proof to allow it to trust the server it is registering against in the form of authentication signatures in the response and possibly even a validated certificate used by the first-hop server. Because of this, Communicator honors an authenticated redirect response from a server in its domain, even if the name does not line up with the SIP URI of the user. However, if Communicator receives a 200 response, the initial registration is complete and login processing continues from here.

In the example login, the server accepts the registration with a 200 OK response, as follows:

```
SIP/2.0 200 OK
ms-keep-alive: UAS; tcp=no; hop-hop=yes; end-end=no; timeout=300
Authentication-Info: Kerberos rspauth=
"602306092A864886F71201020201011100FFFFFFFF5C001B875485F1BC7E66F0006
6537A78", srand="40882645", snum="1", opaque="A7AB18E7", qop="auth",
targetname="sip/srv.contoso.com", realm="SIP Communications Service"
Via: SIP/2.0/TLS 192.168.3.100:2062;ms-received-port=2062;ms-received-cid=2700
From: "Jeremy Los"<sip:jeremy@contoso.com>;tag=59e091cf1e;epid=aa6d968e18
To: <sip:jeremy@contoso.com>;tag=A1F542AB99D66616F9252CB6DF50257F
Call-ID: 2fd39df030554515a412e3aa2964489f
CSeq: 2 REGISTER
Contact: <sip:192.168.3.100:2062;transport=tls;ms-opaque=4d8a610d50;
ms-received-cid=00002700>;expires=7200;+sip.instance="<urn:uuid:6bf396ba-
a7d6-5247-89fb-c13b52f5840d>";
gruu="sip:jeremy@contoso.com;opaque=user:epid:upbza9anR1KJ-8E7UvWEDQAA;gruu"
Expires: 7200
presence-state: register-action="added"
Allow-Events: vnd-microsoft-provisioning,vnd-microsoft-roaming-contacts,vnd-
microsoft-roaming-ACL,presence,presence.wpending,vnd-microsoft-roaming-self,
vnd-microsoft-provisioning-v2
Supported: adhoclistServer: RTC/3.0
Supported: msrtc-event-categories
Content-Length: 0
```

While we are looking at this example, the final 200 OK response has other interesting information to examine. First, the server provides credentials for itself that also prove to the client that the server can be trusted. This proof is especially important for TCP connections, where this is the only means of authentication the client has. The *rspauth* and *targetname* fields in the *Authentication-Info* header provide cryptographic proof that the authenticating server identifies itself with the name specified. Second, the single *Contact* header in the response tells Communicator that only the contact address that was just registered is currently logged on (that is, no other clients are active for Jeremy's account). Third, the *ms-keep-alive* and *Allow-Events* headers provide information to the client to help it understand how to stay connected and synchronized with the server, as well as what services are available. Finally, the *Expires* header tells Communicator how long the registration is valid for. It must be refreshed within 7200 seconds (2 hours) or it will automatically expire and be cleaned up by the server.

Real World: Troubleshooting Client Connections

Troubleshooting the first client connection can be approached in a systematic way. Begin your troubleshooting with Active Directory Users and Computers and Office Communications Server 2007 Management Consoles. Is the user showing that she is enabled? If she is enabled here, you actually have one more place to check, as these views are showing what is configured but not necessarily what is in the database used by Office Communications Server.

Open a command prompt, and navigate to the directory you installed the Office Communications Server Resource Kit Tools to. (You installed the Resource Kit Tools, right?) The default location is C:\Program Files\Microsoft Office Communications Server 2007\Reskit. Typing **dbanalyze /?** provides the available switches, as well as sample syntax. For example, say you are interested in determining if the database includes the SIP-URI of the user you are testing with. (Note that we are not covering the elements of the output here, merely referencing the tool for the purpose of validating the presence of a user in the database.) In this situation, you use the following command:

```
dbanalyze.exe /report:user /user:Jeremy@contoso.com
```

An example of output you might get from running this command follows:

```
Snooper Version: 3.0.6237.0

Report created at 5/30/2007 2:31:00 PM on sip.contoso.com.


User : jeremy@contoso.com
------------------------------------------------
Resource Id         : 5
Home server         : sip.contoso.com
GUID                : 2e324a4b-c048-420f-9c8d-1d86bb9fc266
SID                 : S-1-5-21-3158251299-35245958-1667159398-1173
Display Name        : Jeremy Los
```

```
OptionFlags        : 256
ArchivingFlags     : 0
Enabled            : True
MovingAway         : False
Unavailable        : False
RichMode           : True
Contact Version    : 2
Permission Version : 1
Email              : jeremy@contoso.com
Phone              :
Presence data      :

Contact Groups
--------------
1
Group Number : 1
Display Name : ~
External Uri :


Containers
----------
1
Container Number   : 0
Container Version  : 0
SameEnterprise     : False
Federated          : False
PublicCloud        : False
Everyone           : True
Member User        :
Member Domain      :
...
```

> **Note** For a full example of command output from dbanalyze, see the file dbanalyze-jeremy.txt on the companion CD, in the \Appendixes,Scripts,Resources\Chapter 04 folder.

After you confirm that the user is enabled, also confirm that the Global Settings include the domain you selected for the SIP-URI. This is a common issue for customers who have a SIP-URI that does not match their Active Directory namespace or who have multiple SIP-URIs.

For example, the deployment for Contoso might have used Contoso.local or Contoso.corp as the Active Directory namespace, which would require that we manually add Contoso.com to the list of domains supported by the configuration. If the server is listening with TCP, supported domains are no longer configured by default and therefore must be added. The benefit of adding TCP is that we can use the IP address and a network analyzer in addition to the existing logs. Use the IP address first in the client configuration to eliminate any host name resolution problems. After confirmation, switch to the fully qualified domain name (FQDN) of the server to confirm host name resolution is working and, finally, configure for TLS over TCP with the FQDN of the server. After all of this has been verified, you can add the option of automatic configuration, which requires the DNS SRV records mentioned earlier.

Finally, new to Office Communications Server is the addition of diagnostics in the Office Communications Server Management Console. You can test connectivity and client sign-in, receiving a rather verbose output of the tests and status. If this still fails to provide you with a resolution to your problem, enable the client logs as described previously in this chapter and contact the support services team.

–Thomas Laciano
Program Manager, RTC Customer Experience

Examining What Happens During Login Processing (Step 3)

After registration is complete, a complex set of queries and notifications takes place between the client and the server as Communicator gathers information from the server and the rest of the network. Communicator gathers its own configuration information and then gathers presence information about users on the contact list. To speed things up, Communicator issues the first four subscriptions in parallel and receives the server responses as they come in. For simplicity, the requests and the responses are shown one-by-one, but keep in mind that this ordering is not precisely what is happening at the network level. Requests can be sent out in parallel by the client, and responses can come back in an unrelated order, based on network delays to and from each destination. Figure 4-6 provides an overview of the protocol messages exchanged between Communicator and the server infrastructure during this phase of the login process.

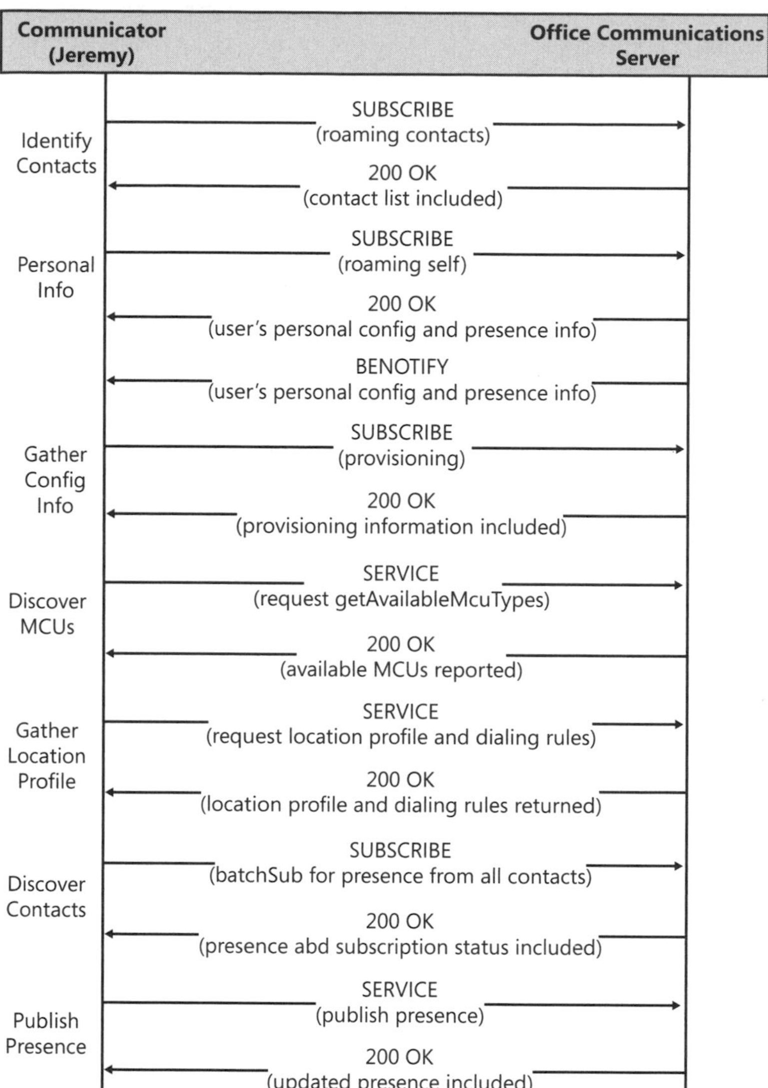

Figure 4-6 Login processing

This subscription allows Communicator to see the contact list, but it also enables it to identify whether contacts are added on other clients with which the user might be logged in. If the contact list changes, the server sends a notification containing the change. A SUBSCRIBE message is sent to the server to initiate the subscription to the contact list, as follows:

```
SUBSCRIBE sip:jeremy@contoso.com SIP/2.0
Via: SIP/2.0/TLS 192.168.3.100:2062
Max-Forwards: 70
From: <sip:jeremy@contoso.com>;tag=9099c0ba1d;epid=aa6d968e18
To: <sip:jeremy@contoso.com>
Call-ID: ecb20da4280142d1b69b920276785d2f
CSeq: 1 SUBSCRIBE
Contact: <sip:jeremy@contoso.com;opaque=user:epid:upbza9anR1KJ-8E7UvWEDQAA;gruu>
User-Agent: UCCP/2.0.6093.0 OC/2.0.6093.0 (Microsoft Office Communicator)
Event: vnd-microsoft-roaming-contactsAccept: application/vnd-microsoft-roaming-
contacts+xml
Supported: com.microsoft.autoextend
Supported: ms-benotify
Proxy-Require: ms-benotify
Supported: ms-piggyback-first-notify
Proxy-Authorization: Kerberos qop="auth", realm="SIP Communications Service",
opaque="A7AB18E7", crand="3b86002b", cnum="1",
targetname="sip/srv.contoso.com", response=
"602306092a864886f71201020201011100ffffffff6150d616a8e990a9b9971b4585bea994"
Content-Length: 0
```

The *Event* header identifies that the request is to get back the contact list (called *roaming contacts*). Other headers (such as the *Supported* and *Proxy-Require* headers) provide optional enhancements or specify capabilities to allow for more functionality to be put to use, specifically protocol optimizations. These optimizations include the use of *BENOTIFY* (which is a best-effort notification that does not require a response to confirm receipt), sending first notifications as part of the response to the subscription request, and automatic server extensions for subscriptions.

The response immediately includes information in the body because both the client and server support *ms-piggyback-first-notify*. This feature allows the information that typically needs to be sent in a subsequent NOTIFY message to simply be sent in the 200 response.

The server accepts the subscription to the contact list with a 200 response in which it also confirms protocol optimizations will be used and specifies that the subscription will be maintained for 41472 seconds (~11.5 hours), as follows:

```
SIP/2.0 200 OK
Contact: <sip:srv.contoso.com:5061;transport=tls>
Authentication-Info: Kerberos rspauth=
"602306092A864886F71201020201011100FFFFFFFF395B434D61013C132B9A488AA61C861D",
srand="1A6EE03C", snum="4", opaque="A7AB18E7", qop="auth", targetname="sip/
srv.contoso.com", realm="SIP Communications Service"
Content-Length: 313
Via: SIP/2.0/TLS 192.168.3.100:2062;ms-received-port=2062;ms-received-cid=2700
From: "Jeremy Los"<sip:jeremy@contoso.com>;tag=9099c0ba1d;epid=aa6d968e18
To: <sip:jeremy@contoso.com>;tag=0A234943
Call-ID: ecb20da4280142d1b69b920276785d2f
CSeq: 1 SUBSCRIBE
```

```
Expires: 41472
Content-Type: application/vnd-microsoft-roaming-contacts+xml
Event: vnd-microsoft-roaming-contactssubscription-state: active;expires=41472ms-
piggyback-cseq: 1
Supported: ms-benotify, ms-piggyback-first-notify
<contactList deltaNum="17" >  <group id="1" name="~" externalURI=""  />
<contact uri="rui@contoso.com" name="" groups="1" subscribed="true" externalURI="" >
<contactExtension>   <contactSettings contactId="0a1d4375-32d1-42b1-be25-41a6720d2dde">
</contactSettings>   </contactExtension>
</contact></contactList>
```

The response contains the user's contact list (also called a *buddy list*). Because the *ms-piggyback-first-notify* extension was supported, the server provides the first notification in the body of the 200 response. Contacts and groups are identified, along with information about what groups they are in and whether they are maintained with an active subscription or just kept in the contact list.

Next, Communicator issues a subscription request for presence information about the user (Jeremy Los in this case), access-level settings that have already been configured by the user to control who has access to what information, and the list of contacts who currently have outstanding subscriptions:

```
SUBSCRIBE sip:jeremy@contoso.com SIP/2.0
Via: SIP/2.0/TLS 192.168.3.100:2062
Max-Forwards: 70
From: <sip:jeremy@contoso.com>;tag=64ecc96946;epid=aa6d968e18
To: <sip:jeremy@contoso.com>
Call-ID: bb8338fdba864da9bc9875dad6dbec7aCSeq: 1 SUBSCRIBE
Contact: <sip:jeremy@contoso.com;opaque=user:epid:upbza9anR1KJ-8E7UvWEDQAA;gruu>
User-Agent: UCCP/2.0.6093.0 OC/2.0.6093.0 (Microsoft Office Communicator)
Event: vnd-microsoft-roaming-selfAccept: application/vnd-microsoft-roaming-self+xml
Supported: com.microsoft.autoextend
Supported: ms-benotify
Proxy-Require: ms-benotify
Supported: ms-piggyback-first-notifyProxy-Authorization: Kerberos qop="auth",
realm="SIP Communications Service", opaque="A7AB18E7", crand="9c81fb7f",
cnum="2", targetname="sip/srv.contoso.com",
response="602306092a864886f71201020201011100ffffffffc33ae8f9e62252efa3320f9e3 99828e9"
Content-Type: application/vnd-microsoft-roaming-self+xml
Content-Length: 174
<roamingList xmlns="http://schemas.microsoft.com/2006/09/sip/roaming-self">
  <roaming type="categories"/>
  <roaming type="containers"/>
  <roaming type="subscribers"/>
</roamingList>
```

The *Event* header identifies the request as a subscription to information that pertains to the user (called *roaming self*). Again, Communicator identifies that it can support several protocol optimizations.

The server accepts the subscription with a 200 OK response. The body of the response contains a list of information about the user, established access levels that contacts have been granted, and users with current subscriptions. These messages are quite large and detailed, and this one does not have much interesting content in it because there are not many contacts or access levels that have been established yet. As the contact list grows and access control settings evolve, this XML document will be expanded. The response shown next is summarized in sections because it is long and actually just repeats information for various access-level containers. Where repetition has occurred, an ellipses (...) is shown with an explanation of what is removed.

On the CD All the protocol messages shown in these examples are on the companion CD, in the \Appendixes,Scripts,Resources\Chapter 04\CD Protocol Logs folder, and can be viewed in their entirety there.

```
SIP/2.0 200 OK
Contact: <sip:srv.contoso.com:5061;transport=tls>
Authentication-Info: Kerberos rspauth=
"602306092A864886F71201020201011100FFFFFFFF1E4469D0C0EA14D4EFE584E6B2FB9CC0",
srand="1FD3FD44", snum="5", opaque="A7AB18E7", qop="auth",
targetname="sip/srv.contoso.com", realm="SIP Communications Service"
Content-Length: 7521
Via: SIP/2.0/TLS 192.168.3.100:2062;ms-received-port=2062;ms-received-cid=2700
From: "Jeremy Los"<sip:jeremy@contoso.com>;tag=64ecc96946;epid=aa6d968e18
To: <sip:jeremy@contoso.com>;tag=9A750080
Call-ID: bb8338fdba864da9bc9875dad6dbec7a
CSeq: 1 SUBSCRIBE
Expires: 51408
Require: eventlistContent-Type: application/vnd-microsoft-roaming-self+xml
Event: vnd-microsoft-roaming-self
subscription-state: active;expires=51408
ms-piggyback-cseq: 1
Supported: ms-benotify, ms-piggyback-first-notify
<roamingData xmlns="http://schemas.microsoft.com/2006/09/sip/roaming-self"
xmlns:cat="http://schemas.microsoft.com/2006/09/sip/categories"
xmlns:con="http://schemas.microsoft.com/2006/09/sip/containers"
xmlns:sub="http://schemas.microsoft.com/2006/09/sip/presence-subscribers">
<categories xmlns="http://schemas.microsoft.com/2006/09/sip/categories"
uri="sip:jeremy@contoso.com">  <category name="calendarData" instance="0"
publishTime="2007-05-04T18:56:32.670" container="32000" version="1"
expireType="static"/>  <category name="calendarData" instance="0"
publishTime="2007-05-04T18:56:32.670" container="100" version="1"
expireType="static"/>  <category name="contactCard" instance="0"
publishTime="2007-05-03T05:40:44.113" container="32000" version="1"
expireType="static">   <contactCard
xmlns="http://schemas.microsoft.com/2006/09/sip/contactcard" >    <identity >
     <name ><displayName >Jeremy Los</displayName></name>    </identity>
</contactCard>  </category>  <category name="contactCard" instance="0"
publishTime="2007-05-03T05:40:44.113" container="400" version="1"
expireType="static">
... (contactCard info repeated for containers 400, 300, 200, 100 and 0)
```

```
  <category name="note" instance="0" publishTime="2007-05-04T18:56:32.670"
container="32000" version="1" expireType="static"/>  <category name="note"
instance="0" publishTime="2007-05-04T18:56:32.670" container="100" version="1"
expireType="static"/>  <category name="state" instance="0" publishTime=
"2007-05-04T18:56:32.670" container="32000" version="1" expireType="static">
   <state xmlns="http://schemas.microsoft.com/2006/09/sip/state"
xmlns:xsi="http://www.w3.org/2001/XMLSchema-instance" manual="false"
xsi:type="aggregateState" >
    <availability >18500</availability>
    <endpointLocation ></endpointLocation>
   </state>  </category>  <category name="state" instance="0"
publishTime="2007-05-04T22:47:48.977" container="400" version="1"
expireType="static">   <state xsi:type="aggregateState" lastActive=
"2007-05-04T22:47:48" xmlns:xsi="http://www.w3.org/2001/XMLSchema-instance"
xmlns="http://schemas.microsoft.com/2006/09/sip/state">
    <availability>18000</availability>
   </state>  </category>
... (state info repeated for containers 300, 200, 100, 3 and 2)

  <category name="routing" instance="0" publishTime="2007-05-04T18:56:28.233"
container="32000" version="1" expireType="static">   <routing
xmlns="http://schemas.microsoft.com/02/2006/sip/routing" name="rtcdefault"
version="1" >
    <preamble xmlns="http://schemas.microsoft.com/02/2006/sip/routing" >
     <flags name="clientflags" value="block" ></flags>
    </preamble>
   </routing>  </category>  <category name="legacyInterop" instance="0"
publishTime="2007-05-03T05:40:44.113" container="32000" version="1"
expireType="static">   <legacyInterop availability="18500" />  </category>
<category name="legacyInterop" instance="0" publishTime=
"2007-05-04T22:47:48.977" container="400" version="1" expireType="static">
<legacyInterop availability="18000" />  </category>

 ... (legacyInterop info repeated for containers 300, 200 and 100)

  <category name="userProperties" instance="0" publishTime=
"2007-05-03T05:40:44.113" container="1" version="1" expireType="static">
<userProperties ><telephonyMode >None</telephonyMode></userProperties>
</category> </categories> <containers
xmlns="http://schemas.microsoft.com/2006/09/sip/containers">  <container
id="32000" version="0"/>  <container id="400" version="0"/>  <container
id="300" version="1">   <member type="user" value="vadim@contoso.com"/>
</container>  <container id="200" version="1">   <member
type="sameEnterprise"/>  </container>  <container id="100" version="1">
<member type="federated"/>  </container>  <container id="3" version="0"/>
<container id="2" version="0"/>  <container id="1" version="0"/>  <container
id="0" version="0">   <member type="everyone"/>  </container> </containers>
<subscribers xmlns="http://schemas.microsoft.com/2006/09/sip/
presence-subscribers"/></roamingData>
```


This user information is stored on the user's home server in the SQL (MSDE) database and is used by the client and server to determine whether subscriptions from other users are accepted and whether messages for the client will be delivered or rejected. This subscription also lets Communicator know if other clients the user might have running on other machines change authorization settings, because the server sends a notification of the changes. This subscription also allows Communicator to be notified when new subscriptions from other users come in, so that the user can decide how to handle them.

After the subscription is initiated, a notification is eventually sent out by the server. An example of that best-effort notification is shown next for reference. (The majority of the XML body was removed for brevity, but it can be viewed from the protocol logs on the companion CD.)

```
BENOTIFY sip:192.168.3.100:2062;transport=tls;ms-opaque=4d8a610d50;ms-
received-cid=00002700 SIP/2.0
Via: SIP/2.0/TLS
192.168.3.1:5061;branch=z9hG4bK0F226A22.4AC8062C;branched=FALSE
Authentication-Info: Kerberos rspauth=
"602306092A864886F71201020201011100FFFFFFFF85D8DA4A3CF277F582B4D4AF1AEBED6",
srand="88553BCA", snum="8", opaque="A7AB18E7", qop="auth",
targetname="sip/srv.contoso.com", realm="SIP Communications Service"
Max-Forwards: 70
To: <sip:jeremy@contoso.com>;tag=64ecc96946;epid=aa6d968e18Content-Length: 7638
From: <sip:jeremy@contoso.com>;tag=9A750080
Call-ID: bb8338fdba864da9bc9875dad6dbec7a
CSeq: 2 BENOTIFY
Require: eventlist
Content-Type: application/vnd-microsoft-roaming-self+xml
Event: vnd-microsoft-roaming-self
subscription-state: active;expires=51410
<roamingData xmlns="http://schemas.microsoft.com/2006/09/sip/roaming-self"
xmlns:cat="http://schemas.microsoft.com/2006/09/sip/categories"
xmlns:con="http://schemas.microsoft.com/2006/09/sip/containers"
xmlns:sub="http://schemas.microsoft.com/2006/09/sip/presence-subscribers">
<categories xmlns="http://schemas.microsoft.com/2006/09/sip/categories"
uri="sip:jeremy@contoso.com">  <category name="state" instance="1"
publishTime="2007-05-04T22:48:10.357" container="2" version="1"
expireType="user">   <state xsi:type="aggregateState"
xmlns:xsi="http://www.w3.org/2001/XMLSchema-instance"
xmlns="http://schemas.microsoft.com/2006/09/sip/state">
    <availability>3500</availability>
   </state>  </category>

...
 </categories></roamingData>
```

Communicator next issues a subscription for provisioning information to help with initial configuration. This subscription is a one-time query (denoted by the *Expires* header, which asks for 0 seconds for the subscription lifetime). This subscription asks for server configuration, meeting policies, and policy settings that Communicator must enforce.

```
SUBSCRIBE sip:jeremy@contoso.com SIP/2.0
Via: SIP/2.0/TLS 192.168.3.100:2062
Max-Forwards: 70
From: <sip:jeremy@contoso.com>;tag=e7c43a41fd;epid=aa6d968e18
To: <sip:jeremy@contoso.com>
Call-ID: 7ea128a6ebe34481b5daa76132607e34
CSeq: 1 SUBSCRIBE
Contact: <sip:jeremy@contoso.com;opaque=
user:epid:upbza9anR1KJ-8E7UvWEDQAA;gruu>User-Agent: UCCP/2.0.6093.0 OC/
2.0.6093.0 (Microsoft Office Communicator)
Event: vnd-microsoft-provisioning-v2
Accept: application/vnd-microsoft-roaming-provisioning-v2+xml
Supported: com.microsoft.autoextend
Supported: ms-benotify
Proxy-Require: ms-benotify
Supported: ms-piggyback-first-notify
Expires: 0
Proxy-Authorization: Kerberos qop="auth", realm="SIP Communications Service",
 opaque="A7AB18E7", crand="e7e65db3", cnum="3", targetname=
"sip/srv.contoso.com", response=
"602306092a864886f71201020201011100ffffffff4dca80cf37e7ee6998209ab5923fc3cd"
Content-Type: application/vnd-microsoft-roaming-provisioning-v2+xml
Content-Length: 242
<provisioningGroupList xmlns=
"http://schemas.microsoft.com/2006/09/sip/provisioninggrouplist">
  <provisioningGroup name="ServerConfiguration"/>
  <provisioningGroup name="meetingPolicy"/>
  <provisioningGroup name="ucPolicy"/>
</provisioningGroupList>
```

The server accepts the one-time provisioning query with a 200 OK response, which contains a rich set of configuration and provisioning information for the client, as follows:

```
SIP/2.0 200 OK
Contact: <sip:srv.contoso.com:5061;transport=tls>
Authentication-Info: Kerberos rspauth=
"602306092A864886F71201020201011100FFFFFFFF506A6B8D20F534E698E78206B898CF44",
srand="F08BB38D", snum="2", opaque="A7AB18E7", qop="auth",
targetname="sip/srv.contoso.com", realm="SIP Communications Service"
Content-Length: 2806
Via: SIP/2.0/TLS 192.168.3.100:2062;ms-received-port=2062;ms-received-cid=2700
From: "Jeremy Los"<sip:jeremy@contoso.com>;tag=e7c43a41fd;epid=aa6d968e18
To: <sip:jeremy@contoso.com>;tag=39420176
Call-ID: 7ea128a6ebe34481b5daa76132607e34
CSeq: 1 SUBSCRIBE
Expires: 0
Content-Type: application/vnd-microsoft-roaming-provisioning-v2+xml
Event: vnd-microsoft-provisioning-v2
subscription-state: terminated;expires=0
ms-piggyback-cseq: 1
Supported: ms-benotify, ms-piggyback-first-notify
<provisionGroupList xmlns=
```

```
"http://schemas.microsoft.com/2006/09/sip/provisiongrouplist-notification">
<provisionGroup name="ServerConfiguration" >
<absInternalServerUrl>http://srv.contoso.com/Abs/Int</absInternalServerUrl>
<organization>Corporation</organization>   <consoleDownloadInternalUrl>
    http://office.microsoft.com/en-us/help/HA101733831033.aspx
   </consoleDownloadInternalUrl>   <consoleDownloadExternalUrl>
    http://office.microsoft.com/en-us/help/HA101733831033.aspx
   </consoleDownloadExternalUrl>   <helpdeskInternalUrl>
    https://srv.contoso.com/conf/int/TShoot.html
   </helpdeskInternalUrl>   <dlxInternalUrl>
    https://srv.contoso.com/GroupExpansion/service.asmx
   </dlxInternalUrl>   <dlxEnabled>true</dlxEnabled>
<ucDiffServVoice>40</ucDiffServVoice>   <ucVoice802_1p>5</ucVoice802_1p>
<ucEnforcePinLock>false</ucEnforcePinLock>   <ucMinPinLength>6
</ucMinPinLength>   <ucPhoneTimeOut>10</ucPhoneTimeOut>
<ucExchangeMWIPoll>3</ucExchangeMWIPoll>   <ucPC2PCAVEncryption>
Support encryption</ucPC2PCAVEncryption>
<ucEnableSIPSecurityMode>High</ucEnableSIPSecurityMode>
<updatesServerEnabled>false</updatesServerEnabled>
<ucLocationProfile >Redmond</ucLocationProfile>   <focusFactoryUri>
    sip:jeremy@contoso.com;gruu;opaque=app:conf:focusfactory
   </focusFactoryUri>
   <voiceMailUri>
    sip:jeremy@contoso.com;opaque=app:voicemail
   </voiceMailUri>
  </provisionGroup>   <provisionGroup name="meetingPolicy"
instanceId="{6B151D61-D98B-4A16-9D6C-8BBB3111228A}" >   <instance>
    <property name="Name"><![CDATA[Default Policy]]></property>
    <property name="AllowIPVideo"><![CDATA[false]]></property>
    <property name="AllowIPAudio"><![CDATA[false]]></property>
    <property name="EnableAppDesktopSharing"><![CDATA[false]]></property>
    <property name="ColorDepth"><![CDATA[256]]></property>
    <property name="AllowAppSharingForExternalMeeting"><![CDATA[None]]></property>
    <property name="RetainPPTForExternalMeeting"><![CDATA[false]]></property>
    <property name="MeetingSize"><![CDATA[10]]></property>
    <property name="EnableDataCollaboration"><![CDATA[false]]></property>
    <property name="AllowPresenterToRecord"><![CDATA[false]]></property>
    <property name=
"AllowPresenterToDelegateRecording"><![CDATA[false]]></property>
   </instance>
  </provisionGroup>   <provisionGroup name="ucPolicy" instanceId=
"{6B41BE99-5C45-41E5-B34C-F6B8D0079E7B}" >   <instance>
    <property name="Name"><![CDATA[Default Policy]]></property>
    <property name="AllowUsersToChangeTeamSettings"><![CDATA[true]]></property>
    <property name="AllowSimultaneousRinging"><![CDATA[true]]></property>
    <property name="MaxTeamMembers"><![CDATA[5]]></property>
    <property name="PhoneRouteUsages">
     <element>
      <![CDATA[CN={C491D082-9CD3-4A41-9A79-9DCEE38670EB},CN=Phone Route
Usages,CN=RTC Service,CN=Services,CN=Configuration,DC=contoso,DC=com]]>
     </element>
    </property>
   </instance>
  </provisionGroup></provisionGroupList>
```

The provisioning information contains information about the Computer Telephony Integration (CTI) gateway for the user (one does not exist in this example) and the Address Book Server (ABS) URL for the user: http://srv.contoso.com/Abs/Int. Additional information about phone integration and the CTI gateway can be found in Chapter 9, "Understanding Remote Call Control Scenario." The Address Book Server URL offers Communicator a location where it can download basic information about enterprise users so that Communicator can search across these names to allow users to quickly add known contacts in the organization.

Note An example of using the Address Book Server information is shown in the "Step 1: Looking Up a Contact" section later in the chapter—which is part of the "Overview of the Presence Sharing Scenario" section. Following that section, the "Examining the Technical Details Behind the Presence Sharing Scenario" section covers the related technical details.

This response contains information about how to find the ABS, which enables fast and remote lookups of the corporate address book, provisioning information, and meeting and unified communications policy settings.

Next, Communicator issues a one-time query to identify which media types the server infrastructure can support for multiparty conferences. It sends a SERVICE request asking for the available multipoint control units (MCUs), to determine the media types that are available (IM, phone, and audio/video).

```
SERVICE sip:jeremy@contoso.com;gruu;opaque=app:conf:focusfactory SIP/2.0
Via: SIP/2.0/TLS 192.168.3.100:2062
Max-Forwards: 70
From: <sip:jeremy@contoso.com>;tag=43cae3a206;epid=aa6d968e18
To: <sip:jeremy@contoso.com;gruu;opaque=app:conf:focusfactory>
Call-ID: 2d7ca35fab1c45d1917bbdf754871b0c
CSeq: 1 SERVICE
Contact: <sip:jeremy@contoso.com;opaque=user:epid:upbza9anR1KJ-8E7UvWEDQAA;gruu>
User-Agent: UCCP/2.0.6093.0 OC/2.0.6093.0 (Microsoft Office Communicator)
Proxy-Authorization: Kerberos qop="auth", realm="SIP Communications Service",
opaque="A7AB18E7", crand="0ca09d1a", cnum="4",
targetname="sip/srv.contoso.com", response=
"602306092a864886f71201020201011100ffffffff4b8520aacbeee71780ccd31c1f2d1675"
Content-Type: application/cccp+xml
Content-Length: 302
<?xml version="1.0"?>
<request xmlns="urn:ietf:params:xml:ns:cccp"
xmlns:mscp="http://schemas.microsoft.com/rtc/2005/08/cccpextensions"
C3PVersion="1" to="sip:jeremy@contoso.com;gruu;opaque=app:conf:focusfactory"
from="sip:jeremy@contoso.com" requestId="17694972">
   <getAvailableMcuTypes/>
</request>
```

The server responds successfully and specifies that audio and video (*audio-video*), data conferencing and application sharing (*meeting*), instant messaging (*chat*), and phone conferencing (*phone-conf*) MCUs are available for use as shown in the body of the 200 OK response, as follows:

```
SIP/2.0 200 OK
Authentication-Info: Kerberos rspauth=
"602306092A864886F71201020201011100FFFFFFFF9C88E2ED809296A76C6F19B1B939F0F8",
srand="87A1E1DD", snum="3", opaque="A7AB18E7", qop="auth",
targetname="sip/srv.contoso.com", realm="SIP Communications Service"
Content-Length: 996
Via: SIP/2.0/TLS 192.168.3.100:2062;ms-received-port=2062;ms-received-cid=2700
From: "Jeremy Los"<sip:jeremy@contoso.com>;tag=43cae3a206;epid=aa6d968e18
To: <sip:jeremy@contoso.com;gruu;opaque=app:conf:focusfactory>;tag=D7146366
Call-ID: 2d7ca35fab1c45d1917bbdf754871b0c
CSeq: 1 SERVICE
Content-Type: application/cccp+xml
<response xmlns="urn:ietf:params:xml:ns:cccp"
xmlns:msacp="http://schemas.microsoft.com/rtc/2005/08/acpconfinfoextensions"
xmlns:msav="http://schemas.microsoft.com/rtc/2005/08/avconfinfoextensions"
xmlns:mscp="http://schemas.microsoft.com/rtc/2005/08/cccpextensions"
xmlns:msci="http://schemas.microsoft.com/rtc/2005/08/confinfoextensions"
xmlns:msdata="http://schemas.microsoft.com/rtc/2005/08/dataconfinfoextensions"
xmlns:msim="http://schemas.microsoft.com/rtc/2005/08/imconfinfoextensions"
xmlns:ci="urn:ietf:params:xml:ns:conference-info"
xmlns:cis="urn:ietf:params:xml:ns:conference-info-separator"
xmlns:msls="urn:ietf:params:xml:ns:msls" requestId="17694972" C3PVersion="1"
from="sip:jeremy@contoso.com;gruu;opaque=app:conf:focusfactory"
to="sip:jeremy@contoso.com" code="success">
  <getAvailableMcuTypes>
   <mcu-types>
    <mcuType>audio-video</mcuType>
    <mcuType>meeting</mcuType>
    <mcuType>chat</mcuType>
    <mcuType>phone-conf</mcuType>
   </mcu-types>
  </getAvailableMcuTypes>
</response>
```

Communicator also queries for its location profile to get dialing rules. It issues another SERVICE request, as follows:

```
SERVICE sip:jeremy@contoso.com;gruu;opaque=app:locationprofile:get;default
SIP/2.0
Via: SIP/2.0/TLS 192.168.3.100:2062
Max-Forwards: 70
From: <sip:jeremy@contoso.com>;tag=43cae3a206;epid=aa6d968e18
To: sip:jeremy@contoso.com;gruu;opaque=app:locationprofile:get;default
Call-ID: 0842328998844bbe9602c6576997f359
CSeq: 1 SERVICE
Contact: sip:jeremy@contoso.com;opaque=user:epid:upbza9anR1KJ-8E7UvWEDQAA;gruu
User-Agent: UCCP/2.0.6249.0 OC/2.0.6249.0 (Microsoft Office Communicator)
```

```
Accept: application/ms-location-profile-definition+xml
Proxy-Authorization: NTLM qop="auth", realm="SIP Communications Service",
opaque="E8DC04B4", crand="d93f8137", cnum="4",
targetname="sip/srv.contoso.com", response="0100000033323839c87cccc75ec0b9fe"
Content-Type: application/ms-location-profile-definition+xml
Content-Length: 2
```

The response shows the dialing plan that is in place that the client should use, and it provides guidance on how extensions listed on a contact should be dialed in the last rule. This chapter simply points out these items. Additional information is provided in later chapters covering telephony and Voice over IP (VoIP).

```
SIP/2.0 200 OK
Authentication-Info: NTLM rspauth="01000000000000000225D5215EC0B9FE",
srand="C8E1D4C1", snum="5", opaque="E8DC04B4", qop="auth",
targetname="sip/srv.contoso.com", realm="SIP Communications Service"
Content-Length: 1277
Via: SIP/2.0/TLS 192.168.3.100:2062;ms-received-port=2062;ms-received-cid=2700
From: <sip:jeremy@contoso.com>;tag=43cae3a206;epid=aa6d968e18
To: <sip:jeremy@contoso.com;gruu;opaque=app:locationprofile:get;default>; tag=D7146366
Call-ID: 0842328998844bbe9602c6576997f359
CSeq: 1 SERVICE
Content-Type: application/ms-location-profile-definition+xml
Server: APP/TranslationService3.0.0.0

<LocationProfileDescription xmlns=
"http://schemas.microsoft.com/2007/03/locationProfileDescription">
<Name>Default</Name>
<Rule><Pattern>^([3-7]\d{4})$</Pattern><Translation>+142570$1</Translation></Rule>
<Rule><Pattern>^([4,5,7,9]11)t?$</Pattern><Translation>+$1</Translation></Rule>
<Rule><Pattern>^9([4,5,7,9]11)$</Pattern><Translation>+$1</Translation></Rule>
<Rule><Pattern>^0$</Pattern><Translation>+14258828080</Translation></Rule>
<Rule><Pattern>^9(\d+)$</Pattern><Translation>+$1</Translation></Rule>
<Rule><Pattern>^(\+?)(\d+)(X|x|EXT)(\d+)$</Pattern><Translation>$1$2;
ext=$4</Translation></Rule>
</LocationProfileDescription>
```

Communicator now uses the contact list that was received during the query for roaming contacts and issues a batch subscription against all contacts. (There happens to be only one in this example, but there could be tens and even hundreds, depending on the user.) The subscription also lists the things that are of interest from the remote contacts (calendar information, notes, presence state, and so on). The batch subscription is sent in the body of a SUBSCRIBE message, as follows:

```
SUBSCRIBE sip:jeremy@contoso.com SIP/2.0
Via: SIP/2.0/TLS 192.168.3.100:2062
Max-Forwards: 70
From: <sip:jeremy@contoso.com>;tag=8024faf8af;epid=aa6d968e18
To: <sip:jeremy@contoso.com>
Call-ID: a1eeb9389b0b445d93eafcf531533371
CSeq: 1 SUBSCRIBE
Contact: <sip:jeremy@contoso.com;opaque=user:epid:upbza9anR1KJ-8E7UvWEDQAA;gruu>
User-Agent: UCCP/2.0.6093.0 OC/2.0.6093.0 (Microsoft Office Communicator)
Event: presence
Accept: application/msrtc-event-categories+xml, application/xpidf+xml,
text/xml+msrtc.pidf, application/pidf+xml, application/rlmi+xml,
multipart/related
Supported: com.microsoft.autoextend
Supported: ms-benotify
Proxy-Require: ms-benotify
Supported: ms-piggyback-first-notify
Require: adhoclist, categoryList
Supported: eventlist
Proxy-Authorization: Kerberos qop="auth", realm="SIP Communications Service",
opaque="A7AB18E7", crand="e396cb73", cnum="5",
targetname="sip/srv.contoso.com",
response=
"602306092a864886f71201020201011100ffffffff664a5be74c5546f938944757f539c2ed"
Content-Type: application/msrtc-adrl-categorylist+xml
Content-Length: 489
<batchSub xmlns="http://schemas.microsoft.com/2006/01/sip/
batch-subscribe" uri="sip:jeremy@contoso.com" name="">
 <action name="subscribe" id="18640544">
  <adhocList><resource uri="sip:rui@contoso.com"/></adhocList>
  <categoryList xmlns="http://schemas.microsoft.com/2006/09/sip/categorylist">
  <category name="calendarData"/><category name="contactCard"/>
  <category name="note"/>
  <category name="services"/>
  <category name="sourcenetwork"/>
  <category name="state"/>
  </categoryList>
 </action>
</batchSub>
```

The server responds with a successful response to the batch subscription in the form of a 200 OK response, as follows:

```
SIP/2.0 200 OK
Contact: <sip:srv.contoso.com:5061;transport=tls>
Authentication-Info: Kerberos rspauth=
"602306092A864886F71201020201011100FFFFFFFF77907E97AFD6725C45B116D563B803E5",
srand="DB5FE03E", snum="6", opaque="A7AB18E7", qop="auth",
targetname="sip/srv.contoso.com", realm="SIP Communications Service"
Content-Length: 1576
Via: SIP/2.0/TLS 192.168.3.100:2062;ms-received-port=2062;ms-received-cid=2700
From: "Jeremy Los"<sip:jeremy@contoso.com>;tag=8024faf8af;epid=aa6d968e18
```

```
To: <sip:jeremy@contoso.com>;tag=EE220080
Call-ID: a1eeb9389b0b445d93eafcf531533371
CSeq: 1 SUBSCRIBE
Expires: 27360
Require: eventlist
Content-Type: multipart/related; type="application/rlmi+xml";start=resourceList;
boundary=f018561c40be4d03b799bff0e31ca241
Event: presence
subscription-state: active;expires=27360
ms-piggyback-cseq: 1
Supported: ms-benotify, ms-piggyback-first-notify--
f018561c40be4d03b799bff0e31ca241Content-Transfer-Encoding: binary
Content-ID: resourceList
Content-Type: application/rlmi+xml
<list xmlns="urn:ietf:params:xml:ns:rlmi" uri="sip:jeremy@contoso.com"
version="0" fullState="false"/>--f018561c40be4d03b799bff0e31ca241Content-
Transfer-Encoding: binaryContent-Type: application/msrtc-event-categories+xml
<categories xmlns="http://schemas.microsoft.com/2006/09/sip/categories"
uri="sip:rui@contoso.com"> <category name="calendarData"/>
<category name="contactCard" instance="0" publishTime=
"2007-05-03T05:37:43.843">
<contactCard xmlns="http://schemas.microsoft.com/2006/09/sip/contactcard" >
<identity >    <name ><displayName >Rui Raposo</displayName></name>
</identity>  </contactCard> </category> <category name="note"/>
<category name="state" instance="1" publishTime="2007-05-04T22:46:17.583">
  <state xsi:type="aggregateState" xmlns:xsi=
"http://www.w3.org/2001/XMLSchema-instance"
xmlns="http://schemas.microsoft.com/2006/09/sip/state">
   <availability>3500</availability>
  </state>
 </category>
 <category name="services" instance="0" publishTime="2007-05-04T22:46:17.583">
  <services xmlns="http://schemas.microsoft.com/2006/09/sip/service">
   <service uri="sip:rui@contoso.com">
    <capabilities>
     <text render="true" capture="true" deviceAvailability="3500" />
     <gifInk render="true" capture="false" deviceAvailability="3500" />
     <isfInk render="true" capture="false" deviceAvailability="3500" />
    </capabilities>
   </service>
  </services>
 </category>
</categories>

--f018561c40be4d03b799bff0e31ca241--
```

The server is actually returning presence information for users that it maintains information for. In this example, the only existing contact, *Rui*, happened to be maintained on the same server, so his subscription is already confirmed (*subscribed="true"*). Because of this, Communicator itself does not need to issue any subscription requests directly. The server can accept all subscriptions locally. If some of the contacts are not maintained on the same server, Communicator manages to send a separate subscription directly to each contact (to which the remote contact's home server responds).

The rich presence schema shows the user's *availability*, *activity*, *displayName*, *e-mail*, *phoneNumber*, *userInfo*, and *devices*. The *availability* section identifies whether the user is busy either because his calendar currently has an appointment or because he manually set his availability. This information is combined, interpreted, and stored in an aggregate numeric value that determines availability. It is worth knowing that these number values are compared to known ranges that Communicator uses to aggregate activity and availability levels into states. The *activity* section is similar and combines information from all workstations to track whether the user is active, idle, or logged out. The *userInfo* section contains global information for the user that is used to compose the underlying data that contacts can view (depending on their level of access). The *devices* section contains a list of devices and the information that each of these devices publish. This information is merged by the server to give a singular view of the user and offer means for connectivity.

Finally, Communicator generates presence information for the client and publishes that information by sending a SERVICE request to the server with an embedded XML *publish* command, as follows:

```
SERVICE sip:jeremy@contoso.com SIP/2.0
Via: SIP/2.0/TLS 192.168.3.100:2062
Max-Forwards: 70
From: <sip:jeremy@contoso.com>;tag=7ae5f901b8;epid=aa6d968e18
To: <sip:jeremy@contoso.com>
Call-ID: d661a29ddb364c61ab1009edbe5e2b95
CSeq: 1 SERVICE
Contact: <sip:jeremy@contoso.com;opaque=user:epid:upbza9anR1KJ-8E7UvWEDQAA;gruu>
User-Agent: UCCP/2.0.6093.0 OC/2.0.6093.0 (Microsoft Office Communicator)
Proxy-Authorization: Kerberos qop="auth", realm="SIP Communications Service",
opaque="A7AB18E7", crand="8ddc94ae", cnum="6", targetname="sip/srv.contoso.com",
response="602306092a864886f71201020201011100ffffffff2a567bb3a6d1ce598e39074
cf9e13419"Content-Type: application/msrtc-category-publish+xml
Content-Length: 1392
<publish xmlns="http://schemas.microsoft.com/2006/09/sip/rich-presence">
<publications uri="sip:jeremy@contoso.com">
  <publication categoryName="device" instance="198826231" container="2"
version="0" expireType="endpoint">
   <device xmlns="http://schemas.microsoft.com/2006/09/sip/device"
endpointId="6BF396BA-A7D6-5247-89FB-C13B52F5840D">
     <capabilities preferred="false" uri="sip:jeremy@contoso.com">
      <text capture="true" render="true" publish="false"/>
      <gifInk capture="false" render="true" publish="false"/>
      <isfInk capture="false" render="true" publish="false"/>
     </capabilities>
     <timezone>00:00:00-06:00</timezone>
     <machineName>OC-CLIENT</machineName>
   </device>
  </publication>
  <publication categoryName="state" instance="817733007" container="3"  version="0"
```

```
expireType="endpoint">  <state xmlns="http://schemas.microsoft.com/2006/09/sip/state"
manual="false" xmlns:xsi="http://www.w3.org/2001/XMLSchema-instance"
xsi:type="machineState">
     <availability>3500</availability>
     <endpointLocation></endpointLocation>
    </state>
   </publication>
   <publication categoryName="state" instance="817733007" container="2" version="0"
expireType="endpoint">
    <state xmlns="http://schemas.microsoft.com/2006/09/sip/state" manual="false"
xmlns:xsi="http://www.w3.org/2001/XMLSchema-instance" xsi:type="machineState">
     <availability>3500</availability>
     <endpointLocation></endpointLocation>
    </state>
   </publication>
  </publications>
</publish>
```

The server accepts this presence publication with a 200 OK response that contains the complete presence document for the user across all devices, after the published presence information for this workstation is taken into account, as follows:

```
SIP/2.0 200 OK
Authentication-Info: Kerberos rspauth=
"602306092A864886F71201020201011100FFFFFFFF7F95AF99B5AA4135D9873CEDF9F8C192",
srand="9D59FA63", snum="7", opaque="A7AB18E7", qop="auth",
targetname="sip/srv.contoso.com", realm="SIP Communications Service"
Content-Length: 7638
Via: SIP/2.0/TLS 192.168.3.100:2062;ms-received-port=2062;ms-received-cid=2700
From: "Jeremy Los"<sip:jeremy@contoso.com>;tag=7ae5f901b8;epid=aa6d968e18
To: <sip:jeremy@contoso.com>;tag=A1F542AB99D66616F9252CB6DF50257F
Call-ID: d661a29ddb364c61ab1009edbe5e2b95
CSeq: 1 SERVICE
Content-Type: application/vnd-microsoft-roaming-self+xml
<roamingData xmlns="http://schemas.microsoft.com/2006/09/sip/roaming-self"
xmlns:cat="http://schemas.microsoft.com/2006/09/sip/categories"
xmlns:con="http://schemas.microsoft.com/2006/09/sip/containers"
xmlns:sub="http://schemas.microsoft.com/2006/09/sip/presence-subscribers">
<categories xmlns="http://schemas.microsoft.com/2006/09/sip/categories"
uri="sip:jeremy@contoso.com">  <category name="state" instance="1"
publishTime="2007-05-04T22:48:10.357" container="2" version="1"
expireType="user">   <state xsi:type="aggregateState"
xmlns:xsi="http://www.w3.org/2001/XMLSchema-instance"
xmlns="http://schemas.microsoft.com/2006/09/sip/state">
    <availability>3500</availability>
   </state>  </category>  <category name="state" instance="268435456"
publishTime="2007-05-04T22:48:10.357" container="2" version="1"
expireType="user">   <state xsi:type="aggregateMachineState"
endpointId="6bf396ba-a7d6-5247-89fb-c13b52f5840d"
xmlns:xsi="http://www.w3.org/2001/XMLSchema-instance"
xmlns="http://schemas.microsoft.com/2006/09/sip/state">
    <availability>3500</availability>
```

```
  </state>  </category>  <category name="state" instance="817733007"
publishTime="2007-05-04T22:48:10.357" container="2" version="1"
expireType="endpoint" endpointId="6BF396BA-A7D6-5247-89FB-C13B52F5840D">
<state xmlns="http://schemas.microsoft.com/2006/09/sip/state"
xmlns:xsi="http://www.w3.org/2001/XMLSchema-instance" manual="false"
xsi:type="machineState" >
    <availability >3500</availability>
    <endpointLocation ></endpointLocation>
  </state>  </category>  <category name="device" instance="198826231"
publishTime="2007-05-04T22:48:10.357" container="2" version="1"
expireType="endpoint" endpointId="6BF396BA-A7D6-5247-89FB-C13B52F5840D">
<device xmlns="http://schemas.microsoft.com/2006/09/sip/device"
endpointId="6BF396BA-A7D6-5247-89FB-C13B52F5840D" >
    <capabilities preferred="false" uri="sip:jeremy@contoso.com" >
     <text capture="true" render="true" publish="false" ></text>
     <gifInk capture="false" render="true" publish="false" ></gifInk>
     <isfInk capture="false" render="true" publish="false" ></isfInk>
    </capabilities>
    <timezone >00:00:00-06:00</timezone>
    <machineName >OC-CLIENT</machineName>
  </device>  </category>  <category name="services" instance="0"
publishTime="2007-05-04T22:48:10.357" container="2" version="1"
expireType="user">
<services xmlns="http://schemas.microsoft.com/2006/09/sip/service">
    <service uri="sip:jeremy@contoso.com">
     <capabilities>
      <text render="true" capture="true" publish="false"
preferredEndpointId="6bf396ba-a7d6-5247-89fb-c13b52f5840d"
deviceAvailability="3500" />
      <gifInk render="true" capture="false" publish="false"
preferredEndpointId="6bf396ba-a7d6-5247-89fb-c13b52f5840d"
deviceAvailability="3500" />
      <isfInk render="true" capture="false" publish="false"
preferredEndpointId="6bf396ba-a7d6-5247-89fb-c13b52f5840d"
deviceAvailability="3500" />
     </capabilities>
    </service>
  </services>  </category>  <category name="state" instance="1"
publishTime="2007-05-04T22:48:10.357" container="3" version="1"
expireType="user">    <state xsi:type="aggregateState"
xmlns:xsi="http://www.w3.org/2001/XMLSchema-instance"
xmlns="http://schemas.microsoft.com/2006/09/sip/state">
    <availability>3500</availability>
  </state>  </category>  <category name="state" instance="817733007"
publishTime="2007-05-04T22:48:10.357" container="3" version="1"
expireType="endpoint" endpointId="6BF396BA-A7D6-5247-89FB-C13B52F5840D">
<state xmlns="http://schemas.microsoft.com/2006/09/sip/state"
xmlns:xsi="http://www.w3.org/2001/XMLSchema-instance" manual="false"
xsi:type="machineState" >
    <availability >3500</availability>
    <endpointLocation ></endpointLocation>
  </state>  </category>  <category name="state" instance="1"
publishTime="2007-05-04T22:48:10.357" container="100" version="1"
expireType="user">    <state xsi:type="aggregateState"
```

```
xmlns:xsi="http://www.w3.org/2001/XMLSchema-instance"
xmlns="http://schemas.microsoft.com/2006/09/sip/state">
    <availability>3500</availability>
   </state>  </category>  <category name="legacyInterop" instance="1"
publishTime="2007-05-04T22:48:10.357" container="100" version="1"
expireType="user">   <legacyInterop availability="3500" />  </category>
<category name="services" instance="0" publishTime="2007-05-04T22:48:10.357"
container="100" version="1" expireType="user">
<services xmlns="http://schemas.microsoft.com/2006/09/sip/service">
    <service uri="sip:jeremy@contoso.com">
     <capabilities>
      <text render="true" capture="true" deviceAvailability="3500" />
      <gifInk render="true" capture="false" deviceAvailability="3500" />
      <isfInk render="true" capture="false" deviceAvailability="3500" />
     </capabilities>
    </service>
   </services>  </category>  <category name="state" instance="1"
publishTime="2007-05-04T22:48:10.357" container="200" version="1"
expireType="user">   <state xsi:type="aggregateState"
xmlns:xsi="http://www.w3.org/2001/XMLSchema-instance"
xmlns="http://schemas.microsoft.com/2006/09/sip/state">
    <availability>3500</availability>
   </state>  </category>  <category name="legacyInterop" instance="1"
publishTime="2007-05-04T22:48:10.357" container="200" version="1"
expireType="user">
   <legacyInterop availability="3500" />  </category>
<category name="services" instance="0" publishTime="2007-05-04T22:48:10.357"
container="200" version="1" expireType="user">
   <services xmlns="http://schemas.microsoft.com/2006/09/sip/service">
    <service uri="sip:jeremy@contoso.com">
     <capabilities>
      <text render="true" capture="true" deviceAvailability="3500" />
      <gifInk render="true" capture="false" deviceAvailability="3500" />
      <isfInk render="true" capture="false" deviceAvailability="3500" />
     </capabilities>
    </service>
   </services>  </category>  <category name="state" instance="1"
publishTime="2007-05-04T22:48:10.357" container="300" version="1"
expireType="user">
   <state xsi:type="aggregateState"
xmlns:xsi="http://www.w3.org/2001/XMLSchema-instance"
xmlns="http://schemas.microsoft.com/2006/09/sip/state">
    <availability>3500</availability>
   </state>  </category>  <category name="legacyInterop" instance="1"
publishTime="2007-05-04T22:48:10.357" container="300" version="1"
expireType="user">
   <legacyInterop availability="3500" />  </category>
<category name="services" instance="0" publishTime="2007-05-04T22:48:10.357"
container="300" version="1" expireType="user">
   <services xmlns="http://schemas.microsoft.com/2006/09/sip/service">
    <service uri="sip:jeremy@contoso.com">
     <capabilities>
      <text render="true" capture="true" deviceAvailability="3500" />
      <gifInk render="true" capture="false" deviceAvailability="3500" />
```

```
      <isfInk render="true" capture="false" deviceAvailability="3500" />
     </capabilities>
    </service>
   </services>  </category>  <category name="state" instance="1"
publishTime="2007-05-04T22:48:10.357" container="400" version="1"
expireType="user">  <state xsi:type="aggregateState"
xmlns:xsi="http://www.w3.org/2001/XMLSchema-instance"
xmlns="http://schemas.microsoft.com/2006/09/sip/state">
    <availability>3500</availability>
   </state>  </category>  <category name="legacyInterop" instance="1"
publishTime="2007-05-04T22:48:10.357" container="400" version="1"
expireType="user">
   <legacyInterop availability="3500" />  </category>
<category name="services" instance="0" publishTime="2007-05-04T22:48:10.357"
container="400" version="1" expireType="user">
   <services xmlns="http://schemas.microsoft.com/2006/09/sip/service">
    <service uri="sip:jeremy@contoso.com">
     <capabilities>
      <text render="true" capture="true" deviceAvailability="3500" />
      <gifInk render="true" capture="false" deviceAvailability="3500" />
      <isfInk render="true" capture="false" deviceAvailability="3500" />
     </capabilities>
    </service>
   </services>  </category> </categories></roamingData>
```


For all users who are not maintained on the same server that the user is, the bulk subscription response tells Communicator to "resubscribe." After Communicator finishes registering and establishing subscriptions for basic user settings and local contacts on its server, it moves into the "logged in" state and allows the user to start issuing commands and viewing presence information.

Understanding Post-Login Processing (Post-Step 4)

To prevent delays because of slower links, Communicator waits to gather presence information for users who are not maintained on the same server until after the client UI is presented and the user is "logged in." Communicator then issues individual subscriptions for all the remaining users by issuing a small set of subscriptions and issuing the next subscriptions as the previous subscriptions complete. The scenarios described do not have additional contacts that are not homed on the same server, so this is not presented in detail. However, a simple subscription dialog is established for each contact, and notifications of presence changes occur directly with the server where the contact is maintained.

At this point, the login process is complete. It is worth understanding that this login section simply establishes connectivity and an authenticated relationship with the infrastructure, gathers information about the user and the Office Communications Server infrastructure, and establishes the subscriptions used to get real-time updates. Additional work is required of Communicator to maintain these subscriptions to prevent them from expiring over time and to refresh the authenticated registration established with the infrastructure. The following sections discuss features and functionality provided by Communicator 2007 after it is logged in.

Understanding How Presence Information Is Shared

To explain how presence information is shared, presence is first defined and explained. Usage examples are explained that involve presence information as the user sees it, based on the steps taken and the feedback Communicator 2007 provides. Finally, the technical steps, decisions, and protocols that are going on in the background are explained to provide a rich experiential understanding that will aid in troubleshooting presence problems and setting presence authorization properly based on your needs.

What Is Presence?

Virtual communication systems must provide the same information that people typically have if they are sitting next to each other or working in the same office. Is the other person there, is she busy, and is she able to talk? Presence information attempts to capture and identify whether a remote user is willing to communicate and what means that user has to communicate. Communicator 2007 and Office Communications Server provide much more than these basics, however. Communicator allows publishing of location on a per-client basis (home, office or custom location) and publishing of custom informational notes (which can be kept in sync with "out of office" e-mail auto-responses from Microsoft Office Outlook). It even ties this in with scheduling information to allow authorized partners to view calendar details. In this way, presence in Office Communications Server is about the ability and willingness to communicate, but it also contains information *about* the partner that goes beyond communication with the partner.

Overview of the Presence Sharing Scenario

This scenario walks Jeremy Los through using Communicator 2007 to gather presence information from Office Communications Server and control the level of access another person has to his presence information. Office Communications Server must have already been installed on the enterprise network, and Jeremy must have already installed Communicator on his workstation and completed a successful login. The overview will show what Jeremy (and his remote contact, Vadim N. Korepin) sees from the Communicator user interface and what steps he and his remote contact take.

Step 1: Looking Up a Contact

Jeremy clicks in the contact search box at the top of the Communicator 2007 window and types in the name of a local colleague he wants to contact, Vadim N. Korepin. Information on Vadim is retrieved and displayed. (See Figure 4-7.) Note that a contact card with information can be shown by clicking the small arrow that appears to the left of the presence icon when you hover over this area with the mouse. From this list, contacts can be called (using a phone or computer on either end, if support is provided) by clicking on the phone icon to the right of the contact name, or an instant message can be sent by simply double-clicking the name.

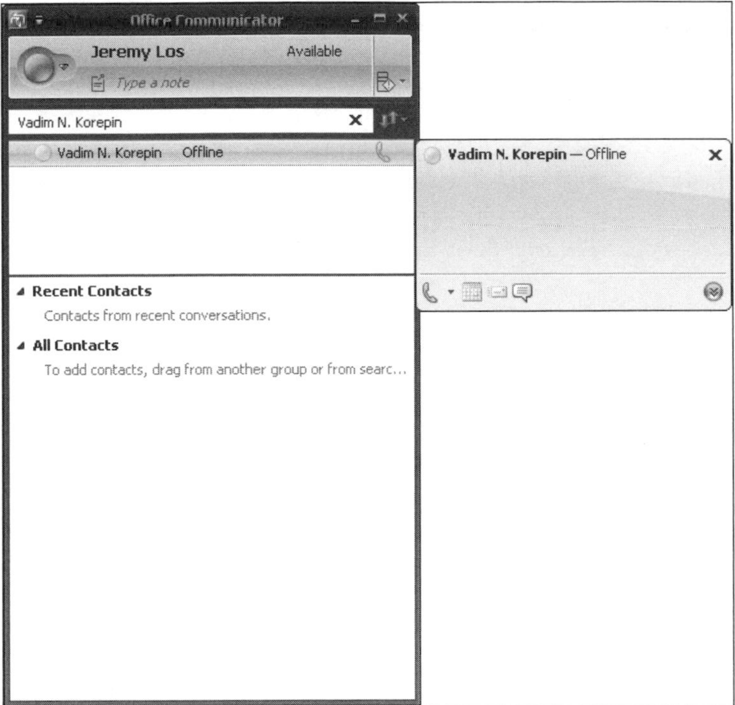

Figure 4-7 Communicator 2007—Contact lookup and contact card

Step 2: Adding a Contact

Because Jeremy works regularly with Vadim, he wants to make Vadim's contact information readily available. He right-clicks the contact listing and selects Add To Contact List, which brings up a menu of contact groups he has set up. Jeremy selects All Contacts to add Vadim to the list of contacts that are readily available on the main Communicator window, as shown in Figure 4-8.

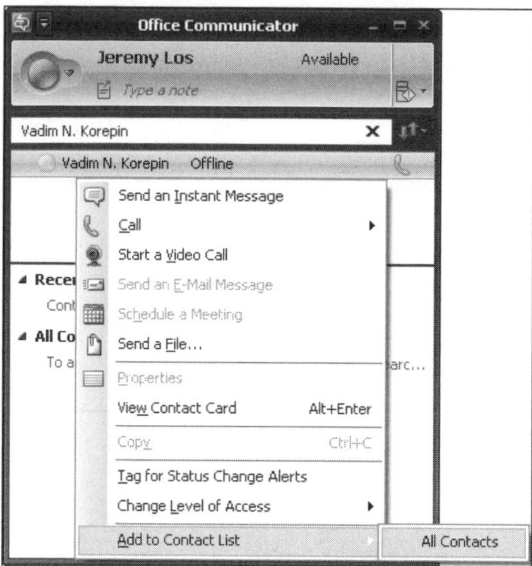

Figure 4-8 Communicator 2007—Adding a contact

Step 3: Receiving an Offline Indication

Jeremy looks on the main Communicator 2007 window and sees that Vadim is currently offline, as shown in Figure 4-9. Jeremy proceeds with other work while waiting for Vadim to become available.

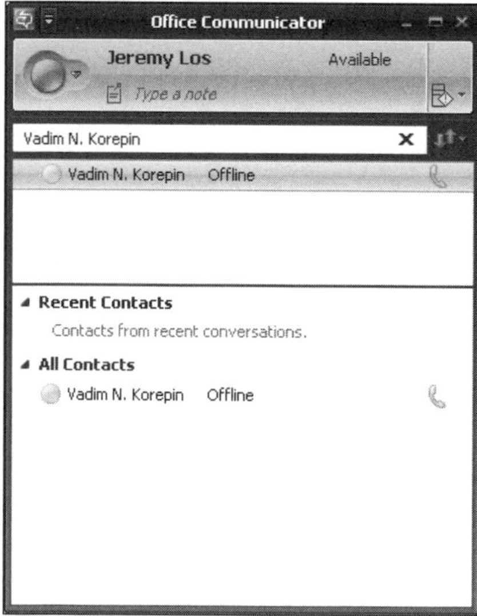

Figure 4-9 Communicator 2007—Contact offline

Step 4: Logging In the Contact and Receiving Updated Presence Information

Vadim logs in to his office workstation when he arrives at work. Vadim receives an alert telling him that Jeremy added him as a contact, as shown in Figure 4-10. Vadim decides to add Jeremy as a contact during authorization, and clicks OK.

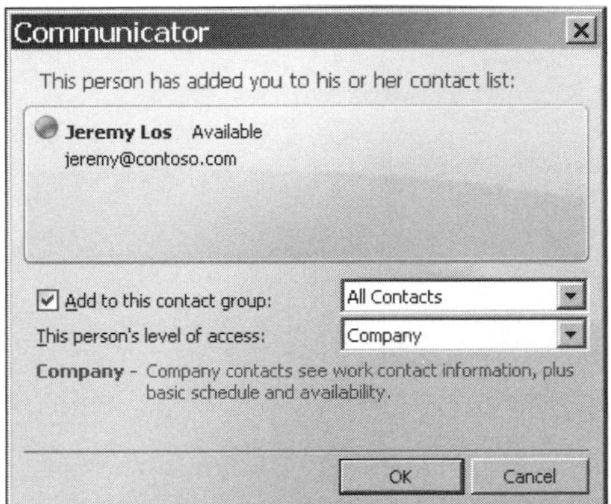

Figure 4-10 Communicator 2007—Added to contact list

Meanwhile, Jeremy receives a notification from Communicator that Vadim has come online, as shown in Figure 4-11.

Figure 4-11 Communicator 2007—Presence update

Step 5: Controlling the Access Level of a Contact

Jeremy has worked previously with Vadim and trusts him with more detailed contact information about himself. He wants to share details from his calendar with Vadim to make sure they stay in sync. Jeremy right-clicks on Vadim's contact listing and Change Level Of Access, and he switches it to Team, as shown in Figure 4-12. This change grants Vadim rights to see details about Jeremy's schedule and availability.

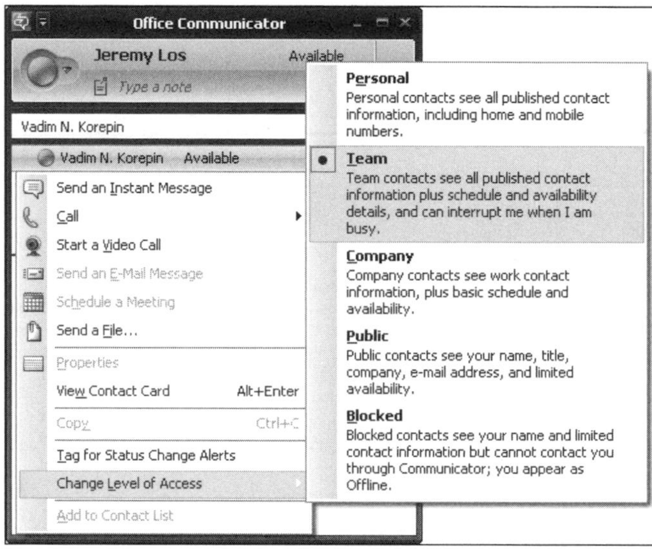

Figure 4-12 Communicator 2007 Control access level

Examining the Technical Details Behind the Presence Sharing Scenario

This section provides technical background on what is happening with Communicator 2007 and the network of Office Communications Servers. Reviewing this section should aid you in understanding the product and thinking through troubleshooting presence-related scenarios later, if the need arises. Presence queries, presence notifications, contact lists, authorization, routing, and the Session Initiation Protocol (SIP) are covered as they relate to these presence scenarios. The following diagram provides an overview of the steps involved in the presence sharing scenario that we will analyze:

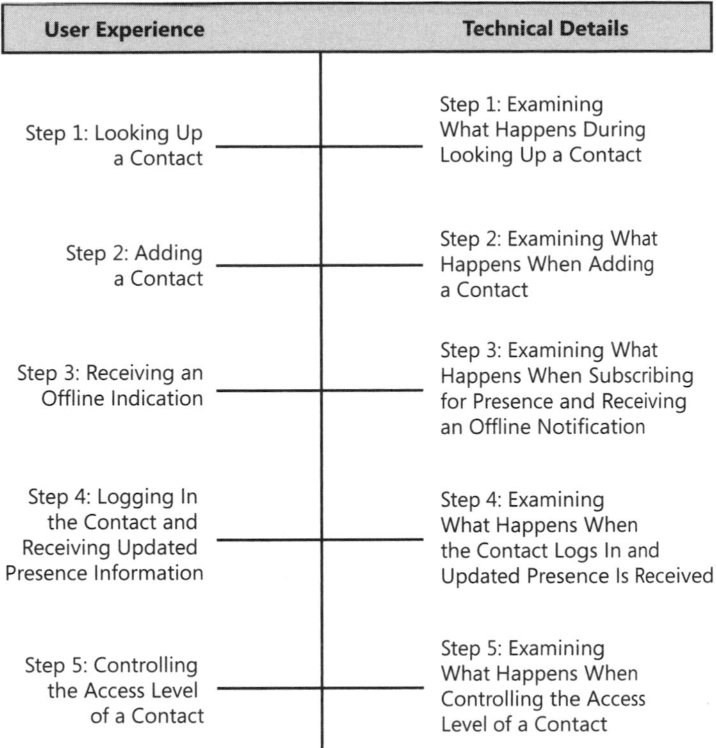

User Experience
Technical Details
Step 1: Looking Up a Contact
Step 1: Examining What Happens During Looking Up a Contact
Step 2: Adding a Contact
Step 2: Examining What Happens When Adding a Contact
Step 3: Receiving an Offline Indication
Step 3: Examining What Happens When Subscribing for Presence and Receiving an Offline Notification
Step 4: Logging In the Contact and Receiving Updated Presence Information
Step 4: Examining What Happens When the Contact Logs In and Updated Presence Is Received
Step 5: Controlling the Access Level of a Contact
Step 5: Examining What Happens When Controlling the Access Level of a Contact

Examining What Happens During Looking Up a Contact (Step 1)

When Communicator is asked to look up a contact, it leverages the contact list it synchronizes with Office Communications Server and the address book that it synchronizes from Outlook on the local machine or the address book that it downloads from the Address Book Server publishing URL. The Address Book Server publishing URL is handed to the client as a result of the subscription step for provisioning and configuration information during login. Step 3 from the "Examining the Technical Details Behind the Login Process" section earlier in the chapter shows the Address Book Server publishing URL received, as follows:

```
<absInternalServerUrl>http://srv.contoso.com/Abs/Int</absInternalServerUrl>
```

With these contact lists combined, Communicator simply indexes the list and is ready to quickly provide search results. As a user types in a contact name, the list is searched by e-mail address, SIP URI, and first/last name. If the name is not recognized and typing pauses, an entry is created (which might or might not be a valid contact at the moment). If an entry exists that is not already in Communicator's list of subscriptions, there is no existing knowledge of the presence information for the new contact entry. This unknown entry results in a presence query, in an attempt to determine if this account exists and, if it does, the contact's presence status.

The presence query that would have been made in the example while looking up Vadim's information is shown next. It involves making a SERVICE request with an XML body that issues a *getPresence* query, as follows:

```
SERVICE sip:vadim@contoso.com SIP/2.0
Via: SIP/2.0/TLS 192.168.3.100:1467
Max-Forwards: 70
From: <sip:jeremy@contoso.com>;tag=81b8232d08;epid=aa6d968e18
To: <sip:vadim@contoso.com>
Call-ID: c31cb9c85d564f15b96a7faf253bd8f0
CSeq: 1 SERVICE
Contact: <sip:jeremy@contoso.com;opaque=user:epid:upbza9anR1KJ-8E7UvWEDQAA;gruu>
User-Agent: UCCP/2.0.6093.0 OC/2.0.6093.0 (Microsoft Office Communicator)
Proxy-Authorization: Kerberos qop="auth", realm="SIP Communications Service",
opaque="E8EA7EDD", crand="fccc07aa", cnum="8",
targetname="sip/srv.contoso.com", response=
"602306092a864886f71201020201011100ffffffff7be3d5766e71b585c2b165da61edf9ee"
Content-Type: application/SOAP+xml
Content-Length: 261

<SOAP-ENV:Envelope xmlns:SOAP-ENV="http://schemas.xmlsoap.org/soap/envelope/">
 <SOAP-ENV:Body>
  <m:getPresence xmlns:m="http://schemas.microsoft.com/winrtc/2002/11/sip">
   <presentity uri="sip:vadim@contoso.com"/>
  </m:getPresence>
 </SOAP-ENV:Body>
</SOAP-ENV:Envelope>
```

The server could respond in several ways to this SERVICE request, as follows:

- **200 OK** In this case, the server network responds with whatever contact and presence information is available for the user. Most enterprises enable presence within the company automatically, but if you go outside of the corporate network to get presence for a remote contact, this is not always the case.
- **404 Not Found** In this case, the server network identifies that the contact did not exist (either locally, remotely, or because the domain could not be routed to).
- **504 Server Time-Out** In this case, a server (probably the Access Edge Server) was unable to forward the message, or a valid remote domain could not be found. This could be because of a network configuration problem, a network outage, or simply because the domain has a typo or does not exist currently.

For any failure cases, the *ms-diagnostics* header should have information about the failure to help you understand whether there is a problem with the URI specified by the user, or whether there is an unexpected issue with the network.

In the example, the server sends a 200 OK response showing Vadim to be offline but sharing some of his contact information, as follows:

```
SIP/2.0 200 OK
Authentication-Info: Kerberos rspauth=
"602306092A864886F71201020201011100FFFFFFFF46E1CA29B5AB2E8D38D0560422E9CC23",
srand="CBB0F6C9", snum="12", opaque="E8EA7EDD", qop="auth",
targetname="sip/srv.contoso.com", realm="SIP Communications Service"
Content-Length: 537
Via: SIP/2.0/TLS 192.168.3.100:1467;ms-received-port=1467;ms-received-cid=A00
From: "Jeremy Los"<sip:jeremy@contoso.com>;tag=81b8232d08;epid=aa6d968e18
To: <sip:vadim@contoso.com>;tag=A1F542AB99D66616F9252CB6DF50257F
Call-ID: c31cb9c85d564f15b96a7faf253bd8f0
CSeq: 1 SERVICE
Content-Type: application/SOAP+xml
<SOAP-ENV:Envelope xmlns:SOAP-ENV="http://schemas.xmlsoap.org/soap/envelope/">
 <SOAP-ENV:Body>
  <m:getPresence xmlns:m="http://schemas.microsoft.com/winrtc/2002/11/sip">
   <presentity uri="vadim@contoso.com"
xmlns="http://schemas.microsoft.com/2002/09/sip/presence"
xmlns:xsi="http://www.w3.org/2001/XMLSchema-instance" >
    <availability aggregate="0" description="" />
    <activity aggregate="0" description="" />
    <displayName displayName="Vadim N. Korepin" />
   </presentity>
  </m:getPresence>
 </SOAP-ENV:Body>
</SOAP-ENV:Envelope>
```

This response not only shows us that the user exists (because the response did not fail), but it provides information about the user's *availability* (how he specified his presence state) and his *activity* (which is programmatically determined). Together, this activity information helps other clients understand whether an online client is really away even though the user indicated that she is "available." The *availability aggregate* and *activity aggregate* values present this information numerically, and a *0* means that the user is unavailable and has no activity information. Additionally, e-mail, phone number, and calendar availability can be provided, but they were not offered in this initial response.

Examining What Happens When Adding a Contact (Step 2)

When Communicator is asked to add a contact, it has two things to do. First, it must update the contact list that is stored on the server. This ensures that other (presumably idle) logged-in clients for this user know to update their contact lists, and it also ensures that future client logins remember that this contact is added. The second thing Communicator must do is set up a subscription with that contact so that she can receive presence information and notifications of presence changes in the future. All subscription requests are time-limited. Communicator does the bookkeeping to keep the subscription continually renewed before it expires each time.

An example of the SERVICE request to update the contact list follows:

```
SERVICE sip:jeremy@contoso.com SIP/2.0
Via: SIP/2.0/TLS 192.168.3.100:1467
Max-Forwards: 70
From: <sip:jeremy@contoso.com>;tag=adb5417230;epid=aa6d968e18
To: <sip:jeremy@contoso.com>;tag=D1972B5B
Call-ID: 46670f6cf7854110888a68bf9d4fef8c
CSeq: 2 SERVICE
Contact: <sip:jeremy@contoso.com;opaque=user:epid:upbza9anR1KJ-8E7UvWEDQAA;gruu>
User-Agent: UCCP/2.0.6093.0 OC/2.0.6093.0 (Microsoft Office Communicator)
Proxy-Authorization: Kerberos qop="auth", realm="SIP Communications Service",
opaque="E8EA7EDD", crand="49aff62c", cnum="13",
targetname="sip/srv.contoso.com", response=
"602306092a864886f71201020201011100ffffffff22e9b5b8a4d8711e7d02c5ffe0af30d7"
Content-Type: application/SOAP+xml
Content-Length: 483
<SOAP-ENV:Envelope xmlns:SOAP-ENV="http://schemas.xmlsoap.org/soap/envelope/">
 <SOAP-ENV:Body>
  <m:setContact xmlns:m="http://schemas.microsoft.com/winrtc/2002/11/sip">
   <m:displayName/>
   <m:groups>1 </m:groups>
   <m:subscribed>true</m:subscribed>
   <m:URI>vadim@contoso.com</m:URI>
   <contactExtension>
    <contactSettings contactId="db48d962-7878-44d6-a469-2f976b7aace3"/>
   </contactExtension>
   <m:externalURI></m:externalURI>
   <m:deltaNum>2</m:deltaNum>
  </m:setContact>
 </SOAP-ENV:Body>
</SOAP-ENV:Envelope>
```

The SERVICE request sends a *setContact* request (in XML) to the server in order to add the Uniform Resource Identifier (URI), *vadim@contoso.com*, to the contact list. It also labels this contact with a *contactId* to reference it specifically in future change notifications. The server confirms the change with a 200 OK response, as follows:

```
SIP/2.0 200 OK
Authentication-Info: Kerberos rspauth=
"602306092A864886F71201020201011100FFFFFFFF7FD058163D53A47D7C264267B9B0BFA8",
srand="563A1C58", snum="17", opaque="E8EA7EDD", qop="auth",
targetname="sip/srv.contoso.com", realm="SIP Communications Service"
Via: SIP/2.0/TLS 192.168.3.100:1467;ms-received-port=1467;ms-received-cid=A00
From: "Jeremy Los"<sip:jeremy@contoso.com>;tag=adb5417230;epid=aa6d968e18
To: <sip:jeremy@contoso.com>;tag=D1972B5B
Call-ID: 46670f6cf7854110888a68bf9d4fef8c
CSeq: 2 SERVICE
Content-Length: 0
```

Next, the server must notify all watchers for the contact list that the contact list has changed. Because Communicator subscribed to the user's contact list during login, it receives a notification of the change that it just made, as follows:

```
BENOTIFY sip:192.168.3.100:1467;transport=tls;
ms-opaque=7c11559fb8;ms-received-cid=00000A00 SIP/2.0
Via: SIP/2.0/TLS
192.168.3.1:5061;branch=z9hG4bK50F66FF8.FD5CCE8F;branched=FALSE
Authentication-Info: Kerberos rspauth=
"602306092A864886F71201020201011100FFFFFFFF010DB5FD2506B119E77AEBF785DD1084",
srand="D5844BEE", snum="18", opaque="E8EA7EDD", qop="auth",
targetname="sip/srv.contoso.com", realm="SIP Communications Service"
Max-Forwards: 70
To: <sip:jeremy@contoso.com>;tag=adb5417230;epid=aa6d968e18Content-Length: 305
From: <sip:jeremy@contoso.com>;tag=D1972B5B
Call-ID: 46670f6cf7854110888a68bf9d4fef8c
CSeq: 3 BENOTIFY
Content-Type: application/vnd-microsoft-roaming-contacts+xml
Event: vnd-microsoft-roaming-contacts
subscription-state: active;expires=48415
<contactDelta deltaNum="3" prevDeltaNum="2" >
 <addedContact uri="sip:vadim@contoso.com" name="" groups="1 "
subscribed="true" externalURI="" >
  <contactExtension>
   <contactSettings contactId="db48d962-7878-44d6-a469-2f976b7aace3" >
   </contactSettings>
  </contactExtension>
 </addedContact>
</contactDelta>
```

As an aside, this notification is only a change notification, which means that it shows only what has changed—not the whole contact list. This efficient means of notification avoids extra parsing and data passing on the network, but it can also run into problems when updates occur from multiple sources at the same time. To avoid this, the *deltaNum* and *prevDeltaNum* fields are used to denote which version of the document this notification was built from. When Communicator sent the original request to add a contact, it specified a *deltaNum* of 2, and this request is indicating that the latest update was built off of this change. If Communicator sent another update that is not processed yet, Communicator can still interpret this notification.

At this point, Communicator has successfully added the contact, received confirmation of the change, and is ready to subscribe to the new contact.

Examining What Happens When Subscribing for Presence and Receiving an Offline Notification (Step 3)

A presence subscription is sent out to the contact of interest (Vadim), as follows:

```
SUBSCRIBE sip:vadim@contoso.com SIP/2.0
Via: SIP/2.0/TLS 192.168.3.100:1467
Max-Forwards: 70
From: <sip:jeremy@contoso.com>;tag=944c2873c1;epid=aa6d968e18
To: <sip:vadim@contoso.com>Call-ID: 85b56acd9b374c70baa50bf89a09b867
CSeq: 1 SUBSCRIBE
Contact: <sip:jeremy@contoso.com;opaque=user:epid:upbza9anR1KJ-8E7UvWEDQAA;gruu>
User-Agent: UCCP/2.0.6093.0 OC/2.0.6093.0 (Microsoft Office Communicator)
Event: presence
Accept: application/msrtc-event-categories+xml, application/xpidf+xml,
text/xml+msrtc.pidf, application/pidf+xml, application/rlmi+xml,
multipart/related
Supported: com.microsoft.autoextend
Supported: ms-benotify
Proxy-Require: ms-benotify
Supported: ms-piggyback-first-notify
Proxy-Authorization: Kerberos qop="auth", realm="SIP Communications Service",
opaque="E8EA7EDD", crand="dc7167ba", cnum="15",
targetname="sip/srv.contoso.com", response=
"602306092a864886f71201020201011100ffffffff6f653032d2c6d18a6b15cf4edf3dfc33"
Content-Type: application/msrtc-adrl-categorylist+xml
Content-Length: 519
<batchSub xmlns="http://schemas.microsoft.com/2006/01/sip/batch-subscribe"
uri="sip:jeremy@contoso.com" name="">
  <action name="subscribe" id="1170624">
   <adhocList>
    <resource uri="sip:vadim@contoso.com">
    <context></context>
   </resource>
  </adhocList>
  <categoryList xmlns="http://schemas.microsoft.com/2006/09/sip/categorylist">
   <category name="calendarData"/>
   <category name="contactCard"/>
   <category name="note"/>
   <category name="services"/>
   <category name="sourcenetwork"/>
   <category name="state"/>
  </categoryList>
 </action>
</batchSub>
```

This request uses the XML body to query for presence information. It is asking for all the presence information on vadim@contoso.com that is available–calendaring information, contact card information, notes, services available, network location (enterprise network, federated network, and so on), and current presence state. The remote contact's home server responds to the request (based on presence authorization).

Examining What Happens During Presence Authorization For our example, the server responds with a 200 OK response containing presence details, as follows:

```
SIP/2.0 200 OK
Contact: <sip:srv.contoso.com:5061;transport=tls>
Authentication-Info: Kerberos rspauth=
"602306092A864886F71201020201011100FFFFFFFF355750633369457F8A07BF7FDEA9B9F3",
srand="A6BCBB5B", snum="20", opaque="E8EA7EDD", qop="auth",
targetname="sip/srv.contoso.com", realm="SIP Communications Service"
Content-Length: 307
Via: SIP/2.0/TLS 192.168.3.100:1467;ms-received-port=1467;ms-received-cid=A00
From: "Jeremy Los"<sip:jeremy@contoso.com>;tag=944c2873c1;epid=aa6d968e18
To: <sip:vadim@contoso.com>;tag=A4F5416B
Call-ID: 85b56acd9b374c70baa50bf89a09b867
CSeq: 1 SUBSCRIBE
Expires: 30384
Content-Type: text/xml+msrtc.pidf
Event: presence
subscription-state: active;expires=30384
ms-piggyback-cseq: 1
Supported: ms-benotify, ms-piggyback-first-notify
<presentity uri="vadim@contoso.com"
xmlns="http://schemas.microsoft.com/2002/09/sip/presence"
xmlns:xsi="http://www.w3.org/2001/XMLSchema-instance" >
 <availability aggregate="0" description=""  />
 <activity aggregate="0" description=""  />
 <displayName displayName="Vadim N. Korepin"  />
</presentity>
```

This response from the remote contact's home server tells us only that the contact is offline. An *availability* and *activity* aggregate of *0* means that the contact is unreachable. Because Vadim has not authorized Jeremy Los to see presence information, very minimal information is shared. (This information is ambiguous; it could be because Jeremy is actually denied access or because Vadim has not authorized him yet.)

Examining What Happens When the Contact Logs In and Updated Presence Is Received (Step 4)

When Vadim logs in, he receives a notification from the server that Jeremy is waiting for presence authorization, because his list of pending watchers includes Jeremy. This was shown in "Examining What Happens During Login Processing (Step 3)" within the "Examining the Technical Details Behind the Login Process" section earlier in this chapter. In Vadim's case, the list the server sends is not empty and instead contacts Jeremy's URI, as follows:

```
SIP/2.0 200 OK...
From: "Vadim N. Korepin"<sip:vadim@contoso.com>;tag=e32b927182;epid=6fe87e039b
To: <sip:vadim@contoso.com>;tag=6C3D0080
Call-ID: 5bf9529db3b14cc08a3bdeeb166f0615
CSeq: 1 SUBSCRIBE
Expires: 47303...
Event: vnd-microsoft-roaming-self...
 ...
<subscribers xmlns="http://schemas.microsoft.com/2006/09/sip/presence-subscribers">
<subscriber user="jeremy@contoso.com" displayName="Jeremy Los"  acknowledged="false"
type="sameEnterprise"/></subscribers>...
```

When Vadim allows Jeremy to see his presence information (and asks to add him as a contact as well), a SERVICE request is sent to the server to acknowledge Jeremy as a subscriber and to change the authorization list. Vadim's clients are all notified that the authorization list changed (to alert inactive clients that might still be logged in).

```
SERVICE sip:vadim@contoso.com SIP/2.0
Via: SIP/2.0/TLS 192.168.3.101:1073
Max-Forwards: 70
From: <sip:vadim@contoso.com>;tag=6e3dba1e93;epid=6fe87e039b
To: <sip:vadim@contoso.com>
Call-ID: 0ea64766096741cd92dd4296d3703988
CSeq: 1 SERVICE
Contact: <sip:vadim@contoso.com;opaque=user:epid:EfpLp1FJKl6EFEzM2Ml2OQAA;gruu>
User-Agent: UCCP/2.0.6093.0 OC/2.0.6093.0 (Microsoft Office Communicator)
Proxy-Authorization: Kerberos qop="auth", realm="SIP Communications Service",
opaque="8FFADC36", crand="d723fdf4", cnum="12",
targetname="sip/srv.contoso.com", response=
"602306092a864886f71201020201011100ffffffff8819cae15eaa9fd62e5730ad9d757ebf"
Content-Type: application/msrtc-presence-setsubscriber+xml
Content-Length: 164
<setSubscribers xmlns=
"http://schemas.microsoft.com/2006/09/sip/presence-subscribers">
 <subscriber user="jeremy@contoso.com" acknowledged="true"/>
</setSubscribers>
```

The request is accepted by Vadim's home server, as follows:

```
SIP/2.0 200 OK
Authentication-Info: Kerberos rspauth=
"602306092A864886F71201020201011100FFFFFFFFC99CE686EDBB3A2B07A9D09CF0F1A936",
srand="17DFA698", snum="18", opaque="8FFADC36", qop="auth",
targetname="sip/srv.contoso.com", realm="SIP Communications Service"
Via: SIP/2.0/TLS 192.168.3.101:1073;ms-received-port=1073;ms-received-cid=C00
From: "Vadim N. Korepin"<sip:vadim@contoso.com>;tag=6e3dba1e93;epid=6fe87e039b
To: <sip:vadim@contoso.com>;tag=A1F542AB99D66616F9252CB6DF50257F
Call-ID: 0ea64766096741cd92dd4296d3703988
CSeq: 1 SERVICE
Content-Length: 0
```

The server sends notification that the list changed and indicates that there was a *contactDelta* because of an *addedContact* event for jeremy@contoso.com, who is now being subscribed to, as follows:

```
BENOTIFY sip:192.168.3.101:1073;transport=tls;
ms-opaque=3f6ee3c2ab;ms-received-cid=00000C00 SIP/2.0
Via: SIP/2.0/TLS
192.168.3.1:5061;branch=z9hG4bK3038528D.91797EAB;branched=FALSE
Authentication-Info: Kerberos rspauth=
"602306092A864886F71201020201011100FFFFFFFF0E7982BDD363E7034027E38D915280AC",
srand="ACCB75D8", snum="17", opaque="8FFADC36", qop="auth",
targetname="sip/srv.contoso.com", realm="SIP Communications Service"
Max-Forwards: 70
To: <sip:vadim@contoso.com>;tag=f64cbe4fb6;epid=6fe87e039b
Content-Length: 165
From: <sip:vadim@contoso.com>;tag=BE9E675E
Call-ID: c1737cc0857a4be4b6fb40aead466060
CSeq: 3 BENOTIFY
Content-Type: application/vnd-microsoft-roaming-contacts+xml
Event: vnd-microsoft-roaming-contacts
subscription-state: active;expires=32134
<contactDelta deltaNum="3" prevDeltaNum="2" >
 <addedContact uri="sip:jeremy@contoso.com" name="" groups="1 "  subscribed="true"
externalURI=""  />
</contactDelta>
```

After authorization is allowed, a more complete view of Vadim's presence is sent to Jeremy through BENOTIFY messages. For brevity, only the content of the message is shown, simply to highlight the availability and capability information that was made available, as follows:

```
<categories xmlns="http://schemas.microsoft.com/2006/09/sip/categories"
uri="sip:vadim@contoso.com">
<category xmlns="http://schemas.microsoft.com/2006/09/sip/categories"
name="contactCard" instance="0" publishTime="2007-05-03T05:37:43.113">
  <contactCard xmlns="http://schemas.microsoft.com/2006/09/sip/contactcard" >
   <identity >
    <name ><displayName >Vadim N. Korepin</displayName></name>
   </identity>
  </contactCard>
 </category>
 <category xmlns="http://schemas.microsoft.com/2006/09/sip/categories"
name="state" instance="1" publishTime="2007-05-04T19:30:25.930">
  <state xsi:type="aggregateState"
xmlns:xsi="http://www.w3.org/2001/XMLSchema-instance"
xmlns="http://schemas.microsoft.com/2006/09/sip/state">
   <availability>3500</availability>
  </state>
 </category>
 <category xmlns="http://schemas.microsoft.com/2006/09/sip/categories"
name="services" instance="0" publishTime="2007-05-04T19:30:25.930">
  <services xmlns="http://schemas.microsoft.com/2006/09/sip/service">
```

```
    <service uri="sip:vadim@contoso.com">
    <capabilities>
     <text render="true" capture="true" deviceAvailability="3500" />
     <gifInk render="true" capture="false" deviceAvailability="3500" />
     <isfInk render="true" capture="false" deviceAvailability="3500" />
    </capabilities>
    </service>
   </services>
  </category>
</categories>
```

The presence information shown here is still simplistic, as it does not integrate with Outlook for calendar details, nor has any note field been set. The device availability is presented as a numeric value that Communicator calculates and interprets to present a textual or graphical indication of a user's presence.

On the CD These protocol messages are part of the complete set of protocol messages on the companion CD for this chapter, in the \Appendixes,Scripts,Resources\Chapter 04\ CD Protocol Logs folder, and you can view them in their entirety there.

Examining What Happens When Controlling the Access Level of a Contact (Step 5)

When the level of access is changed for a given contact, a SERVICE request is sent to tell the server to change the authorization container in which the contact is maintained. These "containers" receive varying levels of detail about presence changes, and all contacts in each container are given the details available for their authorization level. The response and subsequent notification from the server identifying that the list changed are left out here for brevity's sake. These are available on the companion CD for reference, but an example of the SERVICE request follows:

```
SERVICE sip:jeremy@contoso.com SIP/2.0
Via: SIP/2.0/TLS 192.168.3.100:1467
Max-Forwards: 70
From: <sip:jeremy@contoso.com>;tag=0b8629457f;epid=aa6d968e18
To: <sip:jeremy@contoso.com>
Call-ID: 045284d5f9d7439c8df7fb629be00dca
CSeq: 1 SERVICE
Contact: <sip:jeremy@contoso.com;opaque=user:epid:upbza9anR1KJ-8E7UvWEDQAA;gruu>
User-Agent: UCCP/2.0.6093.0 OC/2.0.6093.0 (Microsoft Office Communicator)
Proxy-Authorization: Kerberos qop="auth", realm="SIP Communications Service",
opaque="E8EA7EDD", crand="f4595ce8", cnum="18",
targetname="sip/srv.contoso.com", response=
"602306092a864886f71201020201011100ffffffff2a3751d364162d072028848f060005a5"
Content-Type: application/msrtc-setcontainermembers+xml
Content-Length: 219
<setContainerMembers xmlns=
```

```
"http://schemas.microsoft.com/2006/09/sip/container management">
 <container id="300" version="0">
  <member action="add" type="user" value="vadim@contoso.com"/>
 </container>
</setContainerMembers>
```

Various access levels are defined by the containers. Each container has a predefined level of access to presence information, and contacts can simply be added to or removed from these containers to easily manage the level of information a contact receives. Containers increase complexity for the protocol messages and make it more difficult to understand what the system is doing. However, they simplify managing and authorizing contacts, eliminating authorization as a customization step for each contact.

All the presence information is maintained through subscriptions, which send updates when things change and eventually expire over time if they are not regularly renewed. (Communicator handles this automatically for the user.) The next section shows examples for instant messaging scenarios and talks about the technical details involved.

Understanding Instant Messaging

Instant messaging is already widely in use and fairly well understood. It involves two or more individuals communicating with each other using text messages. However, the point of this section is to explain how instant messaging works and to identify the pieces of the system that enable it. Knowing this should help with troubleshooting messaging problems and make it easier to understand how to build applications and integrate systems that work alongside instant messaging.

Overview of the Instant Messaging Scenario

This example walks Jeremy Los through using his Communicator 2007 client from his office to communicate and interact with coworkers. Instant messaging, sending hyperlinks and emoticons, sharing files, sharing video and audio, and setting up multiple people in a messaging conference are all shown. The scenario shows Jeremy Los interacting with two coworkers, Vadim N. Korepin and Rui Raposo.

Step 1: Opening a Messaging Window

Jeremy double-clicks on Vadim N. Korepin, who is in his contact list, to open a messaging window, as shown in Figure 4-13.

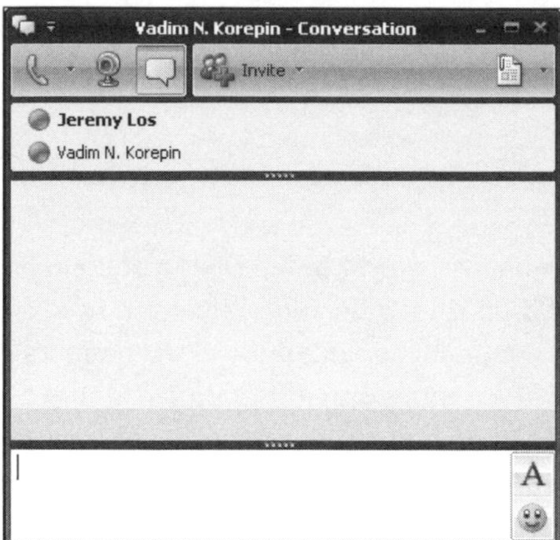

Figure 4-13 Communicator 2007—Messaging window

Step 2: Typing and Sending a Message

Jeremy types the message, "Sorry to hear about the coffee cup :)," into the text box at the bottom of the messaging window, and the message is sent when he hits Enter on the keyboard. This sends a message to Vadim, and Jeremy's message is shown in the current message history window to make tracking the conversation easier, as shown in Figure 4-14.

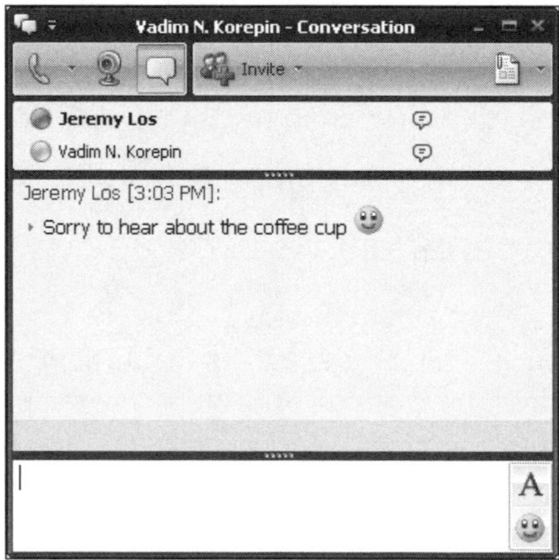

Figure 4-14 Communicator 2007—Message sent

Vadim receives a notification on his desktop, as shown in Figure 4-15, alerting him that Jeremy sent him a message to initiate a new conversation. This notification can be clicked to open the messaging window, or Vadim can open the window directly from the task bar. (It will be blinking to show that an unread message has been received.)

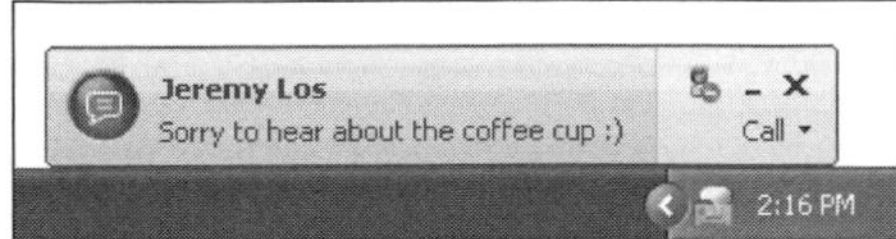

Figure 4-15 Communicator 2007—Message notification

Step 3: Receiving the Message

Jeremy receives the message from his coworker, and it shows up in the message history window, as shown in Figure 4-16.

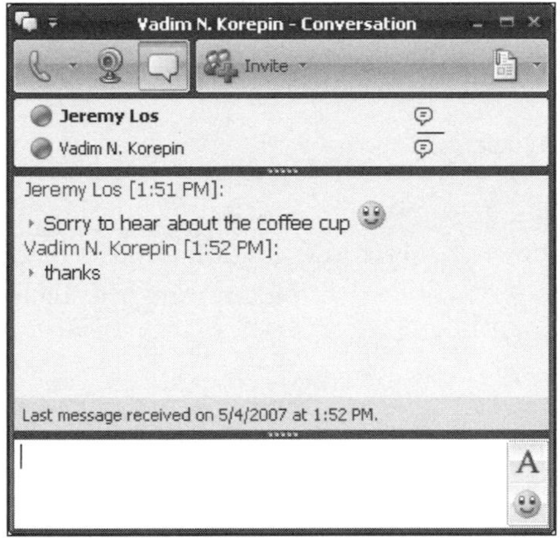

Figure 4-16 Communicator 2007—Receiving a message

Step 4: Sending a Hyperlink

Jeremy sends a hyperlink to an interesting article by pasting the URL into the text box and sending it, as shown in Figure 4-17.

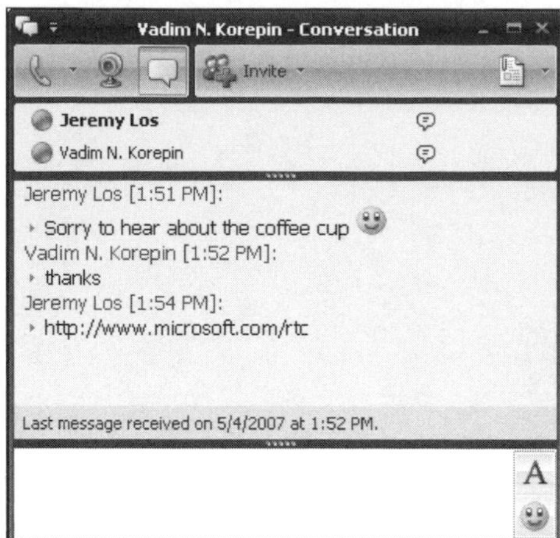

Figure 4-17 Communicator 2007—Sending a hyperlink

Vadim receives the hyperlink, but it has a leading "_" inserted, which prevents it from showing up properly as a hyperlink, as shown in Figure 4-18. More information about what is happening here with content filtering is provided in the next section, "Examining the Technical Details Behind the Instant Messaging Scenario."

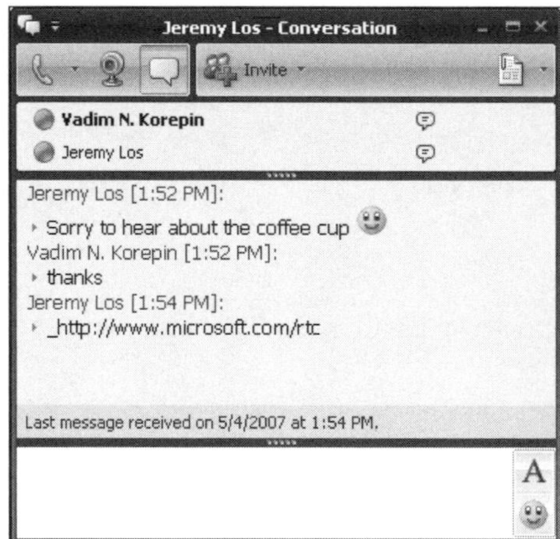

Figure 4-18 Communicator 2007—Receiving a hyperlink

Step 5: Sending a File

Jeremy sends a file by using the file icon button on the top-right of the messaging window and waits for Vadim to accept the file, as shown in Figure 4-19. Vadim receives a similar view where he can accept the transfer and view the file by clicking on the file icon shown in the messaging history after the download completes.

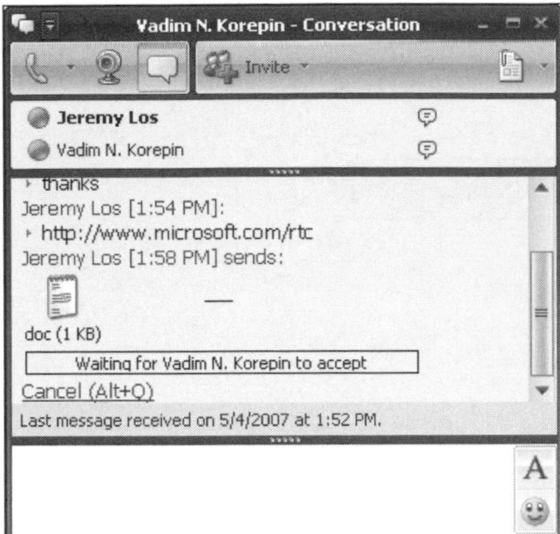

Figure 4-19 Communicator 2007—Sending a file

Step 6: Sharing Video

Jeremy decides to share video, because both he and Vadim have a camera. After they talk briefly, they stop sharing the video session, as shown in Figure 4-20.

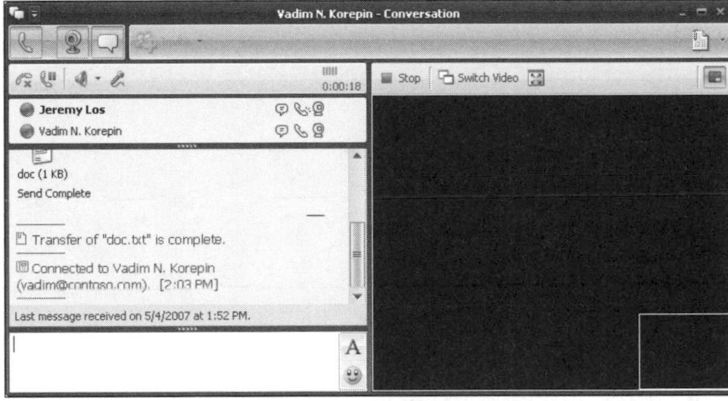

Figure 4-20 Communicator 2007—Sharing video

Step 7: Ending the Conversation

At some point the conversation is complete, so Jeremy closes the window, effectively ending the conversation.

Examining the Technical Details Behind the Instant Messaging Scenario

This section illustrates what is happening with Communicator 2007 and the network of Office Communications Servers at a level of technical detail that should aid in understanding the product and in thinking through how to troubleshoot message scenarios later, if the need arises. We will explore messaging, sending hyperlinks, and message routing in detail. The following diagram provides an overview of the steps involved in the instant messaging scenario that we are analyzing:

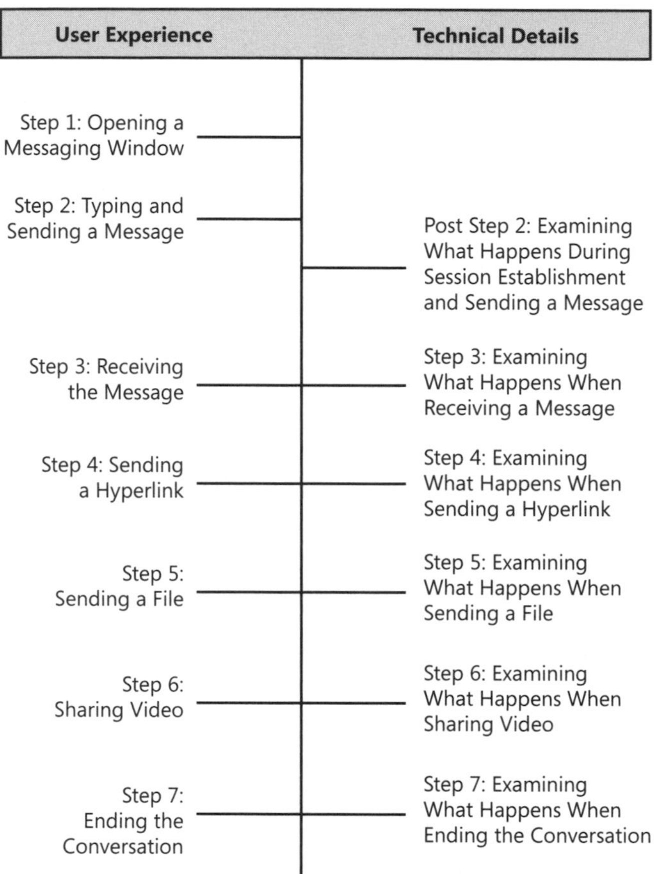

Examining What Happens During Session Establishment and Sending a Message (Post Step 2)

Setting up a conversation at a protocol level is much more involved than it would seem from the user interface. A summary of the protocol messages involved are shown in the diagram shown in Figure 4-21, which also serves as a visual overview of the protocol message flow involved in establishing a messaging session and in sending the first message.

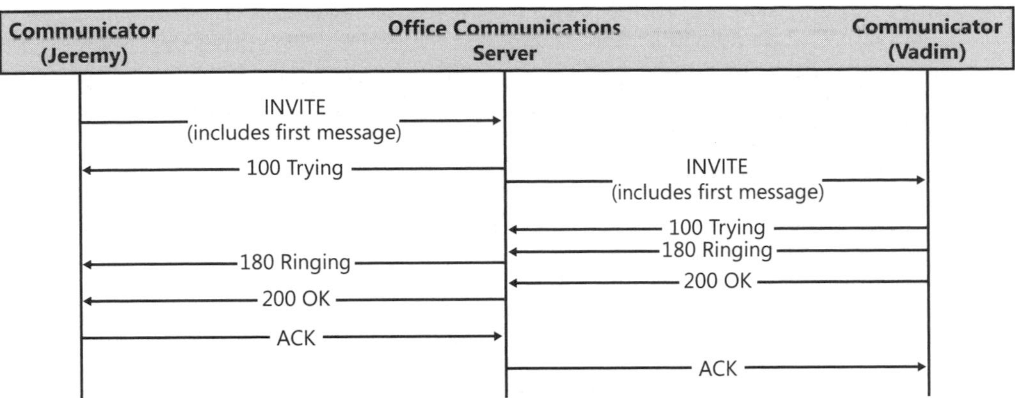

Figure 4-21 Session establishment and sending a message

> **Note** Session establishment using Communicator 2007 works in much the same way that making a phone call through an operator does. The caller (Communicator) first rings the operator (the Office Communications Server Home Server) and asks to be connected to a user. The operator generally tells the caller to hold the line (which is similar to the *100 Trying* message from the server) while he looks up the line associated with the person called (which is similar to the server querying its database). Next the operator makes the connection, and the phone of the person called rings (*180 Ringing* message comes back). Finally, the person called picks up the phone (the *200 OK* message sent from the remote contact) and the call is established.

When the first message is sent–"Sorry to hear about the coffee cup :)"–a messaging session is established at a protocol level. This is initiated by an INVITE message to establish the session. The INVITE actually carries the first message in the session and is base64 encoded into the *ms-body* parameter of the *Ms-Text-Format* header so that it can be presented with the request to start a messaging session.

> **Note** Emoticons are icons that represent sequences of underlying text. For example, the colon and right-parenthesis characters can be typed together as ":)" to make a smile, and this is interpreted and shown as an icon in Communicator. You can select icons within Communicator, but they all are simply represented by text underneath. Sometimes this can result in unintended emoticons, which is something you should be aware of. A text sequence like "Answer:Probably" will actually have the ":P" converted into a smiling face with its tongue sticking out. One unfortunate aspect is that users only see this *after* they send the message, not while they are typing it.

```
INVITE sip:vadim@contoso.com SIP/2.0
Via: SIP/2.0/TLS 192.168.3.100:1467
Max-Forwards: 70
From: <sip:jeremy@contoso.com>;tag=e57383c75b;epid=aa6d968e18
To: <sip:vadim@contoso.com>
Call-ID: d1a1cdc2192048f7a8e9703774cfebcc
CSeq: 1 INVITE
Contact: <sip:jeremy@contoso.com;opaque=user:epid:upbza9anR1KJ-8E7UvWEDQAA;gruu>
User-Agent: UCCP/2.0.6093.0 OC/2.0.6093.0 (Microsoft Office Communicator)
Ms-Text-Format: text/plain; charset=UTF-8;
msgr=WAAtAE0ATQBTAC0ASQBNAC0ARgBvAHIAbQBhAHQAOgAgAEYATgA9AE0AUwAlADIAMABTAGgAZ
QBsAGwAJQAyADAARABsAGcAJQAyADAAMgA7ACAARQBGAD0AOwAgAEMATwA9ADAAOwAgAEMAUwA9ADA
AOwAgAFAARgA9ADAACgANAAoADQA;  ms-
body=U29ycnkgdG8gaGVhciBhYm91dCB0aGUgY29mZmVlIGN1cCA6KQ== Supported: ms-delayed-accept
Supported: ms-renders-isf
Supported: ms-renders-gif
Supported: ms-renders-mime-alternative
Ms-Conversation-ID: AceOhaxSC0KoxENJSUqzhraNmoHCew==
Supported: timerSupported: ms-sender
Roster-Manager: sip:jeremy@contoso.com
EndPoints: <sip:jeremy@contoso.com>, <sip:vadim@contoso.com>
Supported: com.microsoft.rtc-multiparty
Supported: ms-mspms-keep-alive: UAC;hop-hop=yesSupported: ms-conf-invite
Proxy-Authorization: Kerberos qop="auth", realm="SIP Communications Service",
opaque="E8EA7EDD", crand="e870674a", cnum="19",
targetname="sip/srv.contoso.com", response=
"602306092a864886f71201020201011100ffffffff3ee9fabb267878a043ed3695933d69f8"
Content-Type: application/sdp
Content-Length: 205
v=0o=- 0 0 IN IP4 192.168.3.100s=sessionc=IN IP4 192.168.3.100t=0 0
m=message 5060 sip nulla=accept-types:text/rtf application/x-ms-ink image/gif
multipart/alternative application/ms-imdn+xml
```

The body of the message describes more about what capabilities the initiator has, and this is talked about both in the Session Initiation Protocol (SIP) RFC 3261 standard, as well as in Chapter 18, "Background Information," which provides detailed information about SIP.

The first server that receives the message responds with a *100* response, and then the remote client responds immediately to provide a temporary response. However, it does not send a final receipt of confirmation until the invitation is accepted by a user. This three-way handshake establishes the session and allows a negotiation of session information between both clients, as follows:

```
SIP/2.0 100 Trying
Authentication-Info: Kerberos rspauth=
"602306092A864886F71201020201011100FFFFFFFF4CC448BBF8DD25781477D1A85E1D3DBC",
srand="EAE80D89", snum="31", opaque="E8EA7EDD", qop="auth",
targetname="sip/srv.contoso.com", realm="SIP Communications Service"
Via: SIP/2.0/TLS 192.168.3.100:1467;ms-received-port=1467;ms-received-cid=A00
From: <sip:jeremy@contoso.com>;tag=e57383c75b;epid=aa6d968e18
To: <sip:vadim@contoso.com>
Call-ID: d1a1cdc2192048f7a8e9703774cfebcc
CSeq: 1 INVITE
Content-Length: 0
```

The remote client sends a temporary response to confirm that it is waiting for the user to respond to the request, as follows:

```
SIP/2.0 180 Ringing
Authentication-Info: Kerberos rspauth=
"602306092A864886F71201020201011100FFFFFFFF69BE23EA5A0169F00998D21963CEABF6",
srand="44C23DFA", snum="32", opaque="E8EA7EDD", qop="auth",
targetname="sip/srv.contoso.com", realm="SIP Communications Service"
Via: SIP/2.0/TLS 192.168.3.100:1467;ms-received-port=1467;ms-received-cid=A00
From: "Jeremy Los"<sip:jeremy@contoso.com>;tag=e57383c75b;epid=aa6d968e18
To: "" <sip:vadim@contoso.com>;epid=6fe87e039b;tag=5c939f2392
Call-ID: d1a1cdc2192048f7a8e9703774cfebcc
CSeq: 1 INVITE
User-Agent: UCCP/2.0.6093.0 OC/2.0.6093.0 (Microsoft Office Communicator)
Content-Length: 0
```

The remote client confirms that the invitation is accepted and provides session capability information in the body of the message, as follows:

```
SIP/2.0 200 OK
Authentication-Info: Kerberos rspauth=
"602306092A864886F71201020201011100FFFFFFFF885A98EB35E99BF2452E8B1F57D22F91",
srand="B636FA2D", snum="33", opaque="E8EA7EDD", qop="auth",
targetname="sip/srv.contoso.com", realm="SIP Communications Service"
Via: SIP/2.0/TLS 192.168.3.100:1467;ms-received-port=1467;ms-received-cid=A00
From: "Jeremy Los"<sip:jeremy@contoso.com>;tag=e57383c75b;epid=aa6d968e18
To: "" <sip:vadim@contoso.com>;epid=6fe87e039b;tag=5c939f2392
Call-ID: d1a1cdc2192048f7a8e9703774cfebcc
CSeq: 1 INVITE
Record-Route: <sip:srv.contoso.com:5061;transport=tls;ms-role-rs-from;
ms-role-rs-to;ms-opaque=aaB_D3-f9AM9QxeVkHOWddzAAA;lr; ms-route-
sig=aasNJOIb7XhG1fWKA4UvKlDEpMRMM2Fwj8K3gtHgAA>
Contact:
<sip:vadim@contoso.com;opaque=user:epid:EfpLp1FJKl6EFEzM2Ml2OQAA;gruu>
User-Agent: UCCP/2.0.6093.0 OC/2.0.6093.0 (Microsoft Office Communicator)
Require: com.microsoft.rtc-multiparty
Supported: com.microsoft.rtc-multiparty
Supported: ms-sender
Supported: ms-renders-isf
Supported: ms-renders-gif
Supported: ms-renders-mime-alternative
Supported: ms-conf-invite
Content-Type: application/sdp
Content-Length: 222
v=0o=- 0 0 IN IP4 192.168.3.101s=sessionc=IN IP4 192.168.3.101t=0 0
m=message 5060 sip sip:vadim@contoso.coma=accept-types:text/rtf application/
x-ms-ink image/gif multipart/alternative application/ms-imdn+xml
```

This response establishes a few things for the dialog so that communications can begin. First, it establishes that both parties are interested in communicating and that they are able to reach

each other. Second, it establishes routes and contact points for each user. This tells Communicator how to route messages. Communicator uses the *Record-Route* and the *Contact* headers to directly send messages to the end point with which it has established the dialog. The *Record-Route* header contains a signed route that can easily be validated by the server and used to directly route the request. The *Contact* header has a unique identifier (the *epid*, or end-point identifier) that can be used by the home server to route the request to the specific Communicator instance of interest (if multiple instances are logged in). Third, it provides capabilities information through the body to both parties so that the means of communication are known and the interaction can be extended or upgraded as desired. For more details on the body of INVITE messages, refer to Chapter 18.

The initiating client acknowledges the session capabilities and completes the three-way handshake to establish the session, as follows:

```
ACK sip:srv.contoso.com:5061;transport=tls;ms-role-rs-from;ms-role-rs-to;
ms-opaque=aaB_D3-f9AM9QxeVkHOWddzAAA;lr; ms-route-
sig=aasNJOIb7XhG1fWKA4UvKlDEpMRMM2Fwj8K3gtHgAA SIP/2.0
Via: SIP/2.0/TLS 192.168.3.100:1467
Max-Forwards: 70
From: <sip:jeremy@contoso.com>;tag=e57383c75b;epid=aa6d968e18
To: "" <sip:vadim@contoso.com>;epid=6fe87e039b;tag=5c939f2392
Call-ID: d1a1cdc2192048f7a8e9703774cfebcc
CSeq: 1 ACK
Route: <sip:vadim@contoso.com;opaque=user:epid:EfpLp1FJKl6EFEzM2Ml2OQAA;gruu>
User-Agent: UCCP/2.0.6093.0 OC/2.0.6093.0 (Microsoft Office Communicator)
Proxy-Authorization: Kerberos qop="auth", realm="SIP Communications Service",
opaque="E8EA7EDD", crand="e4f67482", cnum="20",
targetname="sip/srv.contoso.com", response=
"602306092a864886f71201020201011100ffffffffc78b87bfa700f1757a4e60fed1847916"
Content-Length: 0
```

This ACK request finalizes the dialog by using the route set provided to test that it works properly. From this point on, the initiating client expects that the dialog is available and the recipient expects that the dialog is established after the ACK arrives as a confirmation that the route set worked in at least one direction. The first line of the request contains the request URI, which is the information used to route the request. This line contains the information that was sent back in the *Record-Route* header from the 200 OK response (including the signature). Additionally, the next routing target (gathered from the *Contact* header in the 200 OK response) is placed in the *Route* header. Additional information on SIP and routing details is provided in Chapter 18.

Note that this section does not discuss messaging sessions with multiple recipients. This is because after more than two people are involved in a session, a conference is created with which all clients interact. Detailed information on conferencing is covered in Chapter 5, "Conferencing Scenario."

Examining What Happens When Receiving a Message (Step 3)

Another message type that you see during interactions is the INFO message. This message is used to send little notifications within an INVITE dialog–to alert the other party when a user is typing a message (before it is sent), for example. Here is an example of the INFO message received by Jeremy from Vadim before his response was sent to signal that he was typing a response. The *KeyboardActivity* data in the body is the key information being passed by this message, as follows:

```
INFO sip:192.168.3.100:1467;transport=tls;ms-opaque=7c11559fb8; ms-received-
cid=00000A00;grid SIP/2.0
Via: SIP/2.0/TLS 192.168.3.1:5061;
branch=z9hG4bKEC902A23.8CE260FA;branched=
FALSE;ms-internal-info="ba9qTQQ5XMtq_uYWsHUg3gqjoqThSM4mD6s150CgAA"
Authentication-Info: Kerberos rspauth=
"602306092A864886F71201020201011100FFFFFFFFC03B6B0D6388E4EE53C6ABA080FFAC55",
srand="53D1DBCD", snum="35", opaque="E8EA7EDD", qop="auth",
targetname="sip/srv.contoso.com", realm="SIP Communications Service"
Max-Forwards: 69
Via: SIP/2.0/TLS 192.168.3.101:1073;ms-received-port=1073;ms-received-cid=C00
From: "" <sip:vadim@contoso.com>;epid=6fe87e039b;tag=5c939f2392
To: "Jeremy Los"<sip:jeremy@contoso.com>;tag=e57383c75b;epid=aa6d968e18
Call-ID: d1a1cdc2192048f7a8e9703774cfebcc
CSeq: 1 INFO
Contact: <sip:vadim@contoso.com;opaque=user:epid:EfpLp1FJKl6EFEzM2Ml2OQAA;gruu>
User-Agent: UCCP/2.0.6093.0 OC/2.0.6093.0 (Microsoft Office Communicator)
Supported: timer
Content-Type: application/xml
Content-Length: 87
<?xml version="1.0"?>
<KeyboardActivity>
 <status status="type" />
</KeyboardActivity>
```

When a message is received (or sent) within a messaging session, a MESSAGE message is used. An example of the MESSAGE received by Jeremy from his coworker (transmitted within the INVITE session by using the same *Call-ID*) is shown next:

```
MESSAGE sip:192.168.3.100:1467;transport=tls;ms-opaque=7c11559fb8;ms-received-
cid=00000A00;grid SIP/2.0
Via: SIP/2.0/TLS 192.168.3.1:5061;branch=z9hG4bK06E6DAB4.5A2D0AB6;
branched=FALSE;ms-internal-info="baj3AsctgNBuSN4A27AfVbksRFndBaLQq2s150CgAA"
Authentication-Info: Kerberos rspauth=
"602306092A864886F71201020201011100FFFFFFFF3D2E62CC853438235B3E6E21C525BA76",
srand="A7C06D90", snum="37", opaque="E8EA7EDD", qop="auth",
targetname="sip/srv.contoso.com", realm="SIP Communications Service"
Max-Forwards: 69
Via: SIP/2.0/TLS 192.168.3.101:1073;ms-received-port=1073;ms-received-cid=C00
From: "" <sip:vadim@contoso.com>;epid=6fe87e039b;tag=5c939f2392
To: "Jeremy Los"<sip:jeremy@contoso.com>;tag=e57383c75b;epid=aa6d968e18
```

```
Call-ID: d1a1cdc2192048f7a8e9703774cfebcc
CSeq: 3 MESSAGE
Contact: <sip:vadim@contoso.com;opaque=user:epid:EfpLp1FJKl6EFEzM2Ml2OQAA;gruu>
User-Agent: UCCP/2.0.6093.0 OC/2.0.6093.0 (Microsoft Office Communicator)
Supported: timer
Content-Type: text/rtf
Content-Length: 242

{\rtf1\ansi\ansicpg1252\deff0\deflang1033{\fonttbl{\f0\fnil\fcharset0 MS Shell
Dlg 2;}{\f1\fnil MS Shell Dlg 2;}}
{\colortbl ;\red0\green0\blue0;}
{\*\generator Msftedit 5.41.15.1507;}\viewkind4\uc1\pard\tx720\cf1\f0\fs20 thanks\f1\par
}
```

Note For privacy purposes, the body of MESSAGE messages is not logged by default, so you usually never see this information in your client or server logs. This option can be enabled only on server logs (not client logs). The registry key to enable this is HKLM\SYSTEM\CurrentControlSet\Services\RtcSrv\Parameters, where the DWORD value of *EnableLoggingAllMessageBodies* must be set to *1*. This registry key causes the server logs to show message bodies after the server is restarted, but it is important to note that this is a *big* security and privacy risk and should be used only for educational purposes on test systems.

In MESSAGE messages, the body contains the textual message ("thanks" in this example) to be transmitted, with formatting information wrapping it to describe the font, color, and so on. Additional details on SIP sessions and how they work are explained in Chapter 18.

Examining What Happens When Sending a Hyperlink (Step 4)

When a hyperlink or Web link (such as http://www.microsoft.com/rtc) is sent as text to another user, many things are happening in the background. First, the message is sent as raw text along with the rest of the message in a MESSAGE message, just as any other text a user might have typed. However, intermediate internal servers, intermediate Access Edge Servers, and the remote client might interpret, alter, or display the message differently based on policy. Office Communications Server 2007 installs with the Intelligent IM Filter active and allows local intranet URLs. However, it inserts a "_" character in front of Internet URLs to prevent it from showing up as an active hyperlink.

An example that shows the IIMFilter server log processing this request is shown next (in place of the protocol message, which would just contain the content shown in the log). This log can be gathered on the server using the logging tool. Additional details on the logging tool are described in this book's Part VI "Technical Reference." The log shown next is summarized where you see ellipses (...) to make it easier to read and to remove information that is not of interest to our example. The log basically tracks the filter, watching message content for clickable URLs and then adding an underscore (_) character to the beginning, as follows:

```
TL_INFO ... ContentType: text/rtf
TL_INFO ... ReadonlyPrefixLength: 0
TL_INFO ... Content:
'{\rtf1\ansi\ansicpg1252\deff0\deflang1033{\fonttbl{\f0\fnil\fcharset0 MS
Shell Dlg 2;}}
{\colortbl ;\red0\green0\blue0;}
{\*\generator Msftedit 5.41.15.1507;}\viewkind4\uc1\pard\tx720\cf1\f0\fs20
http://www.microsoft.com/rtc\par
}'
TL_INFO ... (IIMFilter,IIMFilter.CheckForClickableURL:462.idx(775))( 028F1359 )
http://www.microsoft.com/rtc - URL NOT ignored - SecurityZone = Internet
TL_INFO ... Request modified to convert one or more clickable URLs to unclickable URLs
TL_INFO ... Updated content with ContentType: text/rtf
TL_INFO ... Content:
'{\rtf1\ansi\ansicpg1252\deff0\deflang1033{\fonttbl{\f0\fnil\fcharset0 MS
Shell Dlg 2;}}
{\colortbl ;\red0\green0\blue0;}
{\*\generator Msftedit 5.41.15.1507;}\viewkind4\uc1\pard\tx720\cf1\f0\fs20
_http://www.microsoft.com/rtc\par
}'
TL_INFO ... Proxy request
```

Communicator also has a group policy setting (EnableURL) that it enforces to either display hyperlinks as clickable text or as raw text to require the user to manually copy the text into a browser. All of this is happening simply to allow more control from the network and to prevent bad links from being circulated or accidentally clicked by unsuspecting users.

Examining What Happens When Sending a File (Step 5)

Sending a file to another user involves a few SIP transactions and then a direct connection between Communicator clients to transfer the file. The file transfer does not go through any of the server infrastructure at all other than the negotiation transactions. Figure 4-22 provides an overview of the protocol interactions and the establishment of the direct connection between Communicator clients (for the purpose of transferring the file).

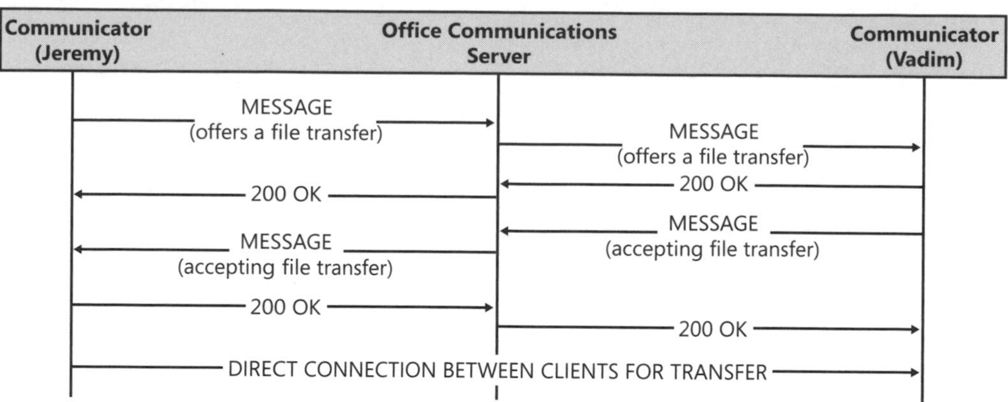

Figure 4-22 File Transfer Handshaking

When Jeremy initiates a file transfer request, the existing session is used and a MESSAGE is sent where the body identifies that a file is available for transfer, as follows:

```
MESSAGE sip:srv.contoso.com:5061;transport=tls;ms-role-rs-from;ms-role-rs-to;
ms-opaque=aaB_D3-f9AM9QxeVkHOWddzAAA;lr;ms-route-sig=
aasNJOIb7XhG1fWKA4UvKlDEpMRMM2Fwj8K3gtHgAA SIP/2.0
Via: SIP/2.0/TLS 192.168.3.100:1467
Max-Forwards: 70
From: <sip:jeremy@contoso.com>;tag=e57383c75b;epid=aa6d968e18
To: "" <sip:vadim@contoso.com>;epid=6fe87e039b;tag=5c939f2392
Call-ID: d1a1cdc2192048f7a8e9703774cfebcc
CSeq: 6 MESSAGE
Route: <sip:vadim@contoso.com;opaque=user:epid:EfpLp1FJKl6EFEzM2Ml2OQAA;gruu>
Contact: <sip:jeremy@contoso.com;opaque=user:epid:upbza9anR1KJ-8E7UvWEDQAA;gruu>
User-Agent: UCCP/2.0.6093.0 OC/2.0.6093.0 (Microsoft Office Communicator)
Supported: timer
Proxy-Authorization: Kerberos qop="auth", realm="SIP Communications Service",
opaque="E8EA7EDD", crand="760faa07", cnum="28",
targetname="sip/srv.contoso.com",
response= "602306092a864886f71201020201011100ffffffff2a46ed40d0acdeacd7bbf79110ea5214"
Content-Type: text/x-msmsgsinvite; charset=UTF-8
Content-Length: 234

Application-Name: File TransferApplication-GUID: {5D3E02AB-6190-11d3-BBBB-
00C04F795683}Invitation-Command: INVITEInvitation-Cookie: 625392Application-
File: doc.txtApplication-FileSize: 28Connectivity: NEncryption: R
```

The body of the message identifies that this is a file transfer request and not a messaging request. The *Application-Name* parameter specifies that a file transfer is offered, and the *Application-File* parameter specifies the name of the file. The file size is also specified so that the recipient knows how much it must transfer. The *Connectivity* parameter identifies whether the client is behind a Network Address Translation (NAT) device or not and an "N" indicates that it is. The *Encryption* parameter identifies whether the sender supports (S) or requires (R) encryption of the transferred file. This information begins the handshake for the file transfer and provides the *Invitation-Cookie* for reference in responding to this offer in a later MESSAGE from the recipient.

> **Note** Office Communications Server 2007 installs with the Intelligent IM Filter active, and it blocks all directly executable binaries and scripts from being transferred. Files with extensions such as *.zip, *.doc, and *.xml are all enabled and allowed by default. To see which extensions are blocked, you can look at the Office Communications Server 2007 MMC snap-in, right-click on the server to select Application Properties, select Intelligent IM Filter, and then move to the File Transfer Filter tab.

For our example, Vadim's Communicator confirms receipt of the MESSAGE offering a file transfer, as follows:

```
SIP/2.0 200 OK
Authentication-Info: Kerberos rspauth=
"602306092A864886F71201020201011100FFFFFFFF74C5A6869E5717FA67441D92794710E5",
srand="F5AE7002", snum="41", opaque="E8EA7EDD", qop="auth",
targetname="sip/srv.contoso.com", realm="SIP Communications Service"
Via: SIP/2.0/TLS 192.168.3.100:1467;ms-received-port=1467;ms-received-cid=A00
From: <sip:jeremy@contoso.com>;tag=e57383c75b;epid=aa6d968e18
To: "" <sip:vadim@contoso.com>;epid=6fe87e039b;tag=5c939f2392
Call-ID: d1a1cdc2192048f7a8e9703774cfebcc
CSeq: 6 MESSAGE
Contact: <sip:vadim@contoso.com;opaque=user:epid:EfpLp1FJKl6EFEzM2Ml2OQAA;gruu>
User-Agent: UCCP/2.0.6093.0 OC/2.0.6093.0 (Microsoft Office Communicator)
Content-Length: 0
```

Next, Vadim's Communicator sends a MESSAGE back when Vadim accepts the file transfer to identify where the file should be sent, as follows:

```
MESSAGE sip:192.168.3.100:1467;transport=tls;ms-opaque=7c11559fb8;ms-received-
cid=00000A00;grid SIP/2.0
Via: SIP/2.0/TLS 192.168.3.1:5061;branch=z9hG4bK9310B3FD.583AF9C8;
branched=FALSE;ms-internal-info="bamr7aJF7hHA-WG_mThfb47YQEs0tYOvnIsl50CgAA"
Authentication-Info: Kerberos rspauth=
"602306092A864886F71201020201011100FFFFFFFE00D15EEBF15E83C6D8C14A42A949B80",
srand="3B024C50", snum="42", opaque="E8EA7EDD", qop="auth",
targetname="sip/srv.contoso.com", realm="SIP Communications Service"
Max-Forwards: 69
Via: SIP/2.0/TLS 192.168.3.101:1073;ms-received-port=1073;ms-received-cid=C00
From: "" <sip:vadim@contoso.com>;epid=6fe87e039b;tag=5c939f2392
To: "Jeremy Los"<sip:jeremy@contoso.com>;tag=e57383c75b;epid=aa6d968e18
Call-ID: d1a1cdc2192048f7a8e9703774cfebcc
CSeq: 4 MESSAGE
Contact: <sip:vadim@contoso.com;opaque=user:epid:EfpLp1FJKl6EFEzM2Ml2OQAA;gruu>
User-Agent: UCCP/2.0.6093.0 OC/2.0.6093.0 (Microsoft Office Communicator)
Supported: timer
Content-Type: text/x-msmsgsinvite; charset=UTF-8
```

```
Content-Length: 302

Invitation-Command: ACCEPTInvitation-Cookie: 625392Request-Data:
IP-Address:Encryption-Key: jdQO/KXdOgzT6pxHI3pG9qc/+HECOZchHash-Key:
bKJQfXeSgWBpFI2LGOHZ/0QveOJwoBwDIP-Address: 192.168.3.101Port: 6891PortX:
11178AuthCookie: 27079318Request-Data: IP-Address:Sender-Connect: TRUE
```

This information tells Jeremy's Communicator that it should connect to the IP address and port specified to send the encrypted file with the key specified. The *AuthCookie* specified is also used on the simple FTP connection between the clients as a handshaking device to disambiguate the session.

Jeremy's Communicator client confirms receipt of the MESSAGE accepting the file transfer, as follows:

```
SIP/2.0 200 OK
Via: SIP/2.0/TLS 192.168.3.1:5061;branch=z9hG4bK9310B3FD.583AF9C8;branched=FALSE;
ms-internal-info="bamr7aJF7hHA-WG_mThfb47YQEs0tYOvnIs150CgAA"
Via: SIP/2.0/TLS 192.168.3.101:1073;ms-received-port=1073;ms-received-cid=C00
From: "" <sip:vadim@contoso.com>;epid=6fe87e039b;tag=5c939f2392
To: <sip:jeremy@contoso.com>;tag=e57383c75b;epid=aa6d968e18
Call-ID: d1a1cdc2192048f7a8e9703774cfebcc
CSeq: 4 MESSAGE
Contact: <sip:jeremy@contoso.com;opaque=user:epid:upbza9anR1KJ-8E7UvWEDQAA;gruu>
User-Agent: UCCP/2.0.6093.0 OC/2.0.6093.0 (Microsoft Office Communicator)
Proxy-Authorization: Kerberos qop="auth", realm="SIP Communications Service",
opaque="E8EA7EDD", crand="bebf384d", cnum="29",
targetname="sip/srv.contoso.com",
response= "602306092a864886f71201020201011100ffffffff4c249327d5a9c2195e194c3235e84318"
Content-Length: 0
```

At this point, Jeremy's Communicator connects directly to Vadim's Communicator (at the IP address and port specified) and begins a simple FTP session where the encrypted file is transferred. The wire protocol is not explained in detail here, but a quick view of what is happening is laid out simply for completeness in the following code sample. (The use of "Jeremy" and "Vadim" in the example actually refers to the Communicator client each is using.)

```
[Jeremy connects to Vadim]
Vadim sends: VER MSN_SECURE_FTP
Jeremy sends: VER MSN_SECURE_FTP
Vadim sends: USR vadim@contoso.com 27079318
Jeremy sends: FIL 28
Vadim sends: TFR
[Jeremy sends binary encrypted data]
Vadim sends: BYE 16777989
Jeremy sends: MAC [signature using hash]
[Jeremy closes the connection]
```

The preceding interaction is simply a minimal handshake on a raw socket to transfer the encrypted file with a signature. After this interaction, the file transfer is complete.

Examining What Happens When Sharing Video (Step 6)

Negotiating an audio and video session can involve a lot of handshaking. The protocol messages that were involved are shown in the diagram shown in Figure 4-23, which serves as an overview for the section. However, only the bodies of the INVITE and 200 OK messages are discussed in detail in this section.

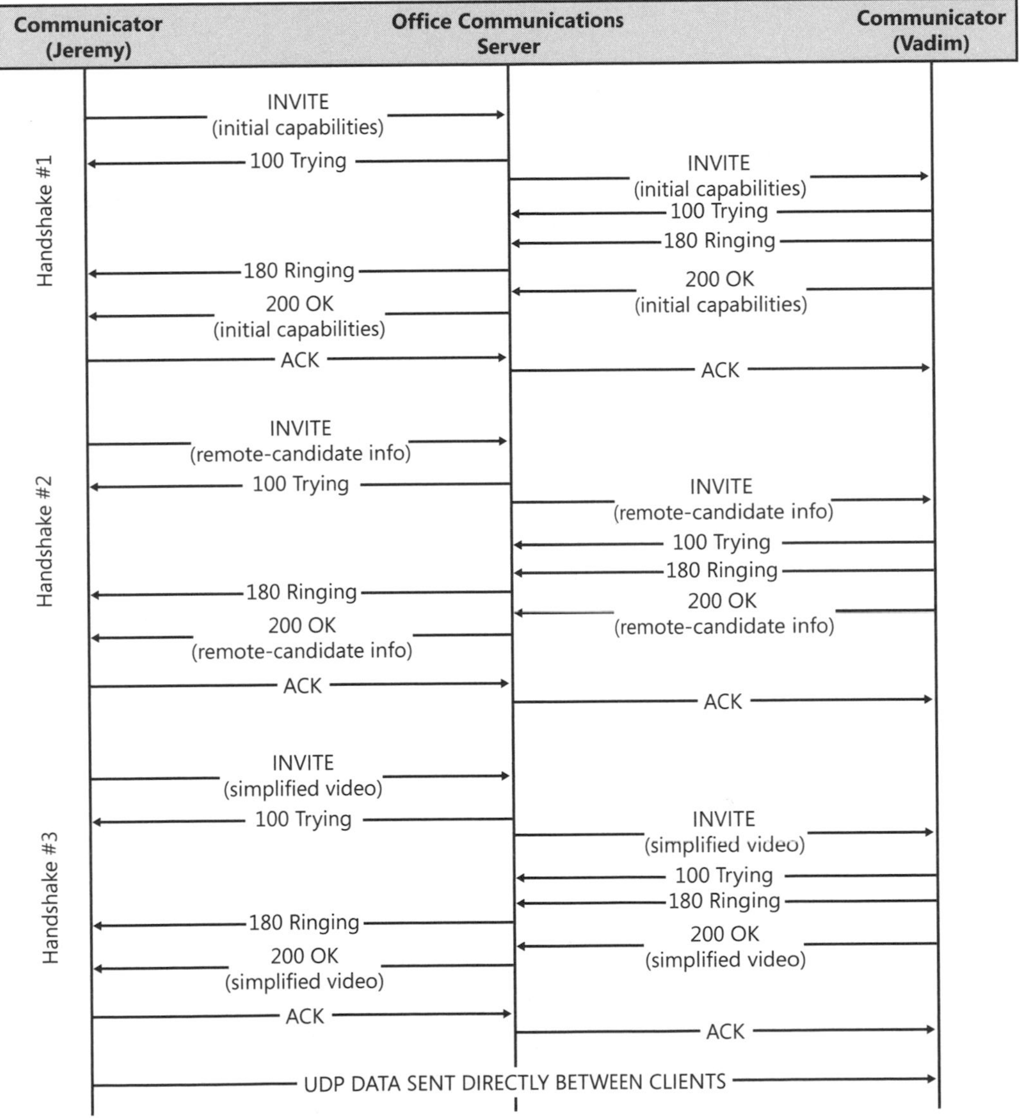

Figure 4-23 Audio and video session handshaking

When video is added to the session, Jeremy's Communicator client negotiates a new session including video and audio by sending an INVITE message for a new session. For brevity, only the protocol message bodies are shown and irrelevant protocol messages are skipped entirely. The body of the INVITE message from Jeremy's Communicator client follows:

```
v=0o=- 0 0 IN IP4 192.168.3.100s=sessionc=IN IP4 192.168.3.100b=CT:99980t=0 0
m=audio 60160 RTP/AVP 114 111 112 115 116 4 8 0 97
101k=base64:WYvabwXemv2PqGEj52+xHzXlpUN+MKRUJ2j2Rra/o/7JGjPiQBJHLM/Gr+xya=
candidate:XAP7A3WqUxk5m9zYTfROszesQz9Jdgvoqu5B5zzqwFw 1 7c99RFukBeRXvntIUMo4CA
UDP 0.830 192.168.3.100 60160 a=
candidate:XAP7A3WqUxk5m9zYTfROszesQz9Jdgvoqu5B5zzqwFw 2 7c99RFukBeRXvntIUMo4CA
UDP 0.830 192.168.3.100 21120 a=cryptoscale:1 client AES_CM_128_HMAC_SHA1_80
inline:OC8ZUW5hfFMjxwMk5GWUARUcuevPVTDjuLAvr93K|2^31|1:1a=
crypto:2 AES_CM_128_HMAC_SHA1_80
inline:UrEdZ6/u+pj+MABtYK7y/3/ZL/JSRjHe3tEjNEGn|2^31|1:1a=maxptime:200a=rtcp:2
1120a=rtpmap:114 x-msrta/16000a=fmtp:114 bitrate=12000a=rtpmap:111
SIREN/16000a=fmtp:111 bitrate=16000a=rtpmap:112 G7221/16000a=fmtp:112
bitrate=24000a=rtpmap:115 x-msrta/8000a=fmtp:115 bitrate=12000a=rtpmap:116
AAL2-G726-32/8000a=rtpmap:4 G723/8000a=rtpmap:8 PCMA/8000a=rtpmap:0
PCMU/8000a=rtpmap:97 RED/8000a=rtpmap:101 telephone-event/8000a=
fmtp:101 0-16a=encryption:optional
m=video 13952 RTP/AVP 121 34 31k=
base64:3QA+RtpnuOd4cCaj/rWBfeW+Hn9AvxcLhLDkB9yVzwJVftCkEcBSL+lBAmOua=
candidate:PVp0w5+rY86zX6Emqm+9zIGUlfTTOU9iEeBBKRfsvks 1 gt+GQX3LSYECKrIM9skhWg
UDP 0.840 192.168.3.100 13952 a=
candidate:PVp0w5+rY86zX6Emqm+9zIGUlfTTOU9iEeBBKRfsvks 2 gt+GQX3LSYECKrIM9skhWg
UDP 0.840 192.168.3.100 50944 a=cryptoscale:1 client AES_CM_128_HMAC_SHA1_80
inline:BsqZIvEl3PQRq4kwE8lRxSeSeDRriKAyS6uPIRBY|2^31|1:1a=crypto:2
AES_CM_128_HMAC_SHA1_80 inline:E3eOmRQAY7c2fSrzR3zrGX8Z1WUI1lGBRxk7GiH2|2^31|1:1a=
maxptime:200a=rtcp:50944a=rtpmap:121 x-rtvc1/90000a=rtpmap:34 H263/90000a=
rtpmap:31 H261/90000a=encryption:optional
```

This INVITE message body asks for an audio/video peer-to-peer conference and offers the media parameters and capabilities for the initiating Communicator client.

The 100 and 180 temporary responses are not shown here for the sake of brevity and because they do not really provide any interesting information. However, the 200 response provides capability information from the recipient, as follows:

```
v=0o=- 0 0 IN IP4 192.168.3.101s=sessionc=IN IP4 192.168.3.101b=CT:99980t=0 0
m=audio 10496 RTP/AVP 114 111 112 115 116 4 8 0 97
101a=candidate:jUpPjJEHNyN3RNHn+LlReOz7YZbWN3BpqnNqJw9KSrA 1
9VE2N1fM/Ug4DHk/KSO/xw UDP 0.830 192.168.3.101 10496 a=
candidate:jUpPjJEHNyN3RNHn+LlReOz7YZbWN3BpqnNqJw9KSrA 2 9VE2N1fM/Ug4DHk/KSO/xw
UDP 0.830 192.168.3.101 53120 a=crypto:2 AES_CM_128_HMAC_SHA1_80
inline:FxTfuRY3zYOR7EPAvnkKjOlOSm4Dwbc/ov1v1qkB|2^31|1:1a=maxptime:200a=
rtcp:53120a=rtpmap:114 x-msrta/16000a=fmtp:114 bitrate=12000a=rtpmap:111
SIREN/16000a=fmtp:111 bitrate=16000a=rtpmap:112 G7221/16000a=fmtp:112
bitrate=24000a=rtpmap:115 x-msrta/8000a=fmtp:115 bitrate=12000a=rtpmap:116
AAL2-G726-32/8000a=rtpmap:4 G723/8000a=rtpmap:8 PCMA/8000a=rtpmap:0
```

```
PCMU/8000a=rtpmap:97 RED/8000a=rtpmap:101 telephone-event/8000a=fmtp:101
0-16a=encryption:optional
m=video 14976 RTP/AVP 121 34 31a=
candidate:1t+HmBqSsE7M8/xGXLbb4U0SG1drKqrEi/RhuqWA5Eo 1 87LtCGRXUnVdv8WaYO+85Q
UDP 0.840 192.168.3.101 14976 a=
candidate:1t+HmBqSsE7M8/xGXLbb4U0SG1drKqrEi/RhuqWA5Eo 2 87LtCGRXUnVdv8WaYO+85Q
UDP 0.840 192.168.3.101 2304 a=crypto:2 AES_CM_128_HMAC_SHA1_80
inline:foe41lE6qfhFItmaGWs13hIJXiAzq98kCZKSJDpB|2^31|1:1a=maxptime:200a=rtcp:2
304a=rtpmap:121 x-rtvc1/90000a=rtpmap:34 H263/90000a=rtpmap:31
H261/90000a=encryption:optional
```

This response confirms that audio and video are available, as well as identifies the media parameters and capabilities for the client.

An ACK message is sent from Jeremy's Communicator client to finish the handshake, but this is not shown because it does not provide any useful additional information.

A second round INVITE is sent next, with the only change being an additional field (*a=remote-candidate*) that is added in the body as shown in the following code sample. (The same is true of the 200 OK response.)

```
...
m=audio 60160 RTP/AVP 114 111 112 115 116 4 8 0 97 101a=
remote-candidate:jUpPjJEHNyN3RNHn+LlReOz7YZbWN3BpqnNqJw9KSrA...
m=video 13952 RTP/AVP 121 34 31
a=remote-candidate:1t+HmBqSsE7M8/xGXLbb4U0SG1drKqrEi/RhuqWA5Eo...
```

Finally, a third round INVITE is sent where the video media is simplified down (the same is true of the 200 OK response) to a single line descriptor, as follows:

```
...
m=video 0 RTP/AVP 34
```

This whole process is simply a way for the two Communicator clients to exchange information about each other that relates to preferences and capabilities. After this session is finally negotiated and created, User Datagram Protocol (UDP) messages are exchanged between the published IPs and ports for each Communicator client as video and audio are shared. This continues until the conference ends based on a user's request.

Examining What Happens When Ending the Conversation (Step 7)

When Jeremy closes the messaging window, Communicator sends a BYE message within the dialog that was established in order to alert Vadim's client that the communication dialog is being closed. An example of the BYE message and the response from Vadim's client are shown here for reference:

```
BYE sip:srv.contoso.com:5061;transport=tls;ms-role-rs-from;ms-role-rs-to;
ms-opaque=aaB_D3-f9AM9QxeVkHOWddzAAA;lr;
ms-route-sig=aasNJOIb7XhG1fWKA4UvKlDEpMRMM2Fwj8K3gtHgAA SIP/2.0
Via: SIP/2.0/TLS 192.168.3.100:1467
Max-Forwards: 70
From: <sip:jeremy@contoso.com>;tag=e57383c75b;epid=aa6d968e18
To: "" <sip:vadim@contoso.com>;epid=6fe87e039b;tag=5c939f2392
Call-ID: d1a1cdc2192048f7a8e9703774cfebcc
CSeq: 8 BYE
Route: <sip:vadim@contoso.com;opaque=user:epid:EfpLp1FJKl6EFEzM2Ml2OQAA;gruu>
User-Agent: UCCP/2.0.6093.0 OC/2.0.6093.0 (Microsoft Office Communicator)
Proxy-Authorization: Kerberos qop="auth", realm="SIP Communications Service",
opaque="E8EA7EDD", crand="58dad80d", cnum="51",
targetname="sip/srv.contoso.com", response=
"602306092a864886f71201020201011100ffffffffec97e0568a70bf53982604eb4d04ebe5"
Content-Length: 0
```

Vadim's Communicator responds to acknowledge that it received the dialog close event, as follows:

```
SIP/2.0 200 OK
Authentication-Info: Kerberos rspauth=
"602306092A864886F71201020201011100FFFFFFFFA46FDE2C8EC5FE1C8E3FBBDC650D58A",
srand="A4C56671", snum="76", opaque="E8EA7EDD", qop="auth",
targetname="sip/srv.contoso.com", realm="SIP Communications Service"
Via: SIP/2.0/TLS 192.168.3.100:1467;ms-received-port=1467;ms-received-cid=A00
From: "Jeremy Los"<sip:jeremy@contoso.com>;tag=e57383c75b;epid=aa6d968e18
To: "" <sip:vadim@contoso.com>;epid=6fe87e039b;tag=5c939f2392
Call-ID: d1a1cdc2192048f7a8e9703774cfebcc
CSeq: 8 BYE
User-Agent: UCCP/2.0.6093.0 OC/2.0.6093.0 (Microsoft Office Communicator)
Content-Length: 0
```

Additional information about the Session Initiation Protocol is discussed in Chapter 18. However, at this point both clients have cleared any remaining state about the communication dialog and if another message is sent by either of them, a new dialog is established.

Note For reference, if Jeremy ends the messaging session before Vadim accepts it, a CANCEL message is sent instead. A BYE is sent on an established session, and a CANCEL is sent if the session is not fully established (that is, the 200 OK and ACK are not completed).

Summary

This chapter shows examples of usage scenarios, including a basic login, some use and control of presence information, and instant messaging. The technical details behind these usage scenarios are discussed, providing insight into how Office Communications Server and Communicator work together to provide useful functionality. Such technical understanding is essential for administrators who need to implement, configure, and troubleshoot Office Communications Server in their enterprises. This chapter also provides the core background on basic server and client operations in terms of discovery, connectivity and communications over the Session Initiation Protocol (SIP) and as such is useful to refer back to as reference material when exploring the other scenario chapters.

Additional Resources

The return code ranges for Office Communicator availability and the activity ranges, based on presence status, are detailed in Appendix B, "Numeric Ranges for Availablity and Activity Levels in Office Communicator." This appendix is on the companion CD in the \Appendixes,Scripts,Resources\Appendix B folder. For product documentation, community tools, frequently asked questions (FAQs), discussion groups, and pointers to up-to-date information on the product and community events, see the Office Communications Server Home Page at *http://www.microsoft.com/livecomm*. Pointers that are mentioned in the chapter are listed here:

- Winerror.exe is part of the Windows Server 2003 Resource Kit Tools, and Lcserror.exe is part of the Office Communications Server 2007 Resource Kit Tools. Both of these can be found at *http://www.microsoft.com/downloads* with a search for either one of the Resource Kit Tools.
- More information on the credentials manager can be found in the Microsoft TechNet article "Windows XP Resource Kit: Understanding Logon and Authentication" at *http://technet.microsoft.com/en-us/library/bb457114.aspx*, in the "Stored User Names and Passwords" section.
- A technical reference for Transport Layer Security (TLS) can be found by searching for the Microsoft TechNet article "TLS/SSL Technical Reference" at *http://technet.microsoft.com*.
- For more detailed information on Kerberos and NTLM, search for the Microsoft TechNet article "Kerberos Authentication Technical Reference" at *http://technet.microsoft.com* or the Microsoft Developer Network (MSDN) article "NTLM Authentication" at *http://msdn.microsoft.com*.
- For information about NTLM, Kerberos, and TLS/SSL, see the Windows Security Collection of the Windows Server 2003 Technical Reference at *http://technet2.microsoft.com/windowsserver/en/library/7cb7e9f7-2090-4c88-8d14-270c749fddb51033.mspx?mfr=true*.

- For information about SIP, see "Session Initiation Protocol [RFC 3261]" at *http://www.ietf.org/rfc/rfc3261.txt?number=3261*. In addition, two useful books about SIP are the following:
  - *SIP: Understanding the Session Initiation Protocol*, Second Edition by Alan B. Johnston (Artech House Publishers, 2003)
  - *SIP Demystified* by Gonzalo Camarillo (McGraw-Hill Professional, 2001)
- There are many useful community-driven Web sites that support Office Communications Server. One that stands out is the LCS Guides site at *http://www.lcs-guides.com*.

On the Companion CD

A full collection of protocol logs is on the companion CD, in the \Appendixes,Scripts,Resources\Chapter 04\CD Protocol Logs folder, for reference. These are useful for seeing example protocol messages and complete message flow. Many of the messages are not discussed here in the book to avoid repeating content and to skip some of the less interesting transactions, but these are all available in a complete form in the sample logs on the CD. You might also find these useful when troubleshooting, for comparison purposes.

In addition, the text file dbanalyze-jeremy.txt on the companion CD, in the \Appendixes,Scripts,Resources\Chapter 04 folder, shows full sample output from the **dbanalyze** command, as explained in the "Real World: Troubleshooting Client Connections" sidebar in this chapter.

Chapter 5
Conferencing Scenarios

In this chapter:

This chapter introduces the conferencing scenarios and capabilities supported by Office Communications Server 2007. The chapter also describes the technical details behind these scenarios, including the conferencing architecture, conference life cycle, and call flow. Finally, the chapter concludes with a discussion of meeting policy and policy enforcement.

Overview of Conferencing Scenarios

Office Communications Server 2007 introduces the capability for enterprise users both inside and outside the corporate firewall to create and join real-time Web conferences hosted on internal corporate servers. These conferences or meetings (which are referred to as *on-premise* conferences) can be scheduled or ad hoc. Attendees of these conferences can communicate using IM, audio, video, application sharing, slide presentations, and other forms of data collaboration. Enterprise users can invite external users without Active Directory Domain Services accounts to participate. Users who are employed by federated partners with a secure and authenticated identity can also join conferences and, if invited to do so, can act as presenters. Conference organizers control access to the conferences they organize by defining access types.

For administrators, Office Communications Server 2007 provides meeting policies, global-level settings, pool-level settings, and user-level settings to allow administrators to control almost every aspect of on-premise conferencing capabilities, such as access control, resource management, conference life cycle management, and so on. The scale-out conferencing architecture based on pools ensures high availability of conferences—if a server supporting a conference fails, the conference is automatically rolled over to another server with the same server role. Moreover, Office Communications Server also supports features that meet common compliance requirements. Basic conference information—such as creation time, activation time, user join, and user leave—are logged in the Call Detail Record (CDR) database. Most data collaboration contents are also recorded in a specific compliance file share.

This unified, server-based conferencing solution provides an alternative to hosted Web conferencing for organizations that require a more secure and controlled collaboration experience.

Understanding Conferencing User Types

In an Office Communications Server conference, all users are authenticated. Authentication is performed either by the front end of an Office Communications Server pool, by a Director if a Director is deployed, or by a federated server. Depending on the type of credentials used for authentication, Office Communications Server supports three types of users: an authenticated enterprise user, a federated user, and an anonymous user.

Understanding Authenticated Enterprise Users

An authenticated enterprise user is an employee of the enterprise hosting the Office Communications Server conference who has the following characteristics:

- Has a persistent Active Directory identity
- Is enabled for communications in Active Directory and in Office Communication Server management, and is assigned a valid Session Initiation Protocol (SIP) Uniform Resource Identifier (URI)
- Is assigned to either a valid Office Communications Server 2007 pool or a Live Communications Server 2005 Service Pack 1 (SP1) pool

Authenticated enterprise users hosted on an Office Communications Server pool can create and participate in an Office Communications Server conference. On the other hand, authenticated enterprise users hosted on a Live Communications Server 2005 SP1 pool cannot create a conference. However, they can participate in an Office Communications Server 2007 conference.

Authenticated enterprise users can be further classified into two categories according to the location from which they access Office Communications Server:

- **Internal User** Internal users connect to Office Communications Server from a location behind the corporate firewall.
- **Remote User** Remote users connect to Office Communications Server from a location outside of the corporate firewall. They include employees working at home or on the road, and other remote workers, such as trusted vendors, who have been granted enterprise Active Directory credentials for their terms of service.

Office Communications Server employs two Integrated Windows Authentication methods to authenticate enterprise users. Internal users are authenticated using either NTLM or Kerberos, depending on the server setting. For remote users, only NTLM is supported because Kerberos requires that the client have a direct connection to Active Directory, which is generally not the case for users connecting from outside of the corporate firewall.

Understanding Federated Users

A federated user is not an employee of the enterprise hosting the Office Communications Server conference. Instead, a federated user is an employee of a federated partner who has the following characteristics:

- Has a persistent identity in the federated partner's Active Directory
- Is enabled for communications in Active Directory and in Office Communications Server management, and is assigned a valid SIP URI
- Is assigned to either a valid Office Communications Server 2007 pool or a Live Communications Server 2005 SP1 pool hosted in the federated partner domain

Federated users are authenticated by the Office Communications Server 2007 or Live Communications Server 2005 SP1 hosted in the trusted federated partner domain. Therefore, they are trusted as authenticated users by the Office Communications Server 2007 server that hosts the conference. Federated users can join conferences, but they cannot create conferences in federated enterprises.

Understanding Anonymous Users

An anonymous user is not an employee of the enterprise hosting the Office Communications Server conference or an employee of a federated partner. Instead, an anonymous user is any user who does not have a persistent Active Directory identity in the enterprise hosting the Office Communications Server or federated partner enterprise.

Anonymous users can connect from the following three locations outside of the corporate firewall:

- An enterprise that deploys Office Communications Server 2007 or Live Communications Server 2005 SP1. However, the enterprise domain is not federated with the enterprise hosting the conference.
- An enterprise that deploys neither Office Communications Server 2007 nor Live Communications Server 2005 SP1.
- The Internet.

Anonymous users are authenticated via Digest authentication. For conferences that allow anonymous users to participate, Office Communications Server generates a conference key. Anonymous users must present the conference key when they join the conference.

> **Note** Anonymous users can join Office Communications Server conferences, but they cannot create conferences on the server.

Understanding Conferencing User Roles

Regardless of authentication types, conference participants fall into one of two user role groups during a conference: presenters or attendees. Office Communications Server 2007 keeps track of user roles for each conference participant. These user roles are used to authorize users to have access to different in-conference functionalities, which are summarized in the following list:

- **Presenter** A user who is authorized to present information at a conference, using whatever media is supported. A presenter is also granted rights to control a conference, such as locking a conference, ending a conference, promoting other participants to the presenter role, removing a user from a conference, or changing the list of in-conference features non-presenter participants can access, and so on.
- **Attendee** A user who has been invited to attend a meeting but who is not authorized to act as a presenter. An attendee can be promoted to presenter by other presenters during a conference.

> **Note** Promotion of user roles is not persistent across different instances of the same conference. If an attendee is promoted to the presenter role during a conference, she has the presenter role until she leaves the conference. The next time the attendee joins the same conference, she will again be assigned the attendee role. Only participants who are designated as presenters by the organizer at conference creation time—that is, they are pre-set presenters—can join a conference with the automatic presenter role. In addition, currently, Office Communications Server does not support demoting a presenter to attendee.

All authenticated enterprise users and federated users can join a conference as pre-set presenters. Anonymous users can join a conference only as attendees. However, once they have joined, anonymous users can be promoted to presenter by any existing presenter in a conference.

In addition, there is an implicit role of organizer:

- **Organizer** The user who creates a conference, whether impromptu or by scheduling.

Every Office Communications Server 2007 conference is associated with an organizer. An organizer must be an authenticated enterprise user. If a user is deleted from the enterprise Active Directory, all Office Communications Server 2007 conferences she organizes are also removed from the back-end database. The content created in conferences organized by such an organizer is also removed through a content expiration feature. An organizer is by definition also a presenter and determines who else can be a presenter. An organizer can make this determination either at the time a meeting is scheduled or after the meeting is under way.

Understanding Conference Security and Access Types

Security has been a top priority for on-premise conferencing. All messaging and media in conferencing are encrypted, using the same security infrastructure as Live Communications Server 2005 SP1. In addition, Office Communications Server 2007 provides additional safeguards for conferencing. These safeguards include the following features:

- Strong authentication using Integrated Windows Authentication and Digest authentication.
- Role-based authorization for conference control.
- Level of access through three predefined access types.
- Policy-based administration to allow administrators to control resource utilization and security. Meeting features are grouped and managed using meeting policies. Administrators control which meeting features a meeting organizer can use during a meeting by configuring and applying specific policies. See the section titled "Understanding Meeting Policy and Policy Enforcement" later in this chapter for more information.

When organizers create a conference, they can set the conference to have one of three access types: open authenticated, closed authenticated, or anonymous allowed.

Understanding the Open Authenticated Conference

An open authenticated conference can be joined by all authenticated enterprise users. They join as attendees unless they have been designated as presenters by the meeting organizer.

An open authenticated conference is suitable in situations where the participant list is dynamic or unknown, such as a brown-bag meeting. Authenticated enterprise users can join any open authenticated meeting hosted on any Office Communications Server pool, even if they are not specifically invited by the conference organizer. This is usually achieved by one user forwarding a conference invitation to another user.

Federated users can join the meeting as attendees if they are invited by the organizer. Federated users are not able to join the meeting as presenters, but they can be promoted to presenter during the meeting (this is currently a client implementation limitation; Office Communications Server does not support creating an open authenticated conference with federated users as pre-set presenters). If you want to prevent federated users from participating in an open authenticated meeting, you can do so by not configuring the Access Edge Server for federation or by disabling the organizer for federation.

Understanding the Closed Authenticated Conference

A closed authenticated conference can be joined only by authenticated enterprise users who are specifically invited by the conference organizer.

Closed authenticated conferences are suitable in situations where tight control of the conference content is required, such as a meeting that discusses confidential company financial information. An authenticated user who is not explicitly invited cannot join a closed authenticated conference, even if the user has conference join information from forwarded invitations.

Federated users can join a closed authenticated conference if explicitly invited. They can join either as attendees or pre-set presenters. Currently, client implementation prevents a user from scheduling a closed authenticated conference with federated users.

Understanding the Anonymous Allowed Conference

Anonymous allowed type conferences have the most relaxed access control. Anonymous allowed conferences can be joined by authenticated enterprise users and federated users, as well as anonymous users, as long as those users have conference join information.

Anonymous allowed conferences are suitable in situations where collaboration between enterprise users and outside users is required, such as a sales meeting that invites potential outside customers.

To create a meeting of this type, the meeting organizer must be authorized to invite anonymous users. Enterprise users and federated users join as attendees unless they have been designated as presenters by the meeting organizer. Anonymous users join only as attendees, although they can be promoted to the presenter role by presenters after they have entered the meeting. To enter a meeting, anonymous users must present a conference key, which they receive in an e-mail meeting invitation, and they must pass Digest authentication.

Table 5-1 summarizes different situations in which users can be allowed into Office Communications Server conferences.

Table 5-1 Conference Access Types (√ means the user can join, whereas × means the user cannot join)

Conference Type	Authenticated Enterprise User		Federated User		Anonymous User	
	Directly Invited	Forwarded	Directly Invited	Forwarded	Directly Invited	Forwarded
Open Authenticated	√	√	√	√	×	×
Closed Authenticated	√	×	√	×	×	×
Anonymous Allowed	√	√	√	√	√	√

Understanding Conferencing Media Types

Office Communications Server 2007 conferences provide rich multimedia experiences. The following sections discuss the four main types of multimedia conferencing: multiparty instant messaging, data collaboration, audio/video, and audio conferencing provider support.

Understanding Multiparty Instant Messaging

Multiparty instant messaging, or group IM, refers to an IM conversation among three or more parties. The Microsoft Windows Messenger 5.x and Office Communicator 2005 clients, along with Live Communications Server 2005 SP1, already support group IM based on establishing a separate connection between each two-user pair engaged in the conversation. In Office Communications Server 2007, a group IM session is implemented as a server-hosted conference with IM modality. This approach is more scalable and offers greater flexibility to participants than a group conversation that is based on a large number of linked peer-to-peer conversations.

The main client for multiparty instant messaging conferences is Office Communicator 2007. A group IM session can be created in one of the following ways:

- By sending an instant message to multiple parties
- By inviting additional parties to a two-person IM conversation
- By sending an instant message to a Microsoft Exchange Server distribution list

Direct from the Source: Group Expansion Web Service

Office Communications Server 2007 provides a group expansion Web service that expands an Active Directory distribution group into a list of users. This expansion allows users to invite one or more individual members of the group to an IM session. Distribution groups of up to 1000 users can be expanded, and an IM session can include as many as 100 members.

The expansion of the following four types of Active Directory distribution groups is supported by the Web service:

- Universal distribution groups that are e-mail enabled
- Global distribution groups that are e-mail enabled
- Universal security groups that are e-mail enabled
- Global security groups that are e-mail enabled

–Hao Yan
Senior Program Manager

Understanding Data Collaboration

Data collaboration conferences are often referred to as *Web conferences*. Office Communications Server 2007 supports a rich mix of data collaboration possibilities, including the following:

- **PowerPoint presentations** Office Communications Server 2007 provides native Microsoft Office PowerPoint support, which includes uploading and sharing slide decks created with PowerPoint, including animations and other rich features.
- **Application and desktop sharing** Sharing applications among multiple participants and giving other participants control of the desktop or application. Administrators can customize the level of sharing or control that is allowed in their organization or disable this feature completely through meeting policy.
- **Microsoft Office Document Imaging (MODI) support** Office Communications Server 2007 also supports uploading and sharing of any document format that supports the MODI print driver. This support provides conference users the ability to share in read-only mode virtually any kind of documents that can be printed to MODI file format, including all Microsoft Office document formats, Adobe PDF format, and HTML file format.
- **Web slides** Sharing URLs to Web pages that can be viewed and navigated independently by all meeting participants.
- **Multimedia content** Office Communications Server supports uploading and sharing media files (such as Flash or Windows Media technology files). The viewing of the media files by all meeting participants can be synchronous (controlled by presenter) or asynchronous (participants view files independently).
- **Handouts** Exchanging files in their native formats among meeting participants.
- **Snapshot slides** Capturing and displaying a static view of (an area of) the user's desktop.
- **Whiteboards** Free-form drawing and writing in a common shared space.
- **Text slides** Writing and sharing text on a virtual whiteboard (separate from the graphical whiteboard features).
- **Annotations** Annotating many types of slides, including PowerPoint slides and MODI document slides.
- **Polling** The ability to create questions and answers and compile and share responses from participants.
- **Q&A** Asking and answering questions during a meeting.
- **In-meeting chat** Peer-to-peer IM within the context of a meeting.
- **Shared notes** The ability to edit and share meeting notes with other participants.

The main client for data collaboration conferences is Office Live Meeting 2007. A data collaboration session can be created in one of the following ways:

- By scheduling a data collaboration conference in Microsoft Office Outlook with the Outlook Conferencing Add-in
- By selecting Meet Now in Office Live Meeting 2007
- By adding data collaboration to an existing IM and audio/video session in Office Communicator 2007

Understanding Audio and Video Conferencing

Office Communications Server 2007 supports multiparty audio/video (A/V) conferencing. Through advanced wideband codecs such as RTAudio and RTVideo, Office Communications Server (through the Audio/Video Conferencing Server role) delivers high-quality audio and video in a conference.

The audio streams from all participants are mixed at the server and broadcasted to all participants. For video, the video stream of the most active speaker is sent to all participants. When deployed on a separate computer, the Audio/Video Conferencing Server can support up to 250 participants within a single session.

The main clients for A/V conferences are Office Communicator 2007 and Office Live Meeting 2007. An A/V conference session can be initiated in the following ways:

- By scheduling a data collaboration conference with audio and video in Outlook with the Outlook Conferencing Add-in.
- By scheduling a conference call with audio and video in Outlook with the Outlook Conferencing Add-in.
- By starting an audio/video conversation with two or more other participants in Office Communicator.

Understanding Audio Conferencing Provider Support

External audio conference participants who have not deployed Office Communications Server can participate through the services of a third-party Audio Conferencing Provider (ACP). The provider enables conferencing over an external Public Switched Telephone Network (PSTN) bridge.

Office Live Meeting 2007 is the main client that supports ACP conferences. It provides user interfaces to control various aspects of the audio conference hosted on an external PSTN bridge, such as mute self, un-mute self, mute all, and so on.

In Office Communications Server 2007, there is no interaction between the VoIP-based audio conference hosted by the Audio/Video Conferencing Server and the ACP conference hosted by external Audio Conferencing Providers. This means in a conference there cannot be some participants using their phones to dial in to the meeting while the rest use their computer audio hardware to join the meeting. When scheduling a conference, the conference organizer needs to make appropriate audio choices.

ACP integration is managed by the Telephony Conferencing Server, which always runs as a separate process on either an Office Communications Server 2007 Standard Edition server or Enterprise Edition front-end server. Integration with the Audio Conferencing Provider occurs by configuring a federated connection with the external service provider, as you would with any other federated partner.

Examining the Technical Details Behind Conferencing Scenarios

In this section, we describe the technical details behind Office Communications Server 2007 conferencing scenarios. First, we introduce the conferencing component architecture. We then discuss the life cycle of a conference. Finally, we reveal more technical details on data collaboration conferences.

Understanding the Conferencing Architecture

Many components participate in an Office Communications Server on-premise conference. They handle functionalities such as authentication, authorization, signaling, conference control, storage, and media mixing and processing. Figure 5-1 shows the logical component architecture for conferencing.

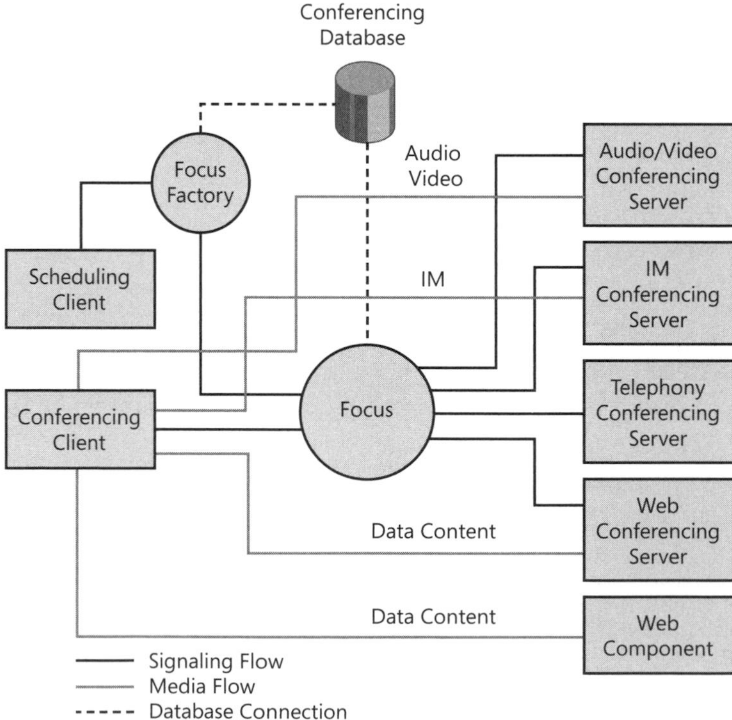

Figure 5-1 Conferencing component architecture

Understanding Conferencing Clients

There are two types of client conferencing applications, scheduling clients and conferencing clients.

- **Scheduling Client** A scheduling client is a client application that handles the creation, modification, or deletion of a conference. The client can also handle the scheduling aspect of a conference, such as start and end time, participant list, and recurrence. Optionally, the client can send invitation notifications for conference participants.
- **Conferencing Client** A conferencing client is a client application that can join and participate in an Office Communications Server conference. The main functionalities of a conferencing client include joining a conference, showing a list of conference participants and their status, and providing a user interface for the user to control different aspects of the conference.

The separation between a scheduling client and a conferencing client is only logical, based on the set of conferencing-related functionalities that each performs. In reality, client applications can have both scheduling and conferencing capabilities. There are three main client applications used for on-premise conferencing hosted by Office Communications Server.

Microsoft Office Live Meeting Console 2007 Microsoft Live Meeting Console 2007 is the primary conferencing client for scheduled Web conferences. It provides support for a full range of modalities that enable participants to have an effective collaborative meeting. Those modalities include the following:

- Data collaboration, such as with PowerPoint presentations, whiteboarding, polling, shared notes, and so on. Microsoft Live Meeting Console is the only client offering that supports application sharing.
- Audio and video. Microsoft Live Meeting Console supports real time multiparty audio and video, complete with active speaker detection and display.
- Audio Conferencing Provider integration. Microsoft Live Meeting Console is the only client offering that supports integration between an Office Communications Server conference and a phone-based audio conference hosted by an outside Audio Conferencing Provider. The console provides user interfaces for users to control the audio conference, such as mute self, mute all, and so on.
- In-meeting chat. Microsoft Live Meeting Console supports peer-to-peer text chat between two conference participants.

Microsoft Office Live Meeting Console 2007 is also a scheduling client. It provides a Meet Now functionality that allows users to create an instant conference and invite other participants from within the conference. The following is a screen shot of the client:

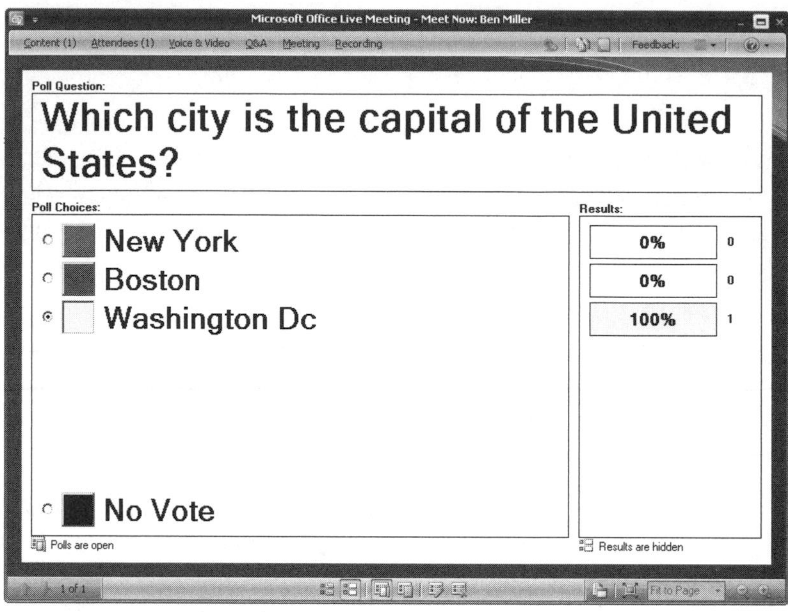

Microsoft Office Communicator 2007 Microsoft Office Communicator 2007 is the primary client application for instant communications and ad hoc collaboration. It provides the following capabilities:

- Multiparty IM conference, based on multiple contacts in a contact list or an Active Directory Distribution Group
- Multiparty audio/video conference
- Seamless escalation from IM and/or audio/video conferences to Microsoft Office Live Meeting Console–based data collaboration conferences

The following image shows a group IM session in the Microsoft Office Communicator 2007 client:

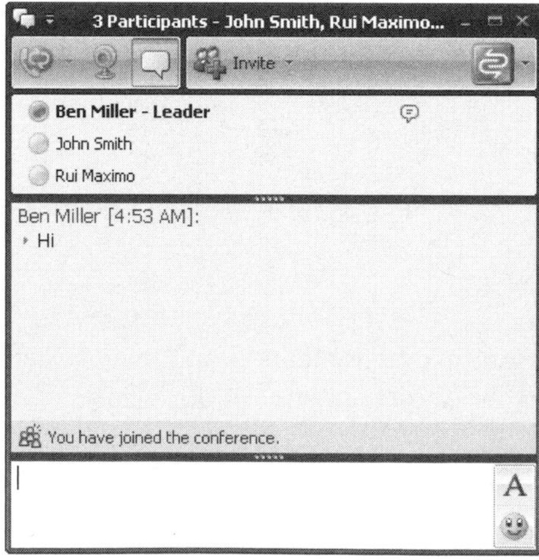

Microsoft Conferencing Add-in for Microsoft Office Outlook The Microsoft Conferencing Add-in for Microsoft Office Outlook is the primary scheduling client. The add-in allows users to use the familiar Microsoft Office Outlook interface for scheduling an Office Communications Server conference. In addition to the usual conference information that Outlook handles—such as meeting start and end time and recurrence—the add-in allows users to apply meeting settings that are specific to an Office Communications Server conference, such as meeting access type, presenter list, and audio information. It also generates a preformatted meeting invitation that contains all the necessary information for joining the conference. The meeting invitation is sent to all the invited participants via e-mail.

Users can schedule two types of conferences:

- **Schedule a Live Meeting** This option schedules a conference that will happen in the Microsoft Office Live Meeting Console 2007 client. All modalities will be provisioned for the conference.
- **Schedule a Conference Call** This option schedules a conference that will happen in the Microsoft Office Communicator 2007 client. Only computer-based audio modality is provisioned at the start of the conference. (Conference participants can add other modalities later.)

The following is a screen shot of the Microsoft Conferencing Add-in for a Microsoft Office Outlook client in action:

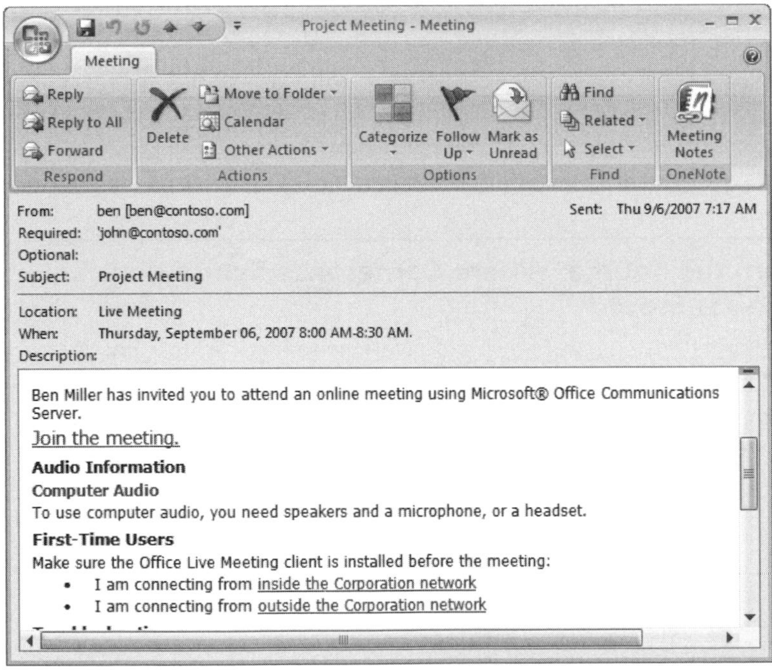

Understanding the Conferencing Database

In the Office Communications Server conferencing architecture, two databases (RTC and RTCDyn) provide storage for conference properties and conference state, respectively. Those databases are hosted in the SQL back-end server.

The RTC database stores persistent user data, including the contact list, access control information, and static conferencing information. Static conference properties are stored in this database from the time the conference is created until the time the conference is deleted from the server. Following is a list of included conference properties:

- Conference identifier. The conference ID along with the SIP URI of the organizer uniquely identifies a conference.
- Conference expiration date. This setting indicates when it is safe for the server to delete the conference automatically.
- Conference access type—for example, open authenticated.
- Conference access key for anonymous users.
- Supported media types.
- A list of meeting participants and their roles.

The RTCDyn database stores transient conference state information, such as the up-to-date participant list and the roles of participants, subscription information, conference lock, and so on. That information is specific to each instance of a conference and is removed when a conference ends. It is, however, important to persist that information in a database during the conference. Doing this ensures high availability for the conference. If one server component fails or stops responding, another server with the same role can easily take over and continue to serve the same conference by using information from the database.

Direct from the Source: Where Conference Scheduling Information Is Stored

The RTC database does not contain conference scheduling information. Supporting a meeting start time and end time, recurrence schedule, and exceptions to recurrence are all important for a prescheduled conference. However, that information is maintained outside of the conferencing database and Office Communications Server. Instead, conference calendar information is maintained by scheduling clients as appropriate. For example, the Microsoft Conferencing Add-in for Microsoft Outlook client saves the time information as part of a Microsoft Exchange Server calendar item.

–Hao Yan
Senior Program Manager, OCS Server

Understanding Focus

The Focus is a conference state server that acts as the coordinator for all aspects of a conference. It is implemented as a SIP user agent that is addressable by using a conference URI. The Focus runs in the User Services module of all front-end servers. A separate instance of the Focus exists for each active conference.

The Focus is responsible for the following tasks:

- Activating conferences
- Enlisting required conferencing servers
- Authenticating participants before allowing them to enter a conference
- Managing conference participant roles and privileges
- Authorizing conferencing control commands from participants based on the conference organizer's meeting policy
- Managing conference state
- Maintaining SIP signaling relationships between conference participants and conferencing servers, providing a conduit for control commands to flow between clients and the conferencing servers
- Accepting subscriptions to conferences, and notifying clients of changes in conference state, such as the arrival and departure of participants and the addition or removal of media

When a new media type needs to be activated for a conference, the Focus also instantiates the conference on the appropriate conferencing server, communicates with the conferencing server about adding a new user, fetches the authorization credentials so that the client can connect to that conference, and then sends the media information to the client. The same sequence is repeated for all clients who want to add this media. When a new media type is added to the conference, the sequence is repeated with the new conferencing server for that media type. By centralizing security enforcement and roster management, the Focus relieves each of the conferencing servers of this duty.

Understanding the Focus Factory

The Focus Factory is an entity that creates, deletes, and modifies meetings in the conferencing database. It is also implemented as a SIP user agent that is addressable by using a Focus Factory URI. When a client application creates a new conference, the client sends a SIP SERVICE message (which carries C3P commands as the message payload) to the Focus Factory. (See the "Understanding the Conferencing Protocols" section for more information about C3P commands.) The Focus Factory creates a new instance of the meeting in the conference database and returns information, including the conference URI, about the newly created conference to the client.

> **Note** The Focus Factory runs in the same process as the Focus.

Understanding Conferencing Servers and the Conferencing Server Factory

Supporting multiparty conferences requires using the *conferencing server* role (also known as an MCU or multipoint control unit). Each type of conferencing server is responsible for managing one or more media types. Office Communications Server 2007 includes four conferencing servers:

- **Web Conferencing Server** Manages conference data collaboration, including native support for Microsoft Office PowerPoint presentations, Microsoft Office document sharing, whiteboarding, application sharing, polling, questions and answers (Q&As), compliance logging, annotations, meeting summaries, handouts, and various multimedia formats. The Web Conferencing Server uses the Persistent Shared Object Model (PSOM), a Live Meeting protocol, for uploading slides to a meeting.
- **A/V Conferencing Server** Provides multiparty IP audio and video mixing and relaying, by using industry standard Real-Time Protocol (RTP) and Real-Time Control Protocol (RTCP).
- **IM Conferencing Server** Enables group IM by relaying IM traffic among all participants. All messages among the participants are routed through the IM Conferencing Server.
- **Telephony Conferencing Server** Responsible for Audio Conferencing Provider (ACP) integration. Supports both dial-out and dial-in, as well as standard third-party call control features such as mute and eject.

A conferencing server consists of two logical pieces: a media controller (MC) and a media processor (MP). The MC on a conferencing server is responsible for managing the control commands between the Focus and a conferencing server. In the Office Communications Server architecture, all conference control commands are sent by clients to the Focus, which then relays these commands to the appropriate conferencing server or servers after verifying that the client that sent the request has the privileges to perform that operation.

Media is exchanged directly between clients and the conferencing server or servers. The media processor is responsible for media management, such as mixing, relaying, and transcoding (direct digital-to-digital translation from one signal encoding format to another). In a Web Conferencing Server, the media processor is a software component that is responsible for managing data collaboration. In an A/V Conferencing Server, the media processor mixes audio streams, switches video streams, and converts the media for clients who are on slow links. Of all the conferencing components, the MP can be the most CPU and network intensive component. In the Office Communications Server conferencing architecture, an MC and MP are co-located on the same machine to simplify deployment.

In a conference, when a media type needs to be added, the Focus requests a conferencing server for that media type through the Conferencing Server Factory. The Conferencing Server Factory is a lightweight logical component responsible for provisioning a conference for a particular media type on a conferencing server. The MCU Factory takes into account the current load on the conferencing servers before assigning a conferencing server to a conference. There is one MCU Factory instance on each front-end server that handles all media types.

Direct from the Source: Office Communications Server 2007 Conferencing Scale

Early in the planning phase of Office Communications Server 2007, we knew a critical decision point would be the size of meetings we supported on the server. After reviewing competitive products, speaking with customers, and mining the experience from our own Live Meeting service, it became clear that the vast majority of meetings were actually small (4 to 6 participants). Digging deeper, we discovered that 80 percent of meetings had fewer than 20 participants and 99.98 percent of meetings had fewer than 100 participants. We then polled customers to see if a figure of around 200 to 250 participants would meet their needs. We found out that it would–with the caveat that there were occasionally larger meetings, such as all-hands meetings, that would exceed this limit. We considered supporting much larger meetings but made the decision to instead focus on the typical information worker meeting (4 to 6 users) and allow room for growth up to 200 to 250 participants. Meetings larger than that would need to take advantage of the Live Meeting hosted service, which can scale beyond 1000 participants in a meeting. Apart from the raw server scaling characteristics of such meetings, it was clear from our own operational experience that it takes dedicated staff and processes to make such large meetings effective. In essence, it is a different solution altogether if done properly.

How We Have Tested That Goal

Our user model for performance testing of conferencing takes into account a number of factors:

- How many users are on the pool
- The effective concurrency rate for meetings
- The media types (mixes) that are available for each meeting
- Where users come from: inside the enterprise, outside the enterprise, federated, or anonymous

To determine the number of meetings we test with, we take the total number of users (for example, 50,000) and multiply by a concurrency rate (for example, 5%). That gives us the number of users we expect to be in a meeting at any given time (in this example, 2500 users). We can then divide this by the number of conferencing servers in the deployment (for example, 2), and that gives us a figure for the number of participants per conferencing server (in this case, 1250). We can then divide that number by the average meeting size (for example, 6), and that gives us the average number of meetings per conferencing server (in this example, ~210). We test a variety of meeting sizes to ensure the server scales appropriately. This calculation represents an average load that we test.

One specific test we do is to ensure that we can indeed support a meeting with up to 250 participants. This includes audio, video, and data. In that test, we run one such large meeting on a given conference server (a multipoint control unit, or MCU). We do not attempt to run multiple such meetings on a single conference server. The reason we don't do this goes back to our data, which indicates that these types of meetings are relatively rare.

No Magic Numbers

When you see numbers like 250 (the largest meeting size), 1250 (the number of users on a single conferencing server), and so on, it can be easy to think that these are hard-coded values. But there really are no such magic numbers in our software. Rather, these numbers represent the capacity we have tested for given a particular user model and a particular set of hardware. (All of this can be found in the Planning Guide for Office Communications Server 2007.) Let me repeat that: you will not find the number 250 hard-coded in our server. We do have a notion of the maximum number of participants in a meeting that is controlled by the administrator through meeting policy. This is an administrator policy that can be set either through the Microsoft Management Console (MMC) or Windows Management Instrumentation (WMI). (More details can be found in the deployment documentation, which can be found at *http://technet.microsoft.com/en-us/library/bb676082.aspx*.)

If you take a look at these policies in MMC, you will note that the default is actually much lower than 250. This is not by accident. It is assumed that users who are allowed to create such large meetings are privileged users and therefore have a nondefault policy. Meeting policies apply to the organizer of the meeting. Some organizers might be allowed to have 200-person meetings; others might be allowed to have only 10 people in a meeting. This is an administrator decision, which our software will enforce.

Pushing the Limits

If 250 is not hard-coded in the server software, you might logically wonder what happens when you exceed this limit. First let me explain how a Conferencing Server manages its load dynamically. When the first user joins a meeting, a conferencing server for the appropriate media type or types is allocated. (See the "Understanding Conferencing Servers and the Conferencing Server Factory" section earlier in this chapter for an explanation of conferencing servers and a list of available types in Office Communications Server 2007.) The conferencing server that is allocated comes from a set of conferencing servers associated with the pool.

In the preceding example, there are two Web conferencing servers in a pool for 50,000 users. Each conferencing server is responsible for managing its load and reporting its ability to host additional meetings. If a conferencing server has exceeded its capacity, it can report this and the pool will allocate a different conferencing server. This is all done in real time at the time of the meeting; we do not reserve resources in advance. We also do not prioritize certain meetings over others when allocating resources. A large 250-person meeting is likely to take up the resources of a single conferencing server, and other meetings will be allocated on other conferencing servers in that pool. So, say that you have a large meeting with 250 people on a single conferencing server and the 251st user tries to join that meeting. If the meeting policy allows this and the conferencing server has spare capacity, the user will be allowed to join. This test is performed for each user that joins, and it is possible for two large meetings to compete for resources on the same conferencing server. Smaller meetings are easier to pack into the same server because each requires fewer resources.

The capacity of the conferencing servers is gated by CPU and memory, for the most part. We test and recommend dual-processor/dual-core servers with 4 GB of memory. If you use more powerful hardware, you will have more capacity and be able to host larger meetings. This is not just theoretical; we deploy larger servers in our Live Meeting service to scale to larger audio/video meeting sizes. You can as well. Our hardware recommendation was chosen based on a reasonable balance of cost vs. typical usage (again, 99.98 percent of meetings have fewer than 100 users). Achieving as many as 1000 participants in a meeting is possible given the right hardware; it simply has not been a goal of the Office Communications Server 2007 release and is not something we directly support at this time.

Keep in mind, though, that there is more than server scale at issue here: do you have the right support and processes in place to make a 1000-user meeting successful? Supporting a meeting of this size typically means having dedicated IT staff on hand to deal with any support calls or "operator assistance" needs, as well as having the infrastructure to manage invitations, follow up on problems, distribute handouts, and so on. You also need to ensure that you have the appropriate network infrastructure in place with the required bandwidth to host such a large meeting.

Proper monitoring and capacity planning will ensure that you have the right hardware to scale to your needs. As your needs change, you can add more conferencing servers (or front-end servers in the consolidated topology) to meet your growing needs.

Recommendations for Larger Meeting Sizes

Here are a few recommendations if you want to push the limit on the meeting size:

- Create a dedicated meeting policy for those (limited) organizers authorized to host such large meetings.

- Ideally, create a dedicated pool for those organizers so that you can dedicate hardware resources particularly for these meetings. This is one form of resource reservation.
- Invest in the support infrastructure needed to make these meetings run smoothly (people, processes, network, and hardware).

– Sean Olson
Principal Group Program Manager, OCS Server

Understanding Web Components

Web Components are the set of ASP.NET applications and virtual directories that are created on Internet Information Services (IIS) during the deployment of Office Communications Server 2007. The Web components support the following functionalities:

- The data collaboration content of a conference is hosted using the *conf* Web component in encrypted format. The Web Conferencing Server instructs clients to download the content through HTTPs and provide an encryption key to the client for decryption.
- The Office Communicator client uses IIS to download Address Book Server files when the client is outside the corporate firewall.
- An ASP.NET application running on top of IIS is used for the Group Expansion Web Service.
- An ASP.NET application running on top of IIS is used for the Web Scheduler Resource Kit tool, which is a Web-based scheduling solution.

Understanding Process and Machine Boundaries for Conferencing Components

Figure 5-2 shows the machine and process boundaries for all the conferencing components that we discussed in previous sections.

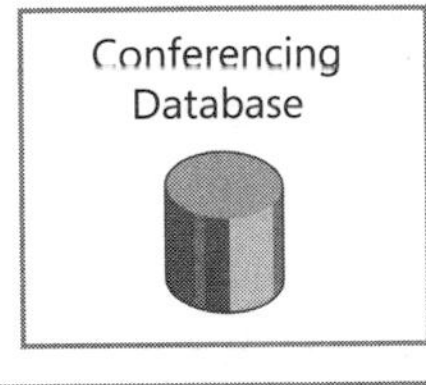

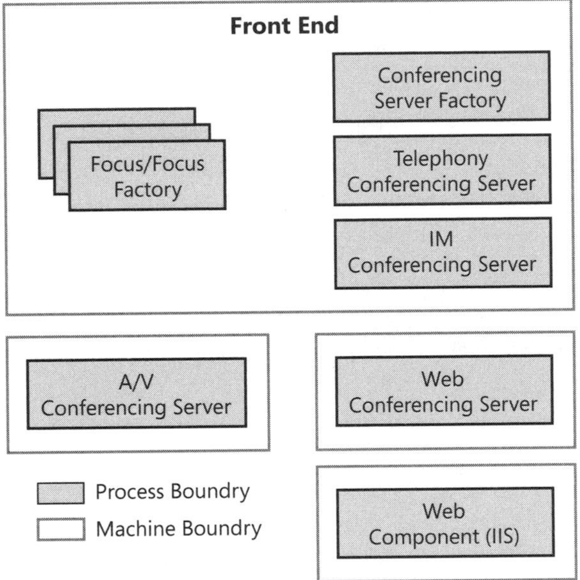

Figure 5-2 Conferencing component process and machine boundary

The Focus, Focus Factory, Conferencing Server Factory, IM Conferencing Server, and Telephony Conferencing Server all run as part of the front-end server. They cannot be separated and installed on different machines.

The Web Conferencing Server and the A/V Conferencing Server can be run on the same machine as the front-end server (in an Office Communications Server 2007 Standard Edition or Enterprise Edition consolidated topology). However, they can also be a separate server role and installed on their own hardware (Office Communications Server 2007 Enterprise Edition expanded topology). This configuration allows enterprises to scale out their Office Communications Server 2007 deployment by deploying as many conferencing servers as necessary to meet their usage model. The host for Web components (IIS) can be installed as part of every Office Communications Server 2007 Standard Edition server or Enterprise Edition consolidated topology server, or as a separate Web farm behind a hardware load balancer in the Enterprise Edition expanded topology.

Understanding Edge Servers

Office Communications Server 2007 allows enterprise users working outside the enterprise network to participate in on-premise conferences. In addition, it also enables enterprise users to invite federated users and anonymous users to participate in on-premise conferences. Enabling conferencing and the ability to share data and media with users outside the corporate firewall requires the following four server roles in the perimeter network:

- **Access Edge Server** Formerly known as the Access Proxy, the Access Edge Server handles all SIP traffic across the corporate firewall. The Access Edge Server handles only the SIP traffic that is necessary to establish and validate connections. It does not handle data transfer, nor does it authenticate users. Authentication of inbound traffic is performed by the Director or the front-end server.
- **Web Conferencing Edge Server** The Web Conferencing Edge Server proxies PSOM traffic between the Web Conferencing Server and external clients. External conference traffic must be authorized by the Web Conferencing Edge Server before it is forwarded to the Web Conferencing Server. The Web Conferencing Edge Server requires that external clients use Transport Layer Security (TLS) connections and obtain a conference session key.
- **A/V Edge Server** The A/V Edge Server provides a single trusted connection point through which inbound and outbound media traffic can securely traverse network address translators (NATs) and firewalls. The industry-standard solution for multimedia traversal of firewalls is Interactive Connectivity Establishment (ICE), which is based on the Simple Traversal Underneath NAT (STUN) and Traversal Using Relay NAT (TURN) protocols. The A/V Edge Server is a STUN server. All users are authenticated to secure both access to the enterprise and use of the firewall traversal service that is provided by the A/V Edge Server. To send media inside the enterprise, an external user must be authenticated and must have an authenticated internal user agree to communicate with him or her through the A/V Edge Server. The media streams themselves are exchanged by using Secure Real-Time Protocol (SRTP), which is an industry standard for real-time media transmission and reception over IP.
- **HTTP Reverse Proxy** Office Communications Server 2007 conferencing support for external users also requires deploying an HTTP reverse proxy in the perimeter network for the purpose of carrying HTTP and HTTPS traffic to the Web components (IIS) for external users.

Figure 5-3 shows the conferencing component architecture with edge servers.

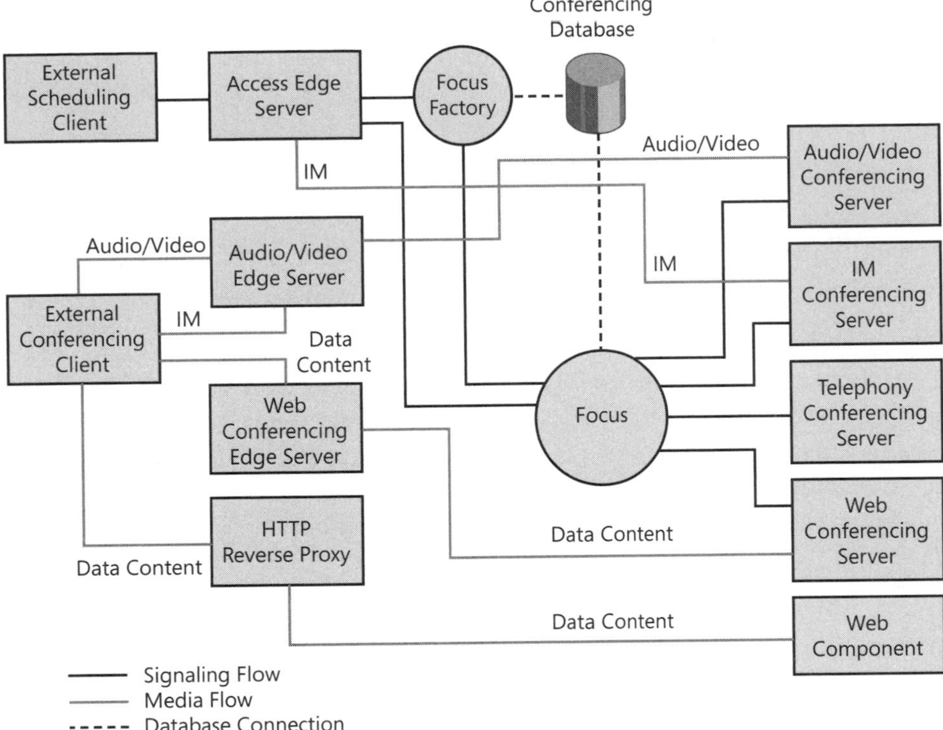

Figure 5-3 Conferencing component architecture with edge servers

Understanding the Conferencing Protocols

This section discusses various protocols for the communication between different components in the conferencing architecture. On a high level, there are two classes of protocols involved in an on-premise conference: signaling and media.

Signaling Protocols *Signaling protocol* refers to protocols that facilitate session establishment, capability exchange, state exchange, and conference control.

Session Initiation Protocol (SIP) is the primary signaling protocol used by Office Communications Server. SIP is the industry-standard protocol described in Internet Engineering Task Force (IETF) RFC 3261, which defines a standard way to perform session setup, termination, and media negotiation between two parties.

The SIP NOTIFY/BENOTIFY methods are used to convey changes in conference state. *Conference state* describes the various entities associated with a conference. It is described using the IETF RFC Conference Event (*http://www.ietf.org/rfc/rfc4575.txt*) package.

Various conference control and state modification tasks are achieved using C3P protocol. C3P stands for *Centralized Conferencing Control Protocol*. It is an XML-based protocol that provides a thin wrapper around the Conference Event package and also provides various media-specific extensions. C3P commands can be carried through SIP INFO or SERVICE methods. In general, C3P commands can be classified into three categories:

- Commands that terminate on the Focus and do not involve conferencing server interaction (for example, renameUser)
- Commands that are authorized by the Focus but are simply proxied to conferencing servers, so no Focus state is modified unless the conferencing server generates a notification (for example, modifyEndpointMedia)
- Commands that are processed by the Focus as well as by conferencing servers (for example, deleteConference, modifyConferenceLock)

The Focus and conferencing servers communicate using C3P and use HTTPS as the carrier protocol for C3P. Clients communicate with Focus and Focus Factory by using SIP INFO or SERVICE methods. SIP INVITE, ACK, BYE, UPDATE, and CANCEL methods are used to establish a signaling dialog between a conferencing client and the Focus. The client signals conferencing servers with the corresponding supported protocols: SIP for the IM Conferencing Server, Telephony Conferencing Server, and A/V Conferencing Server; and PSOM for the Web Conferencing Server.

Media Protocols *Media protocols* refers to protocols that facilitate exchange of specific types of media between clients and a conferencing server.

The Web Conferencing Server uses PSOM, a Live Meeting protocol, for exchanging data collaboration content and control with conferencing clients. The concept of a distributed object is central to PSOM Operations. A distributed object is a set of two interfaces: one interface for the object's client side, and one interface for the object's server side. Protocol messages are mapped to methods of these interfaces. The client interface contains messages sent to the client side of a connection. The server interface contains messages sent to the server side of a connection.

The IM Conferencing Server uses the Session Initiation Protocol for Instant Messaging and Presence Leveraging Extensions (SIMPLE) to communicate with IM conferencing clients. SIMPLE is an open standard defined by IETF RFC 3428 (*http://tools.ietf.org/html/rfc3428*).

RTP/RTCP is standard protocol employed by the A/V Conferencing Server to exchange audio and video streams with conferencing clients. RTP defines a standardized packet format for delivering audio and video over the Internet. RTCP provides out-of-band control information for an RTP flow. In Office Communications Server, all communications are encrypted. The A/V Conferencing Server actually uses the SRTP/SRTCP protocol, which provides encryption over RTP/RTCP.

Figure 5-4 provides an overview of how the various conferencing protocols interact with different Office Communications Server components.

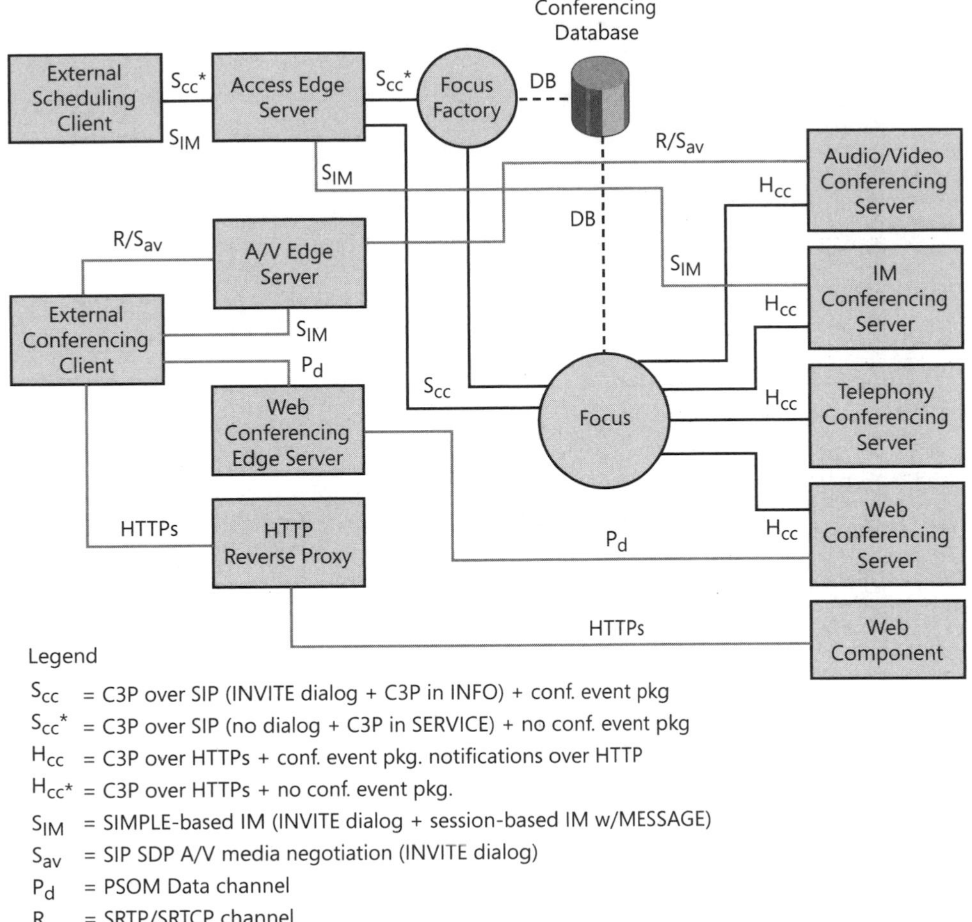

Figure 5-4 Conferencing protocols

Understanding the Conference Life Cycle

Each Office Communications Server conference has the life cycle shown in Figure 5-5. A conference is created by a scheduling client via the Focus Factory. The conference can be activated/joined and deactivated at any time after it is created and after it is cleaned up (has expired) from the server. The conference expires only after the specified expiration date has passed.

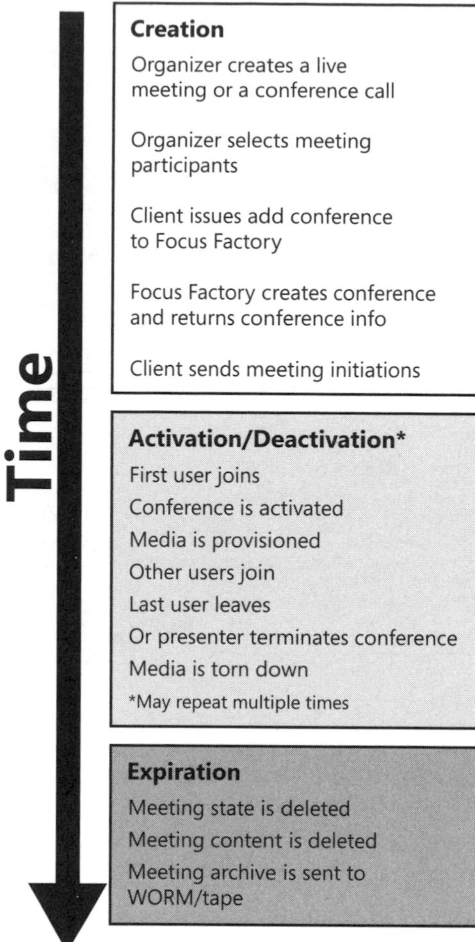

Figure 5-5 Conference life cycle

Understanding Conference Creation

An Office Communications Server 2007 conference can be created in one of the following ways:

- By scheduling a Web conference or conference call from the Microsoft Conferencing Add-in for Microsoft Outlook
- By creating a multiparty IM or A/V conferencing session from the Office Communicator 2007 client
- By using the Share Information Using Live Meeting option in the Office Communicator 2007 client

- By creating an ad hoc meeting by using the Meet Now functionality of the Microsoft Office Live Meeting 2007 client
- By scheduling a Web conference or audio conference by using the Web Scheduler Resource Kit tool

In all the preceding scenarios, the scheduling client communicates with the Focus Factory, which actually creates records in the conferencing database. Only authenticated enterprise users who are home on an Office Communications Server 2007 pool can create conferences. The key inputs to the Focus Factory include the following:

- Organizer SIP URI, which is the SIP URI that identifies the organizer of the conference.
- Conference Id, which is an alpha-numeric string that identifies the conference. The Conference Id has to be unique for the same organizer.
- Subject, which is the subject of the conference. This is used for display in the conferencing client.
- Conference access type, which can be Open/Closed Authenticated or anonymous allowed.
- Conference key, which is an alpha-numeric string that is used to authenticate anonymous users.
- Participant list and roles.
- Expiration time. The scheduling client can specify an optional expiration time at which it is safe to delete the conference completely from Office Communications Server.
- Provisioned conferencing servers. This specifies the type of media that is required in the conference.
- Conferencing server specific information, such as numbers to dial in for the Telephony Conferencing Server.

The key output from the Focus Factory is the conference URI. A conference URI is a globally unique identifier that represents the conference. A sample conference URI is shown here:

```
sip:ben@contoso.com;gruu;opaque=app:conf:focus:id:5D3747C1DEEB684B8962F4078723A65A
```

The *opaque* parameter identifies the type of the resource that has generated or owns this URI. For a conference URI, this is always the Focus component, and hence the *opaque* parameter of the URI always contains the *app:conf:focus* prefix. The conference URI also contains the organizer SIP URI and the conference ID, which together uniquely identify the conference.

The conference URI is used by the scheduling clients to construct a conference join URL. For Microsoft Office Live Meeting Console–based conferences, a *meet:* URL is used. For example:

```
meet:sip:ben@contoso.com;gruu;opaque=app:conf:focus:id:5D3747C1DEEB684B8962F4078723A65A
```

For Microsoft Office Communicator–based audio-only conferences, a *conf:* URL is used. For example:

```
conf:sip:ben@contoso.com;gruu;opaque=app:conf:focus:id:a291a144d9764f38973835f816e52db1
%3Fconversation-id=b2796a94efe040cb9afadc49157557e6
```

Understanding Conference Activation

A conference is activated when the first participant successfully joins the meeting. The first user who joins the meeting can be an enterprise user, a federated user, or an anonymous user. Users are allowed to join the meeting regardless of their presenter or attendee role. A conference can be activated any time after it is created and before it is permanently deleted from the conferencing database.

The following happens when a conference is activated:

1. An instance of the meeting, called the Focus, is created on the Office Communications Server front-end server. This conference instance maintains the following instance-specific pieces of information:
    - A list of participants in the conference that includes the following:
        - Participants connected to the Focus
        - Participants connected to each conferencing server
    - State for each Server
2. A SIP dialog between client and the Focus is established; the conference event subscription/publication is established.
3. The Focus provisions a conferencing server of each required media type in the conference. This information is specified when the conference is created.
4. An *addConference* C3P command is sent to all provisioned conferencing servers. Each conferencing server allocates resources for the conference and becomes ready for the conference.
5. The client establishes a direct connection with each provisioned conferencing server.

Understanding Conference Deactivation

A meeting is deactivated when the Focus instance of the conference is removed from the front-end servers. A conference can be deactivated any time after it is activated in the following ways:

- The organizer or a presenter manually ends the meeting.
- All participants leave the meeting.
- Twenty-four hours (the default) pass since the last participant joined the meeting.

- Ten minutes (the default) pass without an authenticated enterprise user being in the meeting.
- An administrator disables the meeting organizer for Office Communications Server or deletes the meeting organizer's user account from Active Directory.

The following happens when a conference is deactivated:

1. The instance of the conference, the Focus, is removed. All associated instance-specific information is removed from memory and from the RTCDyn conferencing database.
2. All client-Focus dialogs are ended.
3. All conferencing servers involved in the conference receive a *deleteConference* C3P command from the Focus.
4. All client–conferencing server dialogs are ended. All remaining attendees are disconnected. All resources that are allocated for the conference from all conferencing servers are released.

A deactivated conference still exists in the RTC conferencing database and can be reactivated at any time until the meeting expires as described in the following section.

Understanding Conference Expiration

To save disk space and improve performance, Office Communications Server does not store conferences and their content indefinitely. When a conference is created, the conference is given an expiration time. When a conference expires, the conference data record is deleted from the back-end conferencing database and all content data associated with the meeting is deleted. After a meeting expires, no participants, including the organizer, can join the meeting.

The front-end server runs a low-priority expiration thread for the RTC database. When woken up, the thread searches for conferences that meet all of the following criteria:

- There is an expiration time associated with the conference, and the expiration time has passed; or there is no expiration time associated with the conference, and six months have passed since the last recorded conference activation.
- The conference is not currently active.

Any meetings that satisfy the preceding criteria are deleted from the RTC database.

It is up to the scheduling client to specify the expiration time when creating a conference on the server. The expiration time is communicated to each conferencing server that is involved when the conference is activated. Here are some recommendations based on the conference type:

- For one-time scheduled conferences, set the expiration time to be the scheduled end time plus 14 days.

- For recurring scheduled conferences with an end date, set the expiration time to be the scheduled end time of the last occurrence plus 14 days.
- For recurring scheduled conferences without specified end dates, do not set an expiration time or set null as the expiration time.
- For ad hoc IM or A/V conferences, set the expiration time to be eight hours.

> **Note** If no expiration time is specified by the client, the maximum grace period (six months) allowed by the server is used as the expiration time. This maximum allowed grace period is reset whenever a conference is activated. For example, after a conference is activated and deactivated, it will expire in six months. After three months, the meeting is activated again, and then the conference will expire in another six months, not three months.

Similarly, the Web Conferencing Server also runs a low-priority expiration thread similar to the one that runs on the front-end server. When woken up, the thread scans the conference content metadata file share and checks for the expiration time for each conference. The Web Conferencing Server adds a grace period (by default 14 days) on top of the expiration time. It deletes the content folder associated with a conference only if the conference expiration time plus the grace period has passed.

Examining the Technical Details Behind Web Conferencing

In this section, we discuss some technical details of data collaboration conferences and Web conferences. In particular, this section covers technical details of the following scenarios:

- Conferencing client joining the Focus
- Conferencing client joining the Web Conferencing Server
- Conferencing client uploading data content to the Web Conferencing Server
- Conferencing client receiving data content from the Web Conferencing Server and displaying it

Understanding the Client Conference Joining Sequence

A user can join a conference primarily in two ways:

- By clicking the Join link inside the conference invitation e-mail message or the Join link in the IM window in Office Communicator 2007
- By launching Microsoft Office Live Meeting Console and entering the conference join information

Figure 5-6 illustrates the client conference join process.

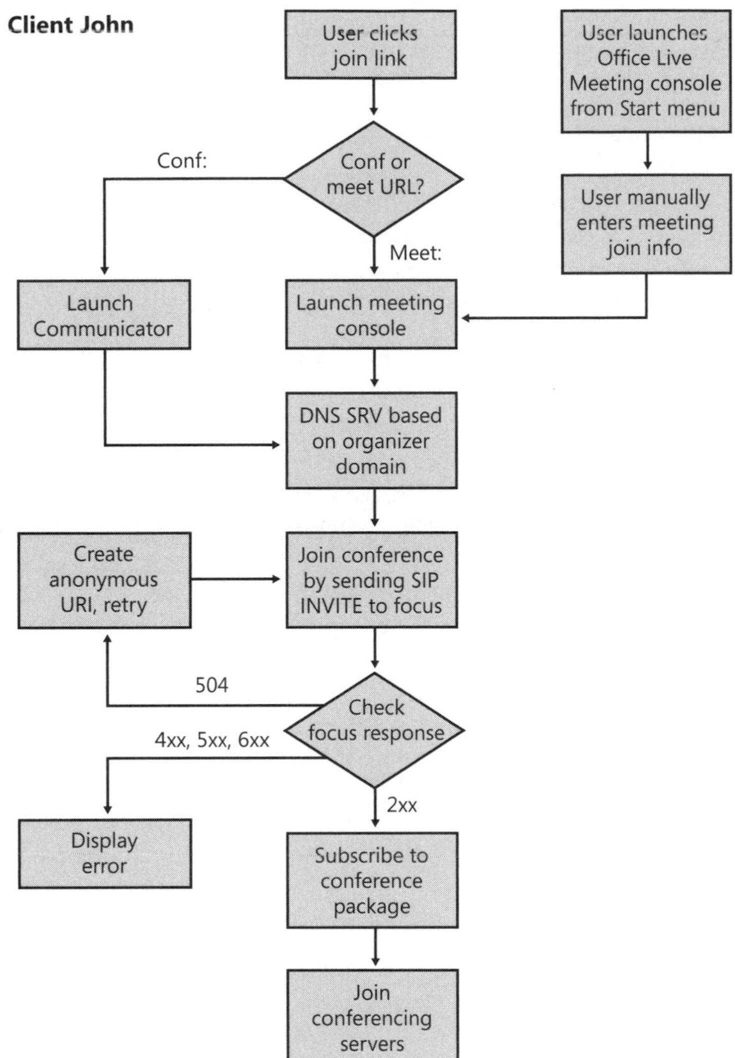

Figure 5-6 Client conference join sequence

Both Microsoft Office Communicator 2007 and Microsoft Office Live Meeting Console 2007 clients register an operating system protocol handler when they are installed. Microsoft Office Communicator 2007 registers a protocol handler for the *conf:* protocol. Microsoft Office Live Meeting Console 2007 registers a protocol handler for the *meet:* protocol. When users click the Join link in an invitation e-mail or in the IM conversation window, the client that will launch depends on the *conf:* or *meet:* prefix of the join URL.

The first step that the conferencing client performs after launch is to discover Office Communications Server for the user, based on the configured user SIP URI in the client. This discovery logic performs a series of DNS SRV queries based on the domain portion of the user's SIP URI. The following four cases could result from the DNS SRV queries:

- An Office Communications Server is found, and it is the server that hosts the conference. In this case, the client sends the join SIP INVITE targeted at the server. The user joins as an enterprise authenticated user.
- An Office Communications Server is found, and the server is federated with the Office Communications Server that hosts the conference. In this case, the client sends the join SIP INVITE targeted at the Office Communications Server 2007 server that hosts the conference. The user is authenticated by the Office Communications Server 2007 server in her own domain, and the SIP INVITE is successfully routed to the Office Communications Server pool that hosts the conference. The user joins as a federated user.
- An Office Communications Server 2007 server is found, and the server is federated with the Office Communications Server 2007 server that hosts the conference. In this case, the client sends the join SIP INVITE targeted at the Office Communications Server 2007 server that hosts the conference. The user is authenticated by the Office Communications Server 2007 server in her own domain. However, the SIP invite cannot be successfully routed because there is no federated link between her own Office Communications Server domain and the conference organizer's Office Communications Server domain (indicated by the SIP 504 response to the SIP INVITE). In this case, the conferencing client will try to join the conference as an anonymous user. The conferencing client must be able to generate a sufficiently unique and random anonymous SIP URI of the form *<ID>@anonymous.invalid* when joining a conference as an anonymous participant.
- An Office Communications Server 2007 server is not found. In this case, the conferencing client will try to join the conference as an anonymous user. The conferencing client must be able to generate a sufficiently unique and random anonymous SIP URI of the form *<ID>@anonymous.invalid* when joining a conference as an anonymous participant.

The SIP INVITE that the client sends has an *addUser* C3P command as the body of the SIP message. Following is an example:

```
INVITE sip:ben@contoso.com;gruu;opaque=app:conf:focus:id:
5D3747C1DEEB684B8962F4078723A65A SIP/2.0
From: <sip:ben@contoso.com>;tag=958d8a3fbc;epid=c5574cd6b6
To: <sip:ben@contoso.com;gruu;opaque=app:conf:focus:id:5D3747C1DEEB684B8962F4078723A65A>
Content-Type: application/cccp+xml
Content-Length: 736

<request C3PVersion="1" to="sip:ben@contoso.com;gruu;opaque=app:conf:focus:id:
5D3747C1DEEB684B8962F4078723A65A" from="sip:ben@contoso.com" requestId="0"> <addUser>
<conferenceKeys confEntity="sip:Ben@contoso.com;gruu;opaque=app:conf:focus:id:
5D3747C1DEEB684B8962F4078723A65A"/>
<ci:user entity="sip:Ben@contoso.com">
<ci:roles>
<ci:entry>attendee</ci:entry>
</ci:roles>
<ci:endpoint entity="{339F927D-6AD4-4090-9104-8414B99EE045}" />
</ci:user> </addUser> </request>
```

The *addUser* request contains the conference URI and the user SIP URI, which must be the same as the SIP To and From URIs, respectively. In addition, it can contain a requested role. The endpoint entity is optional, and the Focus ignores the body of the endpoint entity and just uses the entity URI supplied by the client.

Figure 5-7 shows the server handling logic for such an SIP join INVITE.

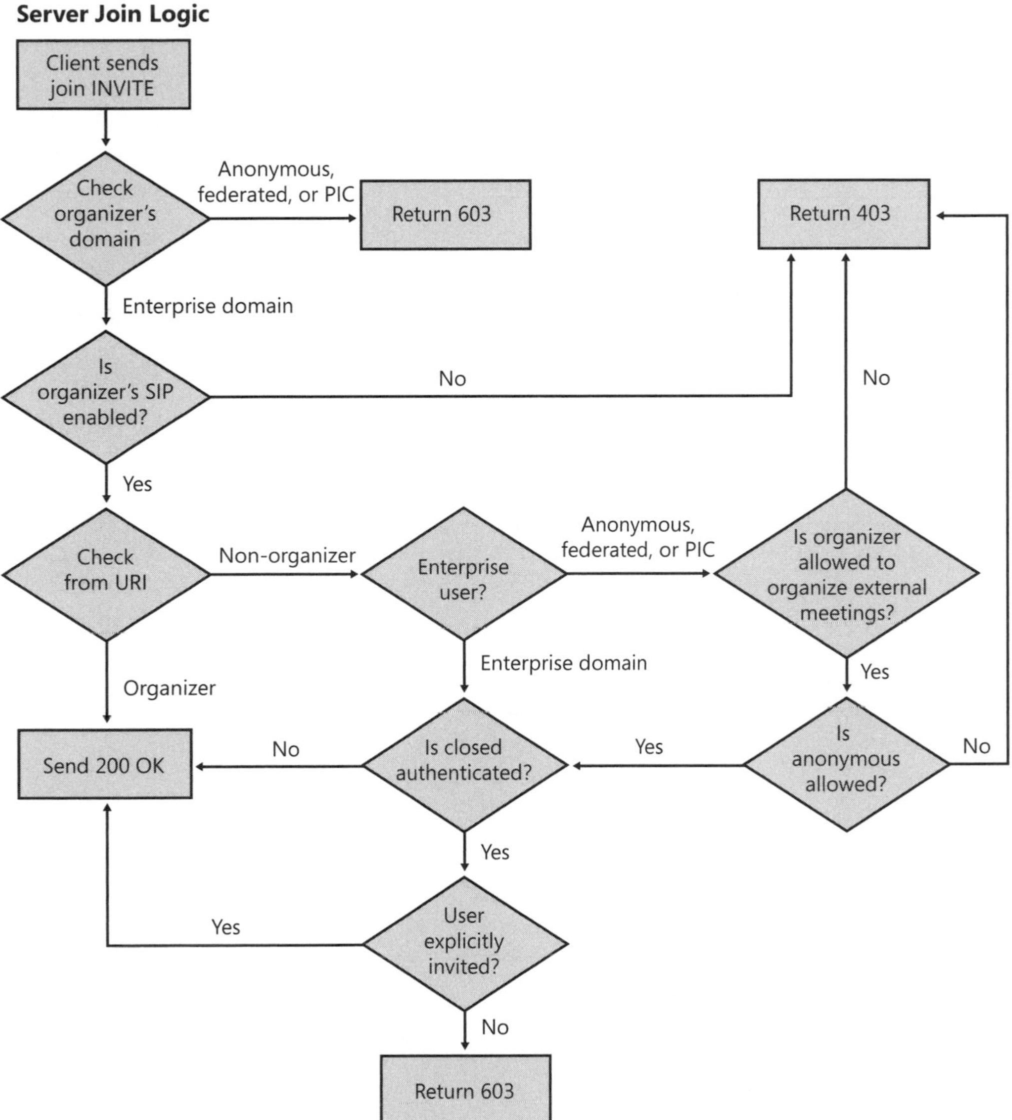

Figure 5-7 Client join sequence, server view

When the *addUser* C3P command is accepted, the Focus responds with the granted role in the 200 response:

```
SIP/2.0 200 Invite dialog created
Contact: <sip:sip.contoso.com:5061;transport=tls>;isfocus
Content-Length: 1095
From: "Ben Miller"<sip:Ben@contoso.com>;tag=958d8a3fbc;epid=c5574cd6b6
To: <sip:Ben@contoso.com;gruu;opaque=app:conf:focus:id:
   5D3747C1DEEB684B8962F4078723A65A>;tag=CC020080
Allow: INVITE, BYE, ACK, CANCEL, INFO, UPDATE
Content-Type: application/cccp+xml

<response requestId="0" C3PVersion="1"
from="sip:Ben@contoso.com;gruu;opaque=app:conf:focus:id:
   5D3747C1DEEB684B8962F4078723A65A" to="sip:Ben@contoso.com" code="success"> <addUser>
<conferenceKeys confEntity="sip:Ben@contoso.com;gruu;opaque=app:conf:focus:id:
   5D3747C1DEEB684B8962F4078723A65A"/>
<ci:user entity="sip:Ben@contoso.com">
<ci:roles>
<ci:entry>presenter</ci:entry>
</ci:roles>
</ci:user> </addUser> </response>
```

At this point, the signaling dialog is successfully established between the joining client and the Focus. The Focus then notifies existing conference participants that the user has joined the conference.

```
NOTIFY sip:157.56.67.50:2383;transport=tls;ms-opaque=02e9ae1f28;
   ms-received-cid=00031600;grid SIP/2.0
To: <sip:Ben@contoso.com>;tag=ccb81c3509;epid=c5574cd6b6
Content-Length: 2373
From:
<sip:Ben@contoso.com;gruu;opaque=app:conf:focus:id:5D3747C1DEEB684B8962F4078723A65A>;tag
=183C0080
Content-Type: application/conference-info+xml
Event: conference
subscription-state: active;expires=3600

<conference-info entity="sip:Ben@contoso.com;gruu;opaque=app:conf:focus:id:
   5D3747C1DEEB684B8962F4078723A65A" state="partial" version="2">
<users state="partial">
<user entity="sip:Ben@contoso.com" state="full">
<display-text>Ben Miller</display-text>
<roles>
<entry>presenter</entry>
</roles>
<endpoint entity="{339F927D-6AD4-4090-9104-8414B99EE045}" msci:session-type="focus"
msci:endpoint-uri="sip:Ben@contoso.com;opaque=user:epid:AD0UTS5Dcl0h9zyK1XWK2AAA;gruu">
<status>connected</status>
</endpoint>
```

After a SIP signaling dialog is successfully established, the conferencing client and the Focus establish a subscription dialog. The client first sends a SIP SUBSCRIBE:

```
SUBSCRIBE sip:Ben@contoso.com;gruu;opaque=app:conf:focus:id:
   5D3747C1DEEB684B8962F4078723A65A SIP/2.0
From: <sip:Ben@contoso.com>;tag=958d8a3fbc;epid=c5574cd6b6
To: <sip:Ben@contoso.com;gruu;opaque=app:conf:focus:id:5D3747C1DEEB684B8962F4078723A65A>
Event: conference
Accept: application/conference-info+xml
Supported: com.cotoso.autoextend
Supported: ms-benotify
Proxy-Require: ms-benotify
Supported: ms-piggyback-first-notify
Content-Length: 0
```

The Focus then processes the subscription. If no corresponding active signaling dialog is found, the Focus fails the subscription. Once the subscription is accepted, the Focus responds to it, and then generates a notification.

```
SIP/2.0 200 OK
Content-Length: 3611
From: "Ben Miller"<sip:Ben@contoso.com>;tag=0dc4a6c3d2;epid=c5574cd6b6
To: <sip:Ben@contoso.com;gruu;opaque=app:conf:focus:id:
   A24F0AA5223B4B478801FA8F60D2191D>;tag=31740080
Expires: 3546
Content-Type: application/conference-info+xml
Event: conference
subscription-state: active;expires=3546
ms-piggyback-cseq: 1
Supported: ms-benotify, ms-piggyback-first-notify
…
```

The subscription dialog is periodically refreshed. The lifetime of the subscription dialog is the same as the lifetime of the signaling dialog. Even though these are two independent dialogs, the Focus terminates the subscription dialog when the signaling dialog is terminated.

After both the signaling and subscription dialogs are established, the conferencing client can receive conference state change notifications, such as another user join, from the Focus. Figure 5-8 illustrates the client focus join sequence.

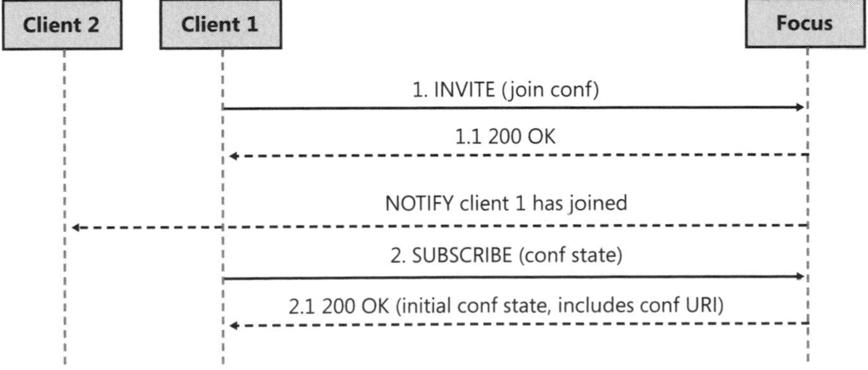

Figure 5-8 Focus join sequence

Understanding the Client Join Sequence to the Web Conferencing Server

The *addUser* C3P command is used by conferencing clients to join themselves to the conferencing servers involved in the conference. The *addUser* command works in two modes: dial-in and dial-out. In dial-in mode, the client sends *addUser* to the conferencing server (with the message being proxied by the Focus) to request permission to create a session with it. In the *addUser* response, the conferencing server responds with connection information that is used by the client to establish signaling and media sessions. In *addUser* dial-out mode, the client requests that the conferencing server initiate the signaling/media session establishment, and hence, the *addUser* command completes only after the session is established.

Conferencing clients use the *addUser* dial-in mode to join the Web Conferencing Server. Figure 5-9 illustrates the flow for a client to join the Web Conferencing Server.

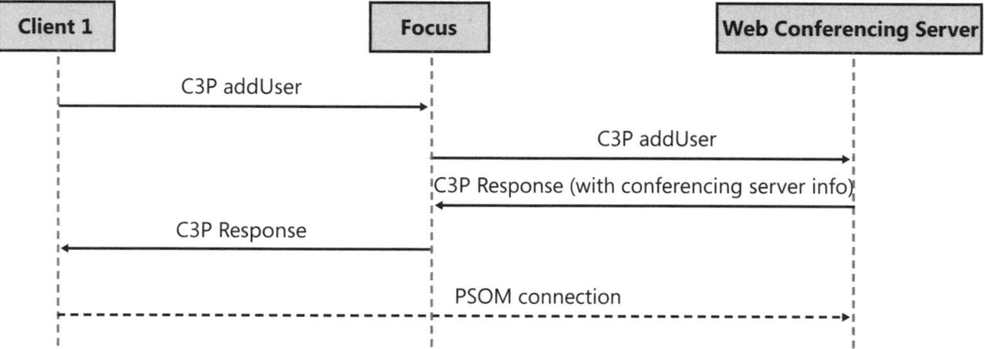

Figure 5-9 Web Conferencing Server join sequence

Some of the notifications that conferencing clients receive from the Focus after they join a conference are about conferencing server URIs. For example:

```
NOTIFY sip:ben@contoso.com SIP/2.0
...
<conference-info xmlns="urn:ietf:params:xml:ns:conference-info"
entity="sip:ben@contoso.com;gruu;
opaque=app:conf:focus:id:5D3747C1DEEB684B8962F4078723A65A"
       state="full" version="5" >
       <conference-description>
        <display-text>Weekly Sales Meeting</display-text>
        <subject>Agenda: This month's goals</subject>
        <conf-uris>
              <entry>
                 <uri>sip:ben@contoso.com;opaque=conf:meeting:
id:5D3747C1DEEB684B8962F4078723A65A</uri>
                 <display-text>meeting</display-text>
                 <purpose>meeting</purpose>
              </entry>
              <entry>
                 <uri>sip:ben@contoso.com;opaque=conf:audio-video:
```

```
id:5D3747C1DEEB684B8962F4078723A65A</uri>
                <display-text>audio video mcu</display-text>
                <purpose>audio-video</purpose>
             </entry>
        </conf-uris>
      </conference-description>
...
</conference-info>
```

To join the Web Conferencing Server, the client then constructs an *addUser* C3P request and sends it to the Focus requesting to dial in to the Web Conferencing Server. The request contains a role that matches the current role of the user in the conference, specifies a joining-method value of *dialed-in*, and also supplies an endpoint that is usually a GUID for the session. The *From* URI of the SIP request must match the *from* attribute of the C3P request. An *mcuUri* attribute must be present in the *addUser* element, and it specifies the MCU (conferencing server) to which this request should be routed. In the case just shown, the Web Conferencing Server URI is as follows:

```
sip:ben@contoso.com;opaque=conf:meeting:conf-id
```

Here is an example of this *addUser* C3P request:

```
INFO ConfURI
To: ConfURI
From: sip:ben@contoso.com;tag=f7588dc66124429ab736;epid=1
...SIP headers..

<request xmlns="urn:ietf:params:xml:ns:cccp" requestId="2"
    from="sip:ben@contoso.com"
    to="sip:ben@contoso.com;gruu;
opaque=app:conf:focus:id:5D3747C1DEEB684B8962F4078723A65A">
 <addUser mscp:mcuUri="sip:ben@contoso.com;opaque=conf:meeting:
id:5D3747C1DEEB684B8962F4078723A65A">
    <conferenceKeys confEntity=" sip:ben@contoso.com;gruu;
opaque=app:conf:focus:id:5D3747C1DEEB684B8962F4078723A65A">
    <user entity="sip:ben@contoso.com">
        <roles>
            <entry>presenter</entry>
            </roles>
            <!-Exactly one endpoint node may be present -->
            < endpoint entity="
               {F43E937E-6C66-4649-9481-13133FCF64FE}">
           <!-Exactly one joining-method and it must be equal
                to dialed-in -->
                <joining-method>dialed-in</joining-method>
                <!-- Optional MCU specific parameters -->
            </endpoint>
        </user>
    </addUser>
  </request>
```

The Focus forwards the dial-in request to the Web Conferencing Server after stamping the request with the originator URI and proper authorization. If the Web Conferencing Server decides to accept the C3P request, it should construct a standard *addUser* response and return it to the Focus, which will then proxy the response to the client.

All conferencing servers must supply contact information that the client can use to connect. For conferencing servers that use SIP as a signaling protocol (such as the A/V Conferencing Server), this takes the form of supplying a SIP *Contact* URI and SIP *To* URI. The SIP *To* URI must always be equal to the *mcuUri* supplied in the *addUser* call. The SIP *Contact* URI refers to the *Conferencing Server* URI (a listening address/port/transport on which the conferencing server is listening and can receive SIP requests). For a Web Conferencing Server that uses PSOM instead of SIP, this takes the form of supplying a suitable URL that the client understands.

Some conferencing servers might supply an authorization token or some other parameter to the client. The semantics of such parameters are a contract between the conferencing server and the client. Following is an sample response to the *addUser* request to join a Web Conferencing Server:

```
From: < sip:ben@contoso.com;gruu;
opaque=app:conf:focus:id:5D3747C1DEEB684B8962F4078723A65A>;
   tag=052B0080
To: <ben:ben@contoso.com>;tag=d1991b44ef;epid=10caaf88e2
...
<response from=" sip:ben@contoso.com;gruu;
opaque=app:conf:focus:id:5D3747C1DEEB684B8962F4078723A65A" to="sip:ben@contoso.com"
responder=" sip:ben@contoso.com;
   opaque=conf:meeting: id:5D3747C1DEEB684B8962F4078723A65A"
   code="success">
<addUser><conferenceKeys confEntity=" ben@contoso.com;gruu;
opaque=app:conf:focus:id:5D3747C1DEEB684B8962F4078723A65A"/>
<user xmlns="urn:ietf:params:xml:ns:conference-info"
entity="sip:ben@contoso.com"><display-text>Hao Yan</display-
text><roles><entry>presenter</entry></roles><endpoint entity="{1D3F15F1-68CA-4EF0-9805-
704EB5795F60}"><joining-method>dialed-in</joining-method><media id="1"><type>meeting</
type><label>meeting</label></media><authMethod xmlns="http://schemas.microsoft.com/rtc/
2005/08/confinfoextensions">
   enterprise</authMethod><accessMethod xmlns="http://schemas.microsoft.com/rtc/2005/08/
confinfoextensions">
   internal</accessMethod>
</endpoint></user><info xmlns="http://schemas.microsoft.com/rtc/2005/08/
cccpextensions"><contact>pod/ben/check/check1.html</contact></info><connection-info
xmlns="http://schemas.microsoft.com/rtc/2005/08/cccpextensions"><entry><key>serverURL</
key><value>https://conference.contoso.com/etc/place/null</value></
entry><entry><key>pw.eName</key><value>sip:ben@contoso.com;gruu;
opaque=app:conf:focus:id:5D3747C1DEEB684B8962F4078723A65A </value></
entry><entry><key>PodName</key><value> ben@contoso.com;gruu;
opaque=app:conf:focus:id:5D3747C1DEEB684B8962F4078723A65A</value></
entry><entry><key>pwuid</key><value>sip:ben@contoso.com</value></
entry><entry><key>sAuthId</key><value>71C00000000000001A36B1629961D219</value></
entry><entry><key>pwrpc.modes</key><value>tls</value></entry><entry><key>pwrpc.port</
```

```
key><value>8057</value></entry><entry><key>pwrpc.authPattern</
key><value>&lt;sAuthId&gt;</value></entry><entry><key>pw.rtcp.enabled</
key><value>false</value></entry><entry><key>pwrpc.tcpEnableSig</key><value>false</
value></entry><entry><key>locale</key><value>en_US</value></
entry><entry><key>directURL</key><value>https://conference.contoso.com:8057</value></
entry><entry><key>pwrpc.pwsURI</key><value>https://conference.contoso.com:8057</value></
entry><entry><key>uType</key><value>pre</value></entry><entry><key>alternativeName</
key><value>conference.contoso.com</value></entry></connection-info></addUser></response>
```

The information included in the C3P response includes the following:

- The Fully Qualified Domain Name (FQDN) or IP address of the Web Conferencing Server and port number.
- The URL for HTTPs content download.
- Access information (FQDN and port) for zero, one, or more Web Conferencing Edge Servers if the client connects from outside of the corporate firewall.
- An authorization cookie for the Web Conferencing Edge Server if the client connects from outside of the corporate firewall. The cookie is base64 encoded. The client needs to present this cookie when establishing a connection with the Web Conferencing Edge Server.
- An authorization cookie for the Web Conferencing Server. This cookie is also encoded in base64. The client needs to present this cookie when establishing a connection with the Web Conferencing Server.
- A unique identifier for the meeting (for example, the Conference URI). This is necessary for the client to identify which conference it is joining when making a connection to the Web Conferencing Server.

Understanding Conference Control

Once a signaling dialog is established with the Focus, clients can send conference control CP commands on the dialog. In general, conference control commands can be classified into three categories:

- Commands that terminate on the Focus and do not involve MCU interaction (for example, renameUser)
- Commands that are authorized by the Focus but are simply proxied to MCU, so no Focus state is modified unless the MCU generates a notification (for example, modifyEndpointMedia)
- Commands that are processed by the Focus as well as by MCUs (for example, deleteConference and modifyConferenceLock)

A typical conference control command operates as follows:

1. The client sends a SIP INFO request to the Focus, with the body containing a C3P command.
2. The Focus validates and authorizes the C3P request.
3. The Focus operates on the C3P request and generates one or more SIP responses back to the client containing C3P pending or a final response.
4. The Focus might proxy or fork the request to one or more conferencing servers as necessary. Responses from the conferencing servers are proxied back to the client except in the forking-command case, where they are consumed by the Focus.
5. All entities maintain C3P transaction timers to control the lifetime of the request.

When the Focus accepts the command from the sender, it usually generates a C3P request to the conferencing servers in the conference and also responds with a SIP 202 Accepted message to the INFO request. When the C3P result is available, the Focus generates another INFO request and sends it to the client. The C3P request might succeed or fail or might succeed/fail after an interim response has been generated. Moreover, a successful C3P request is usually followed by the conferencing servers sending a C3P notification containing the updated conference state. On receipt of this notification, the Focus updates the conference state and generates a notification to all clients.

Figure 5-10 shows the call flow of the C3P *modifyConferenceLock* command. This command is issued when a presenter in the conference tries to lock or unlock a conference in the client. In this case, the command is forked by the Focus and sent to both the A/V Conferencing Server and the Web Conferencing Server.

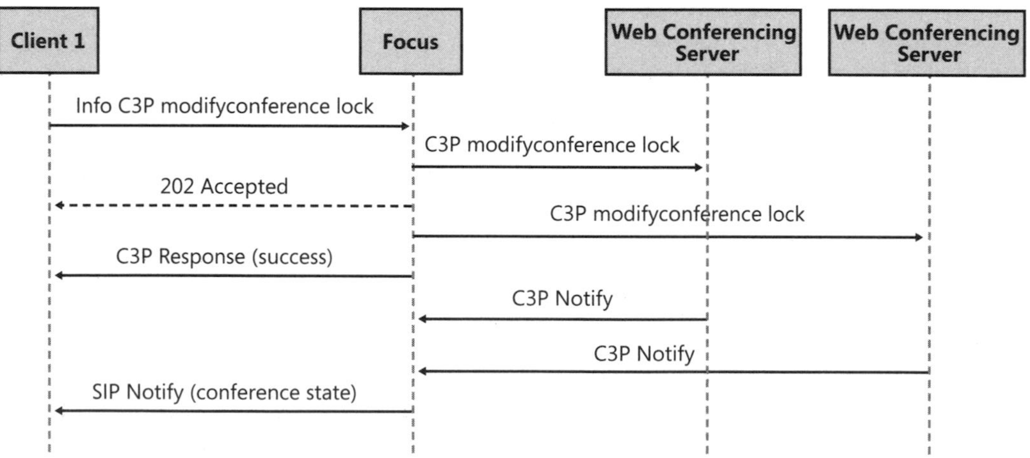

Figure 5-10 Web Conferencing Server join sequence

Understanding Web Conferencing Server Content Management

In Office Communications Server 2007, the Web Conferencing Server stores in-conference data contents and its state information in files. For each Office Communications Server pool, there are two file shares configured:

- Metadata file share, used for storing conference state information and metadata that describes data content.
- Content file share, used for storing user uploaded data content, such as a PowerPoint file. The uploaded contents are encrypted when stored into the content file share.

All Web Conferencing Servers in the pool use these file shares. The file shares are identified using Universal Naming Convention (UNC) paths. They can reside on the same machine as the Web Conferencing Server (as is the case for Office Communications Server 2007 Standard Edition) or on different (dedicated) file servers (as is the case recommended for Office Communications Server 2007 Enterprise Edition).

The file shares are access controlled so that no conferencing client has direct access to them. The metadata share is for Web Conferencing Server internal use only. The Web Conferencing Server needs to have both read and write privileges to the share. The content file share, on the other hand, can be accessed by the conferencing client indirectly via IIS–an IIS virtual directory is created and linked to the content file share when the Office Communications Server Web component is installed so that the client can access the files in the content file share via HTTPs. The Web Conferencing Server requires write privileges to the content file share, whereas IIS requires only read rights to the share.

Figure 5-11 shows the Web Conferencing Server that manages the two file shares.

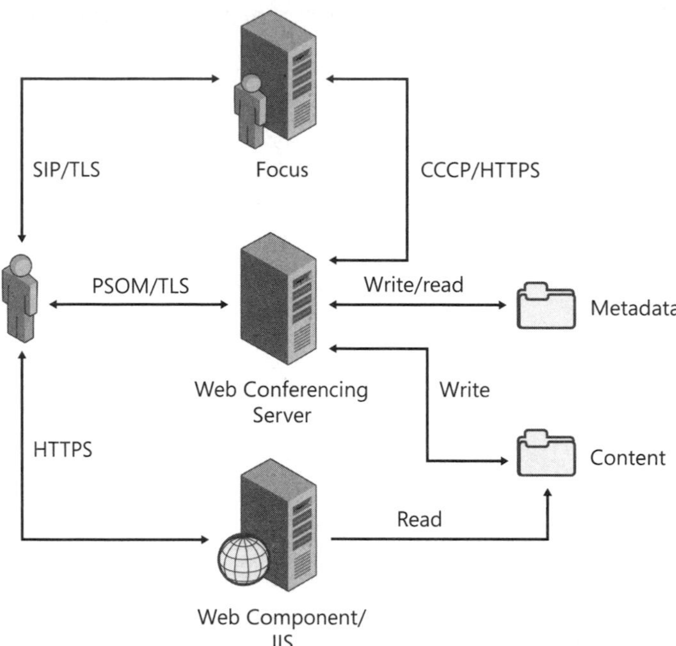

Figure 5-11 Web Conferencing Server content management

When the Web Conferencing Server starts a conference—that is, when it receives an *addConference* command from the Focus—a metadata folder is created for the particular conference under the folder specified by the metadata file share UNC. The metadata file share is structured in the following ways:

- For each organizer, the Web Conferencing Server creates a separate folder under the metadata root folder. The organizer folder name is a computed hash value from the organizer SIP URI.
- For each conference, the Web Conferencing Server creates a separate folder under the organizer sub-folder. The conference folder name is the same as the conference ID.
- Metadata files for a conference are stored under the conference folder. All files except the conference.xml file under the conference folder are encrypted. The conference.xml file contains a randomly generated encryption key for the conference. The key is used to encrypt all other metadata files in the conference. Because sensitive information such as the encryption key is stored under this folder, the administrator should give read and write permissions to this folder just to the users group that runs the Web Conferencing Server.

Figure 5-12 illustrates the metadata folder structure.

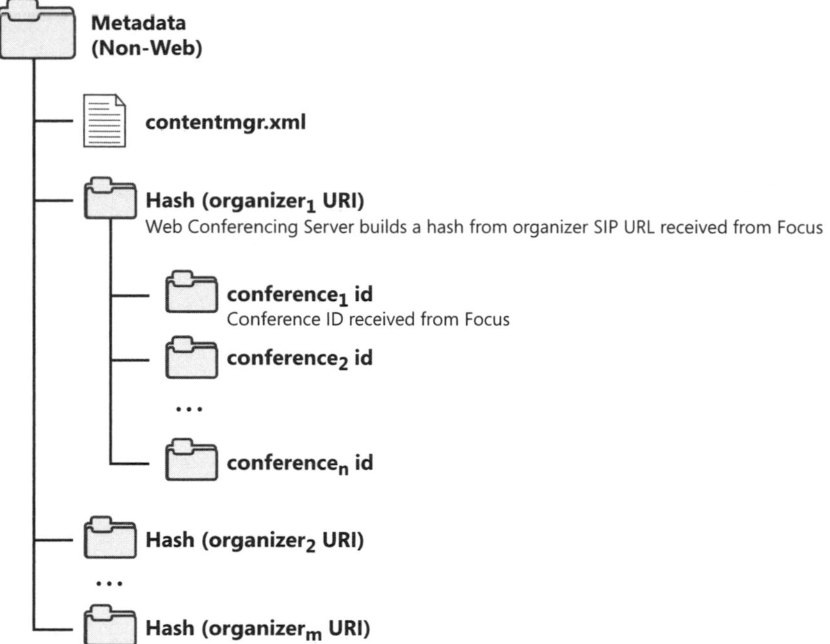

Figure 5-12 Metadata folder structure

> **Note** The contentmgr.xml file is used to coordinate content expiration processes running in multiple Web Conferencing Servers. The expiration process uses a lock/unlock mechanism to ensure that only one server can delete a specific conference folder at any given time.

The content file share is structured the same way as that for the metadata file share. Figure 5-13 illustrates the content folder structure.

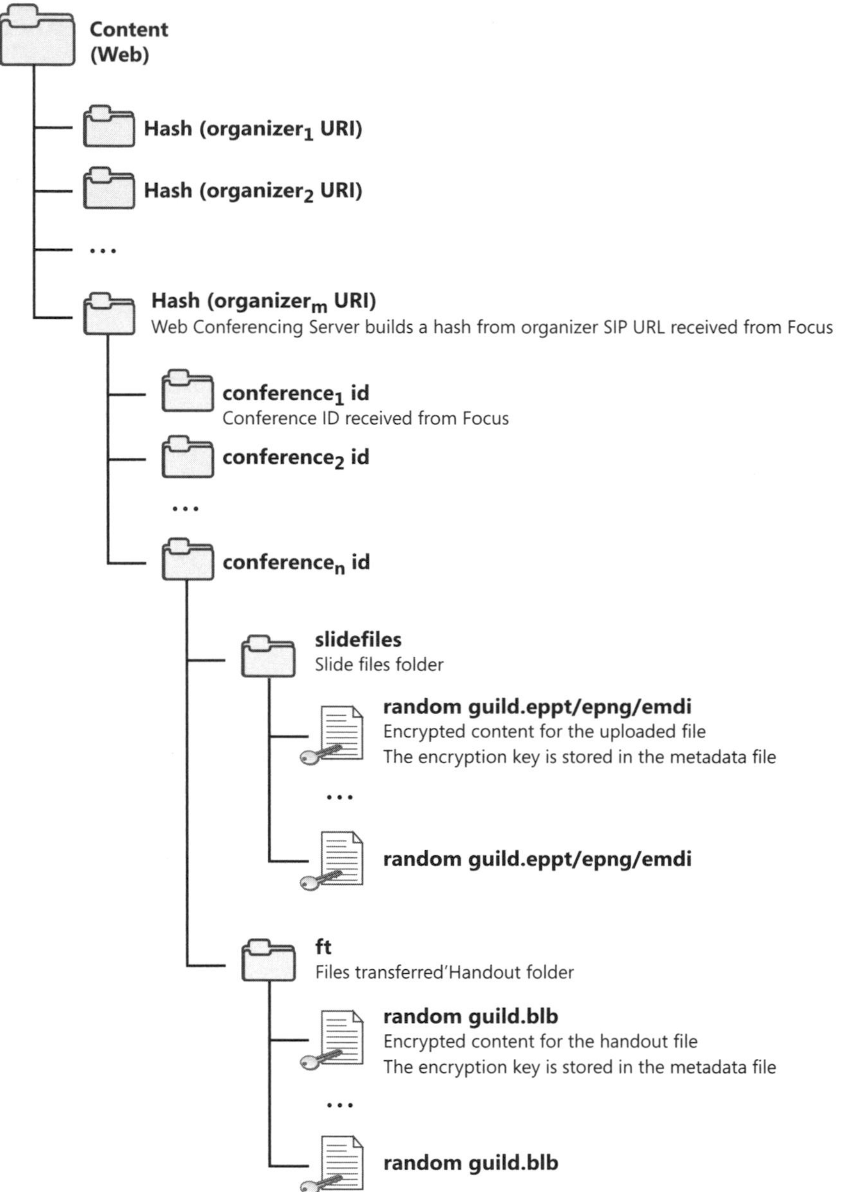

Figure 5-13 Metadata folder structure

This 'Slide Files' folder contains all the user uploaded slide content shared over HTTPS. All files are encrypted using Advanced Encryption Standard (AES) and a randomly generated key (one for each content file). The key is stored in a corresponding metadata file in the corresponding metadata folder. The names of the files are randomly generated to hide the original file name. The generated file name along with the original file name are both stored in the corresponding metadata file. The 'ft' folder stores all the handouts—the files that are natively transferred without any conversion—in encrypted form.

Understanding Web Conferencing Server Content Upload and Download

There are two types of data content in a Web conference: user uploaded and user generated. User uploaded content refers to content that has an origin (either a file or a picture) on the client side and that is uploaded to the Web Conferencing Server by using the PSOM protocol. User uploaded content includes PowerPoint presentation files, MODI documents, handouts, and snapshot slides. User-generated content refers to content that does not come from an original file but instead is created in the conference. These include annotations, Poll content, question-and-answer content, shared notes, text slides, Web slides, and so on.

The upload process is the same for both types of contents. The download process, however, differs. The uploaded content is hosted by the IIS; the Web Conferencing Server sends a URL to the content and an encryption key to clients so that clients can download and decrypt the content. The generated content is downloaded over PSOM.

Figure 5-14 illustrates the flow for uploading and downloading generated content.

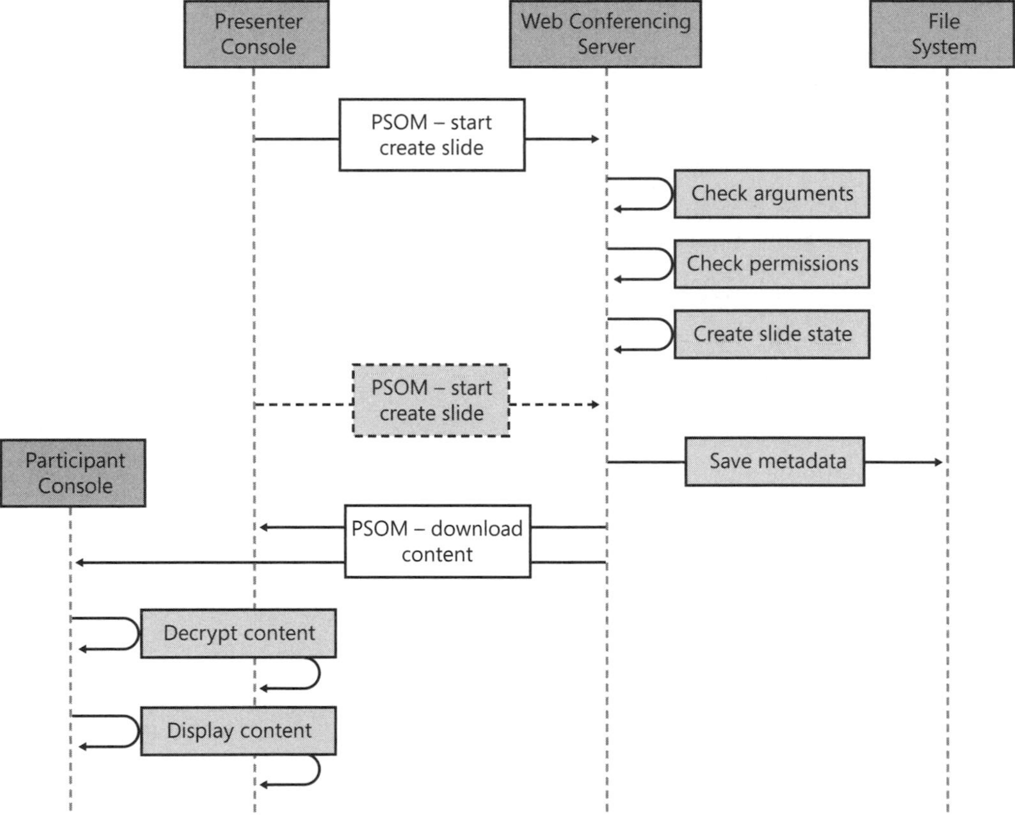

Figure 5-14 Upload and download of generated content

The following happens in sequence in the flow shown in Figure 5-14:

1. Over PSOM, the user creates a slide and its content.
2. The Web Conferencing Server checks the permission for the user (that is, whether the user is allowed to create that particular type of content).
3. The Web Conferencing Server creates the state for the new slide and saves the state on the file system (in the metadata folder for the conference), in encrypted format.
4. The Web Conferencing Server shares back to all clients in the conference the new slide state.

For all generated content except for Poll slides, the content is sent with the first PSOM message that creates the slide. For Poll slides, the content (questions and choices) is sent in a new PSOM message after the initial Create Slide message has been sent. The generated content is saved in the metadata folder as encrypted XML files only. It is not saved in the Content folder of the conference. Following is sample XML metadata for Poll slides (before encryption):

```
<?xml version="1.0" encoding="UTF-8"?>
<POLL>
   <POLLENTITY ID="0AA61051-12BC-A1FF-A98F-A240BCB8ABDB"
          TYPE="QUESTION" TIMESTAMP="5/21/2007 11:39 AM">
   <POLLUSER VALUE="sip:ben@contoso.com"/>
   <POLLCHOICE VALUE="MON"/>
   <POLLCHOICE VALUE="TUE"/>
   <POLLCHOICE VALUE="WED"/>
   <POLLCHOICE VALUE="THU"/>
   <POLLCHOICE VALUE="FRI"/>
   <POLLCHOICE VALUE="SAT"/>
   <POLLCHOICE VALUE="SUN"/>
   </POLLENTITY>
</POLL>
```

Figure 5-15 illustrates the flow for uploading and downloading uploaded content.

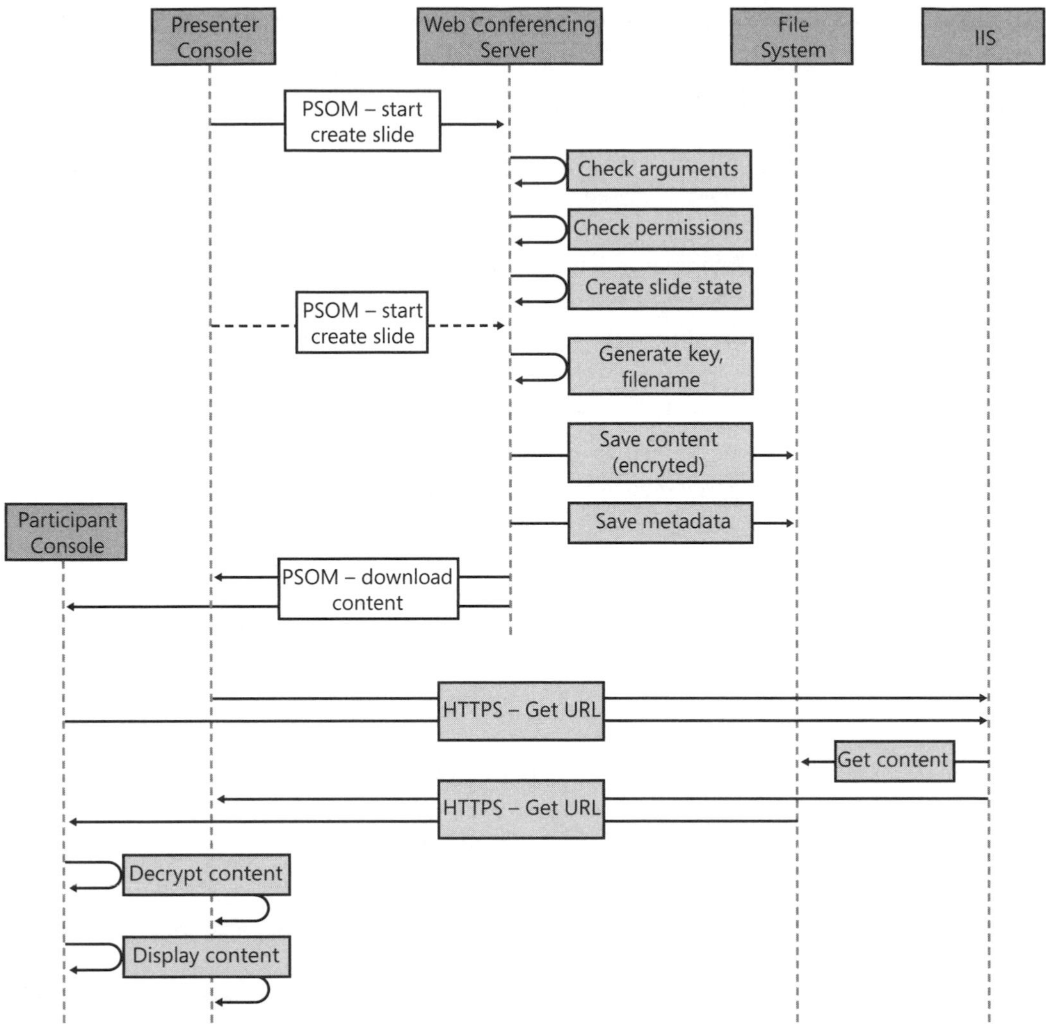

Figure 5-15 Upload and download of uploaded content

The following happens in sequence in the flow just shown:

1. The user starts uploading existing content. A PSOM message is sent from the user's client to the Web Conferencing Server.
2. The Web Conferencing Server checks the permission for the user (that is, whether the user is allowed to create that particular type of content).
3. The user's client prepares the content for upload. The kind of preparation depends on the type of content being uploaded:
   - For PowerPoint presentation files, the client converts each slide into a picture .PNG file, and then packages and compresses both the original .PPT(x) file and all the .PNG files into one .LMP file.

- For Microsoft Office files, the client converts the files into MODI files, and then converts each page of the MODI files into a picture .PNG file. The client then packages and compresses both the MODI .MDI file and all the .PNG files into one .LMP file.
- For handouts, the client just compresses and packages the file into one .LMP file.

4. The client starts sending the .LMP file over a stream to the Web Conferencing Server.
5. The Web Conferencing Server unpacks the .LMP file. For each file that is unpacked, the Web Conferencing Server generates an encryption key and uses it to encrypt the file. The encrypted content file is saved in the content file folder for the conference. The encryption key and metadata information, such as the user SIP URI, are saved in an encrypted metadata XML file under the metadata folder for the conference.
6. The Web Conferencing Server computes the URLs from which the saved encrypted contents can be accessed via HTTPS. This is possible because the Web component sets up a virtual directory that points to the same content file share that the Web Conferencing Server writes to.
7. The Web Conferencing Server sends back to the clients via PSOM the URL and the encryption key for the content files.
8. Each client participating in the conference uses the URL to download the encrypted content from IIS.
9. Using the encryption key, each client decrypts the content and displays it.

Understanding Meeting Compliance

Compliance with regulatory requirements was the motivation for adding IM archiving capabilities to Live Communications Server. Those same requirements apply to certain aspects of an Office Communications Server conference as well. There are two features in Office Communications Server that, when combined, provide compliance for on-premise conferencing.

First, the CDR feature records meeting participation information, including the following:

- The actual start and end time of the Live Server meeting
- The list of participants who attended the meeting

Second, the Meeting Compliance feature running on the Web Conferencing Server, if enabled, records content activities, including:

- A log of any content upload activity, including who uploaded content into the conference and at what time
- The original uploaded content, whether or not it was subsequently deleted and prior to annotation
- Any annotation on any content, or any whiteboard content
- A log of any questions and answers

- A log of any polling activity
- A log of any chat activity
- A log of any native file transfer upload activity

The logs of activities are stored in XML files, and the uploaded contents are saved in the content's original format. Those compliance XML logs and content files are stored in a configurable file share identified by a UNC path. Unlike the metadata and content file shares, the compliance file share stores compliance logs and contents unencrypted. Administrators must be careful when granting permissions to this file share. The Web Conferencing Server needs write permissions, and only authorized users should have read or write permissions.

Figure 5-16 shows the folder structure for the meeting compliance file share. The folder structure is similar to that of the metadata and content file shares. Under each conference ID folder, the content folder stores all content upload activities for uploaded contents, with the original uploaded files going to the content-upload directory. The chat, poll, and QnA folders store XML logs for Chat, Poll, and Q&A activities, respectively.

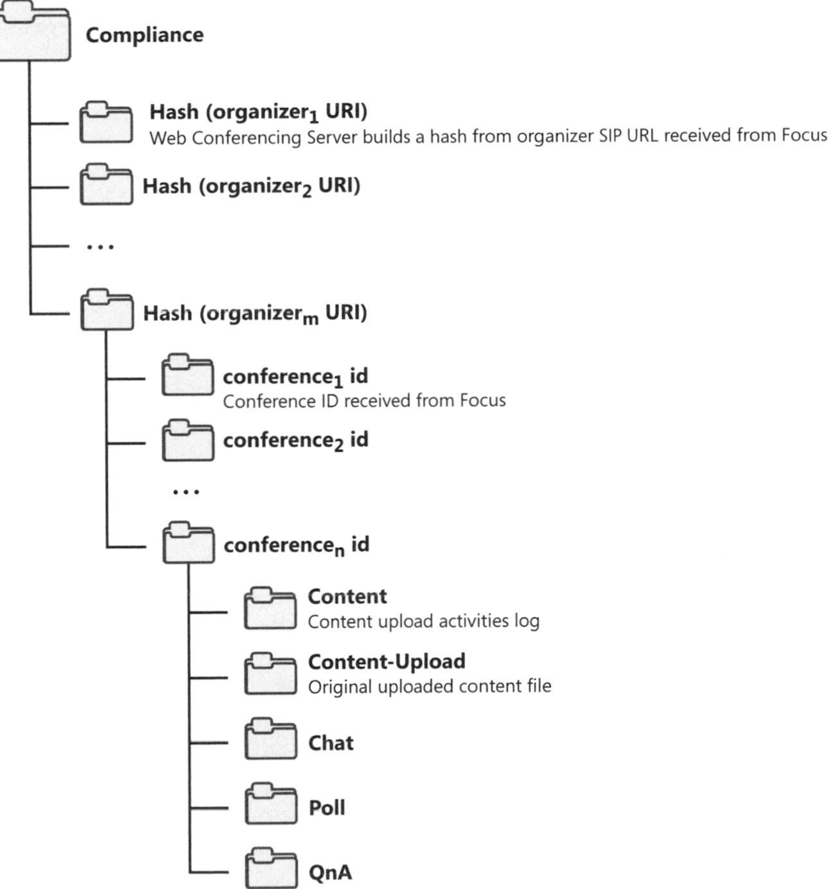

Figure 5-16 Compliance file share folder structure

The following is a sample XML log file for a poll that takes place in a meeting:


```
<?xml version="1.0" encoding="UTF-8"?>
<POLLLOG>
  <POLLENTITY ID="0AA61051-12BC-A1FF-A98F-A240BCB8ABDB"
        TYPE="QUESTION" TIMESTAMP="5/21/2007 11:39 AM">
    <POLLUSER VALUE="sip:ben@contoso.com [Ben]" />
    <POLLQUESTION VALUE="What day is today?" />
    <POLLCHOICE VALUE="MON" />
    <POLLCHOICE VALUE="TUE" />
    <POLLCHOICE VALUE="WED" />
    <POLLCHOICE VALUE="THU" />
    <POLLCHOICE VALUE="FRI" />
    <POLLCHOICE VALUE="SAT" />
    <POLLCHOICE VALUE="SUN" />
  </POLLENTITY>
  <POLLENTITY ID="0AA61051-12BC-A1FF-A98F-A240BCB8ABDB"
        TYPE="CHOICE" TIMESTAMP="5/21/2007 11:39 AM">
    <POLLUSER VALUE="sip:ben@contoso.com [Ben]" />
    <POLLSEQ VALUE="1" />
    <POLLCHOICE VALUE="1" />
  </POLLENTITY>
  <POLLENTITY ID="0AA61051-12BC-A1FF-A98F-A240BCB8ABDB"
        TYPE="CHOICE" TIMESTAMP="5/21/2007 11:39 AM">
    <POLLUSER VALUE="sip:john@contoso.com [John]" />
    <POLLSEQ VALUE="2" />
    <POLLCHOICE VALUE="0" />
  </POLLENTITY>
  <POLLENTITY ID="0AA61051-12BC-A1FF-A98F-A240BCB8ABDB"
        TYPE="CHOICE" TIMESTAMP="5/21/2007 11:39 AM">
    <POLLUSER VALUE="sip:ben@contoso.com [Ben]" />
    <POLLSEQ VALUE="3" />
    <POLLCHOICE VALUE="0" />
  </POLLENTITY>
  <POLLENTITY ID="0AA61051-12BC-A1FF-A98F-A240BCB8ABDB"
        TYPE="CHOICE" TIMESTAMP="5/21/2007 11:39 AM">
    <POLLUSER VALUE="sip:john@contoso.com [John]" />
    <POLLSEQ VALUE="4" />
    <POLLCHOICE VALUE="-1" />
  </POLLENTITY>
  <POLLENTITY ID="0AA61051-12BC-A1FF-A98F-A240BCB8ABDB"
        TYPE="CHOICE" TIMESTAMP="5/21/2007 11:39 AM">
    <POLLUSER VALUE="sip:john@contoso.com [John]" />
    <POLLSEQ VALUE="5" />
    <POLLCHOICE VALUE="0" />
  </POLLENTITY>
```


The administrator can enable and disable the meeting compliance feature on each Office Communications Server pool. The administrator can also set the compliance logging to operate in a *critical* mode. In this mode, new conferences are blocked from starting. Existing conferences are immediately terminated if at any point in time the Web Conferencing Server must access the compliance file share for any reason.

Understanding Web Conferencing Content Tools

The Web Conferencing Server organizes the three content-related file shares in such a way that it is efficient for fast storage and retrieval of content. In addition, both metadata and the content file share contents are stored using strong encryption. These two factors make it difficult for administrators to examine or move the content of a particular conference.

In the Resource Kit tools for Office Communications Server 2007, three tools are provided that help administrators manage the contents in the file shares. Please refer to the Resource Kit tools documentation for instructions on installing and using these tools.

DMInsider.exe For security reasons, a Web Conferencing Server saves conference contents in encrypted format in the content file share. Therefore, even if the user has access to the content file share, the administrator cannot view the actual content. The DMInsider.exe tool helps Microsoft Office Communications Server 2007 administrators find and view conference content managed by the Web Conferencing Server. The tool provides the following main functionalities:

- Ability to list and view content by organizers and by conferences. The content is rendered in the same way as it is rendered in the Microsoft Office Live Meeting Console.
- Ability to list and view XML-based conference compliances logs. The tool can render the compliance content in the same way as it is rendered in the Microsoft Office Live Meeting Console.
- Ability to view statistics about the content file share. The statistics information includes the number of organizers, the number of conferences hosted on a particular file share, and so on.

DMHash.exe The Web Conferencing Server stores the content of conferences by organizers. The content of all conferences organized by one user is stored in the same directory. The directory name is a hash string that is computed based on the organizer's SIP URI. This makes it difficult for administrators to locate the conference content folders for a particular organizer.

The Dmhash.exe tool helps a Microsoft Office Communications Server 2007 administrator generate the hash value for a user URI. The hash value is used to create content folders for each organizer. It is useful for administrators to move a user's conference content when the user's SIP URI is changed.

DMDel.exe The Dmdel.exe tool helps a Microsoft Office Communications Server 2007 administrator find conferences content that is older than a specified date and delete that content.

The Web Conferencing Server, by default, deletes the conference content that has not been activated for roughly 28 days. This tool allows administrators to manually delete inactive conference content on their own time.

Understanding Meeting Policy and Policy Enforcement

Conference features, except for anonymous participation, are grouped and managed using meeting policies. You control which features a conference organizer can use during a conference by configuring and applying specific policies. The conference organizer's meeting policy controls the conference and applies to all meeting participants. The meeting policy of other participants does not affect what the participants can or cannot do in the conference. For example, Ben is configured with a meeting policy that has IP audio enabled and John is configured with a default meeting policy that has IP audio disabled. As an attendee of Ben's meeting, John can use IP audio because the meeting uses Ben's meeting policy. On the other hand, when John organizes a conference, none of the participants in the conference can use IP audio because John's meeting policy applies in that case.

By default, Office Communications Server 2007 has five meeting policy definitions. All meeting policies include the same features, but any or all of the features can be configured differently for each meeting policy. Administrators can assign meeting policy globally—that is, assign one meeting policy for all users hosted on all pools in the same Active Directory forest. Administrators can also assign meeting policy on a per-user basis. In such a case, administrators select a meeting policy for each user as part of the user options. Table 5-2 shows the policy settings that you configure for each policy to manage features.

Table 5-2 Conference Access Types

Policy setting	Description
Policy Name	A name that you specify. We recommend that the name describe the purpose of the policy. The name cannot exceed 256 Unicode characters.
Maximum Meeting Size	The maximum number of participants that an organizer's meeting can admit. An organization can invite more participants than the maximum meeting size, but once attendance reaches the maximum meeting size, no one else can join the meeting. The maximum number is 1000.
Enable Web Conferencing	Enables Web conferencing for users of the policy. If you select this option, you also need to configure the following options: ■ Whether to use native format for Microsoft Office PowerPoint presentation graphics program files ■ Support for program and desktop sharing ■ Support for recording meetings These options are covered later in this table.
Use Native Format For PowerPoint Files	When a user uploads PowerPoint content, it is converted to PNG files that the server renders. PNG files are similar to screen shots. If this option is enabled in a policy (the default), when a presenter makes a slide deck active, each attendee's Microsoft Office Live Meeting 2007 client automatically downloads the Microsoft Office PowerPoint presentation in its native format (.ppt file) as well as the converted PNG files. The PowerPoint data is available only for the duration of the meeting.

Table 5-2 Conference Access Types

Policy setting	Description
Use Native Format For PowerPoint Files	If the policy does not enable this option, when a presenter makes a slide deck active, each Live Meeting 2007 client automatically downloads only the converted PNG files. If you do not use native PowerPoint format, the original source is unavailable and cannot be changed. Attendees also cannot see any active content or animation. Preventing native format increases security because the original source is unavailable and cannot be modified. This option is generally not selected if there are concerns about the bandwidth required to download slides in native mode or if original files should not be shared with participants. If this option is not selected, PowerPoint slides are downloaded as *.png images, which are equivalent to screen shots.
Enable Program And Desktop Sharing	This setting enables presenters in a meeting to share applications or an entire desktop with other participants. If it is selected in a meeting policy, the presenter can allow all participants with Active Directory accounts to take control of the organizer's desktop or a program that is running on the desktop. You can specify the range of colors (color depth) used to display slides and other meeting content, as follows: ■ Gray scale (16 shades) ■ Gray scale (256 shades) ■ 256 colors ■ High color (16 bit) ■ True color (24 bit) The default color depth for displaying slides and other meeting content in the Default Policy and Policy 5 (Low) meeting policies is High Color (16 Bit). For Office Communications Server 2007 and earlier versions, the default for these two meeting profiles was 256 Colors. If you install Office Communications Server 2007 in an environment in which a pre-release version of Office Communications Server 2007 was installed, the default will continue to be 256 Colors for all servers in the environment. You should change the setting for these two policies on all servers in your environment to either True Color (24 Bit), which is recommended for the best meeting experience, or High Color (16 Bit). Original documents are not affected by the color definition settings when viewed outside of a meeting.

Table 5-2 Conference Access Types

Policy setting	Description
Enable Program And Desktop Sharing	You can also change the sharing settings that apply to federated and anonymous users (non–Active Directory users). The following options are available: **Never allow control of shared programs or desktop.** Use this option to specify that users without an Active Directory domain account in your organization cannot take control of a shared program or desktop during meetings organized by users who have been assigned this meeting policy. **Allow control of shared programs.** Use this option to specify that users without an Active Directory domain account in your organization can take control of a shared program, but not a shared desktop, during meetings organized by users who have been assigned this meeting policy. **Allow control of shared programs and desktop.** Use this option to specify that users without an Active Directory domain account in your organization can take control of a shared program or shared desktop during meetings organized by users who have been assigned this meeting policy. Restricting control of shared programs and desktops is generally done to address concerns about who might have access to the shared programs or desktops.
Allow Presenter To Record Meetings	This setting enables internal presenters to record meetings.
Presenter Can Allow Attendees To Record Meetings	If you select the Allow Presenter To Record Meetings option, you can also allow the presenter to allow attendees to record meetings.
Enable IP Audio	This setting enables audio conferencing (Enterprise Voice) over TCP. This option controls whether streaming of audio over the Internet connection is allowed in meetings organized by users who have been assigned this meeting policy. This option is generally not selected if there are concerns about the bandwidth required for IP audio. Enabling IP audio for meetings requires deployment of the appropriate audio hardware, including head sets, microphones, or speakers. Enabling IP audio can affect performance and the Office Communications Server infrastructure.

Table 5-2 Conference Access Types

Policy setting	Description
Enable IP Video	If you select the Enable IP Audio option, you can also enable support for IP video. This option controls whether streaming of video over the Internet connection is allowed in meetings organized by users in this forest who have been assigned this meeting policy. This option is generally not selected if there are concerns about the bandwidth required for video. Enabling IP video for meetings requires deployment of the appropriate video hardware, including webcams or Microsoft Office RoundTable. Enabling IP video can affect performance and the Office Communications Server infrastructure.

Whether a user can invite anonymous users into her conferences is configured outside of the meeting policy. This is because in an enterprise, only a small percentage of users (such as people in the sales department) need to invite external partners or customers into their conference. Enabling anonymous conferences separately from the meeting policy enables customers to specify a global meeting policy for all users in the enterprise, but it only gives selected users the privilege to invite anonymous users. The following configuration options are available for anonymous participation:

- Give permission at the global level to invite anonymous participants to meetings, in which case all users in an Active Directory forest can invite anonymous participants to meetings.
- Deny permission to all users at the global level, in which case no users in the forest can invite anonymous participants to meetings.
- Enforce a meeting policy per user, in which case only individual user accounts configured to allow anonymous participation can invite anonymous participants.

Summary

This chapter introduced basic concepts and scenarios for Microsoft Office Communications Server on-premise conferences. It also described the architecture that supports those conferencing scenarios. The technical details behind Web conferencing show you the life cycle of a typical conference and also explain the client joining process and content management by the Web Conferencing Server. Such technical understanding is essential for administrators who need to implement, configure, and troubleshoot on-premise conferencing in Office Communications Server.

Additional Resources

- Product Documentation: Microsoft Office Communications Server 2007 Technical Overview
- Product Documentation: Microsoft Office Communications Server 2007 Administration Guide

On the Companion CD

The following three Web conferencing content tools mentioned in this chapter are included as part of the Office Communications Server 2007 Resource Kit Tools:

- DMInsider.exe
- DMHash.exe
- DMDel.exe.

You can install the Office Communications Server 2007 Resource Kit tools from the OCS 2007 Resource Kit Tools folder on the companion CD.

Chapter 6

Remote Access Scenarios

In this chapter:

This chapter explains remote access scenarios that are possible with Office Communications Server 2007. Remote access gives users the flexibility to communicate whether they are on the enterprise network or on external networks such as the Internet. The scenarios that will be discussed involve users who are working from an external network outside the enterprise (such as the Internet). There are three primary remote access scenarios and two extended scenarios:

Primary Remote Access Scenarios

- Basic Remote Access (for instant messaging [IM] and presence)
  - Involves remotely using Office Communicator to log in to the enterprise network
  - Requires that the Access Edge Server role is deployed by the enterprise
- Web Conferencing Remote Access
  - Involves using the Live Meeting 2007 client remotely to connect to a data conference
  - Requires that the Access Edge Server and Web Conferencing Edge Server roles are deployed by the enterprise
- A/V Remote Access
  - Involves using Office Communicator remotely for an audio/video conference
  - Requires that the Access Edge Server and A/V Edge Server roles are deployed by the enterprise

Extended Remote Access Scenarios

- Basic Web-Based Remote Access
  - Involves using Office Communicator Web Access 2007 to log in to the enterprise network
  - Requires that an Office Communicator Web Access (CWA) server role is deployed by the enterprise

- Mobile Device Remote Access
  - Involves using Office Communicator Mobile remotely to log in to the enterprise network
  - Requires that the Access Edge Server role is deployed by the enterprise

For almost all remote access scenarios, the Access Edge Server role needs to be deployed. The only exception is the use of Office Communicator Web Access 2007, which involves a Web interface to the Office Communicator client. (See the "Enabling Office Communicator Web Access 2007" section later in this chapter.) The Access Edge Server provides the core functionality for collaboration between internal users and users outside the enterprise firewall. This is true whether the outside users are using Office Communicator, Office Communicator Mobile, or the Office Live Meeting 2007 client. The Access Edge Server provides a single, trusted connection point for both inbound and outbound Session Initiation Protocol (SIP) traffic. Practically all Office Communications Server 2007 components use SIP to provide the basic connectivity and communications channel.

The Web Conferencing Edge Server enables external users using the Live Meeting 2007 client to join enterprise meetings. If the Web Conferencing Edge Server is deployed, enterprise users (whether local or remote) can join meetings, as can users from federated partners or anonymous users (other users who have connectivity to the Web Conferencing Edge Server who don't have accounts defined by the local enterprise Active Directory). Remote access users are authenticated using their domain credentials; federated users are authenticated based on certificate credentials from their organization's Access Edge Server; and anonymous users are authorized by their use of per-meeting conference keys, which are provided to them along with the conference invitation.

The Office Communications Server 2007 A/V Edge Server enables media traversal of firewalls. Users who log in remotely using Office Communicator 2007 require use of the A/V Edge Server for both individual calls and conference calls. The A/V Edge Server is responsible for opening media ports and bridging the external and internal networks safely to allow audio and video sessions for remote users.

Office Communicator Web Access requires its own Web server published through an HTTP reverse proxy independent of the other edge server roles. The other edge server roles can be deployed on separate physical servers within the enterprise edge network (also known as a perimeter network or screened subnet), or they can all be hosted on the same physical server.

This chapter identifies the basic remote access topologies and then explains each of the primary and extended remote access scenarios. An overview of each remote access scenario is shown from the user's perspective, and then the technical details that make the scenario possible are presented.

Understanding Basic Remote Access Topologies

Before examining different remote access scenarios, many examples of the basic remote access topologies are presented to help you see the underlying infrastructure. The extended remote access scenario topologies are presented along with the scenarios themselves in later sections. In a production environment, there are many topology variations that might be useful for an organization to deploy based on its connectivity, collaboration, and availability needs.

Single Edge Server

The simplest installation involves minimizing the hardware required to provide access by consolidating the installation of the Access, Web Conferencing, and A/V Edge Servers on the same physical server in the edge network. (See Figure 6-1.) Firewalls protect the edge network from the external network and protect the enterprise network from irregular access from the edge network. The consolidated edge server bridges the edge network for valid traffic and connects to the internal servers in the organization, which could be a pool of servers or a single, Standard Edition server. Figure 6-1 shows the topology with the next hop as a Standard Edition Director, which can provide authentication and forward requests to the Enterprise Edition pool.

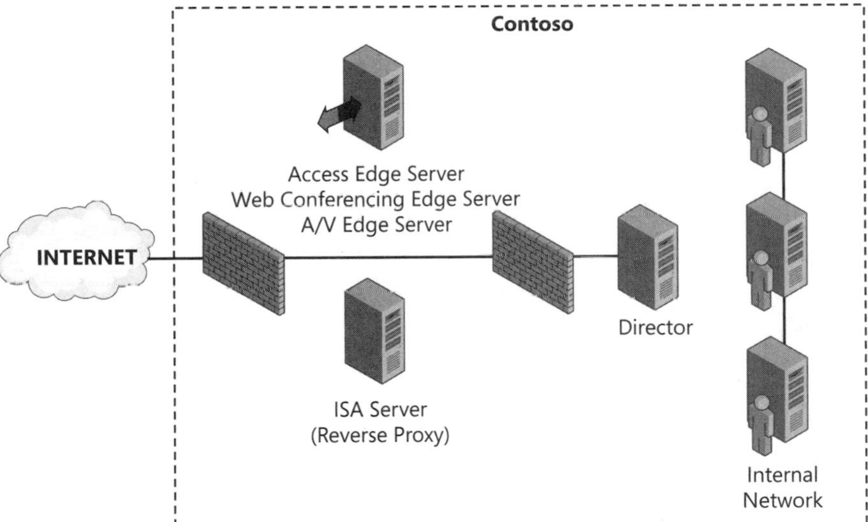

Figure 6-1 Single edge server topology example

For a single edge server topology, remote access Office Communicator clients use Transport Layer Security (TLS) to securely connect to the Access Edge Server from the Internet. The enterprise Access Edge Server is discovered by Office Communicator through Domain Name Service service (DNS SRV) records. This interaction is very similar to how internal clients connect. (See Chapter 4, "Basic IM and Presence Scenarios," for more details on an internal login and the use of DNS SRV records.) However, to prevent anonymous users and network infrastructure on the client's network from listening in on the communications channel, Transmission Control Protocol (TCP) is not offered for clients connecting from external networks. The Access Edge Server has a certificate issued by a well-known certificate authority (CA) that is trusted by Microsoft Windows. This allows non-domain machines outside the enterprise network to easily connect, validate, and trust the Access Edge Server certificate. This trust is necessary to prevent DNS spoofing attacks that could otherwise allow the connecting Office Communicator client to negotiate authentication and pass communications through an undesired intermediary. The Access Edge Server then uses another certificate (issued by a public or private CA) to connect securely to the Director inside the enterprise network. The Director on the internal network actually works through a SIP-based NTLM authentication handshake with Office Communicator (over these established connections) because it has access to the internal Active Directory infrastructure. Note that the Access Edge Server helps protect the internal servers against network-level attacks, validates the SIP network protocol messages that it receives, validates the domain that the client uses to log in, and then forwards requests to the internal Director.

> **Note** For more details on how Office Communicator uses DNS SRV records during remote access and local enterprise logins, refer to Chapter 4. The "Examining the Technical Details Behind the Login Process" section explains which DNS SRV records are queried and how the result is interpreted. For remote access, the *sipexternal.<domain>* host (A) record and the *_sip._tls.<domain>* server (SRV) records are of interest.

Single-Site Edge Topology

The recommended single-site edge topology is similar to the single edge server topology except that in single-site edge topology, the A/V Edge Server is installed on a separate physical server. (See Figure 6-2.) Because the A/V Edge Server is more bandwidth-intensive than the other edge servers, greater scalability is provided by having it installed on its own machine, which alleviates load on the server hosting the Access Edge Server and Web Conferencing Edge Server and provides the most processing and network resources for the A/V Edge Server. Both physical servers reside in the edge network and are insulated by firewalls. The firewall rules for each server can be managed independently to prevent intrusions on one server from affecting the capabilities of the other.

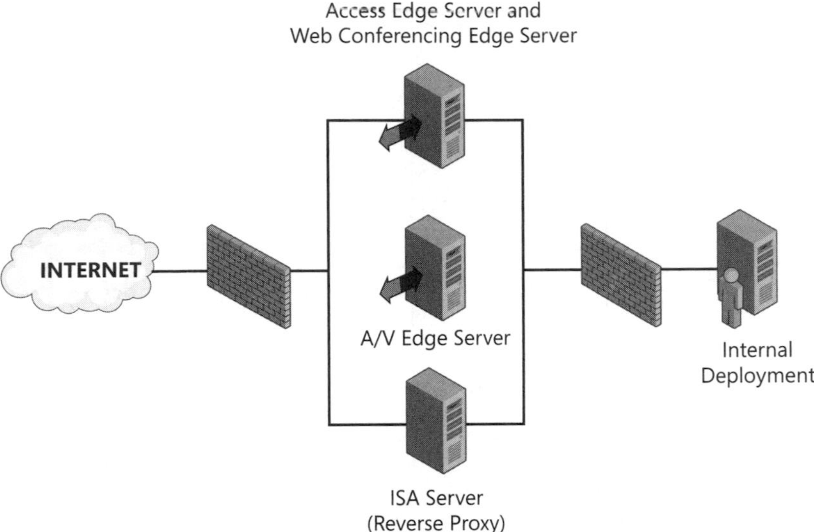

Figure 6-2 Single-site edge topology (recommended)

If the remote Office Communicator client makes use of audio and video conferencing features, the connection point goes through the separate A/V Edge Server. After Office Communicator uses TLS to authenticate with the Access Edge Server, the client then makes a connection to the A/V Edge Server over the Simple Traversal of User Datagram Protocol (UDP) through Network Address Translators (NATs) protocol. (The simplified protocol name is STUN.)

Multisite Edge Topology

The recommended multisite edge topology is similar to single-site edge topology for the primary site; however, for greater scalability, it has a pair of load-balanced Access and Web Conferencing Edge Servers. The remote site simply has A/V and Web Conferencing Edge Servers installed to prevent introducing media session delays by routing media through the local site. (See Figure 6-3.) Because the domain DNS SRV records publish only the main site (for federation and remote access purposes), the SIP traffic from remote Office Communicator clients always travels through the main site with this topology. Because the SIP traffic is not bandwidth intensive like media traffic, the Access Edge Servers can be centrally managed at the main site.

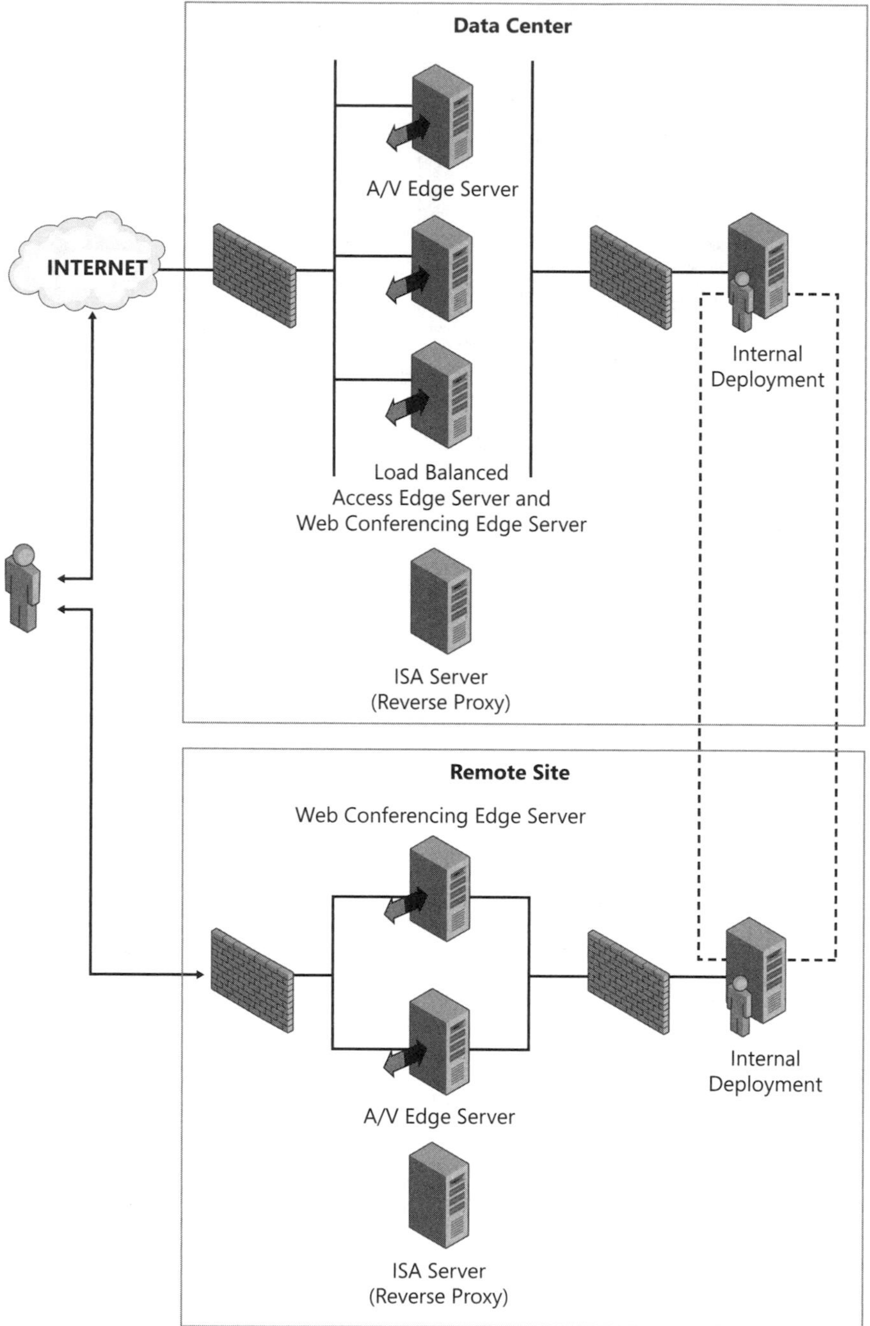

Figure 6-3 Multisite edge topology (recommended)

Understanding Basic Remote Access Scenarios

This section describes the three basic remote access scenarios in detail:

- **Basic Remote Access (for IM and presence)** Involves remotely using Office Communicator to log in to the enterprise network
- **Web Conferencing Remote Access** Involves remotely using the Live Meeting 2007 client to connect to a data conference
- **A/V Conferencing Remote Access** Involves remotely using Office Communicator for an audio/video conference

Understanding Basic Remote Access for IM and Presence

Basic remote access involves the use of Office Communicator to log in from an external network to connect to an Access Edge Server in the enterprise edge network. This scenario does not require the use of a virtual private network (VPN) and is an easy way for enterprise users to connect from home or external sites. The basic remote access scenario involves a user experience that is identical to what is covered in Chapter 4, in the "Understanding the Login Process" section. The topology, shown in Figure 6-4, involves the Office Communicator client connecting via the Access Edge Server to an internal Standard Edition server. For most deployments, this server will actually be a Director that passes the traffic on (after authentication and authorization) to the internal home server (or pool) for the user. The technical details, which vary from what was shown in Chapter 4, are described in the next section.

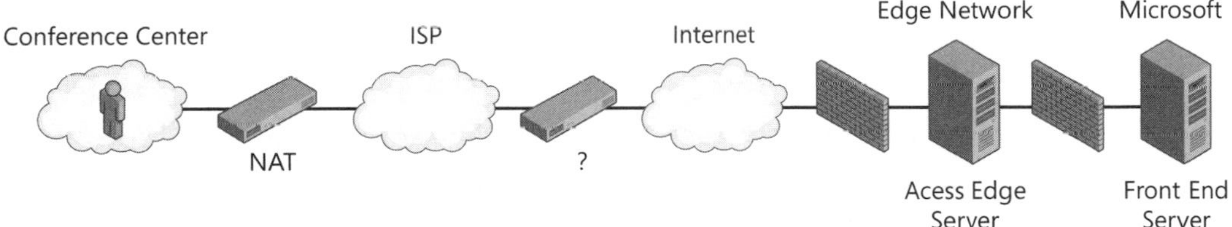

Figure 6-4 Basic remote access scenario/topology

Examining the Basic Remote Access Scenario in Detail

Office Communicator walks through the same logic during a remote access login as it would during a login procedure on an internal network–it simply has no idea what network it is on until some exploration is done through discovery of DNS SRV and host (A) records. These records are used to discover internal and external Office Communications Server contact points. More information about this DNS discovery is shown in Chapter 4, in the "Understanding Client Automatic Configuration and DNS Discovery" section. For basic remote access, two main records are leveraged and these are shown for the example domain contoso.com:

- _sip._tls.contoso.com (SRV record)
- sipexternal.contoso.com (A record)

Once the connection point for basic remote access is identified, Office Communicator always negotiates TLS over a TCP connection. This is mandated by the clients and servers to maintain data privacy and to prevent man-in-the-middle intrusions on the external network. Note that certificate validation can have more problems during remote access—especially if a public CA isn't used to issue the Access Edge Server certificate, because the client might not trust it. Office Communicator clearly identifies this problem with an alert as well as entries in the event log, as well as trace logs (if they are enabled).

The connection point will always be an Access Edge Server for supported topologies, and this server is responsible for performing simple message validation based on the supported enterprise domains and for protecting the enterprise network against network-level and protocol-level attacks. The Access Edge Server also has the ability to filter messages to provide additional functionality or protection. The Access Edge Server tags the messages as remote access requests and passes them to the next-hop internal server (usually a Director role). The following header is added to the request to identify it as being from an external user and to track the name of the Access Edge Server that handled the request:

```
ms-edge-proxy-message-trust: ms-source-type=InternetUser;
ms-ep-fqdn=server22.contoso.local;
ms-source-verified-user=verified
```

The Director (which is either a Standard Edition server or an Enterprise Edition pool server) enforces authentication against Active Directory (using NTLM), validates the user's right to log in to the Office Communications Server infrastructure, and determines whether the user has a right to use remote access. This server supports the rest of the network infrastructure by offloading authentication and potentially larger numbers of requests if a denial of service (DoS) attack is made against the enterprise. The Director then uses its knowledge of the other Office Communications Server 2007 servers to forward requests to the user's home server or pool. From this point, the login is identical to a standard internal network login. However, an additional header is placed in responses to help Office Communicator identify itself as being in a remote access scenario:

```
ms-user-logon-data: RemoteUser
```

The Access Edge Proxy has a distinction in that it tracks *edges* during protocol operations so that it can differentiate messages that are proxied from the outside in and from the inside out. This tracking shows up in the trace logs and can be a point of confusion when an *incoming* message comes from the internal network or an *outgoing* message is headed to the internal network. Messages are logged as they come in and as they are forwarded on, both to and from the internal and external networks.

Understanding Web Conferencing Remote Access

Web conferencing remote access involves use of the Live Meeting 2007 client from a remote network to conduct a meeting or share information with other enterprise or federated users. This section contains an example of a simple conference and presents the technical details that make it possible. Conducting a Web conference is similar to basic remote access for the SIP communications channel, but it also involves the Web Conferencing Edge Server to bridge application-sharing sessions to internal multipoint control unit (MCU) servers that form the conference hub. Additionally, a reverse proxy in the edge network provides access to the internal Web server where conference content is available. Figure 6-5 provides an overview diagram of this topology.

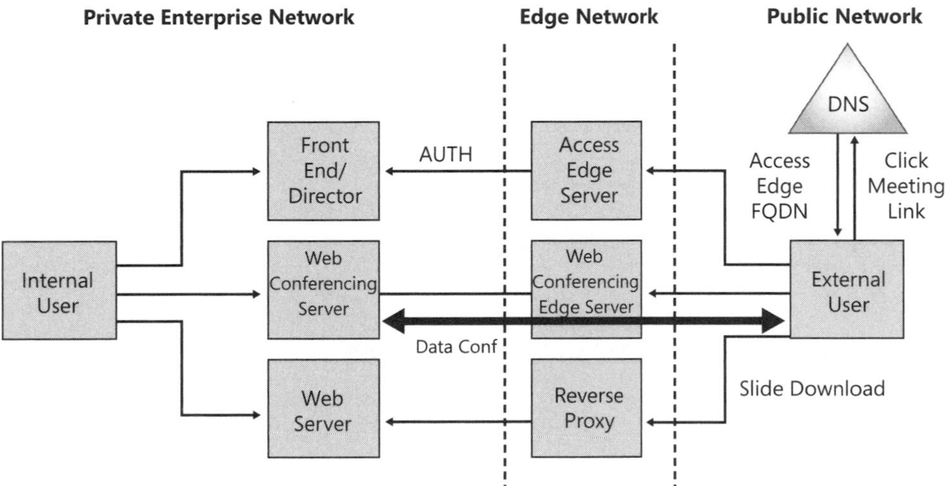

Figure 6-5 Web conferencing remote access scenario/topology

The usage scenario example involves two external users (Vadim N. Korepin and Jeremy Los) who are active contacts with each other. The example assumes that Office Communicator 2007 and Office Live Meeting 2007 clients have been installed on each user's workstation. Additionally, both users are assumed to have already logged in remotely and have been enabled for remote access, for the ability to schedule conferences, and for access to Web conferencing. In this example, Vadim has a desire to share a game of FreeCell he is working on so that he can get Jeremy's advice on what to do next. (Mission-critical applications like this can be extremely time sensitive–especially for the person involved in the game.) This example uses Office Communicator to establish and connect to the conference, but the Live Meeting 2007 client could have also been used to join a scheduled conference either directly or by clicking on a conference URL.

Use Office Communicator to Start a Conference (Step 1)

Vadim N. Korepin opens a session in Office Communicator with Jeremy Los and then uses the sharing button and selects Share Information Using Live Meeting. (See Figure 6-6.) Vadim's Office Communicator launches the Live Meeting 2007 client, which creates the conference and joins it (as shown in Figure 6-7) directly.

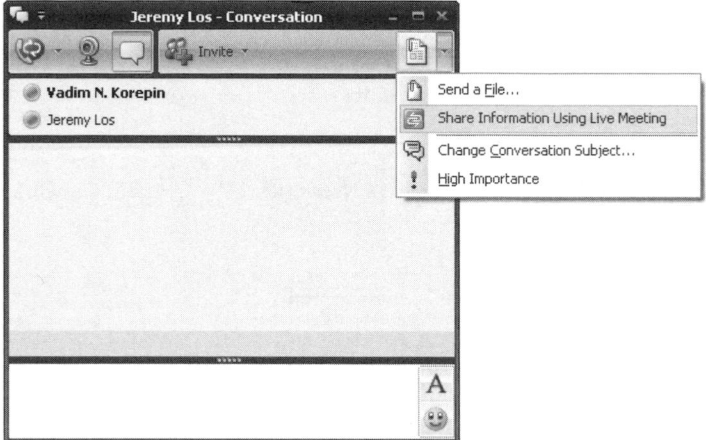

Figure 6-6 Initiating a data conference from Office Communicator

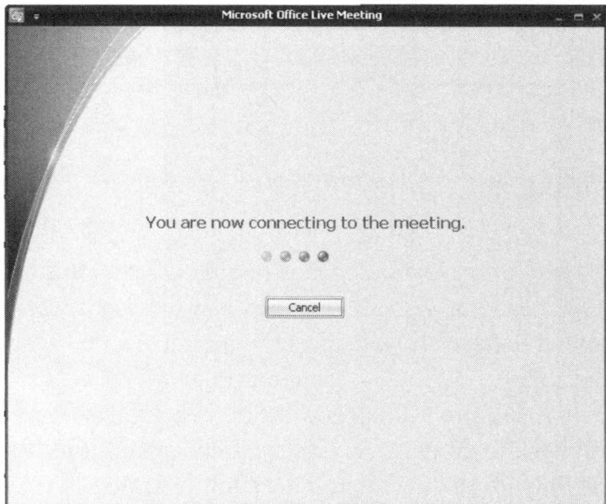

Figure 6-7 Joining a Web Conference with the Live Meeting 2007 client

Accept and Join a Web Conferencing Invitation (Step 2)

At this point, Jeremy sees a message pop up that informs him that Vadim would like to start an application-sharing session. If he accepts the invitation he received in Office Communicator, both his and Vadim's workstations will launch the Live Meeting 2007 client to begin a Web conference. (See Figure 6-7.)

Begin Sharing an Application (Step 3)

Once Vadim and Jeremy are connected to the session, Vadim shares his application by using the Content menu to select Share and finally Share A Program, which shows a list of running programs. From this list, Vadim selects FreeCell.exe. This enables the application to be shared for Jeremy to view so that their analysis can begin. (See Figure 6-8.) From here, application control can be delegated to Jeremy or other applications, tools, and data can be made available.

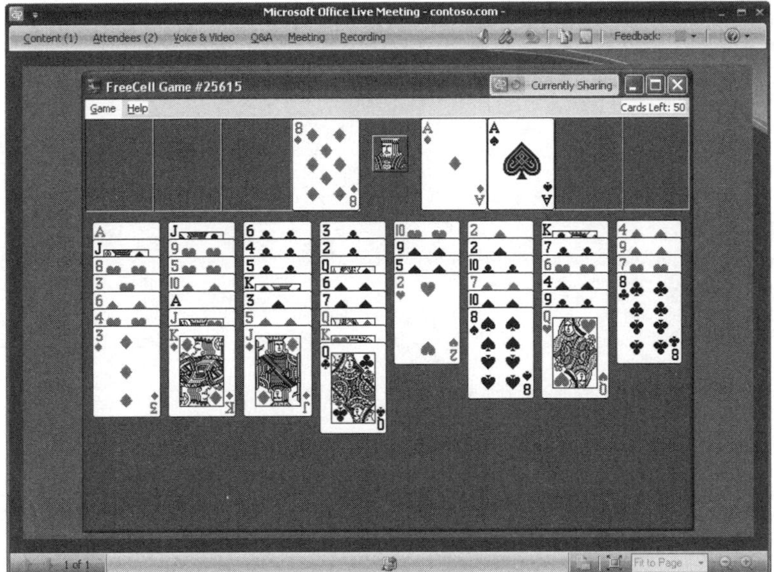

Figure 6-8 Web conferencing session with application sharing

Examining the Web Conferencing Remote Access Scenario in Detail

The primary difference between the internal and remote access Web Conferencing scenarios simply involves Office Communicator logging in through an Access Edge Server and thereby being given the Web Conferencing Edge Server as a data conferencing connection point, as well as being given the HTTP reverse proxy as the URL for establishing a Web-based session. Internally, a local Web Conferencing Server and URL are given to access data conferencing services directly.

When Vadim creates an unscheduled conference and invites Jeremy, Office Communicator makes a SIP SERVICE request asking that a conference be created. The request looks like the following message:

```
SERVICE sip:vadim@contoso.com;gruu;opaque=app:conf:focusfactory SIP/2.0
From: <sip:vadim@contoso.com>;tag=54268ccbd8;epid=0b28f0b0b5 To:
sip:vadim@contoso.com;gruu;opaque=app:conf:focusfactory
CSeq: 1 SERVICE
...
Content-Type: application/cccp+xml
```

```
Content-Length: 1233

<?xml version="1.0"?>
<request xmlns="urn:ietf:params:xml:ns:cccp"
xmlns:mscp=http://schemas.microsoft.com/rtc/2005/08/cccpextensions C3PVersion="1"
to=sip:vadim@contoso.com;gruu;opaque=app:conf:focusfactory from="sip:vadim@contoso.com"
requestId="26587488">
  <addConference>
     <ci:conference-info xmlns:ci="urn:ietf:params:xml:ns:conference-info" entity=""
xmlns:msci="http://schemas.microsoft.com/rtc/2005/08/confinfoextensions">
    <ci:conference-description>
      <ci:subject></ci:subject>
      <msci:conference-id>6CD0FA33C0F133499647246DA968BF6B
          </msci:conference-id>
      <msci:expiry-time>2007-09-25T13:44:34Z</msci:expiry-time>
      <msci:admission-policy>openAuthenticated</msci:admission-policy>
    </ci:conference-description>
    <msci:conference-view>
      <msci:entity-view entity="chat"/>
      <msci:entity-view entity="audio-video"/>
      <msci:entity-view entity="meeting">
      <msci:entity-settings>
        <msdata:settings xmlns:msdata="http://schemas.microsoft.com/rtc/2005/08/
dataconfinfoextensions">
          <msdata:app-viewing-behavior>enableWithFullSharing
              </msdata:app-viewing-behavior>
          <msdata:conferencing-type>collaboration
              </msdata:conferencing-type>
        </msdata:settings>
      </msci:entity-settings>
      </msci:entity-view>
    </msci:conference-view>
    </ci:conference-info>
  </addConference>
</request>
```

This message is sent to the user's URI, but with the additional parameter *;opaque=app:conf:focusfactory*, which specifies that the request is destined for the conference focus factory that is responsible for creating the meeting. In the body of the message, the request also specifies information about the conference to be created. Examples of data in the body of the message include the *msci:conference-id* attribute, which specifies the conference ID that should be used, and the *msci:admission-policy* attribute, which specifies the security level for the meeting (in this case, *openAuthenticated* means that all authenticated users can join, but anonymous Internet users cannot). In the following example, the SERVICE request is responded to with a *200 OK* response that passes back some basic information about the conference that was just created:

```
SIP/2.0 200 OK
From: "Vadim N. Korepin"<sip:vadim@contoso.com>;tag=54268ccbd8;epid=0b28f0b0b5
To: <sip:vadim@contoso.com;gruu;opaque=app:conf:focusfactory>;tag=38971651
CSeq: 1 SERVICE
...
```

```
Content-Type: application/cccp+xml

<response xmlns="urn:ietf:params:xml:ns:cccp" xmlns:msacp=
   "http://schemas.microsoft.com/rtc/2005/08/acpconfinfoextensions"
xmlns:msav="http://schemas.microsoft.com/rtc/2005/08/avconfinfoextensions"
xmlns:mscp="http://schemas.microsoft.com/rtc/2005/08/cccpextensions"
xmlns:msci="http://schemas.microsoft.com/rtc/2005/08/confinfoextensions"
xmlns:msdata="http://schemas.microsoft.com/rtc/2005/08/dataconfinfoextensions"
xmlns:msim="http://schemas.microsoft.com/rtc/2005/08/imconfinfoextensions"
xmlns:ci="urn:ietf:params:xml:ns:conference-info"
xmlns:cis="urn:ietf:params:xml:ns:conference-info-separator"
xmlns:msls="urn:ietf:params:xml:ns:msls" requestId="26587488"
    C3PVersion="1"
from="sip:vadim@contoso.com;gruu;opaque=app:conf:focusfactory"
to="sip:vadim@contoso.com" code="success">
  <addConference>
<conference-info xmlns="urn:ietf:params:xml:ns:conference-info"
entity="sip:vadim@contoso.com;gruu;opaque=app:conf:focus:id:6CD0FA33C0F133499647246DA968BF6B"
 state="partial" version="1"/>
  </addConference>
</response>
```

Next, Vadim's Office Communicator sends a SIP INVITE message to the conference that was just created in order to establish a session and add Vadim as an attendee for the conference:

```
INVITE
sip:vadim@contoso.com;gruu;opaque=app:conf:focus:id:6CD0FA33C0F133499647246DA968BF6B
SIP/2.0
From: <sip:vadim@contoso.com>;tag=80fd98dd31;epid=0b28f0b0b5 To:
<sip:vadim@contoso.com;gruu;opaque=app:conf:focus:id:6CD0FA33C0F133499647246DA968BF6B>
CSeq: 1 INVITE
...
Content-Type: application/cccp+xml
Content-Length: 716

<?xml version="1.0"?>
<request xmlns="urn:ietf:params:xml:ns:cccp"
    xmlns:mscp="http://schemas.microsoft.com/rtc/2005/08/cccpextensions"
    C3PVersion="1"

to="sip:vadim@contoso.com;gruu;opaque=app:conf:focus:id:6CD0FA33C0F133499647246DA968BF6B"
     from="sip:vadim@contoso.com" requestId="0">   <addUser>
<conferenceKeys
confEntity=
"sip:vadim@contoso.com;gruu;opaque=app:conf:focus:id:6CD0FA33C0F133499647246DA968BF6B"/>
<ci:user xmlns:ci="urn:ietf:params:xml:ns:conference-info"entity="sip:vadim@contoso.com">
      <ci:roles>
        <ci:entry>attendee</ci:entry>
      </ci:roles>
      <ci:endpoint entity="{4BB86066-3927-424B-A7DD-2E07FD6B611C}" xmlns:msci="http://
schemas.microsoft.com/rtc/2005/08/confinfoextensions"/>
    </ci:user>
  </addUser>
</request>
```

The conference focus responds with a *200 Invite dialog created* message, shown next, confirming that Vadim is added as a presenter for the conference. Vadim sends back an ACK to confirm (which isn't shown for this example):

```
SIP/2.0 200 Invite dialog created
From: "Vadim N. Korepin"<sip:vadim@contoso.com>;tag=80fd98dd31;
    epid=0b28f0b0b5 To:<sip:vadim@contoso.com;gruu;opaque=app:conf:focus:id:
    6CD0FA33C0F133499647246DA968BF6B>;tag=84670080
CSeq: 1 INVITE
...
Content-Type: application/cccp+xml

<response xmlns="urn:ietf:params:xml:ns:cccp" xmlns:msacp="http://schemas.microsoft.com/
   rtc/2005/08/acpconfinfoextensions"
xmlns:msav="http://schemas.microsoft.com/rtc/2005/08/
avconfinfoextensions" xmlns:mscp="http://schemas.microsoft.com/rtc/2005/08/cccpextensions"
xmlns:msci="http://schemas.microsoft.com/rtc/2005/08/confinfoextensions"
xmlns:msdata="http://schemas.microsoft.com/rtc/2005/08/dataconfinfoextensions"
xmlns:msim="http://schemas.microsoft.com/rtc/2005/08/imconfinfoextensions"
xmlns:ci="urn:ietf:params:xml:ns:conference-info"
xmlns:cis="urn:ietf:params:xml:ns:conference-info-separator"
xmlns:msls="urn:ietf:params:xml:ns:msls" requestId="0" C3PVersion="1"
from="sip:vadim@contoso.com;gruu;opaque=app:conf:focus:id:
    6CD0FA33C0F133499647246DA968BF6B"
    to="sip:vadim@contoso.com" code="success">
  <addUser>
<conferenceKeys confEntity="sip:vadim@contoso.com;gruu;opaque=app:conf:focus:id:
    6CD0FA33C0F133499647246DA968BF6B"/>
    <ci:user entity="sip:vadim@contoso.com">
      <ci:roles>
        <ci:entry>presenter</ci:entry>
      </ci:roles>
    </ci:user>
  </addUser>
</response>
```

Next Vadim's Office Communicator sends a SUBSCRIBE message to the conference in order to receive notifications from the conference as events occur (such as when other users join, and so on):

```
SUBSCRIBE sip:vadim@contoso.com;gruu;opaque=app:conf:focus:id:
    6CD0FA33C0F133499647246DA968BF6B SIP/2.0
From: <sip:vadim@contoso.com>;tag=694f84821b;epid=0b28f0b0b5 To:
  <sip:vadim@contoso.com;gruu;opaque=app:conf:focus:id:
    6CD0FA33C0F133499647246DA968BF6B>
CSeq: 1 SUBSCRIBE
...
Event: conference
Accept: application/conference-info+xml
Content-Length: 0
```

At this point, Vadim's Live Meeting client connects to the Web Conferencing Edge Server after connecting through the HTTP reverse proxy that it was provisioned with during login. His

Office Communicator client sends the invitation, which provides information about the conference that has been established, to Jeremy:

```
INVITE sip:jeremy@contoso.com SIP/2.0 From:
<sip:vadim@contoso.com>;tag=7bf3e5f500;epid=0b28f0b0b5 To: <sip:jeremy@contoso.com>
CSeq: 1 INVITE
...
Content-Type: application/ms-conf-invite+xml
Content-Length: 193

<Conferencing version="2.0">
<focus-uri>sip:vadim@contoso.com;gruu;opaque=app:conf:focus:id:
     6CD0FA33C0F133499647246DA968BF6B</focus-uri>
  <subject></subject>
  <data available="true"/>
</Conferencing>
```

This invitation will be accepted, and Jeremy's Office Communicator and Live Meeting clients will go through the same interactions that Vadim's Office Communicator and Live Meeting client did.

As an aside, if a user were joining anonymously using the Live Meeting client, she would need to authenticate through the use of Digest to pass a hash of the meeting password. This authentication (Digest for anonymous users using conference passwords, and NTLM for enterprise users utilizing remote access) ensures that all servers the user connects to in the edge network can validate the user. This first-level authentication hands back meeting keys that are passed to the Web Conferencing Edge Server to prevent unauthorized access.

Understanding Audio and Video Conferencing Remote Access

Audio and video conferencing remote access enables enterprise users in the external network to share video and audio sessions with internal and other external users. Figure 6-9 shows an example of the topology, with the SIP connections (TLS over TCP) shown as gray lines and the media sessions shown as black lines.

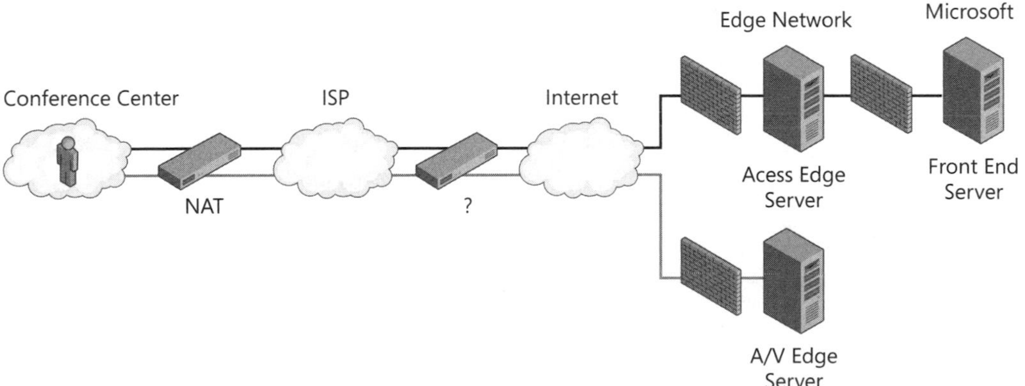

Figure 6-9 Audio/video conferencing remote access scenario/topology

The A/V Edge Server provides a single, trusted connection point through which inbound and outbound media traffic can securely traverse NATs and firewalls. The industry-standard solution for multimedia traversal of firewalls is Interactive Connectivity Establishment (ICE), which is based on STUN and Traversal Using Relay NAT (TURN) protocols. The A/V Edge Server is a STUN server. All users are authenticated to secure both access to the enterprise and use of the firewall traversal service that is provided by the A/V Edge Server. Authenticated users receive a token from the authenticating server, and this token can be used to validate the user's requests of the A/V Edge Server. To send media inside the enterprise, an external user must be authenticated and must have an authenticated internal user agree to communicate with him through the A/V Edge Server. The media streams themselves are exchanged using Secure Real-time Protocol (SRTP), which is an industry standard for real-time media transmission and reception over the Internet Protocol (IP).

Office Communicator remote access forces authentication over the SIP session with the Access Edge Server. Once Office Communicator has logged in and authenticated, it can contact the A/V Edge Server on the public IP address through the use of a secure token that it can retrieve—this is what prevents anonymous and unauthenticated users from leveraging the A/V Edge Server for their own purposes. The A/V Edge Server allocates to the user a port to use on the external/internal interface, and Office Communicator can then invite (through SIP) the recipient by using the internal A/V MCU as a bridge point. The recipient can use a secure token (after authenticating) to register directly with the A/V Edge Server or internal A/V MCU based on the recipient's network location. Finally, media is exchanged over the negotiated ports by using the servers to bridge traffic.

Note The A/V Authentication Service is consolidated with, and provides authentication services for, the A/V Edge Server. Outside users attempting to connect to the A/V Edge Server require an authentication token provided by the A/V Authentication Service before their calls can go through.

Troubleshooting Remote Access

Here are a few tips for troubleshooting Remote Access issues, particularly those associated with the consolidated install (single edge server) topology scenario.

A common issue involves users who are not on the local area network (LAN) being unable to sign in remotely. This problem can occur for either of the following reasons:

- The user has not been provisioned for remote access.
- No users are able to log in remotely.

Checking both of these cases helps to isolate the issue to an individual, or to a group of people when the server infrastructure itself could be causing the problem.

Another common issue that can prevent remote access from functioning properly is when internal and external servers are not able to connect to each other properly. If this happens, use the Office Communications Server 2007 Microsoft Management Console (MMC) on the internal network. Look under global properties, where there are settings that enable the internal servers to see the edge servers. Similarly, on the edge servers there are settings that specify which servers in your internal organization are the next-hop destinations.

For example, consider the situation where the internal servers are not able to route outbound to the appropriate Web Conferencing Servers or Remote Access Servers. In Office Communications Server 2007, there are global properties that specify the list of trusted edge servers. This list must be configured for the internal servers (such as the front-end servers) to allow communication with the Access, Web Conferencing, and A/V Edge Servers. (See Figure 6-10.) If the edge servers are not listed, outbound communication will not be established from the internal servers, leading to internal users failing to send outbound SIP messages or make outbound calls.

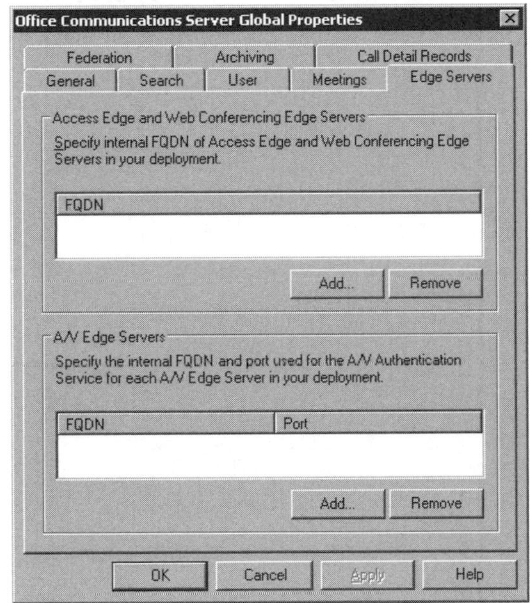

Figure 6-10 Office Communications Server global properties

Understanding Extended Remote Access Scenarios

This section provides some basic information on enabling Office Communicator Web Access 2007 and Office Communicator Mobile Access 2007. An introduction to the basic topology requirements is provided along with some overview information.

Enabling Office Communicator Web Access 2007

Office Communicator Web Access (CWA) is a Web-based replacement for the Office Communicator client and provides a great way to reach alternate operating systems and nondomain workstations without an install process. CWA provides internal and remote access (if a reverse proxy is set up for it) to the Office Communications Server infrastructure by enabling instant messaging and presence capabilities. File transfer, A/V conferencing, whiteboard sessions, and application sharing are not available with CWA like they are with Office Communicator, however. The Web browsers that are supported by Office Communicator Web Access are shown in Table 6-1.

Table 6-1 Supported Browsers for Office Communicator Web Access 2007

Operating System	Browser	Authentication Mechanism
Windows 2000 SP4	Microsoft Internet Explorer 6 SP1	NTLM Kerberos Forms-based Custom
Windows XP SP2	Internet Explorer 6 SP2 Windows Internet Explorer 7	NTLM Kerberos Forms-based Custom
	Mozilla Firefox 2.0.latest	Forms-based Custom
Windows Vista, Enterprise Edition	Internet Explorer 7	NTLM Kerberos Forms-based Custom
	Mozilla Firefox 2.0.0.3 and later	Forms-based Custom
Mac OS X 10.4.9	Apple Safari 2.0.4 Mozilla Firefox 2.0.latest	Forms-based Custom

Office Communicator Web Access 2007 has several new enhancements that weren't present in Office Communicator Web Access 2005, including the following:

- Automatic discovery of local servers in the MMC
- Richer Office Communicator 2007 user interface
- Custom authentication such as single sign-on and two-factor authentication support
- Inbound Voice over Internet Protocol (VoIP) call routing and management

A robust CWA topology can provide support for Web-based access internally and remotely with load-balanced Web servers hosting CWA. (See Figure 6-11.) However, many topologies are supported. Office Communicator Web Access can be deployed in several different topologies:

- A single CWA server for both internal and external users
- Separate CWA servers for internal and external users
- Separate CWA server arrays for internal and external users (as shown in Figure 6-11)

The following topologies *are not supported* for deploying CWA:

- CWA *should not* be deployed in the perimeter network.
- CWA *should not* be installed on a domain controller.

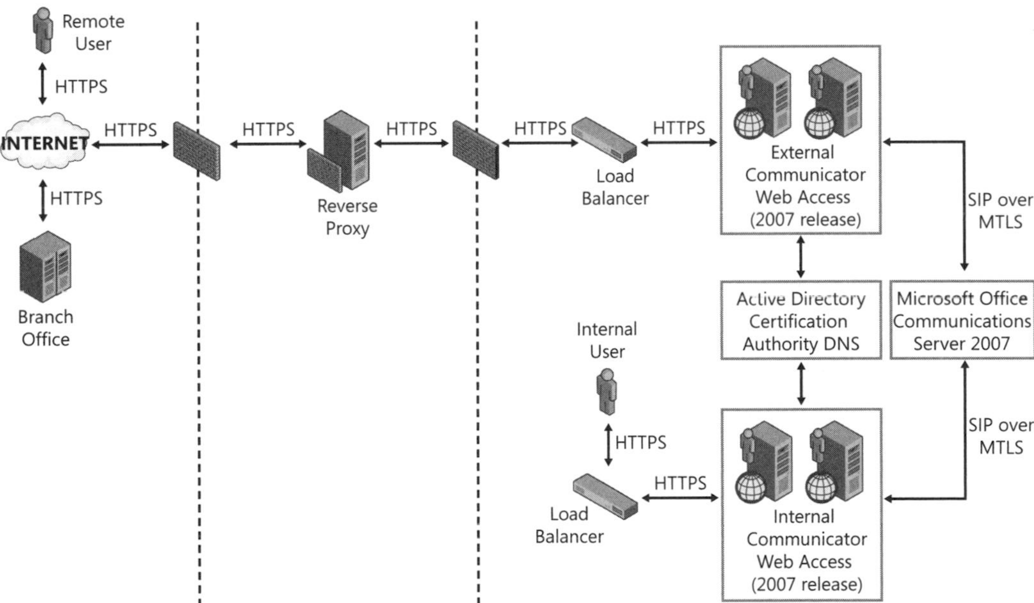

Figure 6-11 Robust Office Communicator Web Access topology

Remote access logins using CWA go through the following process when logging in against the topology shown in the preceding example:

1. The remote user on the public Internet uses her Web browser to connect to the Office Communicator Web Access URL (for example, https://im.contoso.com). This request securely connects through the reverse proxy in the edge network, which routes the connection to the load balancer for the external CWA Web farm.

2. The Web browser verifies the CWA server certificate comes from a trusted CA, and it validates the name that was connected to (for example, im.contoso.com) is represented in the certificate in the Subject Name (SN) or Subject Alternate Name (SAN) fields.
3. CWA authenticates the user, validates the SIP URI, and ensures the user is allowed to log in with remote access. Integrated Windows authentication (Kerberos/NTLM for internal users) or forms-based authentication (NTLM for external users and browsers that don't support Integrated Windows authentication) can be used by CWA to authenticate the user.

Note Forms-based authentication passes the password in clear text, so it should *always* be used with HTTPS in order to encrypt the communications channel. For internal users, this is important, but for external users it is *critical*.

4. The mutual transport layer security (MTLS) server certificate configured for CWA is used to authenticate and encrypt connections between the CWA server and the Office Communications Server 2007 server. This connection will be used to transport the user's SIP-based communications to and from the rest of the Office Communications Server infrastructure.

Direct from the Source: CWA Port Usage

CWA communicates over the following incoming ports:

- TCP port 80 (HTTP) or TCP port 443 (HTTPS)

CWA communicates over the following outgoing ports:

- TCP port 3268 (LDAP) to the Global Catalog (GC) server
- TCP port 389 (LDAP) to the Active Directory Domain Controller (DC)
- TCP port 5061 (MTLS) to the Office Communication Server 2007 server or pool

Byron Spurlock
Microsoft Consultant, Microsoft Consulting Services

Enabling Office Communicator Mobile Access 2007

Office Communicator Mobile Access (COMO) gives users the ability to connect to their Office Communications Server 2007 infrastructure remotely via a phone device. The phone device can be a Pocket PC 5.0/6.0 or a Smartphone 5.0/6.0. COMO gives the user the ability to send an instant message to one or more users (such as distribution lists), publish enhanced presence status, look up users from the enterprise global address book, and initiate phone calls and communicate with Public IM Connectivity (PIC) users and federated partners that are provisioned by the enterprise.

Examining a COMO Topology

COMO leverages the existing Office Communications Server 2007 infrastructure for its functionality. There is not a server role that is specific to COMO—it works just like Office Communicator once it has network connectivity over a wireless data or phone network.

Figure 6-12 illustrates the various ways that Office Communicator Mobile can connect to an Office Communications Server 2007 deployment. COMO clients connect to the internal server or the Access Edge Server based on the network the device is connecting from.

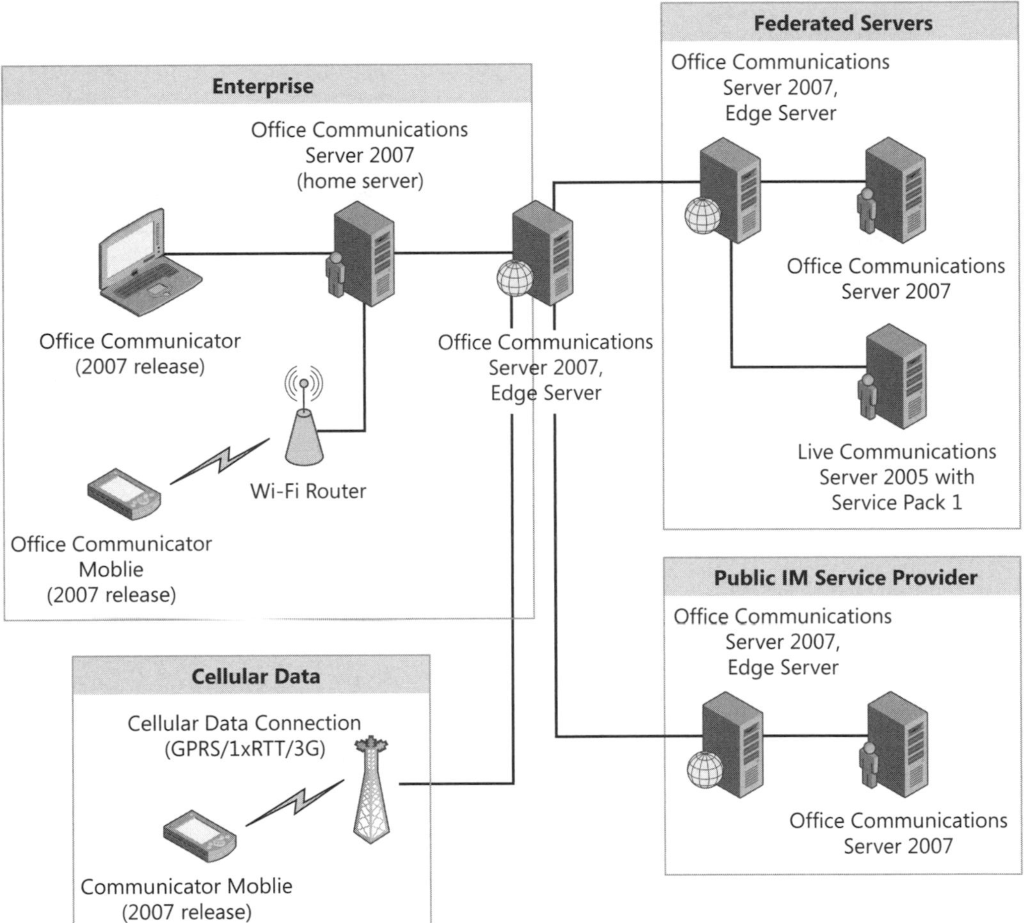

Figure 6-12 Office Communicator Mobile connectivity scenarios/topology

Deploying Certificates for COMO

Once you have decided to deploy COMO in your Office Communications Server 2007 environment, there is a client piece that needs to be installed on the end user's phone device. Specifically, the phone device needs to be able to have a certificate installed on it.

Certificates help keep your network secure by authenticating the Office Communications Server to which Office Communicator Mobile connects. To perform authentication, Office Communicator Mobile requires that the root certificate that is part of the server certificate chain be installed on the device. If your organization uses a public CA, it is likely that the root certificate is already installed on your users' mobile devices.

Figure 6-13 explains the steps that are required when deciding what type of certificate should be installed with COMO.

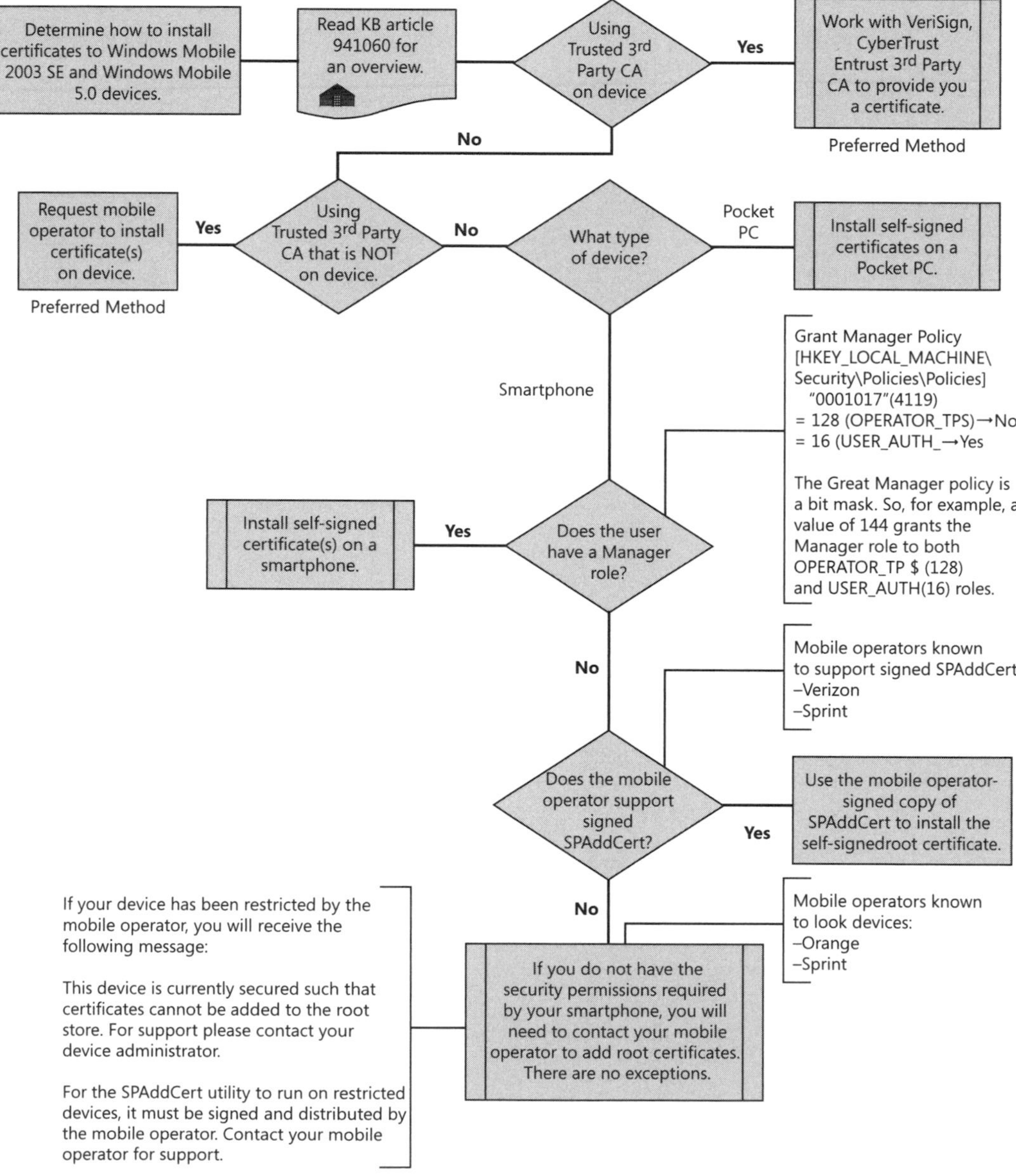

Figure 6-13 Deciding what type of certificate to install for Office Communicator Mobile

Because Office Communicator Mobile acts so much like a standard Office Communicator client, there really isn't much more to it unless problems show up. If there are problems, the easiest way to diagnose issues is to have the user log in with a standard Office Communicator client from the same network to verify that the problem is specific to Office Communicator Mobile. If there are problems, emulators can be downloaded from *http://www.microsoft.com/windowsmobile* by searching for "windows mobile emulator".

Summary

This chapter highlighted remote access and some of the topologies used in the edge network. The consolidated, single-site and the multisite topologies were all identified and briefly explained. In addition, each of the three edge server roles (Access, Web Conferencing and A/V Edge Server roles) were identified along with how they are involved in enabling conferencing and basic remote access capabilities. Finally, Office Communicator Web Access (CWA) and Office Communicator Mobile Access (COMO) were identified as extended remote access tools that provide easier access for many users.

Additional Resources

The following resources contain additional information and tools related to this chapter.

- Pocket Professional from SOTI, available at *http://www.soti.net/default.asp?Cmd=Products&SubCmd=PCPro*
- Windows Mobile Emulator, available for download at *http://www.microsoft.com/windowsmobile* by searching for "windows mobile emulator"

On the Companion CD

- Protocol logs from the Web Conferencing section are available on the CD as OCSLogger_Web_Conferencing.txt, in the \Appendixes,Scripts,Resources\Chapter 06 folder.

Chapter 7

Federation Scenario

In this chapter:

This chapter provides an overview and description of federation in Office Communications Server 2007. The chapter covers the setup and administration of servers, managing users in a Federated environment, understanding Domain Name System (DNS) servers and certificates and their importance, and understanding the technical details behind message flow in a federation.

Understanding Federation

Federation, in its most basic view, is a trust relationship between two entities. If two companies that are separate enterprises need to communicate, they might federate to allow easy access to common data.

Note This method is not the same as Active Directory Federation Services, but it serves the same purpose—that is, allowing two enterprises that do not share a common authentication base to interact with each other.

For example, a manufacturing company and a supply chain partner that sells raw goods to the manufacturing company might federate their enterprises to allow for easy collaboration and access to common applications. Access can be managed in much the same way that access is managed today, because users and groups can be populated with instant messaging (IM) contacts from either enterprise as well. The difference is that there is no common Address Book that contains all the names as the other enterprise. Similar to e-mail, you have to find and enter the name of the target person you are trying to contact into Office Communicator 2007.

In Office Communications Server 2007, the purpose for federation of IM is to enable collaboration between users. Given our example of the manufacturing and the raw materials companies, Bob (an employee of the manufacturing company) needs to confirm details with Alice (an employee of the supply company) of an upcoming contract. Both have Office Communicator, and Bob notes that Alice's presence indicates that she is Available—that is, on line. Bob initiates an IM session with Alice. They both need to review the details in the contract, and Bob initiates a Live Meeting session to share the contract and hash out the final details. Both companies have used federation to enable Bob and Alice to accomplish more and be more productive in their jobs.

A *federated user* is defined as an external user (not a member of your enterprise) who possesses valid credentials and can authenticate to his or her enterprise. Once users authenticate, they are treated very much as if they are a part of your enterprise as far as Office Communications Server 2007 services are concerned. Of course, the behavior can be managed and modified by policies and configuration settings in Office Communications Server 2007.

In this chapter, we will discuss at length and in depth the following federation topologies.

- **Direct Federation** Direct Federation refers to the one-to-one agreement, or trust, that is established between two entities that decide that they want their users to be able to communicate in a common and collaborative way, but not in a fully open and less controlled manner—over the Internet, for example.
- **Enhanced Federation** Federated Partner Discovery (the process by which Enhanced Federation is accomplished) is similar to Direct Federation, but it requires much less administrative effort to establish and maintain. If you are familiar with SRV records in DNS and have used them in Active Directory, you already have an idea as to how this will play out. Please review the section "Understanding Federated Partner Discovery" later in this chapter for more information on SRV records.
- **Federation with Public IM Providers** Federation with public IM providers (Yahoo!, MSN, AOL) will be discussed in this section. We will not go into depth on what public IM is, but we will discuss the technical elements that allow public IM federation to occur between Office Communications Server 2007 and the three public providers mentioned. If you are looking for detail on how public IM works, how to establish it, and how to administer it, you will find those topics covered in Chapter 8, "Public IM Connectivity Scenario."

We will also talk about the user and administrative scenarios and the steps that must be taken to accomplish them.

Administration of federation requires mainly the following prerequisites:

- The use of Public Certification Authority certificates for a common or mutual trust
- Enabling the user for federation

- Applying settings on Access Edge Servers to Allow the Session Initiation Protocol (SIP) domain of the partner
- The fully qualified domain name (FQDN) of the federated partner's Access Edge Server (the Edge Server resides at the perimeter of your enterprise and receives incoming / sends outgoing messages)

Understanding Direct Federation

Direct Federation implies that two enterprises are establishing an explicit trust between each other (see Figure 7-1). This trust says that the enterprises have entered into an agreement in which they will directly share contacts and presence information related to those contacts. This makes it easier for the staff within each of the enterprises to communicate and to determine when a given person is available. Presence information is reflected in applications that are *presence aware* and comply with the requirements of Office Communications Server 2007, and that a federation-enabled user has installed on their desktop. Examples of these are Office Communicator 1.0 (and newer), Microsoft Office Outlook 2003 (and newer), and Microsoft SharePoint 2003 (and newer).

The trust element is established by certificates that ensure that either partner can absolutely confirm that the other end of the established trust is who they say they are, as well as ensuring that the trusted partner domain name is entered on the Allowed tab of the Access Edge Server. We will discuss certificate types that can be used to accomplish this in the section "Understanding the Requirements for and Use of Certificates in Federation" later in this chapter. Also, the options for federation settings will be defined as well.

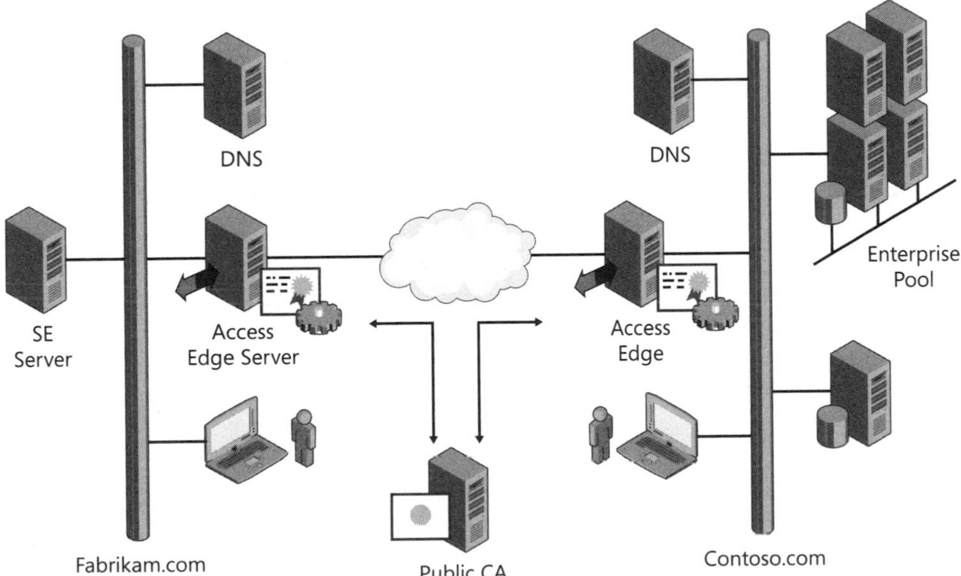

Figure 7-1 Direct Federation—Defined by the FQDN and IP to specific Office Communications Server 2007 enterprises

A Certificate and DNS Name Anomaly To Be Aware Of

The Direct Federation model has administrative overhead because it must be maintained and changes must be communicated to all peers you are federating with. However, this model allows for one name in the certificate for companies with multiple domains. The Allow tab creates a defined relationship between the domain name and SIP FQDN of the Access Edge Server responsible for the SIP conversations:

```
Contoso.com     sip.contoso.com
Contoso.au        sip.contoso.com
Nwtraders.com   sip.contoso.com
```

Why does this matter? Well, Enhanced Federation eliminates this administrative overhead, and uses DNS to determine the SIP FQDN for the requested domain. DNS is treated with tighter rules of logic because it can easily be compromised. So contoso.au for enhanced presence will require a SIP FQDN of *<host>.contoso.au*.

Let's exaggerate the example for illustrative purposes. If I query DNS for an SRV record for the contoso.au domain, I might mentally accept *<host>.contoso.com* because I know the company and it makes sense. However, when performing a comparison of my request to the result, *contoso.com* is as different to *contoso.au* as *hacker.org*. The idea is that I asked for a host that handles the contoso.au domain, and thus only a host record for that namespace will suffice, as I will expect a certificate for contoso.au also.

–Thomas Laciano
Program Manager, OCS Customer Experience

Of the three types of federation, Direct Federation has the most straightforward and simple implementation because there are very few moving parts. That being said, it is, at the same time, the most administratively intensive.

A majority of the work in a Direct Federation model takes place at the Access Edge Server. (The Access Edge Server role provides the same level of functionality as the Access Proxy from Live Communications Server, and more.) It provides a separate, distinct role for incoming communications to be received, and it is an outgoing portal for communications bound for external destinations. As with all roles in Office Communications Server 2007, certificates play an important role in establishing a level of security, trust, and confidentiality. And, as with all roles in Office Communications Server 2007, if you experience any problem with federation, suspect certificates, certificate naming, and DNS as the initial cause–then expand your search for other less relevant causes of difficulty.

A Director is a recommended, but not a mandatory, server role that sits logically between your edge servers and the pool. The role of the Director is to pre-authenticate inbound traffic destined for your internal SIP domains. It's important to differentiate *pre-authenticate* from the type of authentication you are more familiar with–ensuring that a given user's principal and password match that of a known value.

In the case of the Director process, pre-authentication determines whether the SIP domain and/or the user is known to the Director. Using the example shown in Figure 7-1, users in the Contoso.com domain can be pre-authenticated by the Director, but users of Fabrikam.com cannot. Simply, there is a one-way replication from Active Directory to the Director and with only mandatory attributes necessary to pre-authenticate. The Director at this point is authenticating only that the Fabrikam domain is allowed and that the users are recognized and belong to the Fabrikam domain–nothing more. The role of the internal servers is a minor part in federation. The servers, and the way that they operate and support users, still play their roles, but those roles are no different than they would be if the federation did not exist. So they will not be dealt with in this section.

It should be noted that Direct Federation becomes administratively more complex as additional partners are added. The administrative work to manage up to 10 partners can be reasonable, defining the access edges servers and managing certificates for each partner. However, managing much more than this becomes difficult and potentially error prone. And the errors might result in one or both of the following issues:

- Users will not be able to connect with partner users.
- Security problems and issues might arise because of poor configuration.

You can also enable discovery of federation partners and add federated partners to the Allow list. Adding specific partners to the Allow list gives them a higher level of trust. Your Access Edge Server can still discover federated partners other than the ones listed on the Allow list, but specific rules are applied to those partners *not* on the Allow list. Those rules are discussed in the upcoming "Administering Federated Partner Access" section.

Adding a Trusted Federated Partner Domain

To add a trusted federated partner domain and optionally the FQDN of its Access Edge Server, do the following.

1. Log on to the Access Edge Server as a member of the Administrators group or a group with equivalent user rights.
2. Open Computer Management. Click Start, click All Programs, click Administrative Tools, and then click Computer Management.
3. On the Allow tab, click Add.

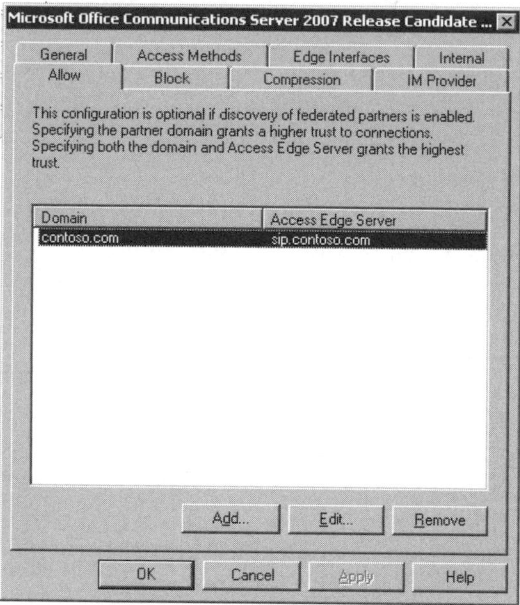

4. In the Add Federated Partner dialog box, do the following:
   - ❑ In the Federated Partner Domain Name box, type the domain of each federated partner domain.

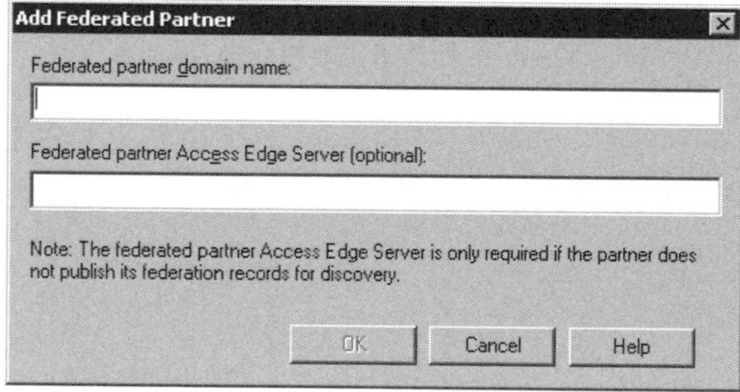

   - ❑ In the Federated Partner Access Edge Server box, optionally type the FQDN of each Access Edge Server that you want to add to your Allow list. Remember if you configure the FQDN of a partner's Access Edge Server and the FQDN changes, you must manually update your configuration for this partner.
   - ❑ Click OK.

Repeat this procedure for each federated partner you want to add to your Allow list, and then click OK.

Understanding Federated Partner Discovery

SRV records play a very important role in Federated Partner Discovery. Compared to Direct Federation, where the path and IP address or fully qualified domain name of the destination federated partner is defined, the Access Edge Server parses the DNS server for any existing SRV records that define potential federated locations (see Figure 7-2).

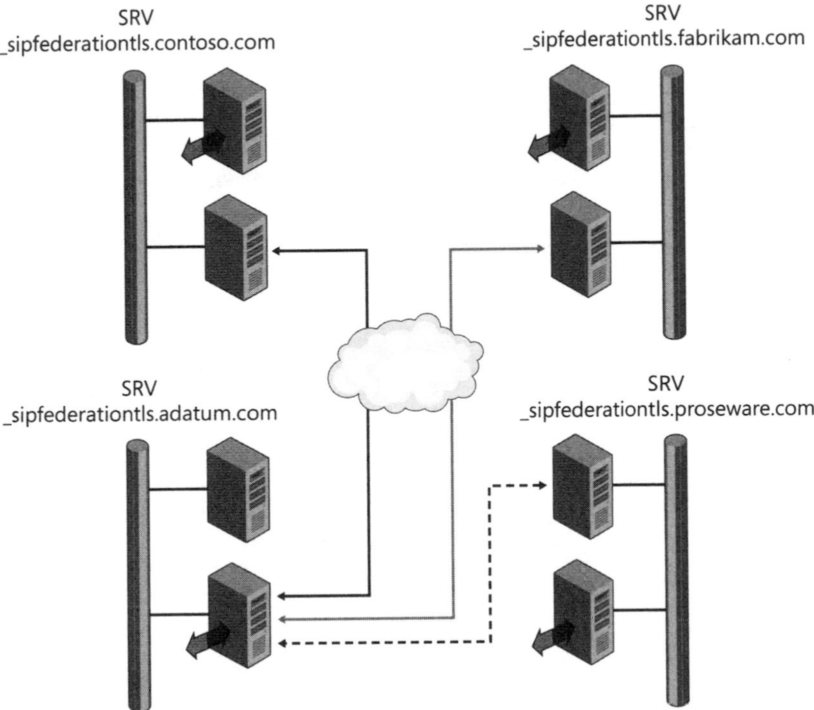

Figure 7-2 Federated Partner Discovery—Access Edge Server queries DNS for SRV records

SRV records are a special type of DNS record that define a service that a server offers. The SRV record defines the name of the server, the protocol, and a port that can be used. For those of you who are familiar with Active Directory, you might recall that SRV records are used to define what domain controllers offer to LDAP, Kerberos, Global Catalog, and so on. In our case, the SRV records define what servers are available to offer federated services. The format of the record is as follows:

```
Service :  _sipfederationtls
Protocol:  _tcp
Priority:  <variable>
Weight:  <variable>
Port:  5061
Target:  access.fabrikam.com
```

Note SRV records are defined by the Internet Engineering Task Force (IETF) Request for Comment (RFC) Document 2782, which you can access at *http://www.ietf.org/rfc/rfc2782.txt*.

There is also an A, or Host, record that ties the SRV record's entry for Host Offering This Service to the actual Access Edge Server–in this case, access.fabrikam.com (see Figure 7-3). Recall that this is the external interface of the edge server, which should have two interfaces. One interface is for the internal communication, and the other is for the perimeter communication.

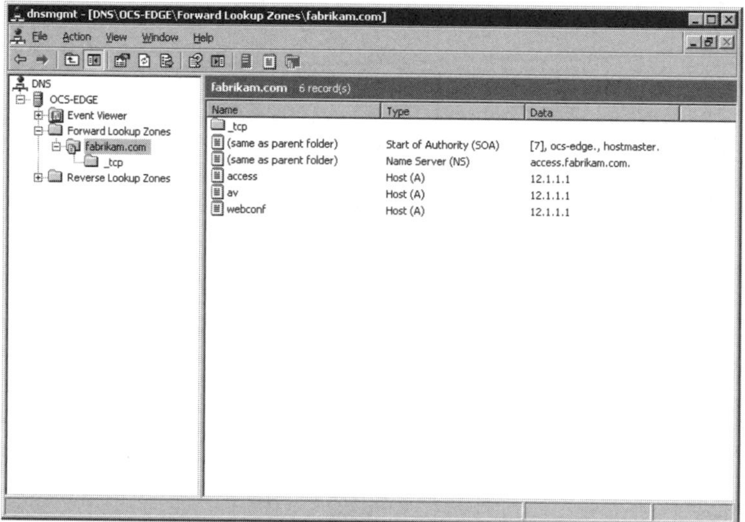

Figure 7-3 DNS SRV records—The A records pointed to by SRV records define names for Office Communications Server 2007 services

The key point in this section is that if we ask DNS for SRV records, it returns records to us that can provide the services of Office Communications Server 2007 federation. This is a very critical step–knowing which servers can provide the necessary services to establish a federated partnership. Once there is clarity as to what is going on with one server, we can then bring in the concept that when an Access Edge Server is configured to look and do a search for other potential federated partners, DNS does most of the work.

The Access Edge Server asks for all the SRV records meeting our federation SRV record criteria, and the DNS server complies with a list of A records for other edge servers that advertise the federation SIP service (see Figure 7-4). It's up to the Access Edge Servers to negotiate a partnership, which we will discuss shortly. The final setup involves heavy use of certificates, allow and deny settings, and DNS configuration. Any of these can complicate the process of troubleshooting, and creating documentation as you go is highly recommended.

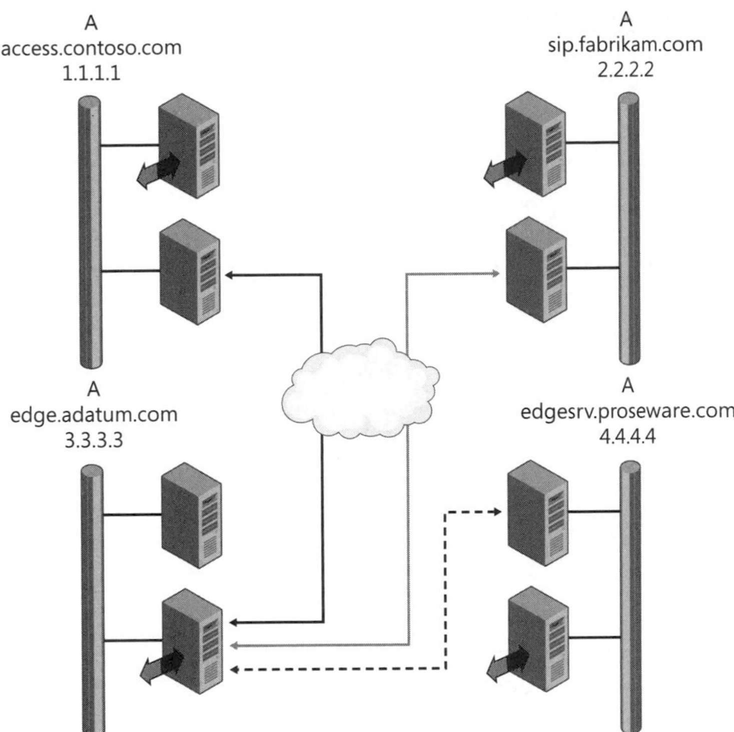

Figure 7-4 Access Edge Server—Finds other Office Communications Server 2007–capable servers through a query to DNS and A record resolution

Note that there are three ways in which Federated Partner Discovery is evaluated and controlled:

- Allow automatic discovery of all federated partners.
- Allow discovery of partners, but assign trust levels via the Allow tab entry.
- Do not allow partner discovery; instead, allow access only to partners or edge servers specifically defined. (This is the method synonymous with Direct Federation.)

To enable discovery of federated partners, do the following:

1. Log on to the Access Edge Server as a member of the Administrators group or a group with equivalent user rights.
2. Open Computer Management. Click Start, click All Programs, click Administrative Tools, and then click Computer Management.
3. In the console tree, expand Services And Applications, right-click Microsoft Office Communications Server 2007, and then click Properties.
4. On the Access Methods tab, select the Allow Discovery Of Federated Partners check box, as shown in the following screen shot:

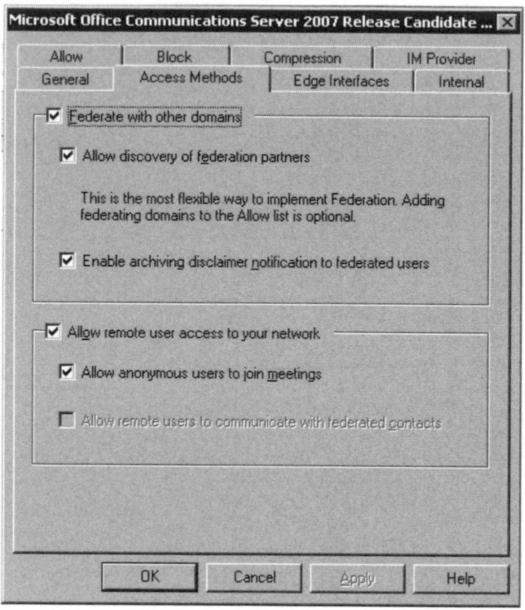

Real World: How Federated Traffic Is Evaluated When Using Automatic Discovery

If you choose to use automatic discovery of federated partners, the Access Edge Server automatically evaluates incoming federated traffic in the following way: If a federated party has sent requests to more than 1000 URIs (valid or invalid) in the local domain, the connection is first placed on the Watch list. Any additional requests are then blocked by the Access Edge Server. If the Access Edge Server detects suspicious traffic on a connection, it limits the federation partner to a low message rate of 1 message per second. The Access Edge Server detects suspicious traffic by calculating the ratio of *#successful* to *#failed* responses.

The Access Edge Server also limits legitimate federated partner connections (unless added to the Allow list) to 20 messages per second. If you know that you will have more than specific 1000 URI requests sent by a legitimate federated partner or a volume of over 20 messages per second sent to your organization, to allow these volumes, you must add the federated partner to the Allow tab. After configuring federation, you can use Office Communications Server 2007 administrative tools to monitor and manage federated partner access on an ongoing basis. For more information, see the Microsoft Office Communications Server 2007 Administration Guide.

–Byron Spurlock
Microsoft Consultant, Microsoft Consulting Services

Understanding Federation with Public IM Providers

Establishing an instant messaging relationship with another enterprise might sound familiar. If you have used the MSN, AOL, or Yahoo! IM client, you've done just this. Office Communications Server 2007 allows establishing what would be seen as a federation between your enterprise environment and one, two, or all three of these IM providers.

Chapter 8 deals specifically with the process and technology of how Office Communications Server 2007 allows you to do this. This chapter won't spend any more time on public IM specifically, but it is important to understand that this chapter is the foundation of how the relationship with public IM providers is established.

Real World: The Three A's of Security

In security practice, three A's define most–if not all–best practices and policy guidance. Those three terms are as follows:

- Authorization
- Authentication
- Auditing (or Accounting)

Let's talk about each of these briefly, as they are rather important in federation, where we are opening ourselves up to a trusted connection where we *think* we know who is connecting to us. But how do we *really* know? That's where the three A's come in.

Authorization

Authorization speaks to the principle that you have been given permissions to access a resource or a place. In networking terms, we can look at file and folder access, which is controlled by Discretionary Access Control Lists (DACLs). These DACLs (or ACLs for short) define *who* can access *what* and what they can do with it. So I might allow you to read only a specific Microsoft Office Word document, but give you Full Control to your Home Directory. Notice that there is no password prompting and no checks (that you know of!) to determine if you are who you say are.

Authentication

When someone attempts to access a system with security controls, it is vital to know who is making the attempt. Modern network servers do this by some type of challenge/response authentication. There are many types of authentication mechanisms, but the most common is the username/password pair. An administrator defines your user account in the system, and you log on using the new username/password pair that you were given. You've now been authenticated, and authorization is then applied to your user object on resources. However, a username/password pair is not the only way to confirm something or someone's identity. We can do it with certificates, which typically use smart cards as the method to carry the certificate, a key fob with a challenge determined by a seed server, or other means to prove you are the person you say you are.

Auditing/Accounting

Auditing/accounting is the last part of the three A's of security. Auditing and accounting are the functions of recording what someone or something does while on the system. Things recorded are file, folder access, application launch, logon, and logoff activity. Typically, on a Windows server we find these events in the Security event log, but only after what we want to have audited is enabled and configured though the Properties/Security tab of the object to be audited. Very little auditing is done that is related specifically to federation. That's not to say that the individual servers can't have auditing enabled!

We'll refer back to these topics as we talk more about how federation works, how we know who is accessing our system, and what restrictions might be imposed on us (or what restrictions we want to impose on others).

–Rick Kingslan
Consultant, Microsoft Consulting Services

Understanding the Requirements for and Use of Certificates in Federation

Certificates are the mechanism that is relied on very heavily to provide authentication in federation–and in all of Office Communications Server 2007. If you have read the initial chapters on the setup and deployment of Office Communications Server, you already know that a lot of certificates are used in the server communication paths. This is not by accident–defense in depth requires that the servers re-affirm that the incoming or outgoing traffic is from trusted sources. Servers have difficulty responding to challenge/response authentication methods, similar to what is presented to a user logging on. Passwords can be compromised, as the typical password is used over and over, from service account to service account. Finally, requirements for secure communication demand strong authentication of the server and encryption of the traffic from client to client so that it is not sent in clear text and easily captured by a man in the middle attack. Though there are other security methods that could be implemented, certificates seem to be well suited for the purpose.

Understanding Subject Alternate Name

There are a multitude of certificate types. There are simple S/MIME certificates for signing and encrypting e-mail. Then there are very complex certificate types that are designed for a specific purpose. These certificates typically have a custom template designed for them that define exactly the fields, the key types and length (the longer the key, the harder to break the encryption), and the method of the hash or signing algorithm. Templates also define whether the certificate will carry and be able to present more than one Subject Name, known also as a *Subject Alternate Name*.

Subject Alternative Name (SAN) is not a feature that is new to Office Communications Server 2007, but it is used quite a bit more in this version. You're strongly encouraged to use the SAN to identify other names that the target server might be known by. It's important to fully understand what this means. A server might have many names that it is known by–for example, edge.contoso.com, access.contoso.com, sip.contoso.com, accessedge, and internaledge. The only way that the conversation between a client and server can be initiated is if the client asks to speak to a name that the server is known by. The client then presents the certificate that is associated with that name (if one exists). As a day-to-day example of what this means, consider the documents we use to identify ourselves. A driver's license or a passport identifies you, but only by a single name. If asked for a driver's license, Bob is identified as Robert on the legal document that he presents. He answers to "Robert," but he is also known as "Bob." Relating this scenario to a certificate with a SAN, the Subject Name (SN) is Robert and there is a SAN entry for Bob.

For our servers that aid in the identification and authentication process, DNS is the typical means to determine what name a server goes by. Common use of A records and PTR (pointer) records provide the most often used DNS functions–forward lookup (A record) and reverse lookup (PTR record). Of course, DNS does not have to be involved at all. If a server is isolated, a HOSTS file is the best choice for providing the name-to-IP-address resolution, and it provides the necessary resolution for certificate SN or SAN lookup. It is possible to have a disconnect between what a server is known by internally and what it is known by in the perimeter. In this case, a HOSTS file can assist in resolving the name conflict, which otherwise might invalidate a certificate.

With certificates, therefore, the most important thing is to plan and define what the names of the servers will be. All people involved in defining the server names should agree, including the network engineers, name resolution management (DNS), and the server build team. Start with an architectural session to design the environment, which will help avoid most misunderstandings. Defining the server environment, communication paths, name resolution, and certificate standards in the planning session before implementation starts–and documenting your decisions in Microsoft Office Visio for mass communication–should be considered mandatory.

> **Tip** If after putting your plan in place, your IM servers don't talk, it's likely to be a DNS/certificate naming conflict or mismatch. Of course, you want to check the obvious, too. Ensure that all switch ports are on and configured correctly. Check the server services for proper state of operation. Recheck your IP configuration. It happens frequently that the obvious is overlooked because so much emphasis is put on certificates and naming—simply because it's newer and therefore less understood.

To illustrate why SAN is important, consider the following: you want to name a given interface two different things based on what it will be used for by distinct groups. "Sip.contoso.com" is a good name for the external interface, but then, so is "access.contoso.com." "sip.contoso.com" is where I want internally known users to connect. "access.contoso.com" is good for my federation interface, and anything else external that wants to connect to my Access Edge Server. It simply defines purpose. And I need only one certificate to do this using the SAN field in conjunction with the Subject Name field. Also, migrations and acquisitions can be eased if the name of the service point changes as little as possible.

From the preceding example, it is evident that creating multiple names for a certificate can often be a good idea. For example, when you have a farm of servers sitting behind a load balancer with a Virtual IP (VIP), the VIP will have a unique name, and it will address each server behind it. And each server behind that load balancer might have a certificate. Each server in a farm of this type might have a copy of the certificate from the first server in the farm. But each of these servers has a unique name as well, not just the name associated with the load balancer. It is possible that you would need to refer to a server as an individual server if the load balancer fails. This is a more likely scenario on the internal network rather than external network, but it is possible nonetheless.

Understanding TLS Certificates

The specific type of certificate that Office Communications Server requires is a Transport Layer Security (TLS) certificate. This is primarily a Web Server Secure Sockets Layer (SSL) certificate, with some differences. (By and large, SSL is being replaced with TLS because it's more flexible and provides much more robust security potential. This seems to be a natural transition, as the TLS 1.0 specification is based on the SSL 3.0 specification.) Certificates of this type are of the public/private key type and require infrastructure to manage them. The subject is too broad to cover in detail here, but a public key infrastructure (PKI) or public certificates will be required. Public Certificate Authorities (CAs) that provide these types of certificates are VeriSign, Thawte, and so on. An alternative to using public certificates is to deploy your own internal PKI by using Windows Server 2003 Certificate Services.

Even if you deploy your own PKI, however, you will require at least some public certificates because federation requires public CA certificates for its external edge. The technology and process in use is related to the discussion on trust. One way that you can decide to trust someone is to have a disinterested third party vouch for them. In this case, you (Contoso) get a certificate from a public CA. You need to set up federation with Fabrikam. They get a public CA certificate. Both parties install the public CA certificates, and the high-level conversation between the two edge servers begins with a confirmation of authenticity and trust. Each of the servers attempts to authenticate the other server's certificate and the information on it. Contoso's certificate says "Contoso.com". How does Fabrikam know that this is true? Fabrikam refers to the authority (the public CA) that issued the certificate because "Contoso.com" is on the certificate as well.

When a certificate is issued, the issuing CA signs the certificate. If another entity needs to know if the certificate was *really* issued by the CA, all that this server needs to do is to retrieve the CA's public key (and verify the signature with the public key). Public/private key pairs are made in such a manner that there is (realistically) only one possible public key for a given private key. And the public CA "signed" (actually, used a small digest hash) the certificate with its private key. And what is the only key that can "read" the signature? The public CA's public key. Once the server has confirmed that this certificate of authenticity was actually issued by the public CA, it's safe to assume that the holder is who they say they are. It's worth mentioning at this point that one further verification is to check certificate revocation lists (CRL) at the CA–just to ensure that the certificate we are verifying has not been revoked for reasons of theft, misuse, fraud, and so on. This process continues–simultaneously–for both servers.

Once the process is done, each server has confirmed who the other is. They now can start talking and federating. However, we still need to provide encryption. TLS is a public/private key technology. But because the keys are so large, it's a waste of CPU power (because encryption is all very complex math) to use the public/private key pair–except to exchange session keys.

Session keys are a specific type of key that the two servers exchange to encrypt/decrypt the traffic between them. One server–Fabrikam for this example–creates a session key, encrypts it with the public key of the intended partner, and then sends it on. Key exchange is complete–and this was 100-percent safe, as the only entity that can open a package that was encrypted with Contoso's public key would be Contoso (the only server that would have the private key).

Real World: Session Keys, Private Keys, and Public Keys

Public/private key encryption is a mathematically intensive algorithm. The numbers used to generate the certificates are derived from a method known as the *Diffie-Hellman key exchange* (named after the inventors of the method). It's an interesting process because it allows two people who do not know or have any reason to trust each other to exchange information and establish trust by the very process. The process of exchanging the keys is blind, and the two participants never have to meet. Diffie-Hellman is known as *asymmetric key cryptography* because the keys held by the subjects involved are not the same. However, because of the intensity of the math involved (involving a lot of very big prime numbers, and the multiplication and division of those numbers) Diffie-Hellman is not practical for encrypting data directly.

But what if we take a very efficient method–known as *symmetric key cryptography* (wherein keys held by the subjects are the same)–and use it? There is one problem with symmetric keys–both individuals involved have the same key, which implies that they know or trust each other. With cryptography, the concept of trust is necessary, and this is where Diffie-Hellman comes in. Bob and Alice were introduced earlier in this chapter. Bob and Alice want to trade information securely, but they don't know each other and have no way to get a symmetric key back and forth securely. If there is one compromise of the symmetric key, all their information is compromised. But if Bob and Alice *each* get a public/private key pair, they can do something very special.

> Let's assume that Bob and Alice have both received key pairs from a public CA. Bob keeps his private key to himself (that's why it's called "private") and sends Alice his public key. She reciprocates and sends Bob her public key. They can do this by e-mail, FTP, courier, carrier pigeon–it really doesn't matter. Now that they have exchanged their public keys, we're ready to do the special part. Bob creates a *session key*. A session key is a symmetric key that has a limited lifetime. In some cases, it is thrown away after every exchange. In other cases, it might persist for much, much longer. But how do you get the session key to Alice so that they can have a much more vibrant conversation?
>
> Bob takes a copy of the session key and encrypts it with Alice's public key. (A cryptographic *envelope* is put around the key, but we're not going to this level of detail.) He then sends the encrypted session key to Alice. Once she receives it, she takes her private key and decrypts the session key. (The magic here is that the *only* key that decrypts something encrypted with someone's *public* key is their *private* key. The sheer complexity virtually guarantees that there is no possibility of key collision.)
>
> Bob and Alice can now have a very pleasant, fast, and efficient private discussion. But where is this in our instant messaging, conferencing application known as Office Communications Server 2007?
>
> It's all in the certificates. They are derived from a public/private key pair. You keep your private key private and make your public key available to literally anyone. And the session key is created by the very processes responsible for managing TLS. The authentication between the servers? DNS and the names on the certificate or certificates presented confirm that you are who you say you are.
>
> *–Rick Kingslan*
> *Consultant, Microsoft Consulting Services*

Comparing Consolidated Topology to Expanded Topology

Access Edge Servers can be set up in a consolidated topology or an expanded topology. The real difference between the two is that the services of Access Edge Servers, Web components, and audio/visual (A/V) components all exist on one server that shares all these roles. In an expanded topology, there are three potential configurations:

- Single-Site Edge Server
  - Access Edge Server and Web Conferencing Server roles are on one server.
  - The Audio/Video Conferencing Server role is on another, separate server.
- Scaled Single-Site Edge Server

- Two or more collocated and load-balanced Access Edge Servers and Web Conferencing Servers are placed.
- Two or more load-balanced Audio/Video Conferencing Servers are placed.

- Multiple-Site Edge Server
  - Two or more Access Edge Servers and Web Conferencing Servers are load balanced and collocated at the primary data center.
  - Two or more Audio/Video Conferencing Server load-balanced servers are collocated at the primary data center.

And, at remote larger locations or secondary data centers, here are the possible configurations:

- Single server with the Web Conferencing Server role, or two or more load-balanced Web Conferencing Servers
- Single server with the Audio/Video Conferencing Server role, or two or more load-balanced Audio/Video Conferencing Servers

What this means in federation is that you have only one set of servers to deal with–one load-balanced array rather than a set of servers for each role.

However, make sure you understand that you can locate Conferencing Web servers and Audio/Video Conferencing servers wherever you want–in the same data center locally or dispersed to different locations to be located with other pools closer to users. But you can have only one farm of Access Edge Servers, at your primary site.

To enable federation in an enterprise, do the following:

1. Go to Global Policy properties.
2. Access the Federation tab.
3. Select the Enable Federation And Public IM Connectivity check box.
4. Specify the FQDN of the next-hop server (Director, load balancer, or Access Edge Server).

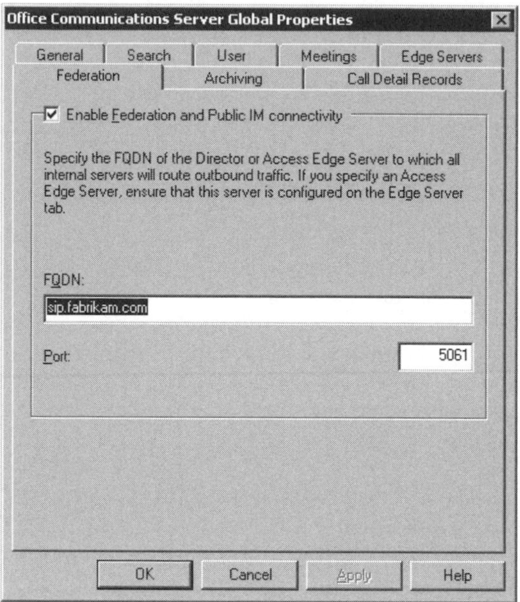

Note The settings just mentioned can be overridden in specific areas of your enterprise. Say, for example, your portion of the enterprise needs to go directly to the Access Edge Server instead of the Director defined in the Global properties. You can redefine this on the Federation tab by entering the correct FQDN.

Why define a global property? As with many settings, the exception is much easier to deal with than defining the multitude of options separately. This configuration affects all default routes for all pools. If we need an exception, it can be defined locally.

Understanding On-Premises Conferencing Rules for Federated and Nonfederated Users

There is more to federation than just allowing our two partner enterprises to exchange instant messages. There are also the conferencing services that allow the two partners to host a meeting on one or the other's infrastructure and allow them to present content such as Microsoft PowerPoint presentations. Externally, this is the LiveMeeting service that Microsoft hosts for customers. There is the ability to host audio/video, such as real-time discussions using microphones, Web cams, or the new Microsoft RoundTable device.

For meetings of this type, there is an allowance made for anonymous users. Each must have a conference invite (made up of a URL/URI with session information, location information, and an invite key) to successfully join the conference.

Although the requirements for federated users with verifiable credentials are not too different, they do have the following characteristics:

- Can attend Open Authenticated meetings
- Can be promoted to the role of Presenter in Open Authenticated meetings
- Cannot participate in Closed Authenticated meetings

Verifiable credentials means that you are an authenticated member of the domain in which the meeting is hosted, or you are an authenticated member of a partner domain. The fact that you must be authenticated to your home domain prevents you from being an authenticated member from a non-domain location (such as a kiosk or another computer not in your company domain).

Configuring and Administering Federation

This section covers how to configure edge servers and user accounts for federation and how to manage federated partner access in an Office Communications Server 2007 environment. We'll also look briefly at how to manage multiple accounts and how to block external domains.

Configuring an Edge Server for Federation

Once the edge servers are set up in the environment, your next step is to configure your organization for federation. The assumption to this point is the edge servers are functioning within the organization and remote access is working. To reach the conclusion that this is happening, you must verify that remote users can contact the edge servers and edge servers can contact the internal Office Communications Server 2007 servers.

Federation provides the organization with the ability to communicate with other organizations' Access Edge Server to share IM and presence. You can also federate and control federation with an audio conferencing provider by using either of the following methods. The process of configuring federation with an organization or an audio conferencing provider is identical.

- **Allow automatic discovery of federated partners** This is the default option during initial configuration of an Access Edge Server because it balances security with ease of configuration and management. For example, when you enable automatic discovery of federated partners on your Access Edge Server, Office Communications Server 2007 automatically evaluates incoming traffic from federation partners and limits or blocks that traffic based on trust level, amount of traffic, and administrator settings.
- **Allow discovery of federated partners** Grant a higher level of trust to specific domains or Access Edge Servers that you specify on the Allow list. For example, if you want to grant a higher level of trust to partners using the SIP domain contoso.com and fabrikam.com, you add these two domains on the Allow tab. Restricting discovery in this way establishes a higher level of trust for connections with the domains or Access Edge Servers that you add to your Allow list, but it still provides the ease of management that is possible by discovering other federation partners that are not listed on the Allow tab.

- **Do not allow discovery of federation partners** Limit access of federated partners to only the domains or Access Edge Servers for which you want to enable connections. Connections with federated partners are then allowed only with the specific domains or Access Edge Servers you add to the Allow tab. This method offers the highest level of security, but it does not offer ease of management. For example, if an FQDN of an Access Edge Server changes, you must manually change the FQDN of the server in the Allow list.

Configuring User Accounts for Federation

You can explicitly manage the user by overriding the Global Settings (in the Office Communications Server snap-in at the Forest node level) or you can manage users as individuals. To configure a user object for federation, the following procedure should be used:

1. Open the Office Communications Server 2007 management console.
2. Expand to pools (Enterprise or Standard).
3. Expand Users, and locate the user.
4. Right-click, select properties, and click the Configure button.
5. Enable federation by selecting the Enable Federation check box.

Administering Federated Partner Access

If you have configured support for federated partners, including an ACP that is providing telephony integration, it is required that you actively manage the lists of external domains that can communicate with the servers in your organization.

The administrator can view a list of the federated domains that have most recently made at least one connection to your Access Edge Server. This list is not all-inclusive, and if numerous domains are hitting your Access Edge Servers, domains that haven't been seen in a while will roll off. To best use this feature, it is highly recommended that DNS-based discovery (via the SRV records) of Access Edge Servers be implemented as the federation configuration method of choice. You can also use Federated Partner Discovery in conjunction with the Allow tab to control domains you specifically will accept; all others will be dropped. (Note the stipulations discussed next that further clarify the rules.) For increased security, explicitly specify the FQDN of a federated partner's Access Edge Server.

When a domain is configured in the Allow list, communications with this domain are assumed to be legitimate. The Access Edge Server does not throttle connections for these domains. In case of DNS-based discovery of federated domains that are not on the Allow tab, connections are not fully trusted and Access Edge Server actively monitors these connections and limits the allowed throughput.

The Access Edge Server marks a connection for monitoring in one of two situations:

- **Suspicious traffic is detected on the connection.** To detect suspicious activity, the server monitors the percentage of specific types of error messages on the connection. A high percentage can indicate attempted requests to invalid users, such as a SPIM (SPAM attack over Instant Messaging) attack. In this case, the connection is placed on a watch list, and the administrator can then take action to explicitly block the offending domain. Also, this type of traffic is throttled to one message per second, as it is much less predictable (in terms of which domain is sending it). Partners are also limited to 20 messages per second unless they are added to the Allow list.
- **Federated party has sent requests to more than 1000 URIs.** When this many URIs are received, they could be valid or invalid, as the sheer volume could be an indication of potential attacks. Again, the domain is placed on a Watch list. Additional requests within a specific time period cause the offending domain to be blocked at the Access Edge Server.

  Two situations may cause the limit of 1000 URIs to be met–one problematic, one probable and expected:

  - **Problematic** The remote party is attempting a directory attack on the local domains.

    If the traffic from this partner is deemed to be legitimate, the sending domain must be added to the Allow tab, as the Access Edge Server has already blocked further connections.
  - **Probable and expected** Valid traffic between the local and federated domains exceeds the limit of 1000 URIs.

  Further traffic from this domain will be dropped. If an administrator knows that the message rate from a given domain will exceed the 1000 URI limit, the sending domain should be added to the Allow list; otherwise, messages beyond the 1000-URI limit will not be accepted.

The information that the Access Edge Server acts on can be viewed administratively in the Office Communications Server 2007 Microsoft Management Console (MMC) on the Access Edge Server. Selecting the Open Federation tab reveals information on Allowed and Open Federated partners (see Figure 7-5).

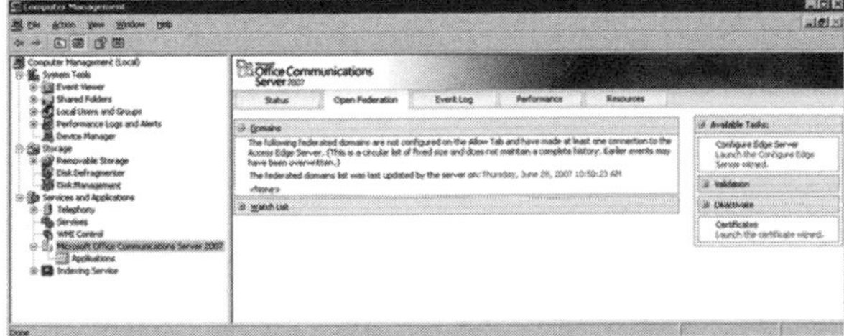

Figure 7-5 Open Federation tab—Usage for federated domains can be viewed and monitored on the Access Edge Server

Managing Multiple User Accounts

It is also possible to manage a large number of accounts as follows:

1. Open Active Directory Users and Computers (ADUC).
2. Select an organizational unit, group, or collection of users.
3. Right-click, and then select Configure Communications Server Users.
4. Select Next on the first page of the Wizard.
5. On the Configure User Settings page, select Federation. Click Next.

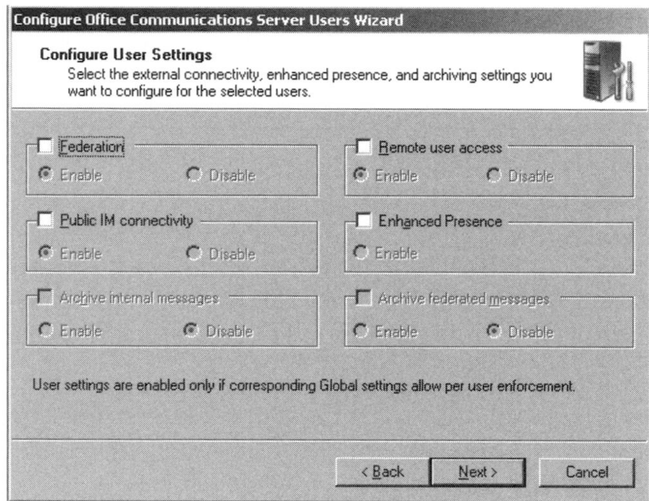

Anonymous (non-authenticated) users are a reality that needs to be considered in an environment where you are accommodating users from domains that there might be a casual relationship with. Whether you will allow anonymous users into your environment, then access to Live Meetings or Audio/Video conferences is a decision that you will need to make. The very concept of anonymous users is unsettling to some administrators and IT security staff, but Office Communications Server 2007 handles the situation with a number of safeguards.

First, users are not completely anonymous. You have to send them an invite for them to access the conference or meeting. Second, they are accessing the edge servers, not your internal environment. In essence, this is little different than allowing a user to access your Web server, except these services are using streaming protocols instead of HTTP. The selections possible for who and how anonymous users can be invited are determined by administrative control, too.

Global properties allow you to set a policy that defines whether the Anonymous User settings are global or per user. Access the global properties by opening the Office Communications Server 2007 management console and right-clicking the Forest node. As shown in Figure 7-6, a fly-out menu allows you to select Properties and then Global Properties.

Figure 7-6 Global Properties—Access to set properties that will be applied to the entire forest

At this point, you are presented with a number of tabs in a dialog box. Select the Meetings tab. (See Figure 7-7.) You have three settings to select from:

- **Allow users to invite anonymous participants** This option allows your users to invite users who are not members of your domain to attend anonymous meetings. Your users will be able to schedule and send invites on behalf of nonmembers, and they can create ad-hoc meetings. Of course, some of the abilities and settings are dependent on the Office Communicator 2.0 client, and this can be controlled administratively as well. Just because users have the ability to send invites does not necessarily mean that they are allowed to.
- **Disallow users from inviting anonymous participants** This option prevents users from inviting users who are not members of your domain (that is, who do not have authentication credentials to your domain–and this includes federated users) to meetings.
- **Enforce per user** This option leaves the administrative capacity to setting if a user can allow an anonymous user at a per-user basis. Though it might seem overly intensive, you can set this option if you intend to grant this ability to only a few people. For example, you can grant this ability to administrative assistants who are responsible for setting up meetings and are generally accountable for sending out external meeting notices–whether they are notices for meetings in your department or notices that the CEO is holding a shareholders' meeting.

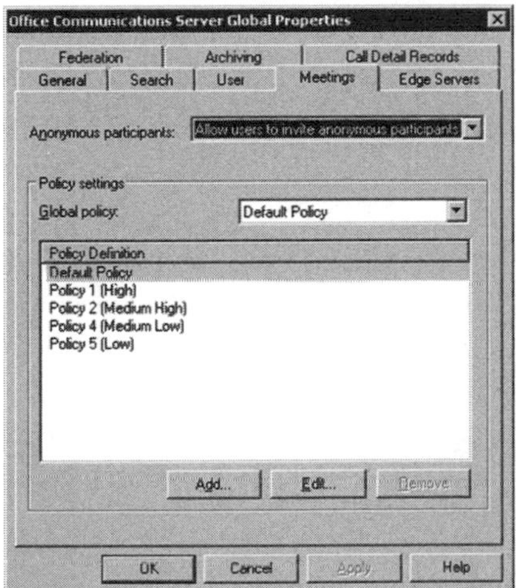

Figure 7-7 User object—Properties of a user in the Office Communications Server 2007 management console

To re-emphasize: Anonymous access still requires specific meeting keys, a URL/URI, and other identifying elements. Anonymous users are anonymous *only* because they do not have authentication credentials for your domain.

Blocking External Domains

Sometimes, because of continued unsolicited instant messages (also known as SPIM) or attempts to compromise security, it's necessary to explicitly block a specific domain. This is accomplished much like an Allow. We use the same beginning dialog box, but we choose the Block tab instead of the Allow tab, as follows:

1. Log on to the Access Edge Server as a member of the Administrators group or a group with equivalent user rights.
2. On an Access Edge Server, open Computer Management.
3. In the console tree, expand Services And Applications, right-click Office Communications Server 2007, and then click Properties.
4. On the Block tab, click Add.
5. In the Add Blocked SIP Domains dialog box, in the SIP Domain box, type the name of the domain to be added to the list of blocked SIP domains. This name should be unique and should not already exist in the Block list for this Access Edge Server. The name cannot exceed 256 characters in length. Click OK.

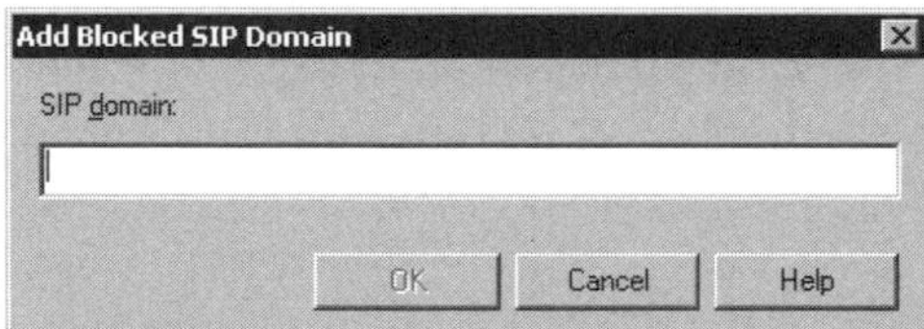

Examining the Technical Details Behind the Federation Scenario

A discussion of how federation is accomplished isn't really complete unless there is an in-depth look at the flow of messages and the protocols that accomplish it. So we're going to look at Session Initiation Protocol (SIP) in federation. Because SIP has been discussed at length in other chapters of this book, we won't spend a lot of time on the nuts and bolts of the protocol. But where necessary, we will re-emphasize some attributes that have been covered elsewhere.

Examining How Clients from Two Federated Domains Get Online and Register Presence

First, note that SIP is a signaling protocol–it uses verbs, or methods, much like SMTP does to talk to server processes. And many of the methods are very clear as to what they are doing when presented to the server process.

The scenario we will examine is one where two federated domains each have a user that wants to use IM with the other user. The domains we will use are Contoso.com and Fabrikam.com. Our users, Kim Akers (kakers@contoso.com) and John Peoples (jpeoples@fabrikam.com) communicate frequently by Office Communicator. They really don't know how the communication occurs, as they need to enter only each other's SIP contact address in Communicator. So it can be seen that to connect with a user in a federated enterprise, you need to have the Access Edge Servers configured correctly to speak to the other enterprise's Access Edge Server. Also, there is no address book service between two federated enterprises, so–again, like SMTP–you need to know what the contact information is for the other person.

John Peoples has entered kakers@contoso.com into his Communicator client, and Kim Akers has entered jpeoples@fabrikam.com into hers. John and Kim are now ready to initiate their communication, but a lot goes on behind the scenes–and this is what we are going to follow. (See Figure 7-8.)

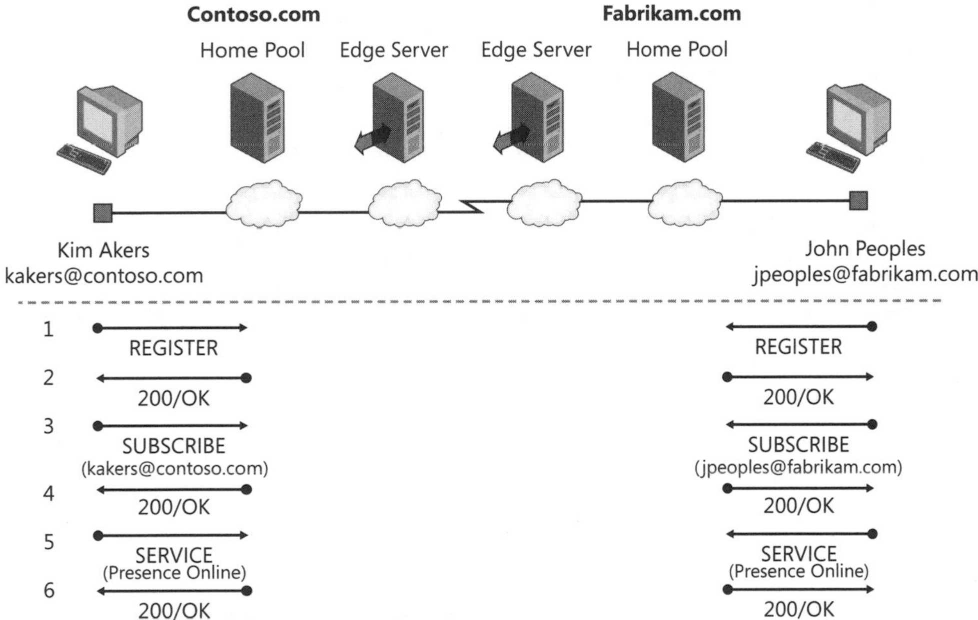

Figure 7-8 Client-to-home server conversation

What you see if you use logging from the pool server (decoded by the snooper.exe tool in the Office Communications Server 2007 Resource Kit tools) and the Access Edge Server is a lot more chatter than the required message elements. A lot of DIAGNOTIC messages and other housekeeping messages ensure that the flow is correct and that the messages are arriving properly. Also, the continued communication between the pool server and the edge server has nothing to do with the maintenance of the communication for Kim and John.

> **Note** The following discussion tracks the most important steps and is not a full step-by-step look at each and every message. Therefore, the following list of steps will skip numbers. The missing steps are typically OK or DIAGNOSTIC messages that don't provide anything more than a simple, "I heard you." Also, to avoid redundancy, the analysis of each type of message is limited unless there was something new to learn or observe in a subsequent message—for example, in a BENOTIFY message.

Step 1—REGISTER sip:contoso.com SIP/2.0

The first part of the message flow begins with the initial discussion of the Communicator client with the home pool server. The client logging in has to register with the pool that it is a member of. This tells the server where the client can be reached. Finally, note that the certificates that were painstakingly prepared are being used to establish TLS.

```
TL_INFO(TF_PROTOCOL) [0]06F4.0CDC::08/22/2007-19:09:27.536.
    00000440 (SIPStack,SIPAdminLog::TraceProtocolRecord:
    SIPAdminLog.cpp(122))
$$begin_record
Instance-Id: 00000280
Direction: incoming
Peer: 10.0.0.24:2065
Message-Type: request
Start-Line: REGISTER sip:vdomain1.com SIP/2.0
From: <sip:kakers@contoso.com>;tag=b801f3431d;epid=5d3080be61
To: <sip: kakers@contoso.com>
CSeq: 2 REGISTER
Call-ID: 091eeac004fb4d94bee8845581203051
Via: SIP/2.0/TLS 10.0.0.24:2065
Max-Forwards: 70
Contact: <sip:10.0.0.24:2065;transport=tls;ms-opaque=57561cdbc3>;methods="INVITE,
MESSAGE, INFO, OPTIONS, BYE,
    CANCEL, NOTIFY, ACK, REFER, BENOTIFY";proxy=replace;
    +sip.instance=
    "<urn:uuid:20C60920-2E75-5AB3-9252-DF040FAD120E>"
User-Agent: UCCP/2.0.6502.502 OC/2.0.6502.502 (Microsoft Office Communicator)
Authorization: Kerberos qop="auth", realm=
    "SIP Communications Service", targetname=
    "sip/pool.contoso.com", gssapi-data=
    "YIIEmQYJKoZIhvcSAQICAQBuggSIMII
<snip of gssapi data>
1y5947WB1ux7FUNWDi6hzm44H9DHWrnglDmYG4jDxmW+razdEP1l1MUXvuAbE=",
    version=3
Supported: gruu-10, adhoclist, msrtc-event-categories
Supported: ms-forking
ms-keep-alive: UAC;hop-hop=yes
Event: registration
Content-Length: 0
Message-Body:
```

Step 3—SUBSCRIBE sip:kakers@contoso.com SIP/2.0

A SUBSCRIBE method is used by the registered user agent to receive notifications on the change of state or other elements. Specifically, the user agent needs to know about events that occur that are of interest, and it establishes event handlers that the client is interested in so that the proper notification is sent when that event is triggered. To terminate a SUBSCRIBE method, there is no corresponding UNSUBSCRIBE method. However, a SUBSCRIBE message is sent with the Expires header field set to 0. Following the conversation in the message flow is simplified by following the *tag* and *epid* fields. Also, note the *User-Agent*. The SUBSCRIBE request is mostly in the last couple of lines.

```
TL_INFO(TF_PROTOCOL) [0]06F4.0CDC::08/22/2007-19:09:27.586.
    00000473 (SIPStack,SIPAdminLog::TraceProtocolRecord:
    SIPAdminLog.cpp(122))
$$begin_record
Instance-Id: 00000284
Direction: incoming
Peer: 10.0.0.24:2065
Message-Type: request
Start-Line: SUBSCRIBE sip:kakers@contoso.com SIP/2.0
From: <sip:kakers@contoso.com>;tag=76293b8509;epid=5d3080be61
To: <sip:kakers@contoso.com>
CSeq: 1 SUBSCRIBE
Call-ID: b6076edf0ea146e594624fe3ae1ba0f7
Via: SIP/2.0/TLS 10.0.0.24:2065
Max-Forwards: 70
Contact: <sip:kakers@contoso.com;opaque=user:epid:
    IAnGIHUus1qSUt8ED60SDgAA;gruu>
User-Agent: UCCP/2.0.6502.502 OC/2.0.6502.502 (Microsoft Office
    Communicator)
Event: vnd-microsoft-roaming-self
Accept: application/vnd-microsoft-roaming-self+xml
Supported: com.microsoft.autoextend
Supported: ms-benotify
Proxy-Require: ms-benotify
Supported: ms-piggyback-first-notify
Proxy-Authorization: Kerberos qop="auth", realm=
"SIP Communications Service", opaque="3A852553",
    crand="c458b6ff", cnum="2", targetname="sip/pool.contoso.com",
    response="602306092a864886f71201020201011100ffffffffc098b3
    7c7b9497ccca0f8eb3b407cd5c"
Content-Type: application/vnd-microsoft-roaming-self+xml
Content-Length: 174
Message-Body: <roamingList xmlns="http://schemas.microsoft.com/2006/09/sip/roaming-
self">
    <roaming type="categories"/><roaming type="containers"/>
    <roaming type="subscribers"/></roamingList>
$$end_record
```

The response to this message is a pair of very verbose "200 OK" messages that informs the client what they are now subscribed for and confirms the events. A snippet of one of those messages is shown next. Note that there is no defined expire time, as the server expects to see a SUBSCRIBE with the *Expires: 0* field to terminate the SUBSCRIBE.

```
<category name="contactCard" instance="0" publishTime="2007-08-22T18:57:41.610"
container="0" version="2" expireType="static">
<contactCard xmlns="http://schemas.microsoft.com/2006/09/sip/
    contactcard" >
<identity >
<name >
<displayName >
Kim Akers</displayName>
</name>
<email >
kakers@contoso.com</email>
</identity>
</contactCard>
</category>
<category name="note" instance="0" publishTime=
    "2007-08-22T19:01:00.317" container="32000" version="1"
    expireType="static"/>
<category name="note" instance="0" publishTime=
    "2007-08-22T19:01:00.317" container="100" version="1"
     expireType="static"/>
<category name="state" instance="0" publishTime=
    "2007-08-22T19:01:00.317" container="32000" version="1"
    expireType="static">
<state xmlns="http://schemas.microsoft.com/2006/09/sip/state" xmlns:xsi="http://
www.w3.org/2001/XMLSchema-instance" manual=
    "false" xsi:type="aggregateState" ><availability >
    18500</availability><endpointLocation ></endpointLocation>
</state>
</category>
<category name="state" instance="0" publishTime=
    "2007-08-22T19:09:05.720" container="400" version="1"
    expireType="static">
```

Step 5—SERVICE sip:kakers@contoso.com SIP/2.0

The SERVICE method is used in this case to turn the presence on for Kim Akers. At this point, Kim can now be seen online and anyone who has her in his contact list will be able to see that she is online (assuming, of course, that she hasn't specifically set her presence as Offline)—and what her current status is.

```
TL_INFO(TF_PROTOCOL) [0]06F4.0CDC::08/22/2007-19:10:04.517.0000055d
(SIPStack,SIPAdminLog::TraceProtocolRecord:
    SIPAdminLog.cpp(122))$$begin_record
Instance-Id: 0000029B
Direction: incoming
Peer: 10.0.0.24:2065
Message-Type: request
Start-Line: SERVICE sip:kakers@contoso.com SIP/2.0
From: <sip:kakers@contoso.com >;tag=446e225cd5;epid=5d3080be61
To: <sip:kakers@contoso.com >
CSeq: 1 SERVICE
Call-ID: a613e9b91a774db4bf65ba293814ad92
Via: SIP/2.0/TLS 10.0.0.24:2065
Max-Forwards: 70
Contact: <sip:kakers@contoso.com;opaque=user:epid:
    IAnGIHUus1qSUt8ED60SDgAA;gruu>
User-Agent: UCCP/2.0.6502.502 OC/2.0.6502.502 (Microsoft Office
    Communicator)
Proxy-Authorization: Kerberos qop="auth", realm=
    "SIP Communications Service", opaque="3A852553",
    crand="87e1e7a1", cnum="11",
    targetname="sip/pool.contoso.com",
    response="602306092a864886f71201020201011100ffffffffdf
    2ec24a2d6d546878a3ddc6ade6690d"
Content-Type: application/msrtc-presence-setsubscriber+xml
Content-Length: 162
Message-Body: <publish
    xmlns="http://schemas.microsoft.com/2006/09/sip/rich-
    presence"><publications uri="sip:kakers@contoso.com">
    <publication categoryName="device" instance="722818101"
     container="2" version="0" expireType="endpoint"><device
xmlns="http://schemas.microsoft.com/2006/09/sip/device"
    endpointId="87AAC0AD-3A90-5901-A799-B4672392F3BF">
    <capabilities preferred="false" uri="sip:kakers@contoso.com">
    <text capture="true" render="true" publish="false"/><gifInk
    capture="false" render="true" publish="false"/><isfInk
    capture="false" render="true" publish="false"/></capabilities>
    <timezone>00:00:00+01:00
    </timezone><machineName>CLIENT</machineName></device>
    </publication><publication categoryName="state"
instance="850482499" container="3" version="0" expireType=
    "endpoint"><state xmlns="http://schemas.microsoft.com
    /2006/09/sip
    /state" manual="false" xmlns:xsi="http://www.w3.org/2001
    /XMLSchema-instance" xsi:type="machineState"><availability>3500</availability>
    <endpointLocation></endpointLocation></state></publication>
    <publication categoryName="state" instance="850482499"
    container="2" version="0" expireType="endpoint"><state>
    xmlns="http://schemas.microsoft.com/2006/09/sip/state"
    manual="false"
    xmlns:xsi="http://www.w3.org/2001/XMLSchema-instance"
    xsi:type="machineState"><availability>3500</availability>
    <endpointLocation></endpointLocation></state></publication>
</publications></publish>
$$end_record
```

This completes the initial "getting online" sequence–Kim Akers is online, and John Peoples is online as well. If John and Kim have each other in their Contacts list (this example assumes that they do), they should be able to see that the other person is online. We've initiated and opened the Office Communicator client, signed into our pool (home) server, and set our current presence status.

Examining Communication from One Federated Enterprise to Another

Now that Kim and John are ready to start a conversation, let's examine the details of adding users to the remote user's pool via the SUBSCRIBE and NOTIFY messages from one enterprise to another across the federated connection. (See Figure 7-9 on the next page.)

> **Note** The following discussion tracks the most important steps and is not a full step-by-step look at each and every message. Also, to avoid redundancy, the analysis of each type of message is limited unless there was something new to learn or observe in a subsequent message.

Step 1—SUBSCRIBE sip:jpeoples@fabrikam.com SIP/2.0

John and Kim are now logged in and signed in to their respective enterprises. Now, the respective users have to be able to get enough information to be able to receive event notifications about their contact records. Because Kim and John have each other's records, the client knows that it has to SUBSCRIBE to the home pool of the other user. The flow begins with a SUBSCRIBE to fabrikam.com via Kim's home pool and Access Edge Servers.

```
TL_INFO(TF_PROTOCOL) [0]05F8.0944::08/22/2007-19:10:01.170.000007fe
    (SIPStack,SIPAdminLog::TraceProtocolRecord:
SIPAdminLog.cpp(122))$$begin_record
Instance-Id: 000000B6
Direction: outgoing;source="internal edge";destination=
   "external edge"
Peer:accessproxy.contoso.com:5061
Message-Type: request
Start-Line: SUBSCRIBE sip:jpeoples@fabrikam.com SIP/2.0
From: "Kim Akers"<sip:kakers@contoso.com>;tag=b5942d9dd9;
    epid=7469ade8c2
To: <sip:jpeoples@fabrikam.com>
CSeq: 1 SUBSCRIBE
Call-ID: f6c1d48ef2084b82b080aedeb3f31707
Record-Route: <sip:accessedge.contoso.com:5061;transport=tls;
    epid=7469ade8c2;lr>;tag=CC4625642D8B2D9A579AD58F130DD603
Via: SIP/2.0/TLS 11.0.0.25:1061;branch=z9hG4bKEEEBA844.0226596C;branched=FALSE;
ms-internal-info="abnlJuPbnBNx-r4dTTJSZtvB0OuVACJlls2H2kKQAA"
ms-asserted-verification-level: ms-source-verified-user=verified
Max-Forwards: 68
Via: SIP/2.0/TLS 10.0.0.20:1504;branch=z9hG4bK27C8ADD2.3872BC78;branched=FALSE;
ms-received-port=1504;ms-received-cid=1600
Via: SIP/2.0/TLS 10.0.0.24:1251;ms-received-port=1251;
ms-received-cid=1F00
  <SNIP>
```

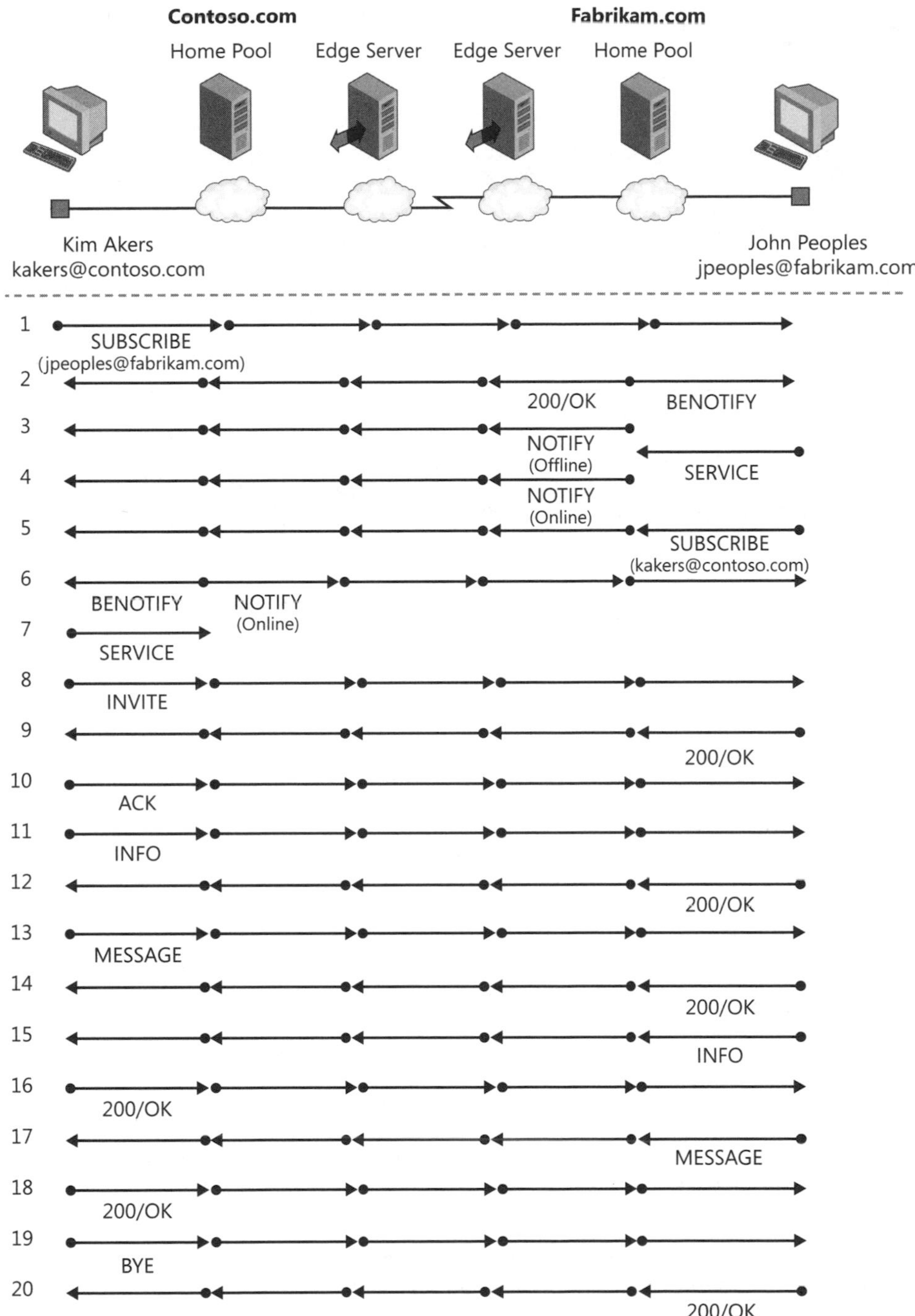

Figure 7-9 Full federation conversation—User-to-user instant messaging

On the Fabrikam.com Access Edge Server, we can find the SUBSCRIBE message as it comes into the server:

```
TL_INFO(TF_PROTOCOL) [0]09B4.0CAC::08/22/2007-19:10:01.537.00000009
    (SIPStack,SIPAdminLog::TraceProtocolRecord:
SIPAdminLog.cpp(122))$$begin_record
Instance-Id: 0000022B
Direction: incoming;source="external edge";destination=
    "internal edge"
Peer: accessedge.contoso.com:1061
Message-Type: request
Start-Line: SUBSCRIBE sip:jpeoples@fabrikam.com SIP/2.0
From: "Kim Akers"<sip:kakers@contoso.com>;tag=b5942d9dd9;
    epid=7469ade8c2
To: <sip:jpeoples@fabrikam.com.com>
CSeq: 1 SUBSCRIBE
Call-ID: f6c1d48ef2084b82b080aedeb3f31707
Record-Route: sip:edgeserver.fabrikam.com:5061;transport=tls;
    epid=7469ade8c2;lr;tag=CC4625642D8B2D9A579AD58F130DD603
<snip>
```

And the DIAGNOSTIC message that is seen right after the preceding message shows that our federation is recognized and the SIP domain has been recognized:

```
TL_INFO(TF_DIAG) [0]09B4.0CAC::08/22/2007-19:10:01.577.0000000d
    (SIPStack,SIPAdminLog::TraceDiagRecord:
SIPAdminLog.cpp(144))$$begin_record
LogType: diagnostic
Severity: information
Text: The message has an Allowed Partner Server domain
SIP-Start-Line: SUBSCRIBE sip:jpeoples@fabrikam.com SIP/2.0
SIP-Call-ID: f6c1d48ef2084b82b080aedeb3f31707
SIP-CSeq: 1 SUBSCRIBE
Peer: accessedge.contoso.com:1061
Data: domain="contoso.com"
$$end_record
```

Step 2—BENOTIFY and OK/200

In this set of actions, a couple of things happen in a quick sequence. If you look at the message flow, you'll see that the home server sends a BENOTIFY message to John Peoples' client, and it also sends a 200/OK message back to Kim Akers. The 200/OK tells her client that you are now subscribed successfully on the Fabrikam.com domain, and much like the SUBSCRIBE just shown, it also indicates what the SUBSCRIBE contained.

The BENOTIFY, though, is a bit different. When a SUBSCRIBE comes in, we're subscribing to the pool on which a user is a member. The home server has to tell the client that this is what happened, and you now have some things to do. The BENOTIFY to John's client looks like this:

```
TL_INFO(TF_PROTOCOL) [0]06F4.0AF8::08/22/2007-19:10:04.507.0000055a
     (SIPStack,SIPAdminLog::TraceProtocolRecord:
SIPAdminLog.cpp(122))$$begin_record
Instance-Id: 0000029A
Direction: outgoing;source="local"
Peer: 11.0.0.25:2065
Message-Type: request
Start-Line: BENOTIFY sip:11.0.0.25:2065;transport=tls;
    ms-opaque=57561cdbc3;ms-received-cid=2D00 SIP/2.0
From: <sip:jpeoples@fabrikam.com>;tag=55D24D67
To: <sip: jpeoples@fabrikam.com >;tag=50d3171d57;epid=5d3080be61
CSeq: 2 BENOTIFY
Call-ID: 63dab314323b44a08637aa1775518841
Via: SIP/2.0/TLS 11.0.0.35:5061;branch=z9hG4bKA56C7273.03AB7EC2;branched=FALSE
    Authentication-Info: Kerberos rspauth="602306092A864886F712010
    20201011100FFFFFFFFC64C8A2A6175A0639CA680B771C00C1F",
    srand="911862A4", snum="14", opaque="3A852553", qop="auth",
    targetname="sip/pool.fabrikam.com", realm="SIP Communications
    Service"
Max-Forwards: 70
Content-Length: 163
Content-Type: application/vnd-microsoft-roaming-contacts+xml
Event: vnd-microsoft-roaming-contacts
subscription-state: active;expires=52019
Message-Body: ----****MESSAGE BODY DELETED****----
$$end_record
```

Steps 3 and 4 are going to respond to the BENOTIFY and initiate a SERVICE method. But just before that, John's home server ensures that his presence is in an offline state. The SERVICE method fires, and John's client notifies the home pool server that he has received the BENOTIFY and that he's ready to communicate. The home pool responds by sending John's presence to contoso.com and will be reflected in Kim's client, and to the state that John indicated when he first signed on.

In Step 5, John initiates a SUBSCRIBE that is destined for the Contoso.com domain and that will accomplish the same set of processes that occurred in Fabrikam when Kim initiated her SUBSCRIBE. Also, the BENOTIFY is sent to Kim and the SERVICE method fires, just as it did for John.

John and Kim are both online, can see each other's presence, and are on the verge of starting the conversation.

Step 8—INVITE sip:test1@vdomain1.com SIP/2.0

Step 8 is the initial INVITE message from Kim Akers to John Peoples—the method used to initiate the actual IM conversation. Note that this is the first message that indicates there is full awareness on the part of both parties, or end points:

```
TL_INFO(TF_PROTOCOL) [0]05F8.0944::08/22/2007-19:10:12.876.00000835
    (SIPStack,SIPAdminLog::TraceProtocolRecord:
SIPAdminLog.cpp(122))$$begin_record
Instance-Id: 000000BA
Direction: incoming;source="internal edge";destination=
    "external edge"
Peer: pool.contoso.com:1504
Message-Type: request
Start-Line: INVITE sip:jpeoples@fabrikam.com SIP/2.0
From: "Kim Akers"<sip:kakers@contoso.com>;tag=af89c73ee3;
    epid=7469ade8c2
To: <sip: jpeoples@fabrikam.com >
CSeq: 1 INVITE
<snip>
EndPoints: <sip:kakers@contoso.com>, <sip:jpeoples@fabrikam.com>
Supported: com.microsoft.rtc-multiparty
<snip>
```

Following the INVITE (in Steps 9 and 10) is an OK that John's client received the INVITE and an ACK back to John that Kim has received the OK to the messaging session. At this point, things are pretty much established.

Why the verbosity of the messaging involved? Remember that SIP is a signaling protocol and, much like ships using a light to send Morse code back and forth, there is no way to know for sure that that the other end really did receive the message unless we respond. Almost everything has an OK associated with it. However, the ACK is unique to INVITE, as this is a three-way handshake process. Also, you should remember that SIP is pretty much a one-sided conversation. It is two clients that have established their *own* message flow. That one responds is merely courtesy and part of the protocol.

Step 12—INFO sip:jpeoples@fabrikam.com;opaque=user:epid:rcCqh5A6AVmnmbRnI5LzvwAA;gruu SIP/2.0

In the world of Office Communications Server 2007 instant messaging, it's this message (step 12) that tells John's client that Kim is typing and also displays the text "Kim is typing a message" in his client.

```
<snip>
Route: <sip:pool.fabrikam.com:5061;transport=tls;ms-role-rs-to;lr>
User-Agent: UCCP/2.0.6502.502 OC/2.0.6502.502 (Microsoft Office Communicator)
Supported: timer
Content-Type: application/xml
Content-Length: 87
Message-Body: <?xml version="1.0"?>
<KeyboardActivity>
 <status status="type" />
</KeyboardActivity>
$$end_record
```

Step 13—MESSAGE sip:jpeoples@fabrikam.com;opaque=user:epid:IAnGIHUus1qSUt8ED60SDgAA;gruu SIP/2.0

Kim has completed typing and is sending her initial message to John. The message text is not seen in the Snooper tool, which shows the following: Message-Body: —****MESSAGE BODY DELETED****—.

```
TL_INFO(TF_PROTOCOL) [0]05F8.0944::08/22/2007-19:10:13.217.000008ba
    (SIPStack,SIPAdminLog::TraceProtocolRecord:
SIPAdminLog.cpp(122))$$begin_record
Instance-Id: 000000C4
Direction: outgoing;source="internal edge";destination=
"external edge"
Peer: accessedge.contoso.com:5061
Message-Type: request
Start-Line: MESSAGE sip:jpeoples@fabrikam.com;opaque=user:epid:
IAnGIHUus1qSUt8ED60SDgAA;gruu SIP/2.0
From: <sip:kakers@contoso.com>;tag=af89c73ee3;epid=7469ade8c2
To: "" <sip:jpeoples@fabrikam.com>;epid=5d3080be61;
tag=4c8535fa6e
CSeq: 2 MESSAGE
Call-ID: 5c2aad6c090241c9bb3b86753b53cee1
Via: SIP/2.0/TLS 11.0.0.25:1061;branch=z9hG4bK75B30E9F.92A6F7E6;branched=FALSE;
ms-internal-info="abEScJuOwN6e6exY40NhVTSh_aIGKSpvfm2H2kKQAA"
ms-asserted-verification-level: ms-source-verified-user=verified
ms-archiving: TRUE
Max-Forwards: 68
Via: SIP/2.0/TLS 10.0.0.20:1504;branch=z9hG4bK58136098.0DBECCED;branched=FALSE;
ms-received-port=1504;ms-received-cid=1600
<snip>
```

The remainder of the message flow involves a series of back-and-forth MESSAGE, 200/OK, and INFO messages. At the end of the session, they end their conversation. Or one person decides to end the session. With the final message that we're going to look at, the BYE method is sent by one person and the session is terminated. (Obviously, the other person can re-establish the communication, which involves most of the steps that we've reviewed in this section.)

Step 19—sip:jpeoples@fabrikam.com;opaque=user:epid:IAnGIHUus1qSUt8ED60SDgAA;gruu SIP/2.0

Oddly, there really isn't all that much that is interesting about this message. We just simply say BYE.

```
TL_INFO(TF_PROTOCOL) [0]05F8.0944::08/22/2007-19:10:31.754.00000923
(SIPStack,SIPAdminLog::TraceProtocolRecord:
SIPAdminLog.cpp(122))$$begin_record
Instance-Id: 000000CA
Direction: outgoing;source="internal edge";destination=
    "external edge"
Peer: edgeserver.fabrikam.com:5061
Message-Type: request
Start-Line: BYE sip:jpeoples@fabrikam.com;opaque=user:epid:
    IAnGIHUus1qSUt8ED6OSDgAA;
gruu SIP/2.0
From: <sip:kakers@contoso.com>;tag=af89c73ee3;epid=7469ade8c2
To: "" <sip:jpeoples@fabrikam.com>;epid=5d3080be61;
    tag=4c8535fa6e
CSeq: 3 BYE
Call-ID: 5c2aad6c090241c9bb3b86753b53cee1
Via: SIP/2.0/TLS 11.0.0.25:1061;branch=z9hG4bKD2EEC434.230ACDF5;branched=FALSE;
ms-internal-info="abBF-BCHJPotZZ4WauGOrWULVm-qEjCs312H2kKQAA"
ms-asserted-verification-level: ms-source-verified-user=verified
Max-Forwards: 68
Via: SIP/2.0/TLS 10.0.0.20:1504;branch=z9hG4bKB5A56090.D7906399;branched=FALSE;
ms-received-port=1504;ms-received-cid=1600
Via: SIP/2.0/TLS 10.0.0.24:1251;ms-received-port=1251;
ms-received-cid=1F00
Route: <sip:assessedge.contoso.com:5061;transport=tls;
    epid=5d3080be61;lr;ms-key-info=jACAANllrITgfVcd4OTHAQEC
    AAADZgAAAKQAAErVfkqSMT4KWRwNZJ9pTueIXj9JstdoDPUx9993-kqbW
    A6eDmg7tjwUXo9W_VhTmuPGcxExiybWGAshIi4C9dNRNXYQEkyEv7Vl0Y
    J1-gEH2ezJXyEclUq3o4RXL5WXqzulCMYmXTt_OwA8gQIeCILVPQY5ty
    ZvZMlqg8pQJ4lkFjqA1Nq1R4LKfdXA4s0lf0M7K2cX-iqosQf6sK-or2G
    Ice7zj2qhcibEOReEXe6YoIWk-nvDeSTmrDMMzR6TKkEltjA6I5BYkU_Cx
    oJ8H9xdLEEjtTWH3Fqn7javve10VaRNywoCNVc_BQOZ8frx5hKv07frixn
    jOuO8FzjthnQA;ms-route-sig=cavUCK1BG4udtUgjn2qUfRLCzTjFdx7R
    j28P9FsQAA>
Route: <sip:pool.fabrikam.com:5061;transport=tls;ms-role-rs-to;lr>
User-Agent: UCCP/2.0.6502.502 OC/2.0.6502.502 (Microsoft Office
    Communicator)
Content-Length: 0
Message-Body:
```

And the subsequent and final OK/200 from jpeoples@fabrikam.com is Step 20:

```
TL_INFO(TF_PROTOCOL) [0]05F8.0944::08/22/2007-19:10:31.764.00000926
(SIPStack,SIPAdminLog::TraceProtocolRecord:
SIPAdminLog.cpp(122))$$begin_record
Instance-Id: 000000CB
Direction: incoming;source="external edge";destination=
    "internal edge"
Peer: edgeserver.fabrikam.com:5061
Message-Type: response
Start-Line: SIP/2.0 200 OK
From: "John Peoples"<sip:jpeoples@fabrikam.com>;tag=af89c73ee3;
    epid=7469ade8c2
To: "" <sip:kakers@contoso.com>;epid=5d3080be61;tag=4c8535fa6e
CSeq: 3 BYE
<snip>
```

Summary

Federation is a very important part of the capabilities in Office Communications Server 2007. Federation is not new, as Live Communications Server also had this ability. But the feature set has been refined and streamlined for a much more configurable and secure solution. In addition, the Audio/Video feature set and the Live Conferencing capabilities all can be launched from the Communicator client, allowing local, federated, and anonymous parties to take part in a variety of communications and collaboration methods. With all these capabilities, Office Communications Server delivers a very rich and compelling solution for intra-enterprise and extra-enterprise solutions.

Finally, as Chapter 8 details, the federation feature sets the stage for a manageable and controllable public Instant Messaging solution. The ability to manage which providers (Yahoo!, AOL, or MSN) your users have access to is a very powerful tool. Again, all of this is available from the Communicator client and Office Communications Server 2007.

Additional Resources

- Office Communications Server 2007 Edge Server Deployment Guide, found at *http://www.microsoft.com/downloads/details.aspx?familyid=ed45b74e-00c4-40d2-abee-216ce50f5ad2&displaylang=en*
- Office Communication Server 2007 Resource Kit Tools (snooper.exe used in this section), found at *http://www.microsoft.com/downloads/details.aspx?familyid=b9bf4f71-fb0b-4de9-962f-c56b70a8aecd&displaylang=en*
- The article "You cannot start the Communications Server 2007 logging and tracing tool from an Access Edge server or from a front-end server," found at *http://support.microsoft.com/kb/941315/en-us*

On the Companion CD

There is no Companion CD content for this chapter.

Chapter 8

Public IM Connectivity Scenario

In this chapter:

Users nowadays can use client software such as Office Communicator 2007 to communicate with users of instant messaging (IM) services provided by the MSN network of Internet services, by Yahoo!, and by AOL. Office Communications Server 2007 provides mechanisms both on the server side and on the user side to control which MSN, Yahoo!, and AOL users can interact with the users in your organization. This allows users to establish connections with one or more of these providers, or to disable existing connections if necessary. Administrators can authorize employees for public IM connectivity on a per-user basis, or they can use a Global policy to configure an enterprise-wide preference. This chapter describes how to implement the public IM connectivity scenario for Office Communication Server.

Why Talk About the Public IM Connectivity Scenario?

Instant messaging, or IM, the ability to transfer text messages in real time over the Internet or a corporate network, has spread from the consumer arena to the workplace. It now is gaining in importance as a means of communication and collaboration not only within the enterprise, but also with the enterprise's suppliers, customers, outsourcing vendors, and other transaction partners. IM is an important component connecting data, platforms, processes, and people so as to increase productivity and save costs.

A recent survey on how we use IM indicates that more than 50 million Americans use IM and that 21 percent, or 11 million of the IM user segment, use it at work. However, though 76 percent of IT executives use IM on the job, only 37 percent are standardized on an enterprise IM application. The Federal Deposit Insurance Corporation (FDIC), which is a U.S. government corporation, warns in Financial Institution Letter (FIL) 84-2004 that the use of public IM rather than enterprise IM can expose companies to security, privacy, and legal liability risks because of ineffective virus protection, lack of effective authentication tools, and transmission of unencrypted data, among other defects.

An increasing number of international, U.S. federal, and state regulations require the review, archiving, production, and audit of business communication (including instant messaging) under shortened regulatory deadlines. By migrating their workers away from the use of insecure public IM networks to an enterprise IM network where security measures are built in, companies can gain increased return on investment as well as greater flexibility to adapt to this challenging regulatory landscape. In addition, the use of an enterprise IM network can support a company's effort to develop and implement an "effective compliance and ethics program" under stricter rules and amendments passed by Congress in 2004 (see "U.S. Sentencing Guidelines Tighten Requirements for Corporate Compliance Programs" found at *http://www.skadden.com/Index.cfm?contentID=51&itemID=943*). Microsoft Office Communications Server 2007 provides a robust IM solution designed to help companies achieve these goals.

Overview of the Public IM Connectivity Scenario

Office Communications Server 2007 provides the means for communicating with users of IM services provided by MSN, AOL, and Yahoo!. Once a connection is established, authorized Office Communications Server users can add contacts, share presence information, and communicate in real time with IM users in these public networks. Note that file transfer, games, formatted text, multimedia, and conferencing will not work over connections between Office Communications Server 2007 and public IM service providers.

Organizations that want to take advantage of public IM connectivity must do the following:

- Obtain separate public IM connectivity service licenses from Microsoft
- Provision the organization's Session Initiation Protocol (SIP) domain using a dedicated Microsoft provisioning Web site

Public IM connectivity licenses cover all three of the supported public IM service providers (MSN, AOL, and Yahoo!), but administrators retain control over which of the providers they enable for their organizations. IM providers are disabled by default when the Edge Server is configured. You can enable one, two, or all three of the public IM service providers if so desired. If desired, administrators can update provisioning information to reflect modification of IM service providers. You can temporarily disable a connection to a provider simply by changing settings in Office Communications Server. However, to permanently disable or enable a connection to an IM provider, use the provisioning process as explained in the "Considerations for Deploying the Public IM Connectivity Scenario" and "Provisioning Federation with a Public IM Service Provider" sections later in this chapter.

As in other federation scenarios, users in your organization can add users of the public IM networks to their allow and block lists in the Office Communicator client. Three scenarios are possible:

- A user of one of the public IM networks added to an allow list can both exchange IM with, and see presence information for, the owner of the list. Use the Personal Information Manager panel, located on the Personal tab on the Options dialog box in Office Communicator to allow and block these lists.

- A public IM user who is not on either an allow list or a blocked list can exchange IM and presence information with an internal user, but the internal user can block all such requests.
- A user added to a block list can neither exchange IM with, nor see presence information for, the owner of the list.

Administrators have full control over who in their organization is authorized for public IM connectivity. Once that permission is granted, however, a user can communicate with all of the public IM service providers enabled for the organization. It is not possible to authorize a user to communicate over one enabled public IM service provider but not over another one.

Administrators can authorize public IM connectivity on a per-user or group basis and change both individual and group authorizations as needed. Administrators can exercise additional control over spim (unsolicited commercial IM, or spam over IM) by setting message filters that further restrict access from unverified users. For more information on message filtering, see the "Security Considerations" section later in this chapter or "Configuring Intelligent IM Filtering" in the "Office Communications Server 2007 Administration Guide."

As with other types of federation, all IM traffic between an organization and a public IM service provider uses an encrypted mutual transport layer security (MTLS) connection. For the purpose of connecting to MSN, AOL, and Yahoo!, an organization must use a certificate from a public certification authority from the list of trusted CAs in Microsoft Windows Server 2003.

> **Note** Microsoft Office Communicator version 1 and version 2 are both supported as clients by Microsoft Office Communications Server 2007. However, if a user has been enabled for 'Enhanced Presence' in the Office Communications Server 2007 user configuration, Office Communicator version 1 will no longer function for this user.

As shown in Figure 8-1, corporate IM users will typically connect to the Home Server, using Office Communicator as a client, whereas federation or external IM users will connect to the Edge Server through a firewall.

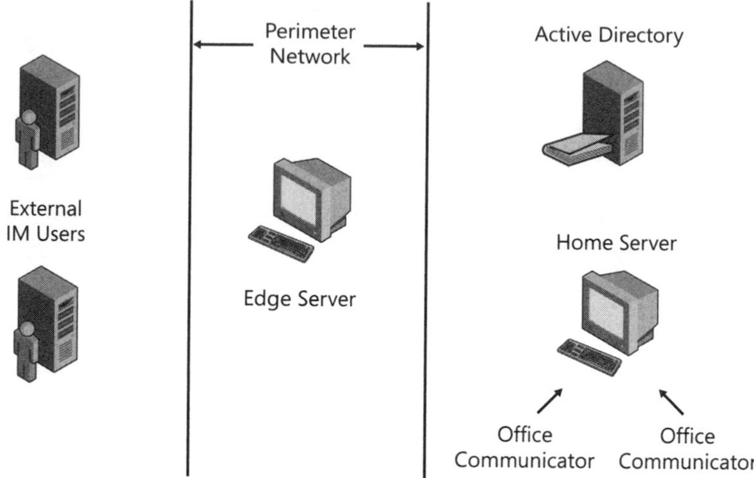

Figure 8-1 Public IM connectivity topology

> **Role of IM Conferencing Server**
>
> The IM Conferencing Server provides server-managed group IM over SIP. The IM Conferencing Server is one of the four conferencing servers in Office Communications Server, and it is installed automatically on the Front End Server. It enables group IM by relaying IM traffic among all participants. When a third participant is added to a peer-to-peer IM conversation, the initiating client invites the IM Conferencing Server to the conversation. From that point, all messages among the participants are routed through the IM Conferencing Server. The IM Conferencing Server is an integral part of the Front End Server and cannot be installed on a separate computer. For more information on group IM, see the "Microsoft Office Communications Server 2007 Technical Overview" document that comes with Office Communications Server 2007.

Considerations for Deploying the Public IM Connectivity Scenario

The following are some considerations that you need to be aware of before implementing the Public IM Connectivity scenario in your enterprise:

- **Acquiring a certificate** Public IM connectivity requires mutual transport layer security (MTLS), using a certificate obtained from a public certification authority. For AOL, client and server Enhanced Key Usage (EKU) is required. For more information, contact an appropriate public certification authority. For more information, see the Knowledge Base article "Unified Communications Certificate Partners for Exchange 2007 and for Communications Server 2007" found at *http://support.microsoft.com/kb/929395*.
- **Acquiring service licenses** Before completing the provisioning form and initiating the request to connect with the public IM service providers, you must first purchase service

licenses, pursuant to the terms and conditions of your Microsoft Volume Licensing agreement. Without first purchasing licenses, the provisioning process will not be completed.

- **Enabling connections to public IM service providers** Each IM service provider with which you want to federate must be enabled and configured on the Edge Server. For more information, see the "Enabling Federation with Public IM Service Providers" section later in this chapter.
- **Authorizing users for public IM connectivity** You can authorize all your enterprise users, certain groups of users, or particular individuals. Users who are not authorized for public IM connectivity can nevertheless be authorized for other types of federation and remote user access. For more information, see the "Enabling User Accounts for Office Communications Server" section in the "Office Communications Server 2007 Administration Guide."
- **Submitting a provisioning request** Your organization and the public IM service provider must exchange network connectivity information in order to activate federation. You perform this exchange by connecting to a Microsoft-hosted provisioning site (*http://r.office.microsoft.com/r/rlidOCS?clid=1033&p1=provision*) and completing a form that initiates a provisioning request.
- **Configuring DNS** If you configure a public provider as described in the "Enabling Federation with Public IM Service Providers" section later in this chapter, the Domain Name System (DNS) Service Record Locator (SRV) record must be published by your partners for you to locate them as Allowed Partners or Discovered Partners. You do not need to publish a DNS SRV record unless you want other enterprises to be able to locate you as one of their Allowed Partners or Discovered Partners. For procedures on configuring DNS for public IM connectivity, see the section "Step 2.2. Configure DNS" in the "Office Communications Server 2007 Edge Server Deployment Guide."

Real World: Role of SRV Records in Office Communicator Sign-On

The Microsoft Office Communicator client enables the user to automatically connect to the appropriate Office Communications Server without actually putting in the server name. Regardless of whether the client is inside the internal network or is working externally, this feature redirects the client and allows it to authenticate and connect to its own Office Communications Server server (in the case of Standard Edition) or home pool (in the case of Enterprise Edition). This feature has a significant DNS dependency. For this to work successfully, the appropriate SRV records should be published both internally and externally.

When the Office Communicator client first starts up and the user tries to connect, Office Communicator always tries to connect to the server or home pool in its same domain, or using the same SIP URI as in the sign-in address. For example, if the sign-in name used is kim.akers@fabrikam.com, Office Communicator looks for the home pool or Office Communications Server server in the same DNS namespace, which is fabrikam.com.

This process is facilitated by usage of DNS SRV records, which ultimately points the client to the FQDN of the home pool or server in the correct domain. The process works the same whether the client is in an internal or external network. The automatic server discovery process follows the steps you see in Figure 8-2.

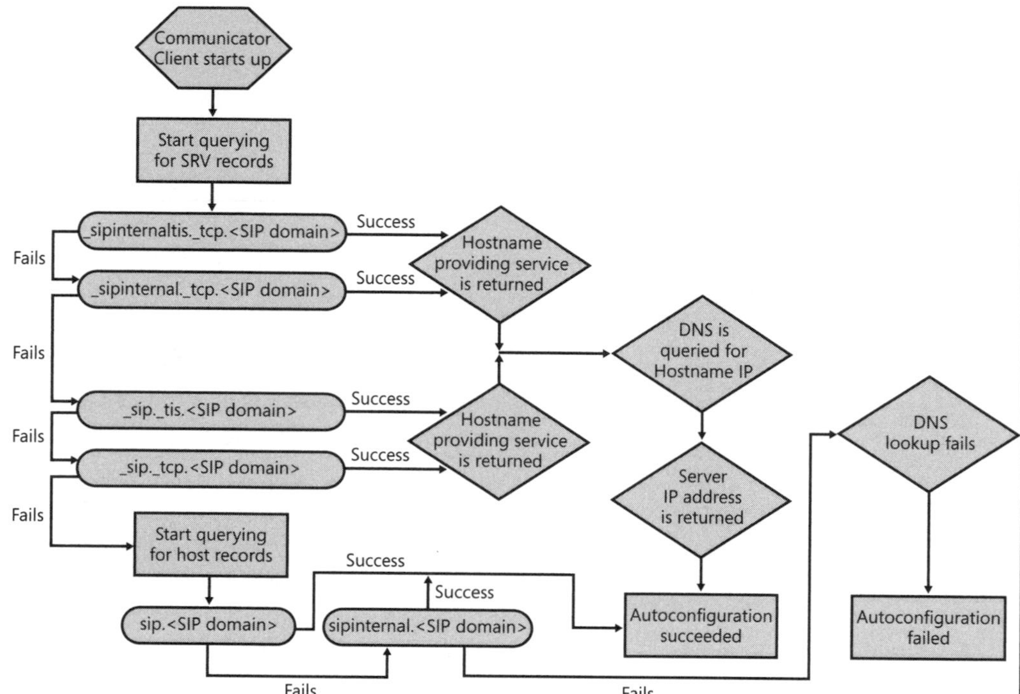

Figure 8-2 Communicator signup

So, in our example, the client starts querying SRV records and, by default, it always tries to use TLS for authentication. If TLS fails, then and only then it falls back to Transmission Control Protocol (TCP).

```
_sipinternaltls._tcp.fabrikam.com
_sipinternal._tcp.fabrikam.com
```

Either of these first two DNS records should be published and available in the internal DNS namespace. So, if by now the client gets the hostname back, it directly connects to the home pool or the Office Communications Server server. Or else, it continues its query process, knowing that it is currently not in the internal network.

```
_sip._tls.fabrikam.com
_sip._tcp.fabrikam.com
```

If either of these queries is a success, the client is redirected to the external edge of the Access Edge Server and subsequently to the internal home pool or the Office Communications Server server. However if it still fails, in a final attempt it tries to look up the host records directly as in the following two examples. If this attempt to configure its settings automatically fails, the Office Communicator will fail and require manual intervention.

```
sip.fabrikam.com
sipinternal.fabrikam.com
```

Figure 8-3 shows an actual network trace, filtered on port 53 to show only DNS queries, which illustrates the same lookup process.

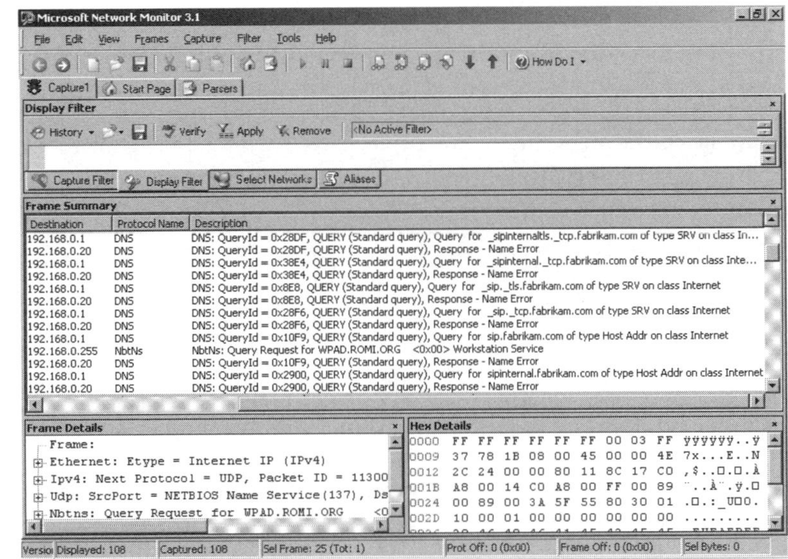

Figure 8-3 Network trace

–Indranil Dutta
Premier Field Engineer

Enabling Federation with Public IM Service Providers

Enabling federation with the public IM service providers is a multi-step process:

- **Provision federation with the IM service providers.** Your organization and the public IM service provider must exchange network connectivity information to activate federation. You perform this exchange by connecting to a Microsoft-hosted provisioning site and completing a form that initiates a provisioning request.

> **Note** Before completing the provisioning form and initiating the request to connect with the public IM service providers, you must have first purchased service licenses for Office Communications Connectivity and installed Office Communications Server, pursuant to the terms and conditions of your Microsoft Volume Licensing agreement. Without first purchasing licenses, the provisioning process will not be completed.

- **Configure DNS on the Edge Server.** If you enable enhanced federation or configure a public or private provider in the IM service providers table, you must do the following:
    - Publish a DNS-SRV record for _sipfederationtls._tcp.<*domain*>, where <*domain*> is the name of your organization's domain, on the appropriate DNS server for the SIP domain hosted by your organization. This DNS server must be publicly accessible.
    - To ensure that DNS-SRV queries are sent to the correct DNS server, provide the internal and external edges of the Edge Server with the address of a DNS server that can resolve internal domains and can forward DNS queries for external domains to public DNS servers.
    - Publish a DNS A record for the Edge Server on an appropriate DNS server. A single record is sufficient for an array of Edge Servers.
- **Obtain a public certificate.** Public IM connectivity requires MTLS, using a certificate obtained from a public certification authority. For more information, contact an appropriate public certification authority.
- **Configure the Edge Server for federation.** Public IM connectivity requires federation to be enabled on the Edge Server.
- **Enable connections to public IM service providers.** Each IM service provider with which you want to federate must be enabled and configured on the Edge Server.
- **Authorize users for public IM connectivity.** You can authorize all your internal users, certain groups of users, or particular individuals. Users who are not authorized for public IM connectivity can nevertheless be authorized for other types of federation and remote user access.

The following sections provide additional details concerning some of the steps just listed. For additional information, see the documentation included with Office Communications Server 2007.

Provisioning Federation with a Public IM Service Provider

The first step in enabling public IM connectivity is to initiate provisioning with one or more of the public IM service providers (MSN, AOL, and Yahoo!).

After you purchase separate service licenses for public IM connectivity, you complete a Web form (*http://r.office.microsoft.com/r/rlidLCS?clid=1033&p1=2&p2=library&p3=provision*) for initiating provisioning requests.

The following information is required to complete the form:

- Master Agreement Number, which identifies your company's Microsoft Business Agreement, which establishes the general terms and conditions of its relationship with Microsoft. Contact your software benefits administrator for this information.

- Enrollment Agreement Number, which identifies your company's purchase of licenses for public IM connectivity. Contact your software benefits administrator for this information.
- Names of your organization's SIP domains.
- The fully qualified domain name (FQDN) of your organization's Edge Server.
- Network administrator contact information.
- Names of the public IM service providers with which you want to federate.

Microsoft will send you an e-mail message confirming that it has received your provisioning information and is in the process of validating the request. Upon validation, Microsoft will send you a second e-mail message verifying that your information has been forwarded to the appropriate public IM service providers and providing an estimate of how long the process is likely to take. If the request is not validated, you will receive an e-mail message explaining how to resolve the issues responsible for the denial.

After validating your Edge Server and SIP domains, Microsoft will forward the information to the public IM service providers with which you want to connect. The public IM service providers will then provision their routing tables to direct instant messages targeting your SIP domains to the Edge Server specified in the form. Once provisioning is complete, each public IM service provider informs Microsoft, which sends you a final e-mail message confirming that the process is complete. After you have received this final message, you can establish a connection from your Edge Server to the public IM service providers to which you want to connect.

After you provision federation with one or more public IM service providers, the next step is to configure your Edge Server for MTLS. This step requires obtaining the necessary certificate from a public certification authority.

Caution Provisioning is complex and involves routing changes to the networks of Microsoft's partners. As a result, provisioning is optimized to work as a single-threaded process. If you want to change provisioning data—specifically, AP FQDN, SIP domains, and the partners to which you want to connect—you must wait until the provisioning request is complete before you submit the changes. If you want to change provisioning data after provisioning has been completed, you need to enter data for all of your existing providers, as well as for any new ones that you want to add. For this reason, please print and save the "Thank you" page that is displayed upon successful submission of your data. This page has the tracking number and a copy of the data that you submitted.

Direct from the Source: End-User Licensing and Auditing

Licensing for public IM on Office Communications Server is really done on an honor system, and through auditing. The public providers get paid based on the number of people using the system, so you should assume they each have their own auditing systems and will identify rampant licensing violations. The details on how Microsoft and the public providers monitor this isn't fully defined, but user counts at every URI using public IM are auditable by the public providers. This sidebar describes a query tool administrators can use to view IM usage data within their organizations.

> **Note** Microsoft's recommendation (because of the lead time on licensing) is that customers purchase lot sizes and then deploy users against those lots.

Querying for Public IM Usage Statistics

Use the public Internet connectivity usage query script Picstats.sql to report statistics related to public IM use–for example, the average number of public IM users on your deployed users' contact lists. This tool is part of the Office Communications Server Resource Kit Tools installation, and you can see a schematic presentation of the data provided by this tool in the "Sample Query Output" section later in this sidebar.

To start public Internet connectivity usage query script Picstats.sql, do the following:

1. On the Windows taskbar, click Start, click Run, type cmd, and then click OK.
2. At the command prompt, type **cd %Program Files%\Microsoft SQL Server\90\Tools\Binn** and then press Enter.
3. Enter the appropriate query script Picstats.sql syntax, and then press Enter.

The syntax for this query script is as follows:

```
osql.exe -E -S <sqlserver>\rtc -d rtc -i picstats.sql
```

Here *<sqlserver>* represents the Microsoft SQL Server instance to connect to. The *-E* flag instructs OSQL to attempt to connect by using Windows Authentication. The default value is to the *rtc* instance on the local computer.

Note that you must be logged on to an account that is in a role that is allowed to run the query script Picstats.sql. For more information, refer to the Readme file in the Office Communications Server Resource Kit Tools installation folder \OCS 2007 Resource Kit Tools, on the companion CD.

Sample Query Output

The following is an example of a valid query script Picstats.sql command:

```
osql.exe -E -S pool-be.contoso.com\rtc -d rtc -i picstats.sql
```

The query script Picstats.sql returns three rows of data based on the contact list information stored within the SQL server associated with your Office Communications Server pool. For more information, see the following sample output and the description following it.

```
PIC Domain   Min Contacts/User   Max Contacts/User   Avg Contacts/User   StDev
Contacts/User
__________   _________________   _________________   _________________

___________________
AOL             1.00                102.00              17.07               13.73
Yahoo!          1.00                4.00                1.80                1.30
MSN             1.00                96.00               16.79               13.56

Users with at least one PIC Contact                   Total Enterprise Users        %
with at least one PIC Contact
___________________________________                   ______________________

   ______________________________
   1000                                               2674                       37.40


Min PIC %/User        Max PIC %/User                  Avg PIC %/User          StDev PIC
%/User
______________        ______________                  ______________

   ________________
0.00                  100.00                          33.52                    34.27
```

The first row in the output shown provides the minimum, maximum, average, and standard deviation in contacts per user for each of the three providers.

The second row provides the number of users with at least one public IM connectivity (PIC) contact, the total number of enterprise users, and the percent and count of users with at least one PIC contact.

The third row is similar to the first row, but it provides a summary number rather than a breakout per provider. This row provides the minimum, maximum, average, and standard deviation in total contacts per user.

Public IM Connectivity Monthly Subscription Licenses

Public IM connectivity monthly subscription licenses are available on a per-user, per-month subscription and are an addition to the Client Access License (CAL). Similar to all online services models, PIC has two licensing components associated with its use: a Services Subscription license (SSL) and a User Subscription license (USL). One PIC SSL is required per company agreement, and one PIC USL is required per user accessing any or all of the public IM service providers.

Pricing for public IM connectivity includes access to all three public IM service providers: Microsoft Network (MSN), America Online (AOL) and Yahoo!. Besides the normal costs that are associated with providing this service, Microsoft pays each provider (MSN, AOL, and Yahoo!) royalties on a per-user, per-month basis.

There is no single or two public IM service provider license available. PIC is sold on a per-user, per-month service agreement; PIC service licenses can be added to a current customer's select, enterprise, or government agreements.

There is no minimum license requirement. Customers can also add licenses at any time. There is no refund or reimbursement for PIC licenses that are not used. PIC service licenses can be added to a current customer's select, enterprise, or government agreements. Customers can pro-rate the months left on their agreements, adding PIC service licenses, but the termination of PIC service must co-terminate with the customer's agreement. For example, if a customer has 17 months left on its current agreement, it has the option to buy 17 months of PIC service.

Microsoft offers volume licensing solutions that scale to meet the needs of small, medium, and enterprise businesses and organizations. Licensing programs provide volume pricing and are designed to save organizations time and money by making the purchase and management of multiple software licenses easier. To view licensing terms, conditions, and supplemental information relevant to the use of products licensed through Microsoft Volume Licensing Programs, visit the Microsoft Volume License Services Web site at *http://r.office.microsoft.com/r/rlidOCS?clid=1033&p1=provision*.

Configuring IM Service Providers

IM service providers include the following:

- Public IM service providers such as MSN, AOL, and Yahoo!. These providers appear in the IM service providers table by default, but they are disabled.
- Private organizations such as data centers, hosting services, and clearing houses.

Important Federating with public or private IM service providers requires enabling federation on the Edge Server.

IM service providers typically, though not necessarily, host multiple SIP domains. Before Office Communications Server, federating with an organization's multiple domains required entering each one explicitly in the direct partner table. Office Communications Server provides two mechanisms that simplify federating with organizations hosting multiple domains:

- The IM service provider table, which requires you to specify an Edge Server but not every domain that it might serve.
- The hosting of multiple domains by including multiple FQDNs in a certificate on the Edge Server.

If your organization requires tighter controls over federation than enhanced federation provides but you do not want to incur the overhead of entering every domain in the direct partner table, you might want to consider configuring the domains in the allowed partners table. For this approach to work, the partner's internal domains must each contain a DNS-SRV record that points to the Edge Server that you list in the IM service providers table.

Note Public IM connectivity allows users in your organization to use IM to communicate with users of instant messaging services provided by public IM service providers, including MSN Internet services, Yahoo!, and AOL. Use the IM Provider tab of the Edge Server Properties dialog box to control the IM service providers that are allowed to federate with your organization. You can add or remove an IM service provider, as well change other settings for any IM service provider (including temporarily blocking the IM service provider). For more information on configuring IM providers, see "Configuring IM Provider Support on Edge Servers" in the "Office Communications Server 2007 Administration Guide."

Table 8-1 summarizes the four main federation options.

Table 8-1 Federation Options

Type of federation	Must specify Edge Server	Must specify domain
Allowed partner server	Yes	Yes
IM service provider table	Yes	No
Discovery of partners	No	No
Allowed partner domain	No	Yes

Important You cannot configure both IM service providers and a default route to a clearing house on the same Edge Server or on an array of Edge Servers. Furthermore, you cannot configure any routing method that requires DNS SRV. If your Edge Server is configured with a default route, or if you want to configure it with a default route, you must first remove the three public IM service providers that populate the IM service providers table when you installed Office Communications Server.

Considerations Involving Public IM Providers

Basic IM and presence work with all public IM providers. However, note the following exceptions to the general rule:

- When an Office Communications Server user sets his presence to Do Not Disturb (DND) in Office Communicator, users on the Yahoo! public IM networks can still send instant messages without knowing that the Office Communications Server user cannot see these messages.

- The public IM networks do not support group IM. As a result, users hosted on the public IM networks (MSN, AOL, and Yahoo!) cannot join IM conferences hosted by Office Communications Server.

Administrators also need to consider how to handle existing accounts on provider networks, public IM connectivity capacity questions, and security issues. These issues are discussed in the following sections.

Considerations Involving Existing Accounts on Provider Networks

Users with existing e-mail accounts will receive an e-mail message notifying them that to continue using IM they must change their e-mail address. Users without IM accounts on a public provider will receive new e-mail accounts. Users' existing public IM contact lists and e-mail messages will be transferred to the new sign-in ID and e-mail address. A user's IM and e-mail contacts will be updated with the user's new sign-in ID. The message will provide a link to a Web page for assistance making the change.

Table 8-2 provides examples of how AOL and Yahoo! screen names are added to contact lists of Office Communications Server users.

Table 8-2 Adding AOL and Yahoo! Screen Names to Contact Lists

Example	User name to be added to Office Communications Server contact list
An Office Communications Server user wants to add AOL user kim.akers@corp.aol.com to the Office Communicator client's contact list.	kim.akers@aol.com
An Office Communications Server user wants to add AOL user kim970 to the Office Communicator client's contact list.	kim970@aol.com
An Office Communications Server user wants to add Yahoo! user kimakers@yahoo.com to the Office Communicator client's contact list.	kimakers@yahoo.com

How the Provider Migrates Existing MSN Accounts

For information on how MSN migrates accounts, see Figure 8-4, which describes the change process.

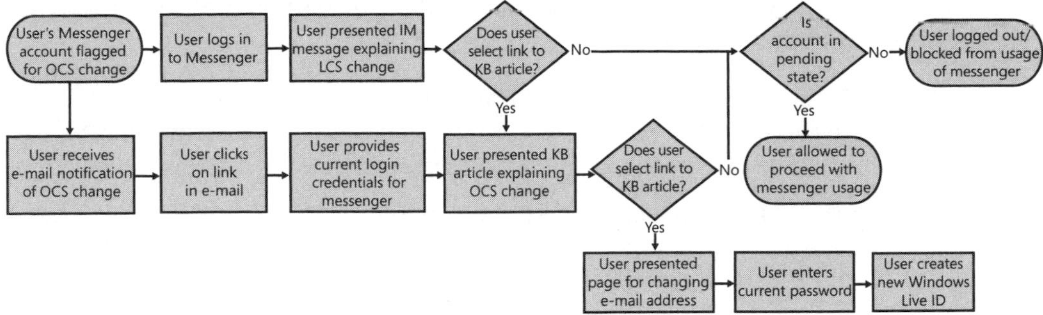

Figure 8-4 Migrating MSN accounts

As shown in Figure 8-4, MSN users who are already using MSN Connect must change their e-mail IDs. Users' existing MSN contact lists and e-mail messages will be transferred to the new sign-in ID and e-mail address. Users' IM and e-mail contacts will be updated with the user's new sign-in ID. Windows Live Messenger Service will work unless your IT administrator has blocked access.

Capacity Planning Considerations

Public IM capacity in Office Communications Server is determined by the bandwidth of the organization's Internet connection. So a T1 connection to public providers provides greater IM access than a 256K connection. Note that SIP, used for IM communication, is particularly capable of supporting large numbers of users. For information on capacity planning, see "Capacity Planning" in the "Office Communications Server 2007 Planning Guide."

Security Considerations

The main security issue with public IM is controlling spim. Controlling spim can be discussed in terms of contacts or message content.

> **Note** All SIP traffic must be carried over the TLS protocol. IP security (IPsec) is not supported. User Datagram Protocol (UDP) is not supported. Compression is done only by TLS negotiation (RFC 2246).

Controlling Spim by Limiting Public Contacts

There are several techniques available to control SPIM by limiting contacts:

- When enabling users for public IM connectivity
- When enabling IM service providers
- When enabling those users on recipients' contact lists only

To limit SPIM when enabling individual users for public IM connectivity, use Active Directory Users and Computers as follows:

1. Log on as a member of the DomainAdmins RTCUniversalServerAdmins group to an Enterprise Edition Server or a server that is a member of an Active Directory domain and that has the Office Communications Server administration tools installed.
2. Open Active Directory Users and Computers. Click Start, click All Programs, click Administrative Tools, and then click Active Directory Users and Computers.
3. In the console tree, expand the Users container or the other organizational unit (OU) that contains the user account for which you want to enable federation, public IM connectivity, or remote user access; right-click the user account name; and then click Properties.
4. On the Communications tab, click the Configure button next to Additional Options.
5. In User Options, under Federation, do the following:
   - To enable the user account for federation, select the Enable Federation check box.
   - To enable the user account for public IM connectivity, select the Enable public IM connectivity check box.
   - To enable the user account for remote access, select the Enable remote user access check box.
6. Click OK twice.

To limit spim when configuring IM provider support on an Edge Server, use the Edge Server Properties dialog box as follows.

1. On the Access Edge Server, open Computer Management.
2. In the console tree, expand Services And Applications, right-click Office Communications Server 2007, and then click Properties. (See Figure 8-5.)

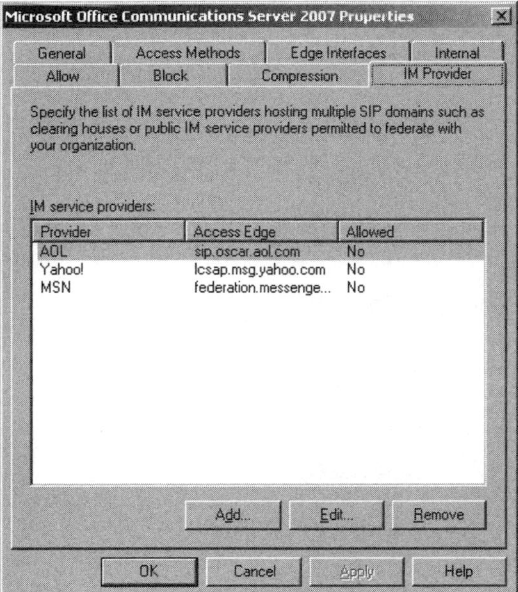

Figure 8-5 IM Provider tab

3. On the IM Provider tab, do one of the following:

   - To view or edit the settings for an IM service provider, in the Edit IM Service Provider dialog box, click the name of the IM service provider, and then click Edit. In the Edit IM Service Provider dialog box, view or change settings, as appropriate, and then click OK.

   - To temporarily block any IM service provider in the list, you can temporarily disable support, click the name of the IM service provider, and then click Edit. In the Edit IM Service Provider dialog box, clear the Allow This IM Service Provider check box and then click OK. This blocks the IM service provider until you later select the check box, but it does not delete the configuration information.

   - To permanently remove an IM service provider from the list, click the name of the server and then click Remove. If you later want to add the IM service provider again, you must use the procedure described previously (in the first bullet) to add the provider and specify all settings.

   - To add an IM provider, click Add. In the Add IM Service Provider dialog box, specify the appropriate options and then click OK.

To limit SPIM when enabling users on recipients' contact lists, use the Add IM Service Provider dialog box to permit IM traffic with contact list items only as follows:

1. On the Access Edge Server, click Start, point to All Programs, point to Administrative Tools, and then click Computer Management.

2. If necessary, expand Services And Applications.
3. Right-click Microsoft Office Communications Server 2007 and then click Properties.
4. On the IM Provider tab, click Add. (See Figure 8-6.)

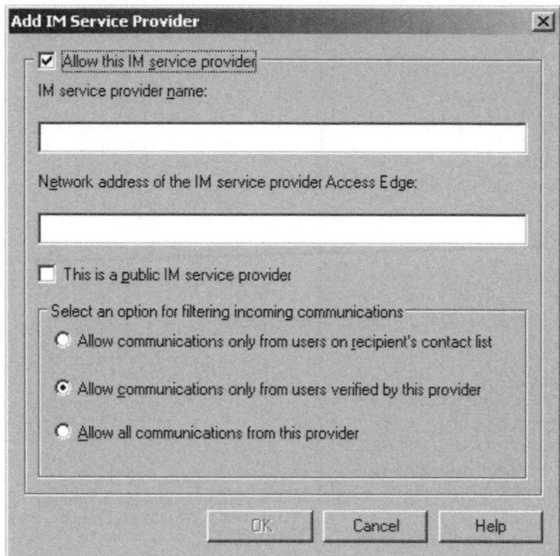

Figure 8-6 Add IM Service Provider dialog box

5. In the Add IM Service Provider dialog box, do the following:
   a. Select the Allow This IM Service Provider check box to enable the new provider.
   b. In the IM Service Provider Name box, type the name of the IM service provider. This name will appear in the Provider column of the IM service providers table.
   c. In the Network Address Of The IM Service Provider Access Proxy box, type the FQDN of the provider's Access Proxy.
   d. Select the This Is A Public IM Service Provider check box only if the provider is MSN, AOL, or Yahoo!
   e. Select an option for filtering incoming communications. To limit IM to users on contact lists, select the option Allow Communications Only From Users On Recipients' Contact List.
6. Click OK.
7. Click OK or Apply to continue.

Controlling SPIM by Limiting Message Content

You can use the Intelligent IM Filter application to protect your Office Communications Server 2007 deployment against harmful instant messages from unknown endpoints outside the corporate firewall. The Intelligent IM Filter provides the following filtering features:

- Enhanced URL filtering
- Enhanced file transfer filtering

To configure URL filtering, do the following:

1. On the Access Edge Server, open Computer Management.
2. In the console tree, expand Services And Applications, right-click Office Communications Server 2007, point to Application Properties, and click Intelligent IM Filter. (See Figure 8-7.)

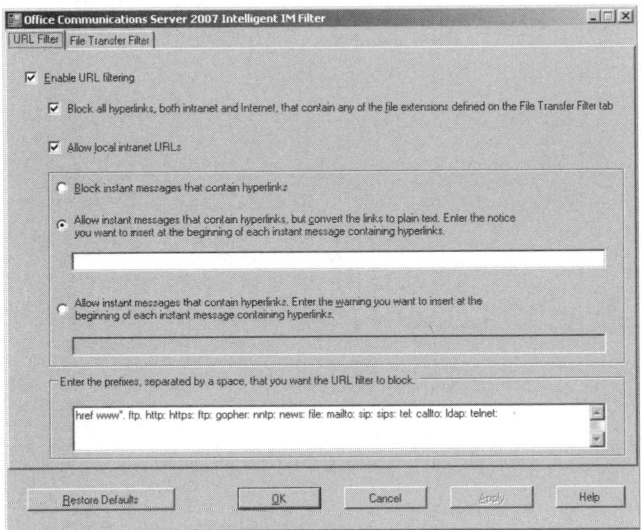

Figure 8-7 Intelligent IM Filter

3. On the URL Filter tab, configure the appropriate settings.

> **Note** It is also possible to access the Intelligent IM Filter by right-clicking either the Enterprise pool or the Standard Edition server.

To configure a file transfer filter, do the following:

1. On the Access Edge Server, open Computer Management.
2. In the console tree, expand Services And Applications, right-click Office Communications Server 2007, point to Application Properties, and click Intelligent IM Filter.
3. On the File Transfer Filter tab, configure the appropriate settings.

Note It is also possible to access the Intelligent IM Filter by right-clicking either the Enterprise pool or the Standard Edition server.

For more information on the Intelligent IM Filter application, see "Configuring Intelligent IM Filtering" in the "Office Communications Server 2007 Administration Guide."

Considerations Involving Media Sharing

Media sharing over a public IM connection is not an issue administrators need to worry about. Users cannot share either audio-visual or binary files over a connection to a public IM provider. Specifically, keep these considerations in mind:

- Between a public IM provider and Office Communications Server, only text and presence information can be exposed.
- Between two Office Communications Servers, sharing of audio-visual or binary files in an IM session is supported.

Enabling Users for Public IM Connectivity

The easiest way to configure multiple users for public IM connectivity is to use the Configure Users Wizard. (See Figure 8-8.) You can access the wizard by using either the Active Directory Users and Computers snap-in or the Office Communications Server Administrative snap-in on an Office Communications Server attached to your SIP domain.

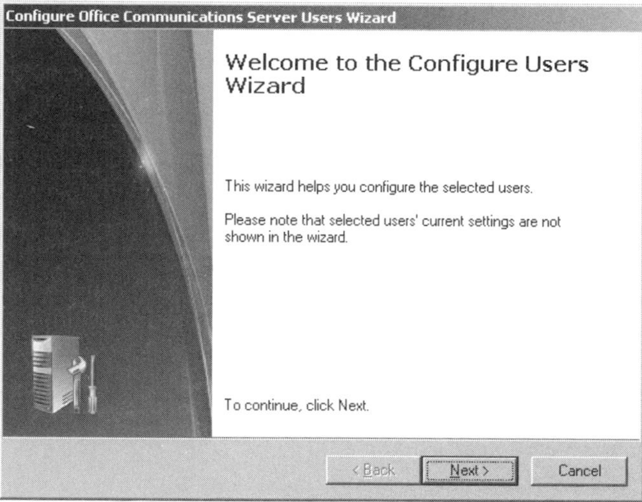

Figure 8-8 Configure Users Wizard

To enable multiple users for public IM connectivity by using the Active Directory Users and Computers snap-in, do the following:

1. If the computer is a domain controller, click Start, point to All Programs, point to Administrative Tools, and then click Active Directory Users And Computers. Otherwise, if the computer is not a domain controller, at the command prompt type **dsa.msc** and press Enter.
2. Go to the folder where your user accounts reside.
3. Do one of the following:
   - Right-click the Users folder or the folder where your user accounts reside, and then click Configure Users to configure all user accounts in this folder.
   - Click the Users folder. In the details pane, select the user or users that you want to configure, and then click Configure Users.
4. On the Welcome To The Configure User Wizard page, click Next.
5. Under Configure User Settings, select Public IM Connectivity.
6. On the Configure Operation Status page, if you want to export the log, click Export to save the XML file.
7. Click Finish.

To enable multiple users for public IM connectivity by using the Office Communications Server administrative snap-in, do the following:

1. Click Start, point to All Programs, point to Administrative Tools, and then click Office Communications Server 2007.
2. In the console tree, expand the forest node.
3. Expand subsequent nodes under the Domains node until you reach the domain that the server or pool resides in.
4. Expand the Standard Edition Servers or Enterprise Pools node.
5. Expand the server or pool.
6. Do one of the following:
   - Right-click the Users folder, and then click Configure Users to configure all user accounts on this server or pool.
   - Click the Users folder, and in the Details pane, select the user or users that you want to configure, and then click Configure Users.
7. On the Welcome To The Configure User Wizard page, click Next.
8. Under Configure User Settings, select Public IM Connectivity.
9. On the Configure Operation Status page, if you want to export the log, click Export to save the XML file.
10. Click Finish.

Note To perform this task, you must be logged on as a member of the RTCDomainUserAdmins group.

You can also enable or disable public IM connectivity for individual users. To configure an individual user for public IM connectivity by using the Active Directory Users and Computers snap-in, do the following:

1. If the computer is a domain controller, click Start, point to All Programs, point to Administrative Tools, and then click Active Directory Users And Computers. Otherwise, if the computer is not a domain controller, at the command prompt type **dsa.msc** and press Enter.
2. Go to the folder where your user accounts reside.
3. Expand the folder.
4. Right-click the user account that you want to configure, and then select Properties.
5. On the Communications tab, make sure that the Enable User For Office Communications Server check box is selected. If it is not, select it now.
6. Enter a sign-in name, and select a server or pool for the user to sign in to. (See Figure 8-9.)

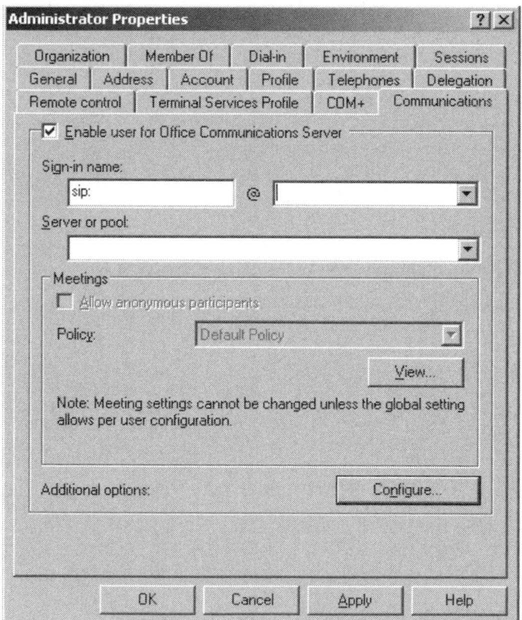

Figure 8-9 Enable User For Office Communications Server

7. Click Configure.

8. Under Federation Settings, select the Enable Public IM Connectivity check box and then click OK.
9. Click OK.

> **Important** An individual user can be authorized for federation, public IM connectivity, remote access, or any combination of the three. Enabling public connectivity for a user does not require disabling federation or remote access.

You can also disable public IM connectivity for one or more users at any time. To do so, follow any of the procedures described previously for enabling public IM connectivity for one or more users, but clear the Enable Public IM Connectivity check box where the procedure says to select it.

Configuring Per-User and Global Settings

When you enable individual user accounts for Office Communications Server 2007 in Active Directory Users and Computers, you can change user account settings to specify the functionality available to each user. For information on the impact of global, group, and individual settings, see "Managing User Accounts" in the "Office Communications Server 2007 Administration Guide."

As shown in the previous sections, settings for user accounts can be configured in different ways. In general, settings can be configured by using the following methods:

- Globally for all users in the forest, using the Office Communications Server 2007 administrative snap-in.
- Individually or in groups, using the Configure Office Communications Server Users Wizard in the Office Communications Server 2007 administrative snap-in or the Active Directory Users and Computers snap-in. After enabling user accounts in Active Directory Users and Computers, using the Configure User Wizards to configure user accounts is recommended–especially for newly enabled user accounts–because it supports configuration of multiple users at a time.
- Individually, using the Communications tab of the user account Properties in Office Communications Server 2007 or Active Directory Users and Computers. This approach is useful if you want to change a small number of settings for a small number of user accounts, or for configuring settings that cannot be configured using the Configure User Wizard.

All three methods are not available for configuration of all settings. Additionally, some of the user account settings that have global settings require that the global setting be configured prior to configuring settings on specific user accounts. Table 8-3 describes which of the methods can be used to configure each of the specific user settings, as well as the global configuration requirements.

Table 8-3 **Configuring Per-User and Global Settings for User Accounts**

User Setting	Description	Global Configuration	Configurable in the Configure Office Communications Server Users Wizard?	Configurable from the Properties, Communications Tab?
Federation	Enables or disables an Office Communications Server 2007 user's ability to communicate with users from other organizations that have an Office Communications Server 2007 deployment and a federated link.	Users cannot be enabled for federation unless federation is enabled at the global level.	Yes, but it takes effect only when federation is enabled at the global level.	Yes, but it takes effect only when federation is enabled at the global level.
Public IM connectivity	Enables or disables an Office Communications Server 2007 user's ability to communicate with users hosted on AOL, Yahoo!, or MSN Internet services.	Users cannot be enabled for public IM connectivity unless federation is enabled at the global level.	Yes, but it takes effect only when public IM connectivity is enabled at the global level.	Yes, but it takes effect only when public IM connectivity is enabled at the global level.
Archiving	Enables or disables archiving of IM conversations of the Office Communications Server 2007 user. This control can be enabled independently for internal conversations and for conversations with users outside your organization.	Yes. At the global level, you can choose to enable archiving for all users, disable archiving for all users, or enable and disable archiving on a per-user basis.	Yes, but only if the global setting is configured to enable and disable archiving on a per-user basis.	Yes, but only if the global setting is configured to enable and disable archiving on a per-user basis.

Table 8-3 Configuring Per-User and Global Settings for User Accounts

User Setting	Description	Global Configuration	Configurable in the Configure Office Communications Server Users Wizard?	Configurable from the Properties, Communications Tab?
Invite anonymous participants to meetings	Enables or disables the ability of Office Communications Server 2007 users in your organization who are meeting organizers to invite participants outside your organization.	Yes. At the global level, you can choose to allow users to invite anonymous participants, disallow users from inviting anonymous participants, or enforce settings at a per-user level.	Yes, but only if the global setting is configured to allow configuration of anonymous participation on a per-user basis.	Yes, but only if the global setting is configured to allow configuration of anonymous participation on a per-user basis.
Meeting policy	Enforces a meeting policy for an Office Communications Server 2007 user who is allowed to organize meetings. The policy specifies aspects of meetings that the organizer can create. The policy name is used to specify which meeting policy to apply.	Yes. At the global level, you can set up one or more meeting policies for specific uses and either select a single global meeting policy to be applied to all users in the forest or specify that the meeting policy is to be applied on a per-user basis.	Yes, if you specify at the global level to apply the meeting policy on a per-user basis.	Yes, if you specify at the global level to apply the meeting policy on a per-user basis.
Enterprise Voice policy	A Voice policy associates phone-usage records with users.	Yes. At the global level, you can set up one or more Voice policies for specific uses and either select a single global Voice policy to be applied to all users in the forest or specify that the Voice policy is to be applied on a per-user basis.	Yes, but only if the global policy is configured to specify Voice policy on a per-user basis.	Yes, but only if the global policy is configured to specify Voice policy on a per-user basis.

The user settings that do not have global settings are configured only at the user level. Table 8-4 shows the configurable user settings that do not use global settings and the configuration methods available for each setting.

Table 8-4 User Settings that Do Not Use Global Settings

User Setting	Description	Configurable in the Configure Office Communications Server Users Wizard?	Configurable from the Properties, Communications Tab?
Enable user for Office Communications Server	Enables an Active Directory user for Office Communications Server 2007.	No	Yes, if an account has been initially enabled in Active Directory Users and Computers and then disabled, it can be re-enabled on the Properties, Communications tab.
Sign-in name	Similar to a user's e-mail address, the sign-in name uniquely defines the user's SIP address as a SIP URI.	No	Yes
Server or pool	FQDN of the Standard Edition server or Enterprise pool where a user's data is stored.	No	Yes
Enhanced presence	Enables or disables enhanced presence, which enables users to control their presence with more granularity. This enables users to create different presence categories and assign data items to the categories. Different views on the categories can be created. With enhanced presence, users can expose different presence states for different categories of contacts.	Yes, but once it is enabled, it cannot be disabled for a user.	Yes, but once it is enabled, it cannot be disabled for a user.

Table 8-4 User Settings that Do Not Use Global Settings

User Setting	Description	Configurable in the Configure Office Communications Server Users Wizard?	Configurable from the Properties, Communications Tab?
Remote user access	Enables or disables a Live Communications user to sign in to Office Communications Server 2007 services from outside the perimeter network of the user's organization without requiring a virtual private network (VPN).	Yes	Yes, as an additional option
PC-to-PC communications only	Enables or disables only PC-to-PC audio communications for the user, but not Remote Call Control or Enterprise Voice. This option does not require deployment of a Remote Call Control server or Unified Messaging.	No	Yes, as an additional option
Remote Call Control	Enables or disables Office Communications Server 2007 user control of a PBX desktop phone by using Microsoft Office Communicator 2007. This option also enables PC-to-PC audio communications.	No	Yes, as an additional option
Enterprise Voice	Enables or disables Enterprise Voice for the user. This option also enables PC-to-PC audio communications.	Yes	Yes, as an additional option
Enable PBX integration	Enables or disables PBX integration for an Enterprise Voice user. This option requires first enabling Enterprise Voice for the user.	No	Yes, as an additional option

Table 8-4 User Settings that Do Not Use Global Settings

User Setting	Description	Configurable in the Configure Office Communications Server Users Wizard?	Configurable from the Properties, Communications Tab?
Line URI (User's phone/device)	URI that uniquely identifies the user's phone line. This URI can be in the form of a SIP URI or a Tel URI.	No	Yes, as an additional option
Remote Call Control server URI	SIP URI that uniquely identifies the Remote Call Control gateway that controls the phone line.	No	Yes, as an additional option

Examining the Technical Details Behind the Public IM Connectivity Scenario

To understand network message flow in the Public IM Connectivity scenario, let's look at two scenarios and the accompanying illustrations of the resulting message flows.

Scenario One: Adding a Contact in Office Communicator 2007

In this scenario, the user enters an account name for a recipient she wants to send instant messages to, performs a search, and adds the recipient account name as a contact. We'll examine seven steps in this process, and these steps are numerically keyed to Figure 8-10. Where possible, each step is illustrated using a corresponding sample SIP message. The illustrative SIP output following the steps is what an admin might see using logging to trace the messages.

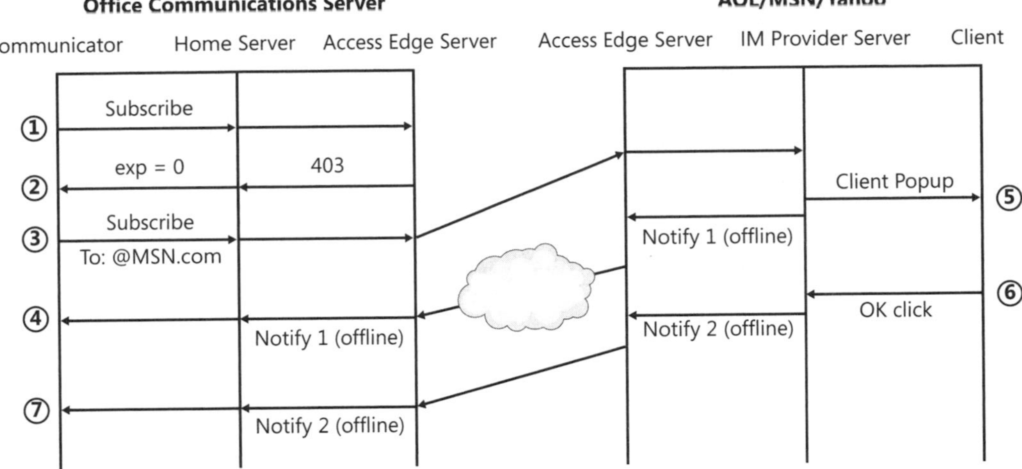

Figure 8-10 Communicator Startup

Step 1: Specify Recipient's Account

The user types in **kim970@msn.com** for a user search. The 'Message Body' shows that the information was sent to the recipient's public IM servers:

```
Start-Line: SUBSCRIBE sip:kim970@msn.com SIP/2.0
From: "PIC Test (pic1)
lcsent01"<sip:pic1@lcsent01.directtaps.net>;tag=dfac414f0f;epid=ce4ccd49ad
To: <sip:kim970@msn.com>
CSeq: 1 SUBSCRIBE
Call-ID: cecb8c21ba01462a90f2f7235673f2b9
Via: SIP/2.0/TLS 10.55.55.22:4231;branch=z9hG4bK0D6A9383.D119DEC5;branched=FALSE
Max-Forwards: 68
Via: SIP/2.0/TLS 10.55.55.33:47696;branch=z9hG4bKC45BE092.1A435385;branched=FALSE;ms-
received-port=47696;
    ms-received-cid=200
ms-user-data: ms-publiccloud=true;ms-federation=true
Via: SIP/2.0/TLS 10.55.55.22:4317;ms-received-port=4317;ms-received-cid=67F00
Contact:
<sip:pic1@lcsent01.directtaps.net;opaque=user:epid:XHiWcZA4TlaDkwMgksvyrQAA;gruu>
User-Agent: UCCP/2.0.6362.0 OC/2.0.6362.0 (Microsoft Office Communicator)
Event: presence
Accept: application/msrtc-event-categories+xml, application/xpidf+xml, text/
xml+msrtc.pidf, application/pidf+xml,
    application/rlmi+xml, multipart/related
Supported: com.microsoft.autoextend
Supported: ms-piggyback-first-notify
Expires: 0
Require: adhoclist, categoryList
Supported: eventlist
Content-Type: application/msrtc-adrl-categorylist+xml
Content-Length: 472
Message-Body: <batchSub xmlns="http://schemas.microsoft.com/2006/01/sip/batch-subscribe"
```

```
uri=
    "sip:pic1@lcsent01.directtaps.net" name=""><action name="subscribe"
id="1008728"><adhocList><resource uri=
    "sip:kim970@msn.com"/></adhocList><categoryList xmlns="http://schemas.microsoft.com/
2006/09/sip/categorylist">
    <category name="calendarData"/><category name="contactCard"/>
    <category name="note"/><category name="services"/><category name="state"/></
categoryList></action></batchSub>
```

Step 2: Recipient's Presence Displayed as Unknown

The account comes up, presence shows as unknown after a short delay, and the information relating to the reason is reflected in the ms-diagnostics "SIPPROXY_E_EPROUTING_MSG_INT_GET_RICH_PRESENCE_FILTERED", indicating that the presence information was filtered.

```
Start-Line: SIP/2.0 403 Forbidden
From: "PIC Test (pic1)
lcsent01"<sip:pic1@lcsent01.directtaps.net>;tag=dfac414f0f;epid=ce4ccd49ad
To: <sip:kim970@msn.com>;tag=C122BE2A56CD774DA0AC6DEC165DB900
CSeq: 1 SUBSCRIBE
Call-ID: cecb8c21ba01462a90f2f7235673f2b9
ms-edge-proxy-message-trust: ms-source-type=EdgeProxyGenerated;ms-ep-fqdn=lcs-ncx-
appool.lcsent01.directtaps.net;
    ms-source-verified-user=verified;ms-source-network=federation
Via: SIP/2.0/TLS
10.55.55.22:4231;branch=z9hG4bK0D6A9383.D119DEC5;branched=FALSE;received=10.154.154.101;
    ms-received-port=1239;ms-received-cid=400
Via: SIP/2.0/TLS 10.55.55.33:47696;branch=z9hG4bKC45BE092.1A435385;branched=FALSE;ms-
received-port=47696;
    ms-received-cid=200
Via: SIP/2.0/TLS 10.55.55.22:4317;ms-received-port=4317;ms-received-cid=67F00
ms-diagnostics: 2;reason="See response code and reason phrase";source="lcs-ncx-
appool.lcsent01.directtaps.net";
    HRESULT="C3E93D80(SIPPROXY_E_EPROUTING_MSG_INT_GET_RICH_PRESENCE_FILTERED)"
Content-Length: 0
Message-Body:
```

Step 3: Recipient's Account Added as a Contact

The user adds the account as a contact, allowing for Rich Presence information to be acknowledged and displayed in the client.

```
Start-Line: SUBSCRIBE sip:kim970@msn.com SIP/2.0
From: "PIC Test (pic1)
lcsent01"<sip:pic1@lcsent01.directtaps.net>;tag=f14fbece50;epid=ce4ccd49ad
To: <sip:kim970@msn.com>
CSeq: 1 SUBSCRIBE
Call-ID: 44047f96df734fc5a6de19b16d3b8376
```

```
Via: SIP/2.0/TLS 10.55.55.22:4231;branch=z9hG4bK59C2C040.5D93021D;branched=FALSE
Max-Forwards: 68
Via: SIP/2.0/TLS 10.55.55.33:47696;branch=z9hG4bK93B4551E.58F79B23;branched=FALSE;ms-
received-port=47696;
    ms-received-cid=200
ms-user-data: ms-publiccloud=true;ms-federation=true
Via: SIP/2.0/TLS 10.55.55.22:4317;ms-received-port=4317;ms-received-cid=67F00
Contact:
<sip:pic1@lcsent01.directtaps.net;opaque=user:epid:XHiWcZA4TlaDkwMgksvyrQAA;gruu>
User-Agent: UCCP/2.0.6362.0 OC/2.0.6362.0 (Microsoft Office Communicator)
Event: presence
Accept: application/msrtc-event-categories+xml, application/xpidf+xml, text/
xml+msrtc.pidf,
     application/pidf+xml, application/rlmi+xml, multipart/related
Supported: com.microsoft.autoextend
Supported: ms-piggyback-first-notify
Content-Type: application/msrtc-adrl-categorylist+xml
Content-Length: 501
Message-Body: <batchSub xmlns="http://schemas.microsoft.com/2006/01/sip/batch-subscribe"
uri=
"sip:pic1@lcsent01.directtaps.net" name=""><action name="subscribe"
id="1008912"><adhocList><resource uri="sip:kim970@msn.com"><context></context></
resource></adhocList><categoryList xmlns="http://schemas.microsoft.com/2006/09/sip/
categorylist"><category name="calendarData"/>
    <category name="contactCard"/><category name="note"/><category name="services"/
><category name="state"/></categoryList></action></batchSub>
```

Step 4: Recipient's Presence Displayed as Offline

Account presence shows as offline, indicating that the Rich Presence is now working as expected and that the contact is offline at the current time.

```
Start-Line: NOTIFY
sip:pic1@lcsent01.directtaps.net;opaque=user:epid:XHiWcZA4TlaDkwMgksvyrQAA;gruu SIP/2.0
From: <sip:kim970@msn.com>;tag=65d68a1bc4
To: <sip:pic1@lcsent01.directtaps.net>;epid=ce4ccd49ad;tag=f14fbece50
CSeq: 1 NOTIFY
Call-ID: 44047f96df734fc5a6de19b16d3b8376
Via: SIP/2.0/TLS 65.54.227.22:19001;branch=z9hG4bK2AAD5BF8.2DEAC26F;branched=FALSE;ms-
internal-info=
    "ca_zFI1fCgvjcqhFOqV_3zHH3WpGMA"
Max-Forwards: 69
ms-asserted-verification-level: ms-source-verified-user=verified
Via: SIP/2.0/TLS 65.54.230.13:8624;branch=z9hG4bKa69bfffe;ms-received-port=8624;ms-
received-cid=38892800
Route: <sip:lcs-ncx-
appool.lcsent01.directtaps.net:5061;transport=tls;epid=ce4ccd49ad;lr>
CONTACT: <sip:kim970@msn.com:5061;transport=tls;maddr=BAYM-TG399.tgw.messenger.msn.com>
CONTENT-LENGTH: 489
EVENT: presence
SUBSCRIPTION-STATE: active
CONTENT-TYPE: application/pidf+xml
Message-Body: <?xml version="1.0" encoding="utf-8"?>
```

```
<presence xmlns="urn:ietf:params:xml:ns:pidf"
xmlns:ep="urn:ietf:params:xml:ns:pidf:status:rpid-status"
xmlns:et="urn:ietf:params:xml:ns:pidf:rpid-tuple"
xmlns:ci="urn:ietf:params:xml:ns:pidf:cipid"
    entity="sip:kim970@msn.com">
  <tuple id="0">
    <status>
      <basic>closed</basic>
    </status>
  </tuple>
 <ci:icon>https://images.edge.messenger.live.com/wlnavbtn.png</ci:icon>
  <ci:display-name>lcs</ci:display-name>
</presence>
```

Step 5: Recipient Receives Notification

User kim970@msn.com gets a popup window that indicates that Office Communicator user 'pic1' has added Kim to her contacts.

Step 6: Recipient Adds a User to Buddy List

User kim970@msn.com adds the Office Communicator user to his buddy list.

Step 7: Recipient's Presence Displayed as Online

Presence shows as online in Office Communicator for kim970@msn.com because a full round trip series of SIP messages from sender to recipient are now being sent and received.

```
Start-Line: NOTIFY
sip:pic1@lcsent01.directtaps.net;opaque=user:epid:XHiWcZA4TlaDkwMgksvyrQAA;gruu SIP/2.0
From: <sip:kim970@msn.com>;tag=65d68a1bc4
To: <sip:pic1@lcsent01.directtaps.net>;epid=ce4ccd49ad;tag=f14fbece50
CSeq: 1 NOTIFY
Call-ID: 44047f96df734fc5a6de19b16d3b8376
Via: SIP/2.0/TLS 65.54.227.22:19001;branch=z9hG4bK2AAD5BF8.2DEAC26F;branched=FALSE;ms-
internal-info=
    "ca_zFI1fCgvjcqhFOqV_3zHH3WpGMA"
Max-Forwards: 69
ms-asserted-verification-level: ms-source-verified-user=verified
Via: SIP/2.0/TLS 65.54.230.13:8624;branch=z9hG4bKa69bfffe;ms-received-port=8624;ms-
received-cid=38892800
Route: <sip:lcs-ncx-
appool.lcsent01.directtaps.net:5061;transport=tls;epid=ce4ccd49ad;lr>
CONTACT: <sip:kim970@msn.com:5061;transport=tls;maddr=BAYM-TG399.tgw.messenger.msn.com>
CONTENT-LENGTH: 489
EVENT: presence
SUBSCRIPTION-STATE: active
CONTENT-TYPE: application/pidf+xml
Message-Body: <?xml version="1.0" encoding="utf-8"?>
<presence xmlns="urn:ietf:params:xml:ns:pidf"
xmlns:ep="urn:ietf:params:xml:ns:pidf:status:rpid-status"xmlns:et=
```

```
  "urn:ietf:params:xml:ns:pidf:rpid-tuple" xmlns:ci="urn:ietf:params:xml:ns:pidf:cipid"
    entity="sip:kim970@msn.com">
  <tuple id="0">
    <status>
      <basic>open</basic>
    </status>
  </tuple>
 <ci:icon>https://images.edge.messenger.live.com/wlnavbtn.png</ci:icon>
  <ci:display-name>lcs</ci:display-name>
</presence>
```

Scenario Two: Sending a Single Message

In this scenario, the user sends a single message to the recipient. Once again, we'll examine some steps in this process, with these steps being numerically keyed to Figure 8-11. And when possible, each step is illustrated using a corresponding sample SIP message.

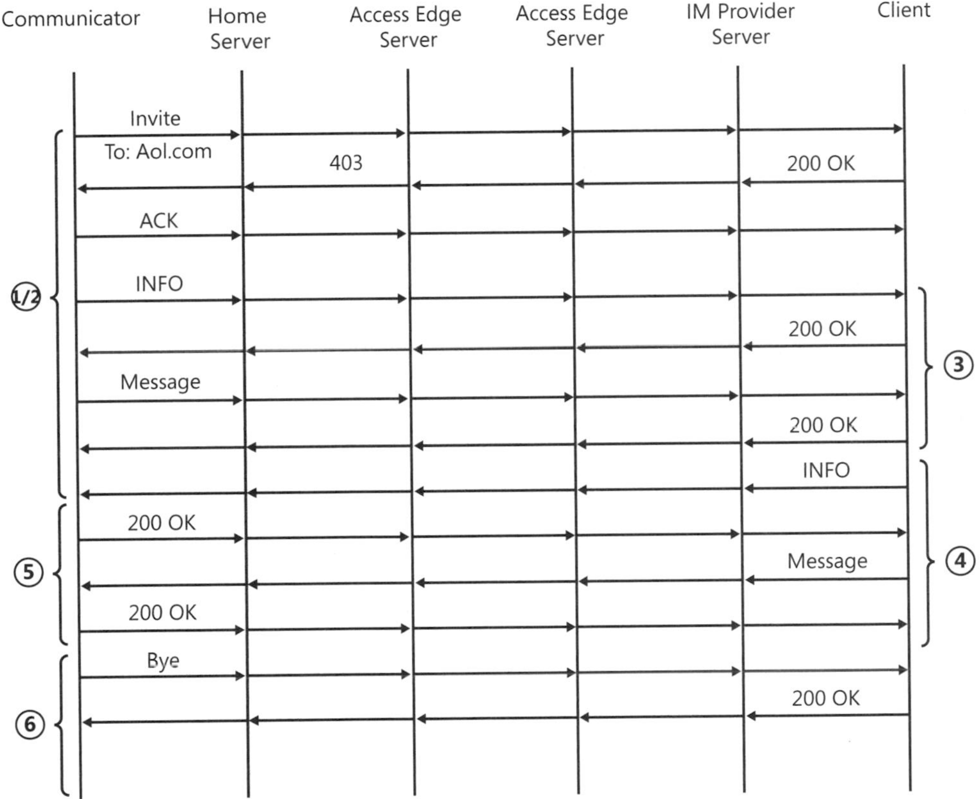

Figure 8-11 Communicator Startup

Step 1: User Selects a Recipient from the Buddy List in Office Communicator

User double-clicks on 'kim970@aol.com' in Office Communicator to initiate a communication with her.

Step 2: User Types a Message to a Recipient

A messaging window opens, and the Office Communicator user types a message to kim970@aol.com.

```
Start-Line: INVITE sip:kim970@aol.com SIP/2.0
From: "PIC Test (pic1)
lcsent01"<sip:pic1@lcsent01.directtaps.net>;tag=d277e1abbb;epid=ce4ccd49ad
To: <sip:kim970@aol.com>
CSeq: 1 INVITE
Call-ID: a9c41d4b12da43e4be363596f309fe4e
Record-Route: <sip:h06-
lct.lcsent01.directtaps.net:5061;transport=tls;lr>;tag=CE46965240D18C4A3635495C069DC843
Via: SIP/2.0/TLS 10.55.55.22:4231;branch=z9hG4bKEC456A32.C97CB7D0;branched=FALSE
Max-Forwards: 68
Content-Length: 201
Via: SIP/2.0/TLS 10.55.55.33:47696;branch=z9hG4bKC2D8526B.D28FDC17;branched=FALSE;ms-
received-port=47696;
    ms-received-cid=200
Via: SIP/2.0/TLS 10.55.55.22:4317;ms-received-port=4317;ms-received-cid=67F00
ms-user-data: ms-publiccloud=true;ms-federation=true
Record-Route: <sip:eepool07.lcsent01.directtaps.net:5061;transport=tls;ms-fe=h05-
lct.lcsent01.directtaps.net;
    ms-role-rs-to;lr>;tag=A520B519F64AB62075583DC8E1FC916C
Contact:
<sip:pic1@lcsent01.directtaps.net;opaque=user:epid:XHiWcZA4TlaDkwMgksvyrQAA;gruu>
User-Agent: UCCP/2.0.6362.0 OC/2.0.6362.0 (Microsoft Office Communicator)
ms-text-format: text/plain; charset=UTF-
8;msgr=WAAtAE0ATQBTAC0ASQBNAC0ARgBvAHIAbQBhAHQAOgAgAEYATgA9AE0AUwAlA

DIAMABTAGgAZQBsAGwAJQAyADAARABsAGcAJQAyADAAMgA7ACAARQBGAD0AOwAgAEMATwA9ADAAOwAgAEMAUwA9A
DAAOwAgAFAARgA9A
    DAACgANAAoADQA;ms-body=aGk=
Supported: ms-delayed-accept
Supported: ms-renders-isf
Supported: ms-renders-gif
Supported: ms-renders-mime-alternative
Ms-Conversation-ID: Acfmq6qEY4LFypq3QkiyeHTKN1rRTg==
Supported: timer
Supported: ms-sender
Supported: ms-early-media
Roster-Manager: sip:pic1@lcsent01.directtaps.net
EndPoints: <sip:pic1@lcsent01.directtaps.net>, <sip:kim970@aol.com>
Supported: com.microsoft.rtc-multiparty
ms-keep-alive: UAC;hop-hop=yes
Supported: ms-conf-invite
```

```
Content-Type: application/sdp
Message-Body: v=0
o=- 0 0 IN IP4 10.55.55.22
s=session
c=IN IP4 10.55.55.22
t=0 0
m=message 5060 sip null
a=accept-types:text/rtf application/x-ms-ink image/gif multipart/alternative application/
ms-imdn+xml

Start-Line: SIP/2.0 200 OK
From: "PIC Test (pic1) lcsent01"
<sip:pic1@lcsent01.directtaps.net>;tag=d277e1abbb;epid=ce4ccd49ad
To: <sip:kim970@aol.com>;tag=1187999459aol
CSeq: 1 INVITE
Call-ID: a9c41d4b12da43e4be363596f309fe4e
Via: SIP/2.0/TLS 10.154.154.6:33660;branch=z9hG4bK81B1A184.E55C7B7D;branched=FALSE;ms-
internal-info="aahcQlfV2sxVHSijae9Oyn6FrB6JjlXHt9jtKVswAA"
Via: SIP/2.0/TLS
10.55.55.22:4231;branch=z9hG4bKEC456A32.C97CB7D0;branched=FALSE;received=10.154.154.101;
    ms-received-port=1239;ms-received-cid=400
Via: SIP/2.0/TLS 10.55.55.33:47696;branch=z9hG4bKC2D8526B.D28FDC17;branched=FALSE;ms-
received-port=47696;
    ms-received-cid=200
Via: SIP/2.0/TLS 10.55.55.22:4317;ms-received-port=4317;ms-received-cid=67F00
Record-Route:
<sip:sip.oscar.aol.com:5061;transport=tls;sag_conn_id=14509788;sag_qid=349;lr>
Record-Route: <sip:lcs-ncx-
appool.lcsent01.directtaps.net:5061;transport=tls;epid=ce4ccd49ad;lr;ms-key-info=

jACAAB63AIzSs4V0rObHAQECAAADZgAAAKQAAEq0o08howd1ofPQstatonzKqkw0xTDqkgxWH_u_jrMEmRFTjHu4
OodKnCTJhs
    5dWtmALBA9QzE6O-Xo0pCckSR6ntVyZSnCjAWZO3snPm2yL0s4nqlcEePfA2pIy1_HjCkIU-
2gr5mUfd9USmP3_p1sHtAO5d1Ic8QnhP-N
    GuWY55EM2SAZRvp7Zgtx6HHKug5Xgb7t-3a7-
qA6y0VBY51q_GmcNj7xcj9uKbMzhGkCjeWOXqCS0Tw6GlSvsNKqdASpsh8bh0wLxSZp
    PgCOn9L73HQq1bJwB_6QkmE0yniNzKX3sSq5w-JjW6vL_FFPjf75bsVtT5sU1xDyINWZVKkA;ms-route-
sig=aa0eCMX_rEFywBlBHQ
    lgewbsiUXbLlXHt94I5_cgAA>;msrrsig=aakgoM1icuCWdSXpbU9QJ6OH6YKuzlXHt94I5_cgAA;
    tag=C122BE2A56CD774DA0AC6DEC165DB900
Record-Route: <sip:h06-
lct.lcsent01.directtaps.net:5061;transport=tls;lr>;tag=CE46965240D18C4A3635495C069DC843
Record-Route: <sip:eepool07.lcsent01.directtaps.net:5061;transport=tls;ms-fe=h05-
lct.lcsent01.directtaps.net;
    ms-role-rs-to;lr>;tag=A520B519F64AB62075583DC8E1FC916C
Contact: <sip:sip.oscar.aol.com:5061;maddr=64.12.162.248;transport=tls>
Ms-asserted-verification-level: ms-source-verified-user=verified
Content-Type: application/sdp
Content-Length: 102
Message-Body: v=0
o=- 0 0 IN IP4 64.12.162.248
s=session
c=IN IP4 64.12.162.248
t=0 0
m=message 5060 sip null
```

```
Start-Line: ACK sip:sip.oscar.aol.com:5061;maddr=64.12.162.248;transport=tls SIP/2.0
From: <sip:pic1@lcsent01.directtaps.net>;tag=d277e1abbb;epid=ce4ccd49ad
To: <sip:kim970@aol.com>;tag=1187999459aol
CSeq: 1 ACK
Call-ID: a9c41d4b12da43e4be363596f309fe4e
Via: SIP/2.0/TLS 10.55.55.22:4231;branch=z9hG4bKA38E2D41.9F92ED13;branched=FALSE
Max-Forwards: 68
Via: SIP/2.0/TLS 10.55.55.33:47696;branch=z9hG4bK668ACE7F.395877BC;branched=FALSE;ms-
received-port=47696;
    ms-received-cid=200
Via: SIP/2.0/TLS 10.55.55.22:4317;ms-received-port=4317;ms-received-cid=67F00
Route: <sip:lcs-ncx-appool.lcsent01.directtaps.net:5061;transport=tls;lr>
Route: <sip:sip.oscar.aol.com:5061;transport=tls;sag_conn_id=14509788;sag_qid=349;lr>
User-Agent: UCCP/2.0.6362.0 OC/2.0.6362.0 (Microsoft Office Communicator)
Content-Length: 0
Message-Body:
```

Step 3: Recipient Receives a Message from a User

The AOL user sees message text in the popup window and status information that says the Office Communicator user is typing.

```
Start-Line: MESSAGE sip:sip.oscar.aol.com:5061;maddr=64.12.162.248;transport=tls SIP/2.0
From: <sip:pic1@lcsent01.directtaps.net>;tag=d277e1abbb;epid=ce4ccd49ad
To: <sip:kim970@aol.com>;tag=1187999459aol
CSeq: 2 MESSAGE
Call-ID: a9c41d4b12da43e4be363596f309fe4e
Via: SIP/2.0/TLS 10.55.55.22:4231;branch=z9hG4bK9309E25C.B523C951;branched=FALSE
Max-Forwards: 68
Via: SIP/2.0/TLS 10.55.55.33:47696;branch=z9hG4bK37466F08.68B7CC23;branched=FALSE;ms-
received-port=47696;
    ms-received-cid=200
Via: SIP/2.0/TLS 10.55.55.22:4317;ms-received-port=4317;ms-received-cid=67F00
Route: <sip:lcs-ncx-appool.lcsent01.directtaps.net:5061;transport=tls;lr>
Route: <sip:sip.oscar.aol.com:5061;transport=tls;sag_conn_id=14509788;sag_qid=349;lr>
User-Agent: UCCP/2.0.6362.0 OC/2.0.6362.0 (Microsoft Office Communicator)
Supported: timer
Content-Type: text/plain; charset=UTF-
8;msgr=WAAtAE0ATQBTAC0ASQBNAC0ARgBvAHIAbQBhAHQAOgAgAEYATgA9AE0AUwAlA

DIAMABTAGgAZQBsAGwAJQAyADAARABsAGcAJQAyADAAMgA7ACAARQBGAD0AOwAgAEMATwA9ADAAOwAgAEMAUwA9A
DAAOwAgAFAARgA
    9ADAACgANAAoADQA
Content-Length: 2
Message-Body: hi

Start-Line: SIP/2.0 200 OK
From: <sip:pic1@lcsent01.directtaps.net>;tag=d277e1abbb;epid=ce4ccd49ad
To: <sip:kim970@aol.com>;tag=1187999459aol
CSeq: 2 MESSAGE
Call-ID: a9c41d4b12da43e4be363596f309fe4e
Via: SIP/2.0/TLS 10.154.154.6:33712;branch=z9hG4bK43E6514E.539273D2;branched=FALSE;ms-
```

```
internal-info="aaoiubm6MQ3y7wu irYnn_hcAGaQdTknPSjtKVswAA"
Via: SIP/2.0/TLS
10.55.55.22:4231;branch=z9hG4bK9309E25C.B523C951;branched=FALSE;received=10.154.154.101;
    ms-received-port=1239;ms-received-cid=400
Via: SIP/2.0/TLS 10.55.55.33:47696;branch=z9hG4bK37466F08.68B7CC23;branched=FALSE;ms-
received-port=47696;
    ms-received-cid=200
Via: SIP/2.0/TLS 10.55.55.22:4317;ms-received-port=4317;ms-received-cid=67F00
Record-Route:
<sip:sip.oscar.aol.com:5061;transport=tls;sag_conn_id=4012686;sag_qid=351;lr>
Contact: <sip:sip.oscar.aol.com:5061;maddr=64.12.162.248;transport=tls>
Ms-asserted-verification-level: ms-source-verified-user=verified
Content-Length: 0
Message-Body:
```

Step 4: Recipient Types a Reply to the User

The AOL user types a message to the Office Communicator user in return.

```
Start-Line: INFO sip:pic1@lcsent01.directtaps.net SIP/2.0
From: <sip:kim970@aol.com>;tag=1187999459aol
To: <sip:pic1@lcsent01.directtaps.net>;tag=d277e1abbb;epid=ce4ccd49ad
CSeq: 2 INFO
Call-ID: a9c41d4b12da43e4be363596f309fe4e
Via: SIP/2.0/TLS sip.oscar.aol.com:5061;branch=z9hG4bK.15d.46cf6eeb.6c72324
Record-Route: <sip:sip.oscar.aol.com:5061;transport=tls;sag_conn_id=14509963;
sag_qid=349;lr>
Contact: <sip:kim970@aol.com:5061;maddr=64.12.162.248;transport=tls>
User-agent: AOL/1.0
Ms-asserted-verification-level: ms-source-verified-user=verified
Max-Forwards: 68
Content-Type: application/xml
Content-Length: 91
Message-Body: <?xml version="1.0"?>
<KeyboardActivity>
 <status status="type" />
</KeyboardActivity>

Start-Line: SIP/2.0 200 OK
From: <sip:kim970@aol.com>;tag=1187999459aol
To: <sip:pic1@lcsent01.directtaps.net>;tag=d277e1abbb;epid=ce4ccd49ad
CSeq: 2 INFO
Call-ID: a9c41d4b12da43e4be363596f309fe4e
Via: SIP/2.0/TLS
10.154.154.16:33589;branch=z9hG4bK9792A2C3.4400EA88;branched=FALSE;received=10.55.55.1;
    ms-received-port=31328;ms-received-cid=600
Via: SIP/2.0/TLS
sip.oscar.aol.com:5061;branch=z9hG4bK.15d.46cf6eeb.6c72324;received=64.12.162.248;
    ms-received-port=9577;ms-received-cid=2100
Contact:
<sip:pic1@lcsent01.directtaps.net;opaque=user:epid:XHiWcZA4TlaDkwMgksvyrQAA;gruu>
User-Agent: UCCP/2.0.6362.0 OC/2.0.6362.0 (Microsoft Office Communicator)
Content-Length: 0
```

```
Message-Body:

Start-Line: MESSAGE sip:pic1@lcsent01.directtaps.net SIP/2.0
From: <sip:kim970@aol.com>;tag=1187999459aol
To: <sip:pic1@lcsent01.directtaps.net>;tag=d277e1abbb;epid=ce4ccd49ad
CSeq: 3 MESSAGE
Call-ID: a9c41d4b12da43e4be363596f309fe4e
Via: SIP/2.0/TLS 10.154.154.16:33589;branch=z9hG4bKA09E3A6E.C8BDC4F0;branched=FALSE
Max-Forwards: 67
ms-edge-proxy-message-trust: ms-source-type=AuthorizedServer;ms-ep-fqdn=lcs-ncx-
appool.lcsent01.directtaps.net;
    ms-source-verified-user=verified;ms-source-network=publiccloud
Via: SIP/2.0/TLS
sip.oscar.aol.com:5061;branch=z9hG4bK.15d.46cf6eeb.6c72325;received=64.12.162.248;
    ms-received-port=9577;ms-received-cid=2100
Record-Route:
<sip:sip.oscar.aol.com:5061;transport=tls;sag_conn_id=14509963;sag_qid=349;lr>
Contact: <sip:kim970@aol.com:5061;maddr=64.12.162.248;transport=tls>
User-agent: AOL/1.0
Content-Type: text/plain; charset=UTF-8
Content-Length: 2
Message-Body: hi

Start-Line: SIP/2.0 200 OK
From: <sip:kim970@aol.com>;tag=1187999459aol
To: <sip:pic1@lcsent01.directtaps.net>;tag=d277e1abbb;epid=ce4ccd49ad
CSeq: 3 MESSAGE
Call-ID: a9c41d4b12da43e4be363596f309fe4e
ms-application-via: backend_token;ms-server=h05-lct.lcsent01.directtaps.net;ms-
pool=eepool07.lcsent01.directtaps.net;
    ms-application=51FB453D-5B9F-45df-83B4-ADD1F7E604A8
Via: SIP/2.0/TLS
10.154.154.16:33589;branch=z9hG4bKA09E3A6E.C8BDC4F0;branched=FALSE;received=10.55.55.1;
    ms-received-port=31328;ms-received-cid=600
Via: SIP/2.0/TLS
sip.oscar.aol.com:5061;branch=z9hG4bK.15d.46cf6eeb.6c72325;received=64.12.162.248;
    ms-received-port=9577;ms-received-cid=2100
Contact:
<sip:pic1@lcsent01.directtaps.net;opaque=user:epid:XHiWcZA4TlaDkwMgksvyrQAA;gruu>
User-Agent: UCCP/2.0.6362.0 OC/2.0.6362.0 (Microsoft Office Communicator)
Content-Length: 0
Message-Body:
```

Step 5: User Receives a Message from the Recipient

The Office Communicator user receives the message and status information that says the AOL user is typing.

Step 6: Conversation Finished

The Office Communicator user closes the IM window, which effectively ends the conversation and is indicated by the 'bye' message.

```
Start-Line: BYE sip:sip.oscar.aol.com:5061;maddr=64.12.162.248;transport=tls SIP/2.0
From: <sip:pic1@lcsent01.directtaps.net>;tag=d277e1abbb;epid=ce4ccd49ad
To: <sip:kim970@aol.com>;tag=1187999459aol
CSeq: 3 BYE
Call-ID: a9c41d4b12da43e4be363596f309fe4e
Via: SIP/2.0/TLS 10.55.55.22:4231;branch=z9hG4bK7CE0B719.C8CE110A;branched=FALSE
Max-Forwards: 68
Via: SIP/2.0/TLS 10.55.55.33:47696;branch=z9hG4bK08021091.03FE3863;branched=FALSE;ms-
received-port=47696;
    ms-received-cid=200
Via: SIP/2.0/TLS 10.55.55.22:4317;ms-received-port=4317;ms-received-cid=67F00
Route: <sip:lcs-ncx-appool.lcsent01.directtaps.net:5061;transport=tls;lr>
Route: <sip:sip.oscar.aol.com:5061;transport=tls;sag_conn_id=14509788;sag_qid=349;lr>
User-Agent: UCCP/2.0.6362.0 OC/2.0.6362.0 (Microsoft Office Communicator)
Content-Length: 0
Message-Body:

Start-Line: SIP/2.0 200 OK
From: <sip:pic1@lcsent01.directtaps.net>;tag=d277e1abbb;epid=ce4ccd49ad
To: <sip:kim970@aol.com>;tag=1187999459aol
CSeq: 3 BYE
Call-ID: a9c41d4b12da43e4be363596f309fe4e
Via: SIP/2.0/TLS 10.154.154.6:33712;branch=z9hG4bK7D675457.97F0C5F5;branched=FALSE;
    ms-internal-info="aa45b3VbBTS4SvYmwjsNPOk2BVBYaX8MX1jtKVSwAA"
Via: SIP/2.0/TLS
10.55.55.22:4231;branch=z9hG4bK7CE0B719.C8CE110A;branched=FALSE;received=10.154.154.101;
     ms-received-port=1239;ms-received-cid=400
Via: SIP/2.0/TLS 10.55.55.33:47696;branch=z9hG4bK08021091.03FE3863;branched=FALSE;ms-
received-port=47696;
    ms-received-cid=200
Via: SIP/2.0/TLS 10.55.55.22:4317;ms-received-port=4317;ms-received-cid=67F00
Record-Route:
<sip:sip.oscar.aol.com:5061;transport=tls;sag_conn_id=4012686;sag_qid=351;lr>
Contact: <sip:sip.oscar.aol.com:5061;maddr=64.12.162.248;transport=tls>
Ms-asserted-verification-level: ms-source-verified-user=verified
Content-Length: 0
Message-Body:
```

Summary

This chapter examined how Office Communications Server 2007 provides the means for communicating with users of instant messaging services provided by MSN, AOL, and Yahoo!. This allows authorized Office Communications Server users to add contacts, share presence information, and communicate in real time with IM users in these public networks. Office Communications Server enables administrators to authorize public IM connectivity on a per-user or group basis and change both individual and group authorizations as needed. Office Communications Server also allows administrators to exercise control over spim by configuring message filters to restrict access from unverified users.

Additional Resources

- "Configuring Intelligent IM Filtering" in the "Office Communications Server 2007 Administration Guide."
- "Enabling User Accounts for Office Communications Server" in the "Office Communications Server 2007 Administration Guide."
- "Configuring IM Provider Support on Edge Servers" in the "Office Communications Server 2007 Administration Guide."
- "Configuring Intelligent IM Filtering" in the "Office Communications Server 2007 Administration Guide."
- "Managing User Accounts" in the "Office Communications Server 2007 Administration Guide."
- "Step 2.2. Configure DNS" in the "Office Communications Server 2007 Edge Server Deployment Guide."
- "Capacity Planning" in the "Office Communications Server 2007 Planning Guide."
- See the Readme file in the Office Communications Server Resource Kit Tools installation folder (\OCS 2007 Resource Kit Tools on the companion CD) for more information about running the Picstats.sql query script.

On the Companion CD

There is no companion CD content for this chapter.

Chapter 9

Understanding Remote Call Control Scenario

In this chapter:

Many standard office environments have workspaces that contain a computer running a Microsoft operating system and Microsoft Office, and a Private Branch eXchange (PBX) or IP PBX phone. Typical information workers perform their daily work using this standard technology environment. In daily workflow, calls are placed to phone numbers of contacts whose contact information is located in Microsoft Office Outlook or the Global Address List, based on data stored by Microsoft Active Directory Domain Services. Without the ability to place a phone call directly from the desktop computer, the user must manually enter a phone number on the desktop phone, while looking at the screen and typing the digits. This is not only inconvenient but also results in calls placed to the wrong destination.

The Remote Call Control (RCC) scenario for Office Communications Server 2007 eliminates the necessity of manually entering phone numbers stored on the computer into a PBX or IP PBX phone. Furthermore, a user's Office Communicator presence state will reflect the fact that she is in a call by changing the presence state to In A Call. This scenario is supported by Live Communications Server 2005 SP1 and by Office Communications Server 2007 with Communicator 2007. This scenario is not supported by Office Communications Server 2007 with Microsoft Office Communicator Phone Edition.

Note Office Communicator Phone Edition is the Internet Protocol (IP) phone solution for Office Communications Server 2007. Chapter 10, "VoIP Scenario," discusses the option to have multiple registered endpoints for the same user on Office Communications Server 2007. For example, one of the endpoints could be a Communicator 2007 application running on a desktop computer, and the other concurrently connected endpoint could be Office Communicator Phone Edition. Both act as VoIP endpoints.

If the user is enabled for RCC and not for Enterprise Voice, such as in the Voice over Internet Protocol (VoIP) scenarios, Office Communicator Phone Edition cannot be used. (For example, it is not possible to establish an outgoing call on Communicator 2007 and let the Office Communicator Phone Edition IP phone make the call.)

The user is able to control his PBX or IP PBX phone by using the Communicator 2007 graphical user interface. If the company has Office Communications Server 2007 Edge Server deployed to allow Remote Access scenarios, it is even possible for the user to control his office desktop phone while he is connected anywhere on the Internet. For example, a user can receive an incoming call on his PBX or IP PBX extension in the office and deflect the incoming call to his mobile phone number by clicking on a small pop-up window that shows the incoming call on Communicator 2007.

In the RCC scenario, the voice media stream of a phone call stays on the existing PBX or IP PBX phone and is not being handled by Communicator 2007. This is one of the major differences between the Remote Call Control scenario and the Enterprise Voice scenarios, as described in Chapter 10.

Why Consider Remote Call Control?

It is reasonable to ask why a company should deploy the RCC scenario when it could take an even bigger step and deploy one of the VoIP scenarios offered by Office Communications Server 2007. After all, today's enterprise IP networks are reliable, provide sufficient service levels, and fulfill VoIP-characteristic requirements. VoIP scenarios using Communicator 2007 offer an even richer set of functionality and better integration into other Microsoft Office applications (such as Microsoft Outlook) than the RCC scenario. In addition, the effort required to integrate with the existing telephone environment so that users can control their existing PBX or IP PBX phones can be eliminated by skipping the RCC step and migrating to VoIP immediately.

Even though we are living in the so-called "VoIP age" and many large enterprises have already replaced their existing Time Division Multiplexing (TDM) PBX with VoIP-based IP PBX, the majority of enterprises are still running TDM PBX systems. Their migration process from TDM to VoIP is delayed for multiple specific reasons. Office Communications Server 2007 offers with the RCC scenario a "lightweight" telephone integration scenario, enabling enterprises to offer computer-to-telephone integration to their users, supplying the ease of a computer telephone (softphone), without migrating their entire telephone environment to VoIP on the IP network.

Real World: Private Branch Exchange

A private branch exchange (PBX) is a communication system that connects phones, faxes, and modems to other extensions within a business or to the public switched telephone network (PSTN). A traditional PBX consists of telephone handsets that are physically wired to a switch located in the same or a nearby building. This traditional approach requires an elaborate wiring system, one that parallels a similar wiring setup for the computers in the building. Furthermore, the traditional PBX assigns a phone number to the port on the PBX where the wire is connected rather than to the person or the telephone device itself. This arrangement results in a labor-intensive process to set up or move an office worker's phone whenever the worker changes offices. These factors and many others combined with the declining costs of computer networking equipment have given rise to the IP PBX, or Internet Protocol PBX. These solutions provide the same functionality as a traditional PBX, often using equipment that so closely resembles its traditional brethren that office workers do not notice a difference. But the total cost of ownership of an IP PBX is substantially lower.

–Paul Tidwell
Software Development Engineer, Microsoft

For all companies that have already migrated to a VoIP platform, mostly in the form of an IP PBX, the main reason to configure the RCC scenario is to provide the ease of integrated telephone functionality in Microsoft Office applications to their users, as most users are already familiar with the look and feel of Communicator 2007 for instant messaging (IM) and presence.

Overview of Remote Call Control Scenario

As shown in Figure 9-1, a user using the RCC scenario has a PBX or IP PBX phone next to his desktop computer running Communicator 2007 enabled for RCC.

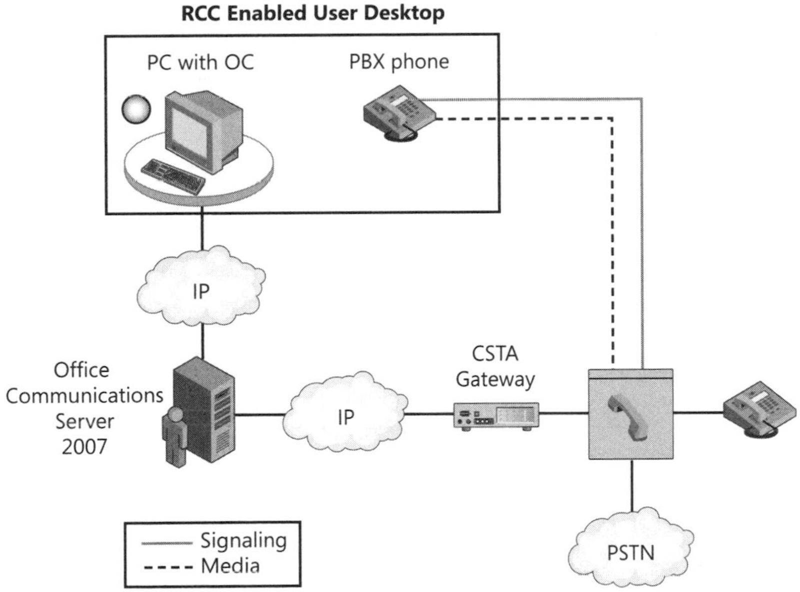

Figure 9-1 System architecture diagram for RCC scenario

Apart from enabling the user's Communicator 2007 for RCC, it is necessary to install at least one Session Initiation Protocol/Computer-Supported Telephony Applications (SIP/CSTA) gateway connected to the existing PBX or IP PBX that also hosts the user's PBX phone or IP PBX phone. CSTA is an international standard set by the European Computer Manufacturers Association (ECMA) to combine network servers in general with PBX or IP PBX environments. There are PBX or IP PBX–specific SIP/CSTA gateways or vendor-neutral SIP/CSTA gateways, such as Genesys Enterprise Telephony Software (GETS) from Genesys, and it is their task to transmit call-related signaling information from the PBX or IP PBX to Communicator 2007 and vice versa. The SIP/CSTA gateway does this by establishing and terminating SIP sessions on the IP network site and converting these messages to CSTA-standard specific messages on the telephone network site to the existing PBX or IP PBX by using PBX/IP PBX-specific CSTA commands, but without handling the voice media stream.

The following functionalities are available with Communicator 2007 if a user is enabled for RCC:

- **Make call** The RCC-enabled Communicator 2007 user can initiate a phone call by clicking on a call menu provided in Communicator 2007 or Microsoft Outlook.
- **Receive call** The RCC-enabled Communicator 2007 user can accept an incoming call that is presented to her in the form of a pop-up window by clicking on the pop-up window. The existing PBX or IP PBX phone will go off-hook, and the speaker phone capabilities will be activated.
- **Caller identification** If the RCC-enabled Communicator 2007 user receives an incoming call, Communicator 2007 will try to resolve the Calling Party Number to a more user-friendly format by presenting the calling party's name. This will be successful only if the phone number can be matched against an entry in Microsoft Outlook, a Communicator 2007 contact, or the Global Address List.
- **Call waiting** If the RCC-enabled Communicator 2007 user is already in a call and receives a second call, Communicator 2007 displays a pop-up window to the user that informs him about this second waiting call.
- **Call hold and retrieve** The RCC-enabled Communicator 2007 user is able to use the conversation window of Communicator to place an existing connection on hold and to retrieve it again. By placing the call on hold, the call is held on the PBX or IP PBX and—if available—music is played to the caller by the existing PBX or IP PBX.
- **Alternate call** The RCC-enabled Communicator 2007 user can handle multiple calls at a time. Each call is represented by a separate communication window. The user can switch between the calls but can have only one active call at a time. The other calls are placed on hold. The number of concurrent calls depends on the existing PBX or IP PBX.
- **Single-step transfer** The RCC-enabled Communicator 2007 user can forward an existing call unannounced to another phone number by clicking on the appropriate transfer button in Communicator 2007. This is one of the Communicator 2007 functionalities that is significantly easier to use than a regular PBX or IP PBX phone.

- **Consultative transfer** The RCC-enabled Communicator 2007 user can place an existing call on hold, establish another call, and later connect the former call with the latter. This is another one of the Communicator 2007 functionalities that is significantly easier to use than a regular PBX or IP PBX phone.
- **DTMF (dual-tone multifrequency) digits** The RCC-enabled Communicator 2007 user can initiate the sending of DTMF digits through the PBX system by using the Communicator 2007 conversation window DTMF dial pad in an active call.

> **Note** This feature is available only if the CSTA gateway supports sending of DTMF tones.

- **Forward to another telephone number** The RCC-enabled Communicator 2007 user can forward an incoming call to another phone number while the call is in a ringing state. This functionality does not work automatically (call forward immediately) and is not available when the Communicator 2007 application is not running.
- **Conversation history** The RCC-enabled Communicator 2007 user can see all of her incoming and outgoing calls in the Conversation History folder in Microsoft Outlook. The user does not receive notifications about calls that come in for the user while Communicator 2007 is not running.
- **Missed call** The RCC-enabled Communicator 2007 user receives Missed Call Notifications in his Outlook Inbox for calls that the user did not answer and that came in while Communicator 2007 was running.
- **Reply with IM** The RCC-enabled Communicator 2007 user can deflect an incoming call by answering with an instant message. This works only if the Calling Party Number can be resolved to a contact in the recipient's Communicator 2007 Contact List.
- **Call notes** The RCC-enabled Communicator 2007 user can type notes in Microsoft Office OneNote directly from the Conversation window in Communicator 2007.

> **Note** The following functionalities were provided with Live Communications Server 2005 SP1 but are no longer provided with Office Communications Server 2007:
>
> - Conference calling
> - Location-based forwarding
> - Setting the Do Not Disturb presence state on a PBX or IP PBX phone
> - Showing display names provided by PBX or IP PBX by CSTA gateway

Even if an Office Communications Server 2007 user is enabled for RCC and the telephone functionalities are limited to a set of call control functionalities of the existing PBX or IP PBX phone, the following VoIP-related features are available as well:

- Make and receive Communicator-to-Communicator audio calls
- Make and receive Communicator-to-Communicator audio/video calls
- Establish a video conversation between two Communicator 2007 clients while audio is handled by the PBX or IP PBX

Note With Communicator 2007 and Office Communications Server 2007, it is in general not possible any longer to place computer-to-phone calls and phone-to-computer calls when the user is enabled for RCC, even if a SIP/PSTN gateway is deployed. Instead, the Enterprise Voice scenario provides exactly this functionality. There is one exception where RCC and Enterprise Voice can be configured for a single user. It is explained in Chapter 10.

By using the functionalities just listed, the audio/video media stream stays on the IP network, as shown in Figure 9-2. It is not possible to make a call to or from the existing telephone environment by using the SIP/CSTA gateway for the audio stream, because the SIP/CSTA gateway cannot convert audio streams from the telephone network into Secure Real-time Transport Protocol (SRTP) media streams as used by SIP-based Office Communications Server 2007.

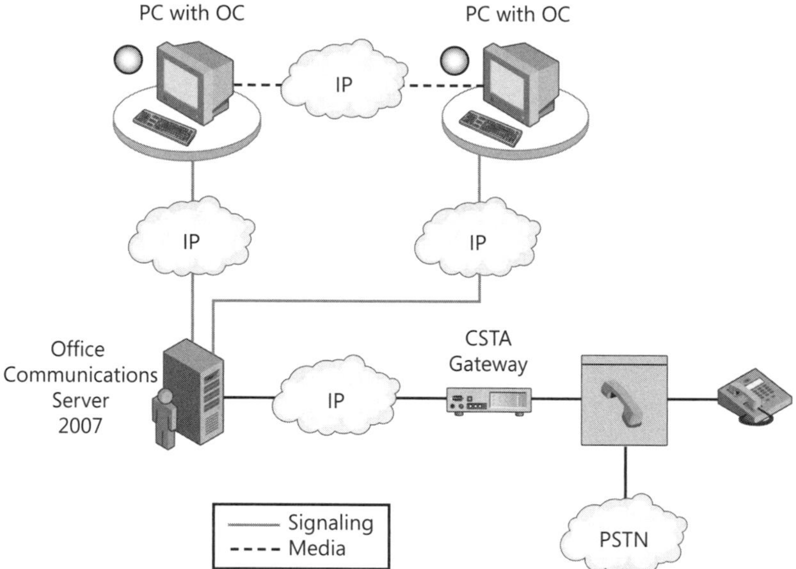

Figure 9-2 Communicator-to-Communicator IP call

Note It is not possible for Communicator 2007 to make a direct SIP call to another SIP endpoint on a different SIP-based IP PBX. Office Communications Server 2007 will proxy SIP messages only to endpoints that are authenticated by the server.

Real World: Unified Communications Using RCC

In the world of Unified Communications, one can be forgiven for overlooking the Remote Call Control (RCC) scenario. With Communicator 2007 and Office Communications Server 2007 supporting such a rich and versatile set of telephony and voice scenarios, RCC is often the forgotten or misunderstood child in this technology family.

What is Remote Call Control?

In everyday terms, RCC enables you to control your PBX desk phone using your laptop or desktop computer, without a cable connecting your computer to the phone. Your desk phone and computer do not need to be in the same country, let alone the same room. RCC does not use Voice over IP (VoIP), nor is there a requirement to have an IP-PBX. This means that there is no need whatsoever to upgrade any of your company's IP network or telephony infrastructure. This is the advantage and lure of RCC: by simply deploying Office Communications Server 2007, Communicator 2007, and (sometimes) a gateway device, you can enable Unified Communications and deliver a useful and innovative solution to your users on a reasonably small budget.

What features does RCC provide?

RCC enables several compelling scenarios. First, users can simply click to call from Communicator 2007 or another presence-enabled application. The user's phone will automatically go off-hook (to speakerphone mode) and dial the number of the intended recipient. This saves the user from performing a directory lookup and typing the number into the phone keypad. Big deal! Now your employees are saving two or three seconds each time they place a call, so now they can spend more time gossiping at the water cooler. Keep reading.

The really great part of RCC is what happens on the other end of that call. For the recipient who is enabled for RCC, several things can happen. When the desk phone rings, the user sees a notification in Communicator 2007 that her phone is ringing–similar to an incoming instant message notification. If the user is at her desk, she can choose to take the call by clicking the Accept Call option in the notification. But if she is not at her desk (perhaps she is online but in a hotel, in a meeting, or in a cafe), she can choose to forward the call to another device, such as a mobile phone. A connection is made, voice mail is averted, and everyone is happy.

Another important benefit of RCC is that a user's presence status automatically changes to On The Phone whenever she is on the phone. This feature has tangible benefits. Wouldn't it be great to know that someone is on the phone before you try calling them? More connections, less voice mail!

What do you need to enable RCC?

To enable RCC, you must have a PBX. If you have a newer PBX, check to see if it supports SIP/CSTA. Major PBX vendors such as Avaya, Cisco, Mitel, and Nortel are shipping PBXs that support native RCC integration with Office Communications Server 2007. If your PBX does not meet this requirement, you need a SIP/CSTA gateway that resides in the path between the Office Communications Server and the PBX to perform the necessary translation.

How does it work?

The mechanism that enables RCC is fairly straightforward. When a user is configured for RCC, he receives two additional pieces of information from Office Communications Server 2007 during the Office Communications Server 2007 registration (sign-in) process. The first piece of information is a "Tel URI", or something that identifies the phone line that the user is allowed to control. The second piece of information is the "RCC URI", or something that identifies the address of the PBX or gateway to which the user will connect. With these two pieces of information, the Communicator 2007 client opens a SIP session with the Call-Control Gateway or PBX. Instead of sending friendly instant messages back and forth, however, Communicator 2007 sends call control (CSTA) messages to the gateway to negotiate features and get the status of the phone line. Communicator 2007 also asks for a "monitor" on the line, which enables Communicator to receive notifications about changes to the status of the line, such as when the user picks up the handset to make a call, or when the line receives an incoming call. This communications channel between Communicator and the gateway or PBX stays open for the duration of the user's session.

What else do I need to do?

Sounds easy, right? As with everything in life, there is fine print. You need to enable each user for RCC. As previously mentioned, this requires setting a unique Tel URI for each user, as well as configuring the RCC URI address, which is usually the same for all users connecting to a particular PBX. Then there is the small matter of phone number normalization.

Phone number normalization

The phone number field in Active Directory is a free-form text field. You probably have numbers specified in different formats and some unusual characters such as parentheses, letters, dashes, and dots thrown in for good measure. A typical phone number in Active Directory might look like this: +1 (803) 201-0333 x10333. User's phone numbers are downloaded into Communicator's local address book by Office Communications Server 2007 Address Book Services. This causes two problems. First, the click-to-call feature from the Communicator 2007 user interface probably will not work unless your PBX understands how to transform this string into a legitimate phone number. Second, reverse number lookup for incoming calls and missed-call notifications fail to match a friendly username to the incoming phone number, because this string is not in the same format as the incoming number on the user phone line.

> There are a few options for fixing the phone number normalization problem. The simplest solution is to change all the phone numbers in Active Directory to a standard format, such as E.164 format. This format looks like this: +18032013333. If doing this is not possible, the next best option is to normalize the phone numbers by using the Office Communications Server 2007 Address Book Service. If that does not work, you might find that the PBX or CSTA gateway has some features or tools that will help. Note that the last option will usually only fix click-to-call scenarios, and it will not enable reverse number lookup functionality. Phone normalization can be a challenging problem to solve, and each case will be slightly different. When in doubt, refer to the documentation for the CSTA gateway or PBX vendor. This topic is usually covered in detail there.
>
> In summary, RCC provides a simple and cost-effective way to enable unified communications for many companies with an older telephony infrastructure. RCC is a great interim step that enhances the feature set of Office Communications Server 2007 investments without requiring an overhaul of the existing telephony system.
>
> *–John Lamb*
> *Principal Consultant, Modality Systems Ltd.*

Technical Details Behind the Remote Call Control Scenario

Communicator 2007 has to send call-related information to and receive call-related information from the telephone environment by using the SIP/CSTA gateway. Therefore, during startup, Communicator 2007 establishes a long-lasting SIP dialog with the SIP/CSTA gateway to transmit call control–related information on incoming calls, on outgoing calls, or in call commands, and it keeps this dialog established. SIP INFO messages are used to send call-related information to and from the SIP/CSTA gateway. The call-related information sits in a set of XML notations, which is the payload of these SIP INFO messages.

In Office Communications Server 2007, ECMA-269 was chosen to implement the application interface for telephone services. This interface enables a softphone application (a computing application) to monitor and control a PBX or IP PBX. ECMA-323 defines the XML schema for those services. ECMA-269 addresses a very broad range of applications. The softphone application implements a profile, which is a small subset of the overall scope of this standard. In Communicator 2007, the SIP implementation follows ECMA Technical Report TR/87.

In Office Communications Server 2007, SIP was chosen to implement the network protocol on the IP side of the SIP/CSTA gateway. ECMA-323 XML messages are tunneled in SIP messages (INVITE and INFO), as shown in the following message example, and they contain the control information for the PBX or IP PBX. This example shows the setup of the long-lasting SIP session with INVITE and responses, which is later used to send the call-related signaling information, as part of a set of XML notations in a SIP INFO message:

```
----------------------------------------------------------------
INVITE to Gateway
CSTA: RequestSystemStatus
----------------------------------------------------------------

INVITE sip:csta-gw01@csta-gw.contoso.com SIP/2.0
Via: SIP/2.0/TCP 10.38.138.183:8759
Max-Forwards: 70
From: "Alice Ciccu" <sip:alice@contoso.com>;tag=1fb5eae7ac;
   epid=a8ae525d8a
To: <sip:csta-gw01@csta-gw.contoso.com>
Call-ID: cedd20b703994209ab6b1e13d4adc8ee
CSeq: 1 INVITE
Contact: <sip:alice@contoso.com:8759;maddr=10.38.138.183;transport=tcp>;
   Proxy=replace
User-Agent: LCC/1.3
Supported: timer
Session-Expires: 1800;refresher=uac
Min-SE: 1800
Content-Disposition: signal;handling=required
Proxy-Authorization: Kerberos qop="auth",
   realm="SIP Communications Service", opaque="16439A15",
   crand="ab9f7b1b", cnum="9",
   targetname="sip/lcs-fe01.contoso.com", response=
        "602306092a864886f71201020201011100ffffffffc
        28e306f3dd4e5f46a187aa3e6084be1"
Content-Type: application/csta+xml
Content-Length: 329

<?xml version="1.0"?>
<RequestSystemStatus xmlns="http://www.ecma-international.org/standards/ecma-323/csta/
ed3"><extensions><privateData><private><lcs:line xmlns:lcs=
"http://schemas.microsoft.com/Lcs/2005/04/RCCExtension">
   tel:75513;phone-context=contoso.com</lcs:line></private>
   </privateData></extensions></RequestSystemStatus>

--------------------------------------------------------------
100 Trying from Gateway
--------------------------------------------------------------

SIP/2.0 100 Trying
Authentication-Info: Kerberos
rspauth="602306092A864886F71201020201011100FFFFFFFFC742986919AF8C
   0BE0FDECD779CD8460", srand="6061FF07", snum="11",
   opaque="16439A15", qop="auth", targetname=
   "sip/lcs-fe01.contoso.com", realm="SIP Communications Service"
Via: SIP/2.0/TCP 10.38.138.183:8759;received=10.37.211.6;
ms-received-port=2141;ms-received-cid=72300
From: "Alice Ciccu" <sip:alice@contoso.com>;tag=1fb5eae7ac;epid=a8ae525d8aTo:
<sip:csta-gw01@csta-gw.contoso.com>
Call-ID: cedd20b703994209ab6b1e13d4adc8ee
CSeq: 1 INVITE
```

```
Content-Length: 0

------------------------------------------------------------
200 OK from Gateway
CSTA: RequestSystemStatusResponse
------------------------------------------------------------
SIP/2.0 200 OK
Authentication-Info: Kerberos
rspauth="602306092A864886F71201020201011100FFFFFFFF5C17289F992E77E
D0349151CC936B961", srand="850C5E3F", snum="12",
   opaque="16439A15", qop="auth", targetname=
   "sip/lcs-fe01.contoso.com", realm="SIP Communications Service"
Via: SIP/2.0/TCP 10.38.138.183:8759;received=10.37.211.6;
   ms-received-port=2141;ms-received-cid=72300
Content-Length: 222
Record-Route: <sip:lcspool01.contoso.com;transport=tcp;
   ms-fe=lcs-fe01.contoso.com;lr;ms-route-sig=aa-
   jWGb9Pd8SAlTDJ76ACeKIIZogGO>
From: "Alice Ciccu" <sip:alice@contoso.com>;tag=1fb5eae7ac;
   Epid=a8ae525d8a
To: <sip:csta-gw01@csta-gw.contoso.com>;tag=hssUA_699671144-5048
Call-ID: cedd20b703994209ab6b1e13d4adc8ee
CSeq: 1 INVITE
Require: timer
Session-Expires: 1800;Refresher=uac
Supported: *,timer
Contact: csta-gw <sip:csta-gw@csta-gw.contoso.com:5060;
transport=tcp>
Allow: INVITE,BYE,CANCEL,ACK,INFO,PRACK,COMET,OPTIONS,SUBSCRIBE,
NOTIFY,REFER,REGISTER,UPDATE
Content-Type: application/csta+xml

<?xml version="1.0" encoding="UTF-16" standalone="no" ?>
<RequestSystemStatusResponse xmlns="http://www.ecma-international.org/standards/ecma-
323/csta/ed3">
<systemStatus>normal</systemStatus></RequestSystemStatusResponse>

------------------------------------------------------------
ACK from client
------------------------------------------------------------
ACK sip:lcspool01.contoso.com;transport=tcp;ms-fe=lcs-fe01.contoso.com;lr;
   ms-route-sig=aa-jWGb9Pd8SAlTDJ76ACeKIIZogGO SIP/2.0
Via: SIP/2.0/TCP 10.38.138.183:8759
Max-Forwards: 70
From: "Alice Ciccu" <sip:alice@contoso.com>;tag=1fb5eae7ac;
   epid=a8ae525d8a
To: <sip:csta-gw01@csta-gw.contoso.com>;tag=hssUA_699671144-5048
Call-ID: cedd20b703994209ab6b1e13d4adc8ee
CSeq: 1 ACK
Route: csta-gw <sip:csta-gw@csta-gw.contoso.com:5060;
   transport=tcp>
User-Agent: LCC/1.3
Proxy-Authorization: Kerberos qop="auth", realm=
   "SIP Communications Service", opaque="16439A15",
   crand="b6b62ff5", cnum="10", targetname="
```

```
   sip/lcs-fe01.contoso.com",
   response="602306092a864886f71201020201011100ffffffffa
   3bbb1a2b1af02f8f55ec392dd96525c"
Content-Length: 0
```

Note Office Communications Server 2007 is not aware that the SIP INVITE message is used to establish a long-lasting SIP dialog for the RCC scenario. Office Communications Server 2007 currently does not support a "long-life" dialog and will terminate the session because of route expiration after 12 to 24 hours. Therefore, Communicator 2007 opens a new dialog (the default is after 30 minutes) with the same SIP/ECMA server (Session Initiation Protocol/European Manufacturers Association) (in this case the SIP/CSTA gateway) before the dialog is expired in Office Communications Server 2007 (regardless of the session timer), and it closes the existing dialog with this device (which is about to expire). Communicator 2007 ensures that events are not lost during the transition.

In the preceding SIP INFO message, Communicator 2007 establishes a logical transport channel and an association between itself, the SIP/CSTA gateway, and the switching system (PBX or IP PBX) to transmit all call-related information between the PBX or IP PBX and Communicator. The logical name of the user is described in the SIP FROM header:

```
----------------------------------------------------------
INFO from client
CSTA: SetForwarding
----------------------------------------------------------

INFO sip:lcspool01.contoso.com;transport=tcp;ms-fe=lcs-fe01.contoso.com;lr;ms-route-
sig=aa-jWGb9Pd8SAlTDJ76ACe
   KIIZogGO SIP/2.0
Via: SIP/2.0/TCP 10.38.138.183:8759
Max-Forwards: 70
From: "Alice Ciccu" <sip:alice@contoso.com>;tag=1fb5eae7ac;
   epid=a8ae525d8a
To: <sip:csta-gw01@csta-gw.contoso.com>;tag=hssUA_699671144-5048
Call-ID: cedd20b703994209ab6b1e13d4adc8ee
CSeq: 4 INFO
Route: csta-gw <sip:csta-gw@csta-gw.contoso.com:5060;transport=tcp>
Contact: <sip:alice@contoso.com:8759;maddr=10.38.138.183;
transport=tcp>;proxy=replace
User-Agent: LCC/1.3Content-Disposition: signal;handling=required
Proxy-Authorization: Kerberos qop="auth", realm="SIP Communications
Service", opaque="16439A15", crand="a4b77dd6", cnum="13", targetname="sip/lcs-
fe01.contoso.com", response=
"602306092a864886f71201020201011100ffffffffb354bf3532a930f8e7c741c
4588d631f"
Content-Type: application/csta+xml
Content-Length: 265

<?xml version="1.0"?>
<SetForwarding xmlns="http://www.ecma-international.org/standards
/ecma-323/csta/ed3"><device>tel:75513;phone-context=contoso.com
```

```
</device><forwardingType>forwardImmediate</forwardingType>
<activateForward>false</activateForward></SetForwarding>

--------------------------------------------------------------
200 OK from Gateway
CSTA: SetForwardingResponse
--------------------------------------------------------------
SIP/2.0 200 OK
Authentication-Info: Kerberos
rspauth="602306092A864886F71201020201011100FFFFFFFF7697AD30
   EC969F34032887CCCD76446E", srand="00D543B4", snum="15", opaque=
   "16439A15", qop="auth", targetname="sip/lcs-fe01.contoso.com",
   realm="SIP Communications Service"
Via: SIP/2.0/TCP 10.38.138.183:8759;received=10.37.211.6;
   ms-received-port=2141;ms-received-cid=72300
Content-Length: 152
From: "Alice Ciccu" <sip:alice@contoso.com>;tag=1fb5eae7ac;
   epid=a8ae525d8a
To: <sip:csta-gw01@csta-gw.contoso.com>;tag=hssUA_699671144-5048
Call-ID: cedd20b703994209ab6b1e13d4adc8ee
CSeq: 4 INFO
Contact: csta-gw <sip:csta-gw@csta-gw.contoso.com:5060;
   transport=tcp>
Allow: INVITE,BYE,CANCEL,ACK,INFO,PRACK,COMET,OPTIONS,SUBSCRIBE,
   NOTIFY,REFER,REGISTER,UPDATE
Supported: *Content-Type: application/csta+xml

<?xml version="1.0" encoding="UTF-16" standalone="no" ?>
<SetForwardingResponse xmlns="http://www.ecma-international.org/standards/ecma-323/csta/
ed3"/>
```

If the Communicator 2007 user wants to establish a phone call to extension 65000, the SIP message as a SIP INFO request looks like this:

```
-----------------------------------------------------------
INFO from client
CSTA: MakeCall
-----------------------------------------------------------
INFO sip:lcspool01.contoso.com;transport=tcp;
ms-fe=lcs-fe01.contoso.com;lr;
ms-route-sig=aa-jWGb9Pd8SAlTDJ76ACeKIIZogGO SIP/2.0
Via: SIP/2.0/TCP 10.38.138.183:8759
Max-Forwards: 70
From: "Alice Ciccu" <sip:alice@contoso.com>;tag=1fb5eae7ac;
   epid=a8ae525d8a
To: <sip:csta-gw01@csta-gw.contoso.com>;tag=hssUA_699671144-5048
Call-ID: cedd20b703994209ab6b1e13d4adc8ee
CSeq: 5 INFO
Route: csta-gw <sip:csta-gw@csta-gw.contoso.com:5060;transport=tcp>
Contact: <sip:alice@contoso.com:8759;maddr=10.38.138.183;
transport=tcp>;proxy=replace
User-Agent: LCC/1.3
Content-Disposition: signal;handling=required
```

```
Proxy-Authorization: Kerberos qop="auth", realm=
"SIP Communications Service", opaque="16439A15", crand=
"bf7e3cd3", cnum="14", targetname="sip/lcs-fe01.contoso.com",
response="602306092a864886f71201020201011100ffffffffec2e8a44b84
ef7850d9c5f595e0d26c6"
Content-Type: application/csta+xml
Content-Length: 303

<?xml version="1.0"?>
<MakeCall xmlns="http://www.ecma-international.org/standards/
ecma-323/csta/ed3"><callingDevice>tel:75513;phone-context=
contoso.com</callingDevice><calledDirectoryNumber>
tel:65000;phone-context=dialstring
</calledDirectoryNumber><autoOriginate>doNotPrompt
</autoOriginate></MakeCall>

------------------------------------------------------------
200 OK from Gateway
CSTA: MakeCallResponse
------------------------------------------------------------
SIP/2.0 200 OK
Authentication-Info: Kerberos rspauth="602306092A864886F71201020201011100FFFFFFFF88C8000
928C70765CA7C6B1F526A9904", srand="11ED47CB", snum="17",
opaque="16439A15", qop="auth", targetname=
"sip/lcs-fe01.contoso.com", realm="SIP Communications Service"
Via: SIP/2.0/TCP 10.38.138.183:8759;received=10.37.211.6;
ms-received-port=2141;ms-received-cid=72300
Content-Length: 303
From: "Alice Ciccu" <sip:alice@contoso.com>;tag=1fb5eae7ac;
   epid=a8ae525d8a
To: <sip:csta-gw01@csta-gw.contoso.com>;tag=hssUA_699671144-5048
Call-ID: cedd20b703994209ab6b1e13d4adc8ee
CSeq: 5 INFO
Contact: csta-gw <sip:csta-gw@csta-gw.contoso.com:5060;transport=tcp>
Allow: INVITE,BYE,CANCEL,ACK,INFO,PRACK,COMET,OPTIONS,SUBSCRIBE,
NOTIFY,REFER,REGISTER,UPDATE
Supported: *Content-Type: application/csta+xml

<?xml version="1.0" encoding="UTF-16" standalone="no" ?>
<MakeCallResponse xmlns="http://www.ecma-international.org/
standards/ecma-323/csta/ed3"><callingDevice><callID>3329005
</callID><deviceID typeOfNumber="dialingNumber">
tel:75513;phone-context=contoso.com</deviceID></callingDevice>
</MakeCallResponse>
```

Setting Up the Remote Call Control Scenario

To set up the RCC scenario, you need to perform the following steps, which should be performed in order and will be explained in detail below:

1. Install the SIP/CSTA gateway, and configure the CSTA interface on the PBX or IP PBX.
2. Configure a user for RCC by doing the following:

   a. Enable the user for RCC in Active Directory.
   b. Configure a Line Server URI (Server Uniform Resource Identifier) and Line URI (Line Uniform Resource Identifier) for the user in Active Directory.
   c. Configure an RCC URI for the user.
3. Configure a route on the Office Communications Server pool for the Server URI.
4. Start Communicator.

The following sections describe these steps in more detail.

Installing the CSTA Gateway and Configuring the SIP/CSTA Interface on the PBX or IP PBX

For integration with the existing telephone environment, a SIP/CSTA gateway is needed. This gateway is connected to the SIP/CSTA interface provided by the existing PBX or IP PBX. It is possible to have multiple SIP/CSTA gateways connected to Office Communications Server 2007, but for a single user, only one SIP/CSTA gateway can be configured. However, only one SIP/CSTA gateway per PBX node is recommended to avoid numbering-plan conflicts.

There are PBX/IP PBX–specific CSTA gateways and vendor-neutral CSTA gateways available on the market. You need to select a CSTA gateway that supports your existing PBX/IP PBX if the PBX/IP PBX doesn't offer a native CSTA interface.

Configuring a User for RCC

To configure a user for RCC, you first need to enable the user for RCC in Active Directory by using the Active Directory Users and Computers Management Console. In the Office Communications Server 2007 Active Directory Snap-In under Advanced Settings, select the configuration option Enable Remote Call Control, as shown in Figure 9-3.

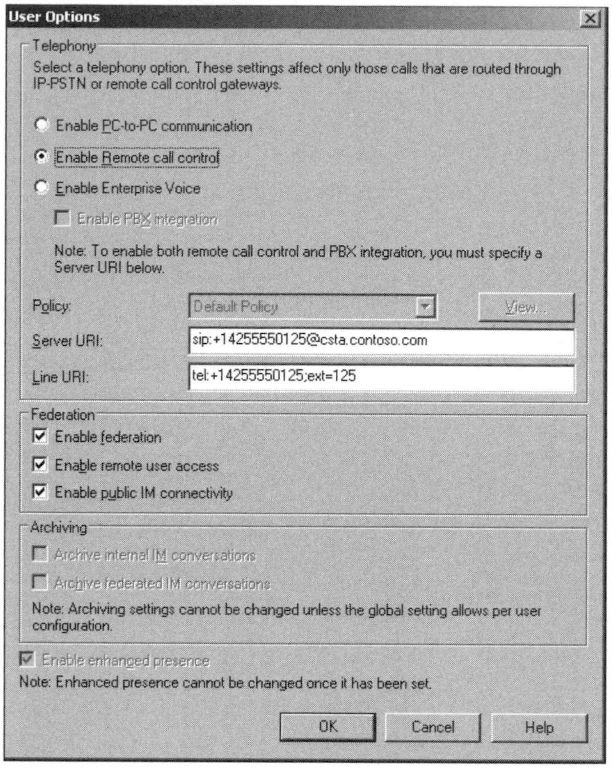

Figure 9-3 Enabling and configuring a user for RCC

You then configure a Server URI for the user. This Server URI points to the SIP/CSTA gateway. Communicator 2007 sends its SIP call control messages to the SIP/CSTA gateway defined in the Server URI field. The syntax of the Server URI entered here must match the requirements of the SIP/CSTA gateway. (Please refer to the documentation provided by the SIP/CSTA gateway vendor.) Here are some examples:

- Sip:+14255550125@gw.csta.contoso.com

  (sip:<E.164 number>@<SIP/CSTA Gateway FQDN>)

- Sip:cstagw@gw.csta.contoso.com

  (sip:<user>@<SIP/CSTA Gateway FQDN>)

The E.164 number is the phone number of the user in E.164 format (+<Country Access Code><Area Code><local number>, such as +14255550125), and the SIP/CSTA Gateway FQDN is the fully qualified domain name of the SIP/CSTA gateway.

Finally, you configure a Line URI for the user. This URI is used to send call control information to and receive it from the existing telephone environment, as Calling or Called Party Number Identification. The syntax must match the requirements of the SIP/CSTA gateway.

(For more information, refer to the SIP/CSTA gateway documentation provided by the SIP/CSTA gateway vendor.) For example, the following syntaxes are common:

- Tel:+14255550125;ext=125

  (Tel:<E.164 number>;ext=<extension>)
- Tel:+14255550125;phone-context=mitel.com

  (Tel:<E.164 number>;phone-context=<SIP/CSTA Gateway name>.<com>)

The E.164 number and the number string following *ext*= must match the number and extension the user has on the existing telephone environment.

> **Note** When you enable a user for PBX integration (also see Chapter 10) as part of the Enterprise Voice scenario, the user can still be enabled for RCC. This is the only exception where a user can be enabled for RCC and for Enterprise Voice at the same time. The Server URI and Line URI fields must be entered as described later in this chapter.

Configuring a Route on the Office Communications Server Pool for Server URI

All SIP traffic from Communicator 2007 always goes through Office Communications Server 2007 and is proxied by the server to the SIP/CSTA gateway. To send SIP INFO call control messages from Communicator 2007 to the SIP/CSTA gateway, the same SIP dialog is used that Communicator 2007 established in its start-up phase by sending a SIP INVITE message to the SIP/CSTA gateway. Communicator 2007 sends its SIP INVITE and SIP INFO call control messages to this SIP/CSTA gateway, which is configured in the Server URI field. This must be the FQDN of the SIP/CSTA gateway. On Office Communications Server 2007, for every Server URI, a route must be configured with the destination address to which Office Communications Server 2007 must proxy SIP call control messages. You can configure this under pool-level settings on the Routing tab, as shown in Figure 9-4.

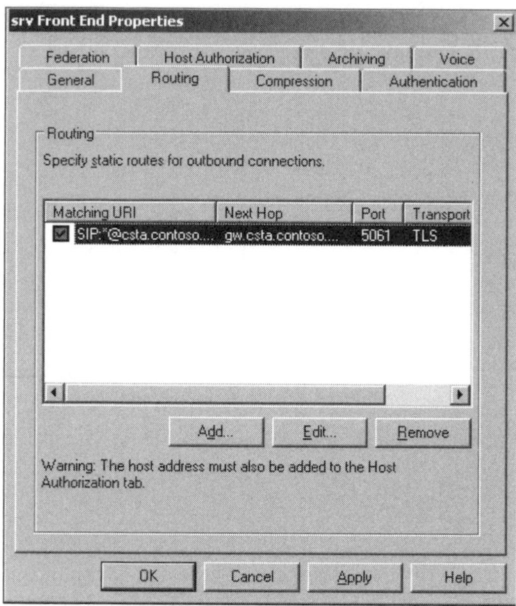

Figure 9-4 Configuring routes for Server URIs

For each route to a SIP/CSTA Gateway Server, the following settings must be configured:

- **Matching URI** The syntax, sip:*@[*CSTA Gateway FQDN*], means that this route will be used for any number (*) configured in the Server URI field of the Active Directory user properties page where the FQDN of the SIP/CSTA gateway Server matches the value entered here.
- **Next hop** This is the FQDN or IP address of your SIP/CSTA gateway.
- **Port** This is the SIP/CSTA gateway that is configured to listen for SIP traffic.
- **Transport protocol** This is the transport protocol that the SIP/CSTA Gateway is configured to use.

Note If Transport Layer Security (TLS) is configured as the transport protocol, the FQDN must be entered in the Next Hop field. If TCP is selected, the IP Address of the CSTA Gateway Server must be entered in the Next Hop field. The FQDN is needed in the TLS mode to allow certificate verification for secure communication. If TLS is not used, a host authorization entry must also be added so that the Office Communications Server treats the CSTA gateway as authenticated.

Note It is possible to have multiple SIP/CSTA gateways configured in the same Office Communications Server 2007 pool.

Starting Communicator 2007

When Communicator 2007 starts, it retrieves its Server and Line URI settings, as well as the RCC-enabled settings through Inband Provisioning. Inband Provisioning transmits configuration settings to the Communicator 2007 client, even when Communicator 2007 has no access to Group Policies stored in Active Directory. Therefore, it is also possible to use RCC when the user is remotely connected to the Office Communications Server 2007 environment on the Internet.

On an incoming call, the PBX or IP PBX rings the user's existing PBX or IP PBX phone and also sends out an incoming call notification to Communicator through the SIP/CSTA gateway, as shown in Figure 9-5, by using a SIP INFO message sent from the SIP/CSTA gateway to Communicator 2007. The user can either answer the incoming call on his PBX or IP PBX phone by picking up the receiver or accept the incoming call on Communicator, which activates the speaker phone functionality on the PBX or IP PBX phone.

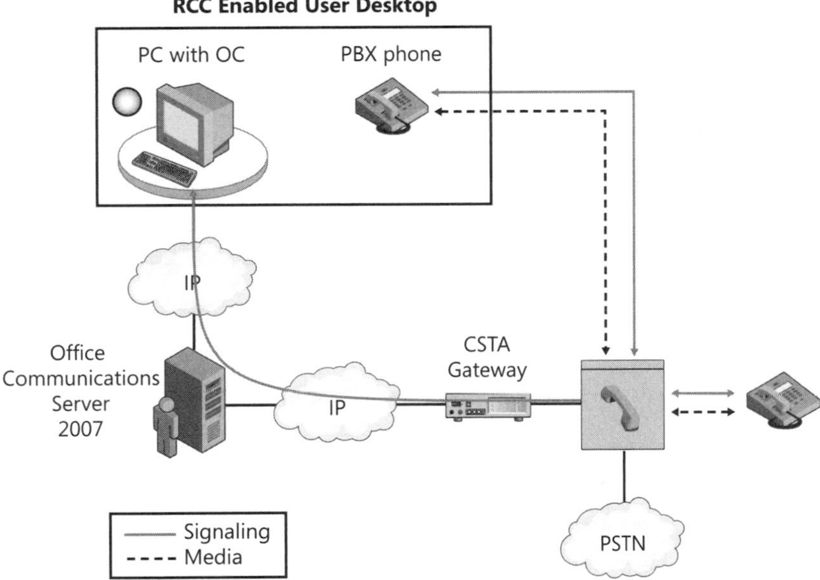

Figure 9-5 Incoming RCC call

To resolve the Calling Party Number to a name, Communicator first applies the number normalization Regular Expressions configured in the Address Book Service on the Office Communications Server 2007 pool on the Calling Party Number. After that, Communicator 2007 matches the current E.164 format normalized Calling Party Number with the phone numbers stored in Active Directory or Outlook contacts. This functionality is called *reverse number lookup*. If Communicator 2007 successfully applies reverse number lookup and finds a name that matches a Calling Party Number, this name is presented to the user in the pop-up window and the Conversation window, instead of the Calling Party Number.

Note Regular Expressions for number normalization can be configured as described in file following file on Office Communications Server Standard Edition or Enterprise Edition:

\\%installation path OCS%\Microsoft Office Communications Server 2007\Web Components\Address Book Files\Sample_Company_Phone_Normalization_Rules.txt

This file also contains examples and an explanation of how to test the phone number normalization rules.

Some CSTA implementations on PBX or IP PBX provide these reverse number lookup functionalities. Thus, instead of or in addition to the Calling Party Number, a display name is transmitted to Communicator on an incoming call. This display name is ignored by Communicator 2007 because it is not possible for Communicator 2007 to verify the name.

Depending on the implementation in the PBX or IP PBX, the Calling Party Number can have the following formats:

- Extension (for example, 1212)
- E.164 format (for example, +14255550125)
- Both (+14255550125;ext=1212)

Note The format of the Calling Party Number entered in the PBX or IP PBX must match the requirements of the SIP/PSTN gateway. Sometimes this is in the E.164 format and sometimes it is not.

If the Calling Party Number string does not contain a number on an incoming call, Communicator 2007 will not apply reverse number lookup.

On an outgoing call initiated on Communicator 2007, Communicator 2007 first applies the Number Normalization regular expression rules (the same rules that were configured for reverse number lookup on incoming calls, which convert a number string to E.164 format) on the number string entered as Called Party Number in Communicator 2007 before sending the request to the SIP/CSTA gateway by using the established long-lasting SIP dialog. This is shown in Figure 9-6.

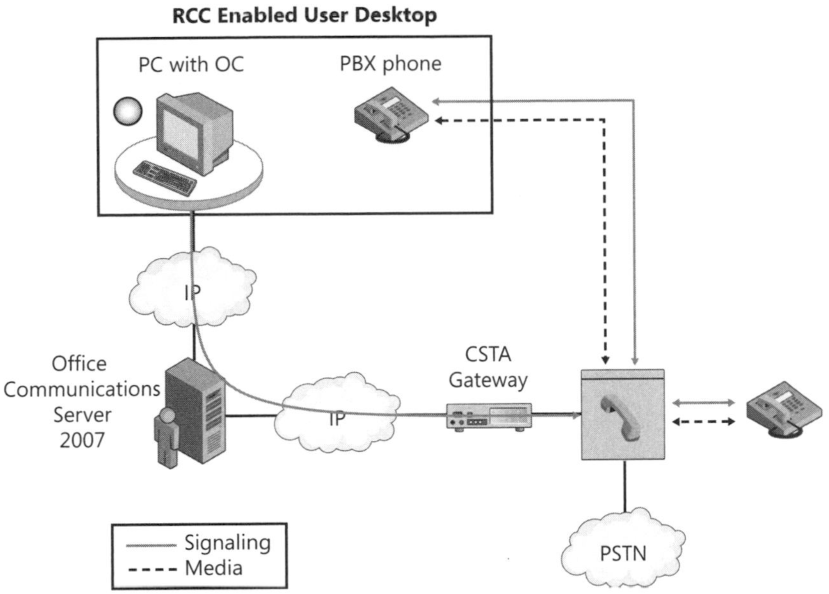

Figure 9-6 Outgoing RCC call

Summary

The RCC scenario is a "lightweight" telephone integration scenario that provides Communicator 2007 users with the ease of computer telephone integration with other business applications, such as Microsoft Outlook. It is not necessary to migrate the existing PBX system to a VoIP-based IP telephone solution at the same time. This chapter provides information on the functionalities of RCC, background information on how the scenario works, the infrastructure that must be set up, and what must be configured on Office Communications Server 2007 to implement the RCC scenario.

Additional Resources

- A description for the Genesys GETS SIP/CSTA gateway can be found here: *http://www.genesyslab.com/products/enterprise_collaboration.asp*
- ECMA-269 information can be found at this site: *http://www.ecma-international.org/publications/standards/Ecma-269.htm*
- ECMA-323 information can be found at this site: *http://www.ecma-international.org/publications/standards/Ecma-323.htm*
- ECMA TR/87 information can be found at this site: *http://www.ecma-international.org/publications/techreports/E-TR-087.htm*

On the Companion CD

- Office Communications Server 2007 user documentation, including the "Enterprise Voice Planning and Deployment Guide," on the companion CD in the \Additional Reading folder. The "Enterprise Voice Planning and Deployment Guide" file is named OCS_VoIP_Guide.doc.

Chapter 10

VoIP Scenarios

In this chapter:

This chapter covers the voice features available in Office Communications Server 2007 and describes how the user experience is seamlessly integrated into the productivity tools of the information worker. The chapter then goes into the technical details of Office Communications Server's Enterprise Voice design. Finally, the server components that are involved to make an Enterprise Voice deployment possible are discussed in detail.

What Is VoIP?

Voice over Internet Protocol (VoIP) refers to the ability of placing and receiving voice calls over the IP network. The call might or might not traverse the Public Switched Telephone Network (PSTN) network. The PSTN network is the traditional telephone network that everyone uses to call friends, family, and colleagues. VoIP is different from Remote Call Control (RCC). RCC is related to controlling the Private Branch eXchange (PBX) phone from a computer running Office Communicator, whereas in VoIP the audio traffic is carried over the IP network. VoIP has the potential of eliminating the need for a PBX network, which most large organizations must deploy and maintain in addition to their IP network. Managing these two independent networks, each with its own idiosyncrasies, requires administrators with various technical backgrounds and skills. Figure 10-1 illustrates the different types of voice networks.

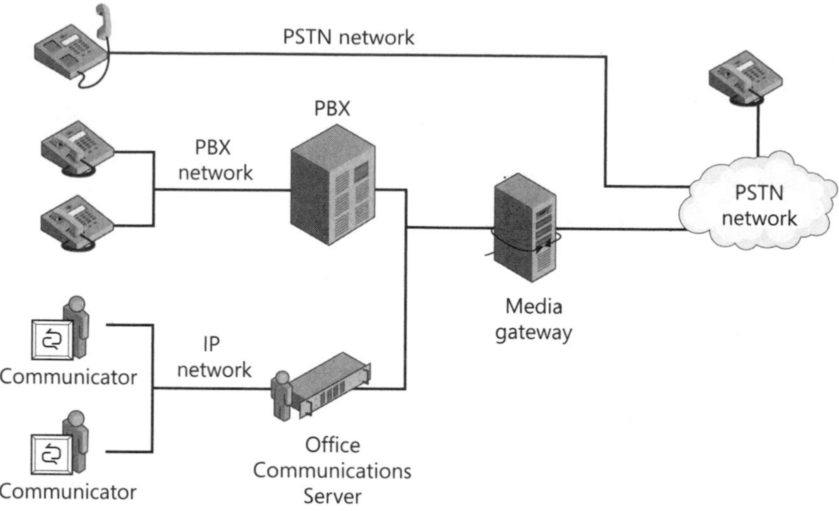

Figure 10-1 PSTN vs. RCC vs. VoIP

VoIP technology promises to deliver on many improvements, such as infrastructure and network consolidation, lower management and toll costs, and better interoperability between systems from different vendors. The VoIP capabilities of Office Communications Server 2007 can replace PBX functionality in many cases and interoperate with existing PBXs in other cases.

Microsoft's VoIP offering, Office Communications Server 2007, provides an integrated user experience where voice communication is integrated into the same applications used by information workers to communicate electronically, such as Microsoft Office 2007, SharePoint 2007, and Exchange 2007. With Office Communications Server 2007, Voice becomes one of many communications modes–e-mail, instant messaging (IM), Web conferencing, file transfer, video–that are accessible from a single consistent user interface. This ease of use encourages user adoption of more advanced features such as call forwarding, call redirection, and multiparty calls, which most users with traditional PBX phones seldom use.

Another important advantage is portability. With Office Communicator 2007 installed on their laptops and an edge server deployed in their organizations' peripheral networks, users have access to their work numbers from anywhere in the world where Internet connectivity is available. This is a powerful proposition given a global economy where more and more workers telecommute. Office Communications Server 2007 makes it possible for information workers to free themselves from the constraints of the office or cubicle.

Overview of VoIP Scenarios

The topics in this section include general VoIP features of Office Communications Server 2007. The next section, "Examining the Technical Details Behind VoIP Scenarios," describes the technical aspects of using these features.

Using Two-Party Calling

With basic two-party calling, one party can dial a number and establish an audio conversation with another party. The user can select a contact from his contact list and click the call icon. A conversation subject can be set so that the called party knows what the call is about. Alternatively, the user can right-click the contact and select a call from the drop-down menu. (See Figure 10-2.) After the user installs Office Communicator, this right-click menu is also available in every Microsoft Office program (Word, Excel, Outlook, and so on) as well as SharePoint. (See Figure 10-3.) This consistent user experience reinforces users' familiarity with making a call.

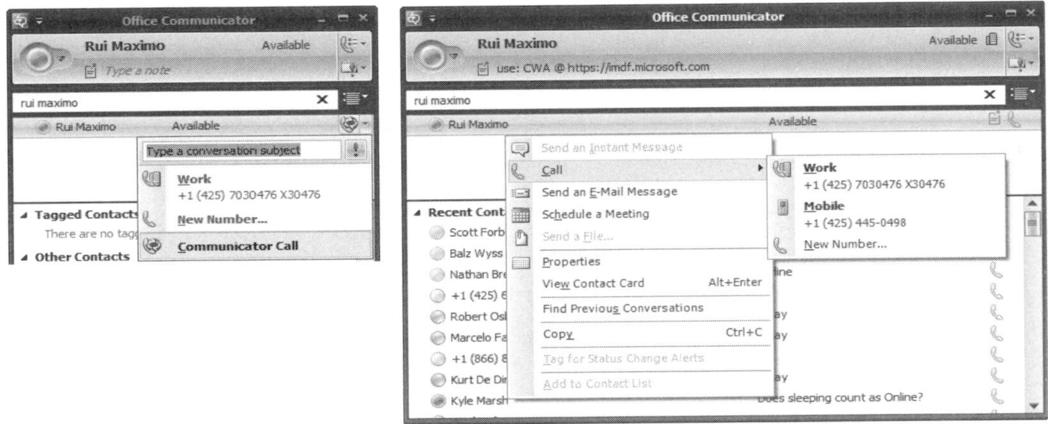

Figure 10-2 Calling from Office Communicator

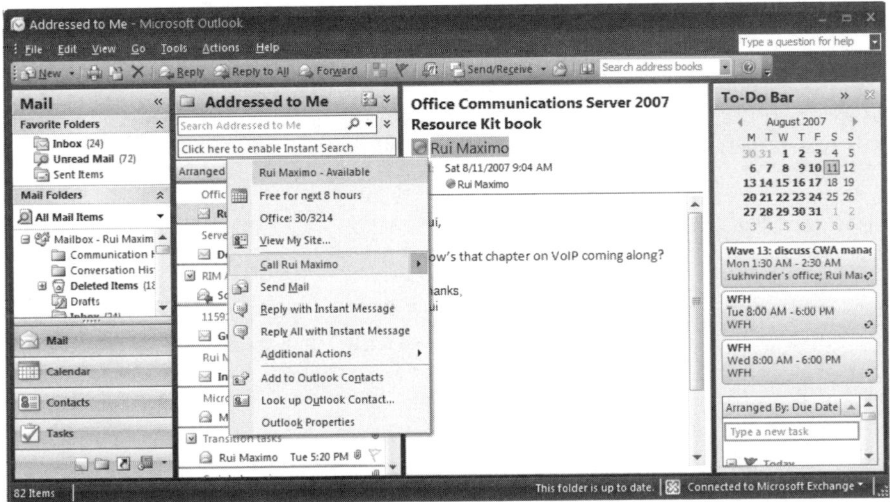

Figure 10-3 Calling from Microsoft Outlook

Calling an internal user is one click away because the caller can dial based on user name by locating the called party in the contact list or performing a search, but what about external users? In the case of external users, the caller will not be able to locate the party to be called by name unless they are added to the Outlook address book by the user. Instead a phone number must be dialed. Dialing from Communicator is as simple as typing the phone number in the search field and pressing the Enter key or clicking the phone icon. (See Figure 10-4.)

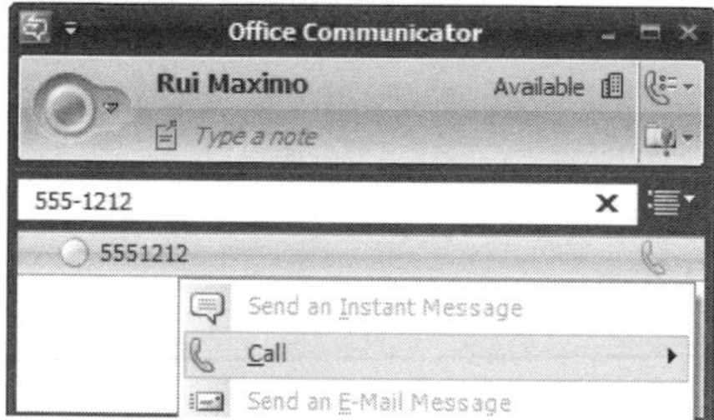

Figure 10-4 Calling external phone numbers

When an internal or external call is placed, Communicator displays an unobtrusive conversation window with visual controls that replace the obscure dial codes of PBX phones, making it much easier for users to discover these features and use them. (See Figure 10-5.) A description of the controls available in the conversation window is described after Figure 10-5.

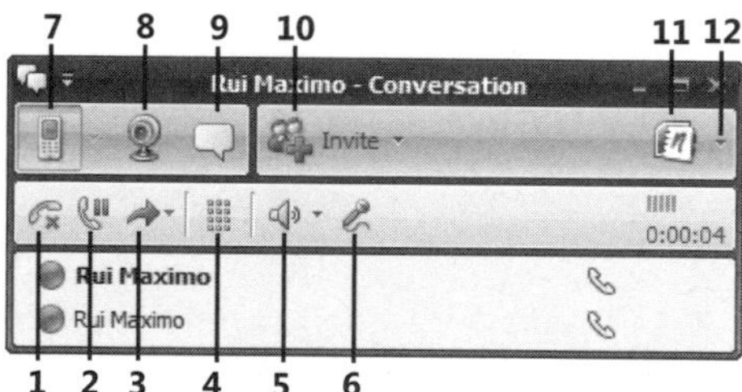

Figure 10-5 Communicator conversation window

The controls shown in Figure 10-5 are numbered to match the following descriptions:

1. End the call.
2. Hold the call.
3. Transfer the call.
4. Expand the standard 3x4 dial pad.

5. Change the volume.
6. Mute the microphone.
7. End the call.
8. Add video to the call.
9. Add IM to the call.
10. Invite additional participants to the call.
11. Take notes associated with the call by using Microsoft OneNote.
12. The down-arrow caret displays a drop-down menu with additional options, such as taking notes, sending a file to the other person the user is talking to, and setting and changing the conversation subject so that the called party gets an indication of the topic the calling party wants to discuss before answering the call. Also, similar to e-mail messages, the caller has the option to set a high-priority importance indicator to the called party.

Note The option for sending a file is available only to two-party conversations.

Once the call is established, the audio comes through the computer speakers and built-in microphone. Although the built-in audio system isn't meant for audio calls, as the other party will likely hear the clicking of the keyboard when typing, the quality is relatively good. For optimal audio quality, use a headset or USB phone.

Configuring Call Deflection

Call deflection refers to the ability of the called party to redirect the calling party to a different phone number before picking up the call. This capability is valuable if you're about to step out for a meeting but need to answer the call, which perhaps is a call you've been expecting. Ideally, the called party is able to redirect the call to her cell phone to take the call while commuting to her next appointment. Redirecting the call from your office phone to your mobile phone is a valuable feature that's possible with Office Communicator 2007. When a call comes in, a toast appears with an accompanying ringing sound. Deflecting the call is as simple as clicking the Redirect caret, and selecting a phone number to forward the call to as shown in Figure 10-6. This is essentially call forwarding on the fly.

Figure 10-6 Communicator incoming call

Another example is the flexibility to receive calls directed to your work number at home. For example, if your home computer doesn't have Communicator 2007 installed, you can still connect using Communicator Web Access (2007 release). Like Communicator 2007, Communicator Web Access (2007 release) also supports call deflection. Similar to Office Communicator, a toast appears on the screen indicating a call is incoming (as shown in Figure 10-7). To deflect the incoming call from your work number to your home number, click on the Redirect caret and select one of the published phone numbers to forward the call to. The caller thinks the call was answered at the office even though the call was forwarded seamlessly to a different number.

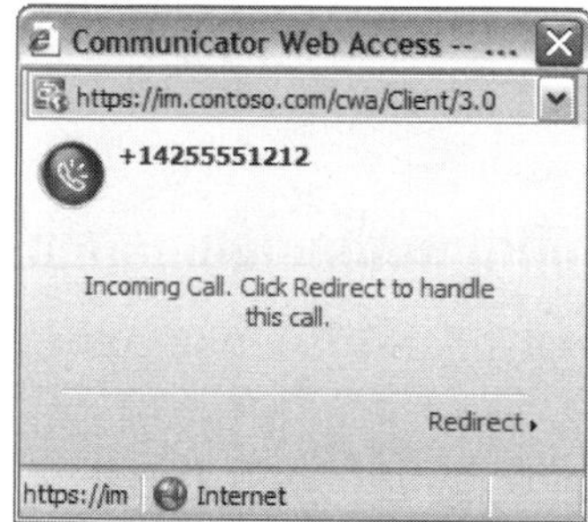

Figure 10-7 Communicator Web Access (2007 release) incoming call

Before an incoming call can be redirected to a predefined phone number, the phone number must be published in the user's settings. Once published, these phone numbers are available for selection in the Redirect drop-down menu. To publish these phone numbers, navigate to the Options dialog box under Tools and select the Phones tab as shown in Figure 10-8.

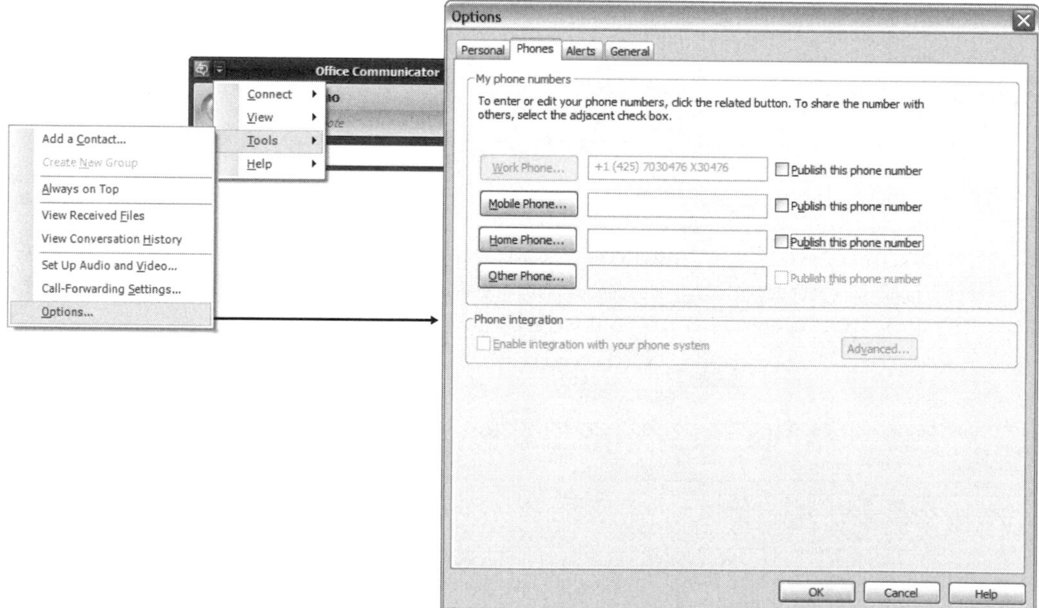

Figure 10-8 Phone options

> **Note** Published phone numbers are visible only to contacts in the Personal and Team access levels.

Configuring Call Forwarding

Call forwarding refers to the feature of configuring your phone to automatically forward incoming calls directly to voice mail, to a contact, or to another phone number published in the user's Phones tab (which was shown in Figure 10-8) without ringing that user's phone. Alternatively, the option to simultaneously ring and forward the call is available. Figure 10-9 shows how to locate these settings to configure them from Communicator.

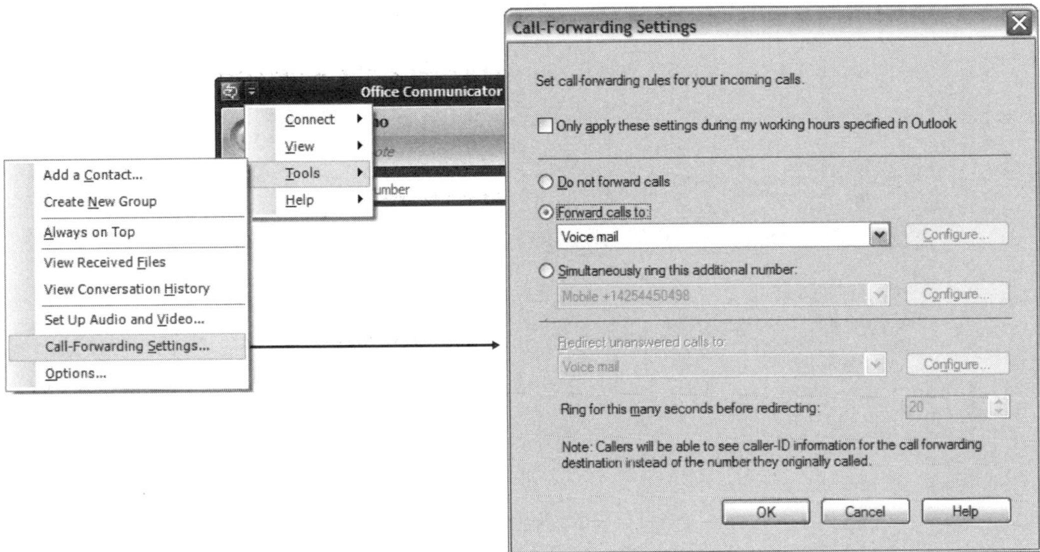

Figure 10-9 Call forwarding settings

Another convenient way of configuring call forwarding is directly from the main Communicator or Communicator Web Access window as shown in Figure 10-10.

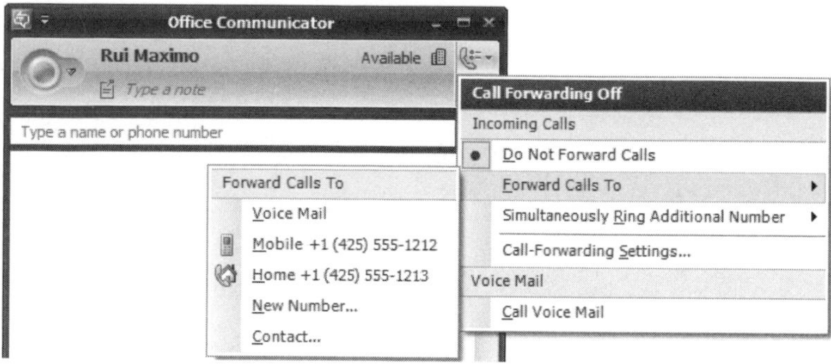

Figure 10-10 Communicator call forwarding settings

Communicator Web Access (2007 release) provides a nearly identical interface for configuring these settings as well. So, if you've already left the office and forgot to configure your call-forwarding settings, it's never too late to do it as soon as you're within reach of any computer with an Internet connection. (See Figure 10-11.)

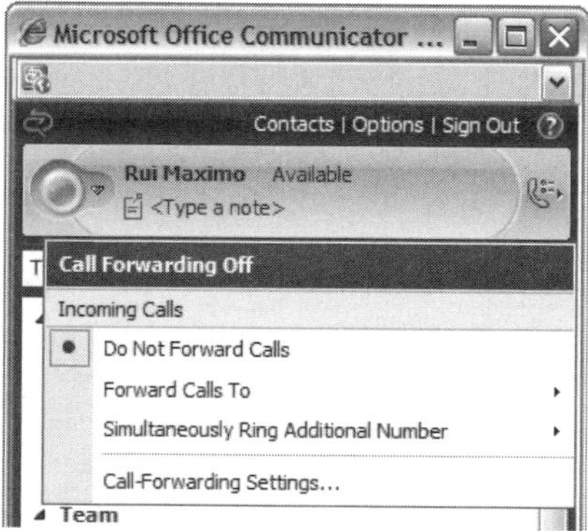

Figure 10-11 Communicator Web Access call-forwarding settings

Using Voice Mail

Voice mail is a required feature of any self-respecting phone system, and Office Communications Server 2007 supports voice mail with Microsoft Exchange Server 2007 Unified Messaging as the voice mail storage application–or in the case where Office Communications Server 2007 is integrated with a supported PBX, Office Communications Server 2007 allows the PBX to handle voice mail. Even if Communicator is not running, calls are routed to the user's voice mail, and the user can later call her voice mail to listen to her messages or retrieve them directly from within her Outlook inbox. Figure 10-12 shows how to call your voice mail directly from within Communicator.

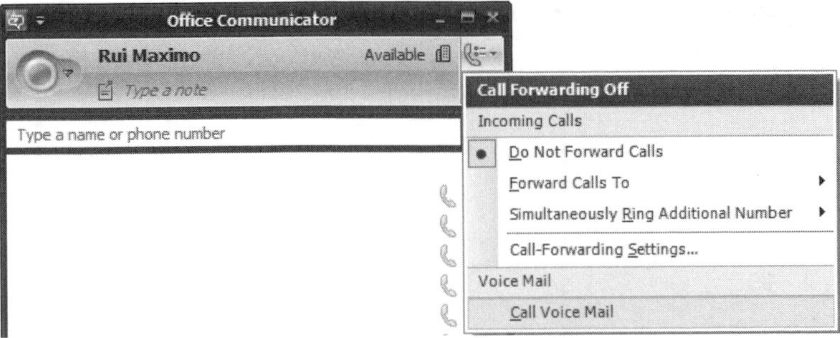

Figure 10-12 Calling voice mail from within Communicator

With Exchange Server 2007 Unified Messaging deployed, users have a rich voice mail experience from within Outlook 2007. Voice messages can be listened to directly from within Outlook. Each voice message is shown as a separate e-mail. The experience of listening to voice mail is similar to reading e-mail messages in Outlook. (See Figure 10-13.)

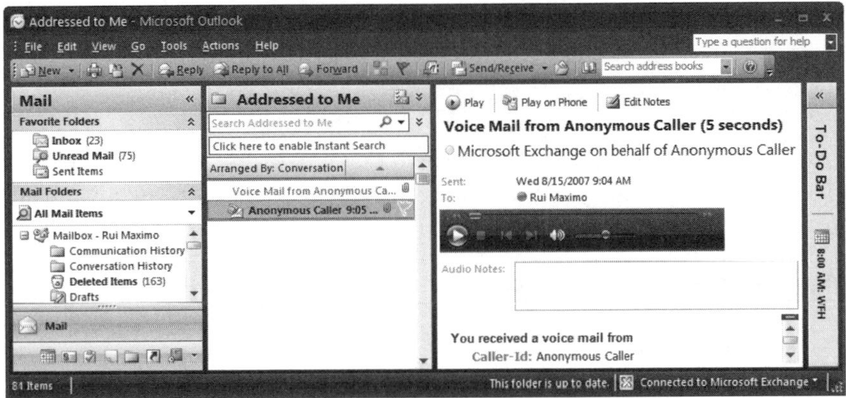

Figure 10-13 Listening to Voice-mail from Outlook 2007

Missed calls are also shown as e-mail notifications showing the caller ID and a link to call back the calling party. (See Figure 10-14.)

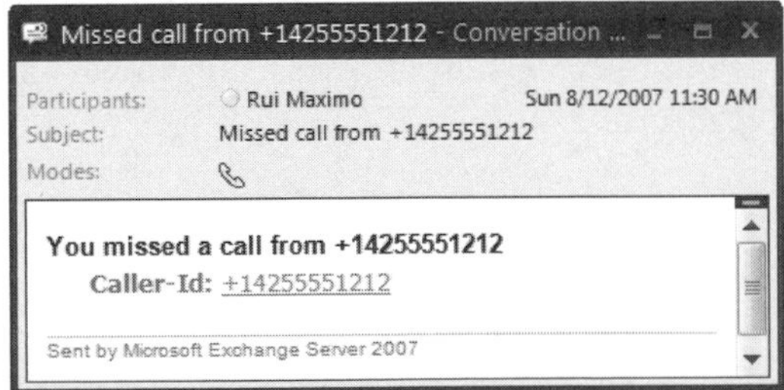

Figure 10-14 Missed call notification from Outlook 2007

In the Conversation History folder in Outlook 2007 is a call log of all outgoing calls made (shown in Figure 10-15). This folder is automatically created by Outlook 2007.

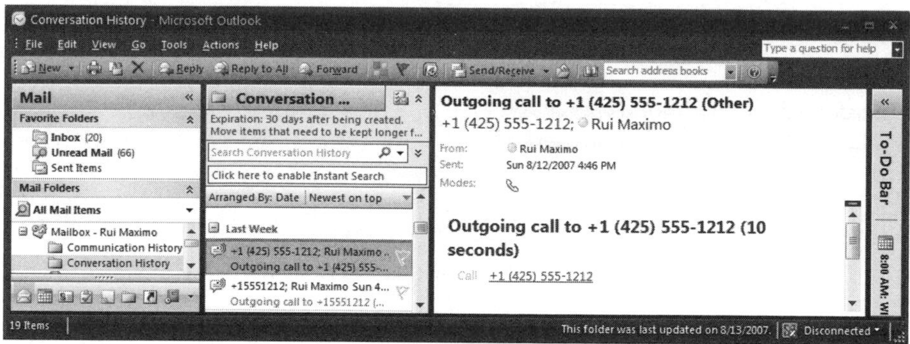

Figure 10-15 Conversation history in Outlook 2007

Using Ad Hoc Conference Calling

An ad hoc conference call occurs when three or more parties participate in the same call. There are multiple ways to establish a conference call. A conference call can be started by adding all the parties at once—such as calling everyone on an e-mail thread or selecting the participants from the contact list in Office Communicator and initiating the call, or adding additional participants to a two-party call in progress. Figure 10-16 shows how to add participants to a two-party call. The peer-to-peer two-party call is changed on the server into a conference call. A focus is started. The focus is directed to one of the available conferencing servers associated with the pool, where the leader is homed to create a conferencing session. The session mixes all the audio feeds before sending the audio back to all the participants.

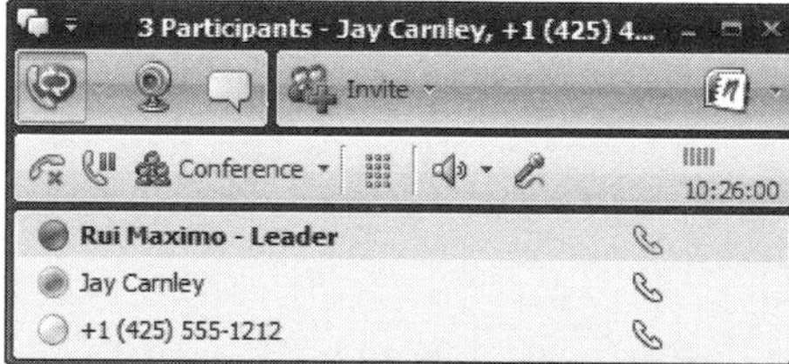

Figure 10-16 Add participants to an existing conversation

Another way of conducting an ad hoc conference call is to select all the participants before beginning the conversation. This approach immediately establishes a conference call instead of escalating from a two-party call. (See Figure 10-17.)

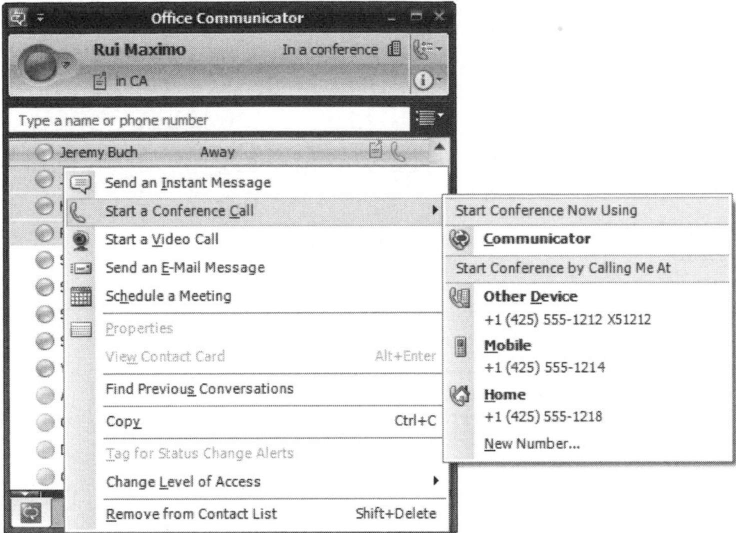

Figure 10-17 Start a conversation with multiple participants

Examining the Technical Details Behind VoIP Scenarios

The components that compose a VoIP topology are illustrated in Figure 10-18. This topology supports the following scenarios: calling and receiving calls outside your organization's network (PSTN), providing external access for users, and receiving voice mail. New server roles come into play when deploying an Enterprise Voice infrastructure. In addition to the basic Office Communications Server home pool, which is either an Office Communications Server 2007 Standard Edition Server or an Enterprise Edition pool, the following server roles are required or recommended.

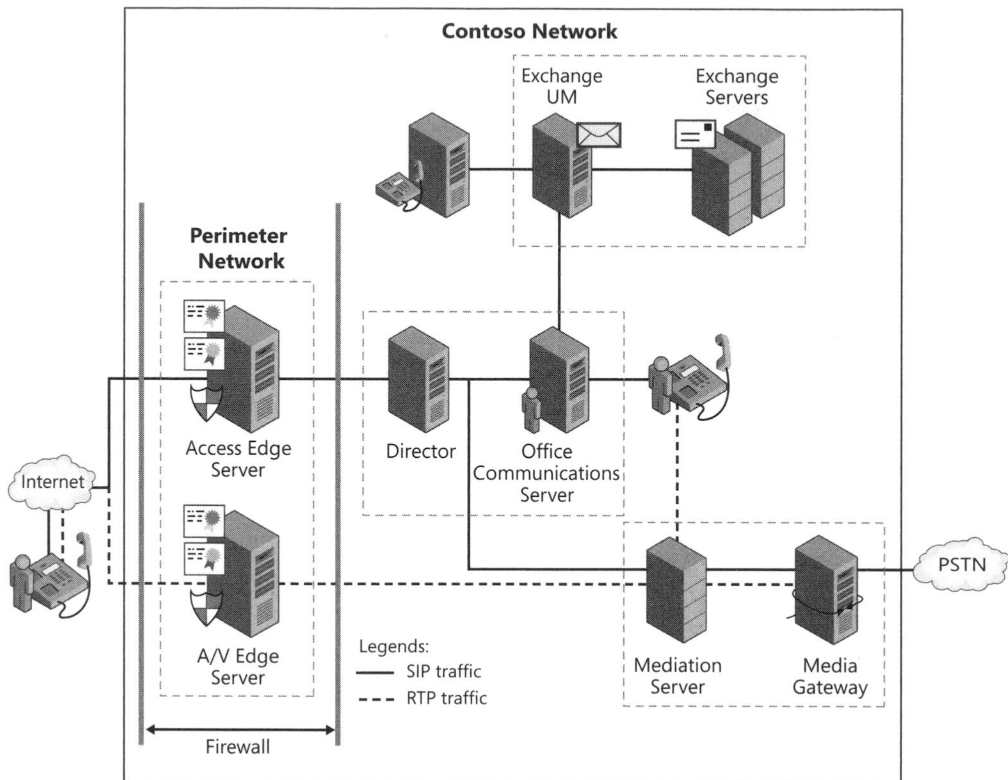

Note: The lines connecting the different server roles represent protocol traffic and do not necessarily represent the number of NICs the server must be configured with.

Figure 10-18 Enterprise voice topology

The elements of the VoIP topology are described in the following list:

- **Media gateway** This is a third-party server solution offered by Microsoft partners.
- **Mediation Server** Depending on the type of media gateway used, this Office Communications Server role is required.
- **A/V Edge Server** This Office Communications Server role is required to allow audio traffic to traverse the corporate firewall for users who are connecting from the Internet.
- **Access Edge Server** If you are giving users remote access to place and receive calls from outside the corporate firewall, the Access Edge Server must also be deployed in addition to deploying an A/V Edge Server. Depending on capacity requirements, it is possible to collocate both the Access Edge Server role and the A/V Edge Server role on the same physical server.
- **Exchange Unified Messaging (UM)** This Microsoft Exchange Server role is required to enable Exchange Server to serve as the voice mail system for Office Communications Server. Exchange UM is also used to provide auto-attendant and call notification service.

- **Monitoring Server** This Office Communications Server role is recommended to collect Call Detail Records (CDRs) for monitoring Quality of Experience (QoE) of calls.
- **Devices** These are VoIP endpoints that are capable of terminating a voice call. This includes Session Initiation Protocol (SIP)-enabled hardware phones as well as softphones such as Office Communicator 2007.

To place calls to and receive calls from outside your organization network, a third-party media gateway is required. The gateway's purpose is to bridge the PSTN network and your corporate IP network. Depending on the type of media gateway used, you might need to deploy an Office Communications Server 2007, Mediation Server to interoperate with the media gateway provided by your vendor. The Mediation Server performs codecs translation between RTAudio and legacy codecs. The following legacy codecs are supported: G.711, G.722.1/SIREN, G.723.1, G.726, and GSM. G.729 is not supported in Office Communications Server 2007. RTAudio is an advanced audio codec used by Office Communications Server. It has been tried and tested in Windows Live Messenger, which serves in excess of one billion voice minutes per month using RTAudio, to provide optimal audio quality over the Internet. Because most media gateways support only SIP over User Datagram Protocol (UDP), the Mediation Server converts SIP over the Transport Layer Security (TLS) used by Office Communications Server to SIP over UDP. There is a one-to-one mapping between the gateway and Mediation Server, as the gateway must be configured to route all incoming calls to the Mediation Server.

To provide users external access, where users can dial and receive calls when connected from outside their corporate network, the following server roles are necessary: Access Edge Server and A/V Edge Server. These server roles must be deployed in the perimeter network.

For voice mail capability, the Microsoft Exchange Server 2007 Unified Messaging (UM) server role is required. In addition to Exchange UM Servers, Exchange Mailbox Servers are required as well to store the voice mail. Office Communications Server 2007 servers connect to the Exchange UM Servers by means of the SIP protocol instead of with MAPI or other protocols. This gives Exchange UM Servers the advantage of being able to scale well in capacity without introducing a lot of hardware. Because SIP is a standard protocol, a second advantage is the potential for third-party vendors of voice mail systems to interoperate with Office Communications Server 2007 servers as an alternative solution. Exchange UM Servers integrate a managed code (.NET) SIP stack that is available as a software development kit (SDK) called Microsoft Unified Communications Managed API SDK, which independent software vendors can take advantage of.

Finally, VoIP-enabled devices that support the SIP protocol with Microsoft's extensions for signaling and the Real-Time Protocol (RTP) for audio are needed to terminate the calls. Microsoft's primary softphone client is Office Communicator 2007; however, Microsoft as well as third-party partners provide a variety of hardphone and softphone options.

As with any telecommunication solution, Office Communications Server 2007 Enterprise Voice must perform the following activities:

- **Outbound routing** Route calls from the organization running Office Communications Server Enterprise Voice to the PSTN
- **Inbound routing** Route calls from the PSTN to the organization's Office Communications Server Enterprise Voice system

These routing activities are enforced by the front-end service in both the Standard Edition Server and Enterprise Edition pool as an integral part of Office Communications Server.

Understanding How Outbound Calls Are Routed

Outbound routing of VoIP traffic in Office Communications Server 2007 is managed by the Outbound Routing component on the front-end server. When a user places a call, the client first attempts to normalize the dialed phone number. It then sends the request to the user's home pool. Based on the permissions allowed in the Voice policy that is assigned to the user, the home pool determines where to route the call. The call (SIP request) is routed to a Mediation Server. The audio portion of the call is routed directly from the client to the Mediation Server. The Mediation Server forwards the call and audio to the media gateway. The media gateway bridges the call to the PSTN. Figure 10-19 illustrates this process, and Figure 10-20 shows the call flow logic. Each of the elements—users, policies, usages, routes, and gateways—is represented as an object in Active Directory and is exposed as a Windows Management Instrumentation (WMI) class at the management application programming interface (API) layer.

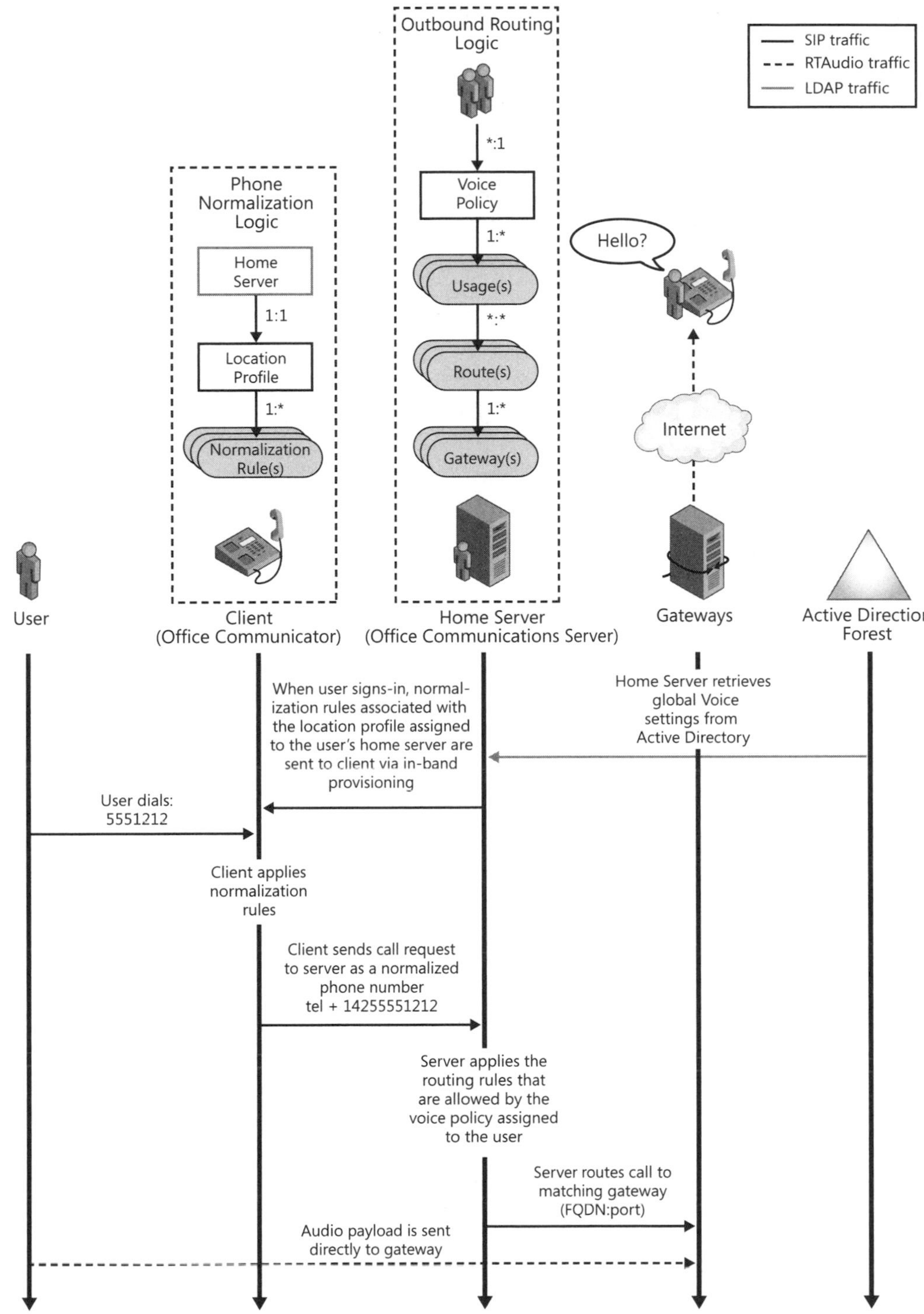

Figure 10-19 Outbound routing logic

Figure 10-20 shows another way to visualize the call flow logic.

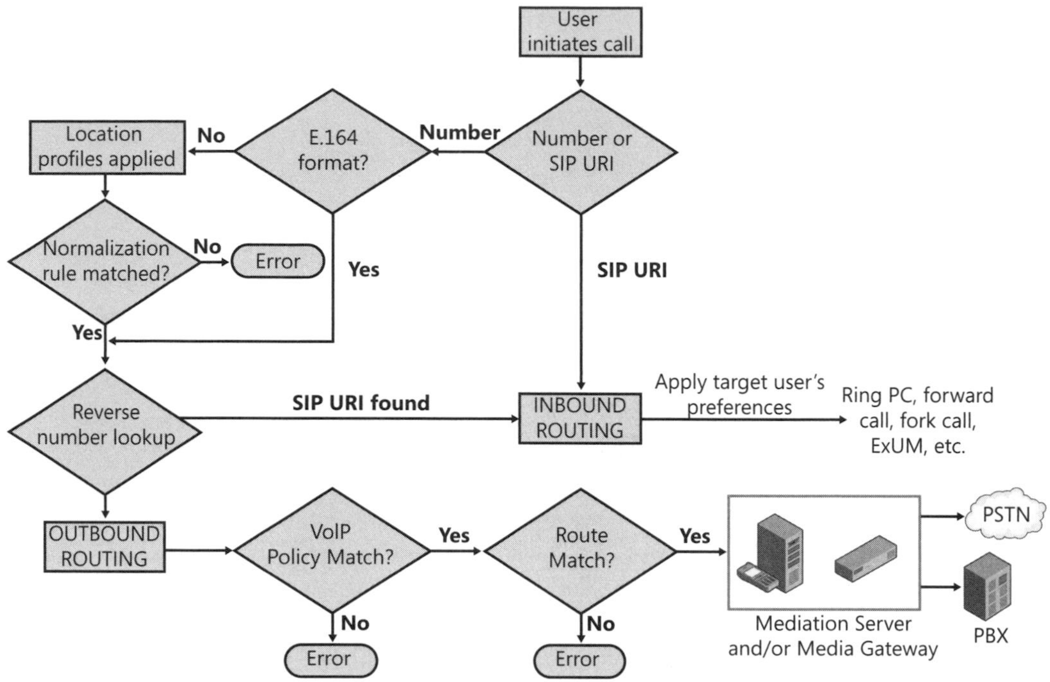

Figure 10-20 Call flow logic

Understanding Voice Policies

Every user enabled for Enterprise Voice is associated by the administrator to a Voice policy. A Voice policy defines the call privileges assigned to a user. The call privileges determine which routes the user is allowed to use. Each user must be associated to a single Voice policy. The number of policies available is created by the administrator.

Each Voice policy contains a setting to allow or disallow users to enable simultaneous ringing and a collection of ordered phone usages. The Voice policy, similar to the Meeting policy, is a logical container of settings defined as an XML document stored in Active Directory. The value of this design is that it can be extended in future versions of Office Communications Server to support additional policy settings without requiring an Active Directory schema extension. For example, if a Voice policy is not associated with any phone usages, this has the effect of preventing users assigned to that policy from making any outbound calls to the PSTN. Such users would be able to dial only internal numbers.

Understanding Phone Usage

A phone usage defines the phone routing privileges users are allowed. A phone usage is a collection of phone routes. It is a string that must be a unique keyword, meaning no other phone usage can have the same name. The administrator can create as many usages as she wants.

Although a Voice policy can be directly associated with a route or a set of routes instead of phone usages, the phone usage keyword is an abstraction used to maintain the association between policies and routes. If policies were directly associated to routes (effectively removing the concept of phone usages) and the administrator modified the name of a route, every policy associated with that route would need to be updated. By using a phone usage, which is an attribute of both a policy and a route to create the association between the policy and the route, the relationship between the policy and route is preserved even if the route's name is changed.

Understanding Phone Routes

A phone route defines how to route a call specified by a phone number to one or more Mediation Servers. The Mediation Server must be configured to route to a specific media gateway. The media gateway then either routes the call directly to the PSTN or it routes the call to an IP-PBX before reaching the PSTN. A route contains a phone number pattern and a list of gateways. This list of gateways includes Mediation Servers if using either basic media gateways or advanced and hybrid media gateways. A route must be assigned to at least one phone usage. This association between the pattern and gateways specifies how to route phone numbers that match that particular pattern.

The pattern specifies a range of phone numbers that it can match. It is defined as a regular expression (regex) that can include and exclude phone numbers. To help build these regular expressions more easily, use the Enterprise Voice Route Helper tool. If the phone number dialed matches the route's regex pattern, the call is routed to one of the gateways defined in the route.

More than one gateway can be listed in the phone route. Office Communications Server routes calls to the gateways in a round-robin fashion as a way to balance the traffic across the gateways. If a gateway fails or is taken out of service for maintenance, Office Communications Server immediately attempts to route the call to another gateway in the route's list. After 10 attempts to route calls to a failed gateway, Office Communications Server subsequently throttles traffic to that gateway until it becomes responsive again. If the gateway continues to fail to respond after an additional 10 attempts, Office Communications Server stops routing calls to that gateway entirely until it becomes responsive .

The list of gateways defined in the route is described by the gateway's fully qualified domain name (FQDN) and the port number that the gateway is listening on. If the phone number does not match the regex pattern, the next route associated with the policy assigned to the user is checked until a match is found. If no match is found, the call cannot be routed and fails to reach its destination. The user receives a notification that the call could not be completed.

Understanding How Inbound Calls Are Routed

Let's examine how Office Communications Server 2007 routes a call originating from the PSTN network to a user in your corporate network. Figure 10-21 illustrates this logic.

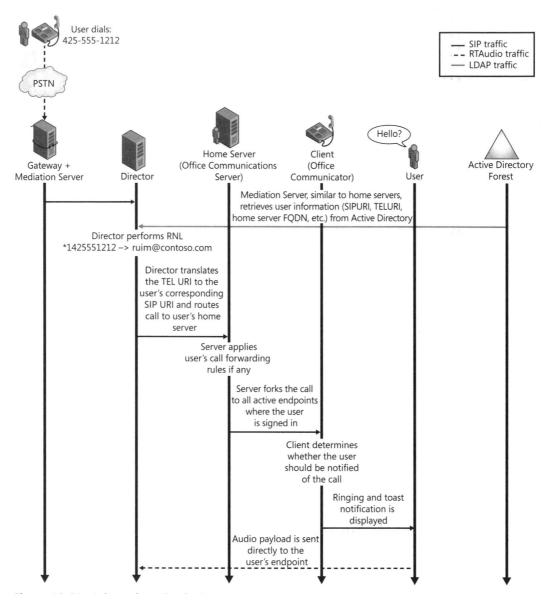

Figure 10-21 Inbound routing logic

Note Inbound calls can originate from another internal user or from a federated partner over a federated link. Before routing the call to a media gateway, Office Communications Server checks whether the phone number matches an internal user's number. If the phone number matches an internal user's number, the TEL URI is replaced by the internal user's SIP URI and routed to that user.

When an outside call originating from the PSTN arrives for a user within your organization, the handoff between the two networks occurs at one of the organization's media gateways. If a Basic Media Gateway or Basic Hybrid Media Gateway is used, the gateway sends the call to the Mediation Server to which it is configured to route to. The Mediation Server routes the signal to the Director it is configured to route to. The Director performs a reverse number lookup (RNL) to determine which user owns the called phone number, referred to as the TEL URI.

> **Note** Although highly recommended in a multi-pool deployment, a Director is not required.

The assignment of the phone number to the user is configured in the *msRTCSIP-Line* attribute of the user's object in Active Directory. If a match is not found, the Director cannot route the request and the call fails. Once a match is found, the TEL URI (for example, +14255551212) is translated into the user's SIP URI (for example ruim@contoso.com). The Mediation Server then determines the FQDN of the user's home pool and routes the SIP request. The SIP request is sent to the user's home pool. The home pool performs additional logic. It applies any call-forwarding rules the user might have set. For example, if the called party is set to simultaneously ring another phone number, Office Communications Server routes the call to the new number in addition to forking the call to all the registered endpoints the called party is signed in to. It drops the call if the user sets his presence to Do Not Disturb*. The only exception to this rule is if the caller is a contact in the called party's Personal or Team access level; then the call notification will be displayed. If the called party answers the call, the audio is routed directly from the Mediation Server to the user's client.

In the case that the called party is not signed in to Office Communications Server, the home pool determines that there are no active endpoints and instead of forking the incoming call to the user's endpoints, it directly routes the call to the user's voice mail server, Exchange Server 2007 Unified Messaging (UM). The user does not need to be signed in to Office Communications Server for voice mail to work. The called party can retrieve his messages once he opens Microsoft Outlook and connects to his Exchange mailbox.

Understanding Normalization

Although the concepts described so far make inbound and outbound calling possible, there are two limitations that must be addressed. First, this routing design works well if there is only a single way to represent a phone number. This is not the case; because the phone number is represented as a string, there are multiple ways to specify the same phone number. For example, the phone number, (425) 555-1212, can be represented in the following ways:

- (425) 555-1212
- 425-555-1212
- +14255551212

- 0014255551212
- 425.555.1212
- 555-1212 (this assumes the area code 425)
- 5551212
- 555.1212
- 51212 (if the number is an internal extension)
- (425) 555-1212 x51212

Although this list is not comprehensive, it demonstrates that the same phone number can be represented as a string in a a variety of ways. It's unlikely that the regex pattern defined in the route will be able to match all these variations. For the pattern matching of the route to work, some form of normalization is necessary. This is the first problem.

Because there are multiple ways to address this issue, the International Telecommunication Union–Telecom (ITU-T) Standardization Committee created the E.164 recommendation. The E.164 recommendation defines the international public telecommunication numbering plan, which specifies a methodology that provides a standardized method for presenting the domestic numbering plans of all countries.

A second problem is that some of the phone number variations are ambiguous. For example, the 555-1212 string assumes a local area. If the user were to dial this number in Redmond, Washington, the area code that should be assumed is 425; however, if the user were to dial this same number in Seattle, Washington, the area code that should be used is 206. To correctly normalize a phone number into E.164 format, a context is necessary to correctly interpret it based on the user's locale. This is the second problem.

To address these two problems, Office Communications Server 2007 exposes the following concepts:

- **Normalization Rules** Normalization rules define a match pattern and a translation pattern. Both patterns are represented as regular expression rules that describe how to translate a given phone number into a well-formatted number in E.164 format. Translating all numbers to E.164 format simplifies the regex defined in the route to match only phone numbers that have already been normalized by the normalization rules.
- **Location Profiles** A location profile is a collection of normalization rules. The location profile defines the collection of rules to apply for a particular region. A region can be a state, province, country, or city that has specific dialing rules. For example, if the user is dialing from Redmond, Washington, the normalization rules for that area code are applied to any phone number the user dials. So if the Redmond user enters, say, an eight-digit number, Communications Server 2007, following a rule in the Redmond location profile, adds the area code 425 when the number is dialed.

The roles these components play in the routing logic of voice communications is illustrated in the Phone Normalization Logic dotted-line box in Figure 10-19 previously. Location profiles and normalization rules are both defined by the administrator in charge of an organization's telephony infrastructure.

Each user is assigned a location profile, and upon dialing a phone number, the ordered list of normalization rules associated with the user's location profile are applied. If a first match to a normalization rule is found, the client translates the phone number into E.164 format before the SIP request is sent to the user's home pool. If a match is not found, the phone number is still sent to the user's home pool, but it is tagged as a dial string because it could not be normalized. The dial string that the client sends to Office Communications Server includes a *phone-context* attribute that specifies the name of the user's location profile. The server attempts to resolve the phone number by using the specified location profile normalization rules.

For example, *INVITE SIP:5551212;phone-context=redmond@contoso.com* is an example of a dial string. The non-normalized phone number is 5551212, and the specified location profile is Redmond.

Office Communications Server 2007 Enterprise Voice enables users to make and receive calls anywhere Internet access is available. They simply sign in to Communications Server and place calls as usual. Regardless of their geographic location, users' dialing patterns can remain the same as long as they are using the same location profile. If the administrator or the user changes the location profile to a different profile, the dialing patterns might change. Office Communications Server uses in-band provisioning to push the normalization rules associated with the location profile assigned to the user. If the user does not select a location profile (Office Communicator Phone Edition) or is not assigned a location profile by the administrator (Office Communicator 2007), the user is assigned a default location profile. This is the default location profile assigned to the user's home pool configured by the administrator. The administrator can assign a location profile to Office Communicator 2007 users who are using group policy.

Communicator caches these normalization rules and is responsible for applying them when a user dials phone numbers. As a result, no matter what their locations might be, Enterprise Voice users are always calling from home.

For example, if the user dials the number, 555-1212, the client runs through the normalization rules it got from the user's home pool. If one of the rules matches, the phone number is normalized. The request is sent to the user's home pool with the normalized phone number. The home pool checks whether the phone number matches any internal user's phone number. If it matches an internal user, the phone number is replaced by the user's SIP URI and is routed to that user's home pool. If a match to an internal user is not found, the home pool performs a route-matching analysis. Once a match is found, the request is routed to one of the gateways listed in the route. The client then sends the audio portion of the call directly to the gateway.

Configuring Global Enterprise Voice Settings

Now that you have a better understanding of the VoIP design of Office Communications Server 2007, this section jumps into the details of configuring VoIP by using the Admin Tools Microsoft Management Console (MMC). The Office Communications Server 2007 Resource Kit also provides useful tools. In particular, the Resource Kit tool Enterprise Voice Route Helper has several advantages currently not available in the Admin Tools MMC.

Direct from the Source: Enterprise Voice Route Helper

Enterprise Voice Route Helper allows you to test the changes before making them persistent. You do eventually want to make changes persistent; otherwise, you are wasting your time.

–Paul Tidwell
Software Development Engineer, Microsoft

Another advantage of Enterprise Voice Route Helper is the ability to simulate the behavior of the system when a particular phone number is dialed. The route taken will be highlighted. Once the administrator is satisfied with her voice configuration, the Route Helper tool can apply the new configuration to Active Directory while maintaining a tracking history of the configurations applied to Active Directory.

The global Enterprise Voice settings can be configured only by administrators who are members of the RTCUniversalGlobalWriteGroup or RTCUniversalServerAdmins groups. Administrator members of the RTCUniversalGlobalReadOnlyGroup group can view the global settings, but they cannot modify them. Inbound routing rules (simultaneous ringing, call forwarding, and so on) are configured by the user.

Configuring Voice Policies

The administrator can create as many Voice policies as desired regardless of whether they are used or not. To create a Voice policy by using the Admin Tools MMC, select the Voice Properties from the forest node, and click the Policy tab. The Policy tab allows administrators to manage their Voice policies. (See Figure 10-22.) Out of the box, a default policy is defined. The administrator can assign all users the same Voice policy or allow users to be assigned a different Voice policy by selecting the Use Per User Policy option from the drop-down list for the Global Policy setting.

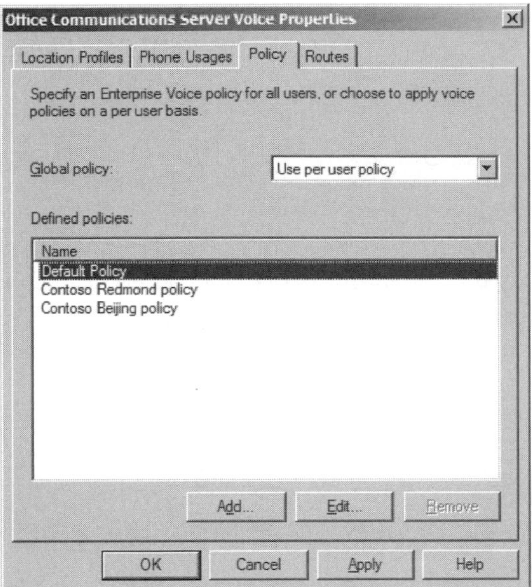

Figure 10-22 Voice policy management

Because Voice policies are associated with phone usages, the administrator also needs to create phone usages to represent routing restrictions. To create a phone usage, navigate to the Phone Usages tab (shown in Figure 10-23). A phone usage consists of a keyword and a description that is used purely for the benefit of the administrator to describe what that phone usage is used for. Out of the box, a default phone usage is defined.

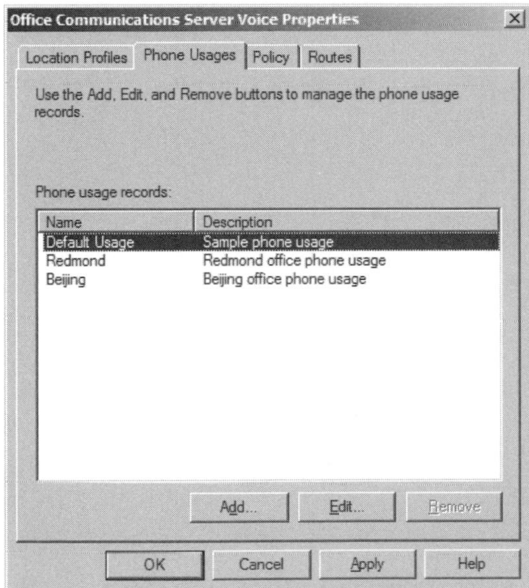

Figure 10-23 Phone usage management

Given the two geographic locations with their own egress to the PSTN in our example, the administrator responsible for this Office Communications Server 2007 deployment defined two Voice policies with associated usages for each office.

Configuring Phone Routes

A phone route assigns defined sets of phone numbers to various media gateways. Consequently, a phone route consists of a name for the route, a description that the administrator creates, a target set of phone numbers expressed in the form of a regular expression (regex), a list of gateways to route phone numbers that match the target regex pattern, and a list of usages. (See Figure 10-24.)

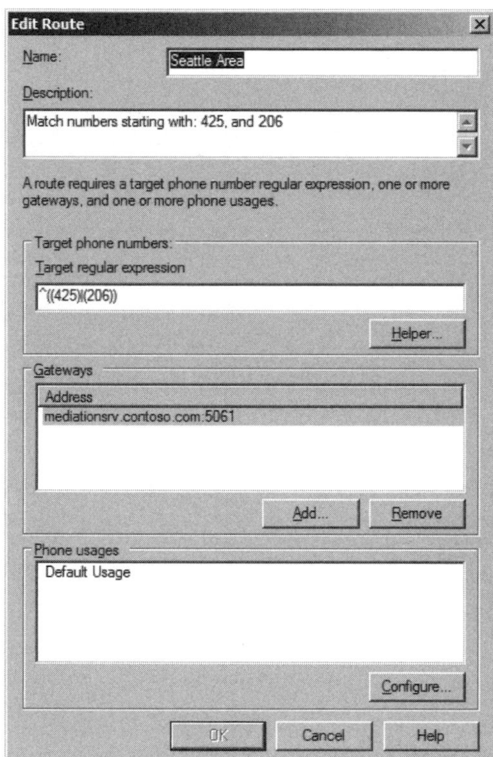

Figure 10-24 Phone route management

The phone usage ties the phone route to the Voice policy (shown earlier in Figure 10-22). Therefore, only users assigned a Voice policy that specifies the same phone usage associated with a phone route can use that route. The list of gateways is specified by its FQDN and the port number to connect to. This FQDN can be the fully qualified name of an advanced media gateway or the fully qualified name of a Mediation Server if you are using a basic media gateway.

Specifying a target regular expression can be a little daunting at first when using the Admin Tools MMC. The Enterprise Voice Route Helper tool provides more assistance in defining phone routes. The user interface simplifies the creation of regular expressions. It automatically translates the regular expressions into plain English in the description field of the route. This makes it easier to understand the meaning of the regular expression. In addition, the Enterprise Voice Route Helper tool offers the ability to test the regular expression before saving it. Figure 10-25 shows the same route defined in Figure 10-24, this time using the Enterprise Voice Route Helper. To view the syntax of the regular expression, click on the Raw tab.

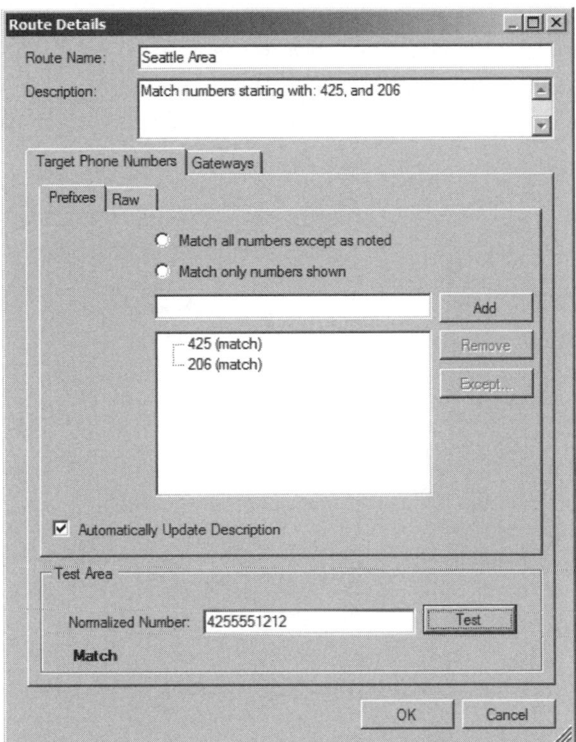

Figure 10-25 Phone route management using Enterprise Voice Route Helper

Another valuable feature of this tool is the ability to test which route(s) are triggered for a given phone number. This feature is particularly useful because it allows administrators to quickly test phone routes. Administrators can simulate the scenario of a user dialing a phone number and see how the call gets routed without applying the phone route in production (that is, in Active Directory). The route that matches is highlighted. The tool even simulates the phone number normalization performed by the client when the user's location profile is specified. This feature is available on the Ad-hoc Test tab.

Configuring Location Profiles

A location profile is a container that holds a name, a description, and a list of normalization rules. Future versions of Office Communications Server can extend the location profile to include additional attributes. The normalization rules associated with a location profile define the dialing patterns for a specific region (location). For example, if the user dials 555-1212, what area code should the system assume? If the user has a location profile with a normalization rule that converts all seven-digit numbers into eleven-digit numbers assuming a country of 1 and an area code of 425, the phone number will be translated to +14255551212. But if a user has a location profile with a normalization rule that adds +1213 to all seven-digit numbers, the phone number will be translated to +12135551212.

Each normalization rule consists of two regular expressions. The first regex is the matching pattern; the second regex is the translation expression. When the user dials a phone number, the client (Office Communicator 2007) immediately runs through the ordered list of normalization rules for the location profile it obtained from the user's home pool. The phone number is translated upon finding the first match.

To manage your location profiles, open the Voice properties at the Active Directory forest node, and select the Location Profiles tab (shown in Figure 10-26). Embedded within this tab is the UI to create/edit normalization rules.

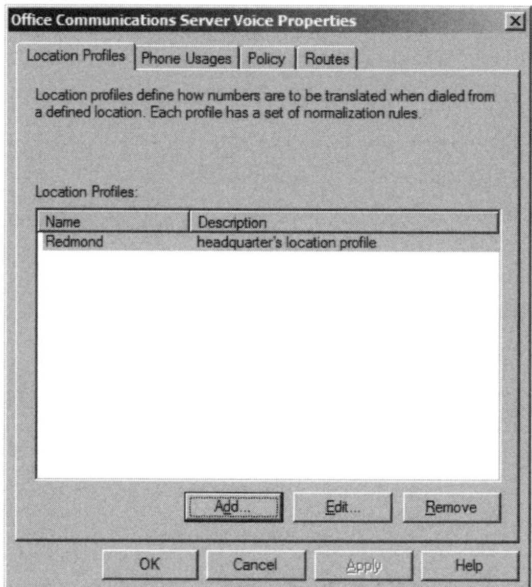

Figure 10-26 Location profile management

The Enterprise Voice Route Helper provides a slightly different user interface, with additional features such as assistance in creating regular expressions, seeing which normalization rules are matched as the user types a phone number, and automatically creating or updating the description of the normalization rule.

A default location profile can be assigned to pools. (See Figure 10-27.) Users inherit the location profile of their home pool if the administrator hasn't assigned a location profile to the user through group policy. If the user is using Office Communicator 2007, the client obtains the user's location profile from his home pool through in-band provisioning. If the user is using Office Communicator Phone Edition, he can select from the list of location profiles available, and the device will obtain the selected location profile from the home pool.

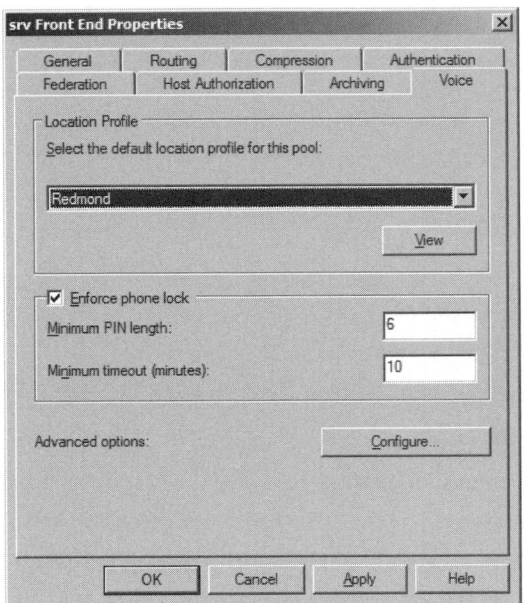

Figure 10-27 Assigning Office Communications Server location profiles

In addition, each Mediation Server is assigned a location profile (as shown in Figure 10-28) because an incoming call from the PSTN might list a phone number that is ambiguous to Office Communications Server. The location profile assigned to the Mediation Server is used to help disambiguate the target phone number.

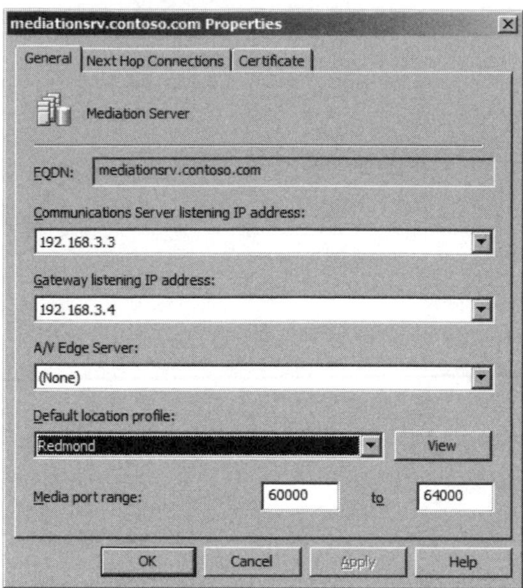

Figure 10-28 Assigning Mediation Server location profiles

Configuring VoIP

VoIP, or Enterprise Voice, requires additional configuration and the deployment of new server roles to support this functionality. Enterprise Voice can be easily added to an existing Office Communications Server 2007 IM and Web Conferencing deployment. Enabling Enterprise Voice involves the following activities covered in the next section:

- Configuring global Voice settings, as covered in the previous section
- Administrating users to be Enterprise Voice enabled
- Deploying media gateways to connect to the PSTN or PBX network
- Deploying a Mediation Server for each corresponding media gateway
- Optionally deploying one or more Monitoring Servers to collect, aggregate, and report Call Detail Records (CDRs)
- Optionally deploying the Deployment Validation Tool to monitor voice quality within and outside the organization's network

Configuring Users for Unified Communications

Configuring users for Unified Communications (UC) is quite simple. Before a user or group of users can be configured for Enterprise Voice, they must be enabled for Office Communications Server and assigned a SIP URI and home pool. A different license agreement than the standard IM or Web Conferencing client access license (CAL) is required before enabling users for Enterprise Voice. Office Communications Server 2007 offers three CALs based on the type of functionality users can be enabled for.

To configure a single user for Enterprise Voice, select the user's Properties from the right-click menu in DSA.MSC or the Admin Tools MMC. Under the Communications tab, select the Configure button to view additional options. In the Telephony section, select the Enable Enterprise Voice Routing option and configure the user's phone number. The option to change the policy selection becomes available so that administrators can specify a different Voice policy. Every Enterprise Voice user must be assigned a Voice policy. This phone number is specified in a valid TEL URI format that is globally unique, meaning no other person has the same phone number extension within the organization. This number is entered in the Line URI field by using the format *tel:<phone>*. These settings are shown in Figure 10-29.

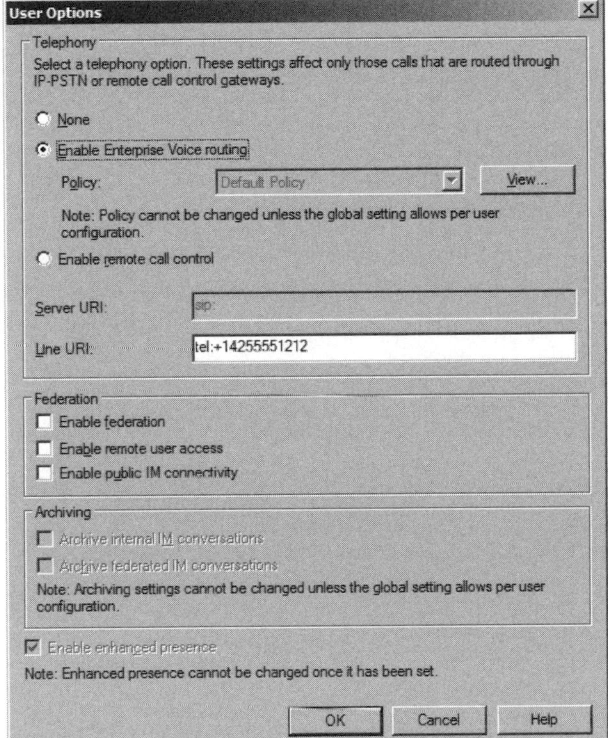

Figure 10-29 Enterprise Voice user properties

If an incorrect format is entered, an error warning is displayed. To specify an extension in addition to the phone number, use the following format: *tel:<phone>;ext=<extension>*. The phone number specified in the Line URI field uniquely associates the user's SIP URI to this TEL URI. This association allows Office Communications Servers to translate between the two URI formats.

By default, the Policy drop-down option is disabled. The global Voice policy is set to the out-of-the-box Default Policy. To be able to modify the policy assigned to the user, the global policy setting must be changed. To access this global policy, navigate to the forest level Voice Properties in the Admin Tools MMC and select the Policy tab. Click the Global Policy drop-down option, and choose Use Per User Policy. This is illustrated in Figure 10-30. Once the global Voice policy is modified, the user's Voice policy can be changed and viewed. When the View button is selected, the phone usage associated with the policy is shown.

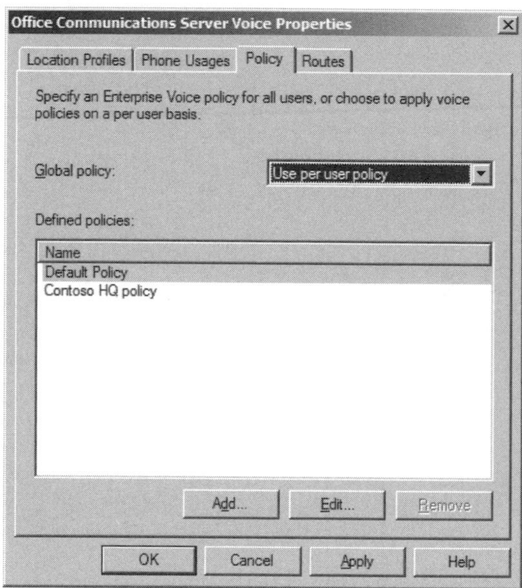

Figure 10-30 Global Voice policy

To configure multiple users at once, a better option is to use the Configure Communications Server Users Wizard. To bulk configure, select all the users to enable for Enterprise Voice from DSA.MSC or Admin Tools MMC, and choose this wizard from the right-click menu (as shown in Figure 10-31).

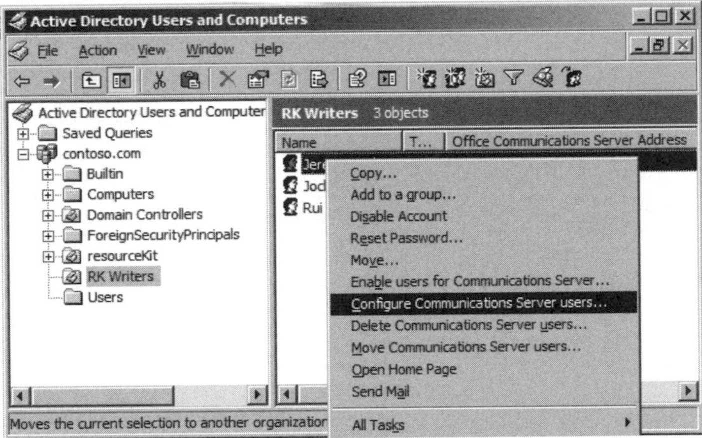

Figure 10-31 Selecting the Configure Communications Server Users Wizard

Because this wizard allows the configuring of all user settings, click Next to arrive at the Enterprise Voice settings. The Enterprise Voice settings to configure are shown in Figure 10-32. The top-level check box, Change Enterprise Voice Settings, must be selected to enable users for Enterprise Voice. The top-level check box indicates that you want to configure the embedded settings. To enable users for Enterprise Voice, the Enable Voice check box must be selected. The policy drop-down list becomes available if the global policy permits it. (See Figure 10-30.) To bulk disable users, select the Change Enterprise Voice Settings check box and leave the Enable Voice check box unselected. This combination of settings effectively prevents users from using Enterprise Voice. Click Next and finally Finish to complete the wizard. The final page of the wizard displays the results of the operation performed. If the wizard indicates that the operation failed for some or all of the users, check whether these users are enabled for Office Communications Server and are assigned a SIP URI and a home pool.

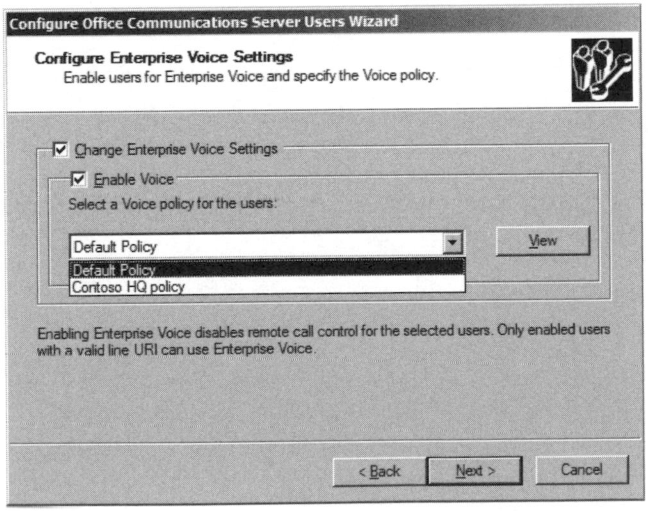

Configure Office Communications Server Users Wizard
Configure Enterprise Voice Settings
Enable users for Enterprise Voice and specify the Voice policy.
Change Enterprise Voice Settings
Enable Voice
Select a Voice policy for the users:
Default Policy
Default Policy
Contoso HQ policy
View
Enabling Enterprise Voice disables remote call control for the selected users. Only enabled users with a valid line URI can use Enterprise Voice.
< Back Next > Cancel

Figure 10-32 Configure Enterprise Voice settings

One important point to keep in mind about using the Configure Office Communications Server Users Wizard is although users might be enabled for Enterprise Voice, unless these users were previously provisioned with a TEL URI that remains unique, they will not be reachable via a phone number if the Line URI field remains blank. The Configure Office Communications Server Users Wizard does not configure the Line URI field because each user must have a unique TEL URI. To bulk configure the Line URI field, you need to resort to using the following Office Communications Server WMI interface: *MSFT_SIPESUserSetting.LineURI*.

Configuring the Media Gateway

The media gateway is a third-party server role offered by Microsoft's partners that is used to convert the signaling portion, SS7, of the PSTN traffic into SIP and the media portion of the PSTN traffic into RTP. Because each media gateway vendor will likely expose its management settings differently, this book will not cover the step-by-step guidelines necessary to configure all the settings of the media gateway. Instead, the administrator should refer to the media gateway vendor's documentation, which is often available online.

Aside from differences in pricing and features, Microsoft differentiates media gateway vendors into three categories that it supports. The first category, referred to as *basic media gateways*, requires the deployment of Office Communications Server, Mediation Server to work with Office Communications Server 2007. Depending on the vendor, installing its media gateway service on the same physical server co-located with the Mediation Server service might be supported. Nevertheless, from a logical perspective, they are considered separate servers. The second category, referred to as *advanced media gateways*, does not require deploying Mediation Servers to interface with Office Communications Server 2007. The third category, referred to as *hybrid media gateways*, consists of a basic media gateway with the functionality of the Mediation Server coexisting on the same physical server. More details are covered in the "Bridging VoIP to the PSTN Network by Using a Media Gateway" section in Chapter 3, "Infrastructure and Security Considerations."

The media gateway must be configured with the Primary Rate Interface/Basic Rate Interface (PRI/BRI) lines allocated by your telecom provider, which connect it to the PSTN network. On the network interface card (NIC) connected to the internal IP network, the gateway should be configured to connect to the Mediation Server if you are using a basic media gateway. To configure the media gateway to send and receive traffic from the Mediation Server, the following settings must be configured:

- **Inbound traffic** A listening port on the media gateway must be configured to listen for incoming traffic from the Mediation Server.
- **Outbound traffic** The media gateway must be configured with the FQDN or IP address of the Mediation Server and the port number it will send outbound traffic to.

This configuration is illustrated in Figure 10-33.

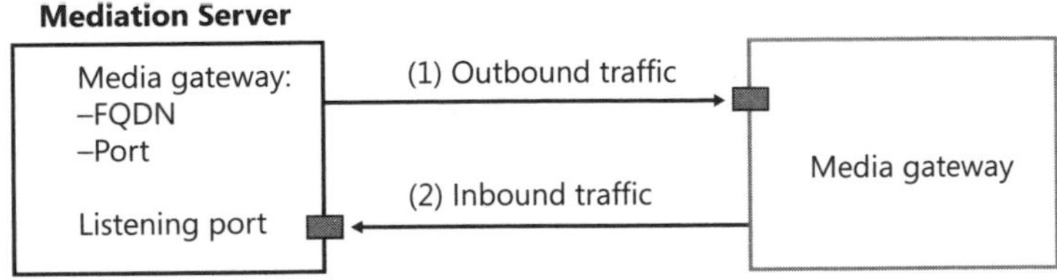

Figure 10-33 Media gateway configuration

Configuring the Mediation Server

The Mediation Server is a server role that is required if you are using a basic media gateway to function with Office Communications Server 2007. Since the majority of basic media gateways support only SIP over TCP or UDP, the Mediation Server extends the security of the Office Communications Server system up to the basic media gateways by translating SIP over TCP/UDP to SIP over MTLS. This is why it is recommended that you deploy a Mediation Server within proximity to its associated media gateway. To prevent internal users from eavesdropping on phone conversations, the network connection between the Mediation Server and media gateway should be placed on a separate network inaccessible to the users. Microsoft's objective is to help media gateway third-party vendors integrate as much of the Mediation Server functionality into the media gateway servers referred to as "advanced media gateways." The objective is to remove the Mediation Server role entirely. This will help reduce the added complexity that deploying and managing another server running the Mediation Server role creates, and consequently it will likely reduce total cost of ownership (TCO). Until third-party media gateway vendors are able to integrate this functionality into their offerings, a Mediation Server is required. The Mediation Server provides the following functions:

- Intermediate signaling (SIP) between Office Communications Servers and the media gateway.
- Transcode RTP media traffic from legacy codecs–such as G.711, G.722.1/SIREN, G.723.1, G.726, and GSM–that are used by media gateways to the Office Communications Server 2007 advanced audio codec, Real-time Audio (RTAudio).
- Acts as an Interactive Connectivity Establishment (ICE) client to enable PSTN-originated media flows to traverse intervening Network Address Translators (NATs) and firewalls.
- Provides management, provisioning, and monitoring for the media gateway to integrate into Office Communications Server's infrastructure of Active Directory, WMI, and MMC.

The Mediation Server installation can be found under the Deploy Other Server Roles option in Office Communications Server 2007 Setup. This is illustrated in Figure 10-34. Office Communications Server 2007 Setup provides a step-by-step set of wizards for installing your Mediation Server.

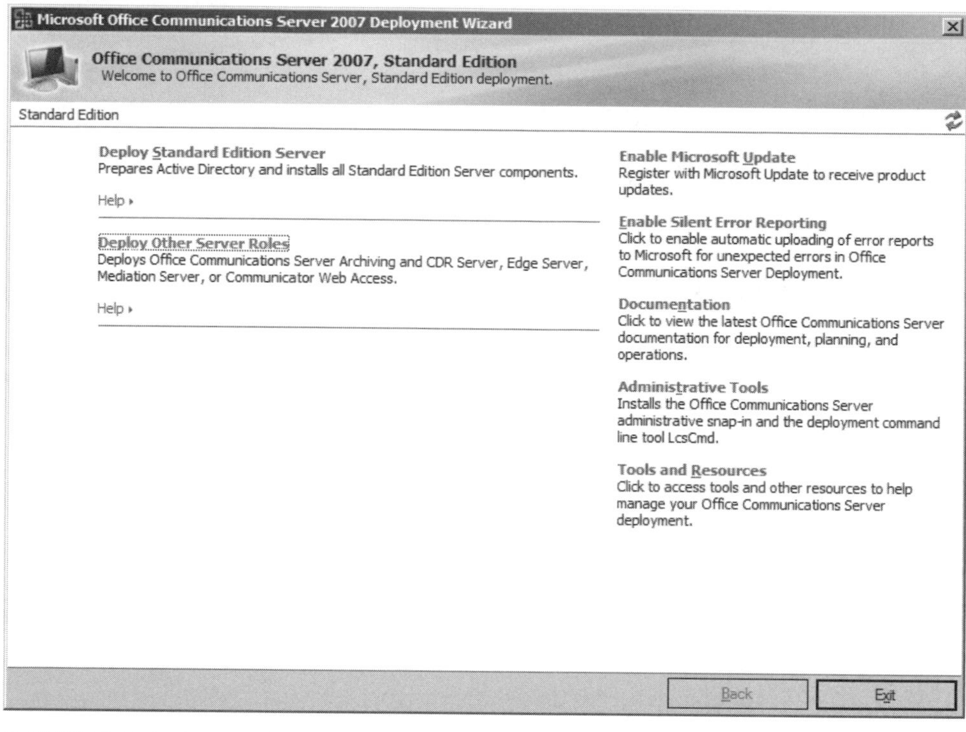

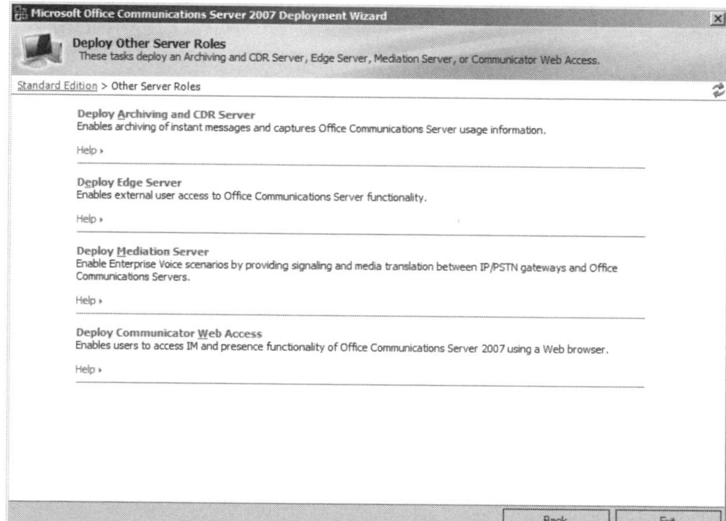

Figure 10-34 Mediation Server Setup

From a configuration perspective, a one-to-one correspondence between Mediation Server and the media gateway is required. That is, one Mediation Server is required for each media gateway deployed. The Mediation Server role must run on a computer that is domain joined to the Active Directory forest where the Office Communications Server 2007 infrastructure is deployed. The Mediation Server must be configured to connect to an Office Communications Server. If a Director is deployed, the Mediation Server can be configured to route calls to the Director; otherwise, the Mediation Server should be configured to route traffic to the home pool closest to it.

Because the Mediation Server is the only Office Communications Server role that connects directly to a basic media gateway, it must be configured to send and receive network traffic to and from the media gateway. The Mediation Server must have at least two NICs configured on the physical computer—one NIC is used for sending and receiving signaling (SIP protocol) traffic from Office Communications Servers as well as audio (RTAudio codec) traffic from internal phone clients, and the other NIC is for sending and receiving signaling (SIP protocol) and audio (G.711 codec) traffic from the media gateway. This is illustrated in Figure 10-35.

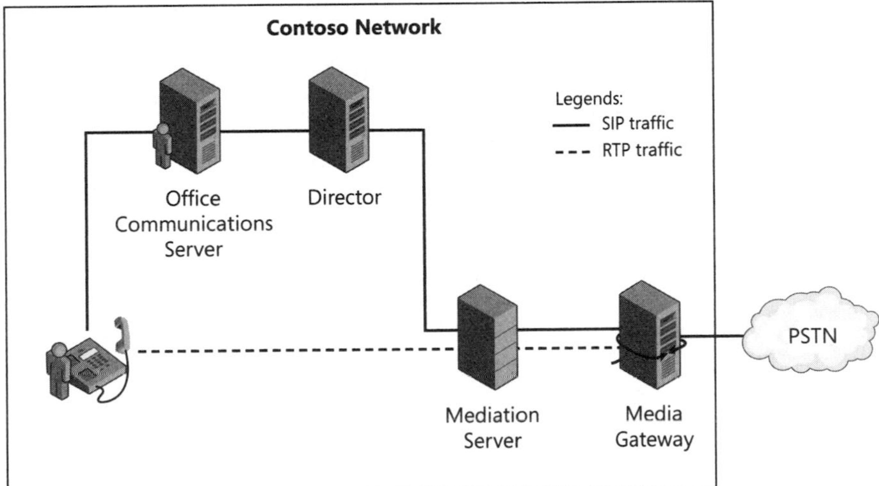

Figure 10-35 Internal call routing

To allow remote users (users connecting from the Internet) who are Enterprise Voice enabled to dial and receive calls from outside the enterprise's network, the administrator must specify the A/V Edge Server that the Mediation Server should connect to for both inbound and outbound calls. For security reasons, the A/V Edge Server does not initiate connections to servers in the corporate internal network. When a remote user dials a phone number, the signaling (SIP) traffic to initiate the call traverses the Access Edge Server to the Director, which routes the request to the user's home pool. The home pool sends the request to the Mediation Server. The Mediation Server forwards the request out to the PSTN through the media gateway. When the call is answered, the Mediation Server needs to establish a connection with the client to obtain the audio portion of the call. The Mediation Server specifies the address of the A/V Edge Server the client should connect to through the signaling channel, and on its end establishes a connection to the A/V Edge Server. The address of the A/V Edge Server is the one the administrator configured the Mediation Server with. Once the client and the Mediation

Server set up a tunnel across the A/V Edge Server, audio can flow through. The Mediation Server forwards this audio to the media gateway. A similar process occurs when the remote user receives a call. This is illustrated in Figure 10-36.

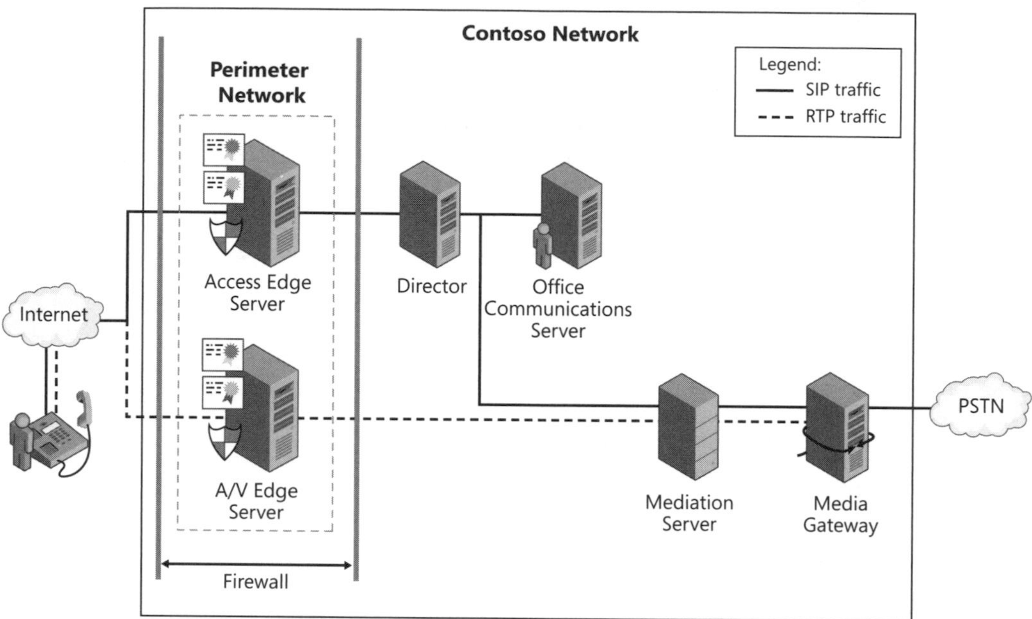

Note: The lines connecting the different server roles represent protocol traffic and do not necessarily represent the number of NICs the server must be configured with.

Figure 10-36 External call routing

Figure 10-37 shows, from the perspective of the Mediation Server, what configuration is necessary to make it work with the other server roles.

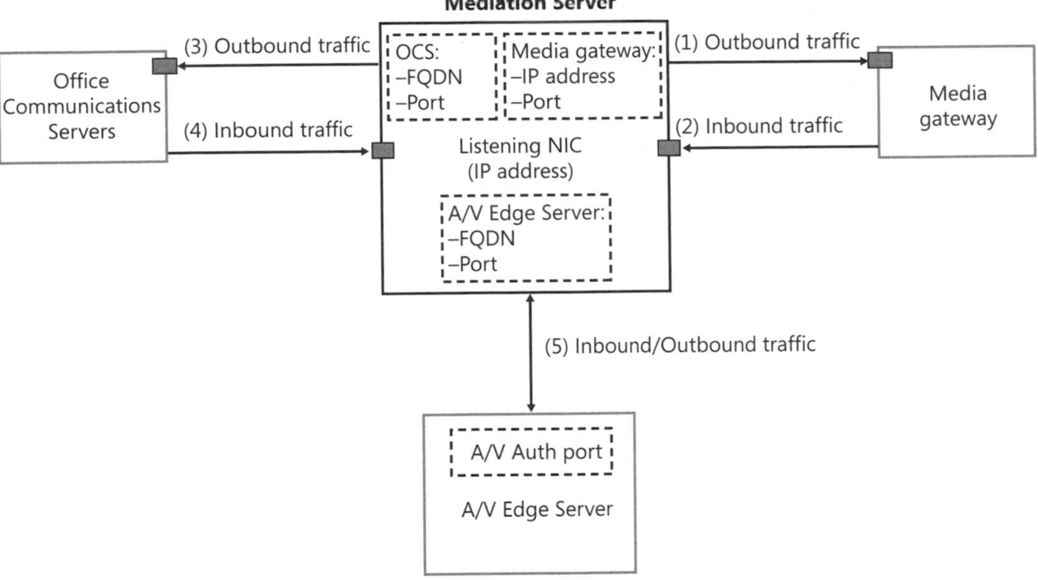

Figure 10-37 Mediation Server configuration

The following are descriptions of the numbers keyed to Figure 10-37:

1. **Outbound traffic to media gateway** The Mediation Server must be configured with the IP address of the media gateway and port number it will send outbound traffic to, which it receives from the Office Communications Server or A/V Edge Server.
2. **Inbound traffic from media gateway** This is the IP address on the Mediation Server that will be used to listen for inbound traffic from the media gateway.
3. **Outbound traffic to Office Communications Server** The Mediation Server is configured with the FQDN and port number of an Office Communications Server to which it will send outbound traffic it receives from the media gateway.
4. **Inbound traffic from Office Communications Server** This is the IP address on the Mediation Server that will be used to listen for inbound traffic from the Office Communications Server.
5. **Inbound/outbound traffic to A/V Edge Server** The Mediation Server is configured with the FQDN and A/V Authentication port number of the A/V Edge Server. The Mediation Server should be configured with a local A/V Edge Server to allow remote users to dial out to the PSTN as well as receive calls originating from outside the user's organization.

To configure the Mediation Server, the administrator must use the Admin Tools MMC. After installing the Mediation Server, open the Admin Tools MMC and locate your Mediation Server by its FQDN. Right-click your Mediation Server, and select Properties (as shown in Figure 10-38).

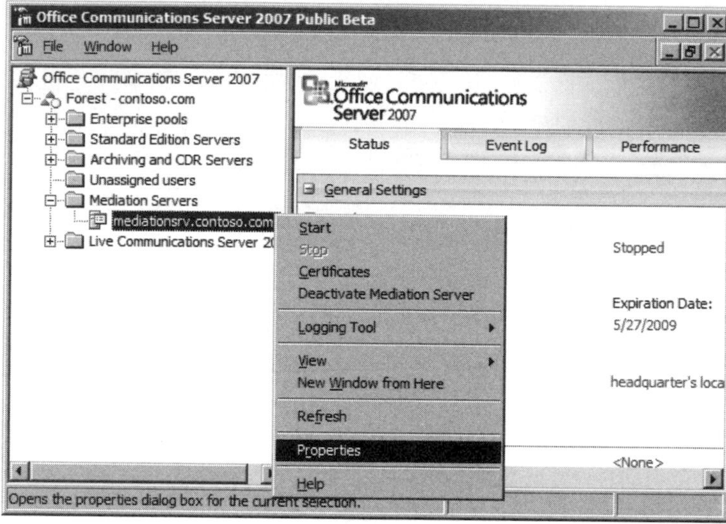

Figure 10-38 Mediation Server properties

The six settings to configure the Mediation Server so that it can route traffic between the Office Communications Server and A/V Edge Server to the media gateway are split between two tabs. These settings are shown in Figure 10-39, and they are numbered to match the logical representation of these settings that was shown in Figure 10-37. The first tab, called the General tab, is used to specify the IP addresses that the Mediation Server listens on for inbound connections (numbered item 4 in Figure 10-39). In addition, the administrator can specify a location profile for the Mediation Server (numbered item 6). The range of media ports used by the Mediation Server is configurable; however, in most cases the default values do not need to be modified. The second tab, called the Next Hop Connections, is where the administrator specifies the outbound connections to the Office Communications Server (numbered item 3) and media gateway (numbered item 1).

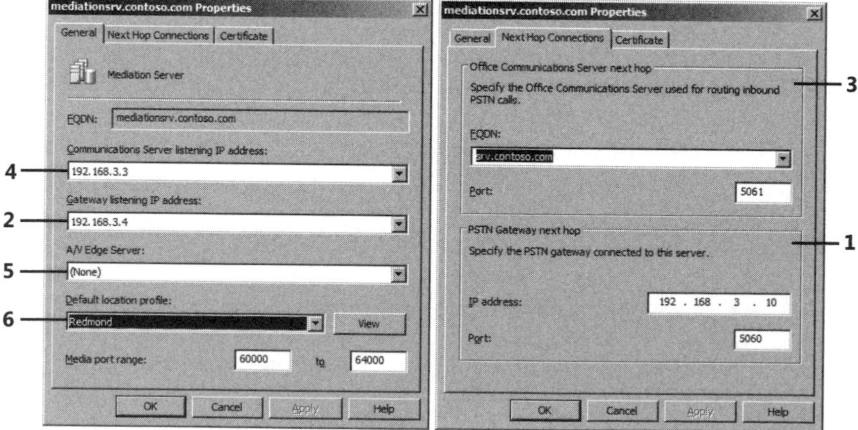

Figure 10-39 Mediation Server configuration

Before the Mediation Server can establish network connections with other Office Communications Servers it interacts with, it must be configured with a server certificate issued by a certificate authority (CA) that is trusted by the other Office Communications Servers. This configuration can be completed from the Certificate tab.

Returning to the configuration of an A/V Edge Server connection in the Mediation Server properties, if the A/V Edge Server drop-down option (shown as 5 in Figure 10-39) is empty, this is because no trusted A/V Edge Servers were configured in the Office Communications Server's global settings at the Active Directory forest level. Once an A/V Edge Server is specified, it becomes visible in the drop-down list of the General tab of the Mediation Server's properties. To configure your A/V Edge Server, navigate to the Global Properties of the forest node in the Admin Tools MMC, and select the Edge Servers tab (shown in Figure 10-40). Click the Add button to specify an A/V Edge Server. The dialog box will prompt you for the FQDN and authentication port number of the A/V Edge Server.

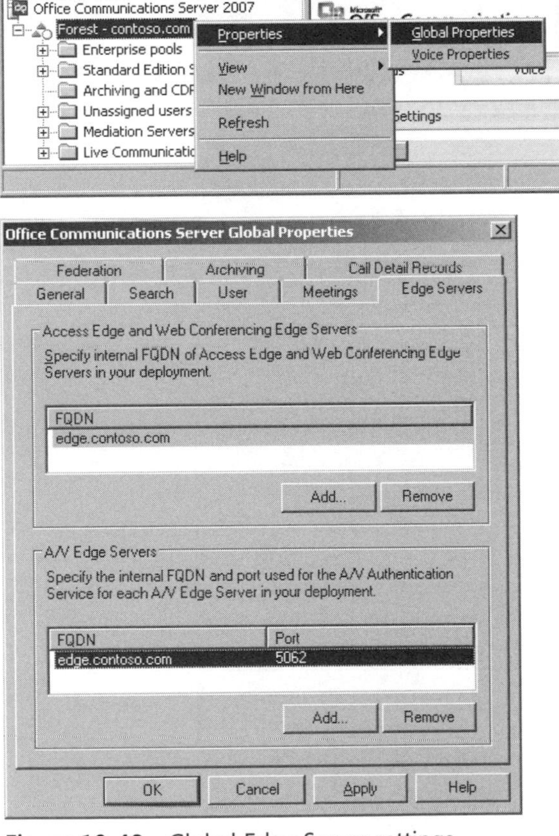

Figure 10-40 Global Edge Server settings

To determine the FQDN and A/V authentication port number of the A/V Edge Server, navigate to the Admin Tools MMC of your A/V Edge Server. The way to get to the Admin Tools MMC of Edge Servers is to right-click My Computer and select Manage. (See Figure 10-41.)

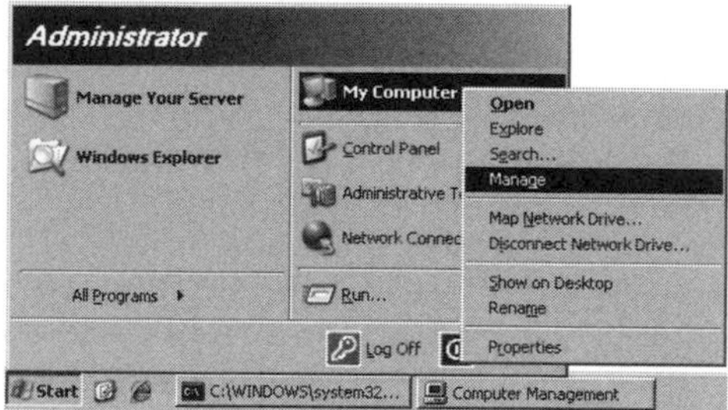

Figure 10-41 Administer A/V Edge Server

Expand the Services And Applications node to reach the Microsoft Office Communications Server 2007 node. Click the plus sign (+) next to Internal Interface Settings in the Status pane to expand it. The information to configure the global Edge Server settings is displayed in the Status pane. (See Figure 10-42.)

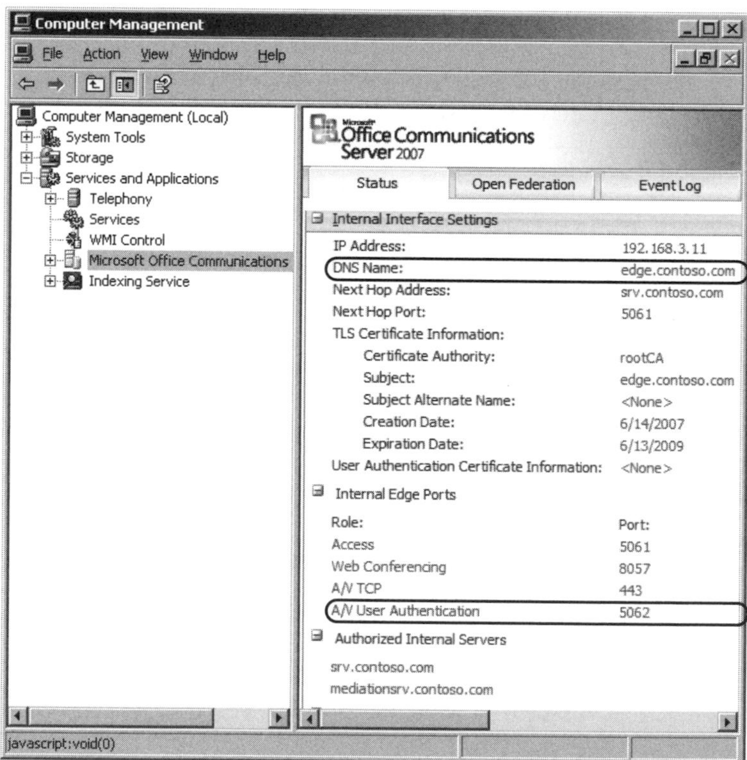

Figure 10-42 A/V Edge Server settings

Once the A/V Edge Server is specified in the global settings, the A/V Edge Server's FQDN and authentication port number are visible in the General tab of the Mediation Server (shown in Figure 10-43).

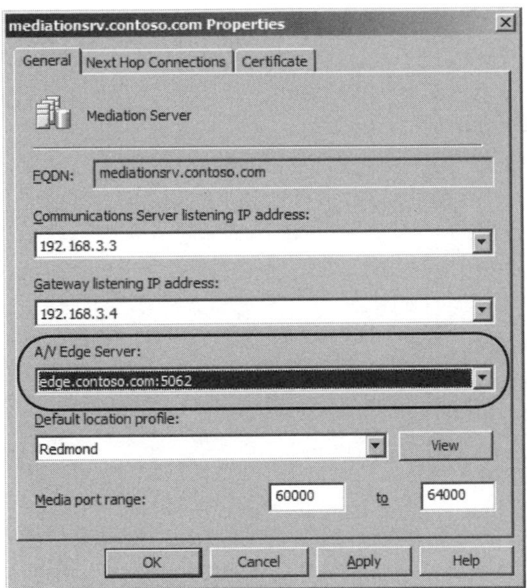

Figure 10-43 A/V Edge Server Setting on the Mediation Server

Configuring the Mediation Server to connect is nearly complete. The Mediation Server is now configured to connect to the A/V Edge Server; however, the A/V Edge Server is not configured to trust incoming network connections from the Mediation Server. To specify the A/V Edge Server to trust the Mediation Server, the administrator must return to the Admin Tools MMC of the A/V Edge Server, select Properties, and navigate to the Internal tab. To add the Mediation Server as an internal server authorized to connect to the A/V Edge Server, click the Add Server button, and specify the FQDN of your Mediation Server (as shown in Figure 10-44).

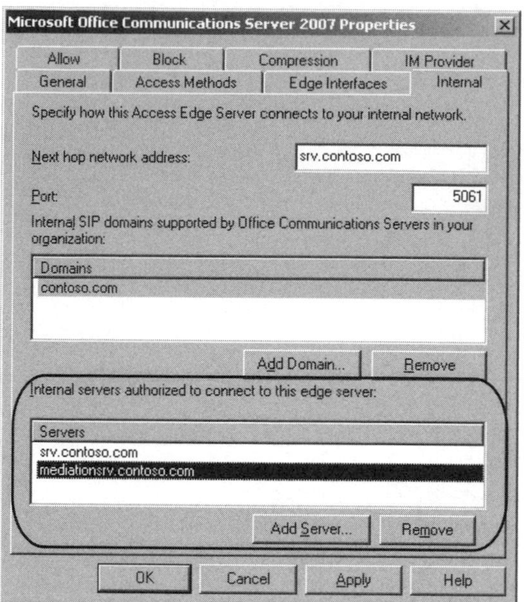

Figure 10-44 Mediation Server configured to connect to the A/V Edge Server

Your configuration of the Mediation Server now allows remote users to place and receive calls when signing in from the Internet.

Configuring the QoE Monitoring Server

Microsoft Office Communications Server 2007 Quality of Experience (QoE) Monitoring Server enables you to perform near real-time monitoring and service assessment of unified communications media. This server role collects Call Detail Record (CDR) metrics from all the Office Communications Servers. The Call Detail Record metrics are routed to the QoE Monitoring Server as SIP traffic. It then analyzes the quality of calls, referred to as Quality of Experience (QoE), and provides root-cause analysis and alarms to administrators.

Quantifying and monitoring the Quality of Experience of all users in all calls is one of the unique differentiations of Office Communications Server 2007. The user endpoints (Office Communicator and Office Communicator Phone Edition) measure the actual experience and generate all relevant metrics of each call, which are collected and aggregated in a CDR by Office Communications Server. The CDRs are sent to the Monitoring Server, which aggregates the data. In total, more than 30 parameters that pertain to quality are logged by each endpoint in a call.

The Monitoring Server provides reporting interfaces that integrate with Microsoft Operations Manager (MOM) 2005 and runs analytics on data that the administrator can use to monitor and proactively remove network bottlenecks. Before the Monitoring Server can be installed, Microsoft Messaging Queue (MSMQ) must be installed.

To install MSMQ on Windows Server 2003, follow these steps:

1. In the Control Panel, double-click Add Or Remove Programs.
2. Click Add/Remove Windows Components in the left pane.
3. In the Windows Components Wizard, select Application Server, and then click Details.
4. Select Message Queuing, click OK, and then click Next to complete the installation.

Note For more information about Microsoft Message Queuing, see the following link: *http://www.microsoft.com/windowsserver2003/technologies/msmq/default.mspx#E3D*.

Configuring the Deployment Validation Tool Server

The Deployment Validation Tool (DVT) provides a very easy and convenient way for checking the quality of calls. This is a resource tool that can help monitor the voice quality of an Office Communications Server Enterprise Voice deployment. Installing DVT is completely optional. It can be used independently or to complement the Monitoring Server.

The Deployment Validation Tool consists of a server, called the Organizer, and multiple clients, called Agents. The Agents are configured similarly to how Office Communicator 2007 is configured. The Agents sign in to Office Communications Server, each with a distinct user account. The Organizer controls the Agents, and the administrator manages the Agents from the Administrative Console. The administrator adds the Agents to the Organizer's roster and can run or schedule recurring tests. The tests are performed between the Agents. The Agents initiate voice calls–both peer-to-peer and conference calls–and then send the results to the Organizer. This helps the administrator test out the voice quality of the Office Communications system without using real users. It helps troubleshoot networks with traffic congestion or poor bandwidth. It's important to properly place Agents in locations where voice quality is likely to degrade or locations that have been reported by users as having poor voice quality.

If setting up an Organizer seems like too much work, another option is to install only Answering Agents. This is a mode that an Agent can run in that does not require the use of an Organizer. An Answering Agent is similar to a bot. Users call the Answering Agent as they would any other contact. The Answering Agent prompts the user to record a message, which it then replays back to the user. This process allows the user to verify the audio quality of the network connection before placing a call to a contact. This is particularly beneficial for remote users who are not sure whether the connectivity at the hotel, customer site, home, café, or wherever they might be will offer sufficient bandwidth for quality audio. This feature requires installing only an Agent. Because the Organizer does not manage this type of Agent, it is not necessary to add it to the roster in the Administrative Console.

When setting up Agents, it's recommended to set up at least a couple of Agents inside the corporate network so that they can initiate calls between each other. Placing Agents in remote branch offices allows monitoring the audio quality across WAN links. If remote access is configured, it's recommended to set up at least one Agent outside the corporate network. Agents can be deployed behind each media gateway. The more Agents that are deployed, the more precisely the administrator can isolate a problem to a specific network segment. A maximum of 16 Agents can be deployed per Organizer.

The Organizer (server) and Agents (clients) must be configured with different SIP URIs that are not used by any existing users. Installing an Agent on the same computer as the Organizer is not recommended. Every time a configuration change is made to either an Agent or the Organizer, the corresponding service must be restarted. To restart the service, navigate to the Services MMC from the Administrative Tools folder. Locate the service, and click the restart button as shown in Figure 10-45.

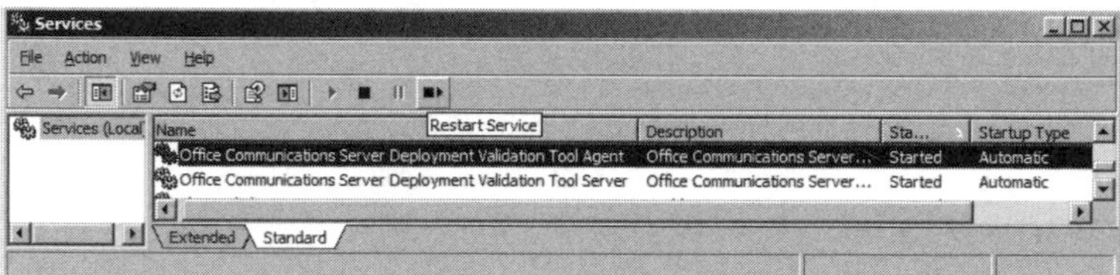

Figure 10-45 DVT services

Configuring the DVT Organizer

To install the Organizer, run the command script **setupserver.cmd**. Alternatively, the command **setup.exe /Server** can be used to install the Organizer. Setup will ask to install Microsoft Visual C++ 2005 SP1 development system Redistributable and .NET Framework 2.0 if they are not installed on the computer. During the installation of the Organizer, Setup will prompt for credentials to run the service under. It's recommended to use an account that is communications enabled. Specify these credentials as shown in Figure 10-46.

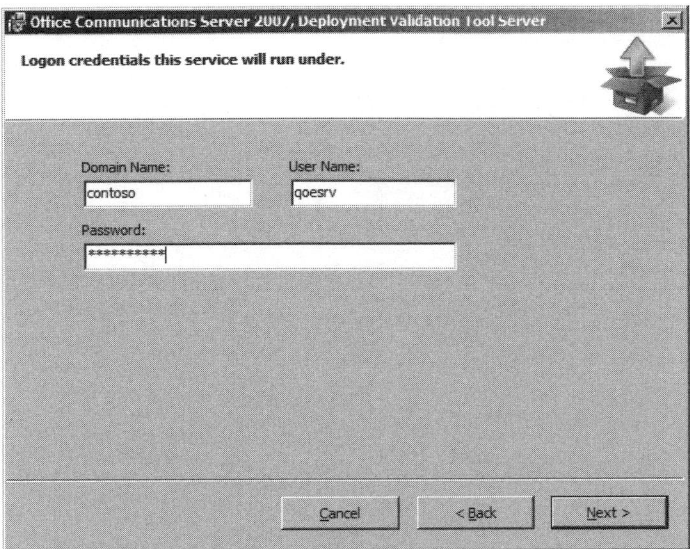

Figure 10-46 Organizer configuration

Note If the Windows Firewall Internet Connection Sharing service is not running during installation, a message indicates an unspecified error (error code 0x80004005) while running Netsh.exe. Click OK in the message box to continue.

Configure the Organizer (server) with a user's SIP URI and credentials. The credentials need to be entered only if you are using a different account than the one specified during the installation of the Organizer. Because the Deployment Validation Tool stores these credentials in plaintext if you are not using the default credentials, for security reasons it's best to use the credentials of the account specified during the Organizer Setup. The configuration (automatic or manual) and connection type (TCP or TLS) should be configured similar to how Office Communicator 2007 is configured. The agent parameters can be ignored, as these are configuration settings for the Agent. These settings are shown in Figure 10-47.

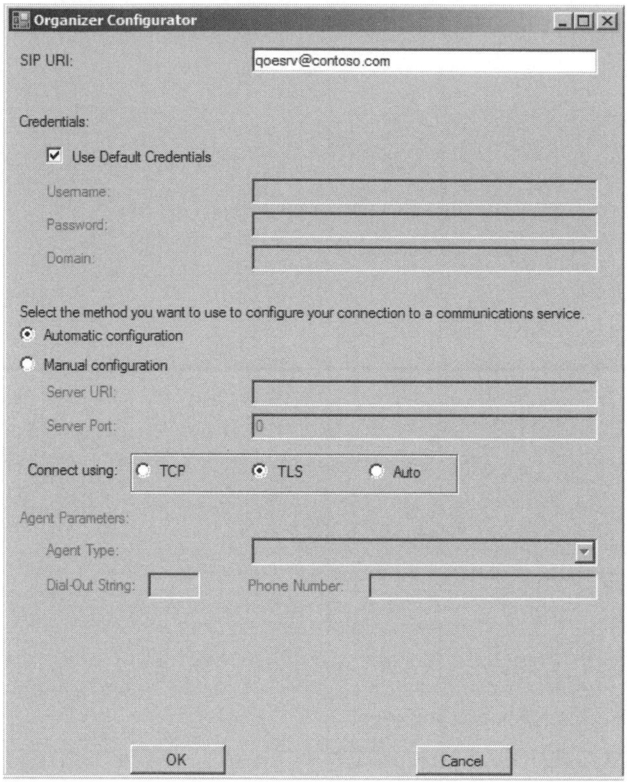

Figure 10-47 Organizer configuration

Setup also automatically installs the Administrative Console during installation of the Organizer. The DVT Administrative Console is where the administrator associates agents to the Organizer to control, and it specifies when to run a test suite and how to report the results.

Configuring the DVT Agent

To install the Agent, run the command script **setupagent.cmd**. Alternatively, the following setup.exe command can be run: **setup /Agent**. The Agent uses Microsoft SQL Server. If SQL Server 2005 Express is not available, Setup will fail to install. DVT comes packaged with SQL Server 2005 Express. To install SQL Server 2005 Express, run the executable **sqlexpr.exe** before continuing with the installation of the Agent. Setup will ask to install Microsoft Visual C++ 2005 SP1 development system Redistributable and .NET Framework 2.0 if they are not installed on the computer. Similar to the Server Setup, the Agent Setup Wizard prompts you for user credentials to run the service as. This user account must be enabled for communications. If the Windows Firewall Internet Connection Sharing service is not running during installation, a message indicates an unspecified error (error code 0x80004005) while running Netsh.exe. Click OK in the message box to continue. The message can be safely ignored.

In the Agent Configurator, Setup prompts you for the account's SIP URI and credentials if you are using a different account than the one used to run the agent. It's recommended not to use a different account because the password will be stored unencrypted. Specify the configuration type—either Automatic or Manual—to Office Communications Server, and specify the connection type—TCP, TLS, or Auto—in the Agent Configurator dialog box. These settings should be similar to the type of settings used by Office Communicator 2007. There are three modes the agent can be configured to behave as:

- **Unified Communication** This type specifies that the Agent should simulate an Office Communicator 2007 client when a user calls it.
- **PSTN** This type specifies that the Agent should simulate a PSTN phone when a user calls it.
- **Answering Agent** This type specifies that the Agent should simulate an answering system when a user calls it. The Agent prompts the user to record her voice and replays it back to the user so that she can evaluate the audio quality of the call.

The phone number of the account used by the Agent is optional except in the case of the Agent configured in the PSTN mode. The phone number should be specified in E.164 format in the Agent Configurator. This dialog box is shown in Figure 10-48.

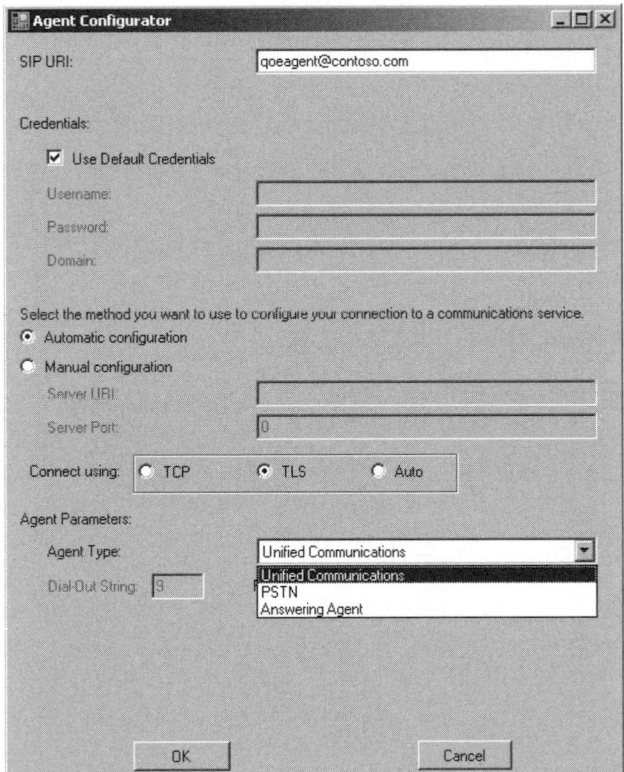

Figure 10-48 Agent configuration

The administrator has the option to return to this dialog box to modify the configuration of the Agent. To access these settings again, click Start, select All Programs, navigate to Deployment Navigation Tool, and click Agent Configurator. Configuration changes do not take effect until the next time the Agent service is restarted.

Managing DVT by Using the Administrative Console

The Administrative Console provides a simple interface to configure DVT. The primary activities an administrator must do are associate Agents to the Organizer, set up and run a test suite, specify how the Administrative Console should alert the administrator, and review results. The Administrative Console provides five tabs to perform these activities:

- **Main** This tab can be used to alert the administrator of any failures.
- **Roster** This tab shows all the Agents that are associated with the Organizer. The Roster shows the status of each Agent.
- **Test Suite** This tab shows all the test cases that the Organizer orchestrates between the registered Agents. It automatically generates a full mesh of test cases for both peer-to-peer and conference calls. The administrator can control each individual test case. The administrator can configure the Organizer to automatically run through the test suite every 60 minutes (the time delay is configurable) or run immediately by clicking the Run Suite button.
- **Reports** This tab reports on the results of the test suite.
- **Alerts** This tab alerts the administrator of all the connectivity results from test suites that have been run. It provides searching functions to query for specific results.

The type of metrics collected by the Agents can be viewed by right-clicking a result entry in the Reports tab and selecting View Details. A Reports Details shows the set of metrics collected and any failure information. The following graphics show an example of a test with no failures and another test with a failure.

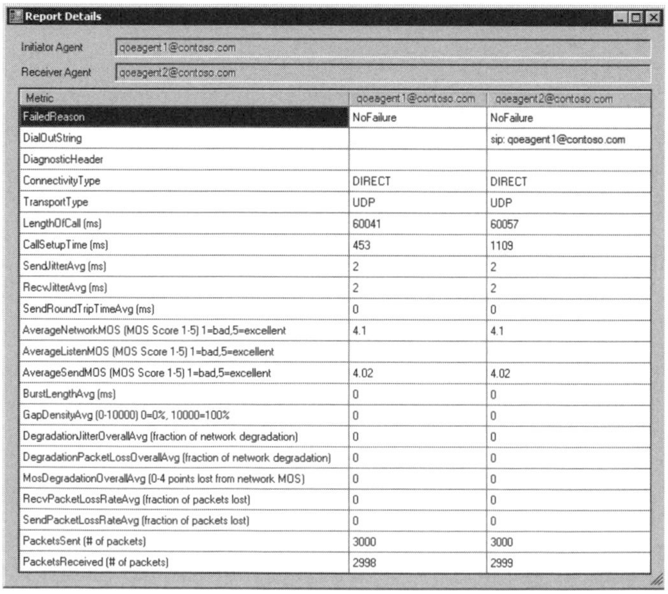

Report Details

Initiator Agent: qoeagent1@contoso.com

Receiver Agent: qoeagent2@contoso.com

Metric	qoeagent1@contoso.com	qoeagent2@contoso.com
FailedReason	NoFailure	NoFailure
DialOutString		sip: qoeagent1@contoso.com
DiagnosticHeader		
ConnectivityType	DIRECT	DIRECT
TransportType	UDP	UDP
LengthOfCall (ms)	60041	60057
CallSetupTime (ms)	453	1109
SendJitterAvg (ms)	2	2
RecvJitterAvg (ms)	2	2
SendRoundTripTimeAvg (ms)	0	0
AverageNetworkMOS (MOS Score 1-5) 1=bad,5=excellent	4.1	4.1
AverageListenMOS (MOS Score 1-5) 1=bad,5=excellent		
AverageSendMOS (MOS Score 1-5) 1=bad,5=excellent	4.02	4.02
BurstLengthAvg (ms)	0	0
GapDensityAvg (0-10000) 0=0%, 10000=100%	0	0
DegradationJitterOverallAvg (fraction of network degradation)	0	0
DegradationPacketLossOverallAvg (fraction of network degradation)	0	0
MosDegradationOverallAvg (0-4 points lost from network MOS)	0	0
RecvPacketLossRateAvg (fraction of packets lost)	0	0
SendPacketLossRateAvg (fraction of packets lost)	0	0
PacketsSent (# of packets)	3000	3000
PacketsReceived (# of packets)	2998	2999

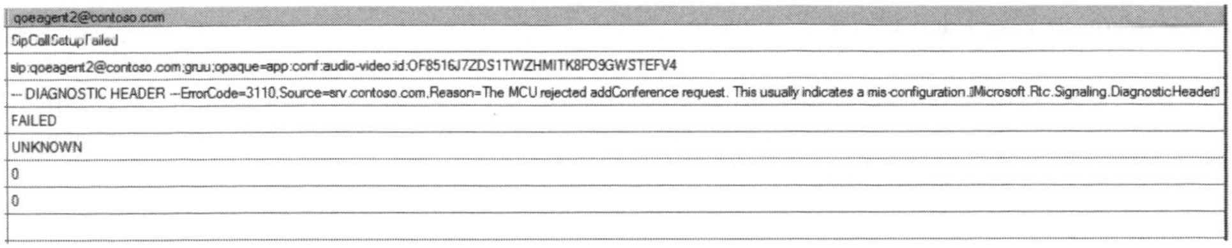

qoeagent2@contoso.com
SipCallSetupFailed
sip:qoeagent2@contoso.com;gruu;opaque=app:conf:audio-video:id:OF8516J7ZDS1TWZHMITK8FO9GWSTEFV4
--- DIAGNOSTIC HEADER ---ErrorCode=3110,Source=srv.contoso.com,Reason=The MCU rejected addConference request. This usually indicates a mis-configuration.Microsoft.Rtc.Signaling.DiagnosticHeader
FAILED
UNKNOWN
0
0

The Deployment Validation Tool is a convenient tool to verify an organization's Enterprise Voice deployment and perform regular check-ups in a dynamic network environment. It is a tool that is relatively easy to install and configure. Administrators should consider adding DVT to their toolsets for managing Office Communications Server Enterprise Voice deployment.

Summary

Office Communications Server 2007 introduces support for VoIP for the enterprise. Although its implementation does not match the rich feature set that IP PBXs offer, Microsoft changes the way users use telephony by conveniently integrating it into the information worker's computing environment for simpler and seamless communication from anywhere with a network connection. Office Communications Server 2007 offers a paradigm shift from how the application has traditionally been used. Now a call can be quickly placed within the context of a Microsoft Office application (Word, Outlook, and so on), Microsoft SharePoint, and third-party applications that integrate with Office Communicator 2007.

With visibility into colleagues' presence, users no longer need to play phone tag. Depending upon the contact's availability, users can choose the form of communication best suited for a particular situation, whether this is e-mail, IM, Web conferencing, or a phone call. Voice calls become an integrated form of communication that is no longer separate from the information worker's primary tool of trade: the computer. Users no longer have to manually bridge the gap between the telephone on their desk and their computer, such as looking up a phone number in their Outlook address book and dialing it from the phone, only to reach a voice mail system.

With Microsoft's Office Communicator 2007, a softphone can also provide a richer user experience than is possible with the 10-digit dial pad of most phones. Advanced features such as call transfer; placing a call on hold, and so on are more easily done by clicking a mouse than pressing * key sequences. Being able to take your office phone with you on the road is a very appealing feature as more and more members of today's workforce have the flexibility to decide where they work from—whether it be the office, a home office, a local restaurant, or wherever they need to be.

Office Communications Server 2007's Enterprise Voice provides a streamlined design so that it is simple to manage while remaining extensible to support future requirements.

Additional Resources

- Microsoft Office Communications Server 2007 Quality of Experience Monitoring Server at *http://www.microsoft.com/downloads/details.aspx?FamilyID=09115944-625f-460b-b09c-51e3c96e9f7e&displaylang=en*
- Office Communications Server 2007 Document: Enterprise Voice Planning and Deployment Guide, found at *http://www.microsoft.com/downloads/details.aspx?FamilyID=24e72dac-2b26-4f43-bba2-60488f2aca8d&displaylang=en*
- Office Communications Server 2007 Telephony Integration, found at *http://download.microsoft.com/download/f/8/8/f8827334-58c6-4cd3-8f68-f4254a7d568c/OCS%20Telephony%20Integration%20WP%20FINAL%20RELEASE.docx*
- Office Communications Server 2007 partners, found at *http://www.microsoft.com/uc/partners.mspx*
- Office Communications Server 2007 Enterprise Voice Route Helper documentation, found at *http://download.microsoft.com/download/d/d/1/dd111a0a-e4b8-41ca-9761-0ab6dec62f08/OCS_ResourceKit_RouteHelper_Guide.doc*
- Office Communications Server 2007 Resource Kit tools, found on the companion CD and also at *http://download.microsoft.com/download/8/9/5/89595bc1-14f6-4dc4-824e-3efcb67ff126/OCSResKit.msi*
- Route Target regular expressions, found at *http://office.microsoft.com/en-us/help/HP102218271033.aspx*
- TEL URI RFC 3966, found at *http://www.rfc-editor.org/rfc/rfc3966.txt*
- .NET Regular Expression Syntax, found at *http://regexlib.com/CheatSheet.aspx*
- Office Communications Server 2007 Document: Microsoft Quality of Experience, found at *http://www.microsoft.com/downloads/details.aspx?familyid=05625af1-3444-4e67-9557-3fd5af9ae8d1&displaylang=en*

On the Companion CD

- Office Communications Server 2007 Resource Kit tools, in the OCS 2007 Resource Kit Tools folder.

Part III
Planning and Deployment

In this part:

Every enterprise IT environment is different, every IP network is different, every enterprise telephone infrastructure is different, and therefore, functionality requirements for a product such as Office Communications Server 2007 vary from enterprise to enterprise as well. Office Communications Server 2007 offers a variety of deployment options and allows enabling of several different scenarios as seen in Part II, "Key Usage Scenarios." And it lets enterprises choose their enterprise-specific level of security, availability, and compliance to regulatory requirements.

All these different options and choices can become overwhelming for administrators who have to define their individual Office Communications Server 2007 deployment strategy based on the enterprise-specific IT environment and IP and telephone network and functionality requirements. It is particularly difficult for administrators who are working for the first time with Office Communications Server 2007. But even administrators who already have experience with Live Communications Server 2005 SP1 deployments and want to enable some new scenarios (such as Conferencing and Enterprise Voice) need to become familiar with the new aspects of the planning and deployment process that result from these new scenarios.

The goal of this part of the book is to walk through the Office Communications Server 2007 planning and deployment process for a fictitious company named Contoso by using the guidelines and structure provided in the "Microsoft Office Communications Server 2007 Planning Guide" and the "Microsoft Office Communications Server 2007 Enterprise Voice Planning and Deployment Guide." In Chapter 12, several deployment guides are used to implement an Office Communications Server 2007 deployment for Contoso. All documents mentioned herein can be found on the CD and are part of the official Office Communications Server 2007 documentation. Many notes, hints, best practices, and recommendations-as well as sample uses for some Office Communications Server 2007 Resource tools-have been added to provide additional value to the reader.

On the CD The Office Communications Server 2007 Resource tools, as well as the official Office Communications Server 2007 documentation, can be found on the CD that accompanies this book. At times throughout these chapters, this set of documents is referred to as the official Office Communications Server 2007 documentation.

Chapter 11

Office Communications Server 2007 Planning Example

In this chapter:

In this chapter, the "Office Communications Server 2007 Planning Guide" and "Office Communications Server 2007 Enterprise Voice Planning and Deployment Guide" will be used to prepare a sample deployment for a fictitious company named Contoso. This sample walk-through provides lots of background information to the user as to why certain deployment decisions have to be taken based on the requirements of the fictitious customer Contoso.

More Info The "Office Communications Server 2007 Planning Guide" and "Office Communications Server 2007 Enterprise Voice Planning and Deployment Guide" are available from this location at Microsoft TechNet Library: *http://technet.microsoft.com/en-us/library/bb676082.aspx*. Both documents are also available on the companion CD in the \Additional Reading folder.

The "Office Communications Server 2007 Planning Guide" is also available from this location at the Microsoft Download Center: *http://www.microsoft.com/downloads/details.aspx?familyid=723347c6-fa1f-44d8-a7fa-8974c3b596f4&displaylang=en*.

The "Office Communications Server 2007 Enterprise Voice Planning and Deployment Guide" is also available from this location at the Microsoft Download Center: *http://www.microsoft.com/downloads/details.aspx?familyid=24e72dac-2b26-4f43-bba2-60488f2aca8d&displaylang=en*.

Contoso is a pharmaceutical company with worldwide operations. Its corporate headquarters are in Chicago, USA; its EMEA (Europe Middle East Africa) headquarters are in Paris, France, with a smaller branch in Madrid, Spain; and its headquarters for the APAC (Asia PACific) region are in Singapore. It is necessary to assess the current existing infrastructure before the deployment strategy can be determined.

Understanding Contoso's Infrastructure

The following information must first be determined by Contoso for the company to properly plan its deployment of Office Communications Server 2007:

- User distribution
- Server infrastructure
- Active Directory infrastructure
- Network infrastructure
- Telephone infrastructure

The sections that follow summarize the pre-deployment environment of Contoso in each of these infrastructure areas.

Understanding Contoso's User Distribution

The number of Office Communications Server 2007 users is one of the key input values for the company's planning process. To be more precise, the value needed here is not the total number of employees in the enterprise and also not the number of potential users, but the number of concurrently connected users in a peak-hour situation. For this condition, the Office Communications Server 2007 infrastructure needs to be dimensioned in order to provide a performance level that is sufficient to deliver all enabled scenarios in a reliable fashion.

Note Office Communications Server 2007 is usually deployed in a data center model, in which users are most often connected to the system from multiple countries or even different time zones. The peak-hour situation (mostly between 10 AM and 12 PM and between 2 PM and 4 PM in standard office environments) can become stretched over longer time periods but lowered in terms of its peak workload in such deployment situations.

Contoso has the distribution of users shown in Figure 11-1 and Table 11-1.

Table 11-1 Contoso User Numbers

Scenario/sites	Employees	Potential Office Communications Server users	Concurrent Office Communications Server users in peak hour
Chicago	100,000	77,000	70,000
Paris	40,000	34,000	30,000
Madrid	550	520	500
Singapore	20,000	17,000	15,000

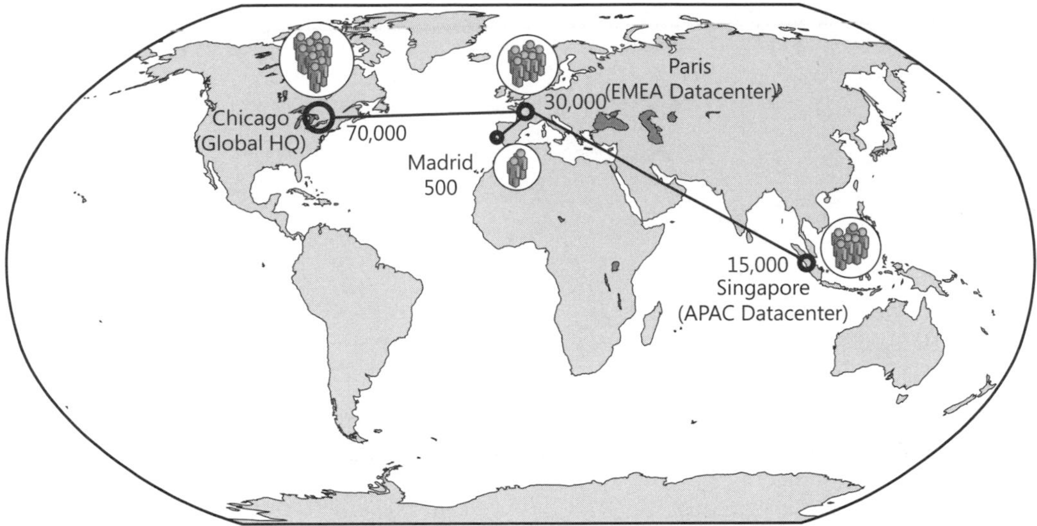

Figure 11-1 Contoso's distribution of users

Apart from the number of users, important parameters of the planning process include the level of reliability of the overall system, the locations for Session Initiation Protocol/Public Switched Telephone Network (SIP/PSTN) gateways, and the placement of Office Communications Server 2007 Mediation Servers. These factors will be covered later in this chapter.

Understanding Contoso's Server Infrastructure

The company already operates data centers for its IT environment in Chicago, Paris, and Singapore, all of which can be used as locations to deploy Office Communications Server roles. All servers operate on Microsoft Windows 2003 R2 with Service Pack 2 (SP2). Domain Name System (DNS) server and global catalog server are deployed for each domain on each site and are fully operational. New server hardware will be ordered as a result of the planning process that meets the requirements of the individual Office Communications Server 2007 deployment guides.

In the Chicago, Paris, and Singapore datacenters, a perimeter network is in place that provides a secure environment for all scenarios that need direct Internet access (Federation, Remote Access, and Public Internet Connectivity). These perimeter network environments are potential sites to place an Office Communications Server 2007 Edge Server.

Contoso has a Microsoft Exchange 2003 Service Pack 2 (SP2) deployment and a pilot installation for Microsoft Exchange 2007 at the Madrid site.

Understanding Contoso's Active Directory Infrastructure

Contoso has a single forest architecture with multiple domains as shown in Figure 11-2.

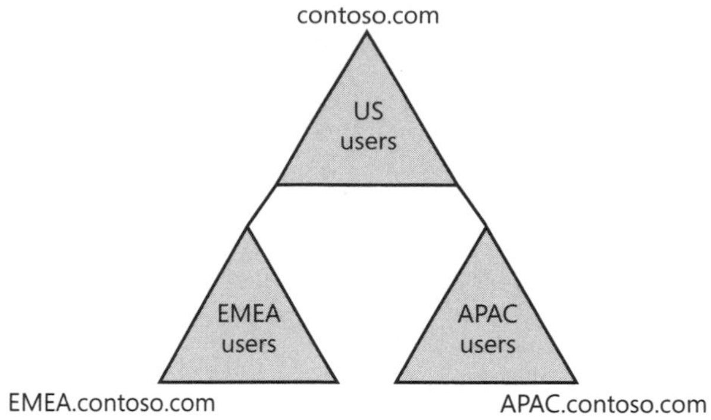

Figure 11-2 Contoso Active Directory infrastructure

Understanding Contoso's Network Infrastructure

Contoso has a switched 100/1000 Mbit/s Ethernet environment in all local area network (LAN) segments in Chicago, Paris, Madrid, and Singapore. The sites are connected with sufficient and redundant wide area network (WAN) links. This topology is shown in Figure 11-3.

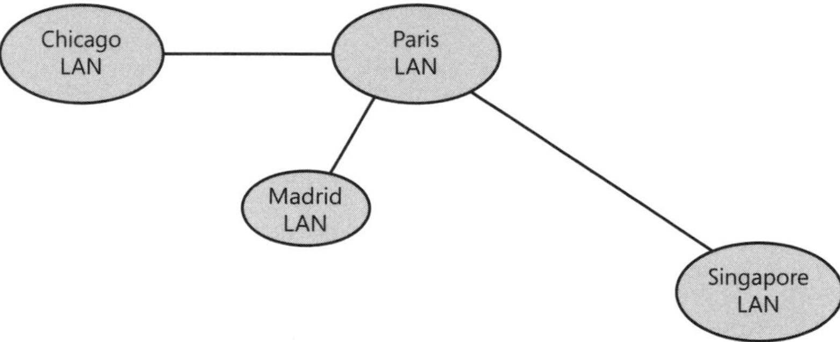

Figure 11-3 Contoso network infrastructure

Understanding Contoso's Telephone Infrastructure

Contoso has on every site a Private Branch eXchange (PBX) network infrastructure based on Time Division Multiplexing (TDM) PBX systems. On each site even multiple PBX nodes are connected with one another and act as one, whereas between sites there are no direct cross-site links in place for telephone calls between the PBX nodes. For voice communication between different sites, the PSTN is used. The architecture is shown in Figure 11-4.

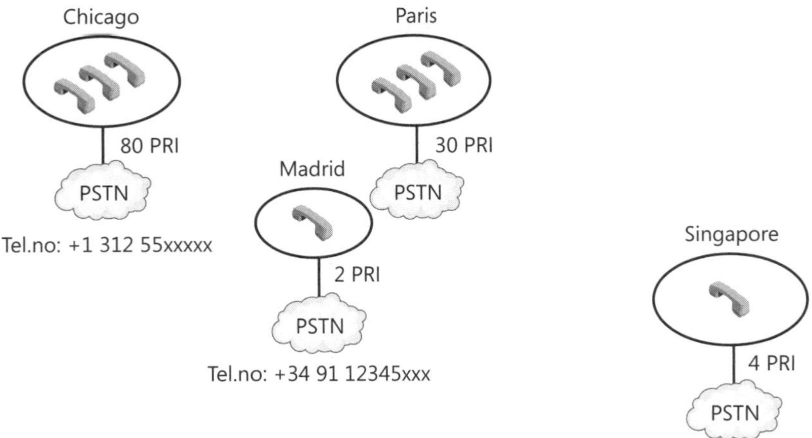

Figure 11-4 Contoso telephone network infrastructure

On each site, there are direct connections with the PSTN and Direct-Inward-Dialing is supported. The PBX systems are connected with multiple Primary Rate Interface (PRI) connections with the PSTN.

Note In general, in the United States a single PRI connection allows 23 concurrent audio connections per PRI (T1 interface), and in Europe and Singapore a single PRI connection allows 30 concurrent audio connections (E1 interface).

The Madrid PBX is already nine years old, and the other PBX systems are between two and five years old.

Defining the Deployment Goals

Before you can plan for an Office Communications Server 2007 deployment, you have to be clear about the deployment goals. Deployment goals are not just the selection of scenarios that will become enabled; you must also be sure that the Office Communications Server 2007 infrastructure complies with the reliability and regulatory requirements of the enterprise.

Defining the Scenario Selection

The available scenarios with Office Communications Server 2007 can be found in Part III, "Planning and Deployment." It is neither necessary to always enable all scenarios, nor is it technically required to always enable selected scenarios for the entire user population. Furthermore, it is possible to enable additional scenarios even after the initial deployment. Office Communications Server 2007 allows you to enable scenarios on a per-user basis.

Contoso wants to enable the scenarios shown in Table 11-2 for its users on the various sites.

Table 11-2 Contoso Selected Scenarios per Site

Scenario/sites	Chicago	Paris	Madrid	Singapore
Instant Messaging (IM) and Presence	✓	✓	✓	✓
Conferencing with Audio/Video	✓	✓	✓	✓
Remote Access Scenario for IM and Presence	✓	✓	✓	✓
Remote Access Scenario for A/V and Conferencing	✓	✓	✓	✓
Federation Scenario	✓	✓	✓	✓
PIC Scenario	—	—	—	—
Phone Control Scenario	—	—	—	—
Enterprise Voice Scenario	✓ (only for 100 users)	-	✓	—

Note Because the PBX in Madrid is already nine years old, it makes sense to investigate whether all PBX users or just a subset of those users can be migrated to Voice over IP (VoIP) by enabling the Enterprise Voice Scenario as part of the Office Communications Server 2007 deployment. The integration of one of the telephone scenarios as presented in Chapter 9, "Understanding the Remote Call Control Scenario," or Chapter 10, "VoIP Scenario," adds another dimension to the planning process, as the existing telephone environment has to be included.

Contoso wants to get experience with the VoIP Scenarios (also known as Enterprise Voice) offered by Office Communications Server 2007. Therefore Contoso management decides that all users in the Madrid office will use the Enterprise Voice Scenario of Office Communications Server 2007 as their primary enterprise telephone solution. Management makes this decision because Madrid has only standard office information worker users, who are able to accomplish their daily work with the feature set that the current 2007 version of Office Communicator and Office Communicator Phone Edition provide.

Important Voicemail functionality is another key functionality for information workers. In Office Communications Server 2007 environments, this functionality is provided by Microsoft Exchange 2007 Unified Messaging (UM) SP1. Exchange UM will be covered in this and the following chapter only from the Office Communications Server perspective. If Microsoft Exchange 2007 is not implemented in your infrastructure, you need to start planning for this by using the planning guidance available with Microsoft Exchange 2007.

Contoso management realizes that by enabling Enterprise Voice for a subset of users those users have to get used to it by exploring its features and discovering the benefits of Unified Communications, such as secure, seamless, multimodal communications. These benefits will outweigh, for Contoso, the potential regression experienced because some previously used telephone feature is no longer available. In addition, Contoso wants to equip about 100 users in the Chicago headquarters with the Enterprise Voice Scenario as a pilot project used in conjunction with the existing PBX system.

Defining the Reliability Requirements

IM, Presence, Conferencing, and VoIP Scenarios have been identified by Contoso as business-critical applications. The importance of these features needs to be factored into the planning process for the Office Communications Server 2007 deployment. Whenever possible, single-point-of-failure situations should be eliminated to achieve high availability of the system and fault tolerance for the most common failure situations.

Remote access scenarios are seen as business critical only for the Chicago and Paris sites, because a larger number of users are frequently working from home and therefore need to have reliable access from remote sites to the Office Communications Server 2007 infrastructure. For the Madrid and Singapore offices, the Remote Access Scenario is not seen as business critical.

Defining the Compliance Requirements

The only requirement in the Contoso enterprise for compliance is that Call Detail Records need to be captured for the Enterprise Voice Scenario in Madrid, Spain. But this is not seen as business critical.

Understanding Contoso's Office Communications Server 2007 Planning Process

The "Microsoft Office Communications Server 2007 Planning Guide" splits the planning process into 12 steps. Some steps might be optional, depending on the selected scenario.

Step 1: Determining Key Planning Decisions

Contoso wants to enable IM, Presence, and On-Premise Conferencing Scenarios for all Office Communications Server 2007 users in the organization. Also all users should be given the capability to remotely log in from the Internet to the internal Office Communications Server 2007 infrastructure by using Office Communicator 2007, Office Communicator Phone Edition, or Live Meeting 2007 even without setting up a virtual private network (VPN) to the enterprise. In Chicago and Madrid, the Enterprise Voice Scenario will be enabled as well, but only for a subset of users (100) in Chicago. Communicator Web Access will not be deployed for now, but Archiving will be deployed in Madrid to capture Call Detail Records.

If you compare now the selection of scenarios by Contoso with the server role requirements presented in "Step 1: Determining Key Planning Decisions" in the "Office Communications Server 2007 Planning Guide," the server roles shown in Table 11-3 need to be deployed.

Note In this stage of the planning process, the following considerations have not been decided yet:

- How often these server roles are required on each site or whether they are required at all
- How many physical machines these roles have to be installed on or whether they need to be installed at all
- Whether multiple server roles can be combined on a single physical machine
- Whether server roles from several sites can be co-located

Most important is that users on the different sites need to have access to these server roles in order to use the selected scenario. For example, there can be only one Access Edge Server role deployed in an entire enterprise but the Access Edge Server role is needed for several scenarios.

Table 11-3 Contoso Server Roles Needed for Scenarios

Scenario/sites	Chicago	Paris	Madrid	Singapore
IM and Presence	Office Communications Server Standard or Enterprise Edition	Office Communications Server Standard or Enterprise Edition	Office Communications Server Standard or Enterprise Edition	Office Communications Server Standard or Enterprise Edition
Conferencing with Audio/Video	A/V Server and Web Conferencing Server	A/V Server and Web Conferencing Server	A/V Server and Web Conferencing Server	A/V Server and Web Conferencing Server
Remote Access Scenario for IM and Presence	Access Edge Server	Access Edge Server	Access Edge Server	Access Edge Server
Remote Access Scenario for A/V and Conferencing	Access Edge Server, Web Conferencing Edge Server, and A/V Conferencing Edge Server	Access Edge Server, Web Conferencing Edge Server, and A/V Conferencing Edge Server	Access Edge Server, Web Conferencing Edge Server, and A/V Conferencing Edge Server	Access Edge Server, Web Conferencing Edge Server, and A/V Conferencing Edge Server
Federation Scenario	Access Edge Server, Web Conferencing Edge Server, and A/V Conferencing Edge Server	Access Edge Server, Web Conferencing Edge Server, and A/V Conferencing Edge Server	Access Edge Server, Web Conferencing Edge Server, and A/V Conferencing Edge Server	Access Edge Server, Web Conferencing Edge Server, and A/V Conferencing Edge Server

Table 11-3 Contoso Server Roles Needed for Scenarios

Scenario/sites	Chicago	Paris	Madrid	Singapore
PIC Scenario	—	—	—	—
Phone Control Scenario	—	—	—	—
Enterprise Voice Scenario	Mediation Server	—	Mediation Server	—

Note If you want to implement Enterprise Voice (as shown in "Step 8: Plan for VoIP" later in this chapter), you also need to have Microsoft Exchange 2007 Unified Messaging SP1 for the Voicemail functionality and the Office Communications Server 2007 Archiving Server role for collecting Call Detail Records. (See "Step 12: Plan for Compliance and Usage Analysis" later in this chapter.)

In "Step 1: Determining Key Planning Decisions" in the "Office Communications Server 2007 Planning Guide," some preliminary decisions on the core architecture (Standard Edition versus Enterprise Edition) are discussed. Because Contoso sees the need for IM, Presence, and Conferencing for all sites, Office Communications Server 2007 Standard Edition is not the right choice for any of the sites. A single server deployment always contains the risk of having a single point of failure. Because Contoso is geographically distributed–with users in Chicago, Paris, Madrid, and Singapore–it is necessary to deploy an Office Communications Server 2007 Enterprise Edition architecture on every site to provide reliable scenario availability on each site. This topology is referred to as *Global Conferencing Deployment with Multisite External Access and Voice.*

Step 2: Select Your Topology

What you've learned from the previous planning step is that on every site an Office Communications Server 2007 Enterprise Edition deployment is necessary according to the deployment goals. However, it is not decided yet which Enterprise Edition deployment option is the appropriate one given the user numbers on each individual site.

Important Enterprise Edition can be deployed as consolidated Enterprise Edition with all Conferencing Server roles installed on the same physical machine as the Front End Server (which is another name for the Office Communications Server 2007 core server role for IM and Presence), or it can be deployed as expanded Enterprise Edition with Conferencing Server roles on dedicated physical machines. This is an important decision because separating the Conferencing Server roles (for example, when conferencing usage exceeds expectations) from a consolidated Enterprise Edition Front End Server requires a new installation of the Front End Server. All Enterprise Edition deployments require a separate Back End Database Server.

Given the number of users on each site and the topology examples in "Step 2: Select Your Topology" in the "Office Communications Server Planning Guide," Contoso's global deployment needs to have the core architecture for each site as shown in Table 11-4.

Table 11-4 Contoso Core Architecture

Scenario/sites	Chicago	Paris	Madrid	Singapore
Number of concurrent users in peak hour	70,000	30,000	500	15,000
Core architecture	Enterprise Edition Expanded Configuration with Clustered Back-End Database	Enterprise Edition Expanded Configuration with Clustered Back-End Database	Enterprise Edition Consolidated Configuration	Enterprise Edition Consolidated Configuration

Note For the core Office Communications Server infrastructure in Madrid, a Standard Edition Server could be deployed instead of an Enterprise Edition Office Communications Server in consolidated configuration. But this would become a potential single point of failure, as the Standard Edition Office Communications Server cannot be deployed in a redundant fashion. Therefore, the Enterprise Edition Server has to be used.

At this point, the number of individual server roles needed to support the designated scenarios is not defined. This will be part of "Step 5: Review System and Network Requirements." When based on the capacity numbers, the number of server roles for consolidated Enterprise Edition Server, Front End Server for expanded Enterprise Edition, as well as Web Conferencing and A/V Conferencing Server will be determined. The Edge Server roles for the Remote Access Scenario and Federation Scenario will be covered in "Step 6: Plan for External User Access." The number and location of Mediation Server roles for the Enterprise Voice Scenario will be handled in "Step 8: Plan for VoIP."

Step 3: Plan Your Deployment Path

"Step 3: Plan Your Deployment Path" in the "Office Communications Server 2007 Planning Guide" covers planning considerations as well as additional information that is relevant when you start the deployment. From a planning perspective, it is necessary to concentrate on aspects of the later deployment, which cannot be changed quickly or might have a significant impact on the enterprise IT environment, delay the deployment, or even make the whole deployment impossible.

For an Office Communications Server 2007 deployment, either a Public Key Infrastructure (PKI) has to be in place or certificates issued by an external Public Certificate Agency can be used. This is necessary because Office Communications Server 2007 authenticates and authorizes any communication between clients. Furthermore, all communication is encrypted.

Therefore, certificates that can be verified against a PKI or an external Public Certificate Agency and contain the correct enterprise-specific validation information have to be issued and installed. If–as in the Contoso case–the Remote Access and Federation Scenarios will be deployed, the certificates for the Edge Server have to be issued by a Public Certificate Agency. This is necessary because it is not possible for external users or federated companies to verify certificates against an enterprise-internal PKI. Any third-party Certificate Agency can be used to issue all certificates–although a Windows 2003 Certificate Agency with auto-enrollment support simplifies Office Communicator Phone Edition deployments.

> **Note** It is recommended that you use the Certificate Wizard, accessible in the Office Communications Server deployment tool or available as an Admin Tool task, to generate and assign the certificates to the server roles you deploy. The Certificate Wizard has logic to generate certificate requests that match the requirements Office Communications Server has for the certificate parameters.

Active Directory is another prerequisite for an Office Communications Server 2007 deployment, as it is the store for user objects and user management information. For an Office Communications Server 2007 deployment, the Active Directory schema has to be extended, which usually requires following a certain enterprise-specific process and varies in preparation time from enterprise to enterprise. In the planning phase, the required administrators for Active Directory in the enterprise should be informed about the additions that need to be applied on the existing schema so that they can approve and prepare the schema expansion well enough ahead of time to avoid delay in the actual deployment. Later in this procedure, the Contoso Active Directory architecture is checked to see whether it complies with one of the supported Active Directory topologies of Office Communications Server 2007.

> **Important** One important planning aspect for Active Directory is the location for the global settings. For Greenfield environments (no previous Live Communications Server deployed), the product provides two options: to use the root domain to store the global settings, or to use the Configuration Naming Context. For deployments that are highly distributed and without reliable connectivity to the root domain, it is recommended that you select the Configuration Naming Context for the location of the global settings. This ensures that any changes affecting the global settings will be available in any remote location through the Active Directory replication mechanisms.

DNS is another key prerequisite for an Office Communications Server 2007 deployment. Throughout the Office Communications Server 2007 deployment, several DNS SRV (DNS Service) records have to be configured. If this process results in significant preparation time in your enterprise, you should read the official deployment documentation for the scenarios you want to deploy and note all required DNS SRV records. This way, you can inform the DNS administrators in your enterprise who are already in the planning phase or–if you have access to the DNS configuration–you can configure the DNS SRV records ahead of time to ensure a quick Office Communications Server 2007 deployment. Details about DNS preparation can be found in "Step 4: Prepare Your Infrastructure" in the "Office Communications Server 2007 Planning Guide" as well as in the individual deployment guides of the official Office Communications Server 2007 documentation.

Office Communications Server 2007 must be deployed on servers that comply with at least the minimum hardware and software requirements for an Office Communications Server 2007 deployment. We will discuss the server hardware requirements in "Step 5: Review System and Network Requirements," but do note now that the servers need to be prepared with Microsoft Windows Server 2003 SP1 (Service Pack 1) or R2 as the operating system. For the Enterprise Edition Back-End Database, we recommend Microsoft SQL Server 2005 SP2 or Microsoft SQL Server 2000 with SP4.

Another potential blocking point for an Office Communications Server 2007 deployment or a potential cause for a delay in the deployment is missing permissions. If you don't have sufficient permissions for all the required configuration steps, you need to get these rights or inform the responsible administrators what they need to configure on your behalf. A table can be found in "Step 4: Prepare Your Infrastructure" of the "Office Communications Server 2007 Planning Guide" that summarizes all required user accounts and access rights you need to have for an Office Communications Server 2007 deployment.

Step 4: Prepare Your Infrastructure

Now that we have checked the general availability and compatibility of Active Directory, DNS, and Certificates for an Office Communications Server 2007 deployment in the previous chapter, you can start with the preparation of these entities to support a smooth Office Communications Server 2007 deployment.

"Step 4: Prepare Your Infrastructure" in the "Office Communications Server 2007 Planning Guide" contains the prerequisites for Active Directory, as well as topologies supported by Office Communications Server 2007. You have to make sure that your designated Office Communications Server 2007 deployment follows one of the recommended topologies.

As shown previously in Figure 11-2, Contoso has a single forest architecture with multiple domains and therefore has a supported Active Directory topology. The domains in which the Office Communications Server 2007 pools will be deployed are mostly dependent on the following:

- **The organization of administrative rights in the company** If multiple domains are administered by different people, the communication effort needed to synchronize between administrators has increased and chances are high that the system will be misconfigured.

- **The availability of Domain Controllers on multiple sites** It is necessary to have on each site Domain Controllers of domains in which Office Communications Server is deployed.

Contoso has Domain Controllers for the contoso.com domain in each of the sites. Therefore, all Office Communications Server 2007 pools will be deployed in the contoso.com domain, and no problems with the delegation of rights/tasks will be encountered. The entire enterprise-wide Office Communications Server deployment will be administered by the administrators in the United States.

The availability of certificates for all server roles is another important prerequisite for an Office Communications Server 2007 deployment. "Step 4: Prepare Your Infrastructure " in the "Office Communications Server 2007 Planning Guide" contains a table with information about where you need to have certificates installed and which information these certificates need to contain in order to allow verification by other server roles against the PKI infrastructure.

As mentioned in the previous chapter, several DNS records have to be configured for the pools as well as for the Edge Server to allow Remote Access, Federation, and PIC Scenarios. You can find in "Step 4: Prepare Your Infrastructure," of the "Office Communications Server 2007 Planning Guide" which DNS records have to be configured. The configuration of DNS records depends on whether the Office Communications Server 2007 topology requires Load Balancer to distribute traffic equally among a number of server roles, because these DNS records have to point to the Load Balancer instead of to the individual server roles fronted by the Load Balancer. The necessity for Contoso to deploy Load Balancer fronting Enterprise Edition Server and Edge Server will be discussed in "Step 7: Plan for Deploying Load Balancers."

The following deployment decisions have an impact on the DNS requirements:

- The list of SIP domains you will manage in that environment.
- Whether you want to enable automatic discovery for clients. With automatic discovery, clients use DNS to resolve the name of the server they have to contact for logon. It is recommended to enable automatic discovery, as it is eliminates the need for manual configuration on the client.

Step 5: Review System and Network Requirements

So far, the planning process for Contoso's Office Communications Server 2007 deployment was based on actual user numbers. It's not just the number of actual users that has an impact on the performance of the system; it is also the scenario usage patterns of the users. All scenarios have to be provided by the same physical servers; therefore, it is necessary to estimate the peak-hour usage of the individual scenarios as part of the planning process. This estimation might be feasible for mature forms of communication such as IM, but it can become challenging in the Conferencing Scenario to estimate the average participant structure of conferences. For instance, it's hard to estimate for Live Meeting 2007 sessions the number of internal participants from the same site, internal participants from another site, remote authenticated participants, or anonymous participants. You would also need to know how many participants joining the conference remotely are doing so over the Internet vs. across federated links. Furthermore, you would need to know the distribution between data-only conferences sharing Microsoft PowerPoint slide decks, data conferences with audio only, or data conferences with both audio and video, for instance when using Microsoft Office Round-Table.

Another dimension of complexity is that even if you would have all the above information concerning conferencing usage patterns, such usage behavior might change because of technology improvements. For example, more people might add video to a Live Meeting as the tool became easier for them to use. The same considerations apply to Enterprise Voice scenarios. For example, although it is possible to estimate the call volume based on usage data reports of the existing telephone system, it is fairly hard to estimate the number of conversations that will contain not only audio, but IM and video as well. So once users become familiar with the usage of all the different modalities to improve their workflow, the scenario usage will shift.

Based on all these considerations, the Unified Communications Product Group decided to define a usage model based on performance-testing experiences in the MSIT (Microsoft IT) environment. This usage model is presented in "Step 5: Review System and Network Requirements" in the "Office Communications Server 2007 Planning Guide."

Important If you have to plan for an Office Communications Server 2007 deployment, take a close look at the numbers in the presented user model. The scenario usage in each enterprise is dependent on its business. Let's assume you need to deploy Office Communications Server 2007 in a consultant agency. Many consultants (more than 50 percent of the user population) are constantly working on projects outside the enterprise and connect remotely from the Internet to the Office Communications Server 2007 deployment. Because the user model assumes that 10 percent of all users will connect remotely, the Edge Server topology has to be adjusted (for example, one additional Web Conferencing Edge Server and one additional A/V Edge Server) as the scenario usage exceeds the tested user model significantly.

Important In general, when usage increases, all server roles that handle media (Web and A/V Edge Server, Web and A/V Conferencing Server, and Mediation Server) should first be offloaded with an additional server role on a separate physical machine to scale out server roles that handle just signaling information. Media requires more server resources than SIP signaling information.

In the case of Contoso, the presented usage model complies with the expected scenario usage that the Office Communications Server 2007 deployment has to support after the installation. The line of business of the enterprise, which is a pharmaceutical company, does not lead to expectations of unusually high numbers of remote users or extensive A/V conferencing usage. Based on the table presented in "Step 5: Review System and Network Requirements," the number of physical servers that have to be deployed for Contoso's Office Communications Server 2007 deployment is shown in Table 11-5. (The Internet Information Service,or IIS, role discussion is beyond the scope of this chapter because it is not an Office Communications Server 2007 server role.)

Table 11-5 Contoso Architecture with Conferencing Server

Scenario/sites	Chicago	Paris	Madrid	Singapore
Number of concurrent users in peak hour	70,000	30,000	500	15,000
Core architecture	Enterprise Edition Expanded Configuration with Clustered Back-End Database	Enterprise Edition Expanded Configuration with Clustered Back-End Database	Enterprise Edition Consolidated Configuration	Enterprise Edition Consolidated Configuration
Number of core servers	6 Front End 2 IIS Servers 1 Back End with SQL cluster	4 Front End 2 IIS Servers 1 Back End with SQL cluster	2 Front End (running all Conferencing Server roles) 1 Back End	4 Front End (running all Conferencing Server roles) 1 Back End
Number of Conferencing Servers	4 Web Conferencing Servers 4 A/V Conferencing Servers	2 Web Conferencing Servers 2 A/V Conferencing Servers	-	-

> **Note** Compare the number of Enterprise Edition Front End Servers in the consolidated configuration as presented in "Step 5: Review System and Network Requirements," in the "Office Communications Server 2007 Planning Guide" (four servers) with the number in Table 11-4 for Madrid (two servers). The reason only two servers are needed for Madrid is that the number of users is pretty low. One single Standard Edition Server is already sufficient for the site in Madrid. However, because in Madrid business critical scenarios such as Conferencing and Enterprise Voice will be enabled, Office Communications Server 2007 in Enterprise Edition in consolidated configuration with two redundant load-balanced Front End Servers has to be deployed.

Now that the number of server roles has been determined, the required server hardware has to be assessed. "Step 5: Review System and Network Requirements," in the "Office Communications Server 2007 Planning Guide" provides the minimum requirements for server hardware for the individual server roles. Contoso orders server hardware that exceeds the minimum requirements in the "Office Communications Server 2007 Planning Guide."

As part of this planning step, the network impact of the different scenarios and their associated usage has to be estimated and, as a result of that, the network has to be prepared. With Live Communications Server 2005 SP1, it was fairly easy to estimate the network impact because mostly IM messages and Presence information had to be transmitted between clients or between clients and a server. Now with the additional scenarios–on-premises Conferencing and Enterprise Voice– IP network administrators will become more challenged to provide a compliant network infrastructure that can handle the following in a reliable and dynamic fashion:

- Audio and Video in peer-to-peer conversations between two Office Communicator 2007 clients
- Audio conferencing conversations using Office Communicator 2007 (intra-enterprise same site, intra-enterprise cross-site, with Remote or Federated users)
- Office Communicator Phone Edition and A/V and data conferences using Live Meeting 2007 in conjunction with Microsoft Office RoundTable

One thing that makes the IP network administration even more difficult is that the bandwidth requirement might shift within the same conversation as media is added and retracted as the conversation flow requires. To prepare the IP network for an Office Communications Server 2007 deployment, you have to estimate the bandwidth requirements based on the scenario usage and you have to make sure that the VoIP-specific requirements–for example, low packet loss, low jitter, and low delay (that is, a delay of less than 150 milliseconds per roundtrip)–will be provided.

Important The "Office Communications Server Planning Guide" contains a table in "Step 5: Review System and Network Requirements" that shows minimum and maximum bandwidth requirements for audio and video as the codec automatically adapts to the performance capacity of the attached devices and network conditions. In general, 45 kilobits per second (kbits/sec) for an audio connection using Wideband RTAudio, 300 kbits/sec for a video connection, and 112 kbits/sec for an application-sharing connection should be calculated for each direction.

Media connections have the biggest impact on the IP network. Media streams flow in an Office Communications Server 2007 deployment between the components as illustrated in Figure 11-5. (Endpoints are Office Communicator 2007, Office Communicator Phone Edition–except for video–and Live Meeting 2007.)

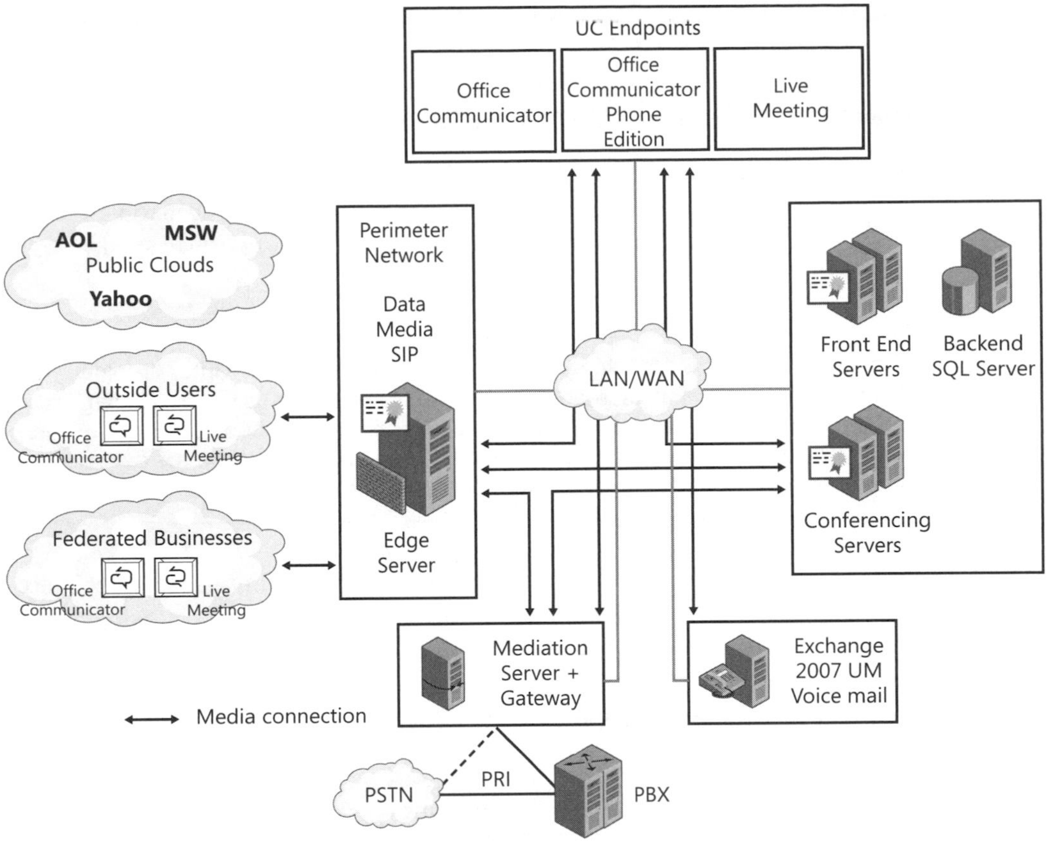

Figure 11-5 Media flows in an Office Communications Server 2007 deployment

To calculate the bandwidth requirements, the number of concurrent connections in a peak-hour situation has to be multiplied with the bandwidth needed, which depends on the codec that is used, as presented in "Step 5: Review System and Network Requirements" in the "Office Communications Server 2007 Planning Guide."

Important Office Communications Server 2007 comes with a media stack that adjusts automatically to the network conditions as soon as the user experience would be affected by negative network effects (loss, jitter, delay, and so on). These effects are compensated for as well as possible by the algorithms in the media stack sitting in each of the applications (Office Communicator 2007, Office Communicator Phone Edition, Live Meeting 2007, A/V Conferencing Server, A/V Edge Server, and Mediation Server). More information about the codecs, as well as information about the algorithms to adapt dynamically to changing network conditions, can be found in the document "Microsoft Quality of Experience" found at *http://www.microsoft.com/downloads/details.aspx?FamilyID=05625AF1-3444-4E67-9557-3FD5AF9AE8D1&displaylang=en*. Additional information is also available from this location on Microsoft TechNet Library in the document "Designing for Adoption: Real-time Audio in the Real World" found at *http://technet.microsoft.com/en-us/bb629431.aspx*.

A sample calculation for the bandwidth requirements on the Edge Server is described in "Step 6: Plan for External User Access."

Step 6: Plan for External User Access

Office Communications Server 2007 provides four different Edge Server topologies for Remote Access Scenarios, the Federation Scenarios, and the PIC Scenarios. You can choose the right topology based on the number of outside connections that the infrastructure has to provide.

On the CD On the CD in the \Appendixes,Scripts,Resources\Chapter 11 folder, you can find Microsoft Office Excel spreadsheet calculations containing the usage model that has been used for performance testing. Based on this usage model, the impact on the Edge Servers on each site is calculated to determine the designated Edge Server topology, the correct number of Edge Server roles, and an example of the bandwidth requirements for the A/V Edge Server.

Because Contoso's site in Madrid has no perimeter network infrastructure to place Edge Server roles in a secure way, Madrid users will use the Edge Server roles deployed in Paris for any Remote Access Scenario. For the Edge Server calculations, the Madrid user numbers have been added to the Paris user numbers. Table 11-6 shows the results (including the number of concurrent participants in Audio, A/V and PowerPoint, and Application Sharing meetings) of the spreadsheet calculations for each of Contoso's sites.

Table 11-6 Contoso Edge Server Calculations

Scenario/sites	Chicago	Paris	Madrid	Singapore
Number of Participants of Meetings through A/V Edge Server (Bandwidth for Conferencing)	528 (184 Mbit/s)	231 (80.3 Mbit/s)	—	114 (39.4 Mbit/s)
Number of Participants of Meetings through Web Conferencing Edge Server	1314	576	—	282
Number of Participants of Meetings through Access Edge Server	1752	765	—	375

Table 11-6 Contoso Edge Server Calculations

Scenario/sites	Chicago	Paris	Madrid	Singapore
Concurrent remote voice access connections for Enterprise Voice user (Bandwidth used)	8 (360 kbit/s)	40 (1.8 Mbit/s)	—	—

On the CD The Excel spreadsheet calculations have also been used to estimate the impact of Remote Office Communicator 2007 or Office Communicator Phone Edition users connected through the A/V Edge Server for Audio and A/V conversations. Table 11-6 shows the results of these calculations in the last row. Because only a few users will be enabled for Enterprise Voice, the impact on the Edge Servers of these users is minor compared to the impact caused by meeting participants using LiveMeeting 2007. The impact of these remote users will be ignored, as they have no significant impact on the design decision for the Edge Server deployment.

By comparing the Contoso global infrastructure to the three datacenters with the supported Edge Server topologies presented in "Step 6: Plan for External User Access," in the "Office Communications Server 2007 Planning Guide," the appropriate topology for Contoso is a *Multisite Edge topology*.

A Multisite Edge topology suggests having at least two load-balanced colocated Access Edge and Web Conferencing Servers with at least two separate load-balanced A/V Edge Servers in the main datacenter and single or multiple load-balanced Web Conferencing and A/V Edge Server roles on dedicated physical machines in each of the remote locations where users require remote access. The Edge Server capacity table in "Step 5: Review System and Network Requirements," in the "Office Communications Server 2007 Planning Guide" shows the capacity numbers for colocated and individual Edge Server roles.

"Step 6: Plan for External User Access," in the "Office Communications Server 2007 Planning Guide" recommends colocating the Access Edge Server with the Web Conferencing Edge Server in the main datacenter (which is Chicago for Contoso) and to have at least two load-balanced physical servers (for performance reasons and for redundancy purposes). All Access Edge connections have to be accumulated, as there can be only one single Access Edge Server location in an Office Communications Server 2007 deployment.

Important In Office Communications Server 2007 deployments, only one location for an Access Edge Server can exist in an entire, global Office Communications Server 2007 deployment. All signaling for all Remote Access Scenarios—even for users homed on other pools that are not colocated with the Access Edge Server—has to enter into the global Office Communications Server 2007 deployment by using the single Access Edge Server deployment. It is possible to have multiple load-balanced Access Edge Servers, but only in one location. The best place to set up the Access Edge Server is at the main datacenter that homes the majority of users with remote access requirements. For Contoso, this is Chicago.

Even though only one Access Edge Server can be deployed in the entire organization, this only means that signaling has to pass through this single location to communicate with the remote users in the Office Communications Server 2007 pool. Media streams will use the Web Conferencing Server and A/V Edge Server that are located physically close to the user's pool. (For example, a user that is homed in the pool in Singapore will use the Singapore Web Conferencing Edge Server and A/V Edge Server.)

According to Table 11-6, the total number of connections (1 connection equals 1 remote participant of an online meeting using LiveMeeting 2007) to the Access Edge Server in Chicago is 1752 plus 765 plus 375, which equals 2892 connections in a peak-hour situation. The number of Web Conferencing connections for Chicago is 1314, as shown in Table 11-6. Neither the number of Access Edge connections nor the number of Web Conferencing connections exceeds the performance parameters for two colocated Access Edge and Web Conferencing Edge Servers according to the values presented in "Step 5: Review System and Network Requirements," in the "Office Communications Server 2007 Planning Guide." According to the same step, to provide sufficient performance to accommodate the number of concurrent A/V Edge Server connections in Chicago (528 according to Table 11-6), Contoso could deploy only one standalone A/V Edge Server role on a dedicated machine However, because the company sees the Remote Access Scenario as business critical and instead wants to eliminate any single point of failure, Contoso decides to deploy two separate load-balanced A/V Edge Servers. This deployment strategy also provides a sufficient buffer for future usage. The Chicago Edge Server deployment is similar to a *Single-Site Edge topology*.

Note The following combinations of Edge Server roles are possible on a single physical machine:

- Consolidated Edge Server with Access Edge Server, Web Conferencing Edge Server, and A/V Edge Server
- Combined Access Edge Server and Web Conferencing Edge Server
- Dedicated Access Edge Server
- Dedicated Web Conferencing Edge Server
- Dedicated A/V Edge Server

The remote access requirements for Paris and Madrid combined is 231 concurrent A/V meeting participants and 576 Web Conferencing participants, as shown in Table 11-6. According to the performance numbers presented in "Step 5: Review System and Network Requirements," in the "Office Communications Server 2007 Planning Guide," this could be accommodated by a single Web Conferencing Server and a single A/V Edge Server. But because the Remote Access Scenario for Paris users is seen as business critical for Contoso, it is necessary to deploy two load-balanced Web Conferencing Edge Servers and two load-balanced A/V Edge Servers for redundancy.

According to the values presented in Table 11-6, the estimations for concurrent meeting participants in Singapore is 114 for meetings containing A/V and 282 for Web Conferencing meetings. Because Contoso does not see the Remote Access Scenario for the Singapore users as business critical and the performance numbers can be accommodated by a single Web Conferencing Edge Server and a single A/V Edge Server, one dedicated server for each Edge Server role will be deployed. It is not possible to colocate the Web Conference Edge Server with an A/V Edge Server, as this combination is not tested and therefore unsupported.

Note If you deploy a consolidated Edge Server with multiple server roles combined on a single physical machine (for example, Access Edge, Web Conferencing Edge, and A/V Edge colocated), a new installation is required if usage numbers increase and the A/V Edge Server role has to be separated from the consolidated Edge Server because of performance reasons. A new installation is required for all separation processes from a consolidated server to dedicated role servers in an Office Communications Server 2007 deployment.

Besides the Office Communications Server 2007 Edge Server, Contoso also needs an HTTP Proxy server, which can be provided based on Microsoft Internet Security and Acceleration (ISA) Server 2006. This server has to be colocated with the Access Edge Server, and it provides the following functionalities to Office Communications Server 2007 users:

- For remote users:
  - Expansion of distribution lists
  - Access to meeting content for LiveMeeting 2007
  - Delivery of the Address Book Server file to the Office Communicator 2007 client
- For federated and anonymous users: access to meeting content for LiveMeeting 2007

A good practice from an ISA perspective would be to use at least one ISA server, but using Caching Array of Redundant Proxy (CARP) would be an even better approach. It's possible to implement only a single ISA server or an ISA server array at the main data center, but doing so might cause performance to suffer for users at other sites. It's also possible to deploy one ISA server at each site that contains these roles, or even better to deploy two ISA servers to eliminate a single point of failure. To reduce the complexity in the Contoso example, only one ISA server at the main data center in Chicago is used.

Important In addition to the Edge Server roles, a *Director* needs to be deployed in Chicago and Madrid. A Director is an Office Communications Server 2007 Standard Edition Server that homes no users. Its purpose is to authorize incoming requests from the Access Edge Server and redirect these requests to the correct Office Communications Server 2007 pool. This offloads the Front-End Server and allows better performance for the pool. It is also a security element because if an attacker got access through the Access Edge Server, he could cause damage only on the Director but not on the pool itself.

To avoid a single point of failure, at least two Directors have to be deployed and load balanced. This is called a *Director array*.

Table 11-7 shows Contoso's final Edge Server deployment.

Table 11-7 Contoso Architecture with Edge Server

Scenario/sites	Chicago	Paris	Madrid	Singapore
Number of concurrent users in peak hour	70,000	30,000	500	15,000
Core architecture	Enterprise Edition Expanded Configuration with Clustered Back-End Database	Enterprise Edition Expanded Configuration with Clustered Back-End Database	Enterprise Edition Consolidated Configuration	Enterprise Edition Consolidated Configuration
Number of Core Servers	6 Front End 2 IIS Servers 1 Back End with SQL cluster	4 Front End 2 IIS Servers 1 Back End with SQL cluster	2 Front End (running all Conferencing Server roles) 1 Back End	4 Front End (running all Conferencing Server roles) 1 Back End
Number of Conferencing Servers	4 Web Conferencing Servers 4 A/V Conferencing Servers	2 Web Conferencing Servers 2 A/V Conferencing Servers	—	—
Edge Server topology	2 Colocated Edge Servers with Access Edge Server and Web Conferencing Edge Server. 2 A/V Edge Servers	2 Web Conferencing Edge Servers 2 A/V Edge Servers	—	1 Web Conferencing Edge Server 1 A/V Edge Server
Director	2 Directors	—	—	—
HTTP Reverse Proxy	1 ISA 2006 or similar reverse proxy server	—	—	—

As part of the Edge Server planning process, not only does the Edge Server topology have to be determined, but the DNS, Certificate, and Firewall configuration requirements (as shown in "Step 6: Plan for External User Access," in the "Office Communications Server 2007 Planning Guide") also have to be prepared.

How It Works: Port Considerations for Firewall Configurations in A/V Edge Server Deployments

The A/V Edge Server enables users to participate in audio and video connections from outside the corporate network–such as when making a point-to-point call, participating in a conference, leaving a voicemail message with Microsoft Exchange UM, or making a PSTN call. Contoso has deployed the A/V Edge Servers with two network interface cards in the perimeter network. The "external" firewall separates the A/V Edge Server from the Internet, and the "internal" firewall separates the server from the corporate network. For the A/V Edge Server to function correctly, the internal firewall must allow traffic to UDP 3478, TCP 443, and TCP 5062 (the A/V authentication port). And the external firewall must allow bi-directional traffic to the following ports: UDP 3478, TCP 443, UDP 50,000–59,999, and TCP 50,000–59,999. No Network Address Translation (NAT) behavior is allowed on either firewall.

These ports on the external edge tend to undergo greater scrutiny because they involve more ports open to the Internet. This sidebar first explains why are there are so many ports and then how these ports are secured from an attack.

Why UDP Ports Are Needed

UDP connections are more resilient to packet loss than TCP. When a UDP packet is lost, the transport delivers subsequent packets without delay. When a TCP packet is lost, the transport holds all subsequent packets because TCP inherently provides a reliable stream of data. This results in increased audio latency as we wait for the lost packet to retransmit and the rest of the TCP stream to "catch up."

Why TCP Ports Are Needed

Although UDP is a more efficient transport, some clients can reach the Internet only via TCP, typically because of a corporate firewall policy. Office Communications Server also supports a TCP media transport in case a UDP path is not available. At the start of each call or conference, the two endpoints use the IETF (Internet Engineering Task Force) ICE (Interactive Connectivity Establishment) protocol to dynamically choose the optimal media path available. This protocol prefers direct media paths over those that go through a media relay, and UDP paths over TCP paths.

Why the Port Range Above 50,000 Is Needed

The A/V Edge Server is an implementation of the IETF STUN (Simple Traversal of User Datagram Protocol through NAT) protocol with TURN (Traversal Using Relay NAT) relay extensions. The standard requires this port range because it cannot assume the remote party has access to the same media relay server. Phone calls often traverse company boundaries, such as a federated VoIP call in Office Communications Server 2007. Calls to standalone SIP devices are another example that one could envision as VoIP technology continues to evolve. The federated company cannot access the local company's A/V Edge Server via UDP3478/TCP443. The 50,000 port range allows media to traverse firewalls in a federated call. It is a port range instead of a multiplexed port to enable efficient relaying of Real-time Protocol (RTP) packets. A multiplexed port requires increased packet inspection and lowers the efficiency of the server. As you'll see in the following section, the port range also increases the security of the A/V Edge Server.

Security Overview

Understanding the technology is not enough. Like most corporations, Contoso's IT department is composed of emerging technology engineers *and* network security engineers. Deploying the technology just described will happen only if it passes a security review. The following section discusses security aspects, first providing a summary of the mechanisms in place and then providing a more detailed description.

Security of A/V Edge Server Auth Port TCP5062 (internal edge only)

Office Communications Server Front-End Servers must provide a validly signed certificate whose subject name matches the FQDN of that server. (The Office Communications Server Front-End Server performs the same check against the A/V Edge Server's certificate.)

The Office Communications Server Front-End Server FQDN must be on a trusted list of the A/V Edge Server. (The Office Communications Server Front-End Server performs the same check against the A/V Edge Server FQDN.)

All SIP signaling is protected with 128-bit Transport Layer Security (TLS) encryption.

Security of UDP3478/TCP443 (internal and external edges)

Port allocation is protected by 128-bit digest "challenge" authentication, using a computer-generated password that rotates every 8 hours. A sequence number and random nonce are used to deter replay attacks. Media relay packaged messages (UDP3478/TCP443) are protected with a 128-bit Hash Message Authentication Code (HMAC) signature.

Security of UDP/TCP 50,000-59,999 (external edge only)

Ports are allocated randomly within the UDP/TCP 50,000–59,999 port range per call. An attacker needs to predict which port is active and complete an attack before the call ends. Incoming traffic is filtered according to the IP addresses of the other endpoint's candidates. Even if an attacker finds a port in use, she must also spoof the correct IP address. These two examples actually make the port range more secure. If all traffic was multiplexed through one port, it would accept traffic from IP addresses of all remote endpoints.

Security of end-to-end media

Media packets are protected with end-to-end Secure Real-Time Protocol (SRTP), preventing any eavesdropping or packet injection. The key used to encrypt and decrypt the media stream is passed over the TLS secured signaling channel.

Details of Security

Let's now dig deeper into the details of port security for the A/V Edge Server.

Security of A/V Edge Server Auth Port TCP5062(internal edge only)

When a user logs in to Office Communicator 2007 or joins a meeting, he first acquires a username/password token from the media relay by sending a SIP SERVICE message over the TLS secured signaling channel. The last leg of this signaling path is a TCP connection from the user's Office Communications Server Front-End Server to the A/V authentication port of the A/V Edge Server. This connection is accepted only on the internal-facing IP address of the A/V Edge Server. Before accepting the SIP SERVICE request, a TLS connection must be set up where both sides validate the following:

1. The other server provides a certificate signed by a trusted authority.
2. The certificate's subject name matches the FQDN of that server.
3. That server's FQDN matches one of the servers on a local trusted server list. (In fact, all servers in the Office Communications Server system perform this series of checks before allowing any communication to or from another Office Communications Server.)

If all three checks pass, the TLS connection is established and the SIP SERVICE command is carried to the A/V Edge Server, which responds with a 200 OK message containing the computer-generated username/password token.

Security of UDP3478 and TCP443 (internal and external edges)

The A/V Edge Server is an enterprise-managed resource, so restricting access to authorized users is important for security and resource considerations. Communication on the UDP3478 and TCP443 ports is allowed only for clients that belong to the corporation managing that A/V Edge Server. A client uses these two ports to allocate UDP and TCP ports within the 50,000 port range for the remote party to connect to. Using the computer-generated username/password obtained via the SIP SERVICE request, the client performs digest authentication against the A/V Edge Server to actually allocate the ports. An initial allocate request is sent from the client and responded to with a nonce challenge message from the A/V Edge Server. The client sends a second allocate containing the username and an HMAC hash of the username and nonce. A sequence number mechanism is also in place to prevent replay attacks. The server calculates the expected HMAC based on its own knowledge of the username and password. If the HMAC values match, the allocate procedure is carried out; otherwise, the packet is dropped. This same HMAC mechanism is also applied to subsequent messages within this call session. The lifetime of this username/password value is a maximum of 8 hours, at which time the client will reacquire a new username/password for subsequent calls.

Security of UDP/TCP 50,000–59,999 (external edge only)

The question arises, "Are 10,000 ports less secure than a couple well-known ports?" One might think so, but actually the answer is no. From an attacker's standpoint, each of those 10,000 ports behaves exactly the same. The more pertinent question is: "How secure is each of those 10,000 ports?"

One consideration is that allocations in this range are chosen randomly. At any given time, it's likely that many of these ports aren't even listening for packets. (Contrast that with a well-known port that an attacker can focus on.) The security mechanism in place on each port is to filter traffic for only those packets that originate from the remote endpoint's IP address. This IP address is communicated over the TLS secured signaling channel, and packets from any other IP addresses are dropped by the A/V Edge Server. In this situation, having a range of ports actually improves security. Because a random port allocation happens for each call, this design forces the attacker to do the following:

- Deduce an active port.
- Break the TLS signaling channel.
- Spoof the remote user's IP address.

And the attacker must do all this in the span of a single call.

Can this port range be reduced? Yes, but doing so limits the degree to which the A/V Edge Server can scale in peak conditions and does not increase security. A reduced port range should factor no less than 6 UDP/TCP ports per user in a peak load condition. Can this port range be eliminated altogether for companies that don't require A/V federation? Unfortunately, this scenario has not been tested and is currently an unsupported configuration.

Security of end-to-end media

Office Communications Server clients perform signaling to the server using 128-bit TLS encryption with validation that the server certificate has a matching FQDN and is signed by a trusted authority. This same mechanism is used by e-commerce sites. To secure the media channel, Office Communications Server uses the IETF SRTP protocol. The mechanism carries out a 128-bit key exchange over the secure signaling channel, which the two endpoints then use to encrypt and decrypt the media stream via 128-bit Advanced Encryption Standard (AES). Even if an attacker can perform a "man in the middle" attack of the media path, no eavesdropping or false packet injection is possible.

Understanding the design features and security mechanisms of the A/V Edge Server will enable a meaningful discussion between the IT engineers deploying Office Communications Server and the security team protecting the corporate network.

–Alan Shen
Senior Program Manager, OCS Customer Experience

Step 7: Plan for Deploying Load Balancers

The main purpose for Load Balancer is to distribute traffic among multiple physical servers that have the same Office Communications Server 2007 server roles installed. With a Load Balancer, it isn't just scalability and extensibility that become possible in the case of a single server failure, but redundancy as well. Contoso needs Load Balancers in the following places:

- Chicago:
  - 1 Load Balancer for the Front-End Server of the pool
  - 1 Load Balancer for the IIS Server
  - 2 Load Balancers for the colocated Access Edge Server and Web Conferencing Edge Server (1 on the side to the Internet, 1 on the internal side)
  - 2 Load Balancers for the A/V Edge Server (1 on the side to the Internet, 1 on the internal side)
  - 2 Load Balancers for the Directors (one facing the Edge Server, one facing the Office Communications Server 2007 pool)
- Paris:
  - 1 Load Balancer for the Front-End Server of the pool
  - 1 Load Balancer for the IIS Server
  - 2 Load Balancers for the Web Conferencing Edge Server (1 on the side to the Internet, 1 on the internal side.)
  - 2 Load Balancers for the A/V Edge Server (1 on the side to the Internet, 1 on the internal side.)
- Madrid: 1 Load Balancer for the consolidated Enterprise Edition Server of the pool
- Singapore: 1 Load Balancer for the consolidated Enterprise Edition Server of the pool

> **Note** Most Load Balancers support the notion of multiple virtual IP addresses. This allows you to use a single physical Load Balancer for multiple server roles. Therefore, the number of Load Balancers just listed is the number of logical Load Balancers that Contoso needs and not necessarily the number of physical Load Balancers.

The Contoso architecture now looks as shown in Table 11-8.

Table 11-8 Contoso Architecture with Load Balancer

Scenario/sites	Chicago	Paris	Madrid	Singapore
Number of concurrent users in peak hour	70,000	30,000	500	15,000
Core Architecture	Enterprise Edition Expanded Configuration with Clustered Back-End Database	Enterprise Edition Expanded Configuration with Clustered Back-End Database	Enterprise Edition Consolidated Configuration	Enterprise Edition Consolidated Configuration
Number of Core Servers	6 Front End 2 IIS Servers 1 Back End with SQL cluster	4 Front End 2 IIS Servers 1 Back End with SQL cluster	2 Front End (running all Conferencing Server roles) 1 Back End	4 Front End (running all Conferencing Server roles) 1 Back End
Number of Conferencing Servers	4 Web Conferencing Servers 4 A/V Conferencing Servers	2 Web Conferencing Servers 2 A/V Conferencing Servers	—	—
Edge Server topology	2 Colocated Edge Servers with Access Edge Server and Web Conferencing Edge Server. 2 A/V Edge Servers	2 Web Conferencing Edge Servers 2 A/V Edge Servers	—	1 Web Conferencing Edge Server 1 A/V Edge Server
Director	2 Directors	—	—	—
HTTP Reverse Proxy	1 ISA 2006 or similar reverse proxy server	—	—	—
Logical Load Balancers	8	6	1	1

Step 8: Plan for VoIP

"Step 8: Plan for VoIP," in the "Office Communications Server 2007 Planning Guide" describes several individual planning steps. In this chapter, you will read only about planning steps that need to be prepared well in advance before the actual deployment takes place (including the selection of the appropriate deployment option, selection of gateways, and location of gateways), as these particular steps need some time for preparation.

> **Note** You should involve your organization's PBX/telephone administrators in this discussion when you plan for VoIP and its integration into the existing telephone environment.

The other planning steps–such as Routing and Normalization rules, location profiles, and number manipulation on gateways–will be discussed in Chapter 12, "Deployment," as they are only configuration options and can be discussed just before the actual deployment happens.

> **Important** If you enable a user for Enterprise Voice, Office Communicator 2007 of Office Communicator Phone Edition becomes the de facto telephone at the desktop for this user. You need to have a USB audio device connected to the PC on which Office Communicator 2007 is running to provide acceptable, echo-free voice quality. By deploying a separate USB audio device (USB headset, USB handset, or USB Bluetooth headset), it becomes possible to direct the normal PC system sounds (for example, beeps on error messages) to the integrated sound board of the PC while the voice media stream for telephone calls will be directed to the external USB audio device. This can be done in the control panel in the sounds application and also in the A/V Tuning Wizard of Office Communicator 2007.
>
> If you decide to even install a USB audio device that complies with the Microsoft Unified Communications (*www.microsoft.com/uc*) specifications, the user can benefit in A/V conversations between Office Communicator 2007 and Office Communicator 2007 users or in conversations using Office Communicator Phone Edition as well as Live Meeting 2007. Users will benefit from the high-fidelity audio quality provided by the devices in conjunction with the media stack of Office Communications Server 2007. The Unified Communications device specification is a technical specification that provides functional, performance, and quality guidelines to ensure devices are optimized for Office Communications Server 2007 and Office Communicator 2007.
>
> High-fidelity audio quality can be provided only on the IP network, because as soon as a call needs to be transferred to the Time Division Multiplexing (TDM) world by using a SIP/PSTN Gateway, a narrowband audio codec will be used in conversations via Mediation Server and SIP/PSTN Gateways. USB handsets with hook functionality provide users a "telephone-like" feeling, because users can just pick up the receiver on an incoming call as they are presently accustomed to doing.
>
> A USB audio device is not needed for Office Communicator Phone Edition because it is a standalone IP phone. "Phone" is actually not the right term, as it is more a PC that looks like a phone, runs the Windows CE operating system, and is an "Office Communicator–like" application. Certificates can be stored on the device so that it can register with Office Communications Server 2007 and participate in secure communications with other Office Communications

Server 2007 endpoints. It is important to know that Office Communicator Phone Edition has not been designed to be used as a "common area phone" in the 2007 release. A user has to sign on with his credentials to get access to the Office Communicator application and its contact list. But what you can do is create a guest user account in Active Directory and use this for a common area phone with limited dialing privileges. You can set the guest user account password to "never expire" in Active Directory, configure the phone not to lock anymore, configure the phone's contact list by using Office Communicator 2007 (log on as the guest user), and finally log on once to the Office Communicator Phone Edition device using the guest account.

An Enterprise Voice–enabled user, for example, can have Office Communicator 2007 installed and registered with Office Communications Server 2007 on her PC and have Office Communicator Phone Edition registered at the same time.

In the 2007 release, Microsoft Office RoundTable is not a standalone SIP endpoint that can register with Office Communications Server 2007. It acts as a USB A/V device in conjunction with Office Communicator 2007 or Live Meeting 2007, or it can be used as a normal conference audio phone by connecting an analog line.

Contoso has a telephone network with multiple TDM PBX nodes on every site. These PBX nodes are not connected via a corporate telephone network. As described earlier in this chapter, Contoso has decided to deploy 100 pilot users for Enterprise Voice in Chicago and wants to enable all 500 users in Madrid. In Madrid, the existing TDM PBX is depreciated, and Madrid users will use Office Communicator 2007 or Office Communicator Phone Edition as their primary voice endpoint. By comparing these requirements with the deployment options in "Step 8: Plan for VoIP," in the "Office Communications Server 2007 Planning Guide," the Departmental Deployment option is the appropriate deployment option for the Chicago site, while the Greenfield Deployment option is the best choice for the Madrid site.

Note Office Communications Server 2007 has a datacenter model architecture. All deployed pools are connected with one another via the wide area network (WAN). By migrating voice users to the Office Communications Server 2007 infrastructure, the former site-oriented telephone model with PBX nodes on every site disappears. After migration of all local PBX nodes to Office Communications Server 2007, Office Communications Server 2007 will act as a worldwide Enterprise Voice solution.

This leads to the fact that the extension model in which every PBX phone had a site-unique extension number cannot be kept anymore. This is because by consolidating user extensions into the Office Communications Server 2007 infrastructure, they won't be unique anymore. (For example, in the Contoso network, extension 11533 can be found in Chicago, Singapore, and Paris.) To avoid conflicts with duplicate extensions, the user's phone numbers must be unique. The only worldwide unique telephone numbering schema is the E.164 format. This is why the user's telephone numbers in the *msRTCSIP-line* attribute in Active Directory has to be entered in E.164 format. Based on this E.164 format number, the match to the user's SIP address is performed whenever needed. The whole transformational process to the E.164 format is transparent to the user, and if it is configured correctly, the user will not even know about it.

The Departmental Deployment option on the Chicago site offers the flexibility for the 100 pilot users to do one of the following two things:

- Replace their existing PBX phone with Office Communicator 2007 by using the same extension number they had before on the PBX
- Get a new extension number from the PBX for the duration of the pilot program, but keep their existing PBX phone. (Ideally the PBX extension should at least be forwarded to the new extension on Office Communications Server 2007 or the PBX should simultaneously ring the PBX extension as well as the user's Office Communicator 2007 extension on an incoming call for the user's PBX extension.)

Figure 11-6 shows this integration scenario for Chicago.

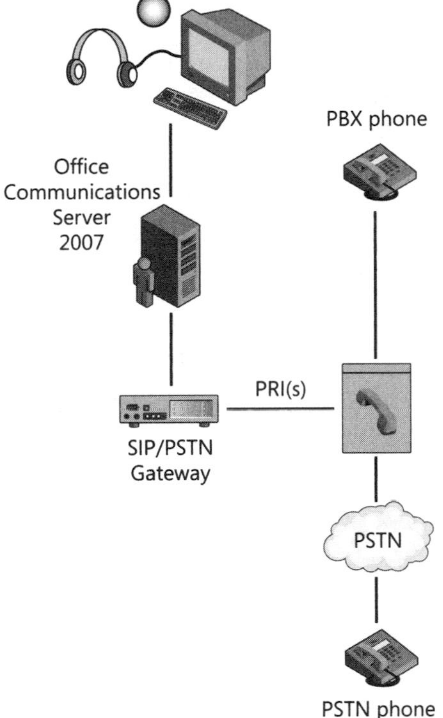

Figure 11-6 Departmental Deployment scenario with existing PBX environment in Chicago

To set up this integration scenario, the following prerequisites need to be prepared:

- **Select an appropriate Media Gateway for the SIP/PSTN connection.** As presented in "Step 8: Plan for VoIP," in the "Office Communications Server 2007 Planning Guide," several kinds of Media Gateways exist: *Basic Gateways* that require a separate Mediation Server, *Basic Hybrid Media Gateways* that run Mediation Server on the Gateway Server, and *Advanced Media Gateways* that support all Office Communications Server 2007 specific requirements (SRTP, TLS, RT audio and RT video codecs, and so on) natively and do not require a Mediation Server at all. Dialogic, AudioCodes, and Quintum are examples of SIP/PSTN Gateway vendors that have Media Gateways certified for Office Communications Server 2007.

- **Prepare the PRI trunk connections in the existing PBX node in Chicago in order to connect the Media Gateway.** A trunk connection off the existing TDM PBX can be used to connect the Media Gateway. You have to make sure that the number of PRI connections serves the usage requirements for concurrent audio connections from the Media Gateway. The protocol on the PRI connections from the PBX has to match at least one of the supported protocols of the Media Gateway. The gateway vendors can help you to decide if your current PBX protocol type is supported by their gateways. On the PBX, a routing has to be configured that routes calls–addressed to extensions on Office Communications Server 2007–from the PSTN or from other PBX extensions to the trunk connection.

For the 100 pilot users in Chicago, Contoso decides that one PRI connection from the PBX (T1 connection = 23 channels) will be sufficient for the pilot users. This means 23 concurrent calls (inbound and outbound) between users on the Office Communications Server 2007 environment and the PBX or the PSTN can be held at the same time. This does not affect the number of concurrent calls on Office Communications Server 2007 between Office Communicator 2007 users, for example, as those IP-to-IP calls do not pass the Media Gateway and do not need audio channels from the gateway. If you want to make calls only on the IP network, you don't need a Media Gateway at all.

Contoso chooses a Basic Media Gateway that needs a separate server for the Mediation Server. The capacity numbers for the Mediation Server presented in "Step 8: Plan for VoIP," in the "Office Communications Server 2007 Planning Guide" confirm that a single Mediation Server running on appropriate hardware is sufficient for this scenario.

> **Note** The Mediation Server should always be placed physically close to a SIP/PSTN Gateway with a good IP network connection between the two entities. The reason for that is because unencrypted media streams have to be passed between the SIP/PSTN Gateway and the Mediation Server.
>
> Also, the Mediation Server should have two network interface cards to separate secure traffic to Office Communications Server from unsecure traffic to the gateway.

On the Madrid site, Contoso chooses to deploy the Greenfield Deployment option. This adds another level of complexity to the planning process, as the existing PBX in Madrid has to be assessed in a more granular way. The Enterprise Voice Scenario of Office Communications Server 2007 is the first release of its kind. Therefore, some functionalities of a traditional PBX will not be provided with this release of Office Communications Server 2007, but they will be provided in subsequent releases (for example, the Boss/Admin solution). However, features will not be provided even in subsequent releases that made sense only in the PBX world but became obsolete following the Unified Communications paradigm (for example, sending display messages on the phone display).

Ideally for an Office Communications Server 2007 deployment, all standard office information workers in the Contoso Madrid office see their daily telephone needs fulfilled with the current telephone feature set of Office Communicator 2007 and Office Communicator Phone Edition. But how about common-area phones, fax machines, elevator phones, alarm systems, and so on that are currently connected to extensions of the existing PBX?

Office Communications Server 2007 does not provide interfaces for these mostly analog extensions in the current release. One option is to configure a trunk connection off the Media Gateway and connect this PRI trunk to the existing TDM PBX or even to a new small PBX. (These PBX systems became very cheap in the past few years.) This way, there are still connections available on the TDM telephone system and not all user requirements have to be solved in the IP world, especially if they can be solved much easier in the TDM world.

Contoso decided to follow this approach, as shown in Figure 11-7, by using a Basic Media Gateway with two PRI connections (E1 connections with 30 channels each, as used previously for the PSTN connection) and one Mediation Server (sufficient according to the Mediation Server Hardware Requirements table presented in "Step 8: Plan for VoIP," in the "Office Communications Server 2007 Planning Guide").

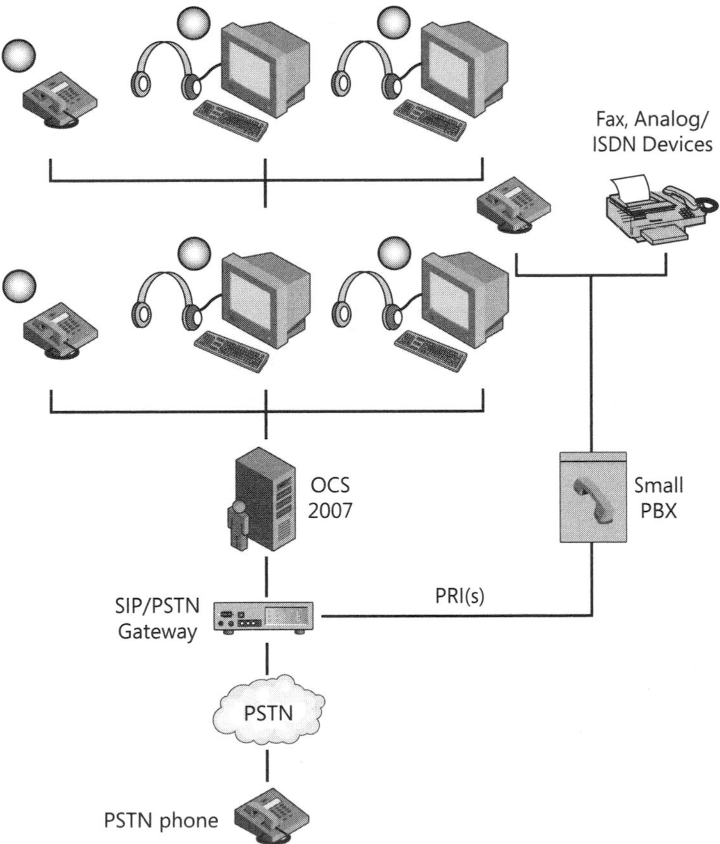

Figure 11-7 Greenfield Deployment scenario with direct PSTN connection

If only a few analog devices have to be connected, certain Media Gateways can already be ordered with analog connections for such purposes—for example, a Media Gateway with 2 PRI connections (to the PSTN) and 8 analog connections (for analog devices).

Important As part of the centralization process to migrate users on local PBX environments to the Office Communications Server 2007 datacenter architecture, the idea might come up to centralize Media Gateways to the PSTN as well. Do not forget in this context that local gateways are not just needed for outbound calls but also for inbound calls. Local phone numbers are usually terminated on the local site by the local PSTN carrier, and if the enterprise does not want to change its phone numbers a local Media Gateway is required. SIP carriers can help you to work around this issue, as they are able to route the local PSTN phone number onto their network and terminate incoming calls as SIP conversations to the enterprise with no geographical dependency. The SIP trunking scenario to external SIP proxies is not supported in the Office Communications Server 2007 release.

Planning for Contoso's Exchange 2007 Unified Messaging Pilot Deployment in Madrid

Contoso is running Exchange 2003 SP2 Server corporate-wide, but a pilot implementation of Exchange 2007 Server in Madrid will be performed as part of the Office Communications Server deployment. Because there are only 500 users in the Madrid location, Contoso has chosen to deploy a single Exchange 2007 Server running four roles: Client Access Server (CAS), Hub Transport (HUB), Mailbox (MBX), and Unified Messaging (UM). The HUB role is required for interoperability with Exchange 2003 Server, and the other roles are required for UM.

Note Exchange 2007 UM is required for the Enterprise Voice Scenario as it is the only supported voicemail system for Office Communications Server 2007. In addition to voicemail functionality, Exchange 2007 UM also provides Subscriber Access (remote voice access to manage the user's Outlook Inbox by using dial-in from any phone) and Auto-Attendant functionality.

Office Communications Server 2007 can store voicemail messages in the form of messages in a user's Exchange 2007 Server mailbox if UM is configured. To support Office Communications Server 2007 features such as the ability to enable an account that is already SIP-enabled for Office Communications Server 2007 for UM, Exchange 2007 SP1 must be installed. The Exchange 2007 UM deployment for Contoso in Madrid is covered in Chapter 12. However, from a planning perspective, Contoso needs the following in place:

- 64-bit server running Windows 2003 64-bit (or R2 64-bit) with SP1.
- 64-bit Exchange 2007 with SP1.

- An Office Communications Server Location profile (must match the FQDN of the Exchange 2007 UM Dial Plan.)
- UM Dial Plan, UM IP Gateway, UM Hunt Group, and UM Mailbox Policy.
- A machine certificate for the Exchange 2007 server (Office Communications Server cannot use the self-signed certificate installed by Exchange), but it must stay in place for Exchange 2007 Server to Server communications.)
- Auto Attendant (with a dedicated number). Auto attendant is used to play a default or customized message to callers when an Office Communications Server user is not available and the call rolls over to Unified Messaging.
- Subscriber Access (also a dedicated number. but it can't be the same number assigned to the auto attendant). Subscriber access is used to retrieve voice messages that are stored in an Exchange 2007 mailbox. The user calls the subscriber access number, enters her Personal Identification Number (PIN), and then plays the messages using Outlook Voice Access.

Important Store contact phone numbers in the same format that the Office Communications Server 2007 Media Gateway uses for incoming phone numbers (typically, E.164 format). This allows an Outlook user to click on thse embedded link in a UM message and directly call the person who left the message. If there is no corporate policy in place for how Outlook stores contact phone numbers, it will be necessary to define one or more normalization rules to account for mismatches.

For example, if a user (Monica 12065550199) from outside Contoso but inside the United States dials a user inside Contoso (Alex 13125550112), the gateway formats the called party number as E.164 (+15035550112). The packet containing the E.164 number then make its way to the Office Communications Server Front-End Server, which will perform a reverse number lookup on it, find a match on Alex's *msRTCSIP-Line* attribute, and route it to all his end points. If Alex doesn't answer, the call, along with the Calling and Called Party Number, information is sent to the Exchange 2007 Server UM for Voicemail functionality. As part of that process, the Calling Party Number is compared to Alex's Outlook contact list. If there is a match, the Calling Party Number is embedded as a link in the message.

If Alex's contacts aren't stored in E.164 format (for example, they just have an area code/number format), Monica's number appears as 2065550199 in the voicemail message. And if there is not a normalization rule configured to handle numbers in that format, the call won't be completed.

Rick Varvel
Microsoft Corporation, Lead Architect

The Contoso architecture after enabling Enterprise Voice in Chicago and Madrid looks like the architecture shown in Table 11-9.

Table 11-9 Contoso Architecture with Enterprise Voice

Scenario/sites	Chicago	Paris	Madrid	Singapore
Number of concurrent users in peak hour	70,000	30.000	500	15,000
Core Architecture	Enterprise Edition Expanded Configuration with Clustered Back-End Database	Enterprise Edition Expanded Configuration with Clustered Back-End Database	Enterprise Edition Consolidated Configuration	Enterprise Edition Consolidated Configuration
Number of Core Servers	6 Front End 2 IIS Servers 1 Back End with SQL cluster	4 Front End 2 IIS Servers 1 Back End with SQL cluster	2 Front End (running all Conferencing Server roles) 1 Back End	4 Front End (running all Conferencing Server roles) 1 Back End
Number of Conferencing Servers	4 Web Conferencing Servers 4 A/V Conferencing Servers	2 Web Conferencing Servers 2 A/V Conferencing Servers	—	—
Edge Server topology	2 Colocated Edge Servers with Access Edge Server and Web Conferencing Edge Server. 2 A/V Edge Servers	2 Web Conferencing Edge Servers 2 A/V Edge Servers	—	1 Web Conferencing Edge Server 1 A/V Edge Server
Director	2 Directors	—	—	—
HTTP Reverse Proxy	1 ISA 2006 or similar reverse proxy server	—	—	—
Logical Load Balancers	8	6	1	1
Media Gateway	1 single T1 PRI Basic Media Gateway	—	1 quad E1 PRI Basic Media Gateway (4 PRI connections: 2 to PSTN, 1 to PBX, and 1 spare)	—
Mediation Server	1 Mediation Server	—	1 Mediation Server	—
Exchange UM	—	—	1 Exchange 2007 UM Server	—

Step 9: Plan for Address Book Server

There are mainly two aspects to cover in this planning step: to provide access to the Address Book file for remote users, and to ensure there is sufficient data storage capacity to store all files that are being produced by the Address Book Server on each Office Communications Server 2007 Front-End Server in the Enterprise Edition or on Standard Edition Server. As already described in "Step 6: Plan for External User Access," an HTTP Reverse Proxy such as Microsoft ISA Server 2006 has to be installed to provide access for the remote users on the Address Book Server. "Step 9: Plan for Address Book Server," in the "Office Communications Server 2007 Planning Guide" contains a table with size estimations for the Address Book Server data files. Considering that hard-disk capacities are still increasing from year to year, the impact on the planning process is low.

Step 10: Plan for High Availability and Fault Tolerance

Apart from the possibility of achieving redundancy in the Office Communications Server 2007 deployment by adding redundant server roles, there are several possibilities to improve the overall system uptime. "Step 10: Plan for High Availability and Fault Tolerance," in the "Office Communications Server 2007 Planning Guide" contains useful information regarding this subject, which is beyond the scope of this chapter.

Step 11: Plan for Database Storage

It is important to plan for database storage because the lack of sufficient storage space can result in the entire system malfunctioning. "Step 11: Plan for Database Storage," in the "Office Communications Server 2007 Planning Guide" provides guidance on the database storage requirements. Contoso's HW for the Office Communications Server 2007 deployment complies with the requirements provided in the "Office Communications Server 2007 Planning Guide."

Step 12: Plan for Compliance and Usage Analysis

Finally, Contoso wants to capture Call Detail Records for the Enterprise Voice Scenario in Madrid, Spain. However, this is not seen as business critical, meaning that according to "Step 12: Plan for Compliance and Usage Analysis," in the "Office Communications Server 2007 Planning Guide," a single-tier Archiving topology running on one physical machine including the SQL Database is sufficient. The final Contoso architecture is shown in Table 11-10.

Table 11-10 Final Contoso Architecture

Scenario/sites	Chicago	Paris	Madrid	Singapore
Number of concurrent users in peak hour	70,000	30,000	500	15,000
Core Architecture	Enterprise Edition Expanded Configuration with Clustered Back-End Database	Enterprise Edition Expanded Configuration with Clustered Back-End Database	Enterprise Edition Consolidated Configuration	Enterprise Edition Consolidated Configuration
Number of Core Servers	6 Front End 2 IIS Servers 1 Back End with SQL cluster	4 Front End 2 IIS Servers 1 Back End with SQL cluster	2 Front End (running all Conferencing Server roles) 1 Back End	4 Front End (running all Conferencing Server roles) 1 Back End
Number of Conferencing Servers	4 Web Conferencing Servers 4 A/V Conferencing Servers	2 Web Conferencing Servers 2 A/V Conferencing Servers	—	—
Edge Server topology	2 Colocated Edge Servers with Access Edge Server and Web Conferencing Edge Server. 2 A/V Edge Server	2 Web Conferencing Edge Servers 2 A/V Edge Servers	—	1 Web Conferencing Edge Server 1 A/V Edge Server
Director	2 Directors	—	—	—
HTTP Reverse Proxy	1 ISA 2006 or similar reverse proxy server	—	—	—
Logical Load Balancers	8	6	1	1
Media Gateway	1 single T1 PRI Basic Media Gateway	—	1 quad E1 PRI Basic Media Gateway (4 PRI connections: 2 to PSTN, 1 to PBX, and 1 spare)	—
Mediation Server	1 Mediation Server	—	1 Mediation Server	—
Exchange UM	—	—	1 Exchange 2007 UM Server	—
Archiving Server	—	—	1 Archiving Server with SQL Database	—

On the CD On the CD, you can find the Office Communications Server Designer tool based on Microsoft Visio 2003, which allows you to create a diagram of your topology (including validation check) before the actual deployment. (This tool is part of the Office Communications Server 2007 Resource Kit tools, which can be installed from the \OCS 2007 Resource Kit Tools folder.) It also allows you to automatically retrieve and display the actual deployment by using its Auto-Discovery functionality. The following illustration shows the architecture of the Singapore pool by using the Office Communications Server Designer tool:

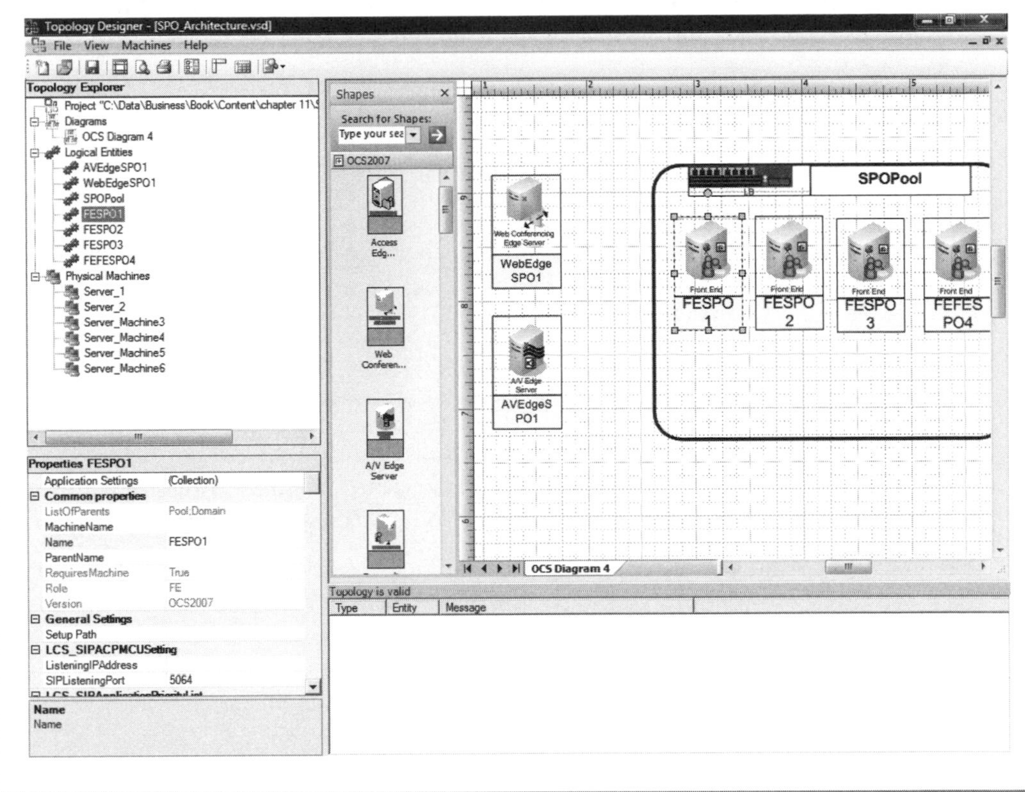

Summary

In this chapter, the example and sample walk through the "Office Communications Server 2007 Planning Guide" should help you become familiar with the information provided by the Planning Guide. The reader aids contain useful tips and tricks to help you find practical ways through your deployment planning. The designed infrastructure contains lots of resources for future usage because its design is optimized for performance and reliability. To reduce complexity, additional server roles such as the Update Server for Office Communicator Phone Edition or the Monitoring Server for Quality-of-Experience have not been described.

Additional Resources

- The Microsoft Unified Communications home page is found at *http://www.microsoft.com/uc*
- Office Communications Server 2007 documentation is available from this location on Microsoft TechNet Library: *http://technet.microsoft.com/en-us/bb629431.aspx*
- "Office Communications Server 2007 Planning Guide" is available from the Microsoft Download Center at *http://www.microsoft.com/downloads/details.aspx?familyid=723347c6-fa1f-44d8-a7fa-8974c3b596f4&displaylang=en*
- "Office Communications Server 2007 Enterprise Voice Planning and Deployment Guide" is available from the Microsoft Download Center at *http://www.microsoft.com/downloads/details.aspx?familyid=24e72dac-2b26-4f43-bba2-60488f2aca8d&displaylang=en*
- "Microsoft Quality of Experience" is available from the Microsoft Download Center at *http://www.microsoft.com/downloads/details.aspx?FamilyID=05625AF1-3444-4E67-9557-3FD5AF9AE8D1&displaylang=en*

On the Companion CD

- Office Communications Server Topology Designer tool. (This tool is part of the Office Communications Server 2007 Resource Kit tools, which can be installed from the \OCS 2007 Resource Kit Tools folder.)
- Three Microsoft Excel calculation sheets for bandwidth estimation for Edge Server, which are in the \Appendixes,Scripts,Resources\Chapter 11 folder.

Chapter 12

Office Communications Server 2007 Deployment Example

In this chapter:

In Chapter 11, "Office Communications Server 2007 Planning Example," a detailed planning process for an Office Communications Server 2007 deployment of a fictitious global company named Contoso was presented. It's been demonstrated how to use the Office Communications Server 2007 Planning Guide and the Office Communications Server 2007 Enterprise Voice Planning and Deployment Guide to design a multi-pool Office Communications Server 2007 deployment with several different scenarios enabled. The aim of the example in this chapter is to develop a deployment path for the entire Contoso architecture. The focus of this chapter will therefore be on the demonstration of all preparation steps that have to be taken before Contoso can be deployed, as well as on the deployment sequence. How to install every individual Office Communications Server 2007 Server role is explained in the various Office Communications Server 2007 deployment guides.

Understanding Contoso's Deployment Process for Office Communications Server 2007

Contoso's deployment of Office Communications Server 2007 is a complex example of an Office Communications Server 2007 deployment created to show the possible difficulties administrators might face when designing the right deployment path for such architecture. In particular, when several scenarios are enabled at one time for such a deployment, the time required can be lowered by first doing all preparation steps–such as developing a server naming convention, preparing Domain Name System (DNS) entries, creating certificates, installing and configuring network interface cards (NICs)–and then proceeding with the actual deployment. This approach saves you from having to come back to the preparation of the environment after each step. The advantage in doing all the server preparation up front is that when you deploy server roles later in your deployment path (for example, when deploying the Edge Server after you have set up the pool), you don't have to ask DNS administrators to do further entries for the Edge Server deployment because you already spoke with them a few days earlier when you deployed the pool. In particular, in large customer environments where multiple administrators are involved, the deployment process will become much smoother. There might be several answers to the questions "Where should I start?" and "What should I do next?" However, in this chapter a deployment path for Contoso is shown that can be seen as the Best Practice guidance for similar Office Communications Server 2007 deployments.

Establishing a Server Naming Convention

At first, it is important to define the naming convention for all servers Contoso wants to deploy. To choose a naming convention that is easily understandable to all organizations involved in the deployment is essential because it decreases the possibility of miscommunication. As Table 12-1 shows, Contoso chooses a naming convention for its servers that easily identifies each of the Office Communications Server 2007 roles and their locations.

Table 12-1 Contoso's Server Naming Convention

Attribute	Naming Convention
Server name	XXXYYYZZ
Server-FQDN (fully qualified domain name)	xxxyyyzz.contoso.com
XXX	Server roles are abbreviated as follows: ■ FRE = Front End Server of an Office Communications Server 2007 Enterprise Edition pool ■ SQL = SQL Database ■ BAE = Back End Server of an Office Communications Server 2007 Enterprise Edition pool ■ IIS = Internet Information Service ■ WCS = Web Conferencing Server in a pool ■ AVC = Audio/Video Conferencing Server ■ DIR = Director (Office Communications Server 2007 Standard Edition) ■ CAW = Co-located Access Edge and Web Conferencing Edge Server ■ AVE = Audio/Video Edge Server ■ MED = Mediation Server ■ HTT = Hypertext Transfer Protocol (HTTP) Reverse Proxy ■ WCE = Web Conferencing Edge Server ■ EXU = Exchange Unified Messaging Server ■ ARC = Archiving Server

Table 12-1 Contoso's Server Naming Convention

Attribute	Naming Convention
YYY	Server locations are abbreviated as follows: ■ CHI = Chicago ■ PAR = Paris ■ MAD = Madrid ■ SPO = Singapore
ZZ	Role number (if this is missing, the server is a Load Balancer)

Note that some exceptions to this naming convention exist for non–Office Communications Server 2007 roles, such as Load Balancers.

Table 12-2 through Table 12-5 show the Server names, IP addresses, and FQDNs for the servers for the four Contoso sites.

Table 12-2 Contoso Server Names for Chicago

Server Role	Server Name	IP Address	Server FQDN
Pool Name	CHIPOOL01	10.18.10.1	chipool01.contoso.com
Load Balancer virtual IP (VIP) for Office Communications Server 2007 Enterprise Edition (EE) Front End Servers	FRECHI	10.18.10.1	frechi.contoso.com
EE expanded Front End Server	FRECHI01	10.18.10.2	frechi01.contoso.com
EE expanded Front End Server	FRECHI02	10.18.10.3	frechi02.contoso.com
EE expanded Front End Server	FRECHI03	10.18.10.4	frechi03.contoso.com
EE expanded Front End Server	FRECHI04	10.18.10.5	frechi04.contoso.com
EE expanded Front End Server	FRECHI05	10.18.10.6	frechi05.contoso.com
EE expanded Front End Server	FRECHI06	10.18.10.7	frechi06.contoso.com
Back End SQL cluster name	SQLCHI01	10.18.10.10	sqlchi01.contoso.com
Back End Nodes	BAECHI01	10.18.10.11	baechi01.contoso.com
Back End Nodes	BAECHI02	10.18.10.12	baechi02.contoso.com
Load Balancer VIP for Internet Information Services (IIS)	IISCHI	10.18.10.15	iischi.contoso.com
IIS	IISCHI01	10.18.10.16	iischi01.contoso.com
IIS	IISCHI02	10.18.10.17	iischi02.contoso.com
Web Conferencing Server	WCSCHI01	10.18.10.20	wcschi01.contoso.com
Web Conferencing Server	WCSCHI02	10.18.10.21	wcschi02.contoso.com
Web Conferencing Server	WCSCHI03	10.18.10.22	wcschi03.contoso.com
Web Conferencing Server	WCSCHI04	10.18.10.23	wcschi04.contoso.com
A/V Conferencing Server	AVCCHI01	10.18.10.24	avcchi01.contoso.com
A/V Conferencing Server	AVCCHI02	10.18.10.25	avcchi02.contoso.com

Table 12-2 **Contoso Server Names for Chicago**

Server Role	Server Name	IP Address	Server FQDN
A/V Conferencing Server	AVCCHI03	10.18.10.26	avcchi03.contoso.com
A/V Conferencing Server	AVCCHI04	10.18.10.27	avcchi04.contoso.com
Director Pool Name	CHIDIRPOOL	10.18.10.32	chidirpool.contoso.com
Load Balancer VIP for Directors (internal-facing pool)	DIRCHI	10.18.10.32	dirchi.contoso.com
Director (internal NIC)	DIRCHI01	10.18.10.30	dirchi01.contoso.com
Director (external NIC)	—	10.18.10.130	—
Director (internal NIC)	DIRCHI02	10.18.10.31	dirchi02.contoso.com
Director (external NIC)	—	10.18.10.131	—
Load Balancer VIP for Directors (external-facing Edge Server)	—	10.18.10.33	dirchiext.contoso.com
Load Balancer VIP for Edge Access Server (internal)	CAWCHI	192.168.10.40	access.contoso.com
Co-located Access Edge Server and Web Conferencing Edge Server (internal NIC)	CAWCHI01	192.168.10.41	cawchi01.contoso.com
Co-located Access Edge Server and Web Conferencing Edge Server (external NIC)	—	64.65.66.3	—
Co-located Access Edge Server and Web Conferencing Edge Server (internal NIC)	CAWCHI02	192.168.10.42	cawchi02.contoso.com
Co-located Access Edge Server and Web Conferencing Edge Server (external NIC)	—	64.65.66.4	—
Load Balancer VIP for Edge Access Server (external)	—	64.65.66.1	sip.contoso.com
Load Balancer VIP for Edge Web Conferencing Server (external)	—	64.65.66.2	wcechi.contoso.com
Load Balancer VIP for A/V Edge Server (internal)	AVECHI	192.168.10.45	avechi.contoso.com
A/V Edge Server (internal NIC)	AVECHI01	192.168.10.46	avechi01.contoso.com
A/V Edge Server (external NIC)	—	64.65.66.16	—
A/V Edge Server (internal NIC)	AVECHI02	192.168.10.47	avechi02.contoso.com
A/V Edge Server (external NIC)	—	64.65.66.17	—
Load Balancer VIP for A/V Edge Server (external)	—	64.65.66.15	avechi.contoso.com
Mediation Server (internal NIC)	MEDCHI01	10.18.10.50	medchi01.contoso.com

Table 12-2 Contoso Server Names for Chicago

Server Role	Server Name	IP Address	Server FQDN
SIP/PSTN Gateway (external to Mediation Server)	—	10.18.10.51	gwychi01.contoso.com
HTTP Reverse Proxy Server (internal NIC)	HTTCHI01	192.168.10.60	httchi01.contoso.com
HTTP Reverse Proxy Server (external NIC)	—	64.65.66.30	httchi01.contoso.com

Table 12-3 Contoso Server Names for Paris

Server Role	Server Name	IP Address	Server FQDN
Pool Name	PARPOOL01	10.17.10.1	parpool01.contoso.com
Load Balancer VIP for EE Front End Servers	FREPAR	10.17.10.1	frepar.contoso.com
EE expanded Front End Server	FREPAR01	10.17.10.2	frepar01.contoso.com
EE expanded Front End Server	FREPAR02	10.17.10.3	frepar02.contoso.com
EE expanded Front End Server	FREPAR03	10.17.10.4	frepar03.contoso.com
EE expanded Front End Server	FREPAR04	10.17.10.5	frepar04.contoso.com
Back End SQL cluster name	SQLPAR01	10.17.10.10	sqlpar01.contoso.com
Back End Nodes	BAEPAR01	10.17.10.11	baepar01.contoso.com
Back End Nodes	BAEPAR02	10.17.10.12	baepar02.contoso.com
Load Balancer VIP for IIS	IISPAR	10.17.10.15	iispar.contoso.com
IIS	IISPAR01	10.17.10.16	iispar01.contoso.com
IIS	IISPAR02	10.17.10.17	iispar02.contoso.com
Web Conferencing Server	WCSPAR01	10.17.10.20	wcspar01.contoso.com
Web Conferencing Server	WCSPAR02	10.17.10.21	wcspar02.contoso.com
A/V Conferencing Server	AVCPAR01	10.17.10.24	avcpar01.contoso.com
A/V Conferencing Server	AVCPAR02	10.17.10.25	avcpar02.contoso.com
Load Balancer VIP for Web Conferencing Server (internal)	WCEPAR	192.167.10.40	wcepar.contoso.com
Web Conferencing Edge Server (internal NIC)	WCEPAR01	192.167.10.41	wcepar01.contoso.com
Web Conferencing Edge Server (external NIC)	—	64.64.66.11	
Web Conferencing Edge Server (internal NIC)	WCEPAR02	192.167.10.42	wcepar02.contoso.com
Web Conferencing Edge Server (external NIC)	—	64.64.66.12	—
Load Balancer VIP for Web Conferencing Server (external)	—	64.64.66.10	wcepar.contoso.com
Load Balancer VIP for A/V Edge Server (internal)	AVEPAR	192.167.10.45	avepar.contoso.com
A/V Edge Server (internal NIC)	AVEPAR01	192.167.10.46	avepar01.contoso.com

Table 12-3 Contoso Server Names for Paris

Server Role	Server Name	IP Address	Server FQDN
A/V Edge Server (external NIC)	—	64.64.66.16	—
A/V Edge Server (internal NIC)	AVEPAR02	192.167.10.47	avepar02.contoso.com
A/V Edge Server (external NIC)	—	64.64.66.17	—
Load Balancer VIP for A/V Edge Server (external)	—	64.64.66.15	avepar.contoso.com
HTTP Reverse Proxy Server (internal NIC)	HTTPAR01	192.167.10.60	httpar01.contoso.com
HTTP Reverse Proxy Server (external NIC)	—	64.64.66.30	httpar01.contoso.com

Table 12-4 Contoso Server Names for Madrid

Server Role	Server Name	IP Address	Server FQDN
Pool Name	MADPOOL01	10.16.10.1	madpool01.contoso.com
Load Balancer VIP for EE Front End Servers	FREMAD	10.16.10.1	fremad.contoso.com
EE consolidated Front End Server	FECMAD01	10.16.10.2	fecmad01.contoso.com
EE consolidated Front End Server	FECMAD02	10.16.10.3	fecmad02.contoso.com
Back End Nodes	BAEMAD01	10.16.10.11	baemad01.contoso.com
Mediation Server (internal NIC)	MEDMAD01	10.16.10.50	medmad01.contoso.com
SIP/PSTN Gateway (external to Mediation Server)	—	10.16.10.51	gwymad01.contoso.com
Exchange Unified Messaging (UM) Server	EXUMAD01	10.16.10.70	exumad01.contoso.com
Archiving Server	ARCMAD01	10.16.10.80	arcmad01.contoso.com

Note It is possible to install only one SQL database in Madrid and store Back End database data as well as the archiving data in the same database.

Table 12-5 Contoso Server Names for Singapore

Server Role	Server Name	IP Address	Server FQDN
Pool Name	SPOPOOL01	10.15.10.1	spopool01.contoso.com
Load Balancer VIP for EE Front End Servers	FRESPO	10.15.10.1	frespo.contoso.com
EE consolidated Front End Server	FECSPO01	10.15.10.2	fecspo01.contoso.com
EE consolidated Front End Server	FECSPO02	10.15.10.3	fecspo02.contoso.com
EE consolidated Front End Server	FECSPO03	10.15.10.4	fecspo03.contoso.com
EE consolidated Front End Server	FECSPO04	10.15.10.5	fecspo04.contoso.com
Back End Nodes	BAESPO01	10.15.10.11	baespo01.contoso.com
Load Balancer VIP for Web Conferencing Server (internal)	WCESPO	192.165.10.41	wcespo.contoso.com
Web Conferencing Edge Server (internal NIC)	WCESPO01	192.165.10.41	wcespo01.contoso.com
Web Conferencing Edge Server (external NIC)	—	64.62.66.11	wcespo01.contoso.com
Load Balancer VIP for A/V Edge Server (internal)	AVESPO	192.165.10.46	avespo.contoso.com
A/V Edge Server (internal NIC)	AVESPO01	192.165.10.46	avespo01.contoso.com
A/V Edge Server (external NIC)	—	64.62.66.16	avespo01.contoso.com

Note The external IP addresses for the Web Conferencing Edge Server and the A/V Edge Server also need an FQDN assigned. This is because there are no external Load Balancers in Singapore, and therefore the external IP addresses have to be in the external DNS.

Preparing the Server Hardware

Each Contoso Server role requires dedicated server hardware, as described in the Office Communications Server 2007 Planning Guide. From a performance perspective, none of the server roles handling media should be installed on virtual machines. When preparing server hardware for an Office Communications Server 2007 deployment, the required number of NICs in each server should be checked. Table 12-6 through Table 12-23, found later in this chapter, show where Contoso needs multiple NICs, as required by the server roles.

Contoso's Deployment Path

Contoso decided to enable several scenarios with a high level of redundancy for its users. This resulted in a high number of individual servers and server roles needing to be deployed. Figure 12-1 through Figure 12-4 provide a graphical view of the target deployment for each of the Contoso sites.

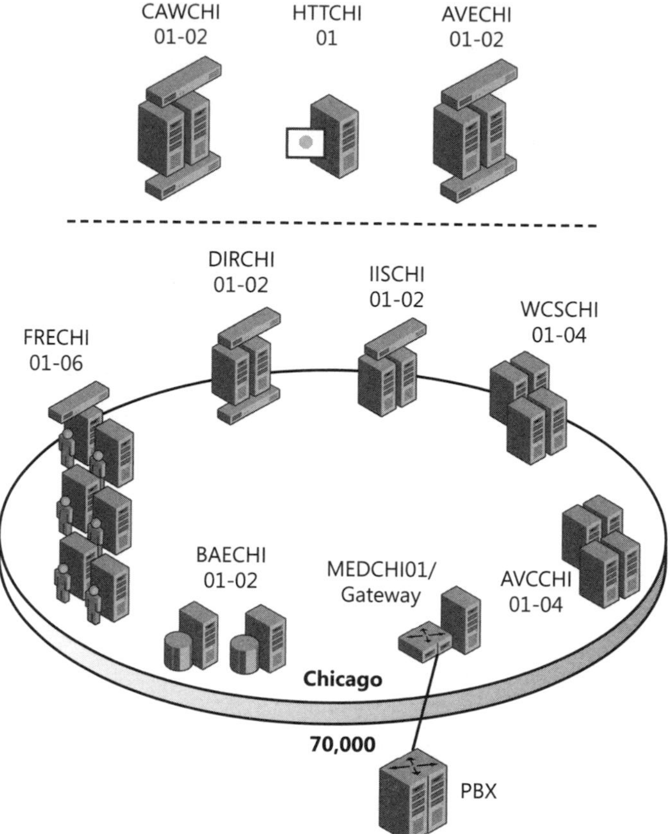

Figure 12-1 Contoso's target architecture in Chicago

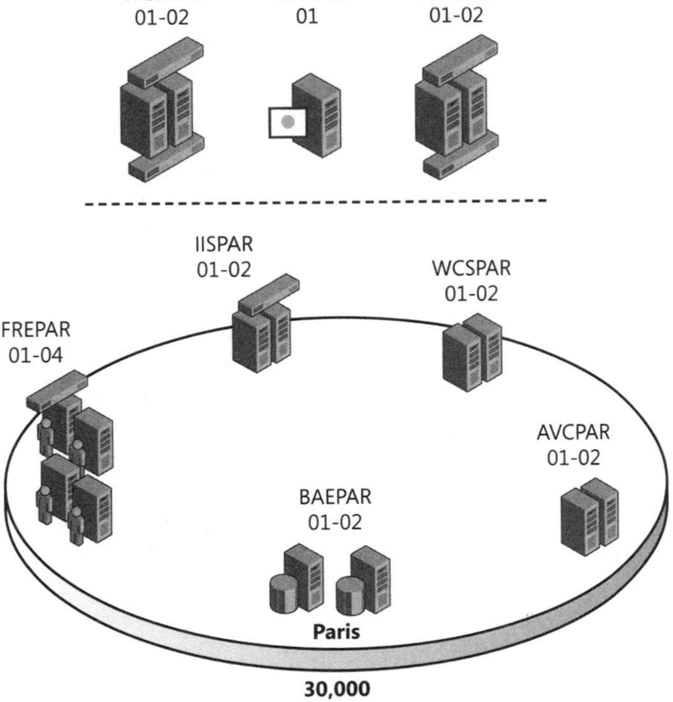

Figure 12-2 Contoso's target architecture in Paris

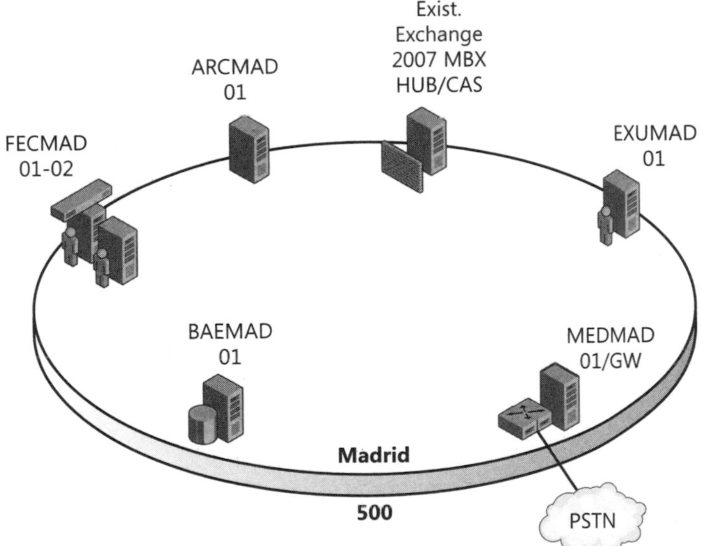

Figure 12-3 Contoso's target architecture in Madrid

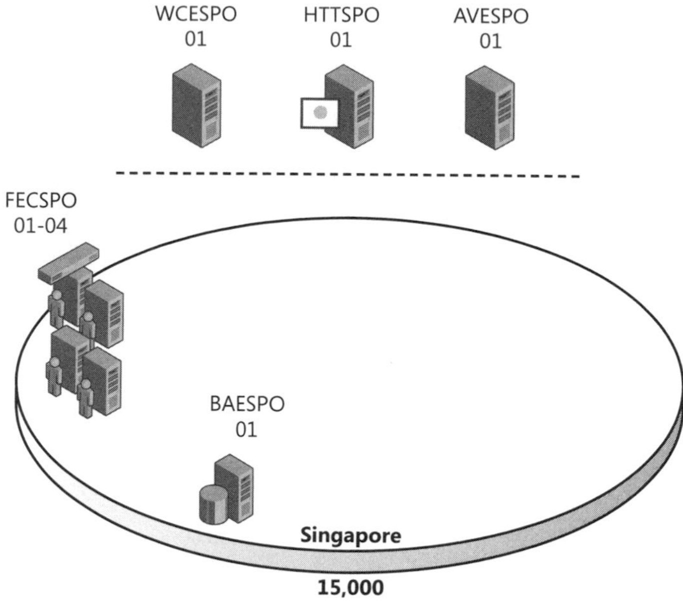

Figure 12-4 Contoso's target architecture in Singapore

Contoso will perform the Active Directory schema update as the initial step for its Office Communications Server 2007 deployment.

Preparing Active Directory

Contoso decided to install the entire Office Communications Server 2007 deployment in a single domain (Contoso.com) because domain controllers are available in each of the sites. The "Office Communications Server 2007 Active Directory Guide" explains in detail the steps that have to be taken to prepare Active Directory for an Office Communications Server 2007 deployment.

> **Important** Active Directory schema updates need to be well-controlled events by the Active Directory administrators because they can affect the entire enterprise's directory infrastructure. Therefore, it is understandable that the Active Directory preparation in an Office Communications Server 2007 deployment has to be coordinated with the Active Directory administrators. Depending on the enterprise and its business, there can be periods where an Active Directory schema update is not allowed by company policy and therefore the Office Communications Server 2007 deployment can be significantly delayed. The effects of such policies on the deployment schedule have to be incorporated into the deployment plan.

Overview of Preparing Firewall Ports, Certificates, NICs, and DNS

In large enterprises, the configurations of DNS, certificates, and firewalls are sometimes organizationally separated from the Office Communications Server 2007administrators who install and configure Office Communications Server 2007 and collaborate with other administrators in the company. Even the setup of servers can be performed by people other than the Office Communications Server 2007 administrators, so clear requirements have to be communicated to each organization within the enterprise to avoid interruptions of the deployment process because of missing prerequisites.

As part of Contoso's Office Communications Server 2007 planning process, the number of individual server roles has been identified as shown in Chapter 11. This allows Contoso to summarize all DNS and Firewall port requirements so that the preparation of the surrounding infrastructure can be done at one time before the actual deployment takes place. Table 12-6 through Table 12-23 summarize all preparations that need to be done for Contoso's Office Communications Server 2007 deployment. In addition to the summary views of the infrastructure requirements for each site, a detailed view with all the infrastructure requirements–including certificate requirements for Chicago–will be shown later in the chapter.

Preparing DNS, Firewall Ports, and Certificates for Chicago Deployment

Table 12-6 provides a summary of Contoso's infrastructure requirements for Chicago.

Table 12-6 Summary of Chicago Infrastructure Requirements

Server Role	Name	External DNS Name (IP Address)	Internal DNS Name (IP Address)	External Firewall Port (Direction)	Internal Firewall Port (Direction)
Edge Server—Access Edge Server (Load Balancer)	CAWCHI	sip.contoso.com VIP = (64.65.66.1) _sip._tls.*domain* (SRV) 443 sip.contoso.com _sipfederationtls._tcp.*domain* (SRV) 5061 sip.contoso.com	access.contoso.com VIP = (192.168.10.40)	443 TCP (Inbound) (Internet → Access Edge Server for Remote User Access) 5061 TCP (Both) (Internet ↔ Access Edge Server for Federation)	5061 TCP (Both) (Office Communications Server 2007 Pool ↔ Access Edge Server)
Edge Server—Web Conferencing Edge Server	CAWCHI	wcechi.contoso.com VIP = (64.65.66.2)	cawchi01.contoso.com (192.168.10.41) cawchi02.contoso.com (192.168.10.42)	443 TCP (Inbound) (Internet → Web Conferencing Edge Server)	8057 TCP (Outbound) (Office Communications Server 2007 Pool → Web Conferencing Edge Server)
Nodes (Access Edge Server/Web Conferencing Edge Server)					
Node1	CAWCHI01	N/A (Not applicable) (64.65.66.3)	cawchi01.contoso.com (192.168.10.41)	N/A	N/A
Node2	CAWCHI02	N/A (64.65.66.4)	cawchi02.contoso.com (192.168.10.42)	N/A	N/A

Table 12-6 Summary of Chicago Infrastructure Requirements

Server Role	Name	External DNS Name (IP Address)	Internal DNS Name (IP Address)	External Firewall Port (Direction)	Internal Firewall Port (Direction)
Edge Server—A/V Edge Server (Load Balancer)	AVECHI	avechi.contoso.com VIP = (64.65.66.15)	avechi.contoso.com VIP = (192.168.10.45)	443 TCP (Inbound) (Internet → A/V Edge Server) 3478 UDP (Inbound) (Internet → A/V Edge Server) 50,000–59,999 TCP & UDP (Both) (Internet ↔ A/V Edge Server)	443 TCP (Outbound) (Internal Net [all IPs] → A/V Edge Server) 3478 UDP (Outbound) (Internal Net [all IPs] → A/V Edge) 5062 TCP (Outbound) (Internal Net [all IPs] → A/V Edge Server)
Nodes (A/V Edge Server)					
Node1	AVECHI01	N/A (64.65.66.16)	avechi01.contoso.com (192.168.10.46)	N/A	N/A
Node2	AVECHI02	N/A (64.65.66.17)	avechi02.contoso.com (192.168.10.47)	N/A	N/A
HTTP Reverse Proxy Server	HTTCHI01	httchi01.contoso.com (64.65.66.30)	httchi01.contoso.com (192.168.10.60)	443 TCP (Inbound) Internet → HTTP Reverse Proxy Server	443 TCP (Inbound) HTTP Reverse Proxy Server → Office Communications Server 2007 Pool
Director (Pool)	CHIDIRPOOL	N/A	chidirpool.contoso.com (10.18.10.32)	N/A	5061 TCP (Both)
Director (Load Balancer)	DIRCHI01	dirchiext.contoso.com VIP = (10.18.10.33)	dirchi.contoso.com VIP = (10.18.10.32)		(Access Edge [internal Load Balancer VIP] ↔ Director [external Load Balancer VIP])
Director Nodes					
Node1	DIRCHI01	N/A	dirchi01.contoso.com (10.18.10.30)	N/A	N/A
Node2	DIRCHI02	N/A	dirchi02.contoso.com (10.18.10.31)	N/A	N/A
EE Expanded Pool	CHIPOOL01	N/A	chipool01.contoso.com (10.18.10.1)	N/A	N/A
EE (Load Balancer)	FRECHI	N/A	frechi.contoso.com VIP = (10.18.10.1) _sipinternal._tcp.*domain* (SRV) 5061 chipool01.contoso.com _sipinternaltls._tcp.*domain* (SRV) 5061 chipool01.contoso.com	N/A	N/A
EE Front Ends					
Node1	FRECHI01	N/A	frechi01.contoso.com (10.18.10.2)	N/A	N/A
Node2	FRECHI02	N/A	frechi02.contoso.com (10.18.10.3)	N/A	N/A
Node3	FRECHI03	N/A	frechi03.contoso.com (10.18.10.4)	N/A	N/A

Table 12-6 Summary of Chicago Infrastructure Requirements

Server Role	Name	External DNS Name (IP Address)	Internal DNS Name (IP Address)	External Firewall Port (Direction)	Internal Firewall Port (Direction)
Node4	FRECHI04	N/A	frechi04.contoso.com (10.18.10.5)	N/A	N/A
Node5	FRECHI05	N/A	frechi05.contoso.com (10.18.10.6)	N/A	N/A
Node6	FRECHI06	N/A	frechi06.contoso.com (10.18.10.7)	N/A	N/A
Mediation Server	MEDCHI01	Session Initiation Protocol (SIP)/Public Switched Telephone Network (PSTN) Gateway (GW) (not in DNS) (10.18.10.51)	medchi01.contoso.com (10.18.10.50)	N/A	N/A
SQL Server 2005 (cluster name)	SQLCHI01	N/A	sqlchi01.contoso.com VIP = (10.18.10.10)	N/A	N/A
SQL Nodes					
Node 1	BAECHI01	N/A	baechi01.contoso.com (10.18.10.11)	N/A	N/A
Node 2	BAECHI02	N/A	baechi02.contoso.com (10.18.10.12)	N/A	N/A
IIS Server (Load Balancer)	IISCHI	N/A	iischi.contoso.com VIP = (10.18.10.15)	N/A	N/A
IIS Nodes					
Node1	IISCHI01	N/A	iischi01.contoso.com (10.18.10.16)	N/A	N/A
Node2	IISCHI02	N/A	iischi02.contoso.com (10.18.10.17)	N/A	N/A
Web Conferencing Array					
Node1	WCSCHI01	N/A	wcschi01.contoso.com (10.18.10.20)	N/A	N/A
Node2	WCSCHI02	N/A	wcschi02.contoso.com (10.18.10.21)	N/A	N/A
Node3	WCSCHI03	N/A	wcschi03.contoso.com (10.18.10.22)	N/A	N/A
Node4	WCSCHI04	N/A	wcschi04.contoso.com (10.18.10.23)	N/A	N/A
A/V Conferencing Array					
Node1	AVCCHI01	N/A	avcchio01.contoso.com (10.18.10.24)	N/A	N/A
Node2	AVCCHI02	N/A	avcchio02.contoso.com (10.18.10.25)	N/A	N/A
Node3	AVCCHI03	N/A	avcchio03.contoso.com (10.18.10.26)	N/A	N/A
Node4	AVCCHI04	N/A	avcchio04.contoso.com (10.18.10.27)	N/A	N/A

Note that in Table 12-6, a total of seven IP addresses are used that point to the same two physical servers (the Access Edge Server and the Web Conferencing Edge Server). Here is a summary to further clarify the addressing scheme for these servers:

- One IP address for the Access Edge VIP (externally) = 64.65.66.1

- One IP address for the Access Edge VIP (internally) = 192.168.10.40
- One IP address for the Web Conferencing Edge VIP (externally) = 64.65.66.2
- Two IP addresses for the Web Conferencing Edge (externally) = 64.65.66.3 and 64.65.66.4 (these addresses are the node addresses and the VIPs point to them)
- Two IP addresses for the Web Conferencing Edge (internally) = 192.168.10.41 and 192.168.10.42 (since no Load Balancing of the Web Conferencing Edge roles is allowed internally)

Table 12-7 through Table 12-9 provide detailed views of the infrastructure requirements for the Access Edge Server and Web Conferencing Edge Server arrays in the Chicago perimeter network. An *array* is a set of servers running the same server roles.

Table 12-7 Details for Chicago—External Load Balancer for Co-located Access Edge Servers and Web Conferencing Edge Servers

Role/Feature	Quantity/Value(s)	Location/Setting	Note/Example
Load Balancer			
Access Edge Server	sip.contoso.com	Perimeter Network	Externally facing hardware Load Balancer with 2 VIPs.
Web Conferencing Edge Server	wcechi.contoso.com		
VIPs			
Access Edge Server VIP (external)	(1) 64.65.66.1	100-Mb Full	Virtual IP Address on the external Load Balancer for array of Access Edge Servers.
Web Conferencing Edge Server VIP (external)	(1) 64.65.66.2	100-Mb Full	Virtual IP Address on the external Load Balancer for array of Web Conferencing Edge Servers.
Ports			
Firewall (external)	443 TCP 5061 TCP	Inbound Bi-directional	Traffic from Internet → Access Edge Server external Load Balancer VIP (sip.contoso.com) and Web Conferencing Edge Server external Load Balancer VIP (wcechi.contoso.com). Traffic to/from Internet ↔ Access Edge Server external Load Balancer VIP (sip.contoso.com).
Certificates			
Certificate Name (CN)/Subject Name (SN)	N/A	N/A	N/A
DNS (Internal)			
(A)	N/A	N/A	N/A

Table 12-7 Details for Chicago—External Load Balancer for Co-located Access Edge Servers and Web Conferencing Edge Servers

Role/Feature	Quantity/Value(s)	Location/Setting	Note/Example
DNS (External)			
(A)	sip.contoso.com	64.65.66.1	
(A)	wcechi.contoso.com	64.65.66.2	

Table 12-8 Details for Chicago—Internal Load Balancer for Co-located Access Edge Servers and Web Conferencing Edge Servers

Role/Feature	Quantity/Value(s)	Location/Setting	Note/Example
Load Balancer			
Note: The internal edges of the Web Conferencing Edge Servers are not load balanced.			
Access Edge	access.contoso.com	Perimeter Network	Internally facing hardware Load Balancer with 1 VIP.
VIPs			
Access Edge VIP (internal)	(1) 192.168.10.40	100-Mb Full	Virtual IP Address on the internal Load Balancer for array of Access Edge Servers.
Ports			
Firewall (internal)	8057 TCP 5061 TCP	Outbound Bi-directional	Traffic from Director external Load Balancer VIP (dirchiext.contoso.com) → Web Conferencing Edge Server Node1 (cawchi01.contoso.com) and Node2 (cawchi02.contoso.com). Traffic to/from Access Edge Server internal Load Balancer VIP (access.contoso.com) ↔ Director external Load Balancer VIP (dirchiext.contoso.com).
Certificates			
CN/SN	N/A	N/A	N/A
DNS (Internal)			
(A)	access.contoso.com	192.168.10.40	
DNS (External)			
(A)	N/A	N/A	N/A

Table 12-9 Details for Chicago—Access Edge Servers and Web Conferencing Edge Servers

Role/Feature	Quantity/Value(s)	Location/Setting	Note/Example
Server			
Edge Server (Access Edge Server/Web Conferencing Edge Server)			
Node1	CAWCHI01	Perimeter Network	Workgroup Servers in the Perimeter Network. Each node is running both the Access Edge Server and Web Conferencing Edge Server roles.
Node2	CAWCHI02	Perimeter Network	
NICs			
Node1 (internal-facing)	(1) 192.168.10.41	100-Mb Full	
Node2 (internal-facing)	(1) 192.168.10.42	100-Mb Full	
Node1 (external-facing)	(1) 64.65.66.3	100-Mb Full	Both the Access Edge Server and Web Conferencing Edge Server roles can be behind a Network Address Translation (NAT) or port-forwarding firewall.
Node2 (external-facing)	(1) 64.65.66.4	100-Mb Full	
Ports			
Firewall (internal)	N/A	N/A	Access Edge Server/Web Conferencing Edge Server array will use ports opened for Access Edge Server internal Load Balancer VIP (access.contoso.com).
Firewall (external)	N/A	N/A	Access Edge Server/Web Conferencing Edge Server array will use ports opened for Access Edge Server external Load Balancer VIP (sip.contoso.com) and Web Conferencing Edge Server external Load Balancer VIP (wcechi.contoso.com).
Certificates			
CN/SN	access.contoso.com	Enhanced Key Usage (EKU): Server/Client	Exportable Machine certificate: Used for Client/Server Transport Layer Security (TLS)/Mutual Transport Layer Security (MTLS).

Table 12-9 Details for Chicago—Access Edge Servers and Web Conferencing Edge Servers

Role/Feature	Quantity/Value(s)	Location/Setting	Note/Example
Subject Alternative Name (SAN)	access.contoso.com sip.contoso.com sip.additionalSIPDomainName.com		First entry in the SAN must match the CN/SN of the certificate.
CN/SN	sip.contoso.com	EKU: Server/Client	Exportable Machine certificate: Used for Client/Server TLS/MTLS.
DNS (Internal)			
(A)	cawchi01.contoso.com	192.168.10.41	This is the internal FQDN of Access Edge Server/Web Conferencing Edge Server (Node1).
(A)	cawchi02.contoso.com	192.168.10.42	This is the internal FQDN of Access Edge Server/Web Conferencing Edge Server (Node2).
DNS (External)			
Note: Access Edge Server/Web Conferencing Edge Server Node1 and Node2 are not directly accessible externally. Use internal IP addresses for managing each node.			
(SRV)	_sip._tls.*domain* _sipfederationtls._tcp.*domain*	_tls for port 443 _tcp for port 5061	Example: _sip Service Location (SRV)[0][0][443]sip.contoso.com Example: _sipfederationtls Service Location (SRV)[0][0][5061]sip.contoso.com

Table 12-10 through Table 12-12 provide detailed views of the infrastructure requirements for the A/V Edge Server arrays in the Chicago perimeter network.

Table 12-10 Details for Chicago—External Load Balancer for A/V Edge Servers

Role/Feature	Quantity/Value(s)	Location/Setting	Note/Example
Load Balancer			
A/V Edge Server	avechi.contoso.com	Perimeter Network	Externally facing hardware Load Balancer with 1 VIP.
VIPs			
A/V Edge Server VIP (external)	(1) 64.65.66.15	100-Mb Full	Virtual IP Address on the external Load Balancer for array of A/V Edge Servers.

Table 12-10 Details for Chicago—External Load Balancer for A/V Edge Servers

Role/Feature	Quantity/Value(s)	Location/Setting	Note/Example
Ports			
Firewall (external)	443 TCP 3478 UDP 50,000–59,999 TCP and UDP	Inbound Inbound Bi-directional	Traffic from Internet → A/V Edge Server external Load Balancer VIP (avechi.contoso.com). Traffic from Internet → A/V Edge Server external Load Balancer VIP (avechi.contoso.com). Traffic to/from Internet ↔ A/V Edge Server external Load Balancer VIP (avechi.contoso.com). If you don't want to open the entire range of ports from 50,000 to 59,999, allow 6 ports for each concurrent external user.
Certificates			
CN/SN	N/A	N/A	N/A
DNS (Internal)			
(A)	N/A	N/A	N/A
DNS (External)			
(A)	avechi.contoso.com	64.65.66.15	

Table 12-11 Details for Chicago—Internal Load Balancer for A/V Edge Servers

Role/Feature	Quantity/Value(s)	Location/Setting	Note/Example
Load Balancer			
A/V Edge Server	avechi.contoso.com	Perimeter Network	Internally facing hardware Load Balancer with 1 VIP.
VIPs			
A/V Edge Server VIP (internal)	(1) 192.168.10.45	100-Mb Full	Virtual IP Address on the internal Load Balancer for array of Access Edge Servers.
Ports			
Firewall (internal)	443 TCP	Outbound	Traffic from Internal Network (all) → A/V Edge Server internal Load Balancer VIP (avechi.contoso.com).
	3478 UDP	Outbound	Traffic from Internal Network (all) → A/V Edge Server internal Load Balancer VIP (avechi.contoso.com).

Table 12-11 Details for Chicago—Internal Load Balancer for A/V Edge Servers

Role/Feature	Quantity/Value(s)	Location/Setting	Note/Example
	5062 TCP	Outbound	Traffic from Internal Network (all) → A/V Edge Server internal Load Balancer VIP (avechi.contoso.com). The internal firewall rule must allow traffic from any computer on the internal network that will be involved in audio/video calls or A/V conferencing to reach the A/V Edge Server internal Load Balancer VIP over all 3 ports.
Certificates			
CN/SN	N/A	N/A	N/A
DNS (Internal)			
(A)	avechi.contoso.com	192.168.10.45	
DNS (External)			
(A)	N/A	N/A	N/A

Table 12-12 Details for Chicago—A/V Edge Servers

Role/Feature	Quantity/Value(s)	Location/Setting	Note/Example
Server			
Edge Server (A/V Edge Server)			
Node1	AVECHI01	Perimeter Network	Workgroup servers in the Perimeter Network. Each node is running the A/V Edge Server role.
Node2	AVECHI02	Perimeter Network	
NICs			
Node1 (internal facing)	(1) 192.168.10.46	100-Mb Full	Set a persistent static route for the internal 10.0.0.0 network.
Node2 (internal facing)	(1) 192.168.10.47	100-Mb Full	Route add –p 10.0.0.0 mask 255.255.0.0 10.0.10.1

Table 12-12 Details for Chicago—A/V Edge Servers

Role/Feature	Quantity/Value(s)	Location/Setting	Note/Example
Node1 (external facing)	(1) 64.65.66.16	100-Mb Full	Must be a publicly addressable IP address. Can be behind a port-forwarding firewall but not translated with NAT.
Node2 (external facing)	(1) 64.65.66.17	100-Mb Full	Note: Default Gateway should be on the external NIC in each node and point to the Internet or you might not get audio on remote Office Communicator 2007/Office Communicator Phone Edition calls.
Ports			
Firewall (internal)	N/A	N/A	A/V Edge Server array will use ports opened for A/V Edge Server internal Load Balancer VIP (avechi.contoso.com).
Firewall (external)	N/A	N/A	A/V Edge Server array will use ports opened for A/V Edge Server external Load Balancer VIP (avechi.contoso.com).
Certificates			
CN/SN	avechi.contoso.com	EKU: Server	Exportable Machine certificate: Used for Client/Server TLS/MTLS.
CN/SN	avechiauth.contoso.com	EKU: Server	Exportable Authorization certificate: Used by the A/V Conferencing Edge Server to create Media Relay Access Server (MRAS) (which is part of the A/V Edge Server) access tokens. Not exposed to the client.
DNS (Internal)			
(A)	avechi01.contoso.com	192.168.10.46	This is the internal FQDN of A/V Edge Server (Node1).
(A)	avechi02.contoso.com	192.168.10.47	This is the internal FQDN of A/V Edge Server (Node2).
DNS (External)			
Note: External NICs in Node1 and Node2 are externally accessible only via the A/V Edge Server (external) Load Balancer VIP; use internal IP addresses for managing each node.			
(A)	N/A	N/A	N/A

Table 12-13 provides a detailed view of the infrastructure requirements for the HTTP Reverse Proxy Server in the Chicago perimeter network.

Table 12-13 Details for Chicago—HTTP Reverse Proxy Server

Role/Feature	Quantity/Value(s)	Location/Setting	Note/Example
Server			
HTTP Reverse Proxy Server	HTTCHI01	Perimeter Network	Workgroup server running ISA 2006 standard edition in the Perimeter Network.
NICs			
Internal	(1) 192.168.10.60	100-Mb Full	
External	(1) 64.65.66.30	100-Mb Full	The HTTP Reverse Proxy Server role can be behind a NAT or port-forwarding firewall.
Ports			
Note: If internal and external facing Internet Security and Acceleration (ISA) Server NICs reside in the perimeter network, port 443 needs to be open inbound from the ISA Server to the Office Communications Server 2007 Enterprise Edition Load Balancer VIP.			
Firewall (internal)	443 TCP	Inbound	Traffic from HTTP Reverse Proxy Server (httchi01.contoso.com) → Office Communications Server 2007 Enterprise Edition Load Balancer VIP (frechi.contoso.com).
Firewall (external)	443 TCP	Inbound	Traffic from Internet → HTTP Reverse Proxy Server (httchi01.contoso.com).
Certificates			
CN/SN	httchi01.contoso.com	EKU: Server	Exportable Machine certificate: Used for Client/Server TLS/MTLS.
SAN	N/A		First entry in the SAN must match the CN/SN of the certificate.
DNS (Internal)			
(A)	httchi01.contoso.com	192.168.10.60	This is the internal FQDN of the HTTP Reverse Proxy Server.
DNS (External)			
(A)	httchi01.contoso.com	64.65.66.30	This is the external FQDN of the HTTP Reverse Proxy Server.

Table 12-14 through Table 12-16 provide detailed views of the infrastructure requirements for the Director Servers in Chicago.

Table 12-14 **Details for Chicago—External Load Balancer for Director Servers**

Role/Feature	Quantity/Value(s)	Location/Setting	Note/Example
Load Balancer			
Director	dirchiext.contoso.com	Internal Network	Externally facing hardware Load Balancer with 1 VIP.
VIPs			
Director VIP (external)	(1) 10.18.10.33	100-Mb Full	Virtual IP Address on the external-facing Load Balancer for array of Director Servers.
Ports			
Firewall (internal)	5061 TCP	Bi-directional	Traffic to/from Access Edge Server internal Load Balancer VIP (access.contoso.com) ↔ Director Server internal Load Balancer VIP (dirchiext.contoso.com).
Certificates			
CN/SN	N/A	N/A	N/A
DNS (Internal)			
(A)	N/A	N/A	N/A
DNS (External)			
(A)	dirchiext.contoso.com	10.18.10.33	

Table 12-15 **Details for Chicago—Internal Load Balancer for Director Servers**

Role/Feature	Quantity/Value(s)	Location/Setting	Note/Example
Load Balancer			
Director	dirchi.contoso.com	Internal network	Internally facing hardware Load Balancer with 1 VIP.
VIPs			
Director VIP (internal)	(1) 10.18.10.32	100-Mb Full	Virtual IP Address on the internal-facing Load Balancer for array of Director Servers.
Ports			
Firewall (internal)	N/A	N/A	N/A
Certificates			
CN/SN	N/A	N/A	N/A
DNS (Internal)			
(A)	dirchi.contoso.com	10.18.10.32	
DNS (External)			
(A)	N/A	N/A	N/A

Table 12-16 **Details for Chicago—Director Server Array**

Role/Feature	Quantity/Value(s)	Location/Setting	Note/Example
Server			
Director Node1 Director Node2	DIRCHI01 DIRCHI02	Internal network Internal network	Domain members on the internal network. Each node is running a copy of Office Communications Server 2007 Standard Edition.
NICs			
Node1 (internal facing) Node2 (internal facing)	(1) 10.18.10.30 (1) 10.18.10.31	100-Mb Full 100-Mb Full	
Node1 (external facing) Node2 (external facing)	(1) 10.18.10.130 (1) 10.18.10.131	100-Mb Full 100-Mb Full	
Ports			
Internal	N/A		
Certificates			
CN/SN	dirchi.contoso.com	EKU: Server	Exportable machine certificate: Used for Client/Server TLS/MTLS. Note: Certficate should be issued for the FQDN of the Director Server internal Load Balancer VIP, not one of the Director Server nodes. Install the same certificate on both nodes.
SAN	N/A		First entry in the SAN must match the CN/SN of the certificate.
DNS (Internal)			
(A)	dirchi01.contoso.com	10.18.10.30	This is the internal FQDN of the Director Server (Node1).
(A)	dirchi02.contoso.com	10.18.10.30	This is the internal FQDN of the Director Server (Node2).
DNS (External)			
Note: Use the Internal NICs for accessing the Director nodes individually.			
(A)	N/A		

Table 12-17 and Table 12-18 provide detailed views of the infrastructure requirements for the expanded Office Communications Server 2007 Enterprise Edition pool in Chicago.

Table 12-17 Details for Chicago—Internal Load Balancer for Office Communications Server 2007 Enterprise Edition Front End Server Pool

Role/Feature	Quantity/Value(s)	Location/Setting	Note/Example
Load Balancer			
Office Communications Server 2007 Enterprise Edition Pool	frechi.contoso.com	Internal network	Hardware Load Balancer with 1 VIP; accessed by way of the Director.
VIPs			
EE Pool VIP (internal)	(1) 10.18.10.1	100-Mb Full	Virtual IP Address on the Load Balancer for the Office Communications Server 2007 Enterprise Edition Front End Servers.
Ports			
Firewall (internal)	N/A	N/A	N/A
Certificates			
CN/SN	N/A	N/A	N/A
DNS (Internal)			
(A)	frechi.contoso.com	10.18.10.1	
DNS (External)			
(A)	N/A	N/A	N/A

Table 12-18 Details for Chicago—Office Communications Server 2007 Enterprise Edition Front End Servers

Role/Feature	Quantity/Value(s)	Location/Setting	Note/Example
Server			
EE Front End Server			
Node1	frechi01.contoso.com	Internal network	Domain member Office Communications Server 2007 Enterprise Edition Expanded Pool. Each Front End Server in the pool is configured exactly the same way. The pool name is CHIPOOL01.
Node2	frechi02.contoso.com	Internal network	
Node3	frechi03.contoso.com	Internal network	
Node4	frechi04.contoso.com	Internal network	

Table 12-18 Details for Chicago—Office Communications Server 2007 Enterprise Edition Front End Servers

Role/Feature	Quantity/Value(s)	Location/Setting	Note/Example
Node5	frechi05.contoso.com	Internal network	
Node6	frechi06.contoso.com	Internal network	
NICs			
Node1 (internal)	(1) 10.18.10.2	100Mb Full	
Node2 (internal)	(1) 10.18.10.3	100Mb Full	
Node3 (internal)	(1) 10.18.10.4	100Mb Full	
Node4 (internal)	(1) 10.18.10.5	100Mb Full	
Node5 (internal)	(1) 10.18.10.6	100Mb Full	
Node6 (internal)	(1) 10.18.10.7	100Mb Full	
Ports			
Firewall (internal)	N/A	N/A	Office Communications Server 2007 Standard Edition (SE) and EE pool Servers never talk directly to the Access Edge Server when a Director is in place.
Firewall (external)	N/A	N/A	N/A
Certificates			
CN/SN	frechi.contoso.com	EKU: Server	Exportable machine certificate: Used for Client/Server TLS/MTLS.
SAN	frechi.contoso.com sip.contoso.com sip.additionalSIPDomainName.com		First entry in the SAN must match the CN/SN of the certificate.
DNS (Internal)			
(A)	frechi01.contoso.com	10.18.10.2	This is the internal FQDN of each EE Front End Server in the pool.
(A)	frechi02.contoso.com	10.18.10.3	
(A)	frechi03.contoso.com	10.18.10.4	
(A)	frechi04.contoso.com	10.18.10.5	
(A)	frechi05.contoso.com	10.18.10.6	
(A)	frechi06.contoso.com	10.18.10.7	

Table 12-18 Details for Chicago—Office Communications Server 2007 Enterprise Edition Front End Servers

Role/Feature	Quantity/Value(s)	Location/Setting	Note/Example
(SRV)	_sipinternal._tcp.*domain* _sipinternaltls._tcp.*domain*	_tcp for port 5061 _tcp for port 5061	Example: _sipinternal Service Location (SRV)[0][0][5061] frechi.contoso.com Example: _sipinternaltls Service Location (SRV)[0][0][5061] frechi.contoso.com
DNS (External)			
(A)	N/A		The Office Communications Server 2007EE Pool is not addressable externally accept via the Access Edge Server/Director Servers

Table 12-19 provides a detailed view of the infrastructure requirements for the Back End SQL cluster in the Chicago pool.

Table 12-19 Details for Chicago—Back End SQL Cluster

Role/Feature	Quantity/Value(s)	Location/Setting	Note/Example
Server			
SQL Server 2005 Cluster	sqlchi01.contoso.com	Internal network	This is the virtual name for the SQL Server 2005 cluster.
Node1	BAECHI01	Internal network	Domain member SQL Server (EE Pool back end).
Node2	BAECHI02	Internal network	Domain member SQL Server (EE Pool back end).
NICs			
Node1 (internal)	(1) 10.18.10.11	100-Mb Full	
Node2 (internal)	(1) 10.18.10.12	100-Mb Full	
Ports			
Internal	N/A		
Certificates			
CN/SN	N/A		
DNS (Internal)			
(A)	sqlchi01.contoso.com	10.18.10.10	This is the internal FQDN of the SQL Server 2005 cluster.
(A)	baechi01.contoso.com	10.18.10.11	This is the internal FQDN of the SQL Server 2005 Node1.
(A)	baechi01.contoso.com	10.18.10.12	This is the internal FQDN of the SQL Server 2005 Node2.

Table 12-19 Details for Chicago—Back End SQL Cluster

Role/Feature	Quantity/Value(s)	Location/Setting	Note/Example
DNS (External)			
(A)	N/A		The SQL Server 2005 server is not addressable externally.

Table 12-20 and Table 12-21 provide detailed views of the infrastructure requirements for the IIS Web Content Server array in Chicago.

Table 12-20 Details for Chicago—Internal Load Balancer for IIS Web Content Server Array

Role/Feature	Quantity/Value(s)	Location/Setting	Note/Example
Load Balancer			
IIS Web Content Server	iischi.contoso.com	Internal network	Hardware Load Balancer with 1 VIP.
VIPs			
EE Pool VIP (internal)	(1) 10.18.10.15	100-Mb Full	Virtual IP Address on the Load Balancer for the IIS Web content servers.
Ports			
Firewall (internal)	N/A	N/A	N/A
Certificates			
CN/SN	N/A	N/A	N/A
DNS (Internal)			
(A)	iischi.contoso.com	10.18.10.15	
DNS (External)			
(A)	N/A	N/A	N/A

Table 12-21 Details for Chicago—IIS Web Content Server Array

Role/Feature	Quantity/Value(s)	Location/Setting	Note/Example
Server			
IIS Web Content Server			
Node1	IISCHI01	Internal network	Domain member IIS Server (Web Content).
Node2	IISCHI02	Internal network	Domain member IIS Server (Web Content).
NICs			
Node1 (internal)	(1) 10.18.10.16	100-Mb Full	
Node2 (internal)	(1) 10.18.10.17	100-Mb Full	
Ports			
Internal	N/A		

Table 12-21 Details for Chicago—IIS Web Content Server Array

Role/Feature	Quantity/Value(s)	Location/Setting	Note/Example
Certificates			
CN/SN	N/A		
DNS (Internal)			
(A)	iischi01.contoso.com	10.18.10.16	This is the internal FQDN of IIS Web Content Server Node1.
(A)	iischi01.contoso.com	10.18.10.17	This is the internal FQDN of IIS Web Content Server Node2.
DNS (External)			
(A)	N/A		The IIS Web Content Server is not addressable externally.

Table 12-22 provides a detailed view of the infrastructure requirements for the Web Conferencing Server array in the Chicago pool.

Table 12-22 Details for Chicago—Web Conferencing Server Array

Role/Feature	Quantity/Value(s)	Location/Setting	Note/Example
Server			
Web Conferencing Server			Each node is a Domain member Web Conferencing Server, and they are all configured identically.
Node1	WCSCHI01	Internal network	
Node2	WCSCHI02	Internal network	
Node3	WCSCHI03	Internal network	
Node4	WCSCHI04	Internal network	
NICs			
Node1 (internal)	(1) 10.18.10.20	100-Mb Full	
Node2 (internal)	(1) 10.18.10.21	100-Mb Full	
Node3 (internal)	(1) 10.18.10.22	100-Mb Full	
Node4 (internal)	(1) 10.18.10.23	100-Mb Full	
Ports			
Internal	N/A	N/A	

Table 12-22 Details for Chicago—Web Conferencing Server Array

Role/Feature	Quantity/Value(s)	Location/Setting	Note/Example
Certificates			
CN/SN	wcschi01.contoso.com	EKU: Server	Exportable machine certificate: Used for Client/Server TLS/MTLS.
CN/SN	wcschi02.contoso.com	EKU: Server	Exportable machine certificate: Used for Client/Server TLS/MTLS.
CN/SN	wcschi03.contoso.com	EKU: Server	Exportable machine certificate: Used for Client/Server TLS/MTLS.
CN/SN	wcschi04.contoso.com	EKU: Server	Exportable machine certificate: Used for Client/Server TLS/MTLS.
SAN	N/A	N/A	
DNS (Internal)			
(A)	wcschi01.contoso.com	10.18.10.20	This is the internal FQDN of Web Conferencing Server Node1.
(A)	wcschi02.contoso.com	10.18.10.21	This is the internal FQDN of Web Conferencing Server Node2.
(A)	wcschi03.contoso.com	10.18.10.22	This is the internal FQDN of Web Conferencing Server Node3.
(A)	wcschi04.contoso.com	10.18.10.23	This is the internal FQDN of Web Conferencing Server Node4.
DNS (External)			
(A)	N/A	N/A	The Web Conferencing Server Array servers are not addressable externally.

Table 12-23 provides a detailed view of the infrastructure requirements for the A/V Conferencing Server array in the Chicago pool.

Table 12-23 Details for Chicago—A/V Conferencing Server Array

Role/Feature	Quantity/Value(s)	Location/Setting	Note/Example
Server			
Web Conferencing Server			Each node is a Domain member A/V Conferencing Server, and they are all configured identically.
Node1	AVCCHI01	Internal network	

Table 12-23 Details for Chicago—A/V Conferencing Server Array

Role/Feature	Quantity/Value(s)	Location/Setting	Note/Example
Node2	AVCCHI02	Internal network	
Node3	AVCCHI03	Internal network	
Node4	AVCCHI04	Internal network	
NICs			
Node1 (internal)	(1) 10.18.10.24	100-Mb Full	
Node2 (internal)	(1) 10.18.10.25	100-Mb Full	
Node3 (internal)	(1) 10.18.10.26	100-Mb Full	
Node4 (internal)	(1) 10.18.10.27	100-Mb Full	
Ports			
Internal	N/A	N/A	
Certificates			
CN/SN	avcchi01.contoso.com	EKU: Server	Exportable machine certificate: Used for Client/Server TLS/MTLS.
CN/SN	avcchi02.contoso.com	EKU: Server	Exportable machine certificate: Used for Client/Server TLS/MTLS.
CN/SN	avcchi03.contoso.com	EKU: Server	Exportable machine certificate: Used for Client/Server TLS/MTLS.
CN/SN	avcchi04.contoso.com	EKU: Server	Exportable machine certificate: Used for Client/Server TLS/MTLS.
SAN	N/A	N/A	
DNS (Internal)			
(A)	avcchi01.contoso.com	10.18.10.24	This is the internal FQDN of A/V Conferencing Server Node1.
(A)	avcchi02.contoso.com	10.18.10.25	This is the internal FQDN of A/V Conferencing Server Node2.
(A)	avcchi03.contoso.com	10.18.10.26	This is the internal FQDN of A/V Conferencing Server Node3.
(A)	avcchi04.contoso.com	10.18.10.27	This is the internal FQDN of A/V Conferencing Server Node4.
DNS (External)			
(A)	N/A	N/A	The A/V Conferencing Server Array servers are not addressable externally.

Table 12-24 provides a detailed view of the infrastructure requirements for the Mediation Server in Chicago.

Table 12-24 Details for Chicago—Mediation Server

Role/Feature	Quantity/Value(s)	Location/Setting	Note/Example
Server			
Mediation	medchi01.contoso.com	Internal network	Domain member running Office Communications Server 2007 Mediation Server role
NICs			
Internal	(1) 10.18.10.50	100-Mb Full	
External	(1) 10.18.10.51	100-Mb Full	Carries unsecured PSTN traffic; allows 64 Kbps per concurrent PSTN call.
Ports			
Internal Network	N/A		
Gateway Network	N/A		
Certificates			
CN/SN	medchi01.contoso.com	EKU: Server	Exportable machine certificate: Used for Server MTLS/SRTP.
SAN	medchi01.contoso.com sip.additionalSIPDomainName.com		First entry in the SAN must match the CN/SN of the certificate.
DNS (Internal)			
(A)	medchi01.contoso.com	10.18.10.50	This is the internal FQDN of the Mediation Server. (Ping resolves to this IP address.)
N/A	Not in DNS, but on internal network	10.18.10.51	This is the IP address used for Mediation Server ↔ SIP/PSTN GW communication. Considered an external interface by the Mediation Server.
DNS (External)			
(A)	N/A		

Important Contoso also installs the Edge Server certificates on the Office Communicator 2007 and Live Meeting 2007 client machines, as they need to have the certificates locally installed for all Remote User Access Scenarios.

Important Mediation Server does not need a certificate for communications with the Media Gateway, as this communication is not encrypted. However, a certificate has to be installed for the secure communication with Office Communications Server 2007.

Preparing DNS and Firewall Ports for the Paris Deployment

Table 12-25 contains the summary view of all infrastructure requirements for the deployment in Paris.

Table 12-25 Summary of Paris Infrastructure Requirements

Server Role	Name	External DNS Name (IP Address)	Internal DNS Name (IP Address)	External Firewall Port (Direction)	Internal Firewall Port (Direction)
Edge Server—Web Conferencing Edge Server	WCEPAR	wcepar.contoso.com Virtual IP Address (VIP) = (64.64.66.10)	wcepar.contoso.com Virtual IP Address (VIP) = (192.167.10.40)	443 TCP (Inbound) (Internet → Web Conferencing Edge Server)	8057 TCP (Outbound) (Office Communications Server 2007 Pool → Web Conferencing Edge Server)
Nodes (Access Edge Server/Web Conferencing Edge Server)					
Node1	WCEPAR01	N/A (64.64.66.11)	cawpar01.contoso.com (192.167.10.41)	N/A	N/A
Node2	WCEPAR02	N/A (64.64.66.12)	cawpar02.contoso.com (192.167.10.42)	N/A	N/A
Edge Server—A/V Edge Server (Load Balancer)	AVEPAR	avepar.contoso.com VIP = (64.64.66.15)	avepar.contoso.com VIP = (192.167.10.45)	443 TCP (Inbound) (Internet → A/V Edge Server) 3478 UDP (Inbound) (Internet → A/V Edge Server) 50,000–59,999 TCP and UDP (Both) (Internet ↔ A/V Edge Server)	443 TCP (Outbound) (Internal Net [all IPs] → A/V Edge Server) 3478 UDP (Outbound) (Internal Net [all IPs] → A/V Edge Server) 5062 TCP (Outbound) (Internal Net [all IPs] → A/V Edge Server)
Nodes (A/V Edge Server)					
Node1	AVEPAR01	N/A (64.64.66.16)	avepar01.contoso.com (192.167.10.46)	N/A	N/A
Node2	AVEPAR02	N/A (64.64.66.17)	avepar02.contoso.com (192.167.10.47)	N/A	N/A

Table 12-25 Summary of Paris Infrastructure Requirements

Server Role	Name	External DNS Name (IP Address)	Internal DNS Name (IP Address)	External Firewall Port (Direction)	Internal Firewall Port (Direction)
HTTP Reverse Proxy Server	HTTPAR01	httpar01.contoso.com (64.64.66.30)	httpar01.contoso.com (192.167.10.60)	443 TCP (Inbound) Internet → HTTP Reverse Proxy Server	443 TCP (Inbound) HTTP Reverse Proxy Server → Office Communications Server 2007 Pool
EE Expanded Pool	PARPOOL01	N/A	parpool01.contoso.com (10.17.10.1)	N/A	N/A
EE (Load Balancer)	FREPAR	N/A	frepar.contoso.com VIP = (10.17.10.1) _sipinternal._tcp.*domain* (SRV) 5061 parpool01.contoso.com _sipinternaltls._tcp.*domain* (SRV) 5061 parpool01.contoso.com	N/A	N/A
EE Front End Servers					
Node1	FREPAR01	N/A	frepar01.contoso.com (10.17.10.2)	N/A	N/A
Node2	FREPAR02	N/A	frepar02.contoso.com (10.17.10.3)	N/A	N/A
Node3	FREPAR03	N/A	frepar03.contoso.com (10.17.10.4)	N/A	N/A
Node4	FREPAR04	N/A	frepar04.contoso.com (10.17.10.5)	N/A	N/A
SQL Server 2005 (cluster name)	SQLPAR01	N/A	sqlpar01.contoso.com VIP = (10.17.10.10)	N/A	N/A
SQL Nodes					
Node1	BAEPAR01	N/A	baepar01.contoso.com (10.17.10.11)	N/A	N/A
Node2	BAEPAR02	N/A	baepar02.contoso.com (10.17.10.12)	N/A	N/A
IIS Server (Load Balancer)	IISPAR	N/A	iispar.contoso.com VIP = (10.17.10.15)	N/A	N/A
IIS Nodes					
Node1	IISPAR01	N/A	iispar01.contoso.com (10.17.10.16)	N/A	N/A
Node2	IISPAR02	N/A	iispar02.contoso.com (10.17.10.17)	N/A	N/A
Web Conferencing Server Array					
Node1	WCSPAR01	N/A	wcspar01.contoso.com (10.17.10.20)	N/A	N/A
Node2	WCSPAR02	N/A	wcspar02.contoso.com (10.17.10.21)	N/A	N/A

Table 12-25 Summary of Paris Infrastructure Requirements

Server Role	Name	External DNS Name (IP Address)	Internal DNS Name (IP Address)	External Firewall Port (Direction)	Internal Firewall Port (Direction)
A/V Conferencing Server Array					
Node1	AVCPAR01	N/A	avcpar01.contoso.com (10.17.10.24)	N/A	N/A
Node2	AVCPAR02	N/A	avcpar02.contoso.com (10.17.10.25)	N/A	N/A

Preparing DNS and Firewall Ports for the Madrid Deployment

Table 12-26 contains the summary view of all infrastructure requirements for the deployment in Madrid.

Table 12-26 Summary of Madrid Infrastructure Requirements

Server Role	Name	External DNS Name (IP Address)	Internal DNS Name (IP Address)	External Firewall Port (Direction)	Internal Firewall Port (Direction)
EE Consolidated Pool	MADPOOL01	N/A	madpool01.contoso.com (10.16.10.1)	N/A	N/A
EE (Load Balancer)	FREMAD	N/A	fremad.contoso.com VIP = (10.16.10.1) _sipinternal._tcp.*domain* (SRV) 5061 madpool01.contoso.com _sipinternaltls._tcp.*domain* (SRV) 5061 madpool01.contoso.com	N/A	N/A
EE Front End Servers					
Node1	FECMAD01	N/A	fecmad01.contoso.com (10.16.10.2)	N/A	N/A
Node2	FECMAD02	N/A	fecmad02.contoso.com (10.16.10.3)	N/A	N/A
Mediation Server	MEDMAD01	Session Initiation Protocol (SIP)/Public Switched Telephone Network (PSTN) Gateway (GW) (not in DNS) (10.16.10.51)	medchi01.contoso.com (10.16.10.50)	N/A	N/A
SQL Server 2005 (non-clustered)	BAEMAD01	N/A	baemad01.contoso.com (10.16.10.11)	N/A	N/A
Exchange 2007 UM, Mailbox Server (MBX), Client Access Server (CAS), and Hub Transport Server (HUB) Server	EXUMAD01	N/A	exumad01.contoso.com (10.16.10.70)	N/A	N/A
Archiving Server	ARCMAD01	N/A	arcmad01.contoso.com (10.16.10.80)	N/A	N/A

Preparing DNS and Firewall Ports for the Singapore Deployment

Table 12-27 contains the summary view of all infrastructure requirements for the deployment in Singapore.

Table 12-27 Summary of Singapore Infrastructure Requirements

Server Role	Name	External DNS Name (IP Address)	Internal DNS Name (IP Address)	External Firewall Port (Direction)	Internal Firewall Port (Direction)
Edge Server—Web Conferencing Edge Server	WCESPO	wcespo.contoso.com (64.62.66.11)	wcespo01.contoso.com (192.165.10.41)	443 TCP (Inbound) (Internet → Web Conferencing Edge Server)	8057 TCP (Outbound) (Office Communications Server 2007 Pool → Web Conferencing Edge Server)
Edge Server—A/V Edge Server (Load Balancer)	AVESPO	avespo.contoso.com (64.62.66.16)	avespo01.contoso.com (192.165.10.46)	443 TCP (Inbound) (Internet → A/V Edge Server)	443 TCP (Outbound) (Internal Network [all IPs] → A/V Edge Server)
				3478 UDP (Inbound) (Internet → A/V Edge Server)	3478 UDP (Outbound) (Internal Network [all IPs] → A/V Edge Server)
				50,000–59,999 TCP and UDP (Both) (Internet ↔ A/V Edge Server)	5062 TCP (Outbound) (Internal Network [all IPs] → A/V Edge Server)
HTTP Reverse Proxy Server	HTTSPO01	httspo01.contoso.com (64.62.66.30)	httspo01.contoso.com (192.165.10.60)	443 TCP (Inbound) Internet → HTTP Reverse Proxy Server	443 TCP (Inbound) HTTP Reverse Proxy Server → Office Communications Server 2007 Pool
EE Consolidated Pool	SPOPOOL01	N/A	spopool01.contoso.com (10.15.10.1)	N/A	N/A
EE (Load Balancer)	FRESPO	N/A	frespo.contoso.com VIP = (10.15.10.1) _sipinternal._tcp.*domain* (SRV) 5061 spopool01.contoso.com _sipinternaltls._tcp.*domain* (SRV) 5061 spopool01.contoso.com	N/A	N/A
EE Front End Servers					
Node1	FECSPO01	N/A	fecspo01.contoso.com (10.15.10.2)	N/A	N/A
Node2	FECSPO02	N/A	fecspo02.contoso.com (10.15.10.3)	N/A	N/A
Node3	FECSPO03	N/A	fecspo03.contoso.com (10.15.10.4)	N/A	N/A
Node4	FECSPO04	N/A	fecspo04.contoso.com (10.15.10.5)	N/A	N/A
SQL Server 2005 (non-clustered)	BAESPO01	N/A	baespo01.contoso.com (10.15.10.11)	N/A	N/A

Contoso's Deployment Path for Chicago

After preparing the server hardware and surrounding infrastructure–such as DNS and firewall configuration–Contoso can begin its Office Communications Server 2007 deployment. Contoso decides to start with the deployment in the Chicago headquarters and follows the deployment path presented in Table 12-28. For each server role deployment, Contoso reads the information in the corresponding Office Communications Server 2007 deployment guides.

Table 12-28 Deployment Path for Chicago

Step	Server	Action
1	SQLCHI01	Install SQL Cluster.
2	BAECHI01	Install SQL Back End.
3	BAECHI02	Install SQL Back End.
4	SQLCHI01	Deploy Office Communications Server 2007 Back End Server.
5	FRECHI	Install pool Load Balancer.
6	FRECHI01	Install FRECHI01.
7		Install one Office Communicator 2007 client to test.
8	FRECHI02	Install FRECHI02.
9	FRECHI03	Install FRECHI03.
10	FRECHI04	Install FRECHI04.
11	FRECHI05	Install FRECHI05.
12	FRECHI06	Install FRECHI06.
13		Test Office Communicator 2007 Client Instant Messaging access first with one or more Front End Servers offline and then with all of them online.
14	DIRCHI	Install inside (pool-facing) Load Balancer Director.
15		Install outside (edge-facing) Load Balancer Director.
16	DIRCHI01	Install DIRCHI01.
17	DIRCHI02	Install DIRCHI02.
18		Test Office Communicator 2007 Client Instant Messaging access first with one Director Server offline and then with all of them online.
19	IISCHI	Install Load Balancer IIS.
20	IISCHI01	Install IISCHI01.
21	IISCHI02	Install IISCHI02.
22	HTTCHI01	Install HTTCHI01.
23		Test Office Communicator 2007 Client Group Expansion and Global Address List download first with one IIS offline and then with both online.
24	WCSCHI01	Install WCSCHI01.
25	WCSCHI02	Install WCSCHI02.
26	WCSCHI03	Install WCSCHI03.

Table 12-28 **Deployment Path for Chicago**

Step	Server	Action
27	WCSCHI04	Install WCSCHI04.
28		Install one Live Meeting 2007 client to test Web Conferencing Servers first with one or more Web Conferencing Servers offline and then with all of them online.
29	AVCCHI01	Install AVCHI01.
30	AVCCHI02	Install AVCHI02.
31	AVCCHI03	Install AVCHI03.
32	AVCCHI04	Install AVCHI04.
33		Test LiveMeeting 2007 and Office Communicator 2007 A/V Conferencing Servers first with one or more A/V Conferencing Servers offline and then with all of them online.
34	CAWCHI	Install internal Load Balancer Access Edge Server/Web Conferencing Edge Server.
35		Install external Load Balancer Access Edge Server/Web Conferencing Edge Server.
36	CAWCHI01	Install CAWCHI01.
37	CAWCHI02	Install CAWCHI02.
38		Test Office Communicator 2007 Client Instant Messaging external access first with one or more Access Edge Servers offline and then with all of them online.
39		Test Live Meeting 2007 client external Web Conferencing Edge Server access first with one or more Web Conferencing Edge Servers offline and then with all of them online.
40	AVECHI	Install internal Load Balancer A/V Edge Server.
41		Install external Load Balancer A/V Edge Server.
42	AVECHI01	Install AVECHI01.
43	AVECHI02	Install AVECHI02.
44		Test Office Communicator 2007 Client A/V Edge Server external access first with one or more A/V Edge Servers offline and then with all of them online.
45		Test Live Meeting 2007 client external A/V Edge Server access first with one or more A/V Edge Servers offline and then with all of them online.
46	MEDCHI01	Install MEDCHI01.
47		Install SIP/PSTN Gateway.
48		Test Office Communicator 2007 client by placing and receiving PSTN calls.

When configuring the Enterprise Voice Scenario in Chicago, Contoso configures Location Profiles, Phone Usages, and Routes that are needed later in the deployment process for the Madrid Enterprise Voice users together with the configuration for the Chicago Enterprise Voice users. The following sidebar explains Contoso's Enterprise Voice configuration.

Working with Enterprise Voice Route Helper

When Contoso starts implementing Enterprise Voice for the users in Madrid and Chicago, it is necessary to configure Enterprise Voice. This involves creating location profiles, phone normalization rules, policies, phone usages, and routes. It can be done using the Office Communications Server 2007 Microsoft Management Console (MMC) snap-in, but it can also be done using the Office Communications Server 2007 Resource Kit utility Enterprise Voice Route Helper.

Enterprise Voice Route Helper enables you to create and test the Enterprise Voice configuration and, when it is correct, upload it to the live environment. It provides a graphical user interface (GUI) to help with the creation of regular expressions used in phone normalization rules and routing. It also can save test cases and rerun them when the configuration changes.

Before you start configuring Enterprise Voice, you need to understand the requirements for making phone calls, who should be able to dial which phone numbers, and the routing of the calls. In the following lists are the requirements identified by Contoso.

Requirements for Madrid

The requirements for Madrid can be summarized as follows:

- Direct-Inward Dialing (DID) range +34 9112345 001 through +34 9112345 999.
- Internal extension to be dialed directly with 3 digits.
- To dial an external national number, first press 0.
- To dial an external international number, first press 000 or +.
- All employees are allowed to dial extensions and to dial nationally.
- Some employees are allowed to dial extensions, dial nationally, and dial internationally.
- Service numbers in Madrid include the following:
  - Helpdesk: 444
  - Travel Service: 666
- Routing:
  - Calls to numbers in the U.S. and Canada should use the PSTN break-out point in Chicago via the Mediation Server in Chicago (MEDCHI01).
  - Calls to numbers in Spain should use the PSTN break-out point in Madrid via the Mediation Server in Madrid (MEDMAD01).
  - Calls to the rest of the world should use the PSTN break-out point in Madrid via the Mediation Server in Madrid (MEDMAD01).

Requirements for Chicago

The requirements for Chicago can be summarized as follows:

- DID range +1 312 55 10001 through +1 312 55 89999.
- Internal extensions to be dialed directly with 5 digits.
- To dial an external local number in Chicago, first press 9 and then 10 digits.
- To dial an external national number (long distance), first press 91 and then 10 digits.
- To dial an external international number, first press 9011 or + and then the country code and number.
- Users have phone numbers stored for their Microsoft Office Outlook Contacts in both E.164 format or just as 10 digits without the leading 91.
- All employees are allowed to dial extensions and national calls.
- Some employees are allowed to dial extensions, dial national, and dial internationally.
- Service numbers in Chicago include the following:
  - Helpdesk: 55555–Should call the helpdesk number in Madrid
  - Travel Service: 666
- Routing:
  - Calls to numbers in the U.S. and Canada should use the PSTN break-out point in Chicago via the Mediation Server in Chicago (MEDCHI01).
  - Calls to numbers in Spain should use the PSTN break-out point in Madrid via the Mediation Server in Madrid (MEDMAD01).
  - Calls to numbers in France, Denmark, and Sweden should use the PSTN break-out point in Madrid via the Mediation Server in Madrid (MEDMAD01).
  - Calls to the rest of the world should use the PSTN break-out point in Chicago via the Mediation Server in Chicago (MEDCHI01).

Creating the Location Profile by Adding Phone Normalization Rules

Let's now go through the Enterprise Voice configuration for Chicago using Enterprise Voice Route Helper. Configuration for Madrid is left up to the reader.

The first step is to create the necessary location profile for Chicago. To do this, right-click in the Location Profile section of Enterprise Voice Route Helper and select New Location Profile, to get the following window:

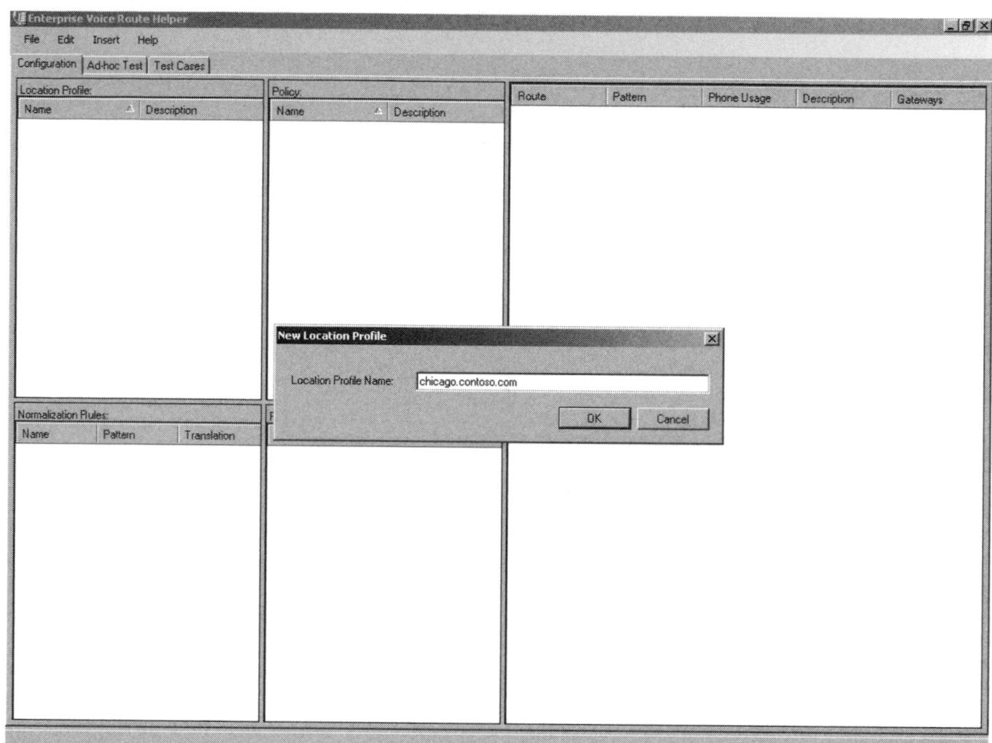

Clicking OK brings up the Location Profile Editor, where we can start adding phone normalization rules:

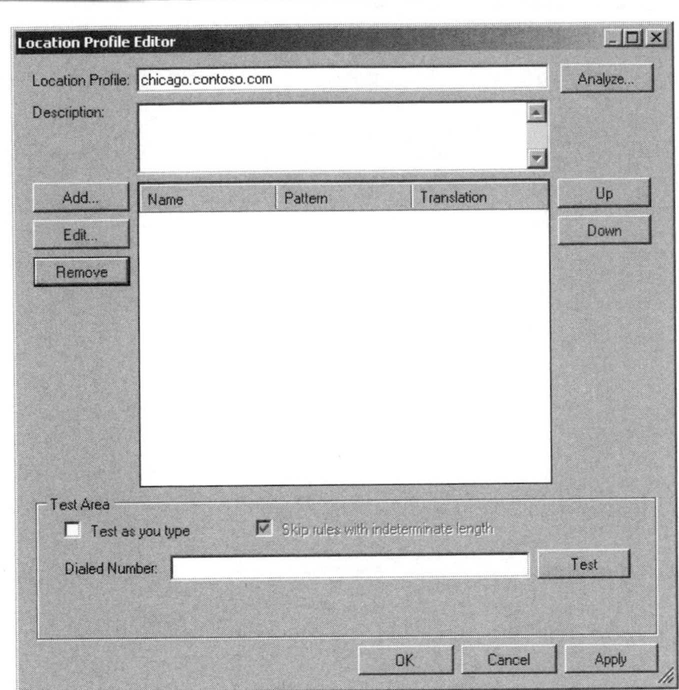

When defining the phone normalization rules, it is important to understand the two main uses of the rules: to convert dialed numbers to the E.164 format, and to enable the Quick Dial experience of the Office Communicator Phone Experience device. The Quick Dial experience entails the device automatically dialing the number when it understands, based on the phone normalization rules, that the last digit in the number has been pressed. It is important to implement phone normalization rules so that users can dial the various number formats without being negatively affected by Quick Dial behaviors–for example, users should be able to dial an external national number without the device starting to dial the number after the last digit in an extension is pressed.

Let's implement the phone normalization rules for Chicago based on the dialing requirements just mentioned. The following screen shot shows the definition of the phone normalization rule that converts extensions in Chicago to the full E.164 phone number:

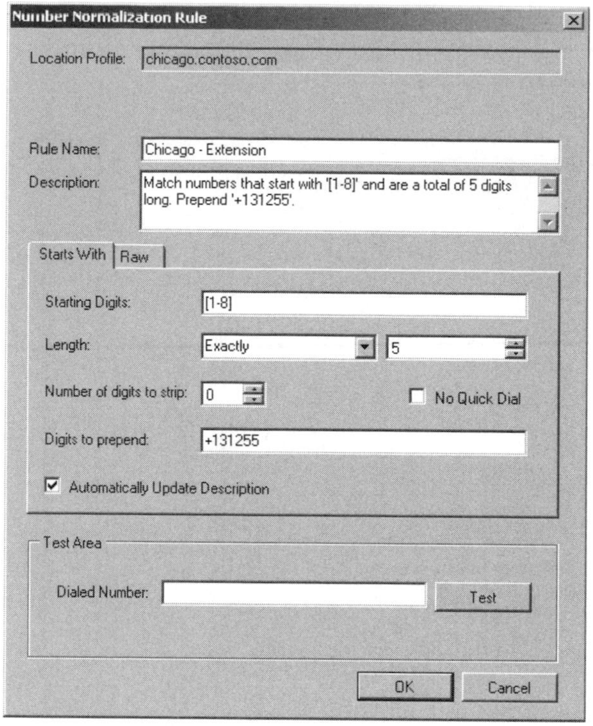

Number Normalization Rule

Location Profile: chicago.contoso.com

Rule Name: Chicago - Extension

Description: Match numbers that start with '[1-8]' and are a total of 5 digits long. Prepend '+131255'.

Starts With | Raw

Starting Digits: [1-8]

Length: Exactly 5

Number of digits to strip: 0

No Quick Dial

Digits to prepend: +131255

Automatically Update Description

Test Area

Dialed Number: Test

OK Cancel

Because the phone normalization rule names need to be unique within the Active Directory forest, all the names have "Chicago -" prepended. Also, please note the string "[1-8]" in the Starting Digits field. The string means any digit in the range 1 through 8 (that is, excluding 0 and 9). The digits 0 and 9 are excluded because they are not part of the DID range. Please also note that the rule is marked as being available for Quick Dial.

All the phone normalization rules used in Chicago are shown in the next screen shot:

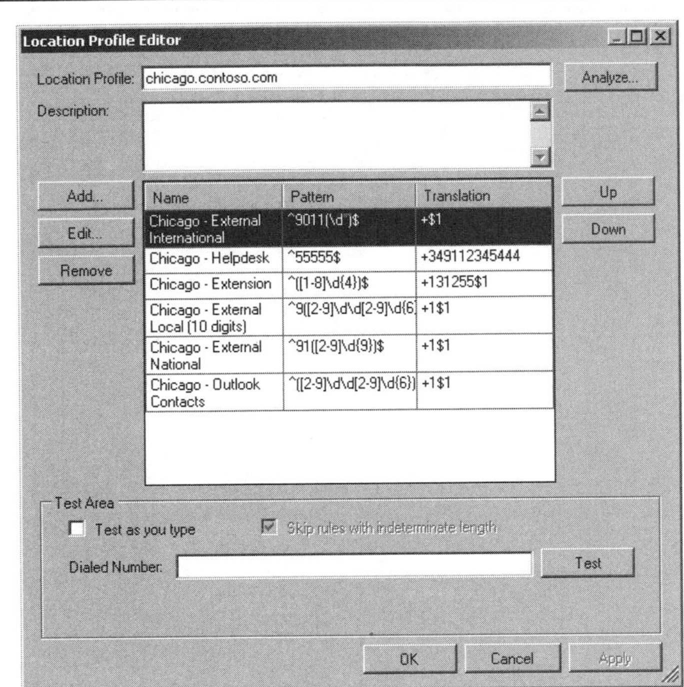

Let's look at the phone normalization rules in more detail. They are listed in Table 12-29 with a comment describing each rule.

Table 12-29 Contoso Normalization Rules

Name	Pattern	Translation	Quick Dial	Example	Comment
Chicago - External International	^9011(\d*)$	+$1	Yes	Dialed: 90114512345678 Translation: +4512345678	Any number starting with 9011 identifies an international number. Strip 9011 and prepend a plus sign (+).
Chicago - Helpdesk	^55555$	+349112345444	Yes	Dialed: 55555 Translation: +349112345444	Direct translation of the helpdesk extension to the E.164 number of the helpdesk in Madrid.
Chicago - Extension	^([1-8]\d{4})$	+131255$1	Yes	Dialed: 12345 Translation: +13125512345	Any extension in Chicago translated to the E.164 number.

Table 12-29 Contoso Normalization Rules

Name	Pattern	Translation	Quick Dial	Example	Comment
Chicago - External Local (10 digits)	^9([2-9]\d\d[2-9]\d{6})$	+1$1	Yes	Dialed: 97735550113 Translated: +17735550113	Dial 9 to get an external line. The 4-digit pattern following uses the fact that in the U.S. 10-digit numbers never have 0 or 1 in the first and fourth digits.
Chicago - External National	^91([2-9]\d{9})$	+1$1	Yes	Dialed: 914255550179 Translated: +14255550179	Long-distance call starts with 91, and then the next digit is not 0 or 1.
Chicago - Outlook Contacts	^([2-9]\d\d[2-9]\d{6})t?$	+1$1	No	Dialed: 4255550179 Translated: +14255550179	Uses the rules mentioned about U.S. 10-digit numbers. The t? pattern at the end means that this rule will not be used for Quick Dial.

To test Quick Dial, you can use the "Test as you type" feature of Enterprise Voice Route Helper by typing a number in the Dialed Number field near the bottom of the window and clicking the Test button. In the following screen shot, the testing of the helpdesk is shown:

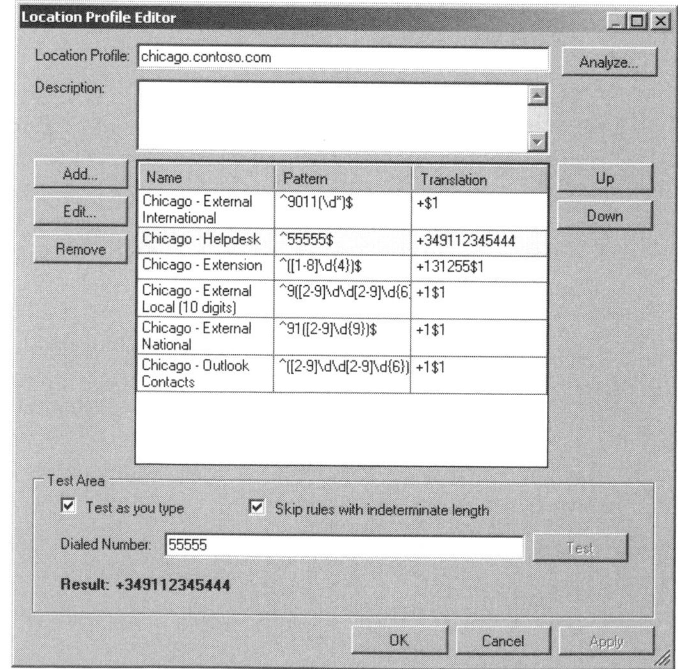

In the following screen shot, the testing of a long-distance number is shown:

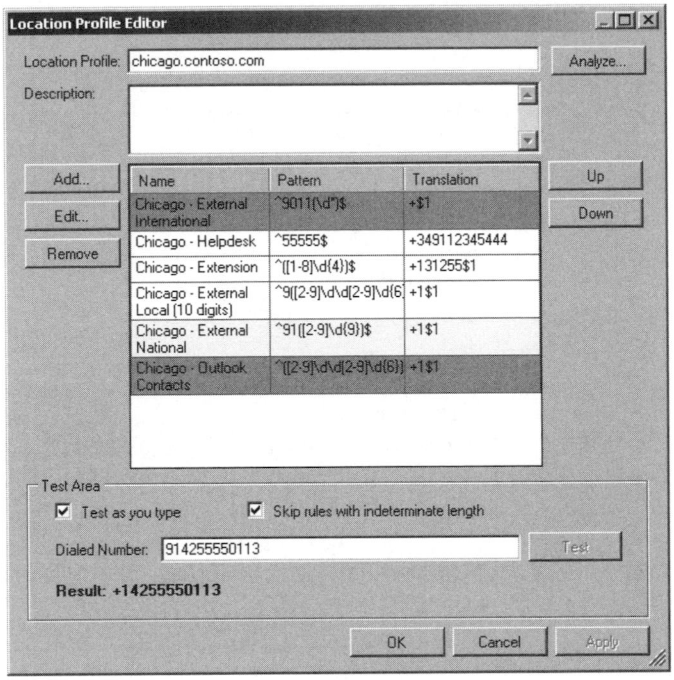

Creating Policies by Adding Phone Usage Records and Routes

In Chicago, there are two types of employees: some are allowed to dial only extensions and nationally, and some are allowed to make local, national, and international calls. Therefore, it is necessary to create two policies, which we'll call *Chicago - Restricted* and *Chicago - Unrestricted*.

A policy contains one or more Phone Usage records. A Phone Usage record contains one or more Routes. These two concepts are used to implement rules about who is allowed to make what kind of phone calls and where the calls should be routed.

For the employees in Chicago, we need four Phone Usage records, which are shown in Table 12-30. The Gateway column specifies the Mediation Server in either Chicago (MEDCHI01) or Madrid (MEDMAD01).

Table 12-30 Contoso Routes

<table>
<tr><th>Phone Usage Name</th><th>Pattern</th><th>Route(s)</th><th>Gateway (Mediation Server)</th><th>Comment</th></tr>
<tr><td>Chicago - Restricted</td><td>^\+1</td><td>Chicago PSTN break-out: Restricted</td><td>MEDCHI01</td><td>All calls to the U.S. and Canada</td></tr>
<tr><td>Madrid - Helpdesk</td><td>^\+349112345444</td><td>Madrid Help-desk</td><td>MEDMAD01</td><td>Calls to the help desk in Madrid</td></tr>
<tr><td>Chicago - Unrestricted</td><td>^(?!((\+34)|(\+45)|(\+33)|(\+46)))</td><td>Chicago PSTN break-out: Unrestricted</td><td>MEDCHI01</td><td>All calls, except calls to Spain (+34), Denmark (+45), France (+33), and Sweden (+46)</td></tr>
<tr><td>Chicago - Unrestricted</td><td>^((\+34)|(\+45)|(\+33)|(\+46))</td><td>Madrid PSTN break-out: Unrestricted</td><td>MEDMAD01</td><td>All calls to Spain, Denmark, France, and Sweden</td></tr>
</table>

The Chicago – Restricted policy contains the following Phone Usage records: Chicago – Restricted (to enable calls to the U.S. and Canada), and Madrid – Helpdesk (to allow calls to the help desk in Madrid). The Chicago – Unrestricted policy contains the Phone Usage record Chicago – Unrestricted.

Testing the Enterprise Voice Configuration

The Enterprise Voice configuration for Chicago is now done. One of the other very nice features of Enterprise Voice Route Helper is the ability to have ad hoc and saved test cases and to run these against the configuration. When testing, it is important to test the phone normalization rules, permissions, and routes. Table 12-31 shows relevant test cases for the Enterprise Voice configuration in Chicago.

Table 12-31 Contoso Routing Test Cases

Dialed Number	Normalized Number	Policy	Expected Route	Comment
90114512345678	+4512345678	Chicago - Unrestricted	MEDCHI01	Allowed to make international calls.
90114512345678	+4512345678	Chicago - Restricted	No route	Not allowed to make international calls.
+4512345678	+4512345678	Chicago - Unrestricted	MEDCHI01	Allowed to make international calls.

Table 12-31 Contoso Routing Test Cases

Dialed Number	Normalized Number	Policy	Expected Route	Comment
+4512345678	+4512345678	Chicago - Restricted	No route	Not allowed to make international calls.
55555	+349112345444	Chicago - Unrestricted	MEDMAD01	Allowed to make help desk calls.
55555	+349112345444	Chicago - Restricted	MEDMAD01	Allowed to make help desk calls.
50116	+13125550116	Chicago - Unrestricted	MEDCHI01	Allowed to make calls to extensions. In real life, this call is routed directly to the Unified Communications–enabled user and not out via the gateway.
50116	+13125550116	Chicago - Restricted	MEDCHI01	Allowed to make calls to extensions. In real life, this call is routed directly to the Unified Communications–enabled user and not out via the gateway.
97735550113	+17735550113	Chicago - Unrestricted	MEDCHI01	Allowed to make local calls.
97735550113	+17735550113	Chicago - Restricted	MEDCHI01	Allowed to make local calls.
4255550179	+14255550179	Chicago - Unrestricted	MEDCHI01	Allowed to make national calls.
4255550179	+14255550179	Chicago - Restricted	MEDCHI01	Allowed to make national calls.

On the CD The sample RouteHelper Configuration file and RouteHelper Testcase file for the Contoso Chicago office are available on the companion CD in the \Appendixes,Scripts,Resources\Chapter 12 folder.

–Jens Trier Rasmussen
Principal Consultant II, Microsoft Corporation

Contoso's Deployment Path for Paris

The next location to be configured after the Chicago deployment in Contoso's Office Communications Server 2007 deployment is Paris. Contoso decides to deploy in the order described in Table 12-32.

Table 12-32 Deployment Path for Paris

Step	Server	Action
1	SQLPAR01	Install SQL Cluster.
2	BAEPAR01	Install SQL Back End.
3	BAEPAR02	Install SQL Back End.
4	SQLPAR01	Deploy Office Communications Server 2007 Back End Server.
5	FREPAR	Install pool Load Balancer.
6	FREPAR01	Install FREPAR01.
7		Install one Office Communicator 2007 client to test.
8	FREPAR02	Install FREPAR02.
9	FREPAR03	Install FREPAR03.
10	FREPAR04	Install FREPAR04.
11		Test Office Communicator 2007 Client Instant Messaging access first with one or more Front End Servers offline and then with all of them online.
12	IISPAR	Install Load Balancer IIS.
13	IISPAR01	Install IISPAR01.
14	IISPAR02	Install IISPAR02.
15	HTTPAR01	Install HTTPAR01.
16		Test the Office Communicator 2007 Client Group Expansion and Global Address List download first with one IIS server offline and then with both online.
17	WCSPAR01	Install WCSPAR01.
18	WCSPAR02	Install WCSPAR02.
19		Install one Live Meeting 2007 client to test the Web Conferencing Server first with one or more Web Conferencing Servers offline and then with all of them online.
20	AVCPAR01	Install AVCPAR01.
21	AVCPAR02	Install AVCPAR02.
22		Test LiveMeeting 2007 and the Office Communicator 2007 A/V Conferencing Server first with one or more A/V Conferencing Servers offline and then with all of them online.
23	WCEPAR	Install internal Load Balancer Web Conferencing Edge Server.
24		Install external Load Balancer Web Conferencing Edge Server.
25	WCEPAR01	Install WCEPAR01.

Table 12-32 Deployment Path for Paris

Step	Server	Action
26	WCEPAR02	Install WCEPAR02.
27		Test the Live Meeting 2007 client external Web Conferencing Server access first with one or more Web Conferencing Edge Servers offline and then with all of them online.
28	AVEPAR	Install the internal Load Balancer A/V Edge Server.
29		Install the external Load Balancer A/V Edge Server.
30	AVEPAR01	Install AVEPAR01.
31	AVEPAR02	Install AVEPAR02.
32		Test the Office Communicator 2007 Client A/V Edge Server external access first with one or more A/V Edge Servers offline and then with all of them online.
33		Test the Live Meeting 2007 client external A/V Edge Server access first with one or more A/V Edge Servers offline and then with all of them online.

Contoso's Deployment Path for Madrid

After the Chicago and Paris deployments, Contoso proceeds with the Madrid deployment by following the deployment path described in Table 12-33.

Table 12-33 Deployment Path for Madrid

Step	Server	Action
1	BAEMAD01	Install BAEMAD01.
2	FREMAD	Install pool Load Balancer.
3	FECMAD01	Install FECMAD01.
4		Install one Office Communicator 2007 client to test.
5	FECMAD02	Install FECMAD02.
6		Test Office Communicator 2007 Client Instant Messaging access first with one or more Front End Servers offline and then with all of them online.
7	MEDMAD01	Install MEDMAD01.
8		Install the SIP/PSTN Gateway.
9		Test the Office Communicator 2007 client by placing and receiving PSTN calls.
10	EXUMAD01	Install EXUMAD01.
11		Test Office Communicator 2007 client access and forward to VoiceMail. Test external access to VoiceMail.
12	ARCMAD01	Install ARCMAD01.
13		Test whether the Archiving Server works by using Office Communicator 2007 Instant Messaging.

Archiving CDR (Call Detail Record) Reporter

Archiving CDR (Call Detail Record) Reporter, an Office Communications Server 2007 Resource Kit tool that is found on the Companion CD for this title, helps you to access and summarize the data from the various tables in the Archiving database. At first, a database has to be selected from which the tool can collect the data:

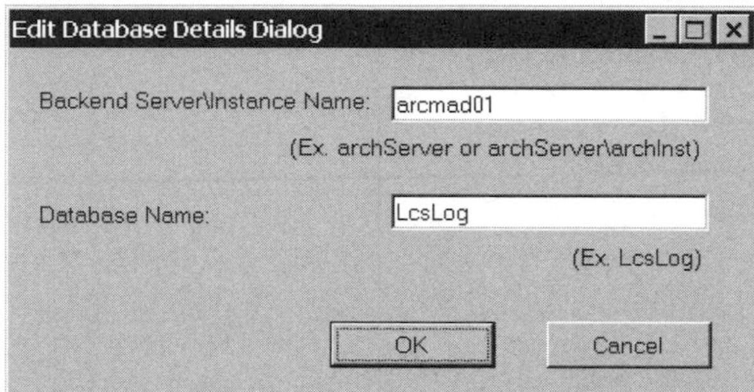

Once opened, the Archiving CDR Reporter tool displays available reports:

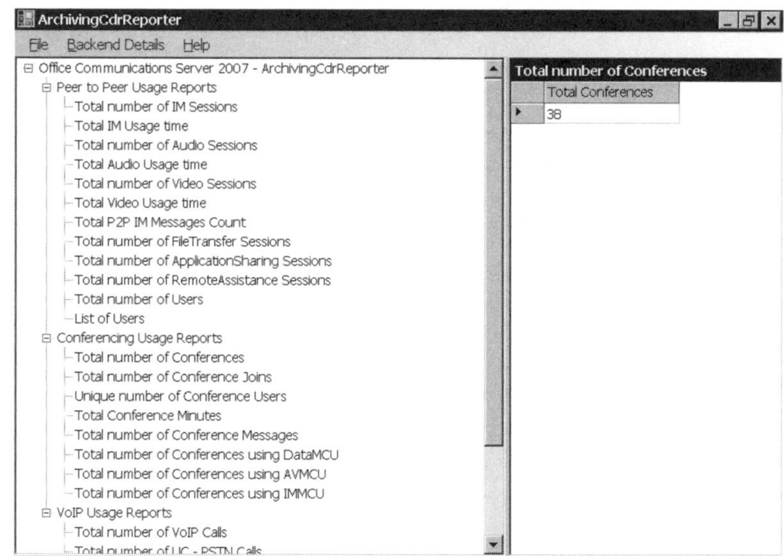

The criteria available in the Archiving CDR Reporter tool include the following:

- Peer to Peer Usage Reports:
  - Total Number of IM Sessions
  - Total IM Usage Time
  - Total Number of Audio Sessions

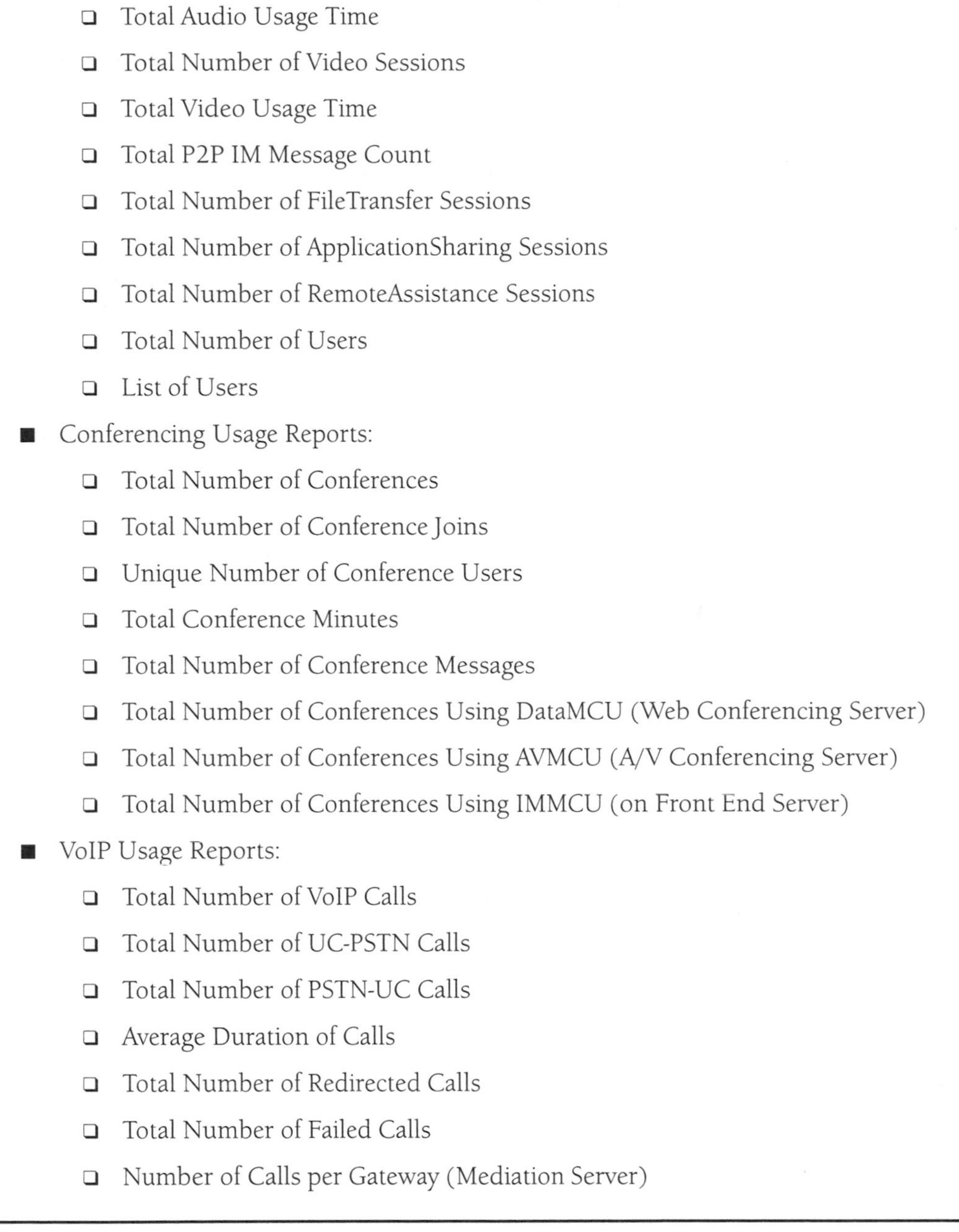

  - Total Audio Usage Time
  - Total Number of Video Sessions
  - Total Video Usage Time
  - Total P2P IM Message Count
  - Total Number of FileTransfer Sessions
  - Total Number of ApplicationSharing Sessions
  - Total Number of RemoteAssistance Sessions
  - Total Number of Users
  - List of Users
- Conferencing Usage Reports:
  - Total Number of Conferences
  - Total Number of Conference Joins
  - Unique Number of Conference Users
  - Total Conference Minutes
  - Total Number of Conference Messages
  - Total Number of Conferences Using DataMCU (Web Conferencing Server)
  - Total Number of Conferences Using AVMCU (A/V Conferencing Server)
  - Total Number of Conferences Using IMMCU (on Front End Server)
- VoIP Usage Reports:
  - Total Number of VoIP Calls
  - Total Number of UC-PSTN Calls
  - Total Number of PSTN-UC Calls
  - Average Duration of Calls
  - Total Number of Redirected Calls
  - Total Number of Failed Calls
  - Number of Calls per Gateway (Mediation Server)

Contoso's Deployment Path for Singapore

The last pool location for Contoso's Office Communications Server 2007 deployment is Singapore. Contoso decides to deploy Office Communications Server 2007 server roles in the order described in Table 12-34.

Table 12-34 Deployment Path for Singapore

Step	Server	Action
1	BAESPO01	Install BAESPO01.
2	FRESPO	Install pool Load Balancer.
3	FECSPO01	Install FECSPO01.
4		Install one Office Communicator 2007 client to test.
5	FECSPO02	Install FECSPO02.
6	FECSPO03	Install FECSPO03.
7	FECSPO04	Install FECSPO04.
8		Test Office Communicator 2007 Client Instant Messaging access first with one or more Front End Servers offline and then with all of them online.
9	HTTSPO01	Install HTTSPO01.
10	WCESPO01	Install WCESPO01.
11		Test the Live Meeting 2007 client external Web Conferencing Server access.
12	AVESPO01	Install AVESPO01.
13		Test the Live Meeting 2007 client and Office Communicator 2007 external A/V Conferencing Server.

Final Contoso Architecture

The final Contoso architecture is shown in Figure 12-5.

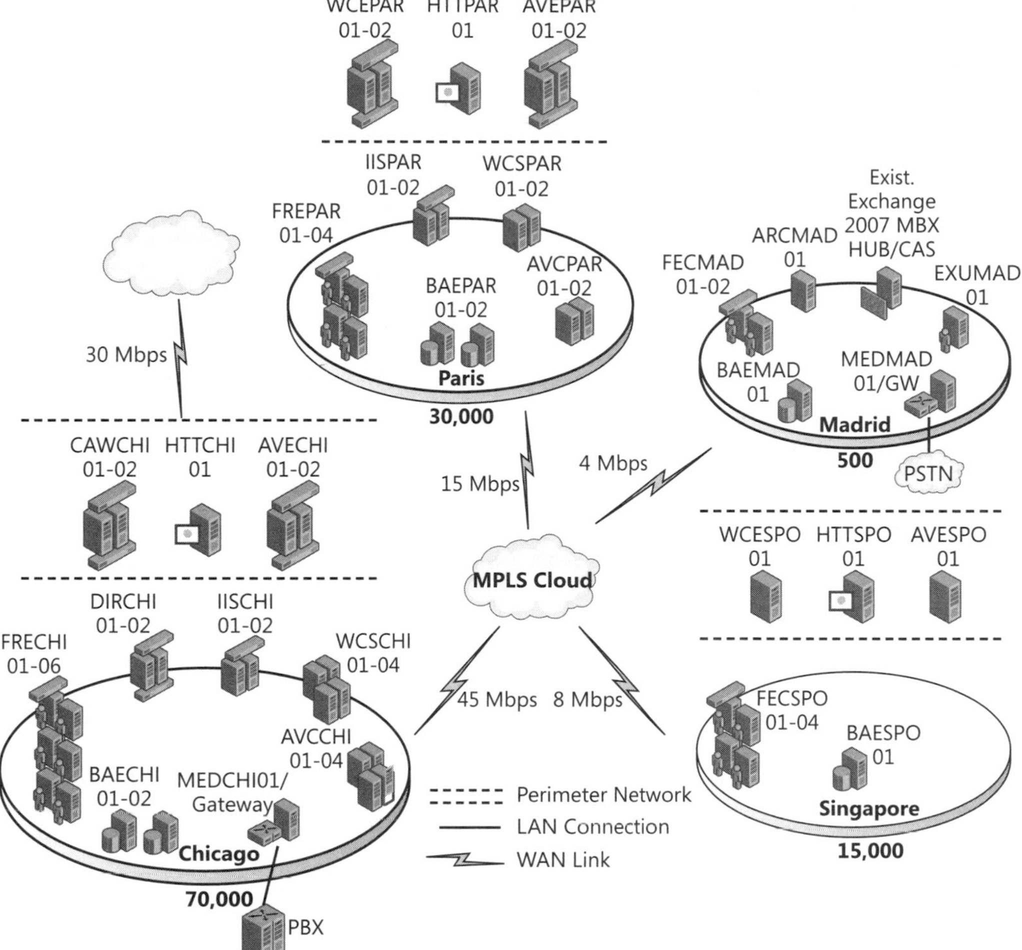

Figure 12-5 Contoso's global Office Communications Server 2007 architecture

It is important to have an architecture diagram that shows the entire Office Communications Server 2007 deployment in an enterprise environment, as it can be used to explain the deployment to other departments that are involved with the deployment or to management. Also, for any technical discussions that require a high-level system overview, diagrams like the one in Figure 12-5 are useful.

Summary

In this chapter, preparation steps as well as a deployment path for the Contoso deployment of Office Communications Server 2007 have been developed. The demonstrated deployment path is not the only possible deployment path for enterprises with similar requirements, IT infrastructure, and geographical distribution of users. However, it contains Best Practice results from previous Office Communications Server 2007 deployments. Therefore, Contoso deployment path can be used for similar enterprise deployments.

Additional Resources

- Office Communications Server 2007 documentation found at *http://technet.microsoft.com/en-us/bb629431.aspx*
- "Office Communications Server 2007 Planning Guide" available from the Microsoft Download Center at *http://www.microsoft.com/downloads/details.aspx?familyid=723347c6-fa1f-44d8-a7fa-8974c3b596f4&displaylang=en*
- "Office Communications Server 2007 Enterprise Voice Planning and Deployment Guide" available from the Microsoft Download Center at *http://www.microsoft.com/downloads/details.aspx?familyid=24e72dac-2b26-4f43-bba2-60488f2aca8d&displaylang=en*

On the Companion CD

- RouteHelper Configuration file (RouteHelperConfiguration_Contoso.rtda), in the \Appendixes, Scripts, Resources\Chapter 12 folder
- RouteHelper Testcase file (RouteHelperTestcases_Contoso.rttc), in the \Appendixes,Scripts,Resources\Chapter 12 folder
- The Archiving CDR Reporter tool, which is included as part of the Office Communications Server 2007 Resource Kit tools, in the \OCS 2007 Resource Kit Tools folder

Part IV
Operations

In this part:

The chapters in this part of the Office Communications Server Resource Kit deal with daily operational tasks such as monitoring, backup and restore, and general administration of the platform. Chapter 13 covers how to monitor Office Communications Server 2007 using event logs, Performance Monitor, and Microsoft Operations Manager 2005, and describes how to monitor and report usage by using call detail records. Chapter 14 provides step-by-step guidance for planning backup and restore of Office Communications Server using the tools included in the platform and also additional tools provided in Microsoft SQL Server 2005. Finally, Chapter 15 examines how to configure global, pool, and server settings for Office Communications Server using both the administration console and the Windows Management Instrumentation (WMI) interface. This chapter also examines how to migrate users from Live Communications Server 2005 Service Pack 1 to Office Communications Server.

Chapter 13

Monitoring

In this chapter:

This chapter provides an overview of how to monitor Office Communications Server by using the Windows Event Logs, Performance Monitor, and Microsoft Operations Manager 2005. The chapter also describes how to monitor and report usage by using Call Detail Records.

Office Communications Server 2007 enables administrators to monitor the health and state of any Office Communications Server through a comprehensive set of events and performance counters associated with every server role. Office Communications Server 2007 currently offers three ways to help monitor the health of Office Communications Servers:

- **Admins Tools** Office Communications Server 2007 offers convenient monitoring views straight from the status pane. A snapshot of each server's configuration, status, event logs, and performance monitor is integrated into the Microsoft Management Console (MMC).
- **Microsoft Operations Manager** The health details of the servers can be monitored by using Microsoft Operations Manager (MOM) 2005. Office Communications Server 2007 makes available a management pack for MOM to easily monitor the health of your Office Communications Server 2007 deployment.
- **Call Detail Records** Office Communications Server 2007 introduces Call Detail Records (CDR) to capture usage records for all types of communication activity on Office Communications Servers.

The sections that follow describe how you can use each of these methods to monitor Office Communications Servers.

Monitoring Office Communications Server by Using the Admins Tools

The Admins Tools for Office Communications Server 2007 is a comprehensive Microsoft Management Console. In addition to providing an interface to configure Office Communications Servers, it provides the following three mechanisms to monitor the status of Office Communications Servers:

- **Status Pane** The status pane (right-hand pane) in the MMC allows monitoring the overall status of all functionalities and settings of your Office Communications Servers. If multiple server roles are installed on the same physical server, a separate tab becomes available to provide a snapshot of each server role.
- **Event Log Tab** The Events tab in the MMC provides a convenient way to monitor recent Office Communications Server events without having to open the Event Viewer MMC in the Administrative Tools folder.
- **Performance Tab** The Performance tab in the MMC provides a convenient way to monitor performance counters for various components of Office Communications Server without having to open the Performance Monitor (PerfMon) MMC in the Administrative Tools folder.

Monitoring Overall Status by Using the Status Pane

The Admin Tools MMC provides a dynamic status pane that shows a snapshot of Office Communications Server services. The status pane shows a high-level status of Office Communications Server services that is useful for monitoring. The status pane is detailed enough to help an administrator quickly troubleshoot a problem with a server.

To view the status of a server, simply select the server from the scope pane on the left side of the Office Communications Server Admin Tools MMC interface (shown in Figure 13-1). Because there is a lot of information to display, the settings are organized logically and grouped in a list that can be expanded by clicking the plus sign (+) next to each group setting.

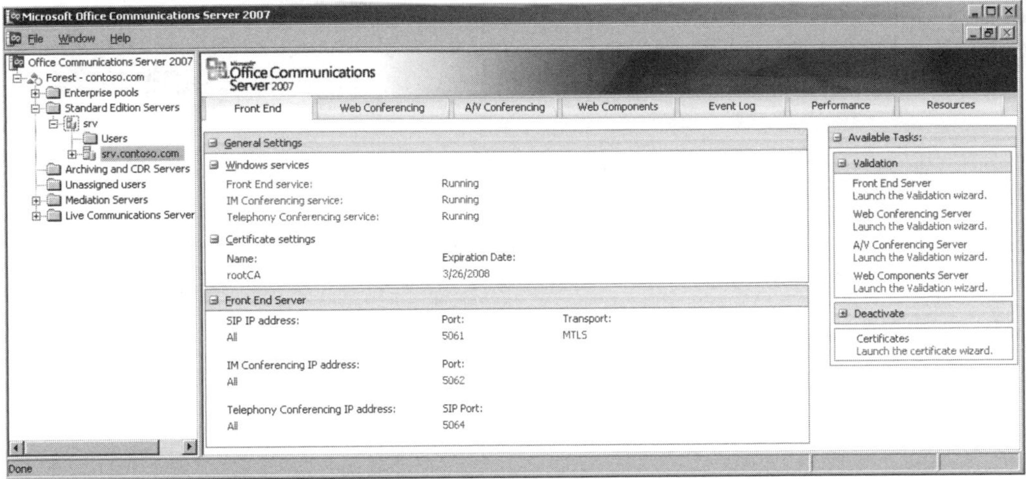

Figure 13-1 Admins Tools server status pane

The Admins Tools MMC can display the status of more than individual servers. It can show the status at the pool level as well as at the Active Directory forest and domain levels.

The status pane for a pool node displays a unique tab specific to pools. This is the Database tab. It provides a convenient interface to query user data from the back-end SQL server. In previous versions, administrators who wanted to examine the user data stored in the SQL database needed to write SQL commands. This interface eliminates this learning curve. The following information can be queried directly from this tab:

- Number of active endpoints logged in to the pool
- Client versions of active endpoints logged in
- Data for a specific user, by specifying the user's SIP URI
- Conference summary reports

The Database tab view is shown in Figure 13-2.

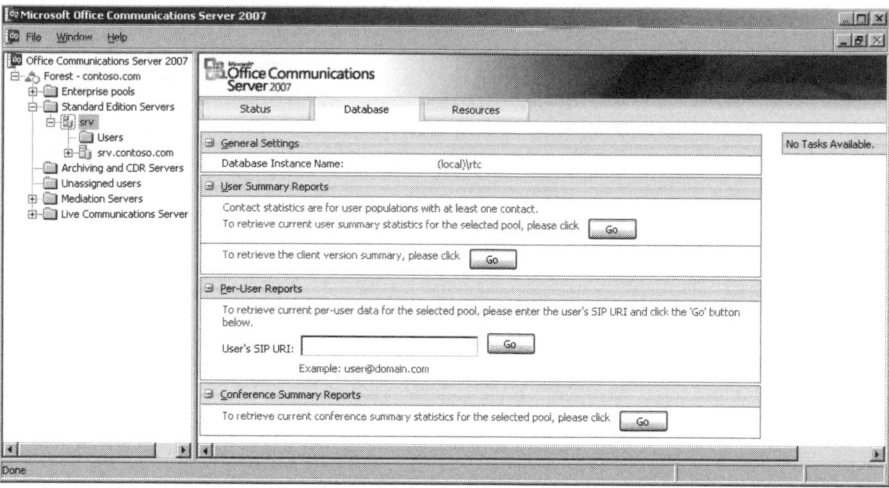

Figure 13-2 Database tab view

When the Forest node is selected, the status pane displays the global settings. Figure 13-3 displays the status pane for the forest node.

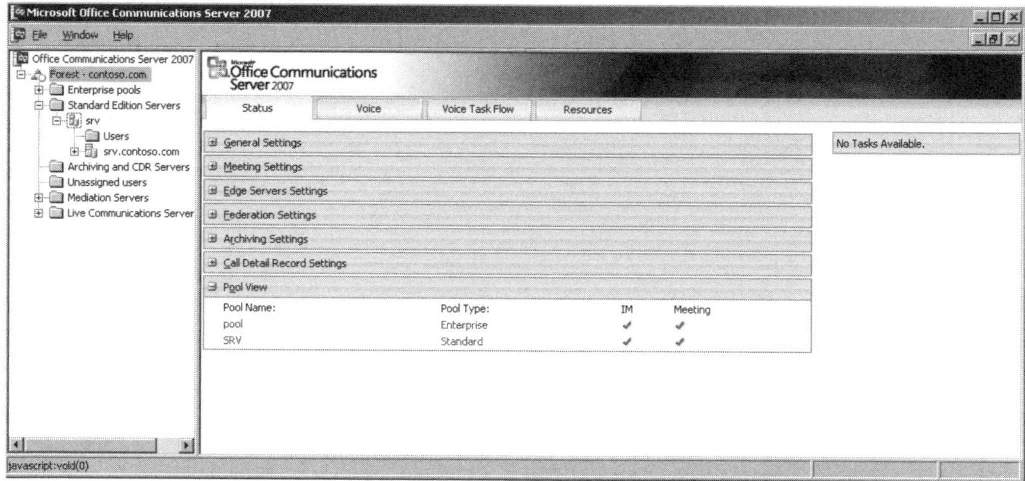

Figure 13-3 Admins Tools forest status pane

To view status at the domain level, the default view must be changed to show Active Directory Domains (as shown in Figure 13-4b). This is done by right-clicking the top node in the scope pane and selecting View Options, which is shown in Figure 13-4a. The Admins Tools MMC must be restarted to view this mode.

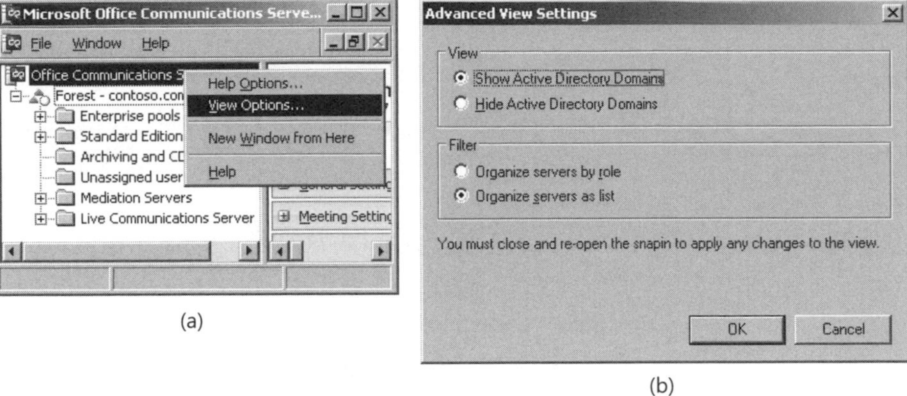

Figure 13-4 Admins Tools domain status pane

In addition to the overall status for a particular functionality or a service, the status pane also provides information about fully qualified domain names (FQDNs) of servers, file URLs, static Internet Protocol (IP) routes, and port numbers that can be used as a reference. It is also an effective display of configuration for the purposes of troubleshooting. The amount of information that is displayed here is sufficient for an overall view of Office Communication Server's status.

Monitoring Events by Using the Event Log Tab

Typically, to monitor events, the administrator launches the Event Viewer MMC, selects the Application log, and filters out all events that are not specific to Office Communications Server. This effort can become tedious and time-consuming. This is no longer necessary. The Admins Tools MMC provides a viewer of Office Communications Server events. The Event Log tab is visible only when a server node is selected in the scope pane. It displays the recent Office Communications Server events for the selected server node. The Event Log tab in the Admins Tools MMC is an integrated event viewer that filters all Office Communications Server–specific events.

Using Event Log Filters

The administrator can further filter events as shown in Figure 13-5.

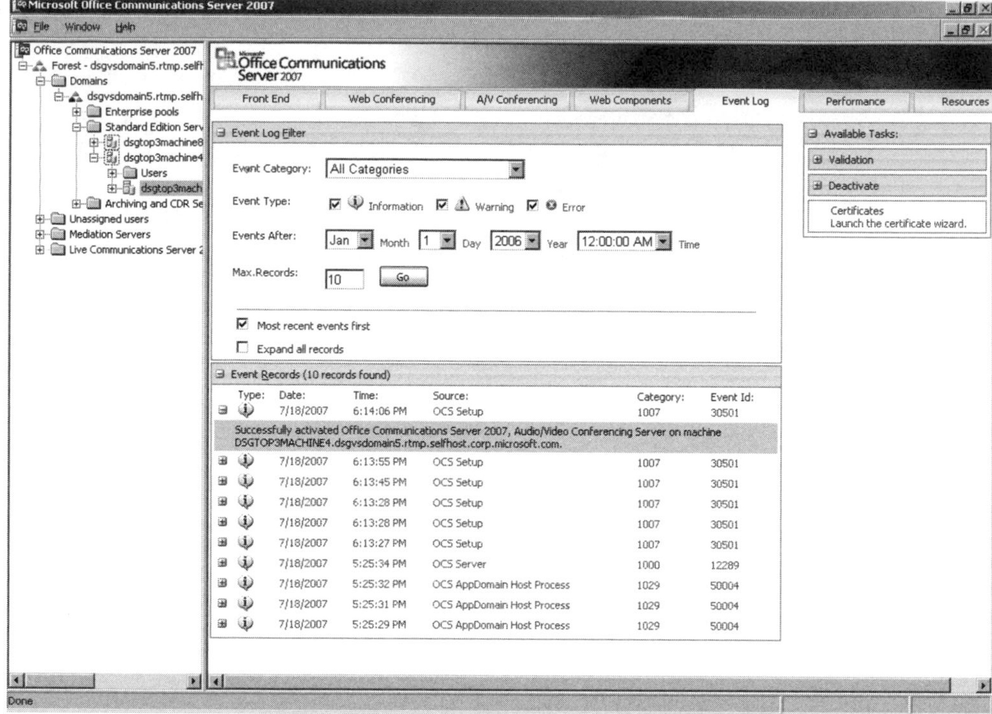

Figure 13-5 Event Log tab showing Event Log filters

You can customize the view of the information displayed in the Event Log tab according to your monitoring requirements by using the following filters:

- Event Category
- Event Type
- Date and Time
- Number of maximum records to display (defaults to 10 records)

The events can be sorted in descending chronological order by selecting the Most Recent Events First option. Deselecting this option will display the events in ascending order.

Understanding Event Categories

The categories map to the different server roles installed on the server. This arrangement makes it easy to hone in on a faulty service. Events for Office Communications Server 2007 are classified in the following categories:

- Front End Components
- Voice Applications
- Server Applications

- IM and Telephony Conferencing
- Archiving and CDR
- Management
- Deployment

Understanding Event Types

The Office Communications Server events are classified as follows:

- **Information** These events are for informational purposes only.
- **Warning** These events can indicate abnormal behavior in some component. Such behavior might require your immediate attention.
- **Error** These events typically indicate a failure in one of the core components or functionality that requires your immediate attention.

The type of events can easily be recognized by their respective icons. For example, the Informational icon is a small blue 'i' on a white background. The warning is a yellow triangle with an exclamation point. The error message is marked by a red circle with an exclamation point.

Monitoring Performance by Using the Performance Tab

The Admins Tools MMC integrates the same functionality of the Performance Monitor (PerfMon) MMC by embedding it within the status pane. This is shown in Figure 13-6.

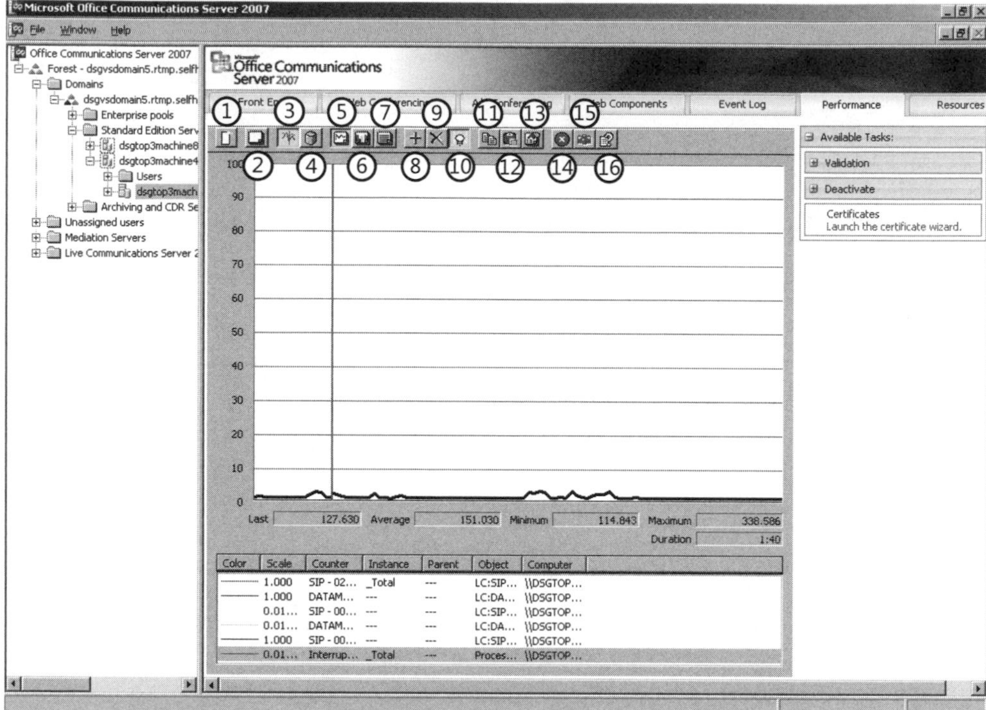

Figure 13-6 Performance Monitor tab

By default, specific performance counters were preselected that will give an overall view of the server's health. By providing over 300 performance counters in Office Communications Server 2007, the engineering team has already done the work of selecting the right set of performance counters that should be monitored.

The performance counters exposed in the MMC are read from the file, ServerPerfMon.xml, at run time. This file includes the performance counters for each server role. The administrator can modify the list of performance counters to monitor by modifying this file. This file is located at

%ProgramFiles%\Common Files\Microsoft Office Communications Server 2007

Note For a list of Office Communications Server performance counters, see Appendix C, on the companion CD in the folder \Appendixes,Scripts,Resources.

Using the Performance Monitor

MMC for Office Communications Server 2007 exposes the standard controls (toolbar buttons) for Performance Monitor. Table 13-1 describes the PerfMon toolbar buttons shown on the toolbar in Figure 13-6 and listed from left to right:

Table 13-1 Performance Monitor Toolbar Buttons

Button	Description	Function
1	New counter set	Removes current counter set from display.
2	Clear display	Clears current display, and restarts counters.
3	View current activity	A toggle switch to toggle between real-time activity and logged data sources. See the View log activity option.
4	View log activity	Allows you to view a logged source of performance data, rather than the real-time activity.
5	View graph	A toggle switch to show a graphed display. You can toggle between a graph, a histogram, and report displays. (See the next two items in this table.)
6	View histogram display	A toggle switch to show histogram data. You can toggle between a graph, a histogram, and report displays.
7	View report display	A toggle switch to show data in report format. You can toggle between a graph, a histogram, and report displays.
8	Add performance counters	You can add any accessible performance counters, including system performance counters, Real-Time Communications (RTC) performance counters, and so on. This option does not add the performance counter to ServerPerfMon.xml.
9	Delete selected performance counters	Deletes selected performance counters from the display. This option does not modify ServerPerfMon.xml.
10	Highlight performance counter	The selected performance counter is highlighted with a thicker line. This option allows for easier viewing. This is a toggle button, so if highlighting is on and the button is selected, highlighting will be turned off.
11	Copy properties	Copies counter path information onto a clipboard so that it can be pasted into another instance of Office Communications Server MMC Status Pane Performance tab or another instance of the System Performance Monitor.
12	Paste counter list	Performs the paste part of a copy-paste operation. (See previous item.)

Table 13-1 Performance Monitor Toolbar Buttons

Button	Description	Function
13	Properties	Displays the system monitor properties for this instance of the MMC Status Pane Performance tab.
14	Freeze display	Freezes the display. This is a toggle button.
15	Update data	If the display is frozen, clicking this button updates the display statically.
16	Help	Help

Note For more information about using the Performance Monitor, see the *Microsoft Windows Server 2003 Performance Guide*, which is one of the volumes of the *Microsoft Windows Server 2003 Resource Kit* from Microsoft Press.

Monitoring Office Communications Server 2007 by Using Microsoft Operations Manager 2005

Microsoft Operations Manager (MOM) 2005 is a comprehensive system monitoring solution to help administrators monitor the performance, availability, and security of Microsoft Windows–based networks and applications, based on the data gathered from events and performance counters collected from the servers. MOM delivers enterprise-class operations management to improve the efficiency of IT operations, and Office Communications Server 2007 integrates with MOM so that administrators can manage their Office Communications Servers directly from the MOM Management Console. The following link provides a product overview of MOM 2005: *http://technet.microsoft.com/en-us/opsmgr/bb498244.aspx*.

The ways in which MOM 2005 helps administrators address server issues include, but are not limited to, the following:

- Alerting administrators by e-mail, instant messaging (IM), and pager when problems occur
- Providing detailed information about potential root causes of a problem
- Suggesting solutions for resolving problems from its knowledge database, which was created by the engineering team

Office Communications Server 2007 offers a management pack that integrates with MOM to monitor specifically Office Communications Server 2007 servers. This management pack is available as a Web download from the Microsoft Download Center (*http://www.microsoft.com/downloads/details.aspx?FamilyId=D04A9EB0-1F67-4535-B865-843621A1B16E&displaylang=en*).

This management pack provides operational knowledge gathered from the expertise of the Microsoft engineering team to help keep Office Communications Server 2007 servers running smoothly. The knowledge necessary to best monitor Office Communications Server 2007 servers is built into the management pack, removing the need for administrators to figure out this work. It includes the rules, criteria, tasks, and views to monitor the events and performance counters of each Office Communications Server role. Before the Office Communications Server 2007 management pack can be used, Microsoft Operations Manager 2005 must be deployed.

To learn more about deploying MOM, refer to the deployment guide for MOM 2005 at *http://www.microsoft.com/technet/prodtechnol/mom/mom2005/Library/ed4712c6-96b5-4241-a2b5-0dfaed30619c.mspx?mfr=true*. After deploying MOM, install the management pack for Office Communications Server 2007 from *http://www.microsoft.com/downloads/details.aspx?FamilyId=D04A9EB0-1F67-4535-B865-843621A1B16E&displaylang=en*.

After installing the management pack, use the Administrator Console for MOM to monitor the activities of Office Communications Server 2007 servers. The Administrator Console offers some of the key elements of the management pack for Office Communications Server 2007 including, but not limited to, computer groups, events, performance counters, alerts, product knowledge, and tasks.

Using Computer Groups

Computers with similar attributes or characteristics are grouped together to target rules for a particular set of computers.

The management pack groups various server roles for Office Communications Server as shown in Figure 13-7. A different set of monitoring rules is defined for each computer group. These rules govern the metrics to collect, the type of alerts to generate, and the type of remedies to suggest.

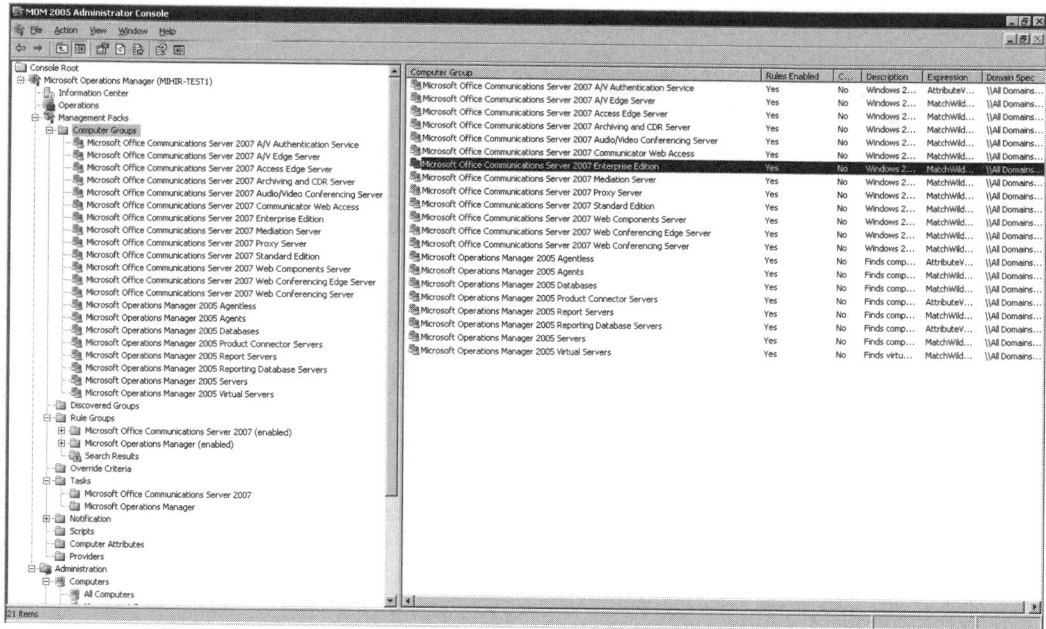

Figure 13-7 MOM Administrator Console

The Office Communications Server 2007 server roles available in the MOM Administrator Console include the following:

- Microsoft Office Communications Server 2007 A/V Authentication Service Computer Group
- Microsoft Office Communications Server 2007 A/V Edge Server Computer Group
- Microsoft Office Communications Server 2007 Access Edge Server Computer Group
- Microsoft Office Communications Server 2007 Archiving and CDR Server Computer Group
- Microsoft Office Communications Server 2007 Audio/Video Conferencing Server Computer Group
- Microsoft Office Communications Server 2007 Communicator Web Access Computer Group
- Microsoft Office Communications Server 2007 Enterprise Edition Computer Group
- Microsoft Office Communications Server 2007 Mediation Server Computer Group
- Microsoft Office Communications Server 2007 Proxy Server Computer Group
- Microsoft Office Communications Server 2007 Standard Edition Computer Group
- Microsoft Office Communications Server 2007 Web Components Server Computer Group

- Microsoft Office Communications Server 2007 Web Conferencing Edge Server Computer Group
- Microsoft Office Communications Server 2007 Web Conferencing Server Computer Group

All of these groups are discovered through registry keys on each computer where a particular server role is installed. Discovery occurs every 15 minutes. (So if you uninstall one, it will take a maximum 15 minutes for MOM to readjust its monitoring.)

Using Events and Performance Counters

Each server logs its events in the local computer's event logs. MOM then collects this event information from these logs and aggregates it to provide an operational view of the system in the Operations Console of MOM. When these metrics cross the thresholds defined in the management pack, an alert is sent to the administrator to warn of potential performance issues.

The management pack has a preselected list of events and performance counters that are monitored by default. The administrator can choose to monitor other events and performance counters in MOM. When enabled, these events and performance counters become visible in the Operations Console.

Using Alerts

MOM calls attention to critical events that require administrator intervention. Alerts are created by rules defined in the management pack. These rules assess the health of the server that is being monitored. MOM enables the administrator to set an alert based on predefined rules, and it notifies the administrator via e-mail or pager notification.

As shown in Figure 13-8, the alerts can be viewed and sorted on various parameters. Every alert contains detailed information about the following:

- Alert severity
- Specific time period in which the alert was generated
- Specific person who owns the alert
- Specific text in the description
- Computer
- Resolution state
- Violated Service Level Agreement
- GUID
- Computer Group

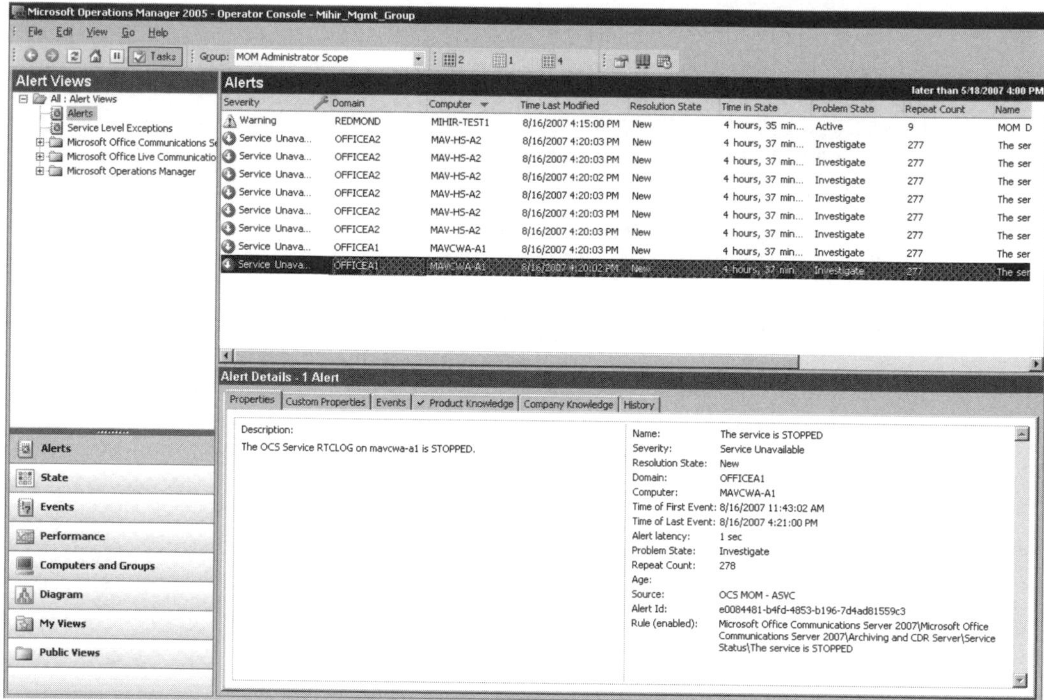

Figure 13-8 Alerts

The management pack provides the built-in expertise, in the context of the specific alerts, to guide administrators in resolving outstanding issues. As shown in Figure 13-9, alerts have built-in product knowledge information and display a detailed description of the problem, a potential cause for that problem, and any recommended resolution for that problem.

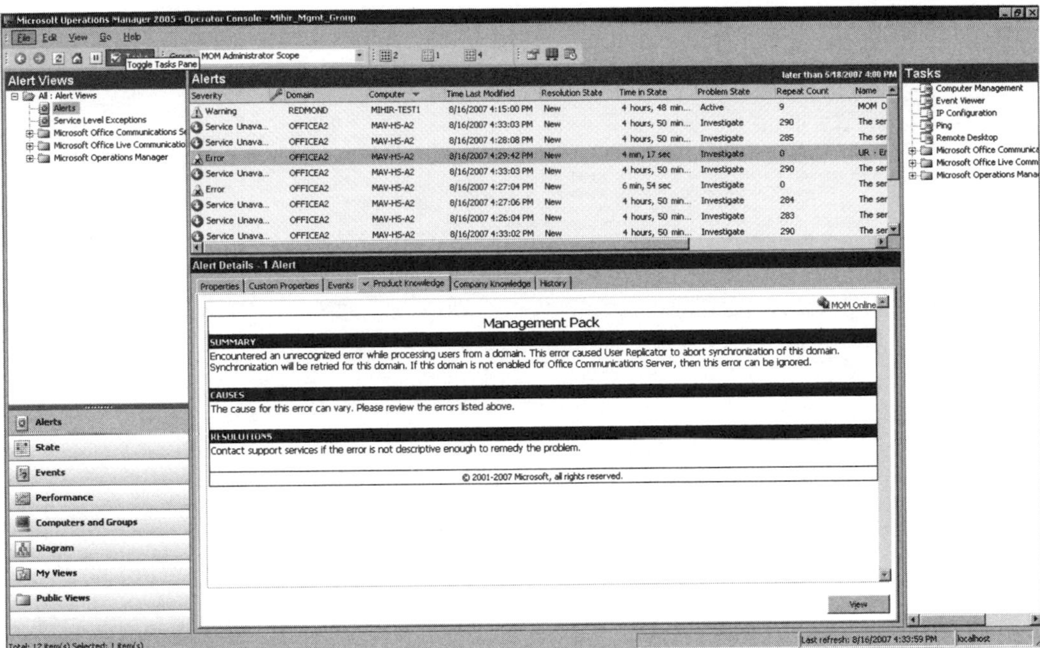

Figure 13-9 Product knowledge base

Using Tasks

MOM enables the administrator to investigate and repair issues from the MOM Operations Console through tasks. As shown in Figure 13-10, the management pack for Office Communications Server 2007 has at least two tasks for every server role that allows the administrator to start or stop a particular service.

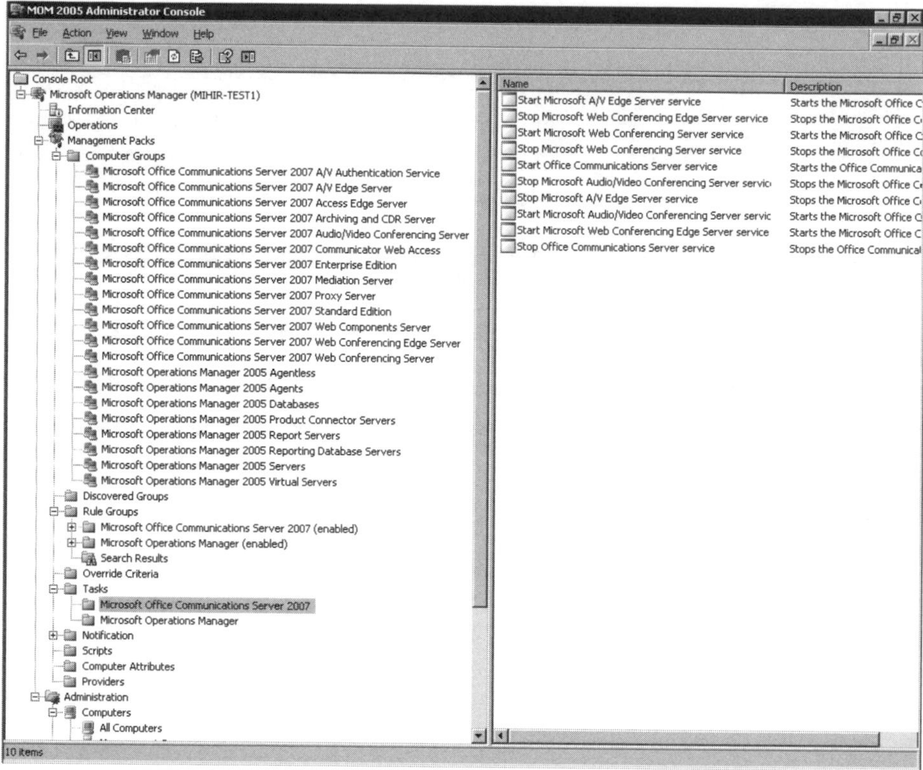

Figure 13-10 Operations Console tasks

Monitoring Office Communications Server Usage by Using Call Detail Records

Office Communications Server 2007 introduces Call Detail Records (CDRs) to capture usage information of various communication and collaboration functionalities. The usage details of instant messaging, conferencing, and Voice-over-Internet-Protocol (VoIP) traffic are collected as CDRs in the database of the Archiving and CDR Server. You can use this data to quantify resource use and to analyze trends in usage of Office Communications Server within your enterprise, and thereby quantify the return on investment (ROI) of your Office Communications Server implementation.

Prerequisites for Deploying the Archiving and CDR Service

Before you deploy the Archiving and CDR service, ensure that your IT infrastructure, network, and systems meet the following infrastructure requirements:

- Message Queuing is installed on the computer that will run the Archiving and CDR service and on all Office Communications Server 2007 servers that you want to archive. Every server in an Enterprise pool must be connected to the Archiving service separately.
- Microsoft SQL Server 2005 Service Pack 1 (SP1) or newer, or SQL Server 2000 with Service Pack 4, is installed on a dedicated database server (SQL Server 2005 SP2 is strongly recommended for Enterprise pools) or on a server running the Archiving and CDR service. Default or named instances are both supported. Windows Integrated Authentication is required.
- Office Communications Server administrative tools are installed on the computer that will run the Archiving and CDR service.

Deploying the Archiving and CDR Service

The Office Communications Server 2007 Archiving and CDR Server architecture consists of the following:

- One or more Office Communications Server servers, hosting an Archiving and CDR Agent, which captures both archiving and CDR details from each server.
- Message Queuing, which enables the Archiving and CDR Agent to communicate with Archiving Services.
- A SQL database for storing IM and meeting content captured by the Archiving and CDR Agent (which acts as the CDR and archiving database server). This database must be installed on a separate dedicated SQL back-end computer and attached to the server or servers running the Archiving and CDR Agent. Optionally, SQL can be collocated on the same computer that is running the Archiving and CDR Agent, but the Archiving and CDR database, which stores all archived content and call detail records information, must be on a dedicated SQL machine not shared by the Enterprise Edition pool.

The Office Communications Server 2007 Archiving and CDR Server can be deployed in the several supported topologies. The topology to use is based on which Office Communications Server servers are being archived and the configuration of the Archiving and CDR service, which is largely determined by your performance and scalability requirements (the number of users targeted for archiving).

For any Archiving and CDR Server deployment, you can choose between two basic topologies:

- **Single-tier** Here the Archiving and CDR Service and the back-end archiving database reside on a single computer.
- **Two-tier** Here the Archiving and CDR Service resides on a dedicated computer, and the back-end database resides on a different dedicated computer.

As a variation of either of these two topologies, you can configure multiple Archiving and CDR Services connecting to the same archiving and CDR back-end database.

> **Note** A Standard Edition server can be collocated with the Archiving and CDR Server, but this configuration is strongly discouraged because of performance limitations.

When you enable the CDR, the Archiving and CDR Agent running on the front-end server captures usage information and sends it to the database by using Microsoft Message Queuing. Office Communications Server 2007 allows you to selectively enable CDRs for any or all of the following through global properties:

- **Peer-to-peer call details** Details of all peer-to-peer sessions, including instant messaging, audio/video, file transfer, and application sharing sessions
- **Conferencing call details** Details of all multiparty sessions, including instant messaging and audio/video sessions, and details of all conferencing sessions conducted using Microsoft Office Live Meeting Console
- **Voice call details** Details of all enterprise voice calls

These settings are turned off by default. You can enable any or all of them from the Office Communications Server 2007 snap-in.

Although the archiving and CDR database is used to store both archived messages for compliance as well as the CDR data, you do not have to enable archiving to enable CDR. The archiving and CDR capabilities can be enabled or disabled independent of each other.

Monitoring Usage

CDRs capture signaling information about all communication sessions on Office Communications Server. You can use this information to monitor common usage information, including but not limited to a count of the usage of a specific functionality, duration of specific sessions, and per-user usage of specific features.

Some of the common usage metrics are as follows:

- Peer-to-peer calls:
  - Total number of instant messaging sessions
  - Total instant messaging usage time
  - Total number of audio sessions
  - Total number of video sessions
  - Total audio usage time
  - Total video usage time
  - Total count of instant messages
  - Total count of File Transfer sessions
  - Total count of Application Sharing sessions

  - Total count of Remote Assistance sessions
  - Total count of users
- Conferencing call details:
  - Total count of conferences
  - Total count of unique conference users
  - Total count of conference minutes
  - Total count of conference messages
  - Total count of conferences organized using Web Conferencing Server
  - Total count of conferences organized using A/V Conferencing Server
- VoIP call details:
  - Total count of enterprise VoIP calls
  - Total count of calls from Office Communicator to PSTN
  - Total count of calls from PSTN to Office Communicator/Unified Communications client
  - Average duration of calls
  - Total count of redirected calls
  - Total count of failed calls
  - Total count of calls per gateway

Reporting Usage Data

Office Communications Server 2007 captures the raw CDR data in the archiving and CDR database. You can use SQL reporting or custom SQL queries to extract any specific information. The schema for the archiving and CDR database is explained in the next section. Office Communications Server 2007 provides a Resource Kit tool named ArchivingCDR Reporter that enables you to capture reports for the predefined set of queries mentioned in the "Monitoring Usage" section earlier in the chapter.

The tool has a configuration file named ArchivingCdrReporter_Config.xml, which can be edited to add custom queries. You can add custom queries to the configuration file and use them to monitor any custom usage information.

New queries can be added to a node under the *<Queries> </Queries>* node—for example:

```
<Query>
<Name>Total number of Users</Name>
<Value>SELECT count(*) as 'Number of Users from users</Value>
</Query>
```

You can export the SQL query reports to a comma-separated value (.csv) file and open it in Microsoft Office Excel to visualize the data in charts, such as those shown in Figure 13-11 and Figure 13-12.

Date	IM Sessions	IM Minutes	IM Count	Audio Sessions	Audio Minutes	Video Sessions	Video Minutes	Conferences	Group IM Messages
29-May	111	715	1128	20	42	1	1		
30-May	319	1868	3100	35	101	5	8	9	48
31-May	2097	11620	16231	151	149	36	38	48	135
1-Jun	2545	12904	18338	144	177	40	57	57	315
2-Jun	2466	13937	20274	172	156	47	57	64	500
3-Jun	1939	11372	13872	127	271	21	8	50	485
4-Jun	131	577	786	7	0	5	0	14	16
5-Jun	168	1207	1768	11	41	0	0	4	0
6-Jun	1812	9681	15404	157	218	58	29	99	14
7-Jun	2502	13705	21231	256	638	108	247	107	0
8-Jun	2391	13727	20246	226	130	136	43	115	0
9-Jun	0	0	0	0	0	0	0	0	0
10-Jun	1617	8888	13200	277	252	111	112	120	508
11-Jun	356	2419	36758	125	233	59	59	144	437
12-Jun	754	5105	8836	207	248	89	76	168	2317
13-Jun	2591	13863	22653	436	360	140	137	292	1300
14-Jun	2638	14552	88873	700	965	323	367	324	970
15-Jun	2799	15816	91215	770	1122	332	443	375	1192
16-Jun	2998	15040	287180	748	840	438	343	479	1894
17-Jun	2595	14653	21387	364	735	166	322	366	908

Figure 13-11 Sample usage report with CDR data displayed in an Excel 2007 table

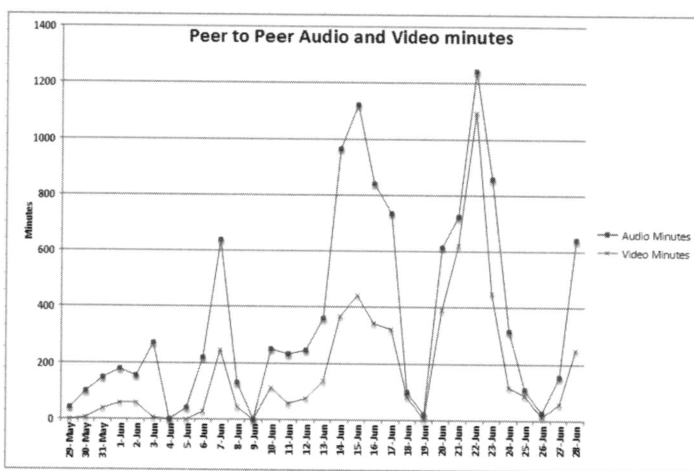

Figure 13-12 Sample usage report with CDR data displayed in an Excel 2007 graph

Database Schema for the Archiving and CDR Database

The raw CDR data is captured in the archiving and CDR database. The following tables describe the schema for the archiving and CDR database.

The static tables shown in Table 13-2 for the Archiving and CDR Server database are used by the other main tables such as those shown in Tables 13-4 and 13-5.

Table 13-2 Static Tables

Table Name	Table Contents
MediaList	Stores the list of different media types
Roles	Stores the type of roles to which conference participants can be as-signed

The supporting tables shown in Table 13-3 are referred to by the main tables for archiving and CDR services.

Table 13-3 Supporting Tables

Table Name	Table Contents
ClientVersions	Stores information about client versions.
Computers	Stores the front-end server host name.
ContentTypes	Stores the available content types for instant messages.
Dialogs	Stores information about the *DialogId* (*CallId*, *FromTag*, and *ToTag*) for each peer-to-peer session. This table is referred to by the Ses-sionDetails table.
Gateways	Stores the list of gateways used for VoIP calls.
Mcus	Stores information about the different conferencing servers (MCUs) and their URIs.
Users	Stores all user URIs.
Phones	Stores all phone numbers/URIs used in VoIP calls.

The tables shown in Table 13-4 are specific to conference CDRs.

Table 13-4 Conference CDR Tables

Table Name	Table Contents
Conferences	Stores information about all the conferences (ConferenceURI and Start and End Times). This table is referred to by the IM Conference ar-chiving tables.
FocusJoinsAndLeaves	Stores information about when each user joins and leaves the conference Focus. Information in-cludes the user's role and client version.
McuJoinsAndLeaves	Stores information about all the conferencing servers (MCUs) involved in a conference and in-formation about when each user joins and leaves each conferencing server.

The tables shown in Table 13-5 are specific to IM Conference archiving.

Table 13-5 IM Conference Archiving Tables

Table Name	Table Contents
ConferenceMessageCount	Stores the message count per user per conference
ConferenceMessageRecipientList	Stores the list of recipients of each message sent in a conference
ConferenceMessages	Archives all the messages sent in a conference

The tables shown in Table 13-6 are specific to peer-to-peer CDRs.

Table 13-6 Peer-to-Peer (P2P) CDR Tables

Table Name	Table Contents
SessionDetails	Stores information about every peer-to-peer session, including start time, end time, from and to user IDs, response code, and message count for each user
FileTransfers	Stores information about file transfer sessions (file name and if it was accepted, rejected, or canceled)
Media	Stores information about media types used in peer-to-peer sessions

The table shown in Table 13-7 contains all messages archived during peer-to-peer sessions.

Table 13-7 Peer-to-Peer (P2P) Archiving Table

Table Name	Table Contents
Messages	Stores messages archived during peer-to-peer (one-to-one) instant messaging sessions

The table shown in Table 13-8 is specific to VoIP CDRs.

Table 13-8 VoIP CDR Table

Table Name	Table Contents
VoipDetails	Stores information about VoIP calls (number of caller, number of called party, who disconnected the call, and what gateway was used). This table refers to the SessionDetails table.

Summary

Administrators can monitor Office Communications Servers from the status pane of the Admins Tools MMC, using the Office Communications Server 2007 management pack for Microsoft Operations Manager 2005, and from the Archiving and CDR Server. The management pack for MOM 2005 offers proactive monitoring of the overall health of the deployment. It provides mechanisms to send alerts as well as knowledge-base information to help resolve issues. Call Detail Records enable administrators to monitor usage data and quantify resource usage for various functionalities offered by Office Communications Server. An administrator can use some or all of these functionalities to proactively monitor Office Communications Server 2007.

Additional Resources

- Microsoft Office Communications Server 2007 Administration Guide, found at *http://technet.microsoft.com/en-us/library/bb676082.aspx*
- Microsoft Office Communications Server 2007 Planning Guide, found at *http://technet.microsoft.com/en-us/library/bb676082.aspx*

On the Companion CD

There is no companion CD content for this chapter.

Chapter 14

Backup and Restore

In this chapter:

As Office Communications Server 2007 becomes a critical service for real-time communications within organizations, it is important to devise a backup and restore plan to ensure that communication remains available to the end users in case of a failure.

This chapter presents step-by-step guidance for planning your backup and restore deployments of Office Communications Server 2007. You can use the recommendations in this chapter for creating a backup and restoration plan tailored for your organization. Multiple tools and programs are available for backing up and restoring data, settings, and systems. This chapter focuses on the use of tools and programs provided with Office Communications Server 2007, as well as components available in Microsoft SQL Server 2005.

Planning for Backup and Restore

An essential component of effective backup and restore operations is establishment of a comprehensive and concise strategy. Typically, an organization's business priorities affect this strategy. Following is a list of some of these priorities:

- **Business continuity requirements** These requirements are driven by the number of business-critical applications that rely on Office Communications Server 2007. If instant messaging (IM), Web conferencing, or Voice over IP (VoIP) is indispensable to continue your organization's business, you must account for it in your backup and restore plan. For instance, if instant messaging is critical to your organization, but Web conferencing is less critical at times of disaster, you can devise your backup and restore strategy accordingly by investing in restoring the components required for instant messaging before any other components.
- **Data completeness** Office Communications Server 2007 stores three main types of data:
  - User data
  - Compliance-related data

- Configuration data

Depending on the need for completeness of this data, you can decide the frequency of backups. For instance, if you back up the user data every 24 hours, a user's contact list or buddy list will be accurate up to the last backup (which could be a day before the data loss).

- **Data criticality** This typically applies to compliance-specific data. If your organization functions in a regulated industry and is mandated by regulations to maintain an up-to-date record of all communications, the data stored by Office Communications Server 2007 is very critical for your organization.
- **Cost constraints** Besides the cost of physical hardware and any backup software costs, you might need to consider implicit costs. These costs typically include, but are not limited to, the cost of lost business (if applicable), cost of re-creating the deployment, administrative cost of backing up data, and so on.

Backup and Restore Requirements

The organization's business priorities should drive the backup and restore requirements. These requirements can be classified as follows:

- **Hardware and software requirements** Specific hardware and software requirements should be determined based on the organization's needs. This includes not only the hardware to be used for backup storage and restoration of specific services, but also any software and network connectivity required to support backup and restoration.
- **Backup and restore tools** The following tools can be used for backing up and restoring Office Communications Server environments:
    - LCSCmd.exe—The Office Communications Server command-line tool to export and import server settings
    - SQL Server Management Studio in SQL Server 2005—Used to back up the Enterprise pool and the Archiving and CDR Server databases
    - SQL Server Management Studio Express in SQL Server 2005 Express Edition—Used to back up databases on Standard Edition Servers
    - NTBackup—File system backup solution available in Microsoft Windows for backing up meeting content and meeting compliance logs
- **Administrative computer** This is the computer that will perform the regular backups. This operation can be performed on an Office Communications Server or a separate administrative computer joined to Active Directory.
- **Recovery time** Depending on the criticality of the system to the organization, the system must be restored within a maximum time period.

- **Backup location** The backup location can be local or remote depending on security and availability requirements. The backup should be stored securely to prevent tampering and privacy risks. If storing the backup in a remote server, network bandwidth constraints and the impact on business use should be taken into consideration.
- **Disaster Recovery Site (if applicable)** In the most extreme cases, loss of a complete site—because of either a total loss of power, a natural disaster, or other issues—can delay or prevent restoration of service at the original site. So use of a separate, secondary site might be a priority to meet the availability requirements of an organization.

Determining What Needs to Be Backed Up

Backup of an Office Communications Server 2007 deployment entails backing up settings and data. This section covers the requirements and options for backing up settings and data required for operation.

Backing Up Settings

Office Communications Server 2007 has three levels of settings:

- Global-level settings, which apply to all computers in the forest
- Pool-level settings, which apply to a pool on a Standard Edition server or to all servers in an Enterprise pool
- Computer-level settings (also referred to as machine-level settings), which are specific to each computer running Office Communications Server 2007

Table 14-1 describes which of the three levels of settings must be backed up for each server role.

Table 14-1 Settings Requirements

Server Role	Settings Required
Standard Edition servers or front-end servers in Enterprise pools Web Conferencing Servers (Enterprise Edition, expanded configuration only) A/V Conferencing Servers (Enterprise Edition, expanded configuration only)	**Global-level, pool-level, and computer-level settings:** Global-level, pool-level, and computer-level settings are backed up from the Standard Edition server or one front-end server so that only computer-level settings are backed up from other front-end servers, each Web Conferencing Server, each A/V Conferencing Server. **For restoration:** In the event of loss of the Active Directory Domain Services, restoration of all three levels is generally required. In the event of an Enterprise pool loss (all front-end servers in an Enterprise pool or the back-end server) or the loss of a Standard Edition server, restoration of pool-level and computer-level settings is generally required. In the event of loss of an individual front-end Server, Web Conferencing Server, A/V Conferencing Server, or Archiving and CDR Server, restoration of computer-level settings is generally all that is required.
Web Components Servers (Enterprise Edition expanded configuration only)	**Pool-level and computer-level settings:** Pool-level settings are backed up from the Standard Edition server or a front-end server so that only computer-level settings are backed up from each Web Components Server. In the event of loss of a Web Components Server, restoration of computer-level settings is generally all that is required.
Mediation Servers Forwarding proxy servers Archiving and CDR Servers	**Global-level and computer-level settings:** Global settings are backed up from the Standard Edition server or front-end server so that only computer-level settings are backed up from each Mediation Server, Archiving and CDR Server, and forward proxy server. In the event of loss of a Mediation Server, Archiving and CDR Server, or forward proxy server, restoration of computer-level settings is generally all that is required.

Table 14-1 Settings Requirements

Server Role	Settings Required
Edge servers	**Computer-level settings:** Computer-level settings are backed up from each edge server. In the event of loss of an edge server, restoration of computer-level settings is all that is required.

If an Office Communications Server has multiple server roles installed, each server role setting must be backed up. The administrator should not assume that because the backup has been completed for a front-end server's settings the settings for the Conferencing Server have also been backed up.

Backing Up Pool and Global Settings

The LCSCmd.exe command-line tool can be used to back up global-level settings, pool-level settings, and computer-level settings. The LCSCmd.exe tool is automatically installed when Office Communications Server 2007 is installed. This tool is also available on any computer where Office Communications Server 2007 Admins tools are installed.

Backing up the settings needed to restore Office Communications Server 2007 requires backing up the following:

- Global-level and pool-level settings. This requires the following:
  - For a Standard Edition server environment, back up these settings on only one Standard Edition server.
  - For an Enterprise pool, back up these settings on only one front-end server.
- Computer-level (machine-level) settings. Back up these settings on each Office Communications Server 2007 server in your deployment.

Tables 14-2 and 14-3 describe the server roles in each configuration that requires backing up of computer-level settings. Table 14-2 also indicates which internal servers require backing up of computer-level settings.

Table 14-2 Internal Servers Requiring Backup of Computer-Level Settings

Servers	Standard Edition Server Environment	Enterprise Pool, Consolidated Configuration	Enterprise Pool, Expanded Configuration
Standard Edition Servers	√		
Front-end Servers		√	√
Directors (optional)		√	√

Table 14-2 Internal Servers Requiring Backup of Computer-Level Settings

Servers	Standard Edition Server Environment	Enterprise Pool, Consolidated Configuration	Enterprise Pool, Expanded Configuration
Web Components Servers			√
Web Conferencing Servers			√
A/V Conferencing Servers			√
Archiving and CDR Servers	√	√	√
Mediation Servers	√	√	√
Forwarding proxy Servers	√	√	√

> **Note** Office Communications Server 2007 is not installed on back-end servers, so you do not need to back up settings for back-end servers.

Table 14-3 indicates which servers in the perimeter network require backing up of computer-level settings, if your deployment includes edge servers.

Table 14-3 Perimeter Network Servers Requiring Backup of Computer-Level Settings

Servers	Consolidated Edge Topology	Single-Site Edge Topology	Scaled Single-Site Edge Topology	Remote Site Edge Topology in a Multiple Site Topology
Access Edge Servers	√	√	√	√
Web Conferencing Edge Servers	√	√	√	√
A/V Edge Servers	√	√	√	√

> **Note** Office Communications Server 2007 is not installed on reverse proxy servers, so you do not need to back up settings for reverse proxy servers.

To export settings, use the LCSCmd.exe command-line tool and the following procedure. Complete this procedure for each server in your deployment, if you are exporting machine-level settings.

To export global and pool-level settings, do the following:

1. Log on to a Standard Edition server or a front-end server in an Enterprise pool, or to a separate computer on which Office Communications Server 2007 administrative tools have been installed (such as a management console), with an account that has RTCUniversalReadOnlyAdmins or equivalent user rights, as well as write permissions for the folder to which settings are to be backed up.
2. Open a command prompt. Click Start, click Run, type **cmd**, and then click OK.
3. At the command prompt, change to the directory containing the LCSCmd.exe tool (by default, <*drive*>:\Program Files\Common Files\Microsoft Office Communications Server 2007).
4. To export both levels of settings (global and pool), do one of the following:
   - To export global-level and pool-level settings in an Enterprise pool to a single configuration file (.xml file), type the following command:

     ```
     lcscmd /config /action:export /level:global,pool /configfile:
     <drive>:\<path>\<filename>.xml /poolname:[name of pool for which settings are to
     be exported]
     ```

   - To export global-level and pool-level settings for a Standard Edition server to a single configuration file (.xml file), type the following command:

     ```
     lcscmd /config /action:export /level:global,pool /
     configfile:<drive>:\<path>\<filename>.xml /poolname [name of Standard Edition
     server, which is used for the pool name]
     ```

   For the drive, specify a separate, removable media or mapped drive to a separate location in a secure location. For example, for an Enterprise pool, type the following:

   ```
   lcscmd /config /action:export /level:global,pool /
   configfile:C:\Backup\OCS1Serversettings.xml /poolname:ocspool1
   ```

   If you prefer to back up each of the two levels of settings to a separate configuration file (xml file), run the command two times, with the following modifications:

   - For the */level* attribute, specify only one of the two setting levels (global or pool) each time you run the command.
   - For the */configfile* attribute, specify a different, unique file name for each level.

   To export the computer-level settings for a server, type the following command:

   ```
   lcscmd /config /action:export /level:machine /configfile:
   <drive>:\<path>\<filename>.xml /fqdn:[FQDN of server from which settings are to be
   exported]
   ```

   For the drive, specify a separate, removable media or mapped drive to a separate location in a secure location–for example:

   ```
   lcscmd /config /action:export /level:machine /
   configfile:C:\Backup\OCS1Serversettings.xml /fqdn:ocspool1server1.contoso.com
   ```

If running this command from the server being backed up (instead of a separate computer serving as a management console), you can omit the */fqdn* attribute (for the fully qualified domain name [FQDN] of the server).

5. After the command completes, open the configuration file you created and verify that it has both levels of settings (global and pool). If you backed up the two levels of settings to separate files, verify that each of the two files contains the level of settings that it should.
6. To store a configuration file on a separate computer or in a secure location other than the location to which you backed it up (a computer or other location that can be accessed if you need to restore the settings), copy it from the backup location to the other computer or location.
7. Verify that the backed-up configuration file is accessible for restoration purposes, including by standby servers if your organization is deploying separate, secondary sites for recovery in the event of site failure.

Backing Up Server Settings

To export the computer-level settings for a server, type the following command:

```
lcscmd /config /action:export /level:machine /configfile: <drive>:\<path>\<filename>.xml /
fqdn:[FQDN of server from which settings are to be exported]
```

For the drive, specify a separate, removable media or mapped drive to a separate location in a secure location–for example:

```
lcscmd /config /action:export /level:machine /configfile:C:\Backup\OCS1Serversettings.xml /
fqdn:ocspool1server1.contoso.com
```

If running this command from the server being backed up (instead of a separate computer serving as a management console), you can omit the */fqdn* attribute (for the FQDN of the server).

Backing Up Data

Office Communications Server 2007 stores data in databases and file shares. These databases and file shares reside on the following servers:

- Standard Edition servers
- Front-end servers in an Enterprise pool
- Back-end servers in an Enterprise pool
- Archiving and CDR Server

Additionally, domain information is stored in the Active Directory Domain Services. Restoration of service can require recovery and restoration of specific data or entire servers.

Table 14-4 describes the specific databases and file shares used by Office Communications Server 2007.

Table 14-4 Data Stored in Databases

Type of Data	Database	Database Location
Persistent user data (such as access control lists [ACLs], contacts, home server or pool data, and scheduled conferences); this includes user contact lists, as well as allow and block lists.	RTC	Standard Edition: SQL Server 2005 Express Edition Enterprise Edition: SQL Server 2005 database on back-end server
Persistent Office Communications Server 2007 global-level, pool-level, and computer-level settings	RTCConfig	Standard Edition: SQL Server 2005 Express Edition Enterprise Edition: SQL Server 2005 database on back-end server
Transient user data (such as endpoints and subscriptions, active conferencing servers, and transient conferencing states)	RTCDyn	Standard Edition: SQL Server 2005 Express Edition Enterprise Edition: SQL Server 2005 database on back-end server
Archiving data and Call Detail Records (CDRs)	LCSLog (default name)	SQL Server database for archiving data and CDRs, which is typically deployed on a separate computer, the Archiving and CDR Server

Tables 14-5 and 14-6 describe the file shares used by Office Communications Server 2007 and where they are located.

Table 14-5 Data Stored in File Shares for Enterprise Edition

Type of Data	File Share	File Share Location
Meeting content (such as Microsoft Office PowerPoint presentations, Q&A logs, polling data, chat data, and uploaded content)	User-specified (UNC path)	Typically created on a separate computer, such as a file server. By default, it is on the front-end server. This file share is often on the same file share as the address book.
Meeting content metadata (XML data that describes the meeting content, such as the date and time that a presentation is uploaded)	User-specified (UNC path)	Typically created on a separate computer, such as a file server. By default, it is on the front-end server. This file share is often on the same file share as the address book.

Table 14-5 **Data Stored in File Shares for Enterprise Edition**

Type of Data	File Share	File Share Location
Meeting content compliance log (XML data that records content upload activities, along with the uploaded meeting content)	User-specified (UNC path)	Typically created on a separate computer, such as a file server. By default, it is on the front-end server. This file share is often on the same file share as the address book.
Address book files	User-specified (UNC path)	Typically created on a separate computer, such as a file server. By default, it is on the front-end server. This file share is often on the same file share as meeting content.

Table 14-6 **Data Stored in File Shares for Standard Edition**

Type of Data	File Share	File Share Location
Meeting content (such as presentations based on the Microsoft Office PowerPoint presentation graphics program, Q&A logs, polling data, chat data, and uploaded content)	<*drive*>:\Program Files\Microsoft Office Communications Server 2007\Web Components\Data MCU Web\Web (default, created automatically during deployment, but can be changed using Microsoft Windows Management Instrumentation, or WMI)	Standard Edition server
Meeting content metadata (XML data that describes the meeting content, such as the date and time that a PowerPoint presentation is uploaded)	<*drive*>:\Program Files\Microsoft Office Communications Server 2007\Web Components\Data MCU Web\Non-Web (default, created automatically during deployment, but can be changed using WMI)	Standard Edition server
Meeting content compliance log (XML data that records content upload activities, along with the uploaded meeting content)	User specified (UNC path)	Standard Edition server
Address book files	<*drive*>:\Program Files\Microsoft Office Communications Server 2007\Web Components\Address Book Files (default, created automatically during deployment, but can be changed using WMI)	Standard Edition server

Backing Up Databases

This section describes the tools and mechanisms that can be used to back up databases in Office Communications Server 2007. Table 14-7 describes database backup utilities.

Table 14-7 Database Backup Utilities

Data to Be Backed Up	Server or Component Requiring Backup	Database Backup Utility
RTC Database	Standard Edition server	Microsoft SQL Server Management Studio Express in SQL Server 2005 Express Edition, to back up the database on the Standard Edition server.
	Enterprise Edition back-end database	SQL Server database backup utilities, such as Microsoft SQL Server Management Studio in SQL Server 2005, to back up the back-end database.
LCSLog database	Archiving and CDR Server	SQL Server 2005 database back-up utilities, as described previously in this table.
RTCConfig	Standard Edition and Enterprise Edition servers	Not applicable; database does not need to be backed up because restoring settings (using the LCSCmd.exe tool, as covered in the procedures in this chapter) restores the required global-level, pool-level, and computer-level settings.
RTCDyn database	Standard Edition and Enterprise Edition servers	Not applicable; transient information that does not need to be backed up.

For the Office Communications Servers that use SQL Server 2005 and SQL Server 2005 Express Edition, only full backups are supported. A full backup is optimal because the data stored by Office Communications Server is typically smaller than the transaction log files and is significantly smaller than those created by line of business (LOB) database applications. Follow the best practices recommended by SQL Server to back up the databases used by Office Communications Servers.

Backing Up File Shares

Backing up file shares requires backing up the following content:

- Meeting data
- Meeting metadata

- Meeting compliance logs

Table 14-8 describes file system backup utilities.

Table 14-8 File System Backup Utilities

Data to Be Backed Up	Server or Component Requiring Backup	Backup Utility
Meeting content, metadata, and meeting compliance log file shares	Meeting content and compliance logs	File share tools and other backup tools, such as NTBackup.
Address book files	None	Not applicable; automatically generated by the User Replicator.

For the location of these files, see Table 14-5 (for Enterprise Edition) and Table 14-6 (for Standard Edition), which show the default locations. Verify that the backed-up file shares are accessible for restoration purposes, including by standby servers if your organization is deploying separate, secondary sites for recovery in the event of a site failure.

Restoring Service

In the event of the loss of one or more databases, servers, pools, or sites, the backed-up data can be used to restore service. Depending on the type of service loss, the restore procedures vary. The potential restore scenarios are described in the following list:

- Loss of the RTC database or a database server (Standard Edition server or, in an Enterprise pool, back-end server). At a minimum, this type of loss requires restoring the database, but it can also require rebuilding the server on which the RTC database resides.
- Loss of a Standard Edition server. At a minimum, this type of loss requires restoring pool-level and computer-level settings, but it can require rebuilding the servers, restoring domain information, and reassigning users.
- Loss of one or more servers in an Enterprise pool (including one or more front-end servers, Directors, Web Conferencing Servers, A/V Conferencing Servers, or Web Components Servers). At a minimum, this type of loss requires restoring computer-level settings for the server, but it can also require rebuilding individual servers or the entire pool, restoring domain information, and reassigning users.
- Loss of Active Directory, as well as loss of a Standard Edition server or all front-end servers. At a minimum, this type of loss requires restoring global, pool, and computer-level settings, but it can also require rebuilding the servers and domain information.
- Loss of the LCSlog database or Archiving and CDR Server. At a minimum, this type of loss requires restoring the database and computer-level settings, but it can also require rebuilding the Archiving and CDR Server.

- Loss of a Mediation Server, forward proxy server, or edge server. At a minimum, this type of loss requires restoring computer-level settings, but it can also require rebuilding the server.
- Loss of a site, including all servers and Active Directory, which might be the result when there is a natural disaster. This type of loss can require switching service to a separate, secondary site (if supported) or rebuilding all servers and components.

The backup and restoration plan can include some or all of the following procedures, as appropriate for your restoration needs:

1. Deciding how to restore service
2. Verifying restoration prerequisites
3. Setting up server platforms
4. Installing restoration tools
5. Restoring data
6. Restoring settings in Standard Edition server environments
7. Restoring settings in Enterprise pool configurations
8. Re-creating Enterprise pools
9. Reassigning users
10. Restoring domain information
11. Restoring a site

Deciding How to Restore Service

To minimize the impact on users, restoration of service should be done in a way that causes the least disruption while still bringing the environment back to an acceptable level of service. An organization's backup and restoration plan should contain criteria for deciding when and how to restore service. In the event of loss of service, the criteria should be used to determine how to resolve the failure. The criteria should help determine whether only data, settings, or a server needs to be recovered or whether the entire infrastructure does.

If you need to restore multiple servers, you must restore them in the appropriate sequence. Table 14-9 indicates the restoration sequence for each type of deployment. Use the sequence shown, skipping any servers (such as edge servers) that are not in your deployment.

Table 14-9 Restoration Sequence for Servers

Servers	Standard Edition Server Environment	Enterprise Pool, Consolidated Configuration	Enterprise Pool, Expanded Configuration
Back-end servers	Not applicable	1	1
Standard Edition servers	1	Not applicable	Not applicable
Front-end servers	Not applicable	2	2
Directors (optional)	Not applicable	3	3
Web Components Servers	Part of Standard Edition server restoration	Part of front-end server restoration	4
Web Conferencing Servers	Part of Standard Edition server restoration	Part of front-end server restoration	5
A/V Conferencing Servers	Part of Standard Edition server restoration	Part of front-end server restoration	6
Archiving and CDR Servers	2	4	7
Mediation Servers	3	5	8
Edge Servers	4 (For any A/V Conferencing Server not collocated, restore each after restoring other Edge servers)	6	9
Forwarding proxy servers	5	7	10
Reassigning users	6	8	11
Restoring domain information	7	9	12

The components (such as a sites, servers, and databases) to be restored determine the sequence in which to restore them. Figure 14-1 summarizes the restoration sequence for restoring the various services.

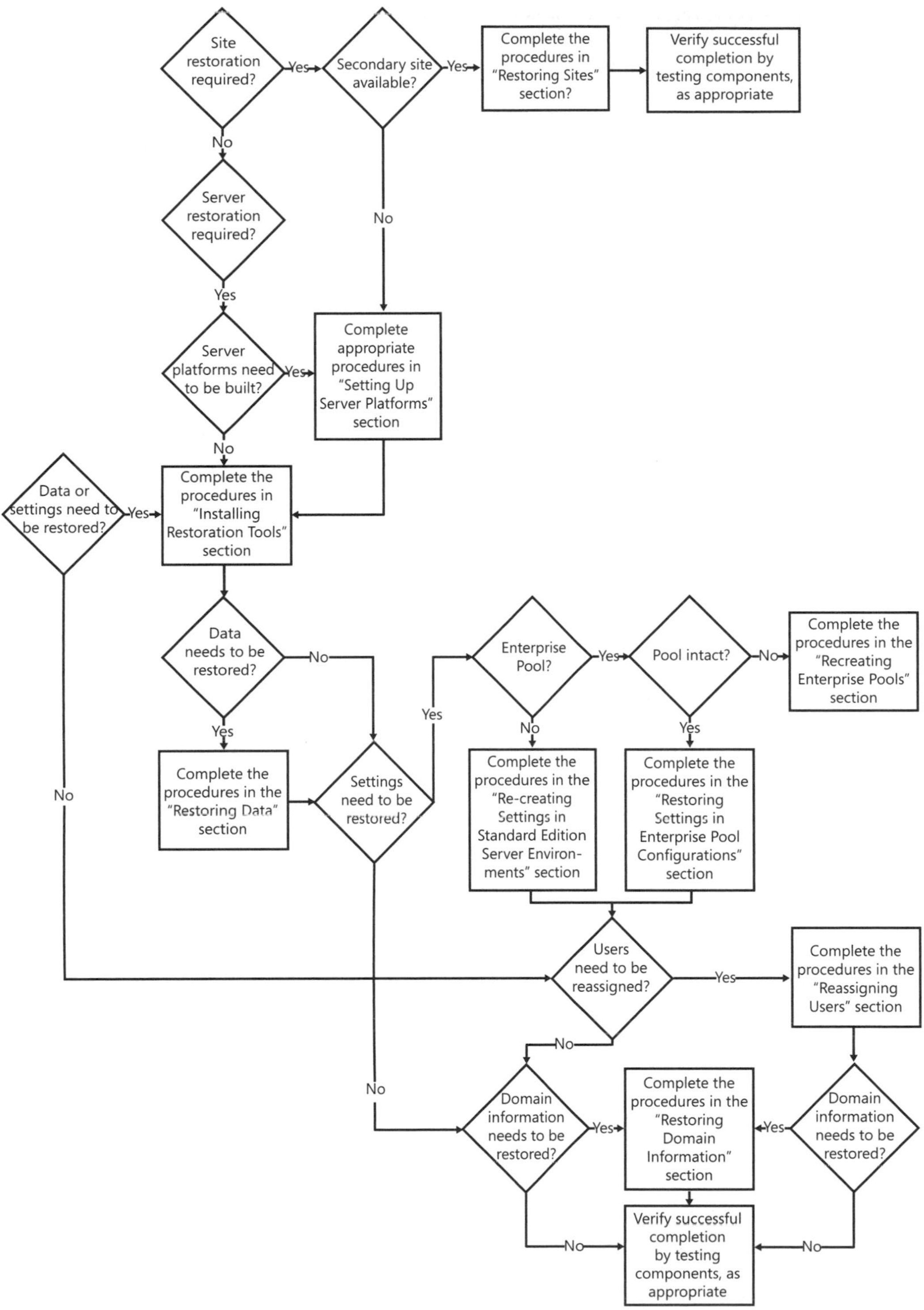

Figure 14-1 Restoration process

Verifying Restoration Prerequisites

Before performing any of the restore procedures, first verify the following prerequisites:

- All required hardware and software for each procedure is available to restore service.
- The backup and restoration plan for your organization is complete, and information from the completed worksheets in Appendix D of this book (or other equivalent information provided by your organization) are available. Appendix D and the worksheets are on the companion CD in the \Appendixes,Scripts,Resources folder.

Setting Up Server Platforms

Typically, a restoration process is required only in the event of a loss of service, so you generally will not need to perform the procedures in this section until then. However, it is necessary to complete some processes in advance, including the following:

- If your backup and restoration strategy includes a requirement to implement a separate, secondary site that can provide recovery capabilities (in the event of the loss of a site, which could be caused by a prolonged power failure or a natural disaster), you need to complete the setup and validation of the standby servers in the secondary site, as covered in the "Restoring Sites" section later in this chapter.
- To ensure that restoration processes work as expected, it is recommended that you test the processes in advance. Your backup and restoration strategy for the organization should identify the testing to be done.

To restore service on any Office Communications Server 2007 server, you first need to set up the hardware and software. This can include any of the following:

- Preparing to use the hardware and software of an existing server for database recovery so that the database can be restored without reinstalling server software
- Recovering an existing server, which requires uninstalling and reinstalling Office Communications Server 2007
- Reinstalling an existing server, which requires reinstalling all software on an existing server
- Rebuilding a server on new hardware, which requires setting up the hardware and installing all software
- Restoring service from standby servers, which requires verifying that the servers are ready to be put into service

Preparing to Use the Hardware and Software of an Existing Server for Database Recovery

On servers using an RTC database or on which an LCSLog database resides, loss of service can be caused by database corruption. Restoring data to the database might be sufficient. If this type of loss occurs, use the following procedure to verify that the operating system and programs installed on the server are operating as they should before proceeding with a database restoration:

1. Log on to the server as a member of the Administrators group.
2. Verify that the required services are running.
3. Check Event Viewer to ensure that no errors exist that would indicate any failures of the database or Office Communications Server.
4. Verify that you can open SQL Server 2005 Express Edition (for Standard Edition server) or SQL Server 2005 (for the back-end server of an Enterprise pool and the Archiving and CDR Server), as appropriate, and that no other software problems are indicated other than the unavailability or corruption of the RTC or LCSLog database. If problems exist that you cannot resolve, refer to the SQL Server 2005 troubleshooting information. (See the following note.) In the worst case, you can uninstall and reinstall the appropriate SQL Server software.

> **Note** To verify that LCSLog and RTC databases exist and that they have valid data, you can open the Management Studio in SQL Server 2005 and run a simple query (for example, **select * from *table_name***). Detailed information on troubleshooting SQL Server 2005 can be found at *http://technet.microsoft.com/en-us/library/ms188314.aspx*.

After you complete these steps, if the server and the software running on it appear to be operable, except for the availability of data in the database, proceed with database restoration, using the information in the "Restoring Databases" section later in this chapter, as appropriate.

If you determine that the server on which the database resides is not operating correctly (and therefore, is not a stable platform for restoring the database), set up the server platform by using one of the other three procedures in this section:

- Recover an existing server by reinstalling and configuring Office Communications Server 2007.
- Reinstall an existing server by reinstalling and configuring the operating system and all other software, including Office Communications Server 2007.
- Rebuild a server on new hardware, including installing and configuring the operating system and all other software.

Recovering an Existing Server

If an Office Communications Server service fails, it might be possible to restore service by uninstalling and reinstalling only Office Communications Server 2007 and then restoring data and settings as necessary. Use the following procedure to recover an existing server without reinstalling the operating system:

1. Log on to the server as a member of the Administrators group.
2. Verify that the required services are running.
3. Check Event Viewer to ensure that no errors exist that indicate use of the current operating system and other programs (other than Office Communications Server 2007) is not advisable.
4. Obtain the deployment plan for your organization that specifies how the server was originally set up. That plan should provide information about the configuration of the server, including the initial configuration of Office Communications Server 2007, which you need to complete the reinstallation of the software.
5. Log on to the server to be recovered or a separate computer (such as a management console) as a member of the RTCUniversalServerAdmins group or a group with equivalent user rights.
6. Deactivate Office Communications Server 2007 by opening Office Communications Server 2007, Administrative Tools, right-clicking the name of the server, pointing to Deactivate, and then clicking the server.
7. Open Services and verify that no services with a name beginning with "Office Communications Server" are running.
8. Uninstall Office Communications Server 2007 on the server to be recovered.
9. Verify that all installation prerequisites have been met.
10. If the server is a Standard Edition server, a back-end server, or an Archiving and CDR Server, verify that you can open SQL Server 2005 Express Edition (for a Standard Edition server) or SQL Server 2005 (for the back-end server of an Enterprise pool and the Archiving and CDR Server), as appropriate, and that no other software problems are indicated other than the unavailability or corruption of the RTC or LCSLog database. If problems exist that you cannot resolve, uninstall and reinstall the appropriate SQL Server software as follows:
    - If you are rebuilding a Standard Edition server, reinstall Office Communications Server 2007, which will reinstall SQL Server 2005 Express Edition.
    - If you are rebuilding a back-end server in an Enterprise pool, install SQL Server 2005.
    - If you are rebuilding an Archiving and CDR Server, install SQL Server 2005.
11. Reinstall Office Communications Server 2007 on the server (as appropriate to the server role to be recovered), completing the setup of all required software, including configuring certificates, starting services, and validating services. You do not need to set up user accounts as part of the basic setup, as the restoration of user accounts is covered by the procedures in the "Reassigning Users" section later in this chapter.

After you complete these steps, if the restored Office Communications Server is operational but does not contain the original data and settings, proceed with restoring the data by using the appropriate procedures in the following sequence (for detailed information about each procedure, refer to the referenced section):

1. Install restoration tools by using the information in the "Installing Restoration Tools" section of this chapter.
2. If the server to which service is being restored is a database server, restore the database by using the information in the "Restoring Databases" section later in this chapter.
3. If required in an Enterprise pool, re-create the Enterprise pool by using the information in the "Re-creating Enterprise Pools" section later in this chapter.
4. Restore settings by using the information in the applicable section of this chapter:
    - "Restoring Settings in Standard Edition Server Environments"
    - "Restoring Settings in Enterprise Pool Configurations"
5. If required, reassign users by using the information in the "Reassigning Users" section of this chapter.
6. If loss of service included loss of Active Directory, restore Active Directory information by using the information in the "Restoring Domain Information" section of this chapter.

If you determine that the server is not operating correctly (and therefore, is not a stable platform), set up the server platform by using the appropriate procedures in the following sections of this chapter to do one of the following:

- Reinstall an existing server by reinstalling and configuring the operating system and all other software, including Office Communications Server 2007.
- Rebuild a server on new hardware, including installing and configuring the operating system and all other software.
- Restore service from standby servers.

Reinstalling an Existing Server

If you have determined that a server loss requires reinstallation of the operating system and other software, and you want to use the same hardware for the deployment, use the following procedure to install and configure the operating system and other software:

1. Obtain the deployment plan for your organization that specifies how the server was originally set up. This plan should provide information about the configuration of the server–including the configuration of the operating system, Office Communications Server 2007, and other programs–which you need to complete the reinstallation of the software.

2. Verify that all deployment prerequisites have been met.
3. Verify that the environment is set up to support the existing server, including preparing Active Directory, configuring Domain Name System (DNS), configuring certificates, setting up load balancers, and configuring routing and other infrastructure components, as applicable (such as would be required if you use different server names or IP addresses for the new server).
4. Install and configure the operating system and all required software, such as SQL Server 2005 (only on a back-end server or Archiving and CDR Server), by using the information in the backup and restoration plan and deployment plans of your organization.
5. Install and configure Office Communications Server 2007 (Standard Edition or Enterprise Edition, as appropriate) and all other required software, as well as configuring certificates, starting services, and validating services. You do not need to set up user accounts as part of the basic setup, as the recovery of user accounts is covered by the procedures in the "Reassigning Users" section of this chapter.

After you reinstall the operating system and all required software, including Office Communication Server 2007 and the appropriate version of SQL Server (if applicable), proceed with restoration of the server by using the appropriate procedures later in this chapter in the following sequence:

1. Install restoration tools by using the information in the "Installing Restoration Tools" section of this chapter.
2. If the server to which service is being restored is a database server, restore the database by using the information in the "Restoring Databases" section of this chapter.
3. If required in an Enterprise pool, re-create the Enterprise pool by using the information in the "Re-creating Enterprise Pools" section of this chapter.
4. Restore settings by using the information in the applicable section of this chapter:
   - "Restoring Settings in Standard Edition Server Environments"
   - "Restoring Settings in Enterprise Pool Configurations"
5. If required, reassign users by using the information in the "Reassigning Users" section of this chapter.
6. If loss of service included loss of Active Directory, restore Active Directory information by using the information in the "Restoring Domain Information" section of this chapter.

If you determine that the server cannot be made to operate correctly (to provide a stable platform) because of hardware problems that cannot be resolved, set up the server on a new platform by using the procedures in the following sections of this chapter to do one of the following:

- Rebuild a server on new hardware, including installing and configuring the operating system and all other software.
- Restore service from standby servers.

Rebuilding a Server on New Hardware

If you have determined that rebuilding a server on new hardware is appropriate, use the following procedure to rebuild the server on new hardware:

1. Obtain the deployment plan for your organization that specifies how the server was originally set up. This plan should provide information about the configuration of the server–including the configuration of the operating system, Office Communications Server 2007, and other programs–which you need to complete the reinstallation of the software.
2. Verify that all deployment prerequisites have been met.
3. Set up hardware for each server to be built, including the computer, network cards, and any additional cards specified in your deployment plan.
4. Set up the environment to support the new server, including preparing Active Directory, configuring DNS, configuring certificates, setting up load balancers, and configuring routing and other infrastructure components, as applicable (such as would be required if you use different server names or IP addresses for the new server).
5. Install and configure the operating system and all required software, such as SQL Server 2005 (only on a back-end server or Archiving and CDR Server), by using the information in the backup and restoration plan and deployment plans of your organization.
6. Install and configure Office Communications Server 2007 (Standard Edition or Enterprise Edition, as appropriate) and all other required software, as well as configuring certificates, starting services, and validating services. You do not need to set up user accounts as part of the basic setup, as the recovery of user accounts is covered by the procedures in the "Reassigning Users" section of this chapter.

After you rebuild the server on new hardware–including installing the operating system, Office Communication Server 2007, the appropriate version of SQL Server (if applicable), and all other required software–proceed with restoration of the server by using the appropriate procedures later in this chapter in the following sequence:

1. Install restoration tools by using the information in the "Installing Restoration Tools" section of this chapter.
2. If the server to which service is being restored is a database server, restore the database by using the information in the "Restoring Databases" section of this chapter.
3. If required in an Enterprise pool, re-create the Enterprise pool by using the information in the "Re-creating Enterprise Pools" section of this chapter.

4. Restore settings by using the information in the applicable section of this chapter:
   - "Restoring Settings in Standard Edition Server Environments"
   - "Restoring Settings in Enterprise Pool Configurations"
5. If required, reassign users by using the information in the "Reassigning Users" section of this chapter.
6. If loss of service included loss of Active Directory, restore Active Directory information by using the information in the "Restoring Domain Information" section of this chapter.
7. In the case of loss of a site, complete the restoration by using the information in the "Restoring Sites" section of this chapter.

Building Standby Servers

If your organization's backup and restoration strategy includes the use of a separate, secondary site to facilitate recovery (in the event of failure), you need to set up the required standby servers.

To deploy one or more standby servers at a secondary site, use the following procedure to build each standby server required by your organization's backup and restoration strategy:

1. Obtain the deployment plan for your organization that specifies how the standby server is to be set up (which should be the same as the way the existing server is set up). This plan should provide information about the configuration of the server–including the configuration of the operating system, Office Communications Server 2007, and other programs–which you need to complete the reinstallation of the software.
2. Verify that all deployment prerequisites have been met.
3. Set up hardware for each standby server to be built, including the computer, network cards, and any additional cards specified in your deployment plan.
4. Set up the environment to support the new server, including preparing Active Directory, configuring DNS, configuring certificates, setting up load balancers, and configuring routing and other infrastructure components, as applicable (such as would be required if you use different server names or IP addresses for the new server).
5. Install and configure the operating system and all required software, such as SQL Server 2005 (only on a back-end server or Archiving and CDR Server), by using the information in the backup and restoration plan and deployment plan of your organization.
6. Install and configure Office Communications Server 2007 (Standard Edition or Enterprise Edition, as appropriate) and all other required software, as well as configuring certificates, starting services, and validating services. The standby server should not be configured with the same pool name as the original server, as covered in the "Restoring Sites" section of this chapter.

7. Install restoration tools on the standby server by using the information in the "Installing Restoration Tools" section of this chapter.

After you complete these steps, use the information in the "Restoring Sites" section of this chapter to complete the deployment and validation of the server to ensure that it is available in the event of a failure. To help ensure that the standby server and other servers at the secondary site are available in case of the loss of the primary site, complete this process as soon as possible after deployment of the primary site.

In the event of a failure, use the information in the "Restoring Sites" section to recover service, as appropriate, including:

- Performing "Step 7. Bring the Secondary Site Online" to restore service in the event of a site failure.
- Performing "Step 8. Restore the Primary Site and Bring It Back Online" to restore the primary site and bring it back online when it is appropriate to do so.

Installing Restoration Tools

The tools required to restore service are the same as those used to back up settings and data:

- LCSCmd.exe, which is used to import settings to the server on which service is being restored. This tool is available on any computer on which you have installed the Office Communications Server 2007 administrative tools (such as a management console). By default, these tools are in the \Program Files\Common Files\Microsoft Office Communications Server 2007 folder on the computer.
- Database tools:
    - To restore databases on Standard Edition servers, use SQL Server Management Studio Express in SQL Server 2005 Express Edition.
    - To restore databases on Enterprise pool back-end servers and Archiving and CDR Servers, use SQL Server Management Studio in SQL Server 2005.
- The appropriate SQL Server program should already be installed on each server that hosts a database, either as a result of the original deployment or rebuilding the server as covered in the "Setting Up Server Platforms" section earlier in this chapter.
- File system management tool or tools used by your organization to restore file shares.

If the required tools are not already installed on each server from which you will be restoring service, install the tools before proceeding.

Restoring Data

If data becomes corrupted, use the information in the following sections to restore it. This includes the following:

- The RTC (user services) and LCSLog (archiving and CDR) databases
- File shares containing meeting content, meeting content metadata, and meeting compliance logs

Restoring Databases

In the event of the loss of an RTC database or an Archiving and CDR Server, you can restore the database to the point of the last backup. If the server on which the database resides needs to be restored also, restore the server first. To restore a server, start with the appropriate procedures in the "Setting Up Server Platforms" section earlier in this chapter.

To restore a database, use the following procedure and the appropriate tool:

- For the RTC database on a Standard Edition server, use SQL Server 2005 Express Edition.
- For the RTC database on a back-end server in an Enterprise pool, use SQL Server 2005.
- For the LCSLog database on the Archiving and CDR Server, use SQL Server 2005.

It is not necessary to restore the RTCConfig database or RTCDyn database.

Complete the following procedure for each database server that requires restoration:

> **Note** The following restoration procedure assumes that you are using Integrated Windows Authentication to access SQL Server 2005.

> **Important** The service account you use to restore the SQL database must be the same one that you used to back up the SQL database.

1. Log on to the servers on which Office Communication Server is installed as a member of the RTCUniversalServerAdmins group or a group with equivalent user rights, and stop all Office Communications Server services that use the database to be restored.
2. Log on to the server on which the database resides as a member of the Administrators group on the local computer or a group with equivalent user rights.
3. On the server, do one of the following:
    - To open SQL Server Management Studio Express, click Start, click All Programs, click Microsoft SQL Server 2005, and then click SQL Server Management Studio Express.
    - To open SQL Server Management Studio, click Start, click All Programs, click Microsoft SQL Server 2005, and then click SQL Server Management Studio.

4. In the console tree, expand the server group, expand the server node, and then expand Databases.
5. Right-click RTC (if restoring the user database) or LCSLog (if restoring the database on the Archiving and CDR Server), point to Tasks, point to Restore, and then click Database.
6. In the Restore Database dialog box, on the General tab, under Destination For Restore, do the following:
   - In the To Database drop-down list, click RTC or LCSLog, as appropriate.
   - Click the button to the right of the To A Point In Time box.
7. In the Point In Time Restore dialog box, under Restore To, click the most recent state possible, and then click OK.
8. In the Restore Database dialog box, on the General tab, under Source For Restore, do one of the following:
   - To select from backup sets in history, click From Database, and then in the drop-down list, click the database backup set from which you want to restore data.
   - To specify one or more tapes or disks as the source for the backup sets, click From Device, and then click the button to the right of the From Device box.
9. Under Select The Backup Sets To Restore, select the backup sets from which you want to restore the database, and then click OK.
10. If you are restoring to an existing database and need to overwrite data in that database, on the Options tab, under Restore Options, do one or more of the following:
    - To overwrite data in the existing database and any related files, select the Overwrite The Existing Database check box.
    - To restore a published database to a server other than the server where the database was created, preserving the replication settings, select the Preserve The Replication Settings check box.
    - To be prompted to start the restoration of each individual backup (for example, if you need to switch tapes for different media sets on a server that has only a single tape drive), select the Prompt Before Restoring Each Backup check box.
    - To make the database available only to members of db_owner, db_creator, and sysadmin, select the Restrict Access To The Restored Database check box.
11. In Restore The Database Files As, verify that the files displayed are correct and, if appropriate, change the path and file name to which database files are to be restored.
12. Under Recovery State, do one of the following:

- To restore the database with the available transaction logs (restore with recovery), click Leave The Database Ready To Use By Rolling Back Uncommitted Transactions.
- To restore the database but leave the database in the restoring state so that you can restore additional transaction logs (restore with no recovery), click Leave The Database Non-operational, And Do Not Roll Back Uncommitted Transactions. If you select this option, the Preserve The Replication Settings option (covered previously in step 10 of this procedure) is not available.
- To restore the database by undoing uncontrolled transactions but saving them in a standby file (restore with standby), click Leave The Database In Read-Only Mode.

13. To start the restoration process, click OK.
14. After the restoration process completes, verify that the restored database is available in the list of databases. To verify the availability of the data in the database, write SQL queries to retrieve specific data.

Repeat this procedure for each back-end server RTC database and LCSLog database that is to be restored in your organization.

Restoring File Shares

In the event of the loss of the file shares containing files related to meeting content, you can restore the file shares to the point of the last backup. This includes the following content:

- Meeting content
- Meeting content metadata
- Meeting content compliance log

You do not need to restore the address book because it is automatically created by User Replicator.

If the server on which each file share is to reside needs to be restored also, restore it first. To restore an Office Communications Server 2007 server on which file shares are to reside, start with the appropriate procedures in the "Setting Up Server Platforms" section earlier in this chapter.

To restore the required file shares, use the file system restoration mechanism and procedures identified in the backup and restoration strategy for your organization.

Restoring Settings in Standard Edition Server Environments

To restore service for a Standard Edition server, use the procedures and guidelines in this section to complete the following steps.

- Step 1. Prepare for restoration of settings
- Step 2. Restore settings
- Step 3. Start services
- Step 4. Validate services

Repeat procedures in the first two steps as appropriate to restore each server in the Standard Edition server environment that requires restoration of settings, and then complete step 3.

Step 1: Prepare for Restoration of Settings

Before restoring settings, you should ensure that servers are ready for restoration. To prepare for restoration of settings, use the following procedure:

1. Set up hardware and software for each server requiring restoration by completing the applicable procedures in the "Setting Up Server Platforms" section earlier in this chapter.
2. If required, restore the RTC database by using the information in the "Restoring Databases" section of this chapter.
3. If required, restore files by using the information in the "Restoring File Shares" section of this chapter.
4. Verify that the configuration file (.xml file) containing the most recently backed up settings is accessible from the computer that you will use to restore settings. This computer can be the server to be restored or a separate computer on which Office Communications Server 2007 administrative tools have been installed (such as a management console). If the configuration file is in a backup location that is not accessible, copy it from the backup location to an accessible location.

Step 2: Restore Settings

To restore settings, you import the required settings to the lost service. In a Standard Edition server environment, this can include the following settings:

- **Global-level settings** Restoration of global-level settings is required only in the event of the loss of Active Directory. If you need to restore global-level settings, you need to do so only once, on a single Standard Edition server.
- **Pool-level settings** Restoration of pool-level settings is required only in the event of the loss of a Standard Edition server. If you need to restore pool-level settings, you need to do so only once, on the Standard Edition server.
- **Computer-level (machine-level) settings** You must restore computer-level settings on each server requiring restoration. This can be a single server or multiple servers, including any of the following:
  - Standard Edition servers

- Archiving and CDR Servers
- Mediation Servers
- Forwarding proxy servers
- Edge servers

To import the required settings, use the LCSCmd.exe command-line tool and the following procedures as appropriate:

- To restore both global-level settings and pool-level settings or only pool-level settings, use the first procedure. If restoration of these settings is required, restore them before restoring any computer-level settings in the Standard Edition environment.
- To restore computer-level settings to a computer in a Standard Edition environment, use the second procedure.

To import global-level and pool level settings in a Standard Edition server environment, do the following:

1. Log on to the Standard Edition server to be restored, or to a computer on which Office Communications Server 2007 administrative tools have been installed, as a member of the RTCUniversalServerAdmins group or a group with equivalent user rights, and stop all Office Communications Server 2007 services (all services that have "Office Communications Server" at the front of the name).
2. Ensure that the required configuration file (.xml file) is accessible.
3. Open a command prompt. Click Start, click Run, type **cmd**, and then click OK.
4. At the command prompt, change to the directory containing the LCSCmd.exe tool (by default, <*drive*>:\Program Files\Common Files\Microsoft Office Communications Server 2007).
5. Import settings by doing one of the following:
   - To restore both global-level and pool-level settings for a Standard Edition server (required in the event of the loss of Active Directory plus the loss of all Standard Edition servers) from a configuration file that contains both levels of settings, type the following command:

     ```
     lcscmd /config /action:import /level:global,pool /restore:true /
     configfile:<drive>:\<path>\<filename>.xml /poolname:[name of computer]
     ```

   - To restore only pool-level settings for a Standard Edition server (required in the event of the loss of a Standard Edition Server but not Active Directory) from a configuration file containing the pool-level settings, type the following command:

     ```
     lcscmd /config /action:import /level:pool /restore:true /
     configfile:<drive>:\<path>\<filename>.xml /poolname:[name of computer]
     ```

For either of these commands, for the drive, specify a separate, removable media or mapped drive to a separate location in a secure location–for example:

```
lcscmd /config /action:import /level:global,pool,machine /restore:true /
configfile:C:\Backup\OCS1Serversettings.xml /poolname:ocsstandardedition1
```

If running the command from a Standard Edition server (instead of a separate computer serving as a management console), you can omit the */poolname* attribute. If you backed up global-level and pool-level settings to separate configuration files (.xml files) and need to restore both levels of settings, run the command once for each level of settings (global and pool) to be imported, with the following modifications:

- For the */level* attribute, specify only one setting level (global or pool) each time you run the command.
- For the */configfile* attribute, specify the name of the file to which the single level of settings was backed up.

6. After typing the command, to start importing settings, press Enter.
7. After importing the settings, verify that the settings are appropriately applied by opening Office Communications Server 2007, Administrative Tools; right-clicking the server name; clicking Properties; and then verifying that both levels of settings are correct.

To import computer-level settings on a computer in a Standard Edition server environment, do the following:

1. Log on to the server to which computer-level settings are to be restored, or to a computer on which Office Communications Server 2007 administrative tools have been installed, as a member of the RTCUniversalServerAdmins group or a group with equivalent user rights, and stop all Office Communications Server 2007 services (all services that have "Office Communications Server" at the front of the name).
2. Ensure that the required configuration file (.xml file) is available.
3. Open a command prompt. Click Start, click Run, type **cmd**, and then click OK.
4. At the command prompt, change to the directory containing the LCSCmd.exe tool (by default, <*drive*>:\Program Files\Common Files\Microsoft Office Communications Server 2007).
5. Import computer-level settings to the server by typing the following command:

```
lcscmd /config /action:import /level:machine /restore:true /
configfile:<drive>:\<path>\<filename>.xml /fqdn:[FQDN of Standard Edition server to
which settings are to be imported]
```

For the drive, specify a separate, removable media or mapped drive to a separate location in a secure location–for example:

```
lcscmd /config /action:import /level:machine /restore:true /
configfile:C:\Backup\OCS1Serversettings.xml /fqdn:ocsstandardedition1.contoso.com
```

The */fqdn* attribute is required only for restoration of a Standard Edition server and only if running the command on a separate computer serving as a management console.

6. After typing the command, to start importing settings, press Enter.
7. After importing the settings, verify that the computer-level settings are appropriately applied by opening Office Communications Server 2007, Administrative Tools; right-clicking the server name; clicking Properties; and then verifying that the settings are correct.

Repeat this procedure for each server in your deployment to which settings are to be restored.

Step 3: Start Services

To complete restoration of service in the Standard Edition server environment, after restoring all required settings, start all applicable services in the following sequence:

1. SQL Server 2005 Express Edition
2. Office Communications Server Archiving and CDR Server service, if required
3. Office Communications Server Front End Service
4. Office Communications Server IM Conferencing Server service
5. Office Communications Server Telephony Conferencing Server service
6. Office Communications Server Web Conferencing Server service
7. Office Communications Server A/V Conferencing Server service
8. Office Communications Server Mediation Server service, if required
9. Office Communications Server Proxy Server service, if required
10. Office Communications Server Access Edge Server service, if required
11. Office Communications Server Web Conferencing Edge Server service, if required
12. Office Communications Server A/V Edge Server service, if required
13. Office Communications Server A/V Authentication Service, if required

Step 4: Validate Services

After starting services, use the Validation Wizard to validate the individual server roles by following these steps:

1. Log on to a computer that is running Office Communications Server 2007 Standard Edition, or to a computer on which the Office Communications Server 2007 Administrative Tools is installed, with an account that is a member of the Administrators group.

2. Open the Office Communications Server 2007, Administrative Tools snap-in. Click Start, point to All Programs, point to Administrative Tools, and then click Office Communications Server 2007.
3. In the console tree, expand Standard Edition Servers, and expand the pool name and role (such as Front Ends).
4. Right-click the FQDN of the restored server, point to Validation, and then click the server role (such as Front End Server) to start the Validation Wizard.
5. Complete the steps in the Validation Wizard.

Repeat this procedure for each of the four primary services (Front End, Web Conferencing, A/V Conferencing, and Web Components).

Next Steps

After you have completed the procedures in this section to restore settings in the Standard Edition server environment, do the following:

- Reassign users, if required, by using the information in the "Reassigning Users" section of this chapter.
- Restore domain information, if required, by using the information in the "Restoring Domain Information" section of this chapter.

Restoring Settings in Enterprise Pool Configurations

To restore service servers in an Enterprise pool configuration, use the procedures and guidelines in this section to complete the following steps.

- Step 1. Prepare for restoration of settings.
- Step 2. Restore settings.
- Step 3. Activate servers (only with a re-created Enterprise pool).
- Step 4. Start services.
- Step 5. Validate server and pool functionality.

Repeat the procedures in the first two steps as appropriate to restore each server in an Enterprise pool environment that requires restoration of settings, and then complete step 3.

Step 1: Prepare for Restoration of Settings

Before restoring settings, you should ensure that servers are ready for restoration. To prepare for restoration of settings, use the following procedure:

1. Set up hardware and software for each server requiring restoration by completing the applicable procedures in the "Setting Up Server Platforms" section earlier in this chapter.

2. If you need to re-create the entire pool, use the information in the "Installing Restoration Tools" section and the "Re-creating Enterprise Pools" section of this chapter to re-create the pool before using the information in step 2 to restore any server settings.
3. If required, restore the RTC database by using the information in the "Restoring Databases" section of this chapter. Restoration of databases is always required if setting restoration is a result of re-creating a pool.
4. If required, restore files by using the information in the "Restoring File Shares" section of this chapter. Restoration of files is always required if setting restoration is a result of re-creating a pool.
5. Verify that the configuration file (.xml file) containing the most recently backed up settings is accessible from the computer that you will use to restore settings. This computer can be the server to be restored or a separate computer on which Office Communications Server 2007 administrative tools have been installed (such as a management console). If the configuration file is in a backup location that is not accessible, copy it from the backup location to an accessible location.

Step 2: Restore Settings

To restore settings, you import the required settings to the lost service. In an Enterprise pool environment, this can include the following settings:

- **Global-level settings** Restoration of global-level settings is required only in the event of the loss of Active Directory. If you need to restore global-level settings, you need to do so only once, on a single front-end server.
- **Pool-level settings** Restoration of pool-level settings is required only in the event of the loss of all front-end servers or a back-end server. If you need to restore pool-level settings, you need to do so only once, on a single front-end server.
- **Computer-level (machine-level) settings** You must restore computer-level settings on each server requiring restoration. This can include a single server or multiple servers, including any of the following:
  - Front-end servers
  - Directors
  - Web Components Servers (Enterprise pool, expanded configuration only)
  - Web Conferencing Servers (Enterprise pool, expanded configuration only)
  - A/V Conferencing Servers (Enterprise pool, expanded configuration only)
  - Archiving and CDR Servers
  - Mediation Servers
  - Forwarding proxy servers
  - Edge servers

To import the required settings, use the LCSCmd.exe command-line tool and the following procedures, as appropriate:

- To restore both global-level settings and pool-level settings or only pool-level settings, use the first procedure below. If restoration of these settings is required, restore them before restoring any computer-level settings in the Enterprise environment.
- To restore computer-level settings to a computer in an Enterprise pool environment, use the second procedure below.

To import global-level and pool-level settings in an Enterprise pool environment, do the following:

1. Log on to the first front-end server to be restored, or to a computer on which Office Communications Server 2007 administrative tools have been installed, as a member of the RTCUniversalServerAdmins group or a group with equivalent user rights, and stop all Office Communications Server 2007 services (all services that have "Office Communications Server" at the front of the name).
2. Ensure that the required configuration file (.xml file) is accessible.
3. Open a command prompt. Click Start, click Run, type **cmd**, and then click OK.
4. At the command prompt, change to the directory containing the LCSCmd.exe tool (by default, <*drive*>:\Program Files\Common Files\Microsoft Office Communications Server 2007).
5. Import settings by doing one of the following:
   - To restore both global-level and pool-level settings for an Enterprise pool (required in the event of the loss of Active Directory plus the loss of all front-end servers) from a configuration file that contains both levels of settings, type the following command:

     ```
     lcscmd /config /action:import /level:global,pool /
     configfile:<drive>:\<path>\<filename>.xml /poolname:[name of pool to which to
     restore server] /restore:true
     ```

   - To restore only pool-level settings (required in the event of the loss of all front-end servers or a back-end server, but not Active Directory) from a configuration file containing the pool-level settings, type the following command:

     ```
     lcscmd /config /action:import /level:pool /
     configfile:<drive>:\<path>\<filename>.xml /poolname:[name of pool to which to
     restore server] /restore:true
     ```

     For either of these commands, for the drive, specify a separate, removable media or mapped drive to a separate location in a secure location–for example:

     ```
     lcscmd /config /action:import /level:global,pool /
     configfile:C:\Backup\OCS1FrontEndServersettings.xml /poolname:ocspool1 /
     restore:true
     ```

If running the command from the front-end server being restored (instead of a separate computer serving as a management console), you can omit the */poolname* attribute. If you backed up global-level and pool-level settings to separate configuration files (.xml files) and need to restore both levels of settings, run the command once for each level of settings (global and pool) with the following modifications:

- For the */level* attribute, specify only one setting level (global or pool) each time you run the command.
- For the */configfile* attribute, specify the name of the file to which the single level of settings was backed up.

6. After typing the command, to start importing settings, press Enter.
7. After importing the settings, verify that the settings are appropriately applied by opening Office Communications Server 2007, Administrative Tools; right-clicking the server name; clicking Properties; and then verifying that both levels of settings are correct.

To import computer-level settings on a computer in an Enterprise pool environment, do the following:

1. Log on to the server to which computer-level settings are to be restored, or to a computer on which Office Communications Server 2007 administrative tools have been installed, as a member of the RTCUniversalServerAdmins group or a group with equivalent user rights, and stop all Office Communications Server 2007 services (all services that have "Office Communications Server" at the front of the name).
2. Ensure that the required configuration file (.xml file) is accessible.
3. Open a command prompt. Click Start, click Run, type **cmd**, and then click OK.
4. At the command prompt, change to the directory containing the LCSCmd.exe tool (by default, <*drive*>:\Program Files\Common Files\Microsoft Office Communications Server 2007).
5. Import computer-level settings to the server by typing the following command:

```
lcscmd /config /action:import /level:machine /configfile:<drive>:\<path>\<filename>.xml
/fqdn:[FQDN of Front End Server to which settings are to be imported] /restore:true
```

For the drive, specify a separate, removable media or mapped drive to a separate location in a secure location–for example:

```
lcscmd /config /action:import /level:machine /
configfile:C:\Backup\OCS1FrontEndServersettings.xml /fqdn:ocspool1frontend.contoso.com
/restore:true
```

The */fqdn* attribute is required only for a front-end server or, in an Enterprise pool, expanded configuration, for the following server roles: Web Components Server, Web Conferencing Server, or A/V Conferencing Server.

6. After typing the command, to start importing settings, press Enter.
7. After importing the settings, verify that the computer-level settings are appropriately applied by opening Office Communications Server 2007, Administrative Tools; right-clicking the server name; clicking Properties; and then verifying that the settings are correct.

Repeat this procedure for each server in your deployment to which settings are to be restored, except the server on which you restored multiple levels of settings (as described in the previous procedure).

Step 3: Activate Servers (Only with a Re-created Enterprise Pool)

To complete the restoration of a front-end server, activate the server by using the following command:

```
lcscmd /server:[<server FQDN>] /action:activate /role:ee [/user:<service account name>] /
password:<pw> /poolname:<name of Enterprise Edition pool to join> [/archserver:<name of
Archiving and CDR Server> /nostart /unregspn /queuename:<name of queue on the Archiving and
CDR service>
```

In this command, *role:ee* is used for the front-end server of an Enterprise pool in the consolidated configuration.

To activate the Web Conferencing Server and the A/V Conferencing Server, use the following command:

```
lcscmd /mcu[:<mcu server FQDN>] /action:activate /role:<datamcu|avmcu> [/user:<service
account name>] /password:<pw> /poolname:<name of Enterprise Edition pool to join> /
nostart:<true|false>
```

In this command, *role:datamcu* is used to activate a Web Conferencing Server role and *role:avmcu* is used to activate an A/V Conferencing Server.

Step 4: Start Services

To complete restoration of service in the Enterprise pool configuration, after restoring all required settings, start all applicable services in the following sequence:

1. SQL Server 2005
2. Office Communications Server Archiving and CDR Server service, if required
3. Office Communications Server front-end server service
4. Office Communications Server IM Conferencing Server service
5. Office Communications Server Telephony Conferencing Server service
6. Office Communications Server Web Components Service
7. Office Communications Server Web Conferencing Server service

8. Office Communications Server A/V Conferencing Server service
9. Office Communications Server Mediation Server service, if required
10. Office Communications Server Proxy Server service, if required
11. Office Communications Server Access Edge Server service, if required
12. Office Communications Server Web Conferencing Edge Server service, if required
13. Office Communications Server A/V Edge Server service, if required
14. Office Communications Server A/V Authentication Service, if required

Step 5: Validate Server and Pool Functionality

If you have re-created the Enterprise pool, run the Validation Wizard from the Office Communications 2007 Server Deployment Wizard to validate the functionality of the pool and servers in the pool. As part of the validation task, you can validate each Enterprise pool server role that you restore, which includes:

- Front-end servers
- Web Conferencing Servers
- A/V Conferencing Servers
- Web Components Servers

Each server role for the topology can also be validated using the Office Communications Server 2007 administrative snap-in.

Next Steps

After you have completed the procedures in this section to restore service to servers in the Enterprise pool, do the following:

- Reassign users, if required, by using the information in the "Reassigning Users" section of this chapter.
- Restore domain information, if required, by using the information in the "Restoring Domain Information" section of this chapter.

Re-creating Enterprise Pools

To re-create a pool, complete the following procedure before doing any other restoration for the pool, including restoring data, adding servers, and restoring settings in the pool. Repeat the procedures in this section for each pool that needs to be re-created.

To re-create a pool, use the LCSCmd.exe command-line tool and the following procedure:

1. Log on to the server as a member of the RTCUniversalServerAdmin and DomainAdmins groups or a group with equivalent user rights.
2. Open a command prompt. Click Start, click Run, type **cmd**, and then click OK.
3. At the command prompt, change to the directory containing the LCSCmd.exe tool (by default, <*drive*>:\Program Files\Common Files\Microsoft Office Communications Server 2007).
4. At the command prompt, type the following command:

```
lcscmd
/forest:<forest FQDN> /action:<action name>
/poolname:<pool name>
/poolbe:<SQL instance name (computer\instance name)>
/refdomain:<domain FQDN> /dbdatapath:<database data file path>
/dblogpath:<database log file path>
/dyndatapath:<dynamic database data path>
/dynlogpath:<dynamic database log path>
/meetingcontentpath:<meeting content UNC path>
/meetingmetapath:<meeting metadata UNC path>
/clean
```

5. After typing the command, to start re-creating the pool, press Enter.

Repeat this procedure for each Enterprise pool in your organization that needs to be created.

After you have completed the procedure in this section to re-create a pool, do the following:

- Restore all required servers in the Enterprise pool configuration by using the information in the "Restoring Settings in Enterprise Pool Configurations" section of this chapter.
- Reassign users, if required, by using the information in the "Reassigning Users" section of this chapter.
- Restore domain information, if required, by using the information in the "Restoring Domain Information" section of this chapter.

Reassigning Users

If restoring users' contact lists and permissions is not a priority, reassigning users to another functioning Office Communications Server is sufficient. This can easily be done through the Move Users Wizard, which is available in the Admins Tools MMC and Active Directory Users and Computers MMC (DSA.MSC).

If restoring users' contact lists and permissions is a priority, in addition to using the Move Users Wizard to reassign the users to another functioning Office Communications Server, the administrator must also restore the data from the failed Office Communications Server. Restoring this data must be performed on the Office Communications Server to which the users are reassigned. Refer to the "Restoring Databases" section for more details.

Restoring Domain Information

The user database (RTC) on Office Communications Server 2007 (Back-End Database) retains a mapping of Active Directory user globally unique identifiers (GUIDs) and security identifiers (SIDs) for every Session Initiation Protocol (SIP)-enabled user. The user's Office Communications settings (SIP URI, remote access, federation, archiving, telephony, Line URI, and so on) are stored in the database. As a result, backups taken of the SQL database contain these mappings and settings.

If Active Directory encounters a problem and global and user settings in Active Directory specific to Office Communications Server 2007 are not restored as part of the service restoration procedure, you might need to restore the RTC database through the steps described in the "Restoring Databases" section of this chapter.

If you need to restore the Active Directory domain, these mappings will change and you will need to export user data using the Office Communications Server user database (RTC), rebuild your Active Directory domain, and import user data back into the database. Though this is a rare occurrence, considering the separate processes and procedures for managing health of Active Directory (as well as the inherent redundancy of Active Directory when more than one domain controller is used per domain), it would be wise to ensure that your processes for recovering Active Directory are up to date.

Restoring Sites

In the event of a failure of an entire site, which can be caused by a natural disaster, all servers in the internal network and perimeter network must be restored. This can be done using one of the following methods:

- Restoring the servers at the original site or another site after the failure by rebuilding servers. You can do this by using the procedures in the "Reinstalling an Existing Server" section or the "Rebuilding a Server on New Hardware" section of this chapter, as appropriate, and restoring servers in the same sequence as in the original deployment.
- Setting up standby servers at a secondary site in advance to provide recovery support, and using them to provide interim support until the primary site is restored. This approach is recommended for optimal site recovery. To help ensure availability of the secondary site, in the event of a catastrophic loss such as a natural disaster, we recommend that the standby servers be located at a separate site at a different geographical location than the primary site. Servers are brought online in the same sequence as in the original deployment.

This section focuses on the second method, setting up a secondary site, which requires deployment of appropriate hardware and software at the secondary site, as well as other preparations and ongoing maintenance of the site. The information in this section is based on using the secondary site as an interim solution until the primary site can be restored. To set up and use a secondary site to support recovery, use the procedures and guidelines in this section to complete the following steps:

1. Determine the recovery support to be provided by the secondary site.
2. Create a deployment plan and restoration strategy for the secondary site.
3. Set up the secondary site.
4. Prepare the primary site to support recovery at the secondary site.
5. Maintain the secondary site.
6. Validate site recovery capabilities by simulating an outage.
7. Bring the secondary site online.
8. Restore the primary site and bring it back online.

> **Note** The following steps describe site restoration for an Enterprise pool. To restore a site for a Standard Edition server deployment, you can use the same procedure steps, modifying them as appropriate (such as using the IP address of the Standard Edition server instead of the virtual IP address of the load balancer). These steps assume that Active Directory is set up with the appropriate configuration to support the secondary site in the same domain as the primary site and that Active Directory remains available and functional in the event of the loss of the primary site.

Step 1: Determine the Recovery Support to Be Provided by the Secondary Site

Using standby servers at a secondary site for recovery helps ensure minimal disruption in the event of failure of services. The secondary site can provide full recovery support or, based on business needs, provide recovery support for only specific functionality. As the first step in preparing for site recovery, you need to determine the level of support that is to be provided by the secondary site, which will determine which servers are to be deployed at the secondary site and how they are to be configured. Ideally, the secondary site provides all the Office Communications Server functionality available at the primary site, but there are several factors that might cause your organization to limit the support provided by the secondary site. Your backup and restoration strategy should specify what is deployed in the secondary site and, if it does not provide full functionality, it should specify why recovery support for specific functionality is not implemented. The determination of what is required at the secondary site is generally made based on the following factors:

- Office Communications Server functionality available at the primary site.
- Business criticality of specific functionality. At a minimum, setting up a secondary site requires support of core services, which are provided by the Standard Edition server or, for an Enterprise pool, by the front-end server and back-end database. Other functional-

ity, such as the A/V Conferencing Server, can be deployed in the primary site but might not have the same level of criticality as core services or might not be fully implemented early in a deployment. The secondary site should reflect the business needs, not simply mirror the primary site. Business criticality can change as the topology and usage change, so your backup and restoration strategy should include periodic reviews of the secondary data site capabilities and whether they match current business needs.

- Cost of the hardware, software, and maintenance for the secondary site. The equipment and software you deploy in the secondary site should be capable of supporting the capacity requirements for your organization, which can mean a significant initial investment in hardware and software, as well as the cost of deploying and maintaining it. Based on business criticality decisions, you might determine that the cost of specific functionality is not justifiable.
- Service availability requirements. Bringing a secondary site online takes time, during which functionality is not available to users in your organization. Bringing core services online can require an hour or more in a large enterprise. Restoring additional functionality increases the downtime. If your organization requires immediate recovery, you might want to limit the functionality that is restored in order to shorten the time required to bring services back online. Or you might want to plan for a staged recovery, with critical functionality brought online at the secondary site first and other functionality introduced on a delayed schedule (such as during off-peak hours).

When using a secondary site for service restoration, all backed-up data and settings must be available at the secondary site. Testing should include restoration of the data and settings from the secondary site.

Step 2: Create a Deployment Plan and Restoration Strategy for the Secondary Site

The deployment plan for the secondary site should match the deployment plan for the primary site, including being in the same domain and having the same network configuration, except for the following:

- It should document only the components required to support the functionality that you determined is required at the secondary site, based on completing step 1 of this section.
- The secondary site should have a pool name that is different than the pool name used for the primary site.
- The _sipinternaltls and _sip_tcp DNS records should be modified to the secondary site.

The backup and restoration strategy should include a schedule and criteria for switching to the secondary site, schedules for performing ongoing maintenance at the secondary site, and assigned responsibilities for performing site restoration procedures at both the primary site and the secondary site.

Step 3: Set Up the Secondary Site

Setting up the secondary site requires first doing the following:

1. Setting up the infrastructure. This includes verifying the setup and configuration of Active Directory, DNS, certificates, load balancers, routing, and other infrastructure components, as specified in the deployment plan.
2. Installing and configuring the required server platforms at the secondary site, using the information in the "Building Standby Servers" section of this chapter.

After the infrastructure is in place and the standby server platforms are installed and configured, prepare them for use by doing the following:

1. On the server that will provide the back-end database for the secondary site, install a new SQL Server database.
2. Create a new Enterprise pool (for example, backuppool.boston.corp.contoso.com), associate it with the new SQL Server instance, and do not select the option to replace existing databases.
3. Set up the front-end servers at the secondary site, and join them to the new Enterprise pool.
4. Set up the other servers required at the secondary site by configuring them to use the new pool.

To help ensure that the secondary site is prepared to be brought online if the primary site fails, you should complete all the setup of the secondary site as soon as possible after deployment of the primary site.

Step 4: Prepare the Primary Site to Support Recovery at the Secondary Site

The only thing required at the primary site is to ensure that the backups are routinely stored at a location accessible by the servers at the secondary site. It is generally recommended that all backups be routinely copied to the secondary site to ensure availability in the event of failure.

Step 5: Maintain the Secondary Site

On an ongoing basis, verify that each standby server is ready to be put into service, which requires the following:

- Evaluating the topology and components of the secondary site to determine if they continue to be appropriate to the business needs. As business directions and usage change, the level of support that is appropriate for the secondary site might require changes to the topology and components of the secondary site.

- Verifying that the infrastructure is ready. This includes verifying the set up and functionality of Active Directory, DNS, certificates, load balancers, routing, and other infrastructure components.
- Reviewing the most recent deployment plan of the primary site and ensuring that it is current (that it matches the actual deployment at the primary site, including installation of all service packs and software updates), including all configuration settings for all servers that are also deployed at the secondary site. This plan should provide information about the setup of each primary site server, including the deployment prerequisites, installation and configuration of the operating system, installation and configuration of Office Communications Server 2007, and installation and configuration of any additional software (such as reverse proxy server software).
- Reviewing the deployment plan of the secondary site, and ensuring that it is current and matches both the most recent deployment plan of the primary site and the actual setup of the servers at the secondary site (including installation of all service packs and software updates). This includes verifying that all software is installed, as appropriate, on each standby server, including the operating system, Office Communications Server 2007, and any additional software required (such as SQL Server 2005 for a back-end server in an Enterprise pool or an Archiving and CDR Server).
- Keep servers running so that they will be ready to be put into service if service is lost at the primary site.

Step 6: Validate Site Recovery Capabilities by Simulating an Outage

To ensure that the secondary site can effectively be brought online in the event of an outage, you should do at least one test to verify that everything works as it should. To do this, you must take the servers at the primary site offline, which you can do by shutting down all the Office Communication Server 2007 servers at the primary site; then use the information in step 7 to bring the secondary site online. After verifying that the secondary site works as required, use the information in step 8 to bring the primary site back online.

As part of the validation process, determine how much time it takes to bring the secondary site online (step 7), as well as to bring the primary site back online (step 8), and incorporate this information in your backup and restoration plan, as appropriate.

Step 7: Bring the Secondary Site Online

In the event of failure of service at the primary site, bring the secondary site online by doing the following:

1. Restore the backup of the RTC database of the primary site to the RTC database of the pool in the secondary site.
2. Modify the _sipinternaltls and _sip_tcp DNS records to point to the pool FQDN of the secondary site. (If using a load balancer, modify the DNS records of the pool in the sec-

ondary site to use the same virtual IP address configured on the load balancer in the original site.)

3. Configure the front-end servers in the new pool created for the secondary site, as specified in the deployment plan, and verify the setup. This can include verifying specific configurations, such as the following:
   - Front-end servers within a pool behind a load balancer must be capable of routing to each other. There can be no Network Address Translation (NAT) device in this path of communication. Any such device will prevent successful interpool communication over RPC.
   - Front-end servers behind a load balancer must have access to the Active Directory environment.
   - Front-end servers must have static IP addresses that can be used to configure them for use with the load balancer. In addition, these IP addresses must have DNS registrations (front-end server FQDNs).
   - Administration computers must be able to route through the load balancer to the pool FQDN, as well as the front-end server FQDN of every front-end server in the pool or pools to be managed. In addition, there can be no NAT device in the path of communication to the front-end servers to be managed (a restriction enforced by the usage of the RPC protocol by DCOM).
4. Use the Office Communications Server 2007 administrative snap-in to move all users to the new pool by using the Force User option.
5. Test connectivity by logging on to Office Communicator from a client computer. Depending on the configuration and situation, you might need to modify configurations to do this. For instance, if the virtual IP address and pool FQDN change, it might be necessary to modify the client configuration unless auto-logon is enabled. It might also be necessary to use the **ipconfig /flushdns** command to flush the DNS cache from the client computers.

Step 8: Restore the Primary Site and Bring It Back Online

When the primary site is ready to return to service, bring it back online.

Note The information describes how to bring the primary site back online after server loss at the primary site. Before starting this step, use the appropriate procedures in the "Setting Up Server Platforms" section to set up the required servers.

If the failure of service at the original site was a temporary condition, such as a power outage, that did not damage the servers, you do not need to do anything except turn the servers back on.

To restore the primary site, after setting up server platforms, do the following:

1. Back up the RTC database from the secondary site, and store it at a location accessible from the primary site.
2. Log on to the front-end server in the primary site, and then use the Office Communications Server 2007 administrative snap-in to deactivate the server roles (as appropriate to your configuration) in the following sequence:

> **Important** Use the log file to verify successful deactivation of each server role (and all deactivation tasks for that server role) before proceeding with deactivation of the next server role.

   - ❑ Microsoft Office Communications Server 2007, Audio/Video Conferencing Server
   - ❑ Microsoft Office Communications Server 2007, Web Conferencing Server
   - ❑ Microsoft Office Communications Server 2007, Web Components Server
   - ❑ Microsoft Office Communications Server 2007, front-end server
3. Expand the pool, right-click Users, and then click Delete Users to remove SIP-enabled users from the pool (after verifying the availability of the database backup in the secondary site pool).
4. Use the Remove Pool Wizard to remove the original pool and corresponding files of the primary site, using the Force option but clearing the Keep Existing Databases option.

> **Important** Use the log file to verify successful removal of the pool and all removal tasks before proceeding to the next step.

5. Use Add/Remove Programs to uninstall each of the server roles (as appropriate to your configuration) in the following sequence:
   - ❑ Microsoft Office Communications Server 2007, Administrative Tools
   - ❑ Microsoft Office Communications Server 2007, Audio/Video Conferencing Server
   - ❑ Microsoft Office Communications Server 2007, Standard Edition server or Microsoft Office Communications Server 2007, Enterprise Edition server
   - ❑ Microsoft Office Communications Server 2007, Web Conferencing Server
   - ❑ Microsoft Office Communications Server 2007, Web Components Server
6. Delete share folders that have been created during pool and server creation for meeting content, meeting metadata, and the address book file store.
7. Use the Office Communications Server 2007 Deployment Wizard to set up all required server roles.

8. Create a new pool with the same pool name as the original primary site, using the default Remove Existing Databases option.
9. Restore the RTC database backup from the secondary site to the same instance of SQL used by the original pool of the primary site (specifying the appropriate instance name if the default was not used originally).
10. With both pools (for the primary site and secondary site) online, use the Office Communications Server 2007 administrative snap-in to move all the users from the secondary site pool to the primary site pool. Do not use the Force option.
11. On the load balancer, disable the front-end servers associated with the pool in the secondary site and configure the front-end servers in the primary site pool as specified in the deployment plan.
12. Modify DNS records to point back to the original primary site pool.
13. Log on to Office Communicator, and verify connectivity to the primary site and functionality of IM, contact groups, and contact lists. Depending on the configuration and situation, you might need to modify configurations to do this. For instance, if the virtual IP address and pool FQDN change, it might be necessary to modify the client configuration unless auto-logon is enabled. It might also be necessary to use the **ipconfig / flushdns** command.

Best Practices

This section describes some best practices that you can follow when backing up and restoring your database environment.

Best Practices for Backup and Restoration

Use the following guidelines as best practices for establishing your backup and restore requirements:

- Perform regular backups at appropriate intervals. The simplest and most commonly used backup type and rotation schedule is a full, nightly backup of the entire SQL database. If restoration is necessary, the restore process requires only one backup tape. In addition, no more than a day's worth of data can be lost.
- Schedule backups when normal Office Communications Server 2007 usage is low. Scheduling backups at times when the server is not under peak load improves server performance and the user experience.

Best Practices for Minimizing the Impact of a Disaster

The best strategy for dealing with disastrous service interruptions (because of unmanageable events such as power outages or sudden hardware failures) is to assume they will happen and plan accordingly.

The disaster management plans you develop as part of your backup and restoration strategy should include the following:

- Keeping your software media and your software and firmware updates readily available.
- Maintaining hardware and software records.
- Monitoring servers proactively.
- Backing up your data regularly, and ensuring the integrity of your backups (test actual backup process to ensure end-to-end integrity).
- Training your staff in disaster recovery, documenting procedures, and implementing disaster-recovery simulation drills.
- Keeping spare hardware available or, if operating under a Service Level Agreement (SLA), contracting with hardware vendors and suppliers for prompt replacements. This can include setting up a separate, secondary site with standby servers that can be brought online quickly.
- Separating the location of your transaction log files (.ldf files) and database files (.mdf files).
- Ensuring your insurance policy is adequate.

Note Many organizations are moving to a model of just-in-time inventories for their IT organizations. They contract with hardware vendors and suppliers, and the contract specifies an SLA of a few hours for delivery of certain pieces of hardware in the event of a catastrophe. The advantage of this method is that it eliminates the need to keep multiple spare servers sitting unused.

Summary

The key to a successful backup and restore plan is setting up a clear process that matches the business requirements of your organization before a failure occurs. Without such a plan, it's likely to be difficult to restore service in an efficient and timely manner under pressure if a failure occurs. Creating a backup and restore plan might involve members from various teams working together in the event of a disaster. It is critical to develop and agree upon a well-thought-out plan in advance. The time to restore a service depends directly on the investments made in backing up the data and defining procedures. Getting the sequence of the restoration steps correct is critical to ensure service is returned to proper functionality. Near-real-time failover when a natural disaster occurs can be achieved by maintaining an active site and a passive site. It is important to align your business priorities with the backup and restoration plan.

Additional Resources

- Microsoft Office Communications Server 2007 Administration Guide, found at *http://technet.microsoft.com/en-us/library/bb676082.aspx*
- Microsoft Office Communications Server 2007 Planning Guide, found at *http://technet.microsoft.com/en-us/library/bb676082.aspx*

On the Companion CD

- Backup and Restoration Worksheets. (See Appendix D in the \Appendixes,Scripts,Resources folder.)

Chapter 15

Administration

In this chapter:

Office Communications Server 2007 has a simple administration model. After you complete your deployment by using the Setup program, which provides wizards to facilitate the configuration of your servers, on-going administration of those servers is performed using the Admin Tools MMC snap-in called Office Communications Server 2007. This management console automatically discovers all the Office Communications Servers joined to Active Directory by querying Active Directory. The only server roles the management console is not able to discover are the Edge Server roles, as they don't publish themselves into Active Directory.

Office Communications Server 2007 also provides a Windows Management Instrumentation (WMI) interface that abstracts the underlying provider whether it is Active Directory, SQL Server, or the WMI repository. This WMI interface simplifies the effort to write management tools and scripts. The Admin Tools management console uses this WMI interface. A graphical representation of this logical structure is shown in Figure 15-1.

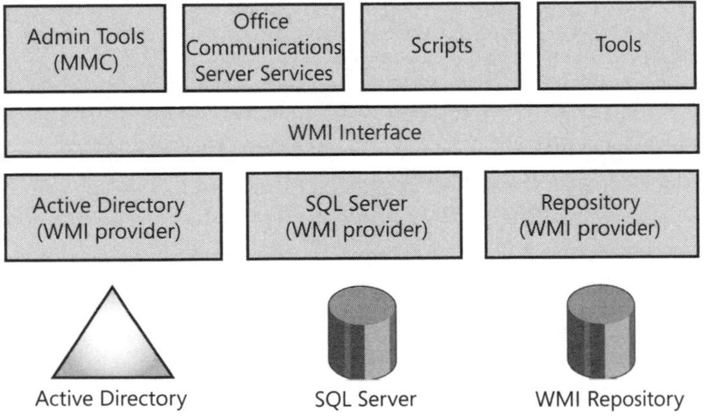

Figure 15-1 Office Communications Server 2007 management model

Note Not all WMI settings are exposed via the Admin Tools MMC. The design philosophy of the Admin Tools MMC is to expose approximately 80 percent of the configurable settings that will be most commonly used by administrators. For more advanced configuration scenarios or less commonly used settings not exposed in the Admin Tools MMC, administrators must use the WMI interface.

The design philosophy behind the Office Communications Server 2007 management infrastructure is to store in Active Directory any information that needs to be available to all servers deployed in the forest, such as global settings and user information. Settings that must be available within the scope of a pool (that is, all servers associated with a pool) are stored in SQL. Server settings (that is, information specific to a server) are stored in the local server's WMI repository. The WMI interface exposes all these settings in an object model representation that provides semantic validation to prevent administrators or developers from creating an invalid state that the system cannot recover from. Office Communications Server 2007 exposes 95 different WMI classes, and the organizational structure of these WMI classes is described in the following section.

Configuring Global Settings

Office Communications Server 2007 leverages Active Directory to store settings that are used by all Office Communications Server 2007 servers deployed within a forest. Office Communications Server 2007 provides two options for storing global settings:

- Global settings can be stored in the Active Directory Configuration Partition. (This option can be used for new installations only.)
- Global settings can be stored in the Active Directory System Container in the root domain partition. (You must use this option if you are already running Live Communications Server.)

When using the System container to store global settings, Office Communications Server 2007 servers connect to root domain domain controllers (DCs) to retrieve this data. When using the configuration container, Office Communications Server 2007 servers connect to their local Global Catalog (GC) servers to obtain global settings. The servers retrieve this data via Windows Management Instrumentation (WMI)–this is not to be confused with user data, which is retrieved via the user replicator (UR) process. (See Figure 15-2.) These global settings are created during the Forest Prep step in Setup.

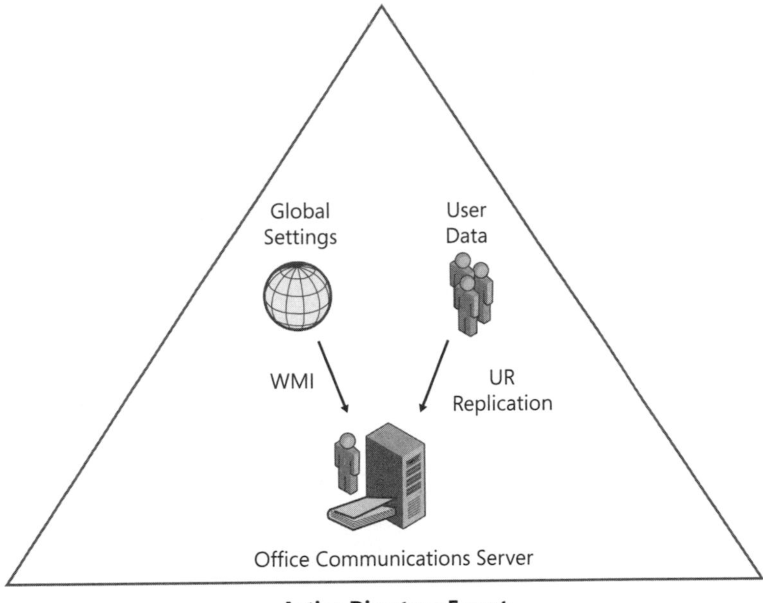

Figure 15-2 WMI and UR services

Global Office Communications Server settings are configurable from the Admin Tools MMC by right-clicking the forest node and selecting Properties. Two settings are available: Global Properties and Voice Properties. (See Figure 15-3.) Voice properties are global settings that are applicable only to Enterprise Voice scenarios.

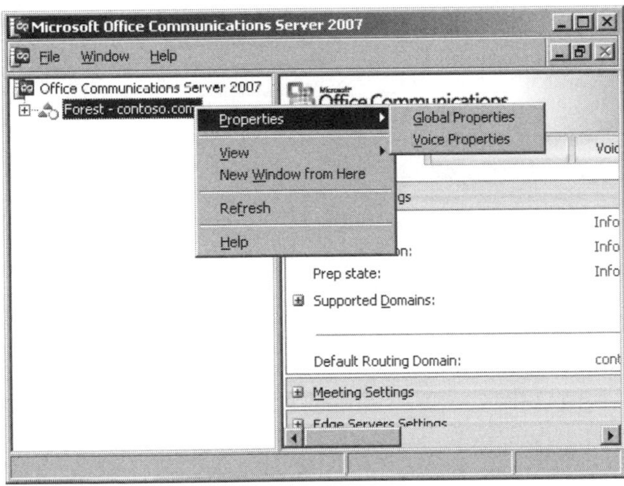

Figure 15-3 Configuring global settings

Office Communications Server 2007 exposes these global settings via WMI. Administrators should access these settings from the WMI interface instead of directly modifying them in

Active Directory via the Active Directory Services Interface (ADSI) or Lightweight Directory Access Protocol (LDAP). The WMI interface builds in a safety measure to prevent setting values that are invalid.

The following WMI classes are used for configuring global settings:

- ***MSFT_SIPDomainData*** This WMI class defines the Session Initiation Protocol (SIP) domains authoritative to the Office Communications Server 2007 servers deployed within the forest. In our example environment, *contoso.com* is the SIP domain. Messages to users with SIP Uniform Resource Identifiers (URIs) of username@contoso.com, where *username* is the name of the user, will be routed internally to the user's home pool server. If a message is addressed to a user with an SIP URI of username@fabrikam.com, for example, the request will be routed outside the organization's network through the federated connection as defined by the administrator in the Federation tab. The Admin Tools MMC exposes the settings from this class in the General tab of Office Communications Server Global Properties. One of the SIP domains must be marked as the default routing domain, as shown in the following screen shot:

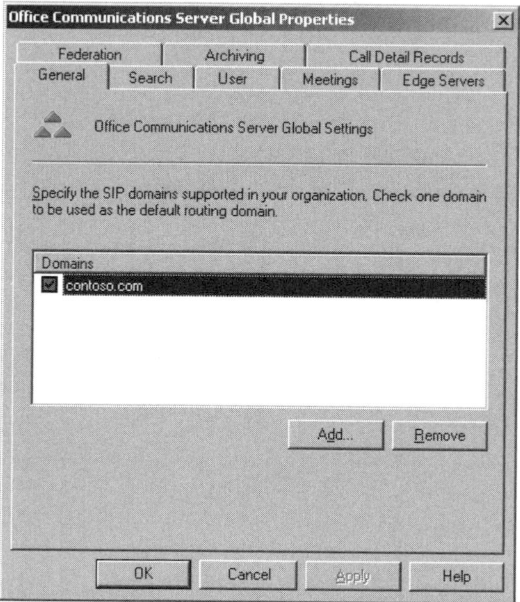

- ***MSFT_SIPESGlobalSearchSetting*** As the class name indicates, all global search settings are configurable via this WMI class. This class is exposed in the Admin Tools MMC in the Search tab, which is shown in the following screen shot:

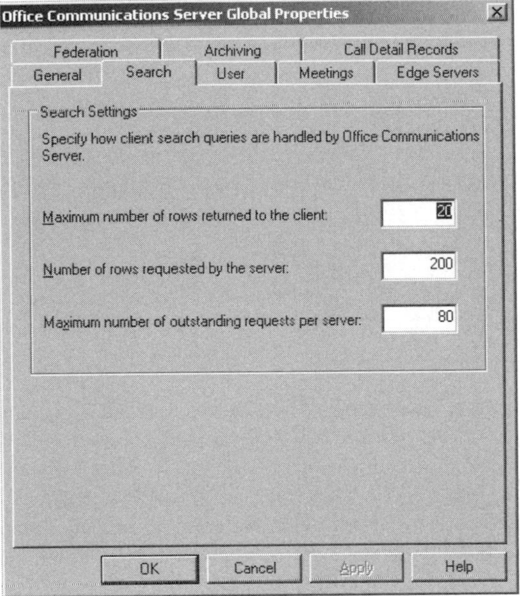

- ***MSFT_SIPESGlobalRegistrarSetting*** This WMI class defines the restrictions for searching the registrar (database) to maintain performance of the system. Part of the configuration settings of this class is exposed in the User tab, which is shown in the following screen shot:

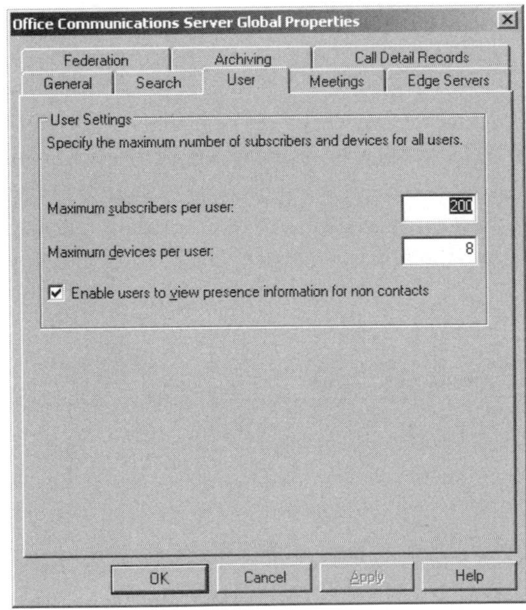

- ***MSFT_SIPGlobalFederationSetting*** This WMI class exposes the global Federation settings. This global configuration setting allows the administrator to centrally disable Federation without going to every server to block Federation traffic in the case of a virus or worm outburst. Also, this class allows the administrator to configure an outbound route for Federation without having to configure this same setting on all Office Communications Server 2007 servers. The Admin Tools MMC displays these settings on the Federation tab, shown in the next screen shot:

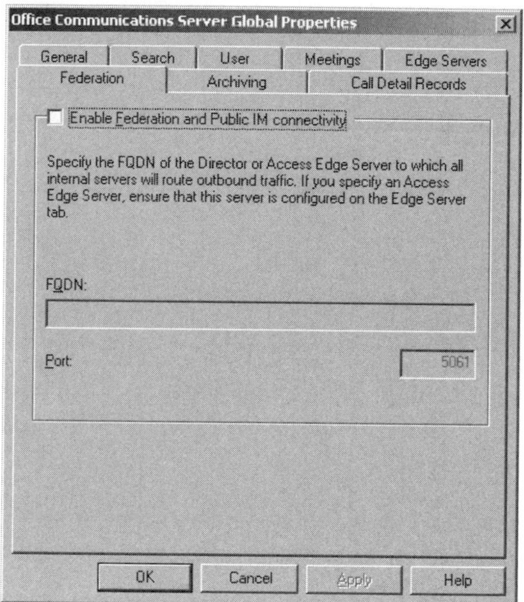

- ***MSFT_SIPGlobalArchivingSetting*** This WMI class exposes the global Archiving settings, and it is enforced by every Office Communications Server 2007 Standard Edition server and Enterprise Edition pool front-end server deployed in the forest that are configured to archive user communications. Settings from this class are available from the Admin Tools MMC in the Archiving tab, which is shown in the following screen shot:

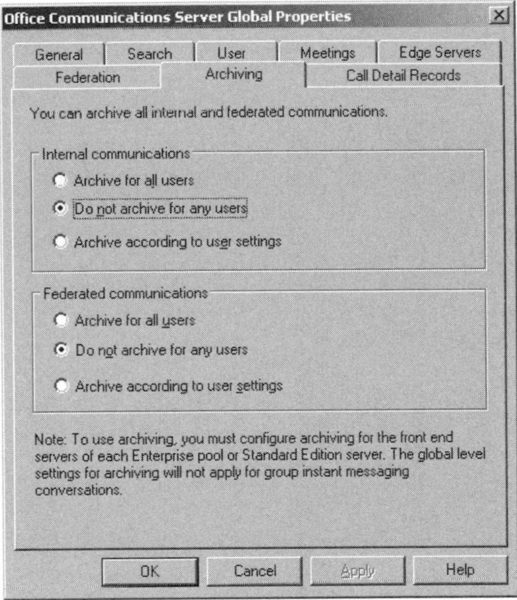

- ***MSFT_SIPGlobalCDRSetting*** This WMI class exposes settings to configure Call Detail Records (CDRs). These settings can be found in the Admin Tools MMC under the Call Detail Records tab, shown in the next screen shot:

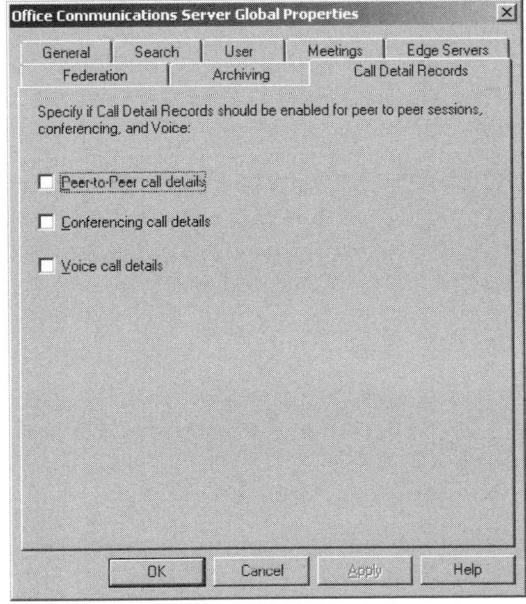

- ***MSFT_SIPEdgeProxySetting*** This WMI class defines the list of trusted Edge Servers. This list includes all Edge Server roles (Web Edge Server, Access Edge Server, A/V Edge Server). This list serves as an added measure of security. Internal Office Communications Server 2007 servers establish MTLS connections with Edge Servers in the organization's perimeter network only if they are registered in this class. The Admin Tools MMC exposes this list of trusted Edge Servers in the Edge Servers tab.

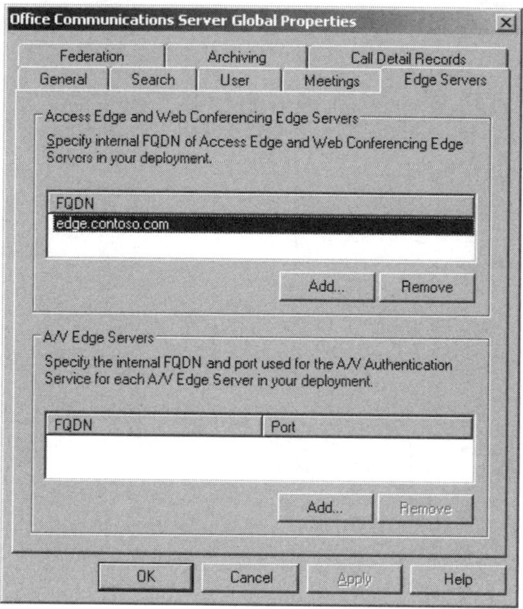

- *MSFT_SIPArchivingServerSetting* This WMI class lists all the Archiving and CDR servers deployed in the forest. This list is exposed in the Admin Tools MMC in the scope pane.
- *MSFT_SIPMCUFactorySetting* This WMI class is not exposed in the Admin Tools MMC. An instance of this class is automatically created for every media type (IM, A/V, Web Conferencing, Telephony) when the pool is created. The MCU Factory is associated with an MCU only when a Conferencing Server of the same media type is activated. Because the IM Conferencing Server role runs on the front-end server, the front-end server is automatically associated with the IM MCU Factory as the IM MCU.
- *MSFT_SIPForwardingProxySetting* This WMI class served a purpose in the Live Communications Server 2003 release, but it's now mostly obsolete and seldom used. As such, it is not exposed in the Admin Tools MMC.

Configuring UC-specific Settings

Office Communications Server 2007 introduces new Enterprise Voice capabilities and scenarios. When a user enabled for Unified Communications (UC) places a call by dialing a phone number, Office Communications Server needs to know how to route the call to the correct destination so that the call reaches the desired party. The administrator must configure this routing logic, configure who is allowed to use this route, and define the different phone number patterns that can be interpreted to use this route. (There's more about how phone routes are defined in Chapter 10, "VoIP Scenario.")

Configuration of these Voice over Internet Protocol (VoIP) settings is exposed by the WMI classes listed next. These settings are also exposed in the Admin Tools MMC in the Voice Properties section located under the forest node.

- ***MSFT_SIPPhoneRouteUsageData*** This WMI class defines a list of usage names created by the administrator. A *usage name* is a friendly name that is associated with a phone route to indicate its intent or usage.
- ***MSFT_SIPPhoneRouteData*** This WMI class defines a phone route. A phone route is composed of a phone pattern that is associated with a Mediation Server (and therefore a media gateway). If a dialed phone number matches the pattern, the route specifies the call to be routed to the associated Mediation Server.
- ***MSFT_SIPLocalNormalizationRuleData*** This WMI class defines a list of 2-tuples. A *2-tuple*, or pair, is composed of a matching regular expression and a transform regular expression. When a user dials a phone number, this number is checked against all the matching regular expressions that are associated with the location profile assigned to the user. If a match is found, the phone number is transformed by the transform regular expression. This process is called *normalization* of the phone number because a phone number can be interpreted in different ways depending on the context (such as country, state, county, city, and so on). These are called local normalization rules. The normalized phone number is then used to match a phone pattern to a phone route, and then it's routed to the correct Mediation Server.
- ***MSFT_SIPLocationProfileData*** This WMI class defines location profiles. A *location profile* is simply a name that describes a collection of normalization rules to translate a phone number into E.164 format.

Configuring Policy-Specific Settings

To ease the administrative burden, instead of requiring administrators to configure each user individually, Office Communications Server exposes the concept of policies. A policy is simply a collection of user-specific settings abstracted by the name of the policy. Once the administrator configures the values of the settings to his or her needs, the administrator can assign users to this policy. If the administrator later modifies settings in the policy, these updates are automatically enforced on all users assigned to this policy without needing to configure each user individually. Office Communications Server introduces two policies: a Meeting policy and a UC policy. The Meeting policy applies to Web Server and A/V Conferencing Server settings. The UC policy configures VoIP-related settings.

The following WMI classes are used for configuring policy-specific settings:

- ***MSFT_SIPGlobalMeetingSetting*** This WMI class defines the default Meeting policy. It actually points to an instance of the class *MSFT_SIPGlobalMeetingPolicyData*.

- ***MSFT_SIPGlobalMeetingPolicyData*** This WMI class lists all Meeting policies created by the administrator. Meeting policies are stored in Active Directory in XML format. You can obtain this raw XML format of the policy by using the class *MSFT_SIPGlobalPolicyXMLData* with the Type field set to Meeting. The Meetings tab of the Global Properties page is shown in the following screen shot:

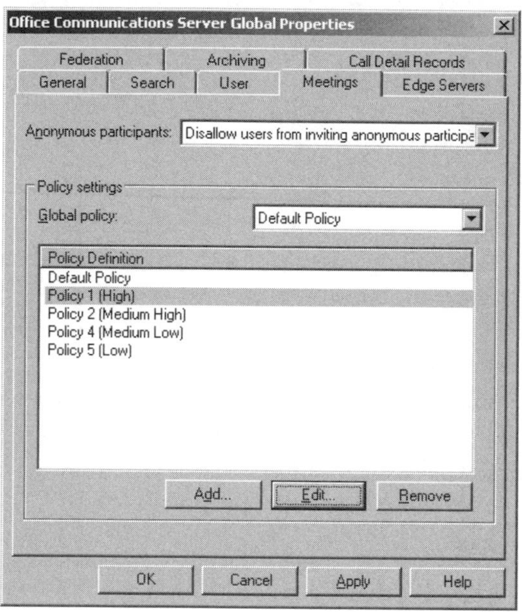

- ***MSFT_SIPGlobalUCSetting*** This WMI class defines the default UC policy. It references one of the UC policies defined in *MSFT_SIPGlobalUCPolicyData*.
- ***MSFT_SIPGlobalUCPolicyData*** This WMI class lists all UC policies created by the administrator. Similar to Meeting policies, these UC policies are stored in XML format in Active Directory. To retrieve the XML version of this policy, use the WMI class *MSFT_SIPGlobalPolicyXMLData* with the Type field set to UC. The Policy tab of the Voice Properties page is shown in the following screen shot:

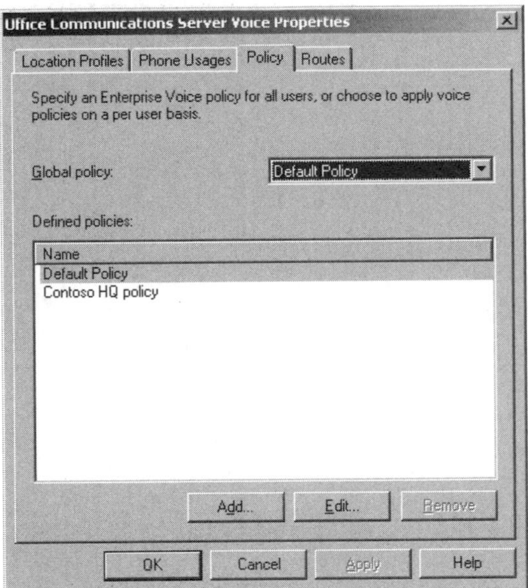

- ***MSFT_SIPGlobalPolicyXMLData*** This WMI class exposes the policy settings in XML format as they are stored in Active Directory.

Configuring Service Connection Point Settings

Each Office Communications Server (with the exception of Edge Server roles) creates a service connection point (SCP) on the corresponding computer object in Active Directory when installed. The SCP marker registers in Active Directory the type of service installed on the computer joined to the Active Directory forest. This makes it possible for administrators and monitoring services (SMS, HP OpenView, IBM Tivoli) to determine what type of services are running on every computer. When the Office Communications Server is uninstalled, the SCP is removed from the corresponding computer object in Active Directory. This is part of Microsoft's best practice standards for Active Directory.

The following WMI classes are used for configuring SCP settings:

- ***MSFT_SIPESServerSetting*** This WMI class defines the SCP for Office Communications Server 2007 Standard Edition servers and Enterprise Edition pool front-end servers. The "ES" in the name of the class stands for "Enterprise Services."
- ***MSFT_SIPMCUSetting*** This WMI class defines the SCP for Conferencing Servers.
- ***MSFT_SIPWebComponentsServerSetting*** This WMI class defines the SCP for Web Components Servers.
- ***MSFT_SIPMediationServerSetting*** This WMI class defines the SCP for Mediation Servers.

Note There is no SCP created for Communicator Web Access Servers.

Configuring Trusted Server Settings

To avoid the scenario of a rogue server inside the organization posing as a legitimate Office Communications Server and therefore gaining access to other users' data, Office Communications Server 2007 uses a trusted server list. This list prevents rogue servers from spoofing as Office Communications Servers. If a server's fully qualified domain name (FQDN) is not listed in the trusted server list, all other Office Communications Servers will not accept mutual transport layer security (MTLS) connections from it.

All internal Office Communications Servers (except Edge Servers) create an entry in the appropriate trusted server list during activation. This is why administrators must be members of the RTCUniversalServerAdmins group to run activation. Rogue users with insufficient permissions are not able to add their server's FQDN to this trusted server list.

This list of trusted servers is not explicitly exposed in the Admin Tools MMC—for example, in a table with the heading "Trusted Servers." However, the scope pane uses the different trusted server lists to populate the tree view. Any server not trusted is not listed in the scope pane. The only exception is Communicator Web Access (CWA) Servers. To view the list of trusted CWA servers, you must open the Communicator Web Access (2007 release) Manager, and all trusted CWA 2007 servers will be listed in the scope pane.

For each type of server role, a different WMI class is used. The following WMI classes are used for configuring trusted server settings:

- ***MSFT_SIPESTrustedServerSetting*** This WMI class defines the list of Office Communications Server 2007 servers to be trusted. The following server roles, when activated, create an entry in this list specifying their FQDN: Standard Edition Servers, Enterprise Edition pool front-end servers, Conferencing Servers, and Mediation Servers.
- ***MSFT_SIPTrustedServiceSetting*** This WMI class defines the list of services trusted by other Office Communications Server 2007 servers. Communicator Web Access Servers, Mediation Servers, and A/V Edge Servers—referred to internally as Media Relay Access Servers (MRAS)—are listed as trusted services. Third-party independent software vendors (ISVs) that want to create SIP servers that are trusted by Office Communications Server 2007 servers must create an entry in this trusted service list.
- ***MSFT_SIPTrustedMCUSetting*** This WMI class, introduced in Office Communications Server 2007, lists all the Microsoft trusted Conferencing Servers (Web Conferencing Server, IM Conferencing Server, A/V Conferencing Server, and Telephony Conferencing Server).
- ***MSFT_SIPTrustedWebComponentsServerSetting*** This WMI class defines the list of trusted Web Components Servers, as its name indicates.

Configuring User-Specific Settings

Office Communications Server 2007 leverages existing user information available in Active Directory, plus it adds more attributes to the user object that are specific to Office Communications. These additional attributes are made available through the schema extension performed during Schema Prep. Such attributes include SIP URI, home server FQDN, Federation setting, Remote User setting, PIC setting, RCC settings, and UC settings.

In addition to the user attributes stored in Active Directory that need to be available to every home server in the forest, the user's home server stores user settings that need to be available only to the user's endpoint (for example, Communicator, which can be considered an endpoint for communications from user to user across various systems). These settings are often large and change more frequently than the user settings stored in Active Directory. Storing these settings in Active Directory would not make the right use of this technology. Storing this data in SQL Server is a more appropriate choice. Settings stored in SQL Server are contacts, contact groups, permissions, and user options (call forwarding rules, notes, and so on).

These Office Communications Server–specific user settings are exposed to administrators via the four WMI classes listed next. Unlike the client application programming interfaces (APIs) offered—such as the UC Communicator Web Access (AJAX) APIs and Communicator APIs—the advantage of these WMI APIs is that the administrator can administer a user's contacts, groups, and permissions without needing to sign in with the user's credentials. These WMI APIs do not expose the full functionality that the client APIs offer, though. For example, an administrator can prepopulate a user's contact list with the peers from her working group or organizational structure.

The following WMI classes are used for configuring user-specific settings:

- ***MSFT_SIPESUserContactGroupData*** This WMI class exposes the user's contact groups.
- ***MSFT_SIPESUserContactData*** This WMI class exposes the user's contact list.
- ***MSFT_SIPESUserACEData*** This WMI class exposes permissions that are applied on the user's contacts.
- ***MSFT_SIPESUserSetting*** This WMI class exposes the user's settings stored in Active Directory and the user's home server SQL Server database.

Configuring Pool Settings

Settings that are specific to the scope of a pool are stored in the SQL Server database. These settings are accessible from the Admin Tools MMC by right-clicking a pool in the tree-view pane and selecting Properties. (See Figure 15-4.) Pool-level settings expose settings that are common to all servers of the same role within the scope of a pool, and they are organized based on roles in the Admin Tools MMC. You'll notice that the same set of sub-property headings (Front End Properties, Web Conferencing Properties, A/V Conferencing Properties) are exposed at the server level with the exception of the Web Component properties. Although the property headings are the same, the settings are different because of the scope level.

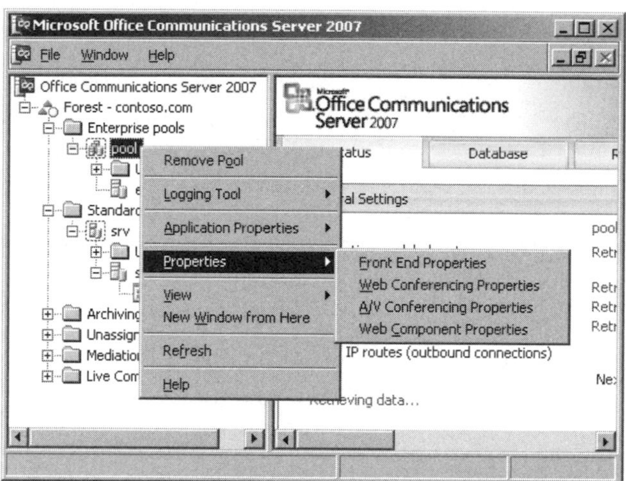

Figure 15-4 Configuring pool settings

The set of pool-level WMI classes is listed next. These classes are explained in the Office Communications Server Software Development Kit (SDK). A convenient way to discover the properties that each of these WMI classes expose is to use the WMI Common Information Model (CIM) Studio tool. This tool is available for free on the Microsoft Web site as part of the WMI Administrative Tools download at *http://www.microsoft.com/downloads/details.aspx?familyid=6430F853-1120-48DB-8CC5-F2ABDC3ED314&displaylang=en*. Using the WMI CIM Studio, you can browse all WMI classes exposed by Office Communications Server 2007 on a computer with the Admin Tools installed.

The following WMI classes (selectively described) are used for configuring pool settings:

- ***MSFT_SIPProxySecuritySetting*** This class is not exposed in the Admin Tools MMC.
- ***MSFT_SIPProxySetting*** The settings from this class are exposed in the Routing and Compression tabs of the Front End Properties.
- ***MSFT_SIPRoutingTableData*** This WMI class is exposed in the pool-level Front End Properties in the Routing tab as shown in the next screen shot. Following is a list of properties in this class:
    - ***InstanceID*** Not directly exposed in the Admin Tools
    - ***Backend*** Used to identify which pool to connect to (not directly exposed in the Admin Tools)
    - ***MatchURI*** Corresponds to the Domain field
    - ***Enabled*** Corresponds to the phone URI check box

- *NextHop* Matches the FQDN or IP Address field
- *NextHopPort* Matches the Port field
- *NextHopTransport* Matches the Transport field
- *ReplacehostinRequestURI* Matches the Replace Host In Request URI check box

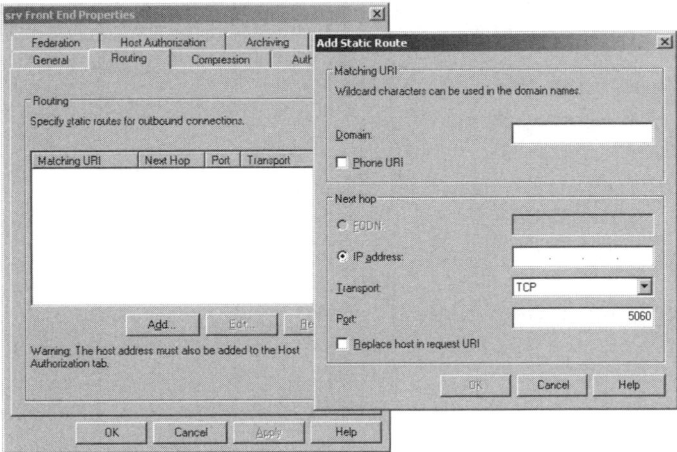

- *MSFT_SIPRemoteAddressData* This class defines the settings shown in the Host Authorization tab of the Front End Properties.
- *MSFT_SIPProxySetting* Properties from this class are exposed on two tabs in the Front End Properties. Tabs covering these settings are the Federation and Compression tabs. The remaining properties are not exposed in the Admin Tools MMC.
- *MSFT_SIPPoolSetting* This is the main class that defines a pool including the pool name, FQDN and type, the default location profile, back-end database server address, the list of servers associated with the pool: front-end servers, Web Conferencing servers, A/V servers, and Web Component servers.
- *MSFT_SIPPoolConfigSetting* This class specifies the Network Address Translation (NAT) settings for a pool.
- *MSFT_SIPUserReplicatorSetting* Settings from this class are no longer exposed in the Admin Tools MMC as the product team discovered that administrators never modified the defaults.
- *MSFT_SIPEsEmSetting* The settings from this class can be found in the General tab of the Front End Properties.
- *MSFT_SIPUCPhoneConfigSetting* The properties of this class are exposed in the Voice tab (shown in the next screen shot) of the Front End Properties of the pool in the Admin Tools MMC.

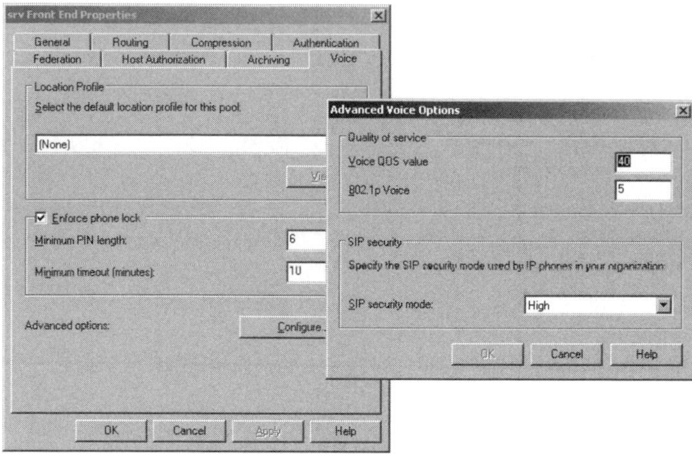

- ***MSFT_SIPMeetingScheduleSetting*** This class defines Web Conferencing settings such as maximum meeting size, maximum number of meetings a user can schedule, the organization name, and the length of time unauthenticated or anonymous users are allowed to remain in a meeting before the meeting starts and after the meeting ends. Part of these settings is shown in the General tab of the Web Components Properties.
- ***MSFT_SIPMeetingInviteSetting*** Properties of this class define administrative settings to configure Web Conferencing invitations sent to users such as the URLs for where users can download the Meeting client; where users can obtain helpdesk; and branding the client. Settings from this class are exposed in the Meeting Invitations tab of the Web Components Properties.
- ***MSFT_SIPAddressBookSetting*** The properties of this class describe the Address Book settings.
- ***MSFT_SIPGroupExpansionSetting*** This class exposes the administrative control to enable expansion of distribution lists in the user's contact list. The settings from this class can be found in the Group Expansion tab of the Web Components Properties.
- ***MSFT_SIPUpdatesServerSetting*** This class defines the URLs for the Update Server.
- ***MSFT_SIPLoadedExtensionModuleElement*** This class defines the status of extension modules installed on the pool.
- ***MSFT_SIPDataComplianceSetting*** This class defines administrative settings for configuring compliance for meeting content. This class is exposed in the Meeting Compliance tab of the Web Conferencing Properties.
- ***MSFT_SIPLoggingToolSetting*** This class defines settings to the logging tool. It is not exposed directly in the Admin Tools MMC.
- ***MSFT_SIPLogSetting*** This class defines Archiving settings as shown in the Archiving tab of the Front End Properties.

You can connect to the local WMI service to perform the following types of operations: query, set, and delete. This requires installing the Admin Tools MMC snap-in on the local computer if it's not an Office Communications Server 2007 server. By default, the Admin Tools snap-in is installed on all Office Communications Server 2007 servers.

Each of these WMI classes requires specifying the back-end server to identify the pool to connect to. The most efficient way to retrieve pool-level settings is to perform a SQL query specifying the back-end server in the following form for an Enterprise Edition pool:

```
'Backend_FQDN\\SQL_Instance_Name'
```

For a Standard Edition server, use the following form:

```
'(local)\\rtc'
```

The following pseudocode illustrates how to query the attributes from the *MSFT_SIPProxySetting* class:

```
If(srv == "Standard Edition")
{
Backend = '(local)\\rtc';
}
If(srv == "Enterprise Edition")
{
Backend = "backend_FQDN\\SQL_Instance_Name';
}
Query = "SELECT * FROM MSFT_SIPProxySetting WHERE Backend =" + Backend;
```

For set operations, specify the back-end attribute as you would any other attribute–for example:

```
Set DefaultRoutingInstance = GetObject("WinMgmts:MSFT_SIPRoutingTableData")
Set NewRoutingInstance = DefaultRoutingInstance.SpawnInstance_
'Populate the properties for new instance.
NewRoutingInstance.DropRouterHeaders = False;
'No escaping required here.
If(srv == "Standard Edition")
{
NewRoutingInstance.Backend = "(local)\\rtc";
}
If(srv == "Enterprise Edition")
{
NewRoutingInstance.Backend = "Backend_FQDN\SQL_Instance_Name";
}
NewRoutingInstance.Put_ 0
```

Direct from the Source: Getting Pool-Level Classes Using WMI

For getting pool-level classes, if you use the select query without the WHERE clause or the Enumerate Instances mechanism provided by WMI, the resulting operation can be very slow. This is because by omitting the WHERE clause, you are asking for all instances of the pool-level class from all pools. This request results in the Office Communications Server WMI provider first discovering all pools and then connecting to each pool and retrieving data for this WMI class from them. If any of these pools are accessed across slow links, the operation takes even longer or might even time out.

Note that the preceding statements are applicable only for pool-level classes. It is safe to omit the WHERE clause for machine-level and global classes.

–Nirav Kamdar
Senior Development Lead, OCS Server

Configuring Server Settings

Settings specific to a server are stored in the local WMI repository that is created when installing a server role. These settings are accessible from the Admin Tools MMC by right-clicking a server in the tree view pane and selecting Properties. (See Figure 15-5.)

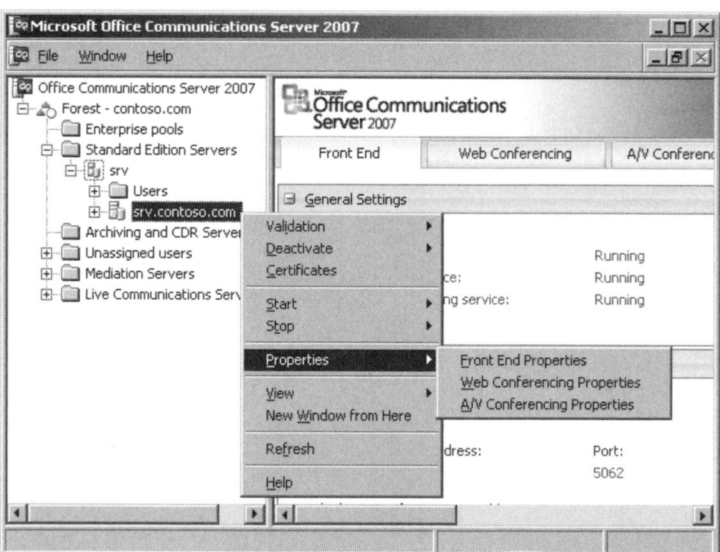

Figure 15-5 Configuring server settings

Notice that when the Conferencing Servers are collocated, as in the case of a Standard Edition Server or Enterprise Edition pool front-end server in a consolidated configuration, the Conferencing Server settings are exposed on the Standard Edition Server or Enterprise Edition pool front-end server. The set of WMI classes exposed by Office Communications Server 2007 is listed next. These classes are explained in the Microsoft Office Communications Server 2007 SDK found at *http://www.microsoft.com/downloads/details.aspx?familyid=7F4CE9C5-9E02-4B99-AA09-360D920D3EE0&displaylang=en.*

Configuring Settings for All Servers

The following WMI classes apply to all server roles:

- *MSFT_SIPServerExtData*
- *MSFT_SIPServerInstalledComponentData*
- *MSFT_SIPRoutingSetting*

Configuring Diagnostic Settings

The following WMI classes apply to all server roles:

- *MSFT_SIPDiagnosticTracingSetting*
- *MSFT_SIPDiagnosticFilterSetting*
- *MSFT_SIPDiagnosticHeader*

Configuring Settings for Standard Edition and Enterprise Edition Servers

The following WMI classes apply only to Office Communications Server 2007 Standard Edition and Enterprise Edition servers:

- *MSFT_SIPListeningAddressData*
- *MSFT_SIPConnectionTablesUpdateTimeSetting*

Configuring Application Server Settings

The following WMI classes apply only to Standard Edition Servers and Enterprise Edition pool front-end servers:

- *MSFT_SIPApplicationSetting*
- *MSFT_SIPApplicationPriorityList*

Configuring Filter Settings

The following WMI classes apply only to Standard Edition Servers and Enterprise Edition pool front-end servers:

- *MSFT_SIPClientVersionFilterSetting*

- *MSFT_SIPClientVersionFilterData*
- *SFT_SIPIIMFilterUrlFilterSetting*
- *SFT_SIPIIMFilterFileFilterSetting*

Configuring Logging Settings

The following WMI classes can be used to configure logging settings:

- ***MSFT_SIPLogOptions*** This WMI class exposes the Archiving and CDR settings on the Standard Edition Servers and Enterprise Edition pool front-end servers, as shown in the following screen shot:

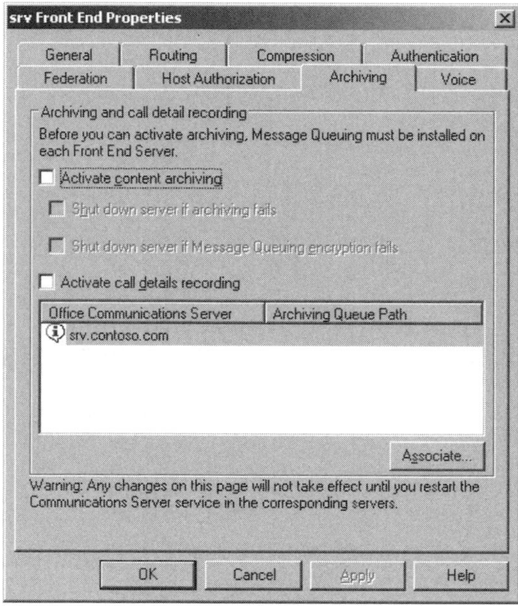

- ***MSFT_SIPLogServiceSetting*** This WMI class defines logging settings that are exposed on the Archiving and CDR server.

Configuring Conferencing Server Settings

The following WMI classes apply only to Conferencing Servers:

- *MSFT_SIPMCUSetting*
- *MSFT_SIPAVMCUSetting*
- *MSFT_SIPIMMCUSetting*
- *MSFT_SIPACPMCUSetting*
- *MSFT_SIPDataMCUSetting*

    - *MSFT_SIPDataMCUCapabilitySetting*
    - *MSFT_SIPDataMCUProxyServerData*
    - *MSFT_SIPDataMCUProxyServerPortSetting*

Configuring Communicator Web Access Server Settings

The following WMI classes apply only to Communicator Web Access servers:

- *MSFT_CWAServerSetting*
- *MSFT_CWASupportedLanguage*
- *MSFT_CWASiteSetting*

Configuring Mediation Server Settings

The following WMI class applies only to Mediation Servers:

- *MSFT_SIPMediationServerConfigSetting*

Configuring Edge Server Settings

The following WMI classes apply only to Edge Servers:

- *MSFT_SIPEdgeServerListeningAddressSetting*
- *MSFT_SIPMediaRelaySetting*
- *MSFT_SIPMediaRelayNetworkInterfaceData*
- *MSFT_SIPDataProxySetting*

Configuring Federation Settings

The following WMI classes apply only to the Access Edge Servers with the exception of the class *MSFT_SIPFederationInternalEdgeListeningAddressSetting*. This class applies to all Edge Server roles:

- *MSFT_SIPFederationPartnerTable*
- *MSFT_SIPFederationNetworkProviderTable*
- *MSFT_SIPFederationInternalEdgeListeningAddressSetting*
- *MSFT_SIPFederationInternalEdgeSetting*
- *MSFT_SIPFederationInternalServerData*
- *MSFT_SIPFederationInternalDomainData*
- *MSFT_SIPFederationExternalEdgeListeningAddressSetting*

- *MSFT_SIPFederationExternalEdgeSetting*
- *MSFT_SIPFederationDeniedDomainSetting*
- *MSFT_SIPEnhancedFederationConnectionLimitsData*
- *MSFT_SIPEnhancedFederationDomainData*

Migrating Users from Live Communications Server 2005 SP1 to Office Communications Server 2007

For those who already have a deployment of Live Communications Server 2005 SP1 and are looking to migrate to Office Communications Server 2007, the migration is straightforward. However, there are a few considerations to keep in mind:

- The impact of migrating users from legacy presence to the enhanced presence model
- Upgrading users' Communicator 2005 client to Communicator 2007
- The possible need to decentralize your deployment to support users in remote offices to do Web conferencing and VoIP

In addition, you need to consider the following issues applicable to any Office Communications Server 2007 deployment:

- Scalability considerations for the new modalities: audio, video, Web conferencing, and VoIP
- The impact of the different modalities on your existing network and the user's experience of Web conferencing, audio and video quality.

Only considerations specific to migrating from Live Communications Server 2005 to Office Communications Server 2007 will be covered in this section. With Office Communications Server 2007, a new presence model is introduced to overcome the shortcomings of the presence model defined in Live Communications Server 2005. Mainly, the Office Communications Server 2007 presence model addresses the issue of large Session Description Protocol (SDP) presence documents sent across the network by shredding this presence document into discrete XML sub-documents. This way a change made, for example, to the Notes field by the user won't result in resending the entire presence document to the home server, as was the case with Live Communications Server 2005. With Office Communications Server 2007, only the sub-document where the Notes field was defined is transmitted to the home server in an SDP envelope. This approach results in a more efficient use of the network as well as resources on the home server. The home server needs to parse only the sub-document instead of the entire presence document.

Another driving factor in changing the presence model in Office Communications Server 2007 is the customers needing to offer a more granular permissions model than the permission model supported in Live Communications Server 2005, which is limited to Allow and

Block. Users want more granularities, and they want to be able to assign varying levels of permissions to contacts. For example, a user might not want to be interrupted during a meeting except by the boss or a particular family member.

The recommended way to upgrade to Office Communications Server 2007 is to perform a side-by-side migration. That is, install a second server installation running Office Communications Server 2007 in the same forest as your Live Communications Server 2005 deployment and migrate the users. The impact on hardware from deploying a second Enterprise Edition pool is significant, because doing this requires duplicating the number of physical servers–one set for Live Communications Server 2005 and another set for Office Communications Server 2007. To minimize this impact, you can deploy the Office Communications Server 2007 Enterprise Edition pool with the minimal set of hardware required–one back-end server and one front-end server. As you migrate users from your Live Communications Server 2005 Enterprise Edition pool to the Office Communications Server 2007 Enterprise Edition pool, you can start decommissioning front-end servers from the Live Communications Server 2005 Enterprise Edition pool and reusing them as front-end servers for the Office Communications Server 2007 Enterprise Edition pool.

Moving users homed on Live Communications Server 2005 to Office Communications Server 2007 can simply be done via the bulk Move Users Wizard. This wizard is accessible from the Admin Tools MMC and the DSA.MSC MMC. If you are using the Admin Tools MMC, the Office Communications Server 2007 version must be used. Select all the users to be moved, right-click, and select the Move Users Wizard as shown in Figure 15-6. If the move process fails, it's likely that either the source server (Live Communications Server 2005) or the destination server (Office Communications Server 2007) is offline and not operational. Verify the service is functioning correctly before attempting the move user process again.

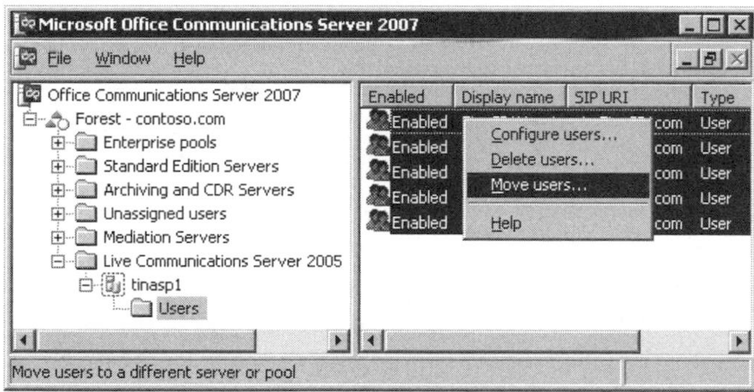

Figure 15-6 Selecting the Move Users Wizard

Users moved to an Office Communications Server 2007 Standard Edition Server or Enterprise Edition pool from Live Communications Server 2005 are not automatically enabled for enhanced presence. They remain in legacy mode until the administrator explicitly enables them. Because users enabled for enhanced presence cannot be returned to legacy presence, the administrator can control the timing for when to enable this feature. Enhanced presence can be enabled from the user's Properties page by clicking the Configure button, which displays the User Options screen (shown in Figure 15-7). To enable users in bulk for enhanced presence, the Configure Users Wizard is an easier choice (shown in Figure 15-8).

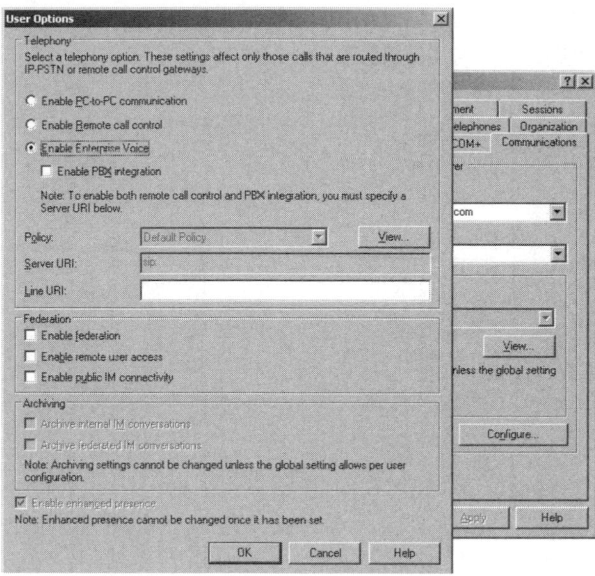

Figure 15-7 User Options screen

Figure 15-8 Configure Users Wizard

The process of migrating users from Live Communications Server 2005 to Office Communications Server 2007 is now complete. You can enable those users for new functionality only available in Office Communications Server 2007, such as UC and Meeting features.

Summary

Office Communications Server 2007 provides two management interfaces out of the box. The Admin Tools MMC offers a graphical user interface (GUI) based on the Microsoft Management Console that integrates with the Windows management infrastructure. The Windows Management Instrumentation (WMI) layer exposed by Office Communications Server 2007 provides a scriptable interface that administrators can use to automate tasks. This WMI interface provides more flexibility and access to additional settings that might not be exposed at the MMC interface. Office Communications Server settings are in three different locations. Global settings are stored in Active Directory. Pool-level settings are stored in a SQL database, and settings specific to a server are stored in the local WMI repository on the server. WMI exposes all these settings in a consistent way by abstracting their storage location. Because of this, administrators do not need to use a different set of API calls depending on where the settings are stored–such as LDAP or ADSI to query Active Directory, structured query language to access the SQL database, and WMI APIs to query the WMI repository.

Migrating users from Live Communications Server 2005 to Office Communications Server 2007 is a straightforward process. By using the Move Users Wizard, administrators can easily migrate those users. As a safety precaution, migrated users are not automatically enabled for enhanced presence. Administrators can decide if and when to enable enhanced presence by running the Configure Users Wizard, such as when all users have migrated to Office Communications Server 2007 or when all user clients are upgraded to a version that supports enhanced presence (Communicator 2007).

Additional Resources

- Office Communications Server 2007 SDK WMI Reference found at *http://msdn2.microsoft.com/en-us/library/bb632199.aspx*

On the Companion CD

- OCS WMI.xlsx, a spreadsheet listing WMI classes supported by OCS 2007, in the \Appendixes,Scripts,Resources folder.

Part V
Technical Troubleshooting and Diagnostics

In this part:

Problems commonly occur when Office Communications Server systems configuration does not match the topology in which they are installed. Additionally, network outages and infrastructure such as firewalls or proxies can introduce problems that were not planned for during initial testing or installation. Identifying helpful diagnostic resources and presenting specific scenario troubleshooting sessions in detail, Part V provides expert guidance and diagnostic frameworks to help efficiently identify and resolve problems.

Office Communications Server and Office Communicator include several tools to help identify and diagnose problems. Event logs are used to identify issues on the server and can now be enabled for the client as well. Both the server and client have the ability to enable diagnostic logs that provide an incredible level of technical detail (sometimes much more information than is necessary to work through a problem). Chapter 16 presents event log examples with explanations and helpful next steps and walks through gathering diagnostic information and putting it to use in general terms.

When involved diagnostics are necessary, Chapter 17 is a helpful reference. This chapter explores a few detailed scenarios—including protocol failures, federation-related errors, and others—to provide the reader expert assistance without the need to spend time contacting support or wait for newsgroup or forum answers.

Chapter 16

Diagnostic Tools and Resources

In this chapter:

This chapter introduces the event logs and diagnostic logging tools that are available in Microsoft Office Communications Server 2007 and Microsoft Office Communicator 2007. Useful diagnostic tools that are available in the Office Communications Server 2007 Resource Kit are identified and explained so as to help build awareness of this toolkit that can be used for diagnosing problems.

Overview of Diagnostic Tools

A variety of tools are available to help diagnose problems. Having an awareness of these tools and how to access them is a step in the right direction. Table 16-1 presents a selection of available tools, the scenarios to which they generally apply (whether they are specific to conferencing or voice applications), and a brief note on what they do and where you can access them.

Table 16-1 Diagnostic Tools for Different Scenarios

Tool Name	Description	Installation Source
Core Scenarios (Basic Presence and Instant Messaging)		
Validation Wizard	Analyzes and validates current configuration and connectivity to detect errors, validate basic end-to-end scenarios, and provide recommendations	Office Communications Server 2007 (in the Deployment Wizard); can also be launched from the server Microsoft Management Console (MMC) snap-in

Table 16-1 Diagnostic Tools for Different Scenarios

Tool Name	Description	Installation Source
Office Communications Server 2007 Logging Tool	Starts and stops server logs as well as filters and displays logs	Office Communications Server 2007; can also be launched from the server MMC snap-in
Event Viewer	MMC snap-in that enables client and/or server event logs to be viewed and examined (snap-in also has an embedded viewer that shows only errors and warnings)	Part of all Microsoft Windows operating systems
Client-LogReader	Script that scans client trace log files to highlight errors, provide protocol summaries, or filter out specific protocol messages	Office Communications Server 2007 Resource Kit Tools
Snooper	Graphical user interface (GUI) for summarizing, searching, and viewing client and server protocol and trace logs; also works for Microsoft Office Communications Server 2005 server logs	Office Communications Server 2007 Resource Kit Tools
Archiving-CDR Reporter	GUI for querying archiving and call detail records	Office Communications Server 2007 Resource Kit Tools
Topology Designer	Provides design, auto discovery, and persistence of topology configuration data	Office Communications Server 2007 Resource Kit Tools

Table 16-1 Diagnostic Tools for Different Scenarios

Tool Name	Description	Installation Source
CheckSPN	Validates service principal names (SPNs) to avoid authentication and topology errors	Office Communications Server 2007 Resource Kit Tools
DbAnalyze	Gathers analysis reports from the Office Communications Server 2007 database	Office Communications Server 2007 Resource Kit Tools
LCSDiscover	Discovers settings for previous and current versions of Live Communications Server 2005 and Office Communications Server 2007	Office Communications Server 2007 Resource Kit Tools
SIPParser	Protocol parser for Session Initiation Protocol (SIP); can be plugged into Network Monitor (Netmon) for viewing unencrypted SIP over Transmissioin Control Protocol (TCP)	Office Communications Server 2007 Resource Kit Tools
SRVLookup	Queries relevant Domain Name System (DNS) Service Record Locator (SRV) records for the specified domain; useful for federation and login diagnostics	Office Communications Server 2007 Resource Kit Tools

Table 16-1 **Diagnostic Tools for Different Scenarios**

Tool Name	Description	Installation Source
Conferencing Scenario		
Network Monitor (Netmon)	Network protocol analyzer used in viewing raw network traffic for media interactions	Part of Microsoft Systems Management Server 2003
Wireshark (formerly Ethereal)	Network protocol analyzer from the open source community	Available on many operating systems; also freely available at *http://www.wireshark.org/*
Quality of Experience (QoE) Monitoring Server	Enables a new server role that helps manage QoE by allowing a view of quality and trends for media connectivity, as well as monitoring and easing the troubleshooting of specific conferencing problem cases	Web download is available at *http://www.microsoft.com/downloads/details.aspx?FamilyID=09115944-625f-460b-b09c-51e3c96e9f7e&displaylang=en*
Enterprise Voice Scenario		
Enterprise Voice Route Helper	GUI for visualization, testing, modification, archiving, and sharing of voice routing configuration data	Office Communications Server 2007 Resource Kit Tools (the user's guide for this tool is available from the Microsoft Download Center; search for "Microsoft Office Communications Server 2007 Enterprise Voice Route Helper User's Guide" at *http://www.microsoft.com/downloads/details.aspx?familyid=cc5bd675-b91b-4339-8b4b-a11378061c95&displaylang=en&tm*)
Deployment Validation Tool (DVT) agents	Enables test endpoints and the ability to schedule tests and report results via Microsoft Operations Manager (MOM) or e-mail	Web download is available at *http://www.microsoft.com/downloads/details.aspx?FamilyID=3596a10d-65cc-4cca-8470-3f23d5ea55b2&DisplayLang=en*

On the CD All tools that are part of Microsoft Office Communications Server 2007 Resource Kit Tools are provided on the companion CD to make them easier to find and use. Pease reference the short document included in the toolset for detailed instructions on how to run each tool. More tools exist in the Microsoft Office Communications Server 2007 Resource Kit Tools than those shown in Table 16-1, for only the primary tools of interest to most readers are highlighted here.

Using Server Setup Logs

Installation is one of the first places in which help may be required if an error occurs. Logs are created in the %TEMP% directory on the machine during installation of the Office Communications Server. The *.log files contain progress and error information from setup and the installer. The *.html files contain clear progress and error information from activation and prep actions. When seemingly silent failures occur during installation, activation, or prep steps during deployment, installation information is the first place to look.

Diagnosing Setup Failures

Setup logs are located under %TEMP% and have either the .log (for Microsoft Installer [MSI] logs) or .html extension (for activation/prep failures). In MSI logs, look for the phrase "value 3" (MSI errors are cryptic, and this is a quick method to locate them). The .html logs are self explanatory and can be expanded to the point of the failure. LcsCmd's "CheckXXState" is usually also very helpful. For example, to check whether the Audio/Video (AV) multipoint control unit (MCU) is activated, you can run LcsCmd /mcu /action:CheckLcServerState /role:AVMCU.

–Nirav Kamdar
Senior Development Lead, OCS Server

Using Event Logs

The Office Communications Server product line has always provided event logs to help identify problems and point out irregularities in the system. In Office Communications Server 2007, there is even a filtered view of server warnings and errors presented in the MMC snap-in as a tabbed overview for each server. Office Communicator 2007 has added the capability to create event logs that can be enabled from the Tools | Options menu item on the General tab by selecting Turn On Windows Event Logging For Communicator, as shown in Figure 16-1. When issues arise, the event log is the first place to turn for high-level guidance on problems that the server or client might have already identified. In general, warnings and errors will be of interest, but informational event logs will not.

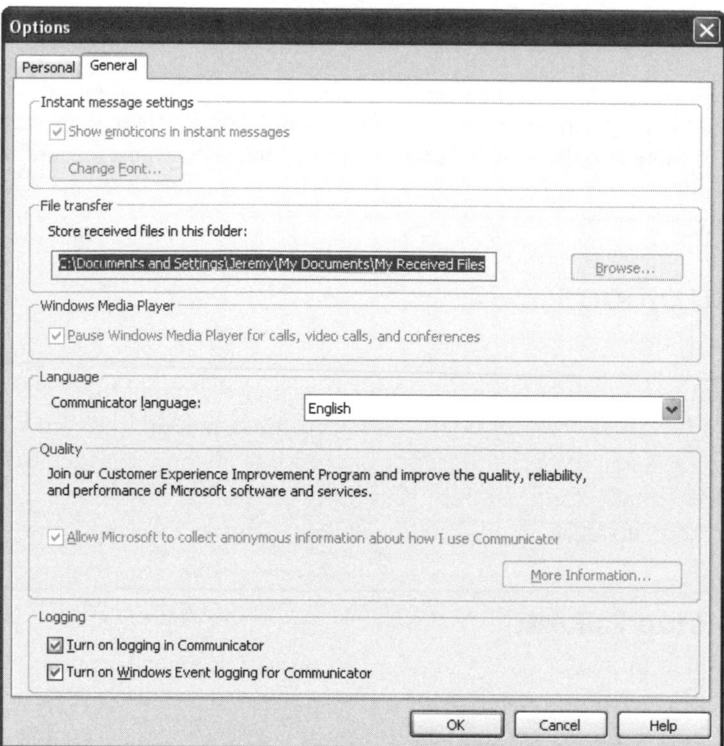

Figure 16-1 Enabling Windows Event Logging For Communicator in Office Communicator

Because the event log has the capability to filter and sort itself, it is not necessary to spend time hunting through the Application Event Log. All events logged by the client show up in the Application Event Log, and all events from servers show up in the Office Communications Server Event Log. The View menu provides the ability to filter by event source; therefore, filtering for Communicator events or a particular server role is possible, as is filtering for only warnings and errors.

Understanding Communicator Events

The following example presents a normal Office Communicator event log along with examples of problematic logs that may show up. Additional information and advice on how to resolve problems are presented with each log.

Example of an Expected Event

Normal event log entries are provided here simply to point out expected log entries so that they can be ignored during troubleshooting. The first log shown is created during every normal Office Communicator login when event logging is enabled.

```
Type: Informational EventID: 1020 Source: Communicator
 Description:
Communicator has enabled event logging.
Information about failed calls will be sent to the Windows event log.
```

Event ID 1020 is useful only for identifying that client event logs are turned on when looking for problematic warnings and errors in the event log.

Examples of Problem Events and Troubleshooting Steps

The detailed tracing log (described in more detail in the following section) is a primary means of understanding the details of problems when they occur, and if event logs are enabled in Office Communicator, it will also create event log entries when there are failures to provide diagnostic information. These entries are incredibly useful for diagnosing login problems. The following examples clearly explain the problem, point at data related to the problem, and explain the steps involved for solving the problem.

This first sample event log message (1007) occurs because Communicator is configured with an invalid server name, IConfiguredAnInvalidServerName.contoso.com. The message explains that Communicator cannot find a server with that name when attempting to resolve the hostname specified using the DNS. As is typical for most events, the actions to be taken next are clearly laid out in the event log Resolution, which greatly aids in resolving the problem.

```
Type: Error EventID: 1007 Source: Communicator
 Description:
Communicator was unable to resolve the DNS hostname of the login server
IConfiguredAnInvalidServerName.contoso.com.

Resolution:
If you are using manual configuration for Communicator, please check that
the server name is typed correctly and in full.  If you are using automatic configuration,
the network administrator will need to double-check the DNS
A record configuration for IConfiguredAnInvalidServerName.contoso.com
because it could not be resolved.
```

The second sample event log error (1015) occurs because Communicator is configured to connect to an invalid port (9999) instead of a valid port (for example, 5061) on the server. The message explains that Communicator is unable to connect (10065 is the code for Windows WSAEHOSTUNREACH error, which means that the host is unreachable on the network). Again, the steps to resolve the problem are laid out in the Resolution section in the event log text.

```
Type: Error EventID: 1015 Source: Communicator
 Description:
Communicator failed to connect to server srv.contoso.com (192.168.3.1)
on port 9999 due to error 10065.  The server is not listening on the
port in question, the service is not running on this machine, the
service is not responsive, or network connectivity doesn't exist.

Resolution:
Please make sure that your workstation has network connectivity.  If you
are using manual configuration, please double-check the configuration.
The network administrator should make sure that the service is running on
port 9999 on server srv.contoso.com (192.168.3.1).
```

The third sample event log error occurs because Communicator cannot validate the certificate credentials presented by the server to which it is connecting. The message explains that Communicator attempted to connect to sipfed.contoso.com, but received a certificate with a Subject Name (SN) that didn't match. This typically occurs because the wrong certificate is installed on the server or an unsupported name is published in the DNS and is used to connect to the server. The Resolution section offers the appropriate steps to take to move forward.

```
Type: Error EventID: 1008 Source: Communicator
 Description:
Communicator could not connect securely to server sipfed.contoso.com
because the certificate presented by the server did not match the expected
hostname (sipfed.contoso.com).

Resolution:
If you are using manual configuration with an IP address or a NetBIOS
shortened server name, a fully qualified server name will be required.
If you are using automatic configuration, the network administrator will
need to make sure that the published server name in DNS is supported by
the server certificate.
```

Some event log messages do not clearly state what needs to happen next, which can occur when the server infrastructure identifies a problem and Office Communicator simply reports the raw data that it receives from the server. Event ID 1000 is used for reporting exactly these types of scenarios, and examples of logs with this event as well as additional information about them are provided in the samples that follow. For event ID 1000, the first number in the technical data (1011 for this example) and the reason text ("Ms-Diagnostics header not provided by previous hop") are linked in that the number is simply an identifier that matches the reason text. It is not another form of error code to be analyzed.

The first sample event log message displays an unexpected failure (diagnostic event 1011 passed back from the server) during federation routing. An error is returned from the remote organization (woodgrovebank.com) by the server sip.woodgrovebank.com, but no diagnostics information is provided. Therefore, the server sipfed.contoso.com adds the ms-diagnostics header to identify the source of the failure. The problem might be transitory and not occur again later (e.g., it is handled by the client and the infrastructure by retrying the request, or a network outage will be resolved at some point), it might be a software bug in the remote implementation, or it might be an invalid request that can't be handled. In the latter case, looking at the transaction details in the Office Communicator tracing logs is the best approach to fully identify the issue.

```
Type: Warning EventID: 1000 Source: Communicator
 Description:
Communicator failed in an unexpected way.  More information is contained
in the following technical data:

1011;reason="Ms-Diagnostics header not provided by previous
hop";source="sipfed.contoso.com";Domain="woodgrovebank.com";PeerServer=
"sip.woodgrovebank.com"

Resolution:
If this error continues to occur, please contact your network
administrator.  The network administrator can use a tool like
winerror.exe from the Windows Resource Kit or lcserror.exe from
the Office Communications Server Resource Kit in order to interpret
any error code listed above.
```

The second sample event log message shows an unexpected failure (diagnostic event 1004) during internal routing. An error is returned by server5.contoso.com because it identifies a problem at the protocol level. In this case, a messaging session or some other interaction must have been in place long enough so that the server signature used to protect and validate the routing information is no longer valid. Servers rotate these keys regularly, and extremely long sessions can come up against this error, but Office Communicator should handle this error by re-establishing the session automatically.

```
Type: Warning EventID: 1000 Source: Communicator
 Description:
...
1004;reason="Route set is no longer valid";source="server15.contoso.com";ErrorType="A key
that was used to
sign the route set is no longer valid"
...
```

The third sample event log message (1013) occurs because the client and the server are not in sync on the current (universal) time. This can happen when the time is set properly but the time zone is set improperly because the system time has not been set to take daylight savings time or simply because the clock is set to the incorrect time. Authentication using Kerberos relies on clock accuracy, so the solution is to check the time and the time zones on the client and then on the server.

```
Type: Warning EventID: 1000 Source: Communicator
 Description:
...
1013;reason="Significant time skew detected during
authentication";source="server6.contoso.com"
...
```

The fourth sample event log message (1010) occurs due to certificate validation problems between two servers. This can happen because the servers are in different organizations and do not have common trust for each other's certificates, the other server's certificate isn't valid due to its name, the certificate has expired, or the remote server isn't using a server certificate. In this case, the problem is actually listed in the *ErrorType* field, which explains that Transport Layer Security (TLS) or Mutually Authenticated TLS (MTLS) was not able to be negotiated quickly enough. This is likely due to some networking problems (slow networks or firewall issues) or because the server went offline during the connection. Steps to resolve the problem would be to explore the remote server and the network path to that server to understand what caused the delay.

```
Type: Warning EventID: 1000 Source: Communicator
 Description:
...
1013;reason="Certificate trust with next-hop server could not be
established";source="sipfed.contoso.com";ErrorType="The peer did
not respond to TLS or MTLS negotiation in a timely manner"
...
```

The fifth sample event log message shows an unexpected failure (diagnostic event 2) with an error code that doesn't provide much explanation. The Windows calculator (calc.exe) can often be used to convert error codes into hexadecimal or decimal numbers so that a tool, such as winerror.exe or lcserror.exe, can provide a descriptive error message. Sometimes, error codes are printed in decimal numbers and need to be converted to hexadecimal numbers to display properly. At other times, a Windows system error message is wrapped with decorations and presented as a hexadecimal error code. If the tools are unable to present an error name and text, try using only the last four hexadecimal digits because it can take a bit of fooling around with calc.exe in scientific mode to back out some error codes. However, for this example, converting the error isn't necessary because it can be interpreted when passed directly to lcserror.exe: "SIPPROXY_E_AUTHENTICATION_LEG <--> The request processing was stopped to continue authentication exchange with the client through challenge response." This error message explains that sometimes the client and server get out of sync with authentication and, though the client thinks its current credentials are still valid, the server needs to prompt for authentication and cannot continue processing the request. In general, this is a harmless warning because the client will establish new credentials and the user is unlikely to even notice a problem.

```
Type: Warning EventID: 1000 Source: Communicator
 Description:
...
2;reason="See response code and reason
phrase";source="sipfed.contoso.com";HRESULT="C3E93D81 (SIPPROXY_E_AUTHENTICATION_LEG)"
...
```

Understanding Server Events

Examples of normal Office Communications Server event logs are presented to avoid confusion, along with examples of problematic logs that might arise. Additional advice on how to resolve problems is presented with each log.

When working through problems in the topology or on specific servers, a good way to minimize the scope or to quickly identify errors is to use the Validation Wizard, which is available as a tool in the Office Communications Server 2007 administration MMC snap-in. This tool checks configuration against connectivity and does the basic validation checks to point out and avoid misconfigurations in Office Communications Server 2007 settings or in network and certificate configurations that relate to the server.

Real World: Using the Validation Wizard

I have an Office Communications Server 2007 Standard Edition server and Office Communications Server 2007 Edge Server deployed. Because I have worked with the product for a long time, I first used the Office Communicator 2007 client to sign in internally. If this did not work, I would check the error message to see whether I could quickly resolve the problem, with DNS and Certificates being the easiest errors to identify. What do you do if that client doesn't work and you aren't able to figure it out? Use the Validation Wizard!

Once one client has successfully logged in, I know that my Standard Edition server is running and accounts are able to log in. I then move to the Edge Server, open Computer Management, Services and Applications, and right-click Microsoft Office Communications Server 2007 to launch Validation for the Edge Server role.

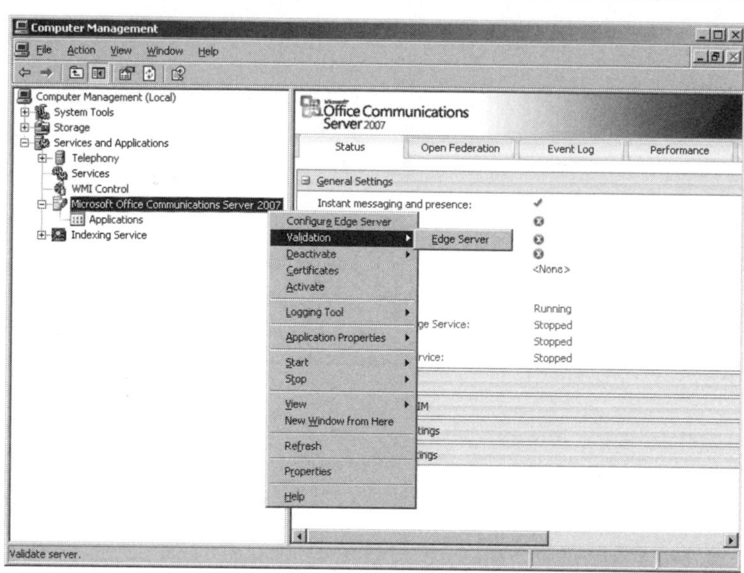

I select the first three checkboxes: Validate Local Server Configuration, Validate Connectivity, and Validate SIP Logon (1-Party) and IM (2-Party).

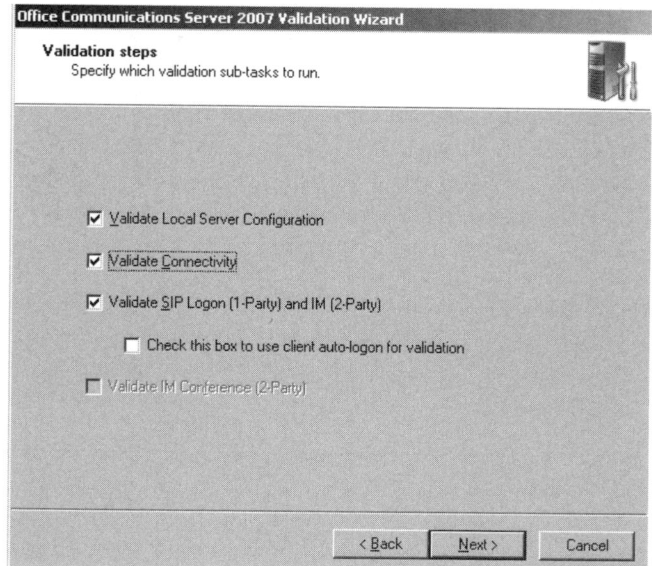

Because I am merely introducing the Validation Wizard here and will not walk through all of the tests, you will not see a Federation test included here.

I start to run the Validation Wizard on the Edge Server and receive errors. I select the View Logs option because logs are created by default in the user's temporary directory. The resulting log page looks like the following figure when opened in Internet Explorer.

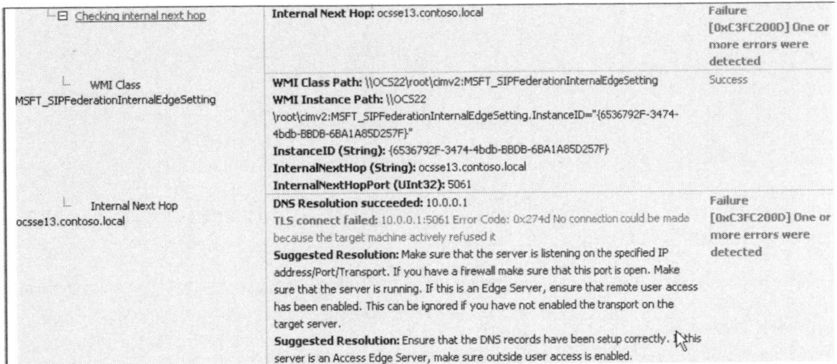

The errors point out problems that I really didn't expect, such as "TLS connect failed: 10.0.0.1:5061 Error Code: 0x274d". No connection can be made because the target machine actively refused it. Please note that the log contains other errors. My experience has taught me to go through all of the errors to find the biggest problem, which in this case is the fact that I cannot connect to the Standard Edition server.

The next step is to run the Validation Wizard on the Office Communications Server 2007 Standard Edition server. I select only the first two options, Validate Local Server Configuration and Validate Connectivity, because my errors are indicative of a server problem and not a logon problem.

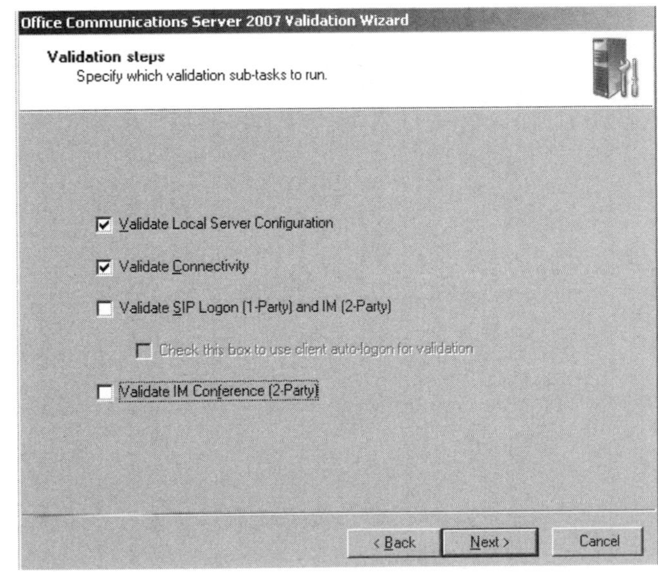

The error received here is so obvious that I don't have to expand it: "Error: Service isn't installed, enabled or started. Please check service installation and configuration".

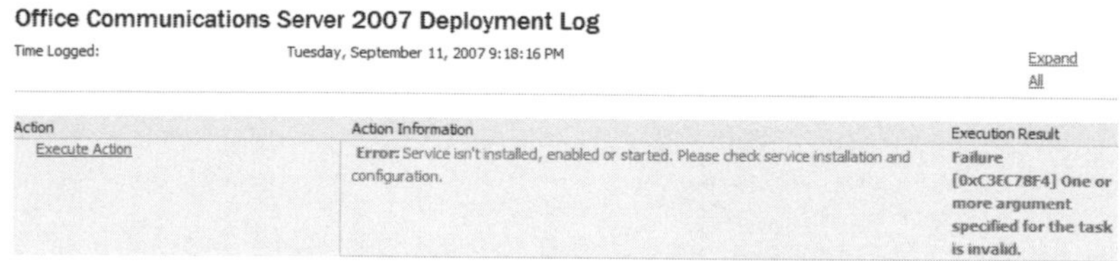

Sure enough, my machines experienced a power failure overnight and when they restarted, I didn't check to make sure that everything was working. I chose to start my validation from the Edge Server with the assumption that everything internally was working properly; because it was not, I took actions to resolve problems for the internal server. I will begin the Validation Wizard testing here and work my way back out to the Edge Server to minimize the number of possible problems.

I have configured my deployment such that I will select all of the options on the Validation Steps page.

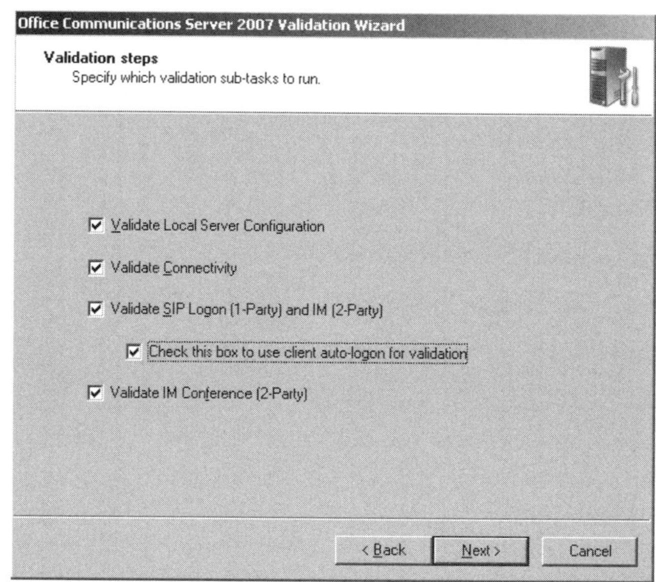

I also have another failure to investigate. Note that now is the time to emphasize the need to select Expand All at the top right of the log file page and scroll through the list. Remember that the first red text is not always the error but is typically a rolling up of the error from the steps contained within it. You will almost always scroll all the way to the bottom of the file.

Checking federation settings	**Default outgoing route for federation:** None available **Suggested Resolution:** Federation is enabled at the forest level. However, no global or default federation servers are available. Ensure that these settings point to a valid server and that the server is running.	Failure [0xC3FC200D] One or more errors were detected
Checking global federation route	**Global Federation Route:** edge.contoso.local	Failure [0xC3FC200D] One or more errors were detected
Global Federation Route edge.contoso.local	**DNS Resolution failure:** No such host is known **Suggested Resolution:** Make sure there are no typos in the Server name. Make sure that the Server name is published in the DNS (A or SRV record) or hosts file entry is configured correctly.	Failure [0xC3FC200D] One or more errors were detected
Checking local federation route	Local Federation Route: None Found	Warning [0x43FC200C] Not all checks were successful
Checking static routes	**No WMI Instance Returned By Query :** select * from MSFT_SIPRoutingTableData **Static route:** None Found	Success
Checking all trusted servers		Failure [0xC3FC200D] One or more errors were detected
Global Federation Route edge.contoso.local	**DNS Resolution failure:** No such host is known **Suggested Resolution:** Make sure there are no typos in the Server name. Make sure that the Server name is published in the DNS (A or SRV record) or hosts file entry is configured correctly.	Failure [0xC3FC200D] One or more errors were detected

I have two problems on which to focus: federation settings are failing, which also includes a DNS error for the name I put into the configuration. I can see here that no records exist. I either failed to enter the correct DNS A record, or I don't have the next hop server of edge.contoso.com. The second problem is that I was not able to sign in one of the two users for whom I provided credentials.

Attempting to login user using Kerberos	**Maximum hops:** 2 **Failed to establish security association with the server:** User jeremy Domain contoso.local Protocol Kerberos Server sip/OCSSE13.contoso.local Target Invalidated **Suggested Resolution:** Check whether the typed password and sign-in name are correct. Check whether the user is present in the AD and enabled for SIP. Check whether the target server is part of the Windows AD domain in which this user account is present. If this is a Kerberos failure check whether the client machine has access to the KDC. In some cases, Kerberos SA negotiation failures may be expected and hence can this error can be ignored.	Failure [0xC3FC200D] One or more errors were detected
Attempting to login user using NTLM	**Maximum hops:** 2 **Failed to establish security association with the server:** User jeremy Domain contoso.local Protocol NTLM Server OCSSE13.contoso.local Target Invalidated **Suggested Resolution:** Check whether the typed password and sign-in name are correct. Check whether the user is present in the AD and enabled for SIP. Check whether the target server is part of the Windows AD domain in which this user account is present. If this is a Kerberos failure check whether the client machine has access to the KDC. In some cases, Kerberos SA negotiation failures may be expected and hence can this error can be ignored.	Failure [0xC3FC200D] One or more errors were detected
Attempting to login user using Kerberos	**Maximum hops:** 2 **Successfully established security association with the server:** User ivo Domain contoso.local Protocol Kerberos Target sip/OCSSE13.contoso.local **User registration succeeded:** User sip:ivo@contoso.com @ Server ocsse13.contoso.com	Success

Notice the information contained in the wizard about user logons. Credentials for Jeremy were passed using both Kerberos and NT LAN Manager (NTLM) and failed, whereas credentials for Ivo passed with Kerberos. The failure for both Kerberos and NTLM is a strong indicator that the password was mistyped (which I did on purpose to create this dialog), but the success of Ivo with Kerberos confirms that there is no authentication problem and, more specifically, no problem with Kerberos.

I corrected the next hop server fully qualified domain name (FQDN) to be ocs22.contoso.local and verified my user credentials.

–Thomas Laciano
Program Manager, Office Communications Server Customer Experience

Examples of Normal Events

For anyone who has looked at the number of events created in the event logs on a server as part of starting up, it can be an overwhelming experience to understand what information is actually useful and what can be ignored. In general, all informational logs can safely be ignored, but examples are provided here to explain some of the detailed information available within them. Warning and error messages are also commonly seen, and some are explained here to alleviate administrator concerns about warnings or errors that aren't fully understood. All server logs will show up in the Office Communications Server Event Log, which can be loaded as a snap-in in the MMC or launched directly as eventvwr.exe, as shown in Figure 16-2.

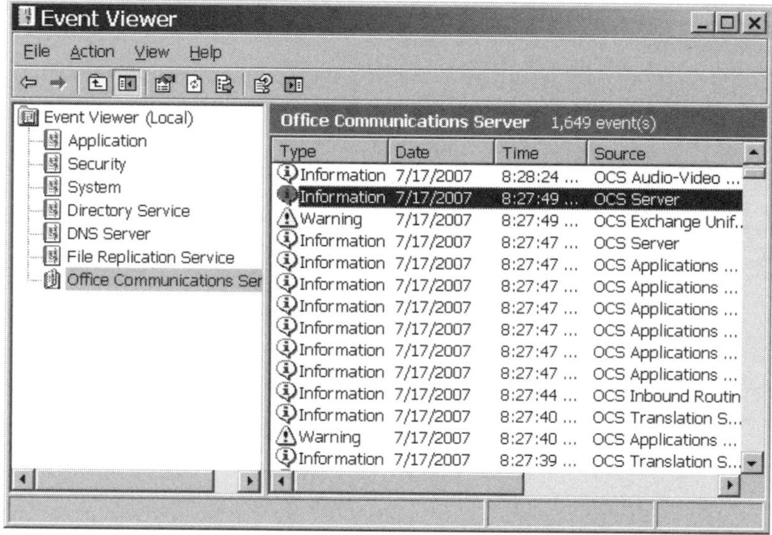

Figure 16-2 Office Communications Server events in Event Viewer

Examples of Normal Informational Events The following startup event log message (Event ID 14426) simply identifies that the registry key was enabled to log message bodies, as shown in Figure 16-3.

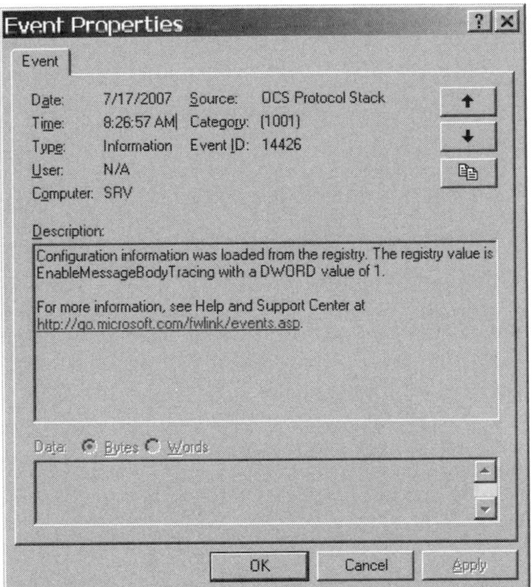

Figure 16-3 Viewing event log entries in Office Communications Server

This isn't a great cause for concern. However, depending on your corporate security policy, it might be a privacy violation to log this type of information in tracing logs; therefore, this type of logging should be used only for short intervals during detailed diagnostic sessions if message bodies are actually required (typically, they are not). Additional information about enabling message body tracing is available in the "Using Client and Server Trace Logs" section later in this chapter.

```
Type: Informational EventID: 14426 Source: OCS Protocol Stack
 Description:
Configuration information was loaded from the registry. The registry
value is EnableMessageBodyTracing with a DWORD value of 1.
```

The next event log message (56001) is similar to several of the first messages in the 56000s, which identify that default settings are being used because they weren't actually stored in the Windows Management Instrumentation (WMI) store. None of these messages are of much concern other than to record the current settings that the server will be using in case of future debugging or to work with Product Support Services (PSS).

```
Type: Informational EventID: 56001 Source: OCS WMI Event Provider
 Description:
The WMI event provider parameter 'initial due time' was not set or
failed to be retrieved. Use the default value.

Initial due time: 300000 milliseconds
```

Several additional settings are shown in other server events during startup, and these are included in the following examples to demonstrate some of the configuration information available and identify the default settings for some potentially interesting detailed configurations. The first event log message shows some of the detailed default configuration used by the SIP stack.

```
Type: Informational EventID: 14413 Source: OCS Protocol Stack
 Description:
Proxy configuration changes were applied successfully.
Request compression on outgoing server to server connections
    [1=yes,0=no]: 0
Accept compression requests from server connections [1=yes,0=no]: 1
Accept compression requests from client connections [1=yes,0=no]: 1
Maximum number of server-to-server connections: 1024
Maximum number of client-to-server connections: 5000
Maximum outgoing TLS connections to the same server: 4
Maximum size of content body for client to server connections: 131072 bytes
Maximum size of content body for server to server connections: 5120000 bytes
```

The second event log message shows some of the detailed default configuration used by the User Services SIP registrar.

```
Type: Informational EventID: 30926 Source: OCS User Services
 Description:
User Services Global Settings configuration applied:
MinRegistrationExpiry: 300.
DefRegistrationExpiry: 600.
MaxRegistrationExpiry: 900.
MinPresenceSubscriptionExpiry: 1200.
DefPresenceSubscriptionExpiry: 28800
MaxPresenceSubscriptionExpiry: 43200
MinRoamingDataSubscriptionExpiry:900
DefRoamingDataSubscriptionExpiry: 43200
MaxRoamingDataSubscriptionExpiry: 86340
NumOfDevicesPerUser: 8
MaxSubscriptionPerUser: 200
AllowPollingForPresence: true
EnableBENotify: true
UserDomainList: false
```

The third event log message shows additional default configuration used by User Services, with the most interesting probably being the maximum contacts that a given user is allowed to maintain.

```
Type: Informational EventID: 30934 Source: OCS User Services
 Description:
Server specific User Services Settings configuration applied:
RedirectMethods: AsAppropriate
MaintenanceHourOfDay: 2
MaxContactsPerUser: 150.
```

As previously mentioned, most informational logs are useful only for backtracking configuration settings of the server after problems are detected or for determining whether the configuration is the same as it was expected to be (based on setting registry keys, WMI configuration, or changes in the user interface [UI]).

Examples of Normal Warning and Error Events Several warning and error event log messages can show up during initial startup of the server, which isn't really a cause for concern. The first event log message warns that a critical application or service has not yet registered with the server. This can occur due to longer startup processing times when the server is booted. As long as the server starts successfully and a subsequent information log identifies that the application finished startup, this log is not of much concern.

```
Type: Warning EventID: 30232 Source: OCS Applications Module
 Description:
Office Communications Server startup is pending.

Some configured critical applications have not yet registered.
Resolution:
For script only applications ensure that the application is available
in the path specified in the MMC, and that no errors are reported by the
Office Communications Server Script-Only Applications Service. For
non-script only critical applications ensure that they are configured to
register on server startup.
```

The next event log message warns that no Exchange Unified Messaging (UM) servers could be found in the domain. This message is a concern only if servers were installed, but this is not a mandatory part of the installation.

```
Type: Warning EventID: 44028 Source: OCS Exchange Unified Messaging Routing
 Description:
Exchange Unified Messaging Routing Application did not find any Exchange
UM servers.

Cause: No Exchange UM servers are configured for SIP traffic or the
RTCSRV service account does not have permission to read Exchange objects
in Active Directory.
Resolution:
Configure one or more Exchange UM servers to handle SIP traffic.
```

The following event log message has an error due to the failure of a service (in this case, the Address Book Server [ABS]) to start up and respond within an expected time frame. Again, this is something that can happen while the server is starting up shortly after the machine boot process when many processes are loading or on slower servers on which a lot of programs are running. As long as subsequent event log messages show that the service eventually started, this message isn't of concern.

```
Type: Error EventID: 12330 Source: OCS Server
 Description:
Failed starting a worker process.

Process: 'C:\Program Files\Office Communications Server 2007\Server\Core\ABServer.exe'
Exit Code: C3E8302D (The worker process
failed to initialize itself in the maximum allowable time.).
Cause: This could happen due to low resource conditions or insufficient
privileges.
Resolution:
Try restarting the server. If the problem persists contact Product Support
Services.

...
```

The next event log message warns that delta files aren't being generated. However, this is normally the case for small servers or test systems because there just aren't enough users. This message can largely be ignored and treated as an informational event log.

```
Type: Warning EventID: 21012 Source: OCS Address Book Server
 Description:
A delta file would be too large in relation to the full file it is based
on.  The delta file will not be generated.

Path: C:\Program Files\Office Communications Server 2007\Web Components
\Address Book Files\D-0909-0926.lsabs
Full File Records:  5
Delta File Records: 3
Cause: A delta file is generated in memory.  If the number of new/updated
contacts plus the number of deleted contacts is greater than a configured
percentage of the number of contacts in the base file, the delta file is
not generated because it would be quicker for the client to just download
the full file.
Resolution:
None needed.
```

Examples of Problem Events and Troubleshooting Steps

Many possible ways exist in which server configurations, network conditions, and invalid requests can create error conditions for the server. A few examples are included in this section both for reference and to explain what is happening.

This first error event occurs because the server didn't have a static IP address. Office Communications Server must be run on a static IP address because doing so will provide the most reliable service if its IP address doesn't change. The SIP records and uses IP addresses during routing, and a change in this address can cause failures for messaging or other active sessions. Under normal conditions, the Dynamic Host Configuration Protocol (DHCP) server (which is in charge of handing out IP addresses) does not change the IP address that it originally assigned to the Office Communications Server, but it can happen, especially across reboots or service windows. The following log helps identify that the IP address on which the server was listening no longer exists, which is an indicator that DHCP was in use.

```
Type: Error EventID: 14336 Source: OCS Protocol Stack Description:
A configured transport has failed to start.

Transport TLS has failed to start on local IP address 192.168.3.104 at
port 5061.Cause: This can occur due to a configuration error, low system resources
or other programs using the specified port. It can also happen if the IP
address specified has become invalid.
Resolution:
Ensure that the IP address specified is valid and that no other program
is listening on the specified port.
```

The second event shows a warning that is logged to alert the administrator that a server certificate (used by Office Communications Server for authentication and encryption with TLS) is close to expiring. Server certificates are valid only for a certain period of time after they are issued and then need to be replaced by a newly issued certificate. This warning helps administrators act before the certificate expires so that an unplanned outage and diagnostics can be avoided.

```
Type: Warning EventID: 14342 Source: OCS Protocol Stack
 Description:
The certificate configured for secure transport will expire soon.

Transport TLS on 192.168.1.103:5061 will expire on Thursday, June 05, 2007
at 09:35 Local Time.  The certificate serial number is attached for
reference.

<attached binary data shows the certificate's serial number>
```

The third event shows an error that will be logged if the administrator doesn't update the certificate, which will prevent the server from starting successfully. The solution for this and the previous log are the same–install a valid certificate for use by the server.

```
Type: Error EventID: 14341 Source: OCS Protocol Stack
 Description:
The certificate configured for secure transport has expired or is not yet
valid.

Transport TLS on 192.168.1.103:5061 will not start.  The certificate
serial number is attached for reference.
Resolution:
Renew the certificate or replace the transport with a new one.

<attached binary data shows the certificate's serial number>
```

Many possible types of events could arise, and all of them cannot be presented here. Use of winerror.exe and/or lcserror.exe from the Windows Server 2003 or Office Communications Server 2007 Resource Kit Tools can help explain any error codes that you come across. However, almost all of these events contain relatively detailed information to help point out the problem, identify specific data related to the problem, and offer solutions or items to investigate.

Note Please see the "Additional Resources" section at the end of this chapter for instructions on obtaining the Windows Server 2003 Resource Kit Tools.

Using Client and Server Trace Logs

Both the Office Communications Server and Office Communicator use the Windows Software Trace Pre-processor (WPP) utility that is part of the operating system. The client manages this itself and dumps logs based on a check box in the UI (which drives one of several registry keys). The server dumps logs based on the tracing tool provided in the MMC snap-in. Though these logs are extremely useful, they also contain a great deal of very detailed information–much of which might not pertain to any problem or issue that is being investigated or analyzed. This section introduces the subject of tracing and offers some basic insights into looking through logs. Other sections on debugging and diagnostics delve into the more technical details included in tracing log files.

Understanding Office Communicator Traces

As of this release, Communicator logging can now be controlled via the General menu inside Tools | Options. Two check boxes on the dialog box control logging and event log messages. Refer to Figure 16-1 earlier in this chapter for a view of the dialog box. All protocol messages for the remainder of this section were captured by enabling logging in Communicator and gathering protocol messages from the log.

Configuring Trace Settings

Values under the registry key HKCU\Software\Microsoft\Tracing\Uccp\Communicator are used for Communicator log configuration. The value EnableFileTracing can be turned on or off by setting it to 0 or 1, respectively. MaxFiles is set to 2 by default, but you can specify that only one file should be created or that many should exist to maintain more history when the log file is recycled. MaxFileSize is set to 0 x 800000 (~8.3 MB) by default and determines how large the log file can get before it is cleared and starts over. FileDirectory determines the directory where log files will be stored and is set to %USERPROFILE%\Tracing by default.

Default settings create the log in %USERPROFILE%\tracing\Communicator-uccp-0.uccplog, which is generally in C:\Documents and Settings\<*username*>\tracing\Communicator-uccp-0.uccplog.

As previously mentioned, default settings create two log files with up to approximately 8.3 MB of logs for each. Once the first file (mentioned earlier) fills up, the second file, Communicator-uccp-1.uccplog is used. Once the second file fills up, its content overwrites the first log file, and the second file will clear itself and add new content until it runs out of space and overwrites the first log file again.

> **Note** Be aware of your logging settings. If logging is run for too long, it can be difficult to find the data of interest, and (if there was a lot of network activity) interesting data might eventually be overwritten. It is important to limit the time when logging is enabled and to avoid logging during actions that create large amounts of traffic (such as an initial login) unless absolutely necessary. For ease of use during an investigative session, increasing the MaxFileSize value (0 x 2000000 allows for ~33.5 MB) and setting MaxFiles to 1 allows larger amounts of data to be analyzed in a single file.

Looking at Trace Files

Your first few attempts at viewing trace files can be an involved process as you learn what to look for and what can be safely ignored. Trace files contain protocol data as well as internal programmer logs that make it more difficult to decipher at first. Using tools such as findstr.exe (or grep.exe/qgrep.exe) makes it easier to scan through trace files if you know what you are looking for. Refer to the "Using ClientLogReader" and "Using Snooper" sections later in this chapter to learn about more advanced tools that can make quick work of these log files. Generally speaking, only very detailed problems require wading through the raw logs, and use of Snooper or ClientLogReader is a much faster way to gather diagnostic information.

> **Note** If logging configuration has been changed to allow it, log files can grow upward of 20MB for an active client. Be aware that logs of this size won't load easily in Notepad and that other editors should be used such as WordPad, Emacs, or VI. Tools like ClientLogReader and Snooper are discussed in later sections of this chapter and are specifically built to interpret and quickly display information from these log files.

The first thing to understand is the structure of the log. An example of one line from the log file follows.

```
07/13/2007|11:13:51.203 A38:82C TRACE ::
CUccSubscriptionEventInfo::GetOperationInfo - enter [0x04356808]
```

The first 10 characters always contain the date, with a "|" character separating it from the next 12 characters that contain the time. A space separates the time and the next field, which is always 7 characters and represents the thread that logged this message (normally a single thread). A space separates the thread ID from the next 5 characters that identify the type of log

(TRACE, INFO, WARN, ERROR). A space, two colons ('::'), and a space then separate the log type from the content of the log. In the previous example, CUccSubscriptionEventInfo::GetOperationInfo - enter [0x04356808] is the content. Because of this rigid formatting, it is much easier to write scripts and tools to parse the log files.

The TRACE log type is generally only of interest to the product development team and product support. INFO logs are informational and can be of interest, but can also provide more detail than necessary and create confusion. WARN logs highlight warnings where a problem might exist, or the issue might be handled by other components. ERROR logs highlight errors, although some of these errors should really be warnings. Therefore, if the ERROR logs don't make much sense, you can probably ignore them. Most problematic errors eventually show up as INFO or ERROR logs that are at least somewhat meaningful and understandable.

On the CD Protocol messages show up as INFO logs. Examples can be seen in the Communicator log files included in the \Appendices,Scripts,Resources\Chapter 04 folder.

All protocol logs have a similar format. An INFO log always precedes the message data, which helps identify it. The following examples for sending and receiving a protocol message are shown for clarity.

```
...
07/13/2007|11:13:51.687 A38:82C INFO  :: Sending Packet - 192.168.1.100:443
(From Local Address: 192.168.1.103:2780) 1719 bytes:
07/13/2007|11:13:51.687 A38:82C INFO  :: <MESSAGE DATA HERE>
...
07/13/2007|11:13:51.828 A38:82C INFO  :: Data Received - 192.168.1.100:443
(To Local Address: 192.168.1.103:2780) 903 bytes:
07/13/2007|11:13:51.828 A38:82C INFO  :: <MESSAGE DATA HERE>
...
```

Looking for the leading INFO trace for Sending Packet or Data Received makes it easier to work through the voluminous data at a protocol level.

Note Please keep in mind that INVITE and MESSAGE messages do not log the body of the message for privacy reasons. Obtaining a full view of the message logging will need to be done on the server. Refer to Chapter 4 for more details on enabling full-message body logging from the server side.

Ignoring Misleading Logs Many logs appear regularly and can be misleading during the first few investigations with client logs. Some of these logs are presented here to make reading them for the first time faster and more effective. Logs that might be confusing are listed in the examples that follow.

```
...
07/13/2007|13:27:53.750 A38:82C ERROR :: SIP_STACK::MapDestAddressToNatInternalAddress
m_pDirectPlayNATHelp is NULL.
Setting *pIsDestExternalToNat to FALSE
...
07/13/2007|11:13:51.203 A38:82C ERROR :: Condition failed with 80ee0058: 'm_lContainerID
!= INVALID_CONTAINER_ID'
...
07/13/2007|11:13:51.687 A38:82C ERROR :: HRESULT failed: 800cce05 = hr. spMimePropSet-
>GetProp
...
07/13/2007|11:33:56.250 A38:82C ERROR :: CSipSubscription::
SubscriptionStateChange already changed to state 3, input state 3
...
07/13/2007|11:33:56.734 A38:82C ERROR :: CUccRichPresenceParser::ParseCategoryInstance -
Instance id is NOT present.
Category note. 0x80ee0058
...
07/13/2007|12:41:45.312 A38:82C ERROR :: REGISTER_CONTEXT::
HandleRegistrationSuccess SetGruuByProviderId failed 80ee0058
...
07/13/2007|12:57:45.859 A38:82C ERROR :: REGISTER_CONTEXT::
HandleRegistrationSuccess - ParseMsUserLogonDataHeader - hr=0x00000000, bRemoteUser=1
...
07/13/2007|11:33:54.531 A38:82C ERROR :: Condition failed with 00000001:
'pos != 0'
...
07/13/2007|11:45:43.156 A38:82C ERROR :: CUccPublication::Publish
[01AD3950] - Publication does not contain any instances
...
```

These logs are listed without much explanation because they are easily red herrings—logs that should really be INFO traces and not ERROR traces. This can be very misleading because a successful login on a production system with many local and federated contacts resulted in 2900 ERROR traces. Working through these logs can be difficult, but working from the end of the log and looking at the log immediately after a failure can help reduce the volume of data that needs to be reviewed.

On the CD To simplify things, the ClientLogReader script or the Snooper tool (which are included on the CD in the Office Communicator Server 2007 Resource Kit Tools) can both help read Communicator 2005 and Communicator 2007 trace logs instead of you having to manually scan through the log file. The Snooper tool, which is detailed in the "Understanding Office Communications Server Traces" section, can be launched from the server MMC and is a viewer for server logs. However, it can also load the client trace file to look at protocol messages in a summary and in full view. The ClientLogReader script is covered in the following "Using ClientLogReader" section.

Using ClientLogReader When some common problems occur, the logs provide useful information. The PERL (Practical Extraction and Report Language) script ClientLogReader from the Office Communications Server 2007 Resource Kit Tools helps tremendously in diagnosing these problems. This tool (also available on the CD) sifts through the client logs and identifies problem records in a meaningful way. The tool can be used to analyze a log file and point out potential problems as well as to show all protocol messages in full or summary mode. The following examples of using the script (with the resulting data trimmed for brevity) introduce the script's capabilities and the output that can be expected.

```
C:\Documents and Settings\Jeremy\Tracing>perl clientlogreader.pl -help

Version: 1.0, Last Update: 07JUN2006

USAGE:
perl clientLogReader.pl [-f fileToProcess] [-protocol] [-protocolSummary]
[-tail]

    fileToProcess - if not specified input is taken from standard input
      the file to process - can contain wildcards
    -protocol - SIP protocol messages will all be output along with hints
    -protocolSummary - SIP protocol messages will have start lines displayed
    -tail - log file will be watched if it grows and/or is recreated
EXAMPLE:
  perl clientLogReader.pl -f lcapi*.log -protocolSummary
  perl clientLogReader.pl -f lcapi*.log -protocol
  perl clientLogReader.pl -f lcapi4.log -tail

Look in the README.txt file for this tool for more help and examples

C:\Documents and Settings\Jeremy\Tracing> perl clientlogreader.pl
-f Communicator-uccp-0.uccplog  WARNING: DNS resolution failed for oldserver.contoso.com
because the
hostname wasn't found (WSANO_DATA)

C:\Documents and Settings\Jeremy\Tracing> perl clientlogreader.pl
    -f Communicator-uccp-0.uccplog -protocol  INFO: Incoming from 192.168.1.100:443 (via
192.168.1.103:2780)
$$$begin-message$$$
...
$$$end-message$$$
INFO: Outgoing to 192.168.1.100:443 (via 192.168.1.103:2780)
$$$begin-message$$$
...
$$$end-message$$$
...

C:\Documents and Settings\Jeremy\Tracing> perl clientlogreader.pl
    -f Communicator-uccp-0.uccplog -protocolSummary  INFO: Outgoing to 192.168.1.100:443
(via 192.168.1.103:2780)
        SUBSCRIBE sip:sip.contoso.com:443;transport=tls;lr;ms-route-
sig=hu4T8Jd65_O8xKIjN1aUGxssauUPBSsbQNNOYHWAAA SIP/2.0
INFO: Incoming from 192.168.1.100:443 (via 192.168.1.103:2780)
        SIP/2.0 200 OK
...
```

The –tail option is not shown in the preceding example, but it allows a log file that is being written by Communicator to be analyzed and its output data to be shown as Communicator runs. This can be especially useful to detect problems or protocol failures daily in the summary view that might otherwise be hidden or go unnoticed.

Understanding Office Communications Server Traces

Server tracing changed significantly with the release of Office Communications Server 2007, and logging can now be initiated and configured, and files can be viewed directly from the MMC. The logging infrastructure is now using WPP instead of the flat-file logging component used in the past. This update results in all client and server traces being logged with the same mechanism and allows remote and interactive logging of server components across the topology. It is now also possible to filter by server component as well as by user and/or server when looking for logs to reduce processing time and the volume of logs created when specific debugging is in process.

The Office Communications Server 2007 Logging Tool can be launched by right-clicking the node that corresponds to the server's short name and selecting Logging Tool | New Debug Session, as shown in Figure 16-4.

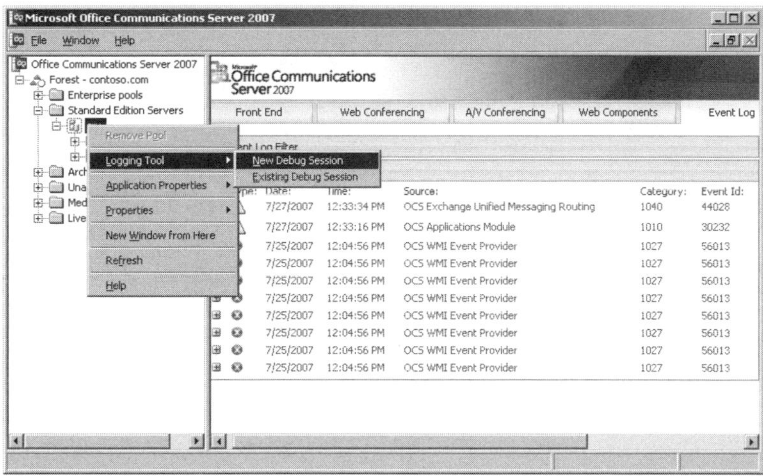

Figure 16-4 Launching the Office Communications Server 2007 Logging Tool

The Logging Tool shown in Figure 16-5 contains a large set of features in one tool to make it easy to learn and then apply across topologies and technologies. The features include:

- Starting and stopping logging
- Enabling/disabling logging individually by server component
  - Enabling various logging types (flags) within each server component
  - Enabling various logging levels within each server component

- Control over logging options
  - Defining specific log file options, such as recycling type and maximum size
  - Formatting information for the log prefix, buffering, and clock resolution
- Enabling real-time monitoring instead of only log-based mechanisms
- Enabling user Uniform Resource Identifier (URI) and server FQDN filtering of protocol logs
- Ability to directly view and analyze the log with the Snooper tool (if the Office Communications Server 2007 Resource Kit Tools have been installed)

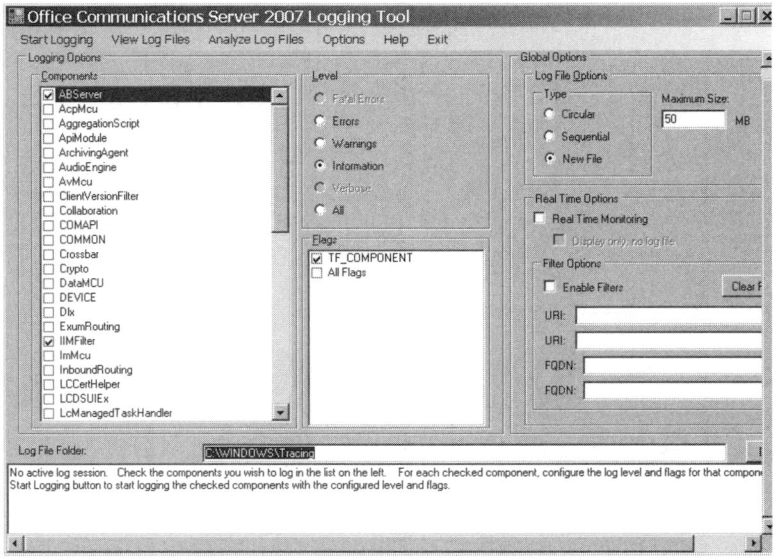

Figure 16-5 Office Communications Server 2007 Logging Tool dialog box

Snooper is included in the Office Communications Server 2007 Resource Kit Tools. It can show protocol summaries and allow full-message text to be displayed. It can load all server and client logs and even allow errors to be identified by looking up user information in the archiving database (if one exists). It can also look up conferencing and presence reports for individual users, conferences, and health reports for MCUs and can display users who have more than a specified number of contacts or permission settings. An example of Snooper with a client log loaded is shown in Figure 16-6. In addition, see the "Using Snooper" section later in this chapter for more information on the capabilities of this tool.

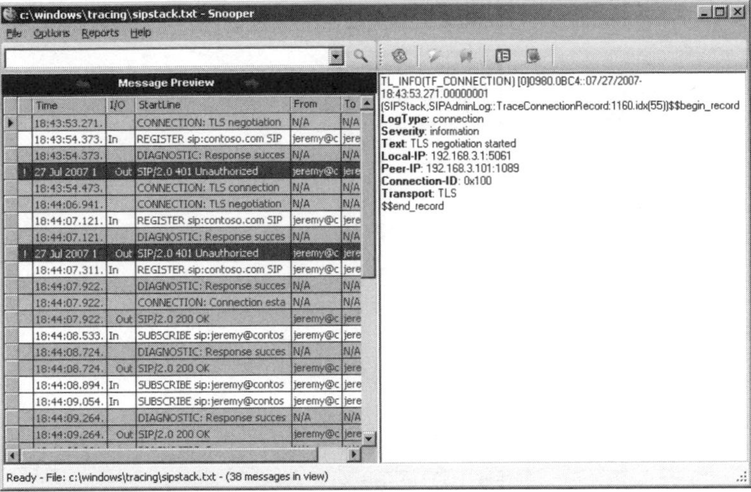

Figure 16-6 Snooper log file analysis and diagnostic tool

Example of Gathering a Server Trace

Once the Office Communications Server 2007 Logging Tool is launched (refer to Figures 16-4 and 16-5), a few steps must be taken to gather a server trace log. In this example, a SIP stack log is collected into a log file. To do this, only the SIPStack component check box should be selected, all levels and flags should be enabled, logging to C:\Windows\Tracing should be left as the default, and no real-time options should be selected (no active display or filtering of the content). For reference, the Flags section identifies subcomponents that log information if they are enabled, thereby allowing protocol, diagnostic information, connection-level, or other details to be logged or ignored (for SIPStack) to prevent the trace logs from being overwhelmed by too much information if a precise area of the server must be investigated. After this configuration is selected, the dialog box should appear as shown in Figure 16-7.

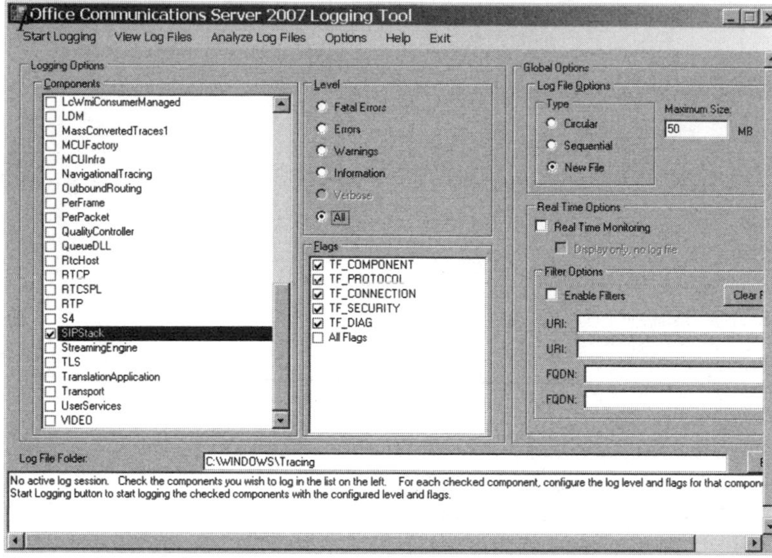

Figure 16-7 Gathering a SIPStack trace with the Office Communications Server 2007 Logging Tool

Once the tracing configuration is set, select the Start Logging menu item to begin logging for the server. If desired, real-time monitoring can be enabled to show the log output in a console as it occurs or to show the console output and log to the log file as normal. Once the network or communication actions of interest are complete, the Stop Logging menu item can be selected to finish logging and prepare the text trace log. Finally, the View Log Files menu item can be used to view the text files (in Notepad), or Analyze Log Files can be used for a summary view of the protocol messages in Snooper (assuming that the Office Communications Server 2007 Resource Kit Tools are already installed). It is worth noting that log files can contain errors and other issues that won't show up in protocol logs, so be aware that the way in which you view the log files can make it easy for you to forget that errors might exist.

Note If the log file has grown upward of 20MB, be aware that logs of this size won't load easily in Notepad and that other editors should be used such as WordPad, Emacs, or VI. Snooper is specifically built to interpret and quickly display information from these log files, but it does not show all of the details that can be seen if the log file is interpreted directly.

The Real-Time Monitoring section can enable a text window that shows the logs as they occur, and filters can be enabled to prevent logs that don't pertain to specific users or servers from showing. This capability is of great utility when working on a busy server because it can reduce the amount of data that scrolls past on the display.

More details and information about the Logging Tool can be found in the product documentation. Most of the remaining features in the Options menu are of interest only during an engagement with product support.

Direct from the Source: Using Trace Filters to Diagnose a Problem on a Busy Server

Logs collected by the Office Communications Server 2007 Logging Tool are valuable, but can quickly become very large on a busy server. For example, a Standard Edition server that hosts thousands of users could log 1MB or more per second of SIP message data. If the problem being investigated requires logging to be enabled for more than a few minutes, the resultant log files might be several GB in size. Such log files are difficult to view and manipulate and might impact server performance due to the disk space that they consume. Fortunately, most problems can be isolated to one or two users or, in the case of an edge proxy, one or two peer servers. The Filter Options supported by the Office Communications Server 2007 Logging Tool can thus be used to greatly reduce the size of log files on a busy server. The following sections discuss problems that have been seen in customers' live deployments of Office Communications Server 2007 and its predecessor, Live Communications Server 2005 with SP1.

Scenario One: Remote User Cannot Log In

In this scenario, a remote user (an employee who is currently located outside the enterprise) has called the help desk of a large company and reported that he cannot log in via the company's edge proxy server. The edge proxy in question not only routes traffic from remote users, but also routes traffic from federated peers and public instant messaging connectivity (PIC) providers. Therefore, hundreds or thousands of SIP messages per second might pass through the edge proxy.

The obvious place to start an investigation into this problem is the edge proxy. Simply running the Office Communications Server 2007 Logging Tool will quickly result in very large log files. Instead, we enter the URI of the affected remote user into the first *URI* field under Filter Options and then select the Enable Filters check box, as shown in Figure 16-8.

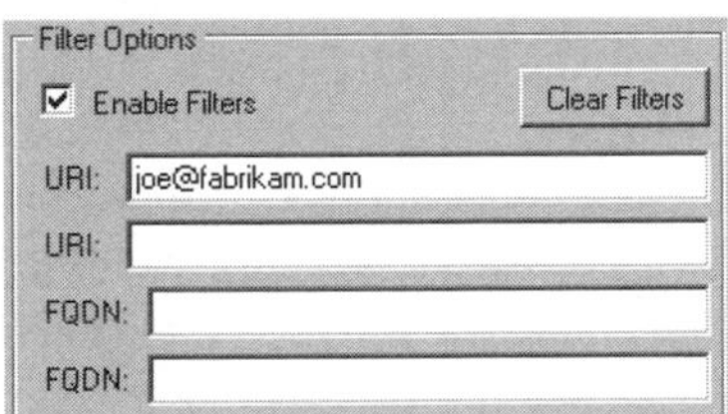

Figure 16-8 Enabling a user URI filter

When logging is started, only SIP messages and related events that contain the user URI of interest appear in the trace log; all other data is ignored, resulting in a small and focused log file. The cause of the problem is typically evident from the failure SIP responses being sent back to the client. For example, the ms-diagnostics field in SIP responses received at the internal edge of the edge proxy from a director might provide a hint as to why a REGISTER or INVITE request has failed.

If the cause of the problem is not evident from the (filtered) log recorded on the edge proxy, then the same procedure can be used to obtain filtered logs on an internal server, such as a director. Simply enter the URI of the affected remote user and enable filters, as in Figure 16-8.

Scenario Two: Incorrectly Configured Firewall Causes Intermittent Failure of IMs to Users in a Federated Partner

In this scenario, one or more users in a large company have called the help desk and reported intermittent failures when sending and receiving instant messages (IMs) from buddies in another company. Routing between the two companies is achieved by federation between their respective edge proxy servers. The local edge proxy routes traffic to many federated partners and PIC providers, so hundreds or thousands of SIP messages per second might pass through the edge proxy.

Simply running the Office Communications Server 2007 Logging Tool on the local edge proxy will quickly result in very large log files. Instead, we enter the FQDN of the edge proxy of the federated partner in the first *FQDN* field under Filter Options and then select the Enable Filters check box, as shown in Figure 16-9.

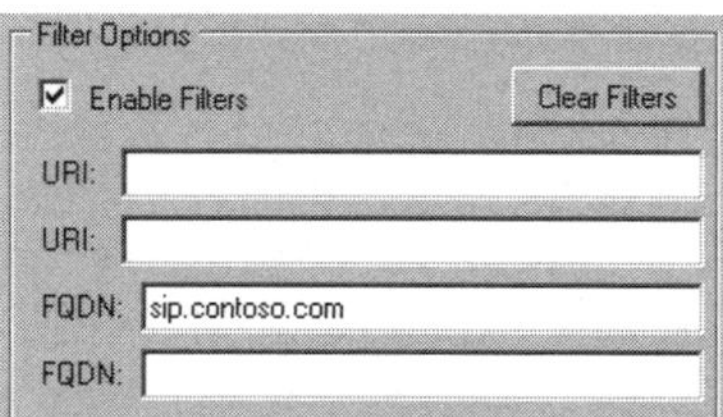

Figure 16-9 Enabling a peer server FQDN filter

When logging is started, only SIP messages and related events that originate from, or are destined to, the FQDN of interest appear in the trace log; all other data is ignored, resulting in a small and focused log file. In this particular scenario, the remote edge proxy server appears to be dropping the MTLS connection for some reason. This manifests itself as TF_CONNECTION and TF_DIAGNOSTIC messages at TL_ERROR level in the trace log. For example:

```
TL_ERROR(TF_CONNECTION) [0]0B90.07F8::09/05/2007-07:06:29.805.00000088
$$begin_record
LogType: connection
Severity: error
Text: Receive operation on the connection failed
Local-IP: 10.0.0.13:1142
```

```
Peer-IP: 10.0.0.10:5061
Peer-FQDN: sip.contoso.com
Peer-Name: sip.contoso.com
Connection-ID: 0x502
Transport: M-TLS
Result-Code: 0x80072746 WSAECONNRESET
$$end_record
TL_ERROR(TF_DIAG) [0]0B90.07F8::09/05/2007-07:06:31.991.0000008d
$$begin_record
LogType: diagnostic
Severity: error
Text: Message was not sent because the connection was closed
SIP-Start-Line: MESSAGE sip:fred@contoso.com;opaque=user:epid:G-
AWNAmf8Vqf8tSG2CexVwAA;gruu SIP/2.0
SIP-Call-ID: a524eda4c75e49e58a3777d0478d49a8
SIP-CSeq: 7 MESSAGE
Peer: sip.contoso.com:5061
$$end_record
```

Furthermore, the MTLS connection is being dropped at a regular interval of every 30 seconds or so.

```
TL_ERROR(TF_DIAG) [0]0B90.07F8::09/05/2007-07:07:01.871.00000094
$$begin_record
LogType: diagnostic
Severity: error
Text: Message was not sent because the connection was closed
SIP-Start-Line: MESSAGE sip:fred@contoso.com;opaque=user:epid:G-
AWNAmf8Vqf8tSG2CexVwAA;gruu SIP/2.0
SIP-Call-ID: 75e49e58a3777d0478d49aa524eda4c8
SIP-CSeq: 9 MESSAGE
Peer: sip.contoso.com:5061
$$end_record
```

The most likely cause of this problem is a firewall that is not correctly configured for SIP traffic, thereby causing it to drop connections when they are idle for 30 seconds. This process is typical of many firewalls and load balancers in which the default configuration assumes a protocol like HTTP rather than SIP.

–Conal Walsh
Senior Software Design Engineer

Using Snooper

The Snooper utility is a tremendous advance for diagnostics when working with the Office Communications Server 2007 product suite and is available as part of Office Communications Server 2007 Resource Kit Tools. Unlike many tools, it has a complete reference manual that is available directly within the tool from the Help | Using Snooper menu. Snooper is capable of viewing logs from the current client and server components as well as Live Communications Server 2005 flat-file server logs. Snooper summarizes protocol messages, identifies diagnostic and connection-level events, and offers full content for any message that is selected. Snooper is also capable of querying the archiving server and other Structured Query Language (SQL) repositories to gather reports containing useful overview and detailed information. Snooper can be run remotely for pools, but Standard Edition servers might have connection errors when logging remotely. If this is the case, Snooper.exe should be run locally on the Standard Edition server.

Snooper enables searches and allows complex queries related to specific fields in the message. For example, if the user jeremy@contoso.com is of interest but only for messages that were sent to vadim@contoso.com, a search such as from:jeremy@contoso.com to:vadim@contoso.com would get the protocol messages of interest. When each message is viewed in detail, the matching text in the protocol message is highlighted. A useful trick for director and access edge server logs is to specify a direction—whether the message is incoming (in) or outgoing (out)—to avoid seeing messages twice. Such a specification might be direction:in. Likewise, to see nonprotocol messages, specifying direction:none allows a view of just these messages (connection events, diagnostic notes, and so forth).

Using Snooper to Jump Into Larger Logfiles

Snooper can be used to quickly find the protocol message that you're interested in. Click the Open In Notepad button in the Snooper toolbar to open the file in Notepad and go quickly to that part of the file. You can then look at the lower-level trace statements for more details.

–CJ Vermette
Software Design Engineer on the Office Communications Server team

Snooper is also capable of building useful reports based on queries against the SQL repositories maintained by Office Communications Server 2007. The Reports menu offers this functionality, and the Error Analysis option allows an archiving server to be queried to gather error reports that have been logged. These records can be filtered by user or by attributes of the error messages and provide an insightful way for information technology (IT) support to identify problems that a user is experiencing without more information or logs from the users themselves. The ability to gather overview information for all errors or specific types of errors allows administrators to proactively look at the errors that have been occurring to predict and resolve problems before many users even end up encountering them. The Analyze Error Reports dialog box is shown in Figure 16-10.

Analyze Error Reports
Archiving SQL Instance (local)\rtc
Archiving Database Lcslog
Search By User
User At Host
Search By Error
Select below attributes for further filtering
Error Status Code
MS-Diagnostic Id
Request Type
Content Type
Filter by Date 07/27/2007 - 12:59:32 PM
OK Cancel

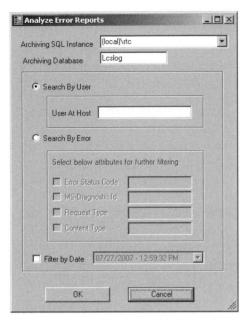

Figure 16-10 Snooper Analyze Error Reports dialog box

The Conferencing And Presence Reports option provides a variety of useful reports that have not been so easily available in the past. Information can be retrieved about users, conferences, MCUs, and diagnostic overview information for the repository. An example of a user query is shown in Figure 16-11. This report contains detailed information about the user, their rights, their contacts and groups, the rich presence information they are publishing, conferences they organized, and conferences to which they are invited.

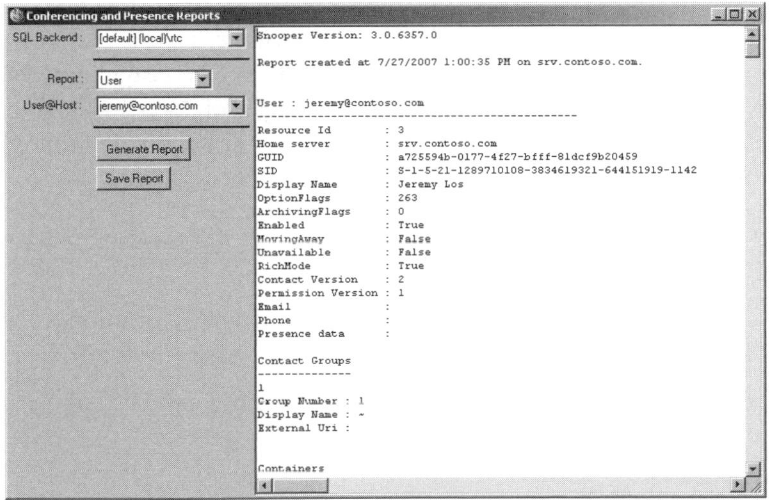

Figure 16-11 Snooper Conferencing and Presence Report for a User

The conference report shows the current settings as well as the current state of the conference that was queried. The schedule for the conference, the invitee list, the media types allowed in the conference, the active MCUs, the active participant list, and the state of each participant are all shown. This information can be helpful when monitoring a running conference or when diagnosing problems for users when they are connecting to or interacting in a conference.

The MCU Health report identifies all MCUs that are present on the server and provides detailed information about them. Their ID, media type, URL, heartbeat status, number of assigned conferences, and number of connected participants are all displayed. An example of this report is shown in Figure 16-12. Heartbeats to the MCU Factory should generally occur within 15 seconds, but the heartbeat to the Focus depends on the activity level of the MCU.

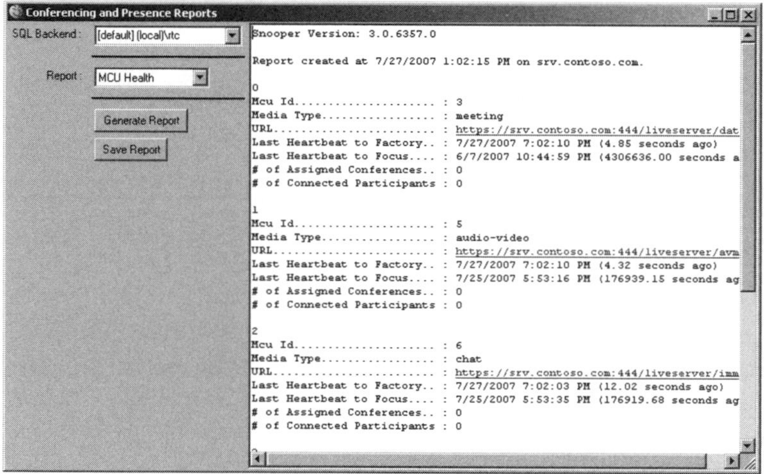

Figure 16-12 Snooper Conferencing and Presence Report for MCU Health

The Diagnostic report identifies overview information about many aspects of the repository in question, but focuses on stats for record counts as well as the size of the database on disk and how this space is allocated across internal records. An example of the report in Snooper is shown in Figure 16-13. The following data are presented in the log, with notes in parentheses to clarify or call out the usefulness of the information.

- Database version (can highlight errors during the update process if the database wasn't updated)
- Database internal statistics along with storage space utilized (helps during maintenance and in understanding what is taking up space if the database grows unreasonably)
  - List of tables in the database along with record count and data/index/total size counts
  - Database size and dynamic database size
  - Files that make up the database (.mdf and .ldf files) plus their sizes and growth

- Server statistics (helps determine server load in terms of storage space and network activity)
  - Distribution of contacts across enterprise servers as well as the percentage of contacts that are outside of the enterprise
  - Number of active endpoints (Communicator clients or otherwise)
- Maintenance, replication, and expiration tasks and the server on which they are scheduled to run
- Number of users with no contacts or permissions (likely idle or have never logged in)
- Presence statistics, all with min, max, average, and standard deviation (helps to get a feel for usage and how users compare with each other in terms of usage)
  - Contacts per user
  - Container member users per user
  - Container member domains per user
  - Cached container members per user
  - Permissions per user
  - Prompted subscribers per user
  - Static publications per user
  - User-bound publications per user
  - Time-bound publications per user
  - Endpoint-bound publications per user
  - Publication data size per user
  - Subscribers per user
  - Category subscriptions per user
  - Endpoints per user
  - Conferences per user
- Overview of activity (quick view of current usage)
  - Number of unique users with endpoints
  - Number of conferences (total and currently active)

> **Note** Generating the Diagnostic Conferencing And Presence Report can create a large amount of load on database servers, so it should be done infrequently during high-activity intervals to prevent creating delays for users. This report effectively locks the database to get a snapshot report, which holds up all traffic on the servers that require a database query from this repository.

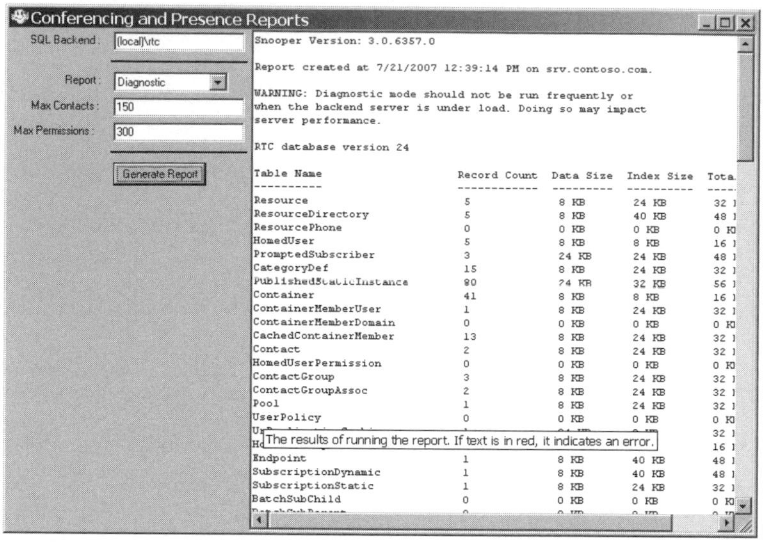

Figure 16-13 Snooper Conferencing and Presence Report for Diagnostics

Overall, Snooper is a helpful resource for gathering information about the configuration and state of servers and users and is a useful tool for scanning logs that have been collected to analyze them. However, it is always good to start by reviewing the event logs and looking at the MMC overviews for each server because many times the problems have already been identified or will be mentioned. Forgetting to look for event log messages before starting an investigation can waste a great deal of time when the error has already been identified and highlighted to make things easier.

Summary

A variety of tools and resources are available for diagnosing problems, and the event log, server and client logs, and MMC diagnostic tools, such as the Office Communications Server Logging Tool and Snooper, all make diagnosing problems easier than it has been in the past. Always check the event log before digging into a diagnostic session as well because the problems it identifies can point out—with no further work—exactly what needs to be done. For more information on how to put these tools and resources to work, please see the other chapters in Part V that describe generic and specific troubleshooting steps for various scenarios.

Additional Resources

- The official Microsoft Office Communications Server Web site is located at *http://office.microsoft.com/en-us/communicationsserver*. Documents, tools, and support information are always available at this location.

- Office Communications Server 2007 Resource Kit Tools are available for download at *http://www.microsoft.com/downloads/details.aspx?familyid=B9BF4F71-FB0B-4DE9-962F-C56B70A8AECD&displaylang=en*. Search for "Office Communications Server 2007 Resource Kit Tools" from *http://www.microsoft.com/downloads*.
- Practical Extraction and Report Language (PERL) downloads are available at *http://www.activestate.com*.
- Windows Server 2003 Resource Kit Tools are available for download at *http://www.microsoft.com/downloads/details.aspx?FamilyID=9d467a69-57ff-4ae7-96ee-b18c4790cffd&DisplayLang=en*. Search for "Windows Server 2003 Resource Kit Tools" from *http://www.microsoft.com/downloads*.
- The Quality of Experience (QoE) Monitoring Server Web download will be available at *http://www.microsoft.com/downloads*, but was not available at the time of this writing.
- Many useful community-driven Web sites support Office Communications Server. One that stands out is the Live Communications Server Guides site at *http://www.lcs-guides.com/*.

On the Companion CD

There is no companion CD content for this chapter.

Chapter 17

Troubleshooting Problem Scenarios

In this chapter:

The Microsoft Office Communications Server 2007 product suite offers a great deal of functionality, connectivity, and control to users and administrators. However, much complex and sophisticated technology is distributed across several machines on a variety of networks with different software components installed on each. The distributed aspects of the product mean that inconsistent local and global settings, network connectivity, and external dependency failures can result in problems with non-obvious root causes. Things can go smoothly when deployments and configuration changes are planned by someone with experience with Office Communications Server 2007, but mistakes and misunderstandings can happen when the product suite is under evaluation or new to the architect or administrator. This chapter is specifically constructed to help architects and administrators through the first deployment and usage hurdles that they might encounter and is also intended to provide a troubleshooting framework that can help experts to explore more detailed problems.

Overview of the Troubleshooting Process

This chapter exists specifically to help identify common problems and to illustrate effective ways to diagnose the source of the problems. This overview section identifies primary technical problem spaces and offers a troubleshooting flowchart to assist with investigations. By exploring and/or ruling out individual technical areas, the complexity of the investigation is reduced and focused effort is possible by working through the troubleshooting flowchart. The remainder of the chapter focuses on problem scenarios and explains common problems along with specific ways to gather information and resolve the problems. For reference, most tools and resources that are used to work through these problems have been described to some level of detail in Chapter 16, "Diagnostic Tools and Resources," as well as the information on where to find these tools and resources.

This chapter contains numerous quotations from various contacts within and around the Office Communications Server 2007 product team. This information comes directly from the experts in and around the team who had specific tips or tricks. Their information is captured here as a compendium of ideas and information for detailed diagnostics and expert troubleshooting.

Identifying Primary Problem Spaces by Technical Area

Office Communications Server 2007 has several primary technical areas and components within it. During troubleshooting, it is desirable to rule out problems in as many of these areas and components as possible to simplify the investigation and help focus on the root cause of the problem. The primary technical areas and components are:

- Deployment and installation errors (which can cause any of the other issues)
- Configuration
  - Dialing rules and routing configuration
  - Domain Name Service (DNS)
  - Local Windows Management Instrumentation (WMI) configuration
  - Active Directory configuration
    - User accounts
    - Servers and infrastructure
  - Conference scheduling and configuration
  - Authorization
    - Per-user presence
    - Account rights (login, remote login, conferencing, federation-capable, and so on)
- Network connectivity
  - Media connectivity
  - Session Initiation Protocol (SIP) connectivity
  - Local or remote outages or firewall configurations
  - Edge network to internal servers and edge network to other federated networks
- Authentication
  - Server Principle Name (SPN) misregistration
  - Disabled or nonexistent user accounts
  - Certificate trust
  - Edge servers that aren't registered in the Active Directory or are without updated knowledge of internal servers
- Session Initiation Protocol (SIP)
- Presence store and associated routing logic
- Software version incompatibilities

When diagnosing a problem, it is helpful to quickly grasp the possible problem areas involved. Try to keep these key areas in mind during the investigation because it can help avoid the escalation of complexity as well as make it easier to approach support staff with a clearly detailed problem statement and idea of the technical areas involved. The next section provides a flowchart to help scope and diagnose problems.

Summary of Troubleshooting Steps

This section provides helpful troubleshooting steps and identifies community and Microsoft resources on the Web to move blocked investigations forward. Information and details that should always be provided when asking for help are also presented to help avoid additional delays in back-and-forth messaging on community and Microsoft forums.

Direct from the Source: Deployment Diagnostics

Figure 17-1 displays the diagnostics and troubleshooting tools that can be used at various stages in the deployment cycle. For example, after configuring Office Communications Server, DNS, and Certificates, you can use the Validation Wizard to ensure that server configuration is correct, verify connectivity to other trusted servers and gateways, and simulate basic sign-on and instant messaging (IM) scenarios.

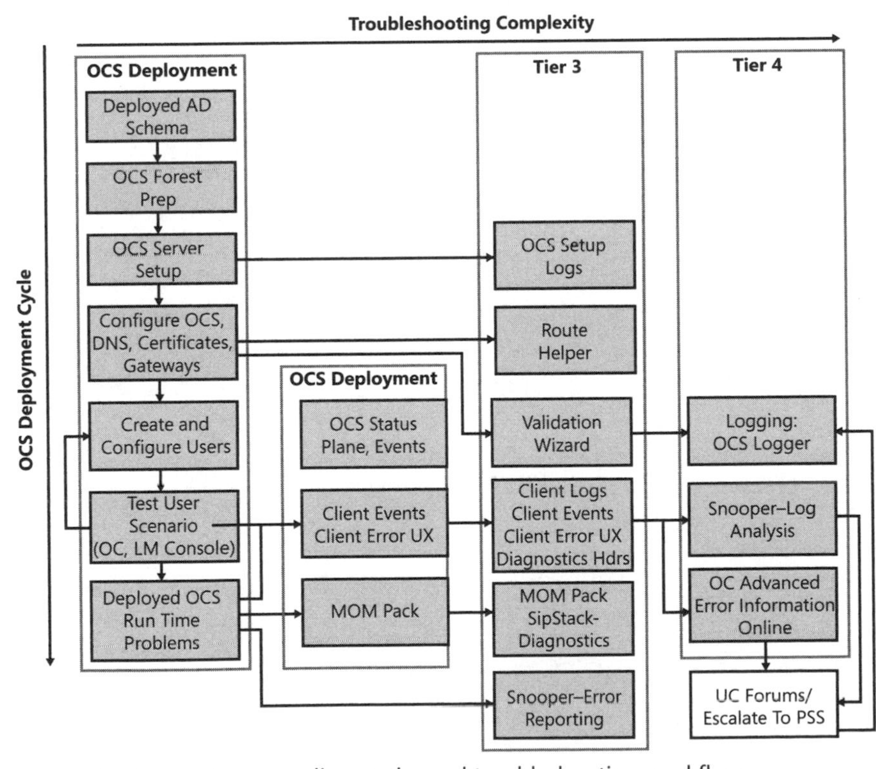

Figure 17-1 Deployment diagnostics and troubleshooting workflow

> You can obtain associated detailed text for each of the tools from the Office Communications Server Technical Reference (OCSLogger, RunTime Diagnostics, Snooper) or the Office Communications Server Administration Guide (Validation Wizard).
>
> *–Amey Parandekar*
> *Program Manager on the Office Communications Server team*

The tools shown in Figure 17-1 are described in Chapter 16 and in the Office Communications Server Technical Reference.

In the previous "Deployment Diagnostics" sidebar, Figure 17-1 identifies deployment steps along with troubleshooting tools and resources to use when something fails, whether during deployment or afterward. Figure 17-2 identifies how to effectively engage community and Microsoft support resources and also covers the procedure involved when following the bottom-right step from Figure 17-1.

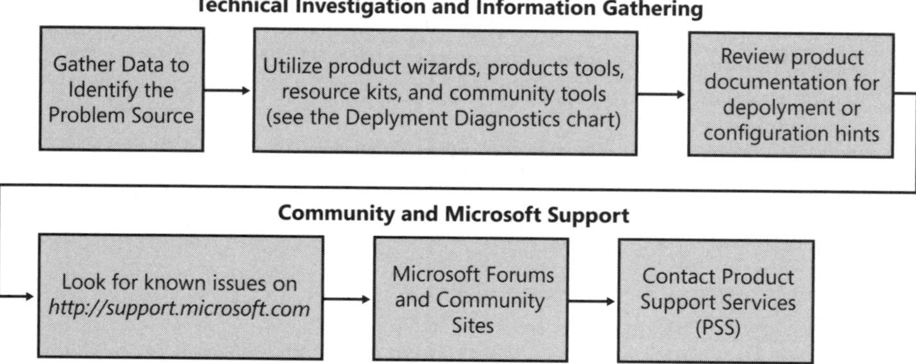

Figure 17-2 Community and Microsoft support

The following outline fleshes out questions to answer when working through the steps identified in Figure 17-2, thereby providing a workflow that minimizes wasted time and effort while getting assistance in pinpointing the root cause of the current problem.

I. Gather data to identify the source of the failure.
   a. Acquire details about error messages and related server and client logs.
   b. Identify when and how the problem occurs.
   c. Attempt to reproduce the problem to be able to verify any potential fixes and to provide a precise description of the problem.
   d. Acquire all related information about the configuration and topology.
      i. Domain names, IP addresses, firewalls, and DNS settings

ii. Windows domain infrastructure, topology deployed, versions of servers and clients

iii. Deployment settings and individual server configurations

iv. Special hardware and software deployed or Active Directory/machine configurations that shouldn't cause problems for Office Communications Server, but aren't specifically mandated by Office Communications Server deployment guides

II. Review product documentation.

a. Before looking for answers on community sites or waiting for answers from others, make sure that related product documentation has at least been reviewed.

b. Find documentation online.

i. Search *http://technet.microsoft.com* for Office Communications Server, or go directly to *http://technet.microsoft.com/en-us/library/bb676082.aspx.*

ii. At least review the Planning Guide, the relevant Deployment Guide documents, and the Technical Reference Guide.

c. Look specifically for deployment steps that were skipped or recommendations that are being ignored. You may want to deal with these items immediately or at least mention them when asking for help to get quick and accurate responses.

III. Browse through the Microsoft Support site.

a. Open *http://support.microsoft.com/* and choose the Select a Product menu to access the site specific to Office Communications Server 2007.

b. Search for keywords or error codes to identify known issues with the product.

IV. Use the Microsoft Forums to view existing answers or ask for community help.

a. Utilize several resources at once to get the best results.

i. Microsoft Forums–Open *http://www.microsoft.com/office/community/en-us/default.mspx* and select from the product list on the left.

ii. Live Communications Server-Guides Community Site–Open *http://www.lcs-guides.com/*

b. Answer your questions immediately by taking the time to look through existing questions and answers, which is the fastest route to solving the problem.

c. Wait for an answer. If the problem hasn't already been solved, post your question and look through other related articles for tips or hints that might apply to this situation.

i. Take notes on error codes and data of interest that is found along with basic information about your topology and configuration.

ii. More information is always better than not enough information. Don't get stuck waiting for a reply that only asks for clarifications on what was posted or data that wasn't provided up front.

iii. Answers will usually be offered within three working days. If no answer is forthcoming within a day or two, try posting more information about the configuration or problem along with any new information from diagnostic investigations to prompt others and identify that the issue is still outstanding.

V. Escalate to Microsoft Product Support Services (PSS).

a. The *http://support.microsoft.com* site contains a link under Need More Help to quickly get in touch with support via e-mail, phone, or instant messaging.

b. Being prepared with existing logs, a full description of the problem, and what investigation has already been explored will speed up the process significantly.

Resolving Common Problem Scenarios

This section identifies scenarios in which problems might be identified, offers pointers and hints as to what the problems might be, and demonstrates how to continue diagnosing the problem for other issues. The primary root causes of problems for existing customers and beta testers have historically been the following:

- Certificate configuration, deployment, or enrollment errors
  - Missing or incorrect parameters (such as Subject Name [SN] or Subject Alternate Name [SAN]) that make it so remote machines can't validate the certificate as being the authority for the DNS name by which the server is recognized
  - Authentication failures due to intermediate or root Certificate Authority (CA) certificates that are missing on the validating user or server machine
  - Inability to configure or utilize a server certificate due to installation in a user store instead of the machine store (which leaves the private key inaccessible to the service)
- Configuration inconsistencies
  - Mismatches between the configuration that was expected and the one that was actually configured
  - Mismatches between the global Active Directory and local server configuration
- Domain Name Service (DNS) problems
  - Servers are unable to reach the DNS zone that publishes the necessary information
  - DNS and certificates don't match up explicitly in a way that allows authentication, client discovery, or the federation to work
- Load balancer configuration

- Ports aren't properly mapped or enabled
- Server shared and private IP addresses are mismatched with the load balancer
- Unsupported configurations are attempted that fail only in certain cases

- Migration or co-existence problems with Office Communications Server 2007 and Live Communications Server 2005
- Quality of Experience (QoE) issues with conferencing over networks
  - Limited resources/bandwidth for necessary traffic
  - Data quality issues (echoing, microphone problems)

Real World: First Verify Connectivity

When troubleshooting Office Communications Server 2007, the network availability and network configuration can play a big part in making things work or in introducing failures. A few potential problems are called out in this sidebar along with tips for efficiently resolving the problems. Always remember to verify connectivity first before proceeding on to more in-depth diagnostics and troubleshooting.

Debugging single client failures when servers are under a load

When a server is experiencing a high volume of traffic, it might be difficult to collect and analyze server logs for a single client failure. Client side logs offered by the Live Meeting console and Office Communicator are a great place to start. These logs are disabled by default, but can be enabled by using regedit.exe to set the following registry keys:

```
...\uccp\Communicator\EnableFileTracing
...\uccp\ConfAPI\EnableFileTracing
...\uccp\LiveMeeting\EnableFileTracing
```

All of these registry entries show up under HKCU\Software\Microsoft\Tracing\..., and each should be set to a DWORD value of 1 to enable them. The registry changes are picked up after the application is exited and restarted. By default, the logs are written to the %USERPROFILE%\Tracing directory.

In case of a SIP failure, try searching for the ms-diagnostics header. If the user is successfully authenticated and is not coming across a federated link, the faulting server often adds information about where the response was generated as well as a reason for the failure. This should aid in the debugging process.

Live Meeting conference join failures

Debugging join failures for Live Meeting console can sometimes be more difficult than debugging Office Communicator sign-in because the console connects to more server roles at join time. The first step in debugging a console join issue is to verify SIP connectivity and user credentials. Two easy ways of verifying SIP connectivity are:

- The Test Connection button on the User Accounts dialog box of the Live Meeting console
- Signing in with the same user from the same machine using Office Communicator

If SIP connectivity appears to be working, yet the client still cannot get into a conference, there is likely an issue with connecting to one of the following roles:

- Web Conferencing (Edge) server
- Web Content download

Try using telnet.exe to establish connections to the ports for these roles, or use Internet Explorer to ensure that the certificates are trusted.

> **Note** In client-side Unified Communications Client Platform (UCCP) logs, the server sends an INFO message containing the fully qualified domain names (FQDNs) that the client should be connecting to.

Debugging connection failures for Edge Server roles

Office Communications Server provides a Validation Wizard to check server configuration and connectivity. The wizard can be accessed from the right-click menu in Computer Management. Even after the Validation Wizard has been run and everything checks out, external conferencing clients might still experience connectivity issues with a Web Conferencing Edge Server. The Web Conferencing Edge Server relies on incoming connections from Web Conferencing Servers in the enterprise network, so the inability of the internal server to connect into the edge network can show up as a failure to connect for an external conferencing user. To check that connections have been established, use netstat.exe on the configured internal port that the Web Conferencing Edge Server is listening on by typing **netstat -aon | findstr 8057**.

–Jeff Reed
Software Design Engineer in Test on the Office Communications Server team

To simplify the scope and remove complexity during investigations, it is always advisable to look for event log errors and warnings that can quickly be checked in the administration Microsoft Management Console (MMC) snap-in for Office Communications Server 2007. These can also be filtered and searched directly from the MMC based on product categories such as Web Conferencing or Voice Applications.

To radically ease diagnostics, install the Office Communications Server 2007 Resource Kit Tools, which enables the use of Snooper inside of the Office Communications Server Logger (which can be launched from the Office Communications Server administration MMC snap-in). Additionally, installing the Archiving Server enables Snooper to use Analyze Errors, which can search for existing errors that have been logged by a specific user or for specific logged error codes. This functionality can radically simplify help desk support as well as determination of what errors are occurring on the network before users actually detect them. Exploring the full functionality available within the Office Communications Server Logger (including Snooper) and leveraging the Archiving Server to track problems that crop up in deployment are easy ways to keep things running smoothly.

Resolving Local and Remote Login Problems and Basic Operational Problems

This section details login and basic operation troubleshooting when using Office Communicator, Communicator Web Access (CWA), and Communicator Mobile. Specific examples of failures as well as the data or troubleshooting steps associated with them are presented and appropriate next steps are identified. Enabling Communicator event logs and using protocol trace logs on the client and server can make most problems readily apparent and even point out helpful next steps.

Direct from the Source: Resolving Mysterious Error Codes

As you are troubleshooting any product, you are inevitably confronted by a mysterious error code. What do you do with this mysterious error code? Microsoft has published a tool named err.exe that is available for download. Search for "Microsoft Exchange Server Error Code Look-up Tool" from *http://www.microsoft.com/downloads*, or download it directly from *http://www.microsoft.com/downloads/details.aspx?familyid=be596899-7bb8-4208-b7fc-09e02a13696c*.

First, disregard the fact that the tool states that it is for use with Microsoft Exchange. This message is included only because the Exchange team published the tool. The tool is NOT Exchange specific. At its most basic level, ERR maps return codes (for example, 0x54F) to symbolic names (such as ERROR_INTERNAL_ERROR). ERR is smart and realizes that you don't always know whether your input value is hexadecimal or decimal. If there's any ambiguity in how the error code is specified, ERR returns multiple results in order to show the hexadecimal (base 16) and decimal (base 10) error code symbolic names. For example, if the command "err.exe 10" was run, the parameter '10' could represent a decimal value of 10 (ERROR_BAD_ENVIRONMENT) or a hexadecimal value of 0x10 (ERROR_CURRENT_DIRECTORY), so running ERR 10 produces both errors. Mapping between symbolic names and error codes goes both ways–you can search for an error code by name as well as by ID, which can be useful when you need an error code for a script or cannot remember the exact name of a symbolic constant. To find an error code by its exact name, preface that name with an equal sign on the command line (err =ERROR_BAD_ENVIRONMENT). The search is case insensitive. ERR doesn't call the operating system (such as via FormatMessage) to look up errors in any way because all of its error codes are kept in internal tables within the binary. This keeps ERR from depending on one operating system or another to produce the right results. In most cases, the symbolic name that is relative to Windows error codes represent the errors associated with the winerror.h table.

–Jason Epperly
Escalation Engineer, Product Support Services

Examples of Resolving Common Office Communicator Problems

Chapter 4, "Basic IM and Presence Scenarios," explains the technical details behind Communicator's login, basic presence, and instant messaging scenarios. Reviewing this information will help to pinpoint problems simply by following along and identifying where the client response or network traffic (from the client trace logs) differs from the logs and technical walk-throughs that are shown.

This section of the chapter presents tips from experts for troubleshooting Office Communicator issues during login as well as information that can be discovered in client trace logs. Chapter 16 covers helpful tools such as ClientLogReader and Snooper and also provides examples of event log messages with appropriate next steps.

Real World: Tips for Troubleshooting the Sign-In Process

The following list presents some tips for troubleshooting the sign-in process, ranging from basic tips to strategies for simplifying the discovery of problems by eliminating complexity.

The basics

- Validate that the user is enabled for IM.
- Validate that the SIP Uniform Resource Identifier (URI) used by the customer to sign in matches the URI configured on the client.
- Determine whether the issue affects one user or all users.
- Test sign-in with an alternate account. (If no other accounts are available, create and enable a test user.)
- Determine whether the issue affects one client machine or all client machines (isolate the machine and the operating system).
- Test sign-in from an alternate machine.
- Test sign-in from a client on either the same network as the server or on a different network than the current client that is failing (thereby isolating potential network infrastructure issues).
- Determine whether the issue also affects a particular version of Office Communicator.

Simplify

To isolate the component that is failing during the sign-in process, it is a best practice to make the sign-in process as simple as possible. Start with an internal client on the local area network (LAN) before testing with a remote user.

How to change to a simple configuration

- Validate that you can resolve the fully qualified name of the server and/or name of the pool (i.e., use ping.exe or nslookup.exe).
- Manually configure the client with the name of the server (Standard Edition) or name of the pool to try and rule out issues with client-side automatic configuration logic.
- If the configuration includes a load balancer, create a host file entry that resolves the fully qualified name of the pool directly to one of the front end servers, using the actual address (not the virtual IP) to try and rule out problems with the load balancer configuration.
- Try to rule out issues with certificates configured on the server and certificate infrastructure (CA, certificate revocation list [CRL]) by configuring Communicator to use Transmission Control Protocol (TCP) to connect to the server (after making sure that the server is configured to allow this type of connection).

–Jason Epperly
Escalation Engineer, Product Support Services

Client trace logs display errors and problems that can occur. Most of this knowledge is embedded within the ClientLogReader tool or Snooper tool in the Office Communications Server 2007 Resource Kit Tools. These useful tools can make the reading of client logs faster and easier when errors aren't clearly identified by the Communicator user interface (UI) or Communicator's event logs (if these have been enabled). With this data, you can more readily understand what to look for outside of protocol messages and thereby ease client troubleshooting. Each case that is described in the sections that follow shows part of an Office Communicator log file and also identifies typical next steps to take to resolve any identified problem.

Note In the following log examples, the date, time, and thread columns have been removed to keep the data succinct and easy to read.

Extracting Errors from Communicator Logs

If you are using Communicator logging to troubleshoot issues, you can extract "error" entries quickly by using FINDSTR. The syntax is as follows:

```
findstr /I error <path to UCCP log file> <output file>
```

For example, you might use the following command:

```
findstr /I error %userprofile%\tracing\Communicator-uccp-0.uccplog errors.txt
```

The errors.txt file contains all log entries tagged as ERROR. You can then find the entry in the source log file and place the error in its proper context. You should then be able to discern what happened before and after the error was thrown.

–Joel Schaeffer
Escalation Engineer, Product Support Services

Resolving Issues That Involve DNS Service Record Locator Queries The following cases show the client doing DNS Service Record Locator (SRV) resolutions as part of automatic configuration in a remote access scenario once the client discovers (through use of the user's SIP URI) where to log in. An SRV query is made against the domain of the user's URI, and then the resolved server name is used to log in. Normally, both internal and external SRV queries are issued at the same time, and the internal result is prioritized if both are received.

Case 1: Success

```
INFO  :: QueryDNSSrv - DNS Name[_sipinternaltls._tcp.contoso.com]
ERROR :: QueryDNSSrv GetDnsResults query: _sipinternaltls._tcp.contoso.com
         failed 0
ERROR :: DNS_RESOLUTION_WORKITEM::ProcessWorkItem ResolveHostName failed
         8007232b
INFO  :: QueryDNSSrv - DNS Name[_sip._tls.contoso.com]
INFO  :: CUccDnsQuery::UpdateLookup - error code=80ee0066, index=0
INFO  :: CUccDnsQuery::CompleteLookup - index=0
INFO  :: CUccDnsQuery::UpdateLookup - error code=0, index=1
INFO  :: CUccDnsQuery::CompleteLookup - index=1
...
TRACE :: SIP_MSG_PROCESSOR::OnDnsResolutionComplete[012CAC60] Entered host
sip.contoso.com
```

In this example, the SIP URI jeremy@contoso.com resulted in two DNS queries:

- _sipinternaltls._tcp.contoso.com–Discovering access to the internal corporate network
  - Failed with the 0x8007232b error, which the LCSError.exe tool (from the Office Communications Server 2007 Resource Kit Tools) shows to be a system error with the description "DNS name does not exist"

- Because the client is on an external network, it is not surprising that resolving the internal service record fails

- _sip._tls.contoso.com–Discovering access through an external network
  - Succeeded as expected and resulted in the host name sip.contoso.com being discovered as the host to which to connect

Note that it's easy to manually verify results shown in the client log by using nslookup.exe, as shown here:

```
C: >nslookup
Default Server:  dns.contoso.com
Address:  7.7.7.1

> set type=srv
> _sip._tls.contoso.com Server:  dns.contoso.com
Address:  7.7.7.1

Non-authoritative answer:
_sip._tls.contoso.com SRV service location:
          priority       = 0
          weight         = 0
          port           = 443
          svr hostname   = sip.contoso.com
```

Case 2: Failure – Invalid DNS Response

```
INFO  :: QueryDNSSrv - DNS Name[_sipinternaltls._tcp.sip.test.contoso.com]
ERROR :: QueryDNSSrv GetDnsResults query: _sipinternaltls._tcp.sip.test.
         contoso.com failed 0
ERROR :: DNS_RESOLUTION_WORKITEM::ProcessWorkItem ResolveHostName failed
         8007232b
INFO  :: QueryDNSSrv - DNS Name[_sip._tls.sip.test.contoso.com]
INFO  :: CUccDnsQuery::UpdateLookup - error code=80ee0066, index=0
INFO  :: CUccDnsQuery::CompleteLookup - index=0
INFO  :: CUccDnsQuery::UpdateLookup - error code=80004005, index=1
INFO  :: CUccDnsQuery::CompleteLookup - index=1
```

In this case, jeremy@sip.test.contoso.com resulted in the preceding queries. The _sipinternaltls._tcp.sip.test.contoso.com record didn't exist (the client stack uses 0x80ee0066 to identify that no record existed), and lcsap.test.contoso.com was returned for the external lookup. However, the result lcsap.test.contoso.com isn't seen as valid (0x80004005 is the E_FAIL error used by the client stack to identify that this result isn't valid) because it doesn't have a strict suffix match with sip.test.contoso.com. It is important to make sure that all server names line up exactly with the domains over which they claim ownership. The server name should be equal to the domain name or directly rooted off of the domain name in question. Some examples are shown in Table 17-1.

Table 17-1 Validation of DNS SRV Query Results

Domain Queried	Published DNS Server Name (certificate must match this name)	Valid?
contoso.com	sip.contoso.com, contoso.com, server7.contoso.com, ocs.contoso.com	**VALID**—All servers either match the domain or have a server name rooted off of the domain in question.
contoso.com	sip.eng.contoso.com	**INVALID**—Server has possible ownership of only eng.contoso.com or sip.eng.contoso.com.
eng.contoso.com	sipserver.eng.contoso.com, eng.contoso.com	**VALID**—All servers either match the domain or have a server name rooted off of the domain in question.
eng.contoso.com	contoso.com, sipeng.contoso.com, sip.contoso.com, sip.woodgrovebank.com	**INVALID**—All servers do not have ownership of the eng.contoso.com domain because they are not either eng.contoso.com or some name directly rooted from it.

Case 3: Failure – No DNS Service Records Exist

```
INFO  :: QueryDNSSrv - DNS Name[_sipinternaltls._tcp.contoso.com]
ERROR :: QueryDNSSrv GetDnsResults query: _sipinternaltls._tcp.contoso.com
         failed 0
ERROR :: DNS_RESOLUTION_WORKITEM::ProcessWorkItem ResolveHostName failed
         8007232a
INFO  :: QueryDNSSrv - DNS Name[_sip._tls.contoso.com]
INFO  :: CUccDnsQuery::UpdateLookup - error code=80ee0066, index=0
INFO  :: CUccDnsQuery::CompleteLookup - index=0
ERROR :: QueryDNSSrv GetDnsResults query: _sip._tls.contoso.com failed 0
ERROR :: DNS_RESOLUTION_WORKITEM::ProcessWorkItem ResolveHostName failed
         8007232a
INFO  :: CUccDnsQuery::UpdateLookup - error code=80ee0066, index=1
INFO  :: CUccDnsQuery::CompleteLookup - index=1
...
ERROR :: gethostbyname failed for host sipinternal.contoso.com, error:
         0x2afc
ERROR :: DNS_RESOLUTION_WORKITEM::ProcessWorkItem ResolveHostName failed
         80072afc
TRACE :: SIP_MSG_PROCESSOR::OnDnsResolutionComplete[012CAC60] Entered host
sipinternal.contoso.com
ERROR :: SIP_MSG_PROCESSOR::OnDnsResolutionComplete - error : 80ee0066
...
ERROR :: gethostbyname failed for host sip.contoso.com, error: 0x2afc
ERROR :: DNS_RESOLUTION_WORKITEM::ProcessWorkItem ResolveHostName failed
         80072afc
TRACE :: SIP_MSG_PROCESSOR::OnDnsResolutionComplete[01D93130] Entered host
sip.contoso.com
ERROR :: SIP_MSG_PROCESSOR::OnDnsResolutionComplete - error : 80ee0066
...
ERROR :: gethostbyname failed for host sipexternal.contoso.com, error:
         0x2afc
ERROR :: DNS_RESOLUTION_WORKITEM::ProcessWorkItem ResolveHostName failed
```

```
        80072afc
TRACE :: SIP_MSG_PROCESSOR::OnDnsResolutionComplete[01D93130] Entered host
sipexternal.contoso.com
ERROR :: SIP_MSG_PROCESSOR::OnDnsResolutionComplete - error : 80ee0066
```

In this case, the SIP URI jeremy@contoso.com resulted in the preceding queries, but neither record is resolved (0x80ee0066 is used by the client stack to mean no record existed). In the absence of these records, Communicator attempts to resolve the hostnames sipinternal.contoso.com, then sip.contoso.com, and finally sipexternal.contoso.com; all of these records fail as well. In this scenario, it is likely that the infrastructure DNS cannot be reached or that the infrastructure is configured incorrectly. Start by using nslookup.exe to determine what DNS server is being used, and change the default server to the publishing point for the domain's DNS SRV records (the server <NewDnsServerName> command changes the default DNS server from the NSLookup command prompt). Failures to resolve the DNS entries directly from the server that should be hosting these service records means that either the DNS service isn't running on that machine or that the entries are configured incorrectly on the server. Failures to resolve the records from intermediate machines could be related to the machines' inability to see the publishing server as an authority or to existing DNS caches holding invalid entries.

Next Steps DNS resolution problems or errors that occur because the resolved records aren't acceptable to the client can be resolved by using the following steps. First, make sure that the necessary DNS SRV and A records exist for the user's domain. Communicator queries DNS SRV based on the domain portion of the user's SIP URI. Therefore, if you want automatic configuration to work, the SRV and A records need to exist for this domain. Secondly, make sure that all record domains match for the user's domain. The DNS SRV record needs to be published for the user's domain, and the server's hostname that the domain SRV record points to needs to have a name suffix that matches the user's domain as well. If either of these do not line up, Communicator does not accept the information that it gathers from DNS. In addition, when Transport Layer Security (TLS) is used, the certificate presented by the server must provide proof of ownership for the server's hostname (as discovered via DNS). Additional information about these problems is provided in the "Resolving Issues That Arise from Certificate Negotiation Failures" section that follows.

Resolving Issues That Arise from Certificate Negotiation Failures The following logs demonstrate cases in which certificate validation failed on the client, which can occur when Communicator uses TLS and isn't able to validate the server's certificate.

Case 1: Certificate Name Does Not Match DNS Name

```
TRACE :: SIP_MSG_PROCESSOR::OnDnsResolutionComplete[01D87BA0] Entered host
sipserver.contoso.com
...
ERROR :: SECURE_SOCKET: negotiation failed: 80090322
```

In this case, Communicator received the SEC_E_WRONG_PRINCIPLE failure message (0x80090322), which means that the name to which the client connected isn't listed as a valid name in the server certificate. By looking back in the trace log, you can see the name of the server that the client was connected to (shown earlier). Make sure that this name is listed in the server certificate. This failure can also happen when an IP address is improperly used to identify the server when using TLS. The hostname needs to be used so that it can be matched against the name in the certificate.

Case 2: Root CA Certificate Is Missing the Server EKU

```
ERROR :: SECURE_SOCKET: negotiation failed: 80090349
```

In this case, Communicator received the SEC_E_CERT_WRONG_USAGE failure message (0x80090349), which means that the server certificate does not have rights to be used as a server certificate. The root CA certificate does not have the Server Authentication usage listed in its Enhanced Key Usage (EKU). This failure means that the right to be used as a server certificate cannot be inherited by the server's certificate, and therefore the client doesn't trust this certificate to act as a server. Make sure that the server certificate and all CA certificates have either no EKU field listed in them (meaning all rights are allowed) or each contain the Server Authentication EKU.

Case 3: Server Certificate Is Not Issued by a Trusted CA

```
ERROR :: SECURE_SOCKET: negotiation failed: 80090325
```

In this case, the TLS negotiation failed because the server certificate isn't trusted. The SEC_E_UNTRUSTED_ROOT error code appears (0x80090325) because the root CA isn't trusted. This can happen if an enterprise CA is used to issue the certificate, but the client isn't part of the domain or has not yet added trust for this CA. The root CA certificate must be present in the list of Trusted Root Certification Authorities, preferably for the client workstation's machine store. However, simply putting the root CA certificate in the user's store as a Trusted Root Certificate Authority is sufficient.

Note Please keep in mind that any intermediate CA certificates should be placed in the list of Intermediate Certification Authorities. By default, Windows servers are configured to hand out the root and intermediate CA certificates along with the server certificate to avoid certificate authentication problems. To date, not explicitly placing Intermediate Certificate Authorities in a trusted store has been an issue only during certificate authentication with the only Public IM Connectivity provider that has a non-Windows edge server and isn't configured to send intermediate CA certificates during TLS negotiation.

Next Steps If problems validating or negotiating certificates arise, validation of the client and/or server configuration is required. Problems validating the certificate name can come up when the client uses an IP address instead of the hostname to identify the server. The client might also be using a valid hostname that resolves to an IP address for a server, but that server doesn't have the original hostname listed in its certificate. The server certificate might not be issued properly, such as when it or one of its issuing CAs doesn't have a server EKU, although this is rare. If the server is issued by a private CA for the enterprise, non-domain clients can fail to validate the certificate because they don't trust it. This situation can be resolved by installing the issuing root certificate on the client machine. If certificates have expired, use lcserror.exe from the resource kit or winerror.exe from the Windows resource kit to interpret any error codes into strings for detailed information about any failure.

Resolving Issues Associated with Status Unknown The following logs demonstrate cases in which contacts have a presence of "status unknown" and the logs identify what has occurred.

Case 1: User Does Not Exist – 404 (Not Found)

```
INFO  :: SIP/2.0 404 Not Found...
ms-diagnostics: 1003;reason="User does not
exist";source="srv.contoso.com";TargetUri=james@woodgrovebank.com
...
TRACE :: CUccSubscription::SavePresentityInFailedMap uri:  james@woodgrovebank.com, this
000AD580
```

In this case, the presence request received a 404 – Not Found response. The 404 – Not Found response in SIP is used by domain authority registrars to identify that contacts cannot be reached because they don't exist. Additional information can be found in the protocol message where the 404 response is returned by looking at the ms-diagnostics header because it displays a short reason description, the server that is the source of the message, and the user URI in question.

If the contact does exist, verify that no error exists in the contact address, validate the configuration in the owning domain, and ensure that connectivity between the domains exists. The source of the 404 response also provides a great deal of information. If the domain that owns the user is returning the 404 response, then their configuration should be checked; however, if the local domain is returning the 404 response for a remote domain, then routing on the local domain might not be enabled for remote domains.

Case 2: User Unreachable – 504 (Service Unavailable)

```
INFO  :: SIP/2.0 504 Server time-out
...
ms-diagnostics: 1014;reason="Unable to resolve DNS A
record";source="sip.contoso.com";LookupFQDN="sip.woodgrovebank.com"
```

In this case, the presence request received a 504 – Service Unavailable response. This response in SIP is used by servers to identify that the message is unable to be sent due to connectivity issues, lack of routing rules, or the DNS SRV records that are used to determine where the request should next be routed. Additional information can be found in the protocol message where the 504 response is returned by looking at the ms-diagnostics header, which shows a description of the reason for the failure, the server that identified the failure, and data related to the specific failure (in this case, the name of the remote server that needs to be resolved).

The subscription request is not able to be delivered; therefore, these contacts do not show presence information because they cannot be reached. This generally occurs because of network infrastructure or because an e-mail address that is used as a presence contact does not yet support Office Communications Server 2007 federation.

Resolving Issues That Involve Connectivity Failure The following logs identify problems with connectivity to the server. They typically happen during login while the client is initially establishing its connectivity to the server. These problems can occur because of firewalls, because the server is not listening or not running, or because of temporary network or DNS failures.

Case 1: Connection Timed Out

```
ERROR :: ASYNC_SOCKET::OnConnectReady - Error: 10060 dest: 7.7.7.52:5061
```

In this case, the client received a WSAETIMEDOUT (10060) error while trying to establish a connection to the server. This typically happens if the server isn't running on the specified IP address or if the port in question is being blocked by a firewall, proxy, or other network infrastructure (even local client firewall software).

Direct from the Source: Diagnosing Connection Failures (Load Balancers and Firewalls)

When diagnosing connection issues, my first guess is that a load balancer is involved, especially if the connections close at regular intervals (5 minutes is a popular default). When a network device like a load balancer causes connection problems, both servers will see that the other end has closed the connection. The Winsock error code for the remote host closing the connection is WSAECONNRESET (10054 in decimal, 2746 in hexadecimal, or 0x80002746 as a HRESULT in the logs). In a network trace, both sides will see a TCP segment with the RST (TCP 'reset') flag set. In defense of load balancers, most are optimized for Web traffic that has short-lived connections (unlike connections between Office Communications Server servers); therefore, the default length of time before a load balancer assumes that a connection is "dead" tends to be lower than the value needed by the Office Communications Server.

For firewall issues, the Winsock WSAETIMEDOUT error code (10060 in decimal, 274C in hexadecimal, or 0x8000274C as a HRESULT in the logs) is usually a good indicator. As firewalls tend to drop the network packets they are blocking, connection attempts that fail will simply time out. If you know that the IP address being tried is correct and that the server at the other end is running, you can be more confident that a firewall is blocking the traffic.

–James Undery
Software Design Engineer II

Case 2: Server Name Does Not Exist

```
INFO  :: QueryDNSSrv - DNS Name[_sip._tls.contoso.com]
ERROR :: QueryDNSSrv GetDnsResults query: _sip._tls.contoso.com failed 0
ERROR :: DNS_RESOLUTION_WORKITEM::ProcessWorkItem ResolveHostName failed
         8007232b
```

In this case, the client received the DNS_ERROR_RCODE_NAME_ERROR system error (0x8007232B or 0x232B), which means that there is no DNS record for the name being queried. The client fails to resolve the hostname to which it is trying to connect. This can happen if the server name is typed incorrectly or if, during automatic configuration, the SRV record exists and points to a hostname that doesn't have a corresponding DNS A record to resolve the hostname to an IP address.

Case 3: Failed to Authenticate

```
INFO  :: REGISTER sip:contoso.com SIP/2.0
...
INFO  :: SIP/2.0 401 Unauthorized
...
ERROR :: SIP_MSG_PROCESSOR::CompleteSAProcessingAndGetAuthHeader
InitializeSecurityContext failed: 0x8009030e
...
INFO  :: REGISTER sip:contoso.com SIP/2.0
...
INFO  :: SIP/2.0 401 Unauthorized
...
ERROR :: SIP_MSG_PROCESSOR::CompleteSAProcessingAndGetAuthHeader
InitializeSecurityContext failed: 0x80090311
... (more REGISTER and 401 handshaking) ...
ms-diagnostics: 1000;reason="Final handshake
failed";source="OCSSE13.contoso.local";HRESULT="C3E93EC3
    (SIP_E_AUTH_UNAUTHORIZED)"
...
ERROR :: OUTGOING_TRANSACTION::ProcessAuthRequired-Too many 401/407s seen.
    Failing the session
```

The client received a few different errors during this sequence. The first is the SEC_E_NO_CREDENTIALS error (0x8009030E), which can be expected because the client initially tries to log in anonymously. The second is the SEC_E_NO_AUTHENTICATING_AUTHORITY error (0x80090311), which means that credentials are used from the desktop and that the Active Directory that is specified for the credentials isn't able to be reached or is unknown (also not a surprise for many environments). The final error (as shown in the ms-diagnostics header) is the SIP_E_AUTH_UNAUTHORIZED error, which is generated from the server when the user's credentials are invalid. This error can happen because the password, SIP URI, or account name is typed incorrectly, the account is disabled, the password has expired, or underlying Active Directory connectivity problems exist with the server.

Direct from the Source: Diagnosing Problems with Group Expansion Failures

For help diagnosing Group Expansion failures when using Communicator, use Internet Explorer (IE) to navigate to *https://<webfqdn>/GroupExpansion/Int/service.asmx* (replace *<webfqdn>* with the server FQDN that you are using, such as: srv.contoso.com). Using IE, select the Tools, then Internet Options, then Advanced menu item, and then uncheck Show Friendly HTTP Error Messages so that any internal failures also show up in IE on the bottom left of the window.

Communicator obtains the Group Expansion URLs (which are a pool-level setting) through in-band provisioning:

- Internal clients use *https://<internalwebfqdn>/GroupExpansion/Int/service.asmx.*
- External clients use *https://<externalwebfqdn>/GroupExpansion/Int/service.asmx.*

Whenever a user wants to expand a directory list (DL), the Group Expansion URLs are connected. Debugging DL expansion failures involves directly accessing these URLs from within IE so that errors come up front (Internet Information Services [IIS] errors, access errors, proxy errors, or service failures or crashes).

Fully qualified domain names

When a pool is created, the administrator must mention the Web farm FQDN that he will use in the deployment. Two FQDNs must be mentioned here: InternalWebFqdn and ExternalWebFqdn.

`InternalWebFqdn` is used by intranet clients. This FQDN is either the same as the SIP server (Standard Edition case) or the pool load balancer (Enterprise Edition case #1), or it can be different (Enterprise Edition case #2 in which IIS servers are deployed behind a separate load balancer for scalability purposes).

`ExternalWebFqdn` is used by remote clients. This is the FQDN of the reverse proxy (or farm) in the DMZ. The reverse proxy, in turn, proxies requests to the internal Web components server.

–Kiran Kulkarni
Software Design Engineer II, OCS Product Group

Direct from the Source: Certificate Issues

What do you do if you see a 401 Unauthorized error in a Validation Wizard or a The Client Did Not Supply A Certificate error in the event log that causes conferencing to fail?

- Check to see whether the certificate has the correct subject name (Pool FQDN).

- Check whether your certificate has Client Authentication EKU. If it does, ensure that the Root Certificate and all intermediate certificates have Client Authentication EKU enabled as well. Otherwise, this causes the servers to return a 401 Unauthorized error.
- If this doesn't help, check out the "Too Many Trusted Root CAs Can Affect Office Communications Server Operations" issue in the Office Communications Server release notes, and follow the resolution described within.
- Any changes from this list require a computer reboot.

–Sankaran Narayanan
Senior Software Design Engineer, OCS Server

Real World: Useful Database Query for Contact Lists

We used various diagnostic stored procedures internally while developing and deploying the back-end database used by Office Communications Server. One of these procedures returns aggregate statistical information about the nature of the contact lists maintained by all users that are homed in the database. The following command can be executed with osql.exe or with SQL Management Studio against the Real-Time Communications (RTC) database of an Office Communications Server back-end SQL instance:

```
exec DiagShowContactDistribution
```

Executing this command returns information such as the following:

```
MinNumContacts MaxNumContacts AvgNumContacts StdNumContacts
-------------- -------------- -------------- ---------------
1              250            45             37.59

ModeNumContacts CountWithMode
--------------- -------------
28               985

BucketCriteria NumSamples  Percent  Histogram           CumulativePercent
-------------- ----------- -------- ------------------- -------------------
<=           5 3237        5.4      xx                  5.4
<=          25 17840       29.6     xxxxxxxxxxxx        35.0
<=          50 18971       31.5     xxxxxxxxxxxxx       66.5
<=          75 10196       16.9     xxxxxxx             83.5
<=         100 4953        8.2      xxx                 91.7
<=         125 2377        3.9      xx                  95.6
<=         150 1206        2.0      x                   97.7
<=         175 682         1.1                          98.8
<=         200 350         0.6                          99.4
<=         300 381         0.6                          100.0
all others     0           0.0                          100.0
```

This result displays min/max/average/std deviation/mode as well as a graphical histogram of the distribution of the number of contacts maintained by each user. Of course, it is worth noting that the use of stored procedures is not officially supported by Microsoft because these procedures might change or be withdrawn entirely as the product is updated.

–Shaun Cox
Principal Development Manager, OCS Server

Direct from the Source: Multi-Party IM Establishment Failures

When attempting to bring multiple users into an instant messaging session, several causes for failures are possible. Some tips and potential causes are called out here:

- Use the Validation Wizard to check the status of servers and connectivity. It should report success.
- All .NET quick fix engineerings (QFEs) should be installed. (Failing to install them could result in communication failure between components. The Knowledge Base list is available in the release notes.)
- If you have an Enterprise Edition Pool, the appropriate ports should be open on the load balancer (443, 444). Check your destination network address translation (DNAT) settings.

–Sankaran Narayanan
Senior Software Design Engineer, OCS Server

Examples of Resolving Common Communicator Web Access Problems

Certificates are the most common problem for a CWA server/client connection. Customers using a single Standard Edition server for Office Communications Server could configure the server to listen only on TCP (not the default, as was the case with Live Communications Server 2005). However, CWA attempts to create a Mutual TLS (MTLS) connection to Office Communications Server that will fail due to the lack of a proper MTLS listener.

The other problem encountered with certificates and multiple servers is not using the computer FQDN of the server as the subject name for CWA. This specific use of the FQDN is required due to the necessary MTLS connection that will be established. To have clients use a simpler URL for connecting to the CWA server, you might issue a second certificate solely for the HTTPS listener or use a certificate with Subject Alternative Name. Remember that the subject name must be included in the *Subject Alternative Name* field and that it should also be the first one in the *Subject Alternative List* field.

Resolving Conferencing Problems Involving Sharing Files and A/V

This section presents a few conferencing tips and provides information and pointers for recognizing common problems that administrators encounter with conferencing. Figure 17-3 shows a detailed view of a Standard Edition server with everything on the same box. This image is based on a graphic provided by Kiran Kulkarni from the Office Communications Server product team and displays the steps that Microsoft Office Outlook and the Meeting Console must work through as part of scheduling and joining a meeting. Relationships are spelled out between Communicator and the server technology as well as how various servers and technology interact with each other. This diagram can be very useful when trying to determine all of the interactions and connections that must be in place when troubleshooting conferencing.

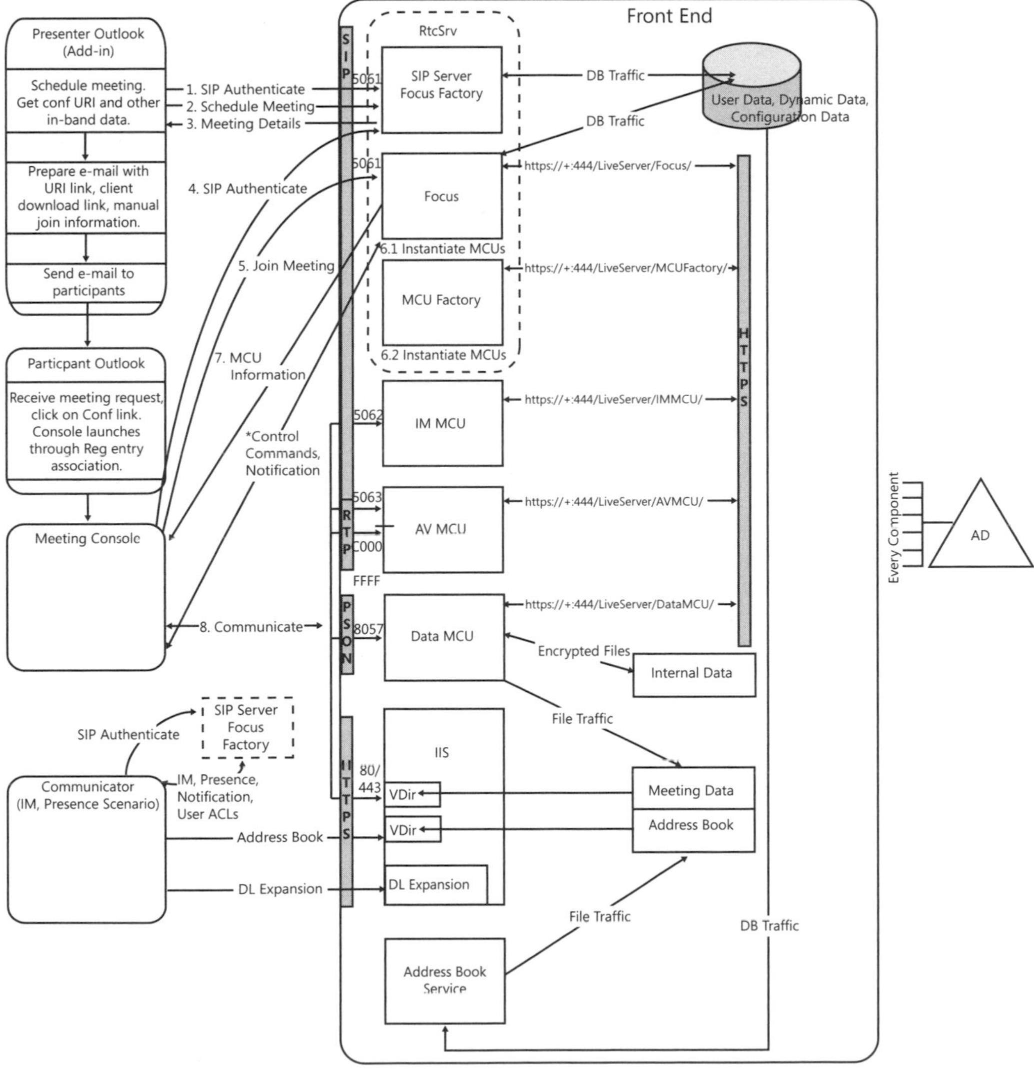

Figure 17-3 Inside a live server box

Direct from the Source: Inside a Live Server Box

Figure 17-3 presents an example of a Standard Edition server with everything on the same box. It illustrates the interactions between clients and services as well as some of the inner workings of the Office Communications Server 2007 systems.

–Kiran Kulkarni
Software Design Engineer II, OCS Product Group

Real World: Tips for Audio and Video Conferencing

The following tips are useful for gathering more details related to audio and video conferencing.

Determining metrics from a point-to-point conferencing session

In some circumstances, it might be helpful to determine metrics from a point-to-point conferencing session. This may hold true when poor video or audio is observed on either side. To gather basic statistics from a point-to-point conferencing session, you can do the following:

- Enable Communicator logging
- Start the conferencing session, communicate, and then terminate the session
- Open the log file (by default, Communicator-uccp-0.uccplog), and search for the text VQReportEvent
- Beginning at <VQReportEvent xmlns="ms-rtcp-metrics">,
    - copy/paste the text into an editor ending at </VQReportEvent>, and
    - then save it as VQReportEvent.xml
- Double-click VQReportEvent.xml to view the report

In the report, you will find items such as SIP URIs, IP configuration, and ports used, as well as the video and audio drivers used during the conversation. You will also see statistics such as jitter, packet loss, video resolution, bit rate, frame rate, and more.

Viewing session description protocol session information

To properly set up a video conference session, some parameters must be passed between endpoints to set up the session. The protocol used for this session setup is called the Session Description Protocol (SDP).

To view SDP information for a session, do the following:

- Enable Communicator logging.

- Start the conferencing session, communicate, and then terminate the session.
- Open the log file (by default, Communicator-uccp-0.uccplog), and search for the text Content-Type: application/sdp.

Inside of the SIP packet containing this entry, you will see an SDP session description. Each line is in the format <type>=<value>. Types of interest include:

- "o", originator–Usually includes the IP address of the initiator or receiver of the session
- "m", media name and transport address–Either "audio" or "video" with various parameters of each media type
- "a", attribute line–Used for all other configuration parameters of the session (e.g., codecs, bit rate)

See RFC 4566 (*http://www.ietf.org*) for details and a full description of each SDP type.

–Joel Schaeffer
Escalation Engineer, Product Support Services

Examples of Resolving Common Conferencing Problems

The most commonly encountered server-side problem is that content download does not work in Web conferences, which is caused by IIS not having a server certificate configured that enables HTTPS. A manual certificate configuration step is required after installation for content download to work properly.

Real World: Investigating Content Download Issues

One of the most common problems we've seen when the console is connected to a conference hosted on a data multipoint control unit (MCU) is the failure to download the content of a PowerPoint/Word document or the content of an uploaded file. In almost all of these cases, the problem is not in the data MCU but in how IIS and the client IE are configured.

The problem

How can you recognize the problem? There are two ways to recognize the download problem, and in both cases, you start by connecting the console to a meeting.

- The first way to reproduce the problem is to upload a PowerPoint document (Content->Share->Add File To Meeting->View). Once the document is uploaded, the main console window displays a gray background with an error message: "Content failed to download due to a problem with the Conference Center configuration. Contact your administrator."

- The second way to reproduce the problem is to upload a file using the Handouts feature (see the Handouts button in the toolbar). Once you have uploaded a file, try to download it. A message box pops up with the following error message: "Download failed."

In both cases, the failure is induced by the same configuration problem that you might encounter in an IIS server and/or IE on the client/console machine.

Summary of steps to follow

What's next? In summary, these are the steps to follow:

1. Reproduce the problem and get a URL from the console trace file.
2. Check whether the data MCU uploaded the file.
3. Check and fix the client IE (Web proxy issue).
4. Check and fix the IIS server (server is not running).
5. Check and fix the IIS server certificate (server is not configured to do HTTPS).

Let's look at these steps in detail.

Step 1: Grab console tracing information

Let's reproduce the problem by uploading a document (the first bullet under the heading "The problem" in this sidebar).

You must first take a look into the console trace file, which can be found in C:\Documents and Settings\<user>\Local Settings\Temp. You can easily access this folder by running cd /d %temp% in the command console.

In this folder, you'll find few console trace files (run in command console: dir pwconsole-debug*.txt). In Notepad, open the most recent trace file. At the end of the file, you should find a trace line generated by the Downloaded::addRequest() method that looks like the following:

```
[MC] 21:06:10:064 GMT [THREAD 4888]  [I] Downloader::addRequest()
    - Found previously failed request, will not download https://srv.contoso.com/
etc/place/null/FileTree/IE6HRFPCBJ3K1CCUC1
    HH75UPN8Q/6a24bb55f381433285cc878baa11ed3a/slidefiles/
    xc75dbd0baa6a.epng
```

This trace line indicates that the console failed to download the content from a specific URL. The URL is printed at the end of the trace line, starting with HTTPS. When debugging the problem, please copy the URL from the actual log for use later in the investigation during Step 2.

Step 2: Was the file uploaded?

The next step is to check whether the file was uploaded by the data MCU. The file is uploaded in 99% of the cases, but let's double-check before going further with our investigation. To do this check, you must go on the machine on which the IIS runs, where you will open the IIS Management Console by clicking Start, then Administrative Tools, and then Internet Information Services (IIS) Manager.

Open the nodes in the left panel tree, Internet Information Services, then <server machine>, then Web Sites, then Default Web Services and there should be a node with a name that matches the URL obtained from the console traces at the end of Step 1 (the "etc" portion of the URL). From that point in the URL on, you can continue to open the nodes in the IIS Management console: Etc, then Null, then FileTree, then <organizer-guid>, then <consoleguid> and then sidefiles. Please note that you get the <organizer-guid> and <consoleguid> from the URL that you copied at the end of Step 1 (in our example, the <organizeguid> is IE6HRFPCBJ3K1CCUC1HH75UPN8Q and the <con-ferenceguid> is 6a24bb55f381433285cc878baa11ed3a). Click the sidefiles node, and you should see a list of files in the right-panel list. One of these files should be the .epng file from the end of the URL (in our example, the file is xc75dbd0baa6a.epng).

If the .epng file is not there, then there is likely a bug. You should contact PSS to report the problem observed with the data MCU. That's all you can do, and you don't need to read further!

If the file is there, the data MCU was able to upload the file, and your problem exists in the IIS and/or client IE. Keep reading this chapter!

Step 3: Is the Web proxy the problem?

In a test topology, your IIS server is usually not published in the DNS. If your IE client is configured to resolve the Web HTTP URL by using a Web proxy, IE reports a failure when you pass in a URL like the one you obtained from the console trace file because the server FQDN cannot be resolved (in our case, the server FQDN is srv.contoso.com).

Open IE and go to Tools, then Internet Options, then Connections, and then LAN Settings. You now have two options:

- Uncheck the Automatically Detect Settings and Use A Proxy Server ... check boxes.

  If you want to keep the Use A Proxy Server ... box checked (so that you still have access to external Web sites from the client machine), you must click Advanced. In the Exceptions list, add the IIS server FQDN (in our case, srv.contoso.com).
- Save the changes by clicking OK.

To verify that all is well, let's see whether IE can browse for our URL. Open IE, and paste in the URL that you copied from the trace file. Change it from https to http, remove everything after the server FQDN (the URL in IE will now look like *http://srv.contoso.com*), and then browse for it. If you see a page that says "Under construction," then you have properly configured IE. If you don't see this page (you will probably see a page with the message, "Internet Explorer cannot display the webpage"), you must look at the IIS management console (opened in Step 2) as well because the server is probably not running.

Let's assume that you saw the "Under construction" page. Change the URL from http to https (the URL in IE will look like *https://srv.contoso.com*). If you see a page that says "Under construction," then the IIS server is already configured for HTTPS. The console problem should be fixed as well, and you don't need to go further with this document. If you don't see this page (you will probably see a page with the message "Internet Explorer cannot display the webpage"), then the IIS server is running but is not configured for HTTPS. You must take a look at the IIS server configuration.

To double-check that all is well, open the IE, paste in the entire URL you obtained from the console trace file, and browse for it. You should now see a dialog box asking you whether you want to download the file, which means that everything is fine (click Cancel in the dialog box). The console is expected to run properly, and you should see the conference content in its main window.

You should read the following paragraphs only if you determined that the IIS server is not running or is not configured for HTTPS.

Step 4: Is IIS running?

Let's first make sure that IIS is running. In the same IIS Management console that you opened in Step 2, take a look at the <machine>, <default web site> icons in the left-panel tree. These icons should not have any small red circles drawn on top of them, for these circles indicate that you have a big problem within IIS. First, try to restart IIS by right-clicking the machine icon. From the context menu, select All Tasks, then Restart IIS, which should restart IIS. Hopefully, everything will then be clean. If you still see the red marks, I advise you to reinstall IIS and then reinstall the servers. If the problem persists, you should contact PSS.

From this point onward, we'll assume that the IIS is running just fine.

Step 5: Is IIS configured for TLS?

Let's make sure that IIS is configured to listen to TLS/HTTPS requests. Note that the URL you copied from the console trace file is an HTTPS address (it starts with https://). When the console downloads the conference content, it does so by using HTTPS, and therefore the server must be configured to accept such requests. IIS does not accept such requests by default, and there is a chance that you forgot to configure your IIS for TLS/HTTPS.

To check whether IIS is allowed to accept HTTPS requests (and listens to port 443), you must access the same IIS management console (opened in Step 2) and right-click

Default Web Site. Select Properties, then select Directory Security and then Server Certificate. Follow the steps in the wizard. In the second wizard step, select Assign An Existing Certificate. (You must first have installed a Web certificate on the server machine. Check the deployment guide to see how you can obtain one.) Select the certificate in the third step, and keep the port set to 443 in the fourth step. Save the settings by clicking Finish in the wizard and then clicking OK on the Properties page. IIS should now be configured for HTTPS (you don't need to restart the service). To confirm that everything is working, repeat the procedures listed in the "Step 3: Is the Web Proxy the Problem?" section in which you tried the HTTPS URL. IE should be able to display the "Under construction" page even when the URL starts with https://.

You should now have a console that displays the uploaded content.

–Vlad Eminovici
Senior Development Lead

If client configuration is not as expected, then other problems can arise:

- Failure to schedule meetings
- Inability to see the Meet Now button in the Live Meeting console
- Failure to join meetings

The majority of the remaining conferencing errors are simply related to users' attempts to do things that their meeting policy does not allow:

- Inability to schedule a Web conference (Enable Web Conferencing)
- Inability to schedule a conference call (Enable IP Audio)
- Inability to start application sharing (*Enable Program And Desktop Sharing*)
- Inability for anonymous users to join
    - The Organize Meetings With Anonymous Participants Right is not allowed
    - The default meeting type in the Office Outlook conferencing add-in is set to Open Authenticated

Real World: Simple Way to Set Maximum Attendees

There is a simple way to set the maximum number of attendees that your end users can invite to Office Communications Server Audio/Video/Web conferences in Office Communicator and Live Meeting client. Launch the Office Communications Server MMC. Right-click the Forest, click Properties, and select Global Properties. Select the Meetings tab, select the meeting policy you'd like to modify, and then click Edit. Change the *Maximum Meeting Size* field to the desired value.

The maximum meeting size number applies to both Audio/Video/Web conferences through the Live Meeting client as well as Audio/Video conferences conducted through Office Communicator. Though 250 attendees per session has been the design goal for Office Communications Server conferences, a number of other consideration points must be taken into account during the planning/architectural phase of your deployment. Refer to the Office Communications Server Planning Guide documentation for more details. You certainly do not want to assign a meeting policy that allows a meeting size of 250 attendees to all of your users, given the 5 percent concurrency model on Office Communications Server's MCUs. Be sure to create various meeting policies and assign the appropriate meeting policy to each user and group based on their needs and job functions.

–Ali Rohani
Technical Specialist, Unified Communications, Canada

Resolving Management and Configuration Problems

This section contains several quotations from contacts in and around the product team on how to resolve setup, installation, management, and configuration issues. Common problems are also identified and discussed.

Real World: Use the Validation Wizard Often

Whenever I deploy an Office Communications Server, I run the Validation Wizard as soon as the service is running, even if I know that the server is not configured correctly yet. The .html log file that is generated provides good information about any problems with configuration, connectivity, user logon, IM, and the ability to perform conferencing. I can read through the errors, fix whatever I can, and then run the Validation Wizard again. In many cases, I might receive a different set of errors that can help me reconfigure the server. I can repeat this procedure until the validation comes up green and my server is in good working order.

Sometimes, the error points me to a different location than the local machine. For example:

- I run validation on an Access Proxy using a new user account to test logon and IM. The log file shows:

```
SIP/2.0 403 Forbidden
...
ms-diagnostics: 4003;reason="From URI not enabled for remote access"
...
```

I go to Active Directory, enable the user account for remote user access, and run the wizard again. I receive no error this time, so I know that my Access Proxy is configured for remote user access correctly.

- I run validation on a Standard Edition server. A "TLS connect failed" error appears to a different Office Communications Server. I can go to that server in the Office Communications Server snap-in and view its properties. I see that the SIP service is not started, so I start it remotely. Running validation again shows that connectivity to all servers is working.
- I run validation on a front-end server. I get the following errors:

```
Error: One or more pool hosted users are enabled for federation,
remote access or public IM connectivity, but global federation is
disabled.
Federation: Disabled
```

I go to the Global Properties settings in the Office Communications Server snap-in, assign a valid Access Proxy to enable federation, and run the validation again. I receive no errors this time, so I know that my default federation settings are correct.

–Les Viger
Software Design Engineer in Test, OCS Server

Examples of Resolving Common Management and Configuration Problems

Various services can sometimes fail to start, and this problem can be difficult to understand or resolve. The interface for starting and stopping services usually provides no more information about the failure than that it failed to start, but the event log is the first place to look for more information.

Direct from the Source: Diagnosing Service Start Failures

This is probably the single most common failure that people encounter. Some useful hints are the following:

- Look through the event logs (not just the last event that was logged).
- Make sure that the server was activated successfully.
- Make sure that the server certificate is configured.
- Use runas.exe to impersonate the service account, and then make sure that the Active Directory and back-end Structured Query Language (SQL) are accessible.

It is also worth mentioning that when things go wrong, Office Communications Server services usually throw more than one event log. Generally speaking, the first event log contains the most information, but it is beneficial to go through all of the error event logs. I often see people look at the top-most event log and give up because it is a very general event log that might not point out enough details on its own to completely identify the problem.

–Nirav Kamdar
Senior Development Lead, OCS Server

Direct from the Source: Diagnosing AD/SQL/WMI Failures

Active Directory, SQL database, and Windows Management Instrumentation (WMI) failures are typically reported during service startups. Use wbemtest.exe to access the class about which the service is complaining. It is beneficial to access one class from each of the three Office Communications Server repositories (Active Directory, SQL, and local WMI repositories). The following is one set of samples:

- **AD:** *select * from MSFT_SIPGlobalDomainData*
- **SQL:** *select * from MSFT_SIPProxySetting where BackEnd="<BackendSQLInstance>"*
- **LOCAL WMI:** *select * from MSFT_SIPRoutingSetting*

Note that the SQL query can be executed only on roles that belong to a pool (therefore, it won't work on Archiving Server, Access Edge Server, and so forth). Similarly, the Active Directory query won't work on an Access Edge Server. Also, the class referenced in the local WMI query must be changed for Archiving Server and Access Edge Server because this class is installed on all roles except these two.

–Nirav Kamdar
Senior Development Lead, OCS Server

Direct from the Source: Diagnosing Active Directory Errors

If you receive an Active Directory error (whose symbolic name starts with ERROR_DS_*, for example, ERROR_DS_NO_SUCH_OBJECT) during deployment, the first thing to check is which account credentials are being used. Run whoami.exe /groups, and make sure that the RTCUniversalServerAdmins group shows up in your access token. If it does, remember to use the Windows Server 2003 Resource Kit Tools Nltest.exe and NetDiag.exe to rule out problems with Domain Controllers (DCs) and the local machine network.

```
Nltest. exe /DsGetDC:[Root Domain FQDN] /GC
Nltest. exe /DsGetDC:[Root Domain FQDN] /PDC
Nltest. exe /DsGetDC:[Local Domain FQDN] /PDC
NetDiag.exe
```

The root and local domain FQDNs (shown in the following example as [Root Domain FQDN] and [Local Domain FQDN]) must be replaced with the root DC FQDN for the top-level domain and DC FQDN for the domain from which you are running the commands. Examples of domain names might be contoso.com for the root domain and eng.contoso.com for the local domain, with the command sequence being:

```
Nltest. exe /DsGetDC:contoso.com /GC
Nltest. exe /DsGetDC:contoso.com /PDC
Nltest. exe /DsGetDC:eng.contoso.com /PDC
NetDiag.exe
```

–Yong Zhao
Software Developer on the Office Communications Server team

Direct from the Source: Diagnosing Setup Failures

Setup logs are located under %temp% and have the .log extension (for Microsoft Installer Package [MSI] logs) or.html extension (for activation/prep failures). In MSI logs, look for the phrase "value 3" (MSI errors are cryptic, and this is a quick method to locate them). The .html logs are self explanatory and can be expanded to the point of the failure. LcsCmd's CheckXXState is also usually very helpful. For example, to check whether the AV (Audio/Video) MCU is activated, you can run LcsCmd /mcu /action:CheckLcServerState /role:AVMCU.

–Nirav Kamdar
Senior Development Lead, OCS Server

Real World: Installation and Tool Tips

The following tips can help with install/uninstall issues as well as provide useful information you should know when working with some of the Office Communications Server tools and with the Office Communications Server Resource Kit Tools.

Installation and uninstallation tips

Always uninstall the Office Communications Server product by using Control Panel->Add/Remove Programs. If the uninstall fails, then resolve the error that is thrown and try to uninstall again. If the uninstall still fails, then use the Microsoft Discussion Groups as the next-best solution (go to *http://www.microsoft.com/office/community/en-us/default.mspx*, and select the appropriate product from the list on the left). Ultimately, you might need to use the LcsVerifyClean.vbs script in the Office Communications Server 2007 Resource Kit Tools to clean up the installation. Never use any other cleanup utilities or manually clean up the state (registry, file system, WMI, SQL, permissions, and so forth).

MSI install/uninstall failures throw errors in the Application Event Log. You can use that information along with the log of installation/uninstallation to diagnose the problem yourself.

Tool tips

On 64-bit machines, launching the 32-bit MMC snap-in requires a switch, such as compmgmt.msc -32 or wrtcsnap2.msc -32 or dsa.msc -32.

Many Office Communications Server 2007 Resource Kit Tools now have a dependency on the Service Pack 1 C Run-Time Libraries (CRTs). If you don't install the SP1 CRTs, then running the application might result in a Failed To Initialize Properly message. If this happens, install SP1 CRTs from *http://www.microsoft.com/downloads* by searching for *Microsoft Visual C++ 2005 SP1 Redistributable Package*. Both x86 and x64 versions should be available. The direct link to the x86 download is *http://www.microsoft.com/downloads/details.aspx?FamilyID=200B2FD9-AE1A-4A14-984D-389C36F85647&displaylang=en*.

If the component that you want to trace does not appear in the OCSLogger components list, click Advanced Options->Additional Components. Click the empty space under executable files. Type the name of the file that you want to trace (such as wsipsetp.dll for LcsSetupCustomActions), and click OK. LcsSetupCustomActions should now appear in the components list.

–Nirav Kamdar
Senior Development Lead, OCS Server

Resolving Telephony Problems

This section contains a tip on exporting dial plans as well as a list of the major problems encountered with Microsoft Office Communicator Phone Edition and how to resolve them. Office Communicator Phone Edition is a business-use Voice over Internet Protocol (VoIP) phone containing new voice communication capabilities that are not available with traditional desktop phones. For example, with Communicator Phone Edition you can:

- Make outbound audio calls to phone users, answer inbound phone calls, and make VoIP calls. In short, you can do everything you can do today with your regular phone, and then some.

- Set call-handling options to forward calls to another number or contact so that you can receive calls on your mobile phone when you're not in the office.
- Keep a record of all phone conversations in Outlook.
- Move seamlessly from the same familiar Communicator-like context to the Communicator Phone Edition interface.
- Make calls from wherever you are, regardless of whether you are inside or outside a firewall.

Real World: Exporting Dial Plans

Did you know that you can export your Office Communications Server Enterprise Voice dial plan (Location Profiles, Policies, Phone Usage, and Routes) out of your test environment and import them into your Office Communications Server production servers? Here how it's done:

1. If you defined your Location Profiles, Policies, Phone Usage, and Routes through the Route Helper tool, proceed to Step 2. If you used the Office Communications Server MMC, launch the Enterprise Voice Route Helper tool (part of the Office Communications Server 2007 Resource Kit), and click File->Reload. Proceed to Step 2.
2. From the Route Helper tool, click File and select Export Routing Data (RTDA format) to save your data. Copy your RTDA file over to your production server, and launch the Route Helper tool on that server. Click File, and select the Import Routing Data option. Point to the copied RTDA file, and click OK. To add these dial plans to the Office Communications Server, click File and select Upload Changes.

–Ali Rohani
Technical Specialist, Unified Communications, Canada

Examples of Resolving Common Telephony Problems

The following sections identify the most commonly encountered telephony problems and offer tips on how to resolve them.

Communicator Phone Edition Log-in I cannot sign in with the Communicator Phone Edition. I receive the "Cannot connect to server or server name is incorrect" error message.

- Validate that your domain name is correct.
- Ensure that Dynamic Host Configuration Protocol (DHCP) is configured to provide the DNS server address as part of the DHCP response.
- Ensure that the DNS has SRV records for SIP service.
- Ensure that the SIP server is reachable from the Communicator Phone Edition LAN.

- None of the above solutions work? Refer to the "Communicator Phone Edition Unexpected Behavior" section later in this chapter.

I cannot sign in to the Communicator Phone Edition. I receive the "Cannot validate server certificate" error message.

- Ensure that either time.windows.com is accessible or that Network Time Protocol (NTP) is configured with appropriate SRV records created in the DNS.
- Ensure that PKIenrollment objects are created on Active Directory to point to CA or CA delegate.
- If PKI enrollment is not enabled, ensure that caAttribute for the CA container has appropriate root certificates.
- None of the above solutions work? Go to Generic Behavior – Communicator Phone Edition is behaving erratically.

I cannot sign in to the Communicator Phone Edition. I receive the "User name or password is invalid" error message.

- Make sure that your username and password are correct.
- If you change your password on the device before the server attempts to re-authenticate, the device cannot sign in to the server and is therefore left on the sign-in screen. Enter your old password in the *Password* field, and press Sign in.
- If your domain password has changed and the server attempts to re-authenticate, the device returns to the sign-in screen. Enter your new password in the *Password* field, and press Sign in.
- Make sure that the time on your phone is correct if Kerberos is enabled in your system.
- Make sure that either the Windows Internet Naming Service (WINS) server is enabled or that DHCP option 119 provides the DNS suffix search list if Kerberos authentication is being used on the server.
- None of the above solutions work? Refer to the "Communicator Phone Edition Unexpected Behavior" section later in this chapter.

I cannot sign in to the Communicator Phone Edition. I continue to see the "Device does not have a valid IP address" error message.

- Make sure that the Ethernet cable is connected to the first port on the back of the device (shown as a LAN picture).
- Check that your device is properly connected to a switch or router.
- Make sure the switch outlet has proper connectivity to your network and DHCP server.
- Make sure that DHCP is enabled in your system.

- Go to the About page on the sign-in screen, and check whether the virtual local area network (VLAN) has been misconfigured.
- Try connecting the Ethernet wire directly to the wall port.
- None of the above solutions work? Refer to the "Communicator Phone Edition Unexpected Behavior" section later in this chapter.

I configured my device and left for the day. This morning, the device is showing a login prompt.

- Your software upgrade might have occurred last night, which caused the phone to reset.
- Your password might have expired.
- None of the above solutions work? Refer to the "Communicator Phone Edition Unexpected Behavior" section later in this chapter.

I am trying to log in for the first time on Communicator Phone Edition, and I do not see a Personal Identification Number (PIN) option.

- Ensure that the PIN is enabled on the Office Communications Server (pool level-> FrontEnd Properties->VoIP tab).

I am trying to register my fingerprint, but the Communicator Phone Edition does not seem to recognize my swipes.

- Try to swipe your finger slowly (do not press hard) with just one slow swipe.
- Click Use Pin Configuration on the menu bar, and then click Use Finger Print Configuration on the menu bar. Try the finger swipe again.
- If it still does not work after repeated attempts, refer to the "Communicator Phone Edition Unexpected Behavior" section later in this chapter.

I used my fingerprint as an unlock mechanism, but my finger swipe is not being recognized on each attempt. My phone is locked, and I am stuck.

- Try to do a full-length, clean fingerprint swipe very slowly and easily.
- Repeat the previous step a few times. If your finger swipe still goes unrecognized, then use a small pin or toothpick to press the small pinhole button on the back of your phone between the universal serial bus (USB) and headset connectors. This procedure returns you to the factory defaults.

How should I restore my device to factory defaults?

- Use the small PIN to press the small pinhole button on the back of your phone between the USB and headset connectors. This returns you to the factory defaults.

My screen calibration seems incorrect, and I cannot click anything on the screen.

- The settings menu contains an option to recalibrate your device.

Placing Calls with Communicator Phone Edition I entered digits, but I do not see the dialed digits.

- Make sure that you are in call view or contacts view.
- Touch the screen input once to make sure that the text box is in focus.

I am pressing the Help button, but nothing is happening.

- Are you signed into the Office Communications Server service?

As soon as I call <xyz>, the call is shown as active and on hold.

- "Hold" is merely a button and not a state. If you want to put the call on hold you can use the Hold button that is displayed during the call.

Before I complete dialing, the call is becoming initiated with an invalid number

- Your dialing plan probably has overlapping rules that cause one rule to override another. Remove any overlap rules, or reconfigure the dial plan to remove any conflicts.
- None of the above solutions work? Refer to the "Communicator Phone Edition Unexpected Behavior" section later in this chapter.

I called someone, but there is no speech path.

- Are you traversing a firewall? If so, make sure that the Media Relay Access Server (MRAS) is configured correctly.
- Do you have an internal firewall? If so, make sure that the User Datagram Protocol (UDP) ports on the internal firewall are open for communication.
- Press Hold and then press Restore to determine whether the speech path is re-created.
- None of the above solutions work? Refer to the "Communicator Phone Edition Unexpected Behavior" section later in this chapter.

Voice Mail/Missed Calls/Call Logs on Communicator Phone Edition My device does not show Call Logs, Missed Calls, or Voice Mails.

- Make sure that Exchange Client Access Server (CAS) servers are installed.
- Make sure that the Exchange autodiscover service is configured.
- Make sure that appropriate DNS entries are created for the autodiscover service.
- Make sure that a SAN is added to the certificate on Exchange for appropriate validation.

Conference Call with Communicator Phone Edition I am trying to add a participant to an existing voice call, but I continue to see the word "Connecting" on display.

- Make sure that AV MCUs are configured in the network.
- Make sure that VoIP is enabled on the AV MCUs.
- Make sure that the Communicator Phone Edition user is enabled for Unified Communications (UC).
- None of the above solutions work? Refer to the "Communicator Phone Edition Unexpected Behavior" section later in this chapter.

Communicator Phone Edition Unexpected Behavior

- Power-cycle your device.
- From the Settings menu, click About, and then click Send Logs.

Summary

This chapter contains a large number of tips and practical guidance directly from the Office Communications Server 2007 product, support, and consulting teams. When working through a problem, start with the guidance provided at the beginning of the chapter: attempt to simplify the scenario and gather as much information as possible about what is occurring. Look at event logs and trace logs from the client or server, validate network connectivity, and validate that servers are operational and configured as expected. Use of the Validation Wizard is very helpful in this regard, and many problems can be found easily before they are actually encountered.

Additional Resources

- The official Microsoft Office Communications Server Web site is located at *http://office.microsoft.com/en-us/communicationsserver*. Documents, tools, and support information are always available at this location.
- Office Communications Server 2007 Resource Kit Tools are available for download at *http://www.microsoft.com/downloads/details.aspx?familyid=B9BF4F71-FB0B-4DE9-962F-C56B70A8AECD&displaylang=en*. Search for "Office Communications Server 2007 Resource Kit Tools" from *http://www.microsoft.com/downloads*.
- Practical Extraction and Report Language (PERL) downloads are available at *http://www.activestate.com*.
- Windows Server 2003 Resource Kit Tools are available for download at *http://www.microsoft.com/downloads/details.aspx?FamilyID=9d467a69-57ff-4ae7-96ee-b18c4790cffd&DisplayLang=en*. Search for "Windows Server 2003 Resource Kit Tools" from *http://www.microsoft.com/downloads*.

- The Quality of Experience (QoE) Monitoring Server Web download will be available at *http://www.microsoft.com/downloads*, but was not available at the time of this writing.
- Many useful community-driven Web sites support Office Communications Server. One that stands out is the Live Communications Server Guides site at *http://www.lcs-guides.com/*.

On the Companion CD

There is no companion CD content for this chapter.

Part VI
Technical Reference

In this part:

Part VI is divided into two chapters. Chapter 18 describes what is happening "under the hood" when you use Office Communications Server 2007 and Office Communicator 2007. This chapter provides an overview of the Session Initiation Protocol (SIP) that is used to help establish communication sessions; the authentication technologies that are used to help establish secure communications; how requests are routed through the network inside and outside the enterprise; and, finally, some security concepts that should be considered.

Chapter 19 provides an overview of the architecture and the internal components that make up the Office Communications Server 2007. Office Communications Server 2007 differs from previous versions in that its architecture is comprised of distributed server components. This chapter describes each of the internal components that make up the Office Communications Server 2007, including the core, presence, conferencing, and voice components.

Chapter 18

Office Communications Server 2007 Fundamentals

In this chapter:

This chapter provides a more in-depth discussion of six fundamental areas for Office Communications Server 2007 technology. This chapter covers the Session Initiation Protocol (SIP), SIP routing, the Globally Routable User-Agent URI (GRUU), enhanced presence, authentication, and security.

SIP is the protocol used between the server and the clients to establish communication sessions between client endpoints. Clients and servers need to use a standard protocol so that they know how to communicate with each other. SIP routing is the means of ensuring that communication sessions are established with the right people at the right locations. Office Communications Server 2007 uses routing logic to route all requests inside and outside the enterprise. The GRUU is an extension of SIP that is specifically designed to implement reliable routing to a specific device for an end user.

Presence is a combination of a user's ability and willingness to communicate. Live Communications Server 2005-enabled client applications to publish and subscribe to basic presence information such as name, e-mail address, and presence state (such as online, offline, or busy). Enhanced presence is an infrastructure element that enables client applications to publish and subscribe to extended, or enhanced, presence information. With enhanced presence, client applications can subscribe to more granular presence information such as calendar information or device state, and they can choose which presence information to publish and whom to publish to.

Authentication is the process of determining if someone is in fact who he says he is. Because SIP is used to communicate with people over the Internet, it is important for users to know who they are communicating with. Knowing this helps users protect themselves from malicious users, and it helps enterprises protect their sensitive data.

Finally, the last part of this chapter introduces some security features of Office Communications Server 2007 that should be considered before you begin your deployment.

Understanding Session Initiation Protocol

As described in RFC3261, there are many applications that use the Internet and that require the creation and management of a session, where a *session* is considered an exchange of data between an association of participants. The implementation of these applications is complicated by the practices of participants: users might move between endpoints, be addressable by multiple names, and communicate in several different media (sometimes simultaneously). Numerous protocols have been authored that carry various forms of real-time multimedia session data, such as voice, video, or text messages. SIP works in concert with these protocols by enabling Internet endpoints (called *user agents*) to discover one another and to agree on a characterization of a session they want to share. For locating prospective session participants and for other functions, SIP enables the creation of an infrastructure of network hosts to which user agents can send registrations, invitations to sessions, and other requests. SIP is an agile, general-purpose tool for creating, modifying, and terminating sessions that works independent of underlying transport protocols and without dependency on the type of session that is being established.

SIP is an application-layer control protocol that can establish, modify, and terminate multimedia sessions. Participants can be invited to already-existing sessions using SIP. Media can be added to or removed from an existing session. SIP transparently supports name mapping and redirection services, which means users can maintain a single, externally visible identifier regardless of their network location.

SIP is lightweight, providing five main functions for establishing and terminating multimedia communications as defined in RFC3261:

- **User location** The determination of the end system to be used for communication
- **User availability** The determination of the willingness of the called party to engage in communications
- **User capabilities** The determination of the media and media parameters to be used
- **Session setup** The "ringing," which is the establishment of session parameters at both called and calling parties
- **Session management** Includes transfer and termination of sessions, modifying session parameters, and invoking services

SIP provides primitives that can be used to implement different services. For example, SIP can locate a user and deliver an opaque object to his current location. If this primitive is used to deliver a session description written in Session Description Protocol (SDP), for example, the endpoints can agree on the parameters of a session.

SIP can be used with other Internet Engineering Task Force (IETF) protocols to build a complete multimedia architecture. Typically, these architectures include protocols such as the Real-Time Transport Protocol (RTP) for transporting real-time data and providing quality of service (QoS) feedback, the Real-Time Streaming Protocol (RTSP) for controlling the delivery of streaming media, the Media Gateway Control Protocol (MEGACO) for controlling gateways to the Public Switched Telephone Network (PSTN), and the Session Description Protocol (SDP) for describing multimedia sessions. Although SIP can be used with other IETF protocols to build a complete multimedia architecture, the basic functionality and operation of SIP does not depend on any of these protocols.

Figure 18-1 shows an architecture diagram illustrating how SIP fits into the Transmission Control Protocol/Internet Protocol (TCP/IP) networking stack.

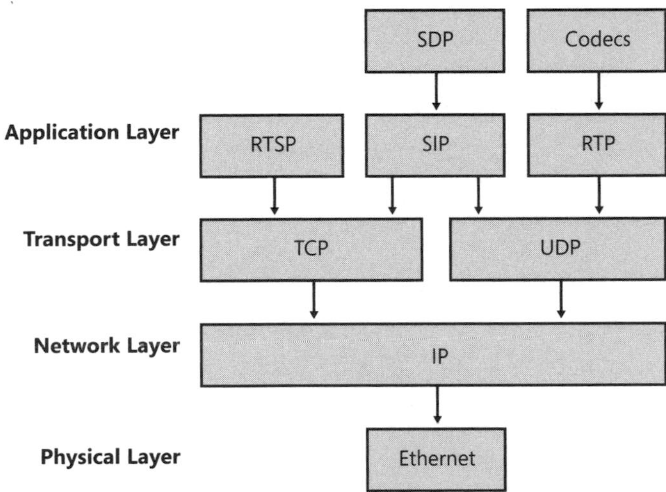

Figure 18-1 How SIP fits into the TCP/IP networking stack

How Office Communications Server 2007 and Office Communicator 2007 Use SIP

Office Communications Server 2007 and Office Communicator 2007 use SIP to register client endpoints, fetch and publish presence information, and help establish communications sessions, such as Instant Messaging, multiparty conferencing, and Voice over Internet Protocol (VoIP) between clients. Office Communications Server acts as a User Agent Server (UAS) and proxy, and it responds to the SIP requests issued by the client as well as forwards them from one client to another.

Common SIP Verbs

In SIP, there are commonly used verbs, which are shown in the following list:

- REGISTER
- SUBSCRIBE and NOTIFY
- SERVICE
- INVITE and MESSAGE
- ACK
- CANCEL
- BYE

REGISTER is used for endpoint registration. INVITE, ACK, CANCEL, and BYE are used for session establishment. MESSAGE is used for exchanging messages and within the session. SUBSCRIBE and NOTIFY are used for watching someone's presence. SERVICE requests are used for changing your information, such as your contact list and presence information. The following sections describe each of the verbs in more detail.

REGISTER

The first step a user takes when using an instant messaging application such as Office Communications Server 2007 is to log in. When a user signs in to her instant messaging application, for instance, her client sends a REGISTER request to the server. Additionally, if the user changes locations–from her desktop to her laptop, for example–the new client sends a REGISTER request to let the server know that she has changed locations.

The following data flow diagram (Figure 18-2) shows an example of a client registering to her Office Communications Server 2007 server. You see the user logging in and the server challenging the client for authentication credentials. In this example, the client has requested to use Kerberos authentication. More details on authentication technologies, including NTLM and Kerberos, are discussed later in this chapter in the "Overview of NTLM and Kerberos" section.

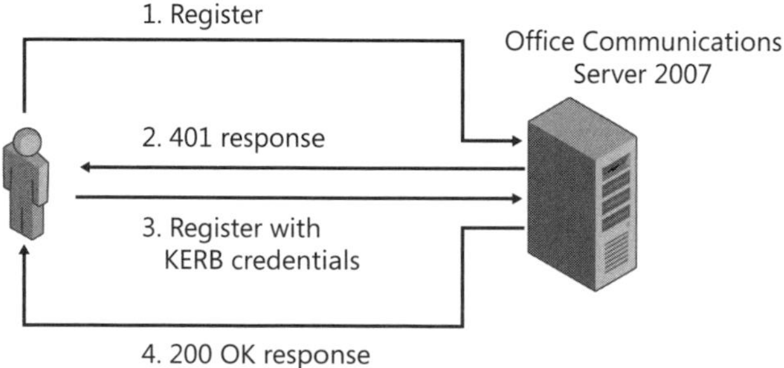

Figure 18-2 Data flow diagram for registration

The client first sends a REGISTER request to the server. The following block of code is an example of a REGISTER packet. Notice that the *From* and *To* headers are the same and the GRUU identifies the endpoint where the client is logging in. More details about the GRUU are covered later in this chapter in the "Understanding the Globally Routable User Agent URI" section.

```
REGISTER sip:example.com SIP/2.0
From: Callee <sip:callee@example.com>;tag=calee1111;epid=01010101
To: Callee <sip:callee@example.com>
Call-ID: REG1111@192.0.1.1
CSeq: 1 REGISTER
Supported: gruu-10
Contact: <sip:callee@192.0.1.1:1111;msopaque=1111>; proxy-
replace;+sip.instance="<urn:uuid:4b1682a8-f968-5701-83fc-7c6741dc6697>"
Via: SIP/2.0/TLS 192.0.1.1:1111;branch=z9hG4bK1111
...
```

After receiving a REGISTER request, Office Communications Server can do one of the following:

- **Query** If a *Contact* header is *not* present, the request is deemed to be a query for the list of registrations for all endpoints of the user.
- **Remove a registration** If an *Expires:0* header is present, the request is deemed to delete any existing registration for the user endpoint specified in the *epid* parameter of the *From* header in Live Communicator 2005 or the *+sip.instance* parameter of the *Contact* header in Office Communicator 2007. Live Communicator 2005 and Office Communicator 2007 also supply this *epid* parameter for backward compatibility.
- **Add or update a registration** If a *Contact* header is present with a non-empty value other than "*", Office Communications Server updates any existing registration for the user endpoint or adds a new registration if no previous registration is present.

After removing, adding, or updating a registration or querying the server, you will typically receive a response with a "200 OK" message. Otherwise, the server will return an error response. More details on common error responses can be found later in this chapter in the "Common SIP Responses" section.

SUBSCRIBE and NOTIFY Requests

SUBSCRIBEs and NOTIFYs are used for watching for event notifications from the server. They are used for presence as well as the user's own data, such as in-band provisioning information, contact lists, and specifying who the user wants to allow to watch his presence. Figure 18-3 shows an example data flow of a client subscribing to get the presence status of his contacts.

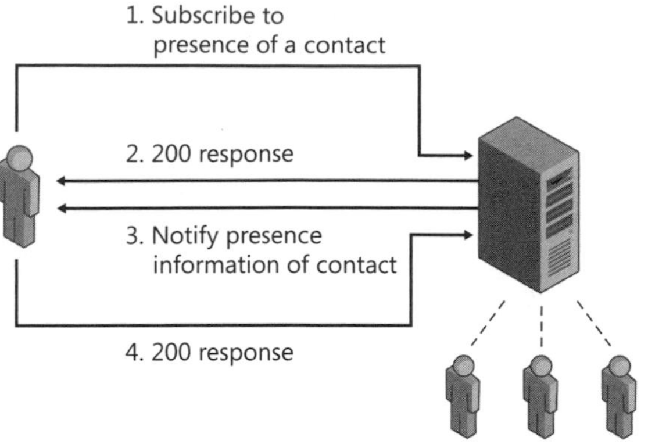

Figure 18-3 SUBSCRIBE and NOTIFY data flow diagram

SUBSCRIBE is used by the user to subscribe to information from the server that is dynamic in nature–that is, the information can change as a result of updates made by other users or as a result of administrative functions. NOTIFY is used by the server to notify users that information they had previously subscribed to has changed and to deliver the updated information.

Typically, Office Communicator will respond to the NOTIFY request with a "200" response. However, if Office Communicator responds to the NOTIFY message with a "404," "480," or "481" response, Office Communications Server assumes that the corresponding subscription is invalid and deletes the subscription from its records.

SERVICE

SERVICE requests are used when you want to change your information on the server as well as create and modify conferences. For example, if you want to add or change your presence information, the client sends a SERVICE request to the server to perform this operation. Figure 18-4 shows a typical dataflow from the client to the server for the SERVICE requests. The (SOAP) envelope inside the SERVICE requests tells the server what the client is requesting the server to do. SOAP is a protocol for exchanging XML-based messages. For details about SOAP, see *http://msdn2.microsoft.com/en-us/library/ms995800.aspx*.

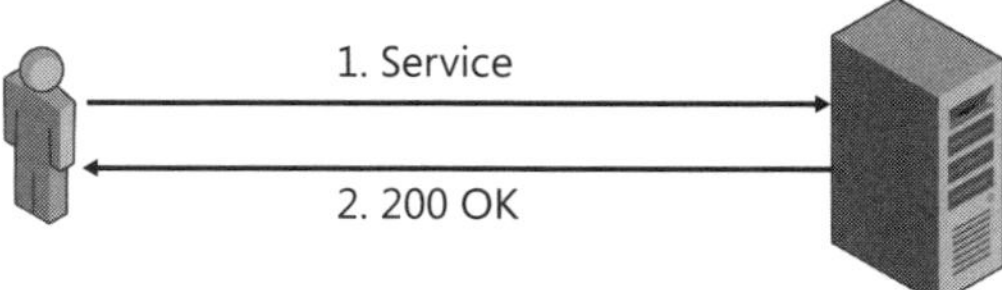

Figure 18-4 Sample SERVICE request

After Office Communicator sends a valid SERVICE request, Office Communications Server responds to the user with one of the following responses: "100 Trying," "200 OK," or "4xx error." If the initial response is "100 Trying," Office Communications Server responds with a "200 OK" or a "4xx error" message when it completes the processing.

The SOAP/XML envelope in the body of the SERVICE request describes the service to be executed by Office Communications Server. You can use a SERVICE request to do things such as control access control entries (ACEs), modify your contact list and groups, set your own presence, and retrieve presence information.

INVITE and MESSAGES

The INVITE request helps establish sessions for client-to-client communication, as well as establish sessions with the A/V Conferencing Server and the IM Conferencing Server. For instance, when User A wants to send an instant message to User B, User A's client sends an INVITE request to User B.

Office Communications Server follows the guidelines provided in RFC 3261 to allow its users to create and manage an INVITE dialog (by using INVITE, ACK, CANCEL, and BYE messages). Office Communications Server does not consume any of these messages itself in a normal scenario, except in some error cases where Office Communications Server is forced to intervene and respond to these messages.

A Microsoft Office Communicator 2007 user uses the INVITE dialog to establish various types of sessions with other users. The user negotiates what type of session she wants to create in the SDP payload of the SIP INVITE request. These sessions can be one of the following types:

- Instant messaging (IM)
- Audio and video
- Application sharing
- Whiteboarding

With the exception of instant messaging, these session types are peer-to-peer sessions. Only the SIP signaling (SIP messages related to an INVITE dialog) traverses the Office Communications Server. The media itself is peer-to-peer communications based on the information exchanged between the users in the SDP. The server does not validate or otherwise consume or modify this SDP information.

IM sessions are not peer-to-peer communications because the user sends the IM text to the destination user in the body of SIP MESSAGEs proxied through Office Communications Server. Office Communications Server does not process the contents of a MESSAGE request (or any other client-specific requests) in any special way compared to other general SIP requests. It tries to proxy them as usual to the destination based on the registration information of the target user or the routing information present in the request.

ACK

An ACK request is used in a three-way handshake, similar to TCP. If User A sends an INVITE to User B, User B accepts the session and sends a "200 OK" response back to User A. Then User A's client responds with an ACK. This is the three-way handshake process to establish a session between endpoints.

CANCEL

A CANCEL request is used to cancel a session establishment process. For example, if User A sends an INVITE to User B but then decides not to go through with the call, User A's client then sends a CANCEL request to User B.

BYE

A BYE request is used to terminate a session. For example, if User A and User B have established a call session and now User A has decided to hang up, Users A's client sends a BYE request to User B.

Common SIP Responses

Following a SIP request, the server sends a SIP response back to the client. The SIP responses are almost a one-to-one mapping to HTTP responses. In general, the following SIP responses will be sent back to the client:

- Informational
- Success
- Redirection
- Client error
- Server error
- Global failure

Informational

This response ranges from 100 to 199. This response class indicates that the server is trying to process the client's request.

Success

This response ranges from 200 to 299. This response class indicates that the request was received and processed.

Redirection

This response ranges from 300 to 399. This error class indicates that a response is being redirected to another server.

Client Error

This response ranges from 400 to 499. This error class indicates that a client error occurred, such as the server challenged with a password and the password is bad.

Server Error

This response ranges from 500 to 599 and represents an error that occurred on the server, such as the server might be down and not responding.

Global Failure

This response ranges from 600 to 699 and represents global errors.

Understanding SIP Routing

When sending SIP requests to Office Communications Server, a series of routing decisions are made by the server in order to route the requests to the right person or the right location. How the server decides this depends on the types of requests and the given topology. The server uses the information in the headers in each of the requests to know how to route the request through the network.

Overview of SIP Routing Concepts

Office Communications Server uses the header information found in the packets to know how to route packets through the network to the right user or the right location. The headers that are primarily used for routing in SIP are record-route headers, route headers, via headers, and contact headers. Routing signatures are placed in the headers to guarantee integrity of the messages. The following sections describe each of these headers and routing signatures in more detail.

Record-Route Headers

A server that proxies a message can add its own fully qualified domain name (FQDN) or IP address to the record-route header to indicate that it wants to remain in the signaling path for all subsequent SIP traffic in the current session. For example, for security reasons, an Office Communications Server 2007 Access Edge Server inserts its FQDN into all requests that establish a session originating from a corporate branch office; it does this to ensure that all subsequent messages in the established session have to go back through it before crossing the branch office firewall.

Route Headers

Route headers consist of a list of FQDNs or IP addresses of all entities in the path of a request. Upon receiving a message, each Office Communications Server removes its own FQDN or IP address from the list and forwards the message to the next Uniform Resource Identifier (URI) in the list.

Via Headers

The via header or headers contain FQDNs or IP addresses of the client and all Office Communications Servers that have handled a request. Via headers are used to direct responses back to a client by using the same path by which it was sent, but in the opposite direction. A server can also inspect the via header to determine whether it has previously handled a request.

Contact Headers

A user's address, as opposed to the address of the SIP server on which the user is hosted, is stored in the contact header. A server redirecting a message can write the address of the intended recipient in a contact header returned in a response to the client. Subsequently, the client can contact the recipient directly without having to go through the server.

Route Signatures

Office Communications Server uses route signatures to guarantee integrity of the messages flowing through the network. Without route signatures, the server would have no way to verify that the route the packets took through the network was not compromised by an attacker. Office Communications Server uses a cryptographic signature to verify that the packets did actually come through every hop that was expected.

Office Communications Server signs routing information in the *Record-Route+Contact* header and the via headers. The signing is performed on the edges of the server network trusted for supplying routing information on connections that are not trusted for routing and on Access Edge Servers on connections to federated domains. When signing the *Record-Route+Contact* header, the signature is placed in the route URI so that it is retained in the dialog state by the clients and echoed back in route headers in each request in the dialog. When a request is received from an untrusted network boundary (such as client or federated), Office Communications Server uses the route signature contained in the route URI to verify that the route path has not been tampered with.

Direct from the Source: Routing Logic

Figure 18-5 shows an example topology with a mixture of federated users, extranet clients, and intranet clients, as well as multiple pools and multiple front-end servers.

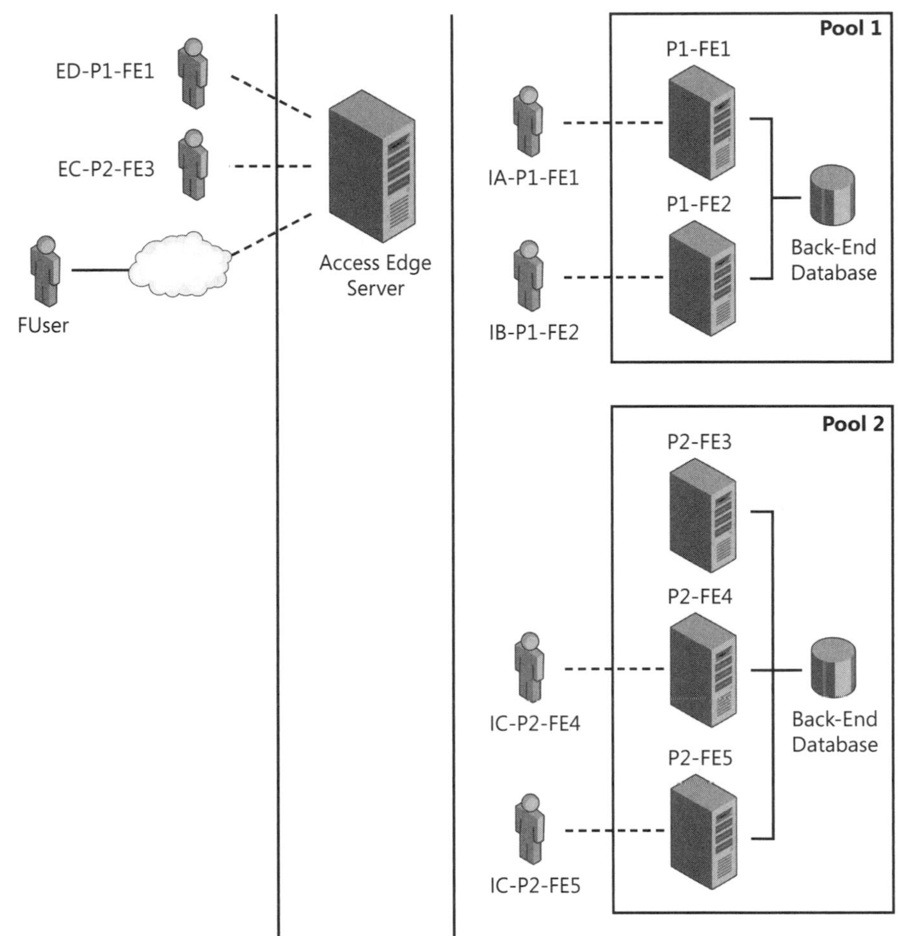

Figure 18-5 Sample topology

In the diagram, we have a sample topology with a federated user (FUser) and some extranet users (such as ED-P1-FE1) and intranet users (such as IA-P1-FE1). Federated users typically belong to another organization that is a peer of the enterprise. It can also be a user from the public cloud, such as Yahoo!, MSN, or AOL. These users do not belong to the enterprise but are able to get presence information and start communications with users within that enterprise. Their requests come in through an Access Edge Server. The extranet users are remote enterprise users that connect through an Access Edge Server. The intranet users are users located within the enterprise. Each of the extranet users and intranet users belongs to different pools in the enterprise. You can see which pools each user belongs to in the diagram in Figure 18-5. For example, ED-P1-FE1 is an extranet user, User D, who belongs to Pool 1. FE stands for "Front End" and refers to the server that each of these users is logged on to. For instance, ED-P1-FE1 is logged on to Front-End Server 1.

An overview of the routing logic for enterprise and federated users is provided in the "Detailed Routing Logic in the Enterprise" and "Detailed Federation Logic" sections that follow. First, we introduce a few SIP routing concepts.

Detailed Routing Logic in the Enterprise

We will use the sample topology provided in Figure 18-5 (shown earlier) for the purposes of this discussion. This discussion includes any user in that topology except for FUser (federated user). Routing can vary depending on the request that comes in, who it is from, and who it is intended for. The following sections explain in more detail the routing logic for the different requests. All requests are first redirected to the home server of the user specified in the *From* header for logging and registration purposes, and then the destination logic applies.

REGISTER Requests from Extranet Users

When a REGISTER request comes in from an extranet user such as user ED, it arrives at the Access Edge Server. The REGISTER request is deterministically forwarded to one of the front-end servers, called a *director*. The request is then authenticated on that server, and a security association (SA) is established. At this point, one of two things can happen:

- If the REGISTER request comes from a user that belongs to the same (director) pool, a registration record is created in the pool. In this case, the route would have been ED-P1-FE1 to Access Edge Server to P1-FE1.
- If the REGISTER request comes from a user that belongs to a different internal pool, the REGISTER request is again deterministically forwarded to a front-end server in that pool. So, in this case, the routing logic would have been EC-P2-FE3 to Access Edge Server to P1-FE2 to P2-FE3. In this case, the SA was established in P1-FE2.

REGISTER Requests from Intranet Users

If the REGISTER request comes from an intranet user such as IA, one of the following two things can happen:

- If the REGISTER request comes from a user that belongs to the same pool, a registration record is created in the pool. In this case, the route would have been IA-P1-FE1 to P1-FE1.

- If the REGISTER request comes from a user that belongs to a different pool, the REGISTER request is redirected to a different pool via a "301" response. So, in this case, the routing logic is IA-P1-FE1 to P2-FE3 to "301" response to P1-FE1.

SUBSCRIBE Requests from Extranet Users

When a SUBSCRIBE request comes in from an extranet user such as user ED, it arrives at the Access Edge Server. The SUBSCRIBE request is deterministically forwarded to one of the front-end servers (director). Most likely, the SA would have been established by a prior REGISTER request. At this point, one of the following two things can happen:

- If the SUBSCRIBE request is destined for a user in the director pool, a subscription dialog is created in the pool. In the case that ED-P1-FE1 is subscribing to User B, the route is ED-P1-FE1 to Access Edge Server to P1-FE1.
- If the SUBSCRIBE request is for a user in an internal pool, the SUBSCRIBE request is again deterministically forwarded to a front-end server in that pool. In the case that ED-P1-FE1 is subscribing to User C, the routing logic would have been ED-P1-FE1 to Access Edge Server to P1-FE1 to P2-FE3. The SUBSCRIBE request was routed to one of the front-end servers in Pool2, where User C is homed.

SUBSCRIBE Requests from Intranet Users

If the SUBSCRIBE request comes from an intranet user such as IA, it comes in at the front-end server where the client is logged in. One of the following two things can happen:

- If the SUBSCRIBE request is destined for a user in the same pool, the subscribe operation is done on that server. In the case that IA-P1-FE1 subscribes to its roaming contacts, the routing logic is IA-P1-FE1 to P1-FE1.
- If the SUBSCRIBE request is destined for a user in a different pool, the SUBSCRIBE request is deterministically forwarded to a front-end server in that pool. In the case that IA-P1-FE1 subscribes to user C, the routing logic would have been IA-P1-FE1 to P1-FE1 to P2-FE4.

SERVICE Requests from Extranet Users

When a SERVICE request comes in from an extranet user such as user EC, it arrives at the Access Edge Server. The SERVICE request is deterministically forwarded to one of the front-end servers. Most likely, the SA would have been established by a prior REGISTER request. At this point, one of the following two things can happen:

- If the SERVICE request is destined for a user in the director pool, the service operation is done on that pool. In the case that EC-P2-FE3 adds a new contact, the routing logic is EC-P2-FE3 to Access Edge Server to P1-FE2 to P2-FE3.

- If the SERVICE request is for a user in an internal pool, the SERVICE request is again deterministically forwarded to a front-end server in that pool. In the case that EC-P2-FE3 issues a *get presence* request for User A, the routing logic is ED-P1-FE1 to Access Edge Server to P1-FE1 to P2-FE3 to P1-FE1.

SERVICE Requests from Intranet Users

If the SERVICE request comes from an intranet user such as IA, it comes in at the front-end server where the client is logged in. One of the following two things can happen:

- If the SERVICE request is destined for a user in the same pool, the request is processed on the same server. In the case that IB-P1-FE2 deletes an existing contact, the routing logic is IB-P1-FE2 to P1-FE2.
- If the SERVICE request is for a user in a different pool, the SERVICE request is deterministically forwarded to a front-end server in that pool. In the case that IB-P1-FE2 issues a *get presence* request for EC-P2-FE3, the routing logic would have been IB-P1-FE2 to P1-FE2 to P2-FE3.

INVITE Requests from Extranet Users

When an INVITE request comes in from an extranet user, it arrives at the Access Edge Server. The INVITE request is deterministically forwarded to one of the front-end servers. Most likely, the SA would have been established by a prior REGISTER request. At this point, one of the following three things can happen:

- If the INVITE request is destined for a user in the director pool, the INVITE request is routed to a particular endpoint by using the Multiple Point of Presence (MPOP) routing logic. In the case that ED-P1-FE1 sends an INVITE to User B (user B has only 1 endpoint, IB-P1-FE2, which is logged in to P1-FE2), the routing logic is ED-P1-FE1 to Access Edge Server to P1-FE1 to IB-P1-FE2.
- If the INVITE request is for a user in an internal pool, the INVITE request is deterministically forwarded to a front-end server in that pool. In the case that ED-P1-FE1 sends an INVITE to User C (User C has three endpoints–IC-P2-FE4, IC-P2-FE5, and EC-P2-FE3–and assumes that EC-P2-FE3 wins MPOP logic), the routing logic is ED-P1-FE1 to Access Edge Server to P1-FE1 to P2-FE5 to P2-FE3 to Access Edge Server to EC-P2-FE3.
- If the INVITE request is for a user in a federated domain, it is routed back to the Access Edge Server via static routes. In this case, if EC-P2-FE3 sends an INVITE to FUser, the routing logic is EC-P2-FE3 to Access Edge Server to P1-FE2 to P2-FE3 to P1-FE2 to Access Edge Server...to FUser.

INVITE Requests from Intranet Users

If the INVITE request comes from an intranet user such as IA, it comes in at the front-end server where the client is logged in. One of the following two things can happen:

- If the INVITE request is destined for a user in the same pool, the request is routed to a particular endpoint by using the MPOP routing logic. In the case that IA-P1-FE1 invites User B, the routing logic is IA-P1-FE1 to P1-FE1 to P1-FE2 to IB-P1-FE2.
- If the INVITE request is for a user in a different pool, the INVITE request is deterministically forwarded to a front-end server in that pool. In the case that IA-P1-FE1 invites user C, the routing logic is IA-P1-FE1 to P1-FE1 to P2-FE5 to P2-FE3 to Access Edge Server to EC-P2-FE3.

NOTIFY Sent to Extranet User

If a user changes presence, a NOTIFY request needs to be sent to a watcher who might be an extranet user. For example, if IC-P2-FE5 changes its presence and EC-P2-FE3 is one of its watchers, the routing logic is P2-FE5 to P2-FE3 to P1-FE2 to Access Edge Server to EC-P2-FE3.

NOTIFY Sent to Intranet User

If a user adds a new contact from one of its endpoints, a roaming delta NOTIFY request is sent to all of its other endpoints. In the case that IC-P2-FE4 and IC-P2-FE5 are the endpoints of the same user C and both of them have roaming subscriptions, and IC-P2-FE4 adds a new contact and a roaming delta NOTIFY request is sent to IC-P2-FE5, the routing logic is P2-FE4 to P2-FE5 to IC-P2-FE5.

Detailed Federation Logic

Again, we will use the sample topology provided in Figure 18-5 for the purposes of this discussion. This discussion includes all requests coming into the enterprise from a federated user. Routing can vary depending on the type of request. The following sections explain in more detail the routing logic for the different requests.

REGISTER Request

When a REGISTER request comes into the Access Edge Server, all requests are blocked. The Access Edge Server returns a "403 Forbidden" response. This is because Office Communications Server 2007 does not allow federated users to register with its server.

SUBSCRIBE Request

When a SUBSCRIBE request comes in from a federated user, it arrives at the Access Edge Server. The SUBSCRIBE request is deterministically forwarded to one of the front-end servers. At that point, one of the following two things can happen:

- If the SUBSCRIBE request is destined for a user in the director pool, a subscription record is created in that pool. In the case that FUser is subscribing to User A, the routing logic is FUser to Access Edge Server to P1-FE2.
- If the SUBSCRIBE request is for a user in an internal pool, the SUBSCRIBE request is deterministically forwarded to a front-end server in that pool. In the case that the FUser subscribes to user C, SUBSCRIBE is routed to one of the front-end servers in Pool2, where user C is homed. The routing logic is FUser to Access Edge Server to P1-FE2 to P2-FE4.

SERVICE Requests

When a SERVICE request comes in from an FUser to the Access Edge Server, the Access Edge Server blocks the request. The reason for this is that Office Communications Server 2007 does not support SERVICE requests from federated networks.

INVITE Requests

When an INVITE request comes in from a federated user, it arrives at the Access Edge Server. The invite request is deterministically forwarded to one of the front-end servers. At that point, one of the following two things can happen:

- If the INVITE request is destined for a user in the director pool, the INVITE request is routed to a particular endpoint using MPOP routing logic. In the case that FUser sends an INVITE to User A and User A has only one endpoint, IA-P1-FE1, the routing logic is FUser to Access Edge Server to P1-FE2 to P1-FE1 to IA-P1-FE1.
- If the INVITE request is for a user in an internal pool, the SUBSCRIBE request is deterministically forwarded to a front-end server in that pool. In the case that the FUser sends an INVITE to User C (User C has three endpoints–IC-P2-FE4, IC-P2-FE5, and EC-P2-FE3–and assumes that EC-P2-FE3 wins the MPOP logic), the routing logic is FUser to Access Edge Server to P1-FE2 to P2-FE5 to P2-FE3 to Access Edge Server to EC-P2-FE3.

NOTIFY Sent to a Federated User

If a user changes its presence, a NOTIFY request is sent to the watcher, FUser. In the case that IB-P2-FE2 changes its presence and FUser is one of its watchers, the routing logic is P1-FE2 to Access Edge Server to...to FUser.

–Dhigha Sekaran
Senior Software Developer Lead

Understanding the Globally Routable User Agent URI

The Globally Routable User-Agent URI (GRUU) is an extension of SIP that is currently defined in an Internet-Draft, available at *http://tools.ietf.org/id/draft-ietf-sip-gruu-13.txt*. The GRUU is specifically designed to implement reliable routing to a specific device for an end user. Though a plain SIP URI such as janedoe@contoso.com is a URI that refers to a user, a GRUU is a URI that refers to a specific device. The Communicator client running on each user's computer will have its own GRUU that allows other applications to route messages specifically to that device. A GRUU can be used within multiple separate SIP dialogs to reach the same device. This works not just for client applications but also for server applications (for example, the Mediation Server, which was discussed in Chapter 2, "Server Roles").

The GRUU is widely applied across the server to solve a variety of problems, including but not limited to Enterprise Voice call transfer or conference escalation scenarios, which require the ability to establish a new dialog with a specific endpoint. The GRUU is also used to address scenarios where one endpoint in a dialog is server based and, therefore, the *To/From* header in the dialog cannot be resolved to a specific endpoint. In the original SIP standard, it was not possible to construct a URI that could be routed to and from anywhere (including the Internet) and reach a specific device or user agent.

In previous versions, the server used a proprietary extension called an End-Point Identifier (EPID) to address a specific user agent. In Office Communications Server 2007, the GRUU replaces the EPID where possible. Office Communications Server 2007 supports backwards compatibility with EPIDs, but to the degree possible all new applications and clients should use the GRUU instead.

The GRUU is a SIP URI that *generally* follows the form shown here:

```
sip:<user>@<domain or FQDN>;opaque=<private>;grid=<optional cookie>;gruu
```

Here is an example:

```
sip:janedoe@contoso.com;opaque=user:epid:qIIWS2j5AVeD_HxnQdxmlwAA;gruu
```

The *opaque* parameter in combination with the address of record (AOR) make this URI unique even though the prefix of the URI is still the standard user address. The *gruu* parameter specifies that this URI has all the properties of a GRUU and can be used with multiple separate SIP dialogs to reach the same UA (device). The *grid* parameter is optional and is inserted by a user agent instance when the user agent uses the GRUU to route to itself. If the *grid* parameter is included in a request, it helps the user agent instance determine the context of the request.

Understanding GRUU Creation

The server is responsible for creating a GRUU and returning it to the client through the SIP registration mechanism if the client requests one at registration time. The GRUU returned to the client during the registration process is not managed or exposed to the administrator in any way. This process is handled entirely by the User Services module and can be inspected only by examining the registration database itself. For details about the User Services module, see Chapter 19, "Microsoft Office Communications Server 2007 Internals." The GRUU can be used anywhere you would normally use a URI.

How the GRUU Is Used by Office Communications Server

The GRUU is used by Office Communications Server in the following ways:

- Communicator 2007 clients request and receive a GRUU at registration time that they will use in their *Contact* header for all subsequent SIP dialogs, such as Enterprise Voice calls, conferencing, and so on.
- Live Meeting 2007 uses one aspect of GRUU known as the "sip.instance" to create a unique identifier for each meeting client in a conference. This is necessary because the meeting client does not actually register with the server and therefore cannot obtain a genuine GRUU from the server for use in its SIP *Contact* header.
- The client uses the GRUU of the Media Relay Access Server (MRAS) application (co-located with the A/V Conferencing Server) to send requests to the MRAS without necessarily having to know the FQDN of the server or be able to directly connect to the MRAS. The client learns the MRAS application's GRUU through in-band provisioning. (The A/V Conferencing Server uses the MRAS application GRUU that is configured in WMI.)
- Enterprise Voice endpoints send their QoS metric reports to a GRUU, which identifies the metrics collection point. (The Mediation Server and A/V Conferencing Server use the collection point GRUU configured in WMI.)
- The voice-mail server (generally Microsoft Exchange Server's Unified Messaging) for a given user will be identified by a GRUU. The client learns this GRUU through in-band provisioning (for itself) and through presence (for someone else). An application running on the server, ExUM Routing, resolves the GRUU to a specific Exchange Unified Messaging server that handles user voice mailboxes. An application can be written that resolves the GRUU for non–Microsoft Exchange voice-mail systems.
- Pools use GRUU to address other pools for batched subscriptions.
- The Mediation Server uses GRUU to identify different outbound gateways that are connected to the Mediation Server. This allows Office Communications Server to send messages to a single FQDN/port on the Mediation Server and have the messages routed correctly to the proper outbound IP-PSTN gateway. (This GRUU is not exposed in any way to the client; it is used only for server-to-server communications.)
- During conference creation, the client addresses the Focus Factory by using a GRUU that is composed in part by the meeting organizer's SIP URI. This Focus Factory GRUU

is sent to the client via in-band provisioning. The Focus Factory is the central policy and state manager for a conference and acts as the coordinator for all aspects of the conference. For details about the Focus Factory, see Chapter 19, "Microsoft Office Communications Server 2007 Internals."

- Conferences are identified using a GRUU that is constructed from the organizer's SIP URI. This GRUU is routable within the SIP network and allows conference requests to be routed to the appropriate Conference Focus. The Conference Focus is the central policy and state manager for a conference and acts as the coordinator for all aspects of the conference. For details about the Conference Focus, see Chapter 19, "Microsoft Office Communications Server 2007 Internals."

Understanding Enhanced Presence

Office Communications Server 2007 provides the infrastructure to enable client applications to publish and subscribe to extended, or enhanced, presence information. The enhanced presence infrastructure includes categories and containers. Categories are individual pieces of presence information, such as status, location, note, contact information, or calendar data. Containers are logical buckets into which clients publish instances of various categories of presence information. (See Tables 18-1 and 18-2.) When change occurs, clients can publish an individual category instance instead of an entire presence document, as is the case with Live Communications Server 2005.

Table 18-1 Types of Presence Information in Office Communications Server 2007

Presence Information	Detailed Description
Basic Presence (Always Visible)	Displays the following presence information: ■ Available ■ Inactive ■ Away ■ Busy (Inactive) ■ Busy ■ Do Not Disturb ■ Offline ■ Unknown ■ Blocked
Name/E-mail	Name E-mail address
Basic Contact Information	Title Company

Table 18-1 Types of Presence Information in Office Communications Server 2007

Presence Information	Detailed Description
Detailed Contact Information	Work phone Work address Office number SharePoint site Free/Busy schedule Notes (for example, out of office) Notes (personal)
Additional Numbers	Mobile phone Home phone Other phone
Location	Current location Time away Working hours

Table 18-2 Examples of Presence Containers in Office Communications Server 2007

Container	Description	Can See
Personal	Family and friends who can contact you at any time	Name/E-mail address Basic contact information Detailed contact information Additional numbers Location
Public	General public whom you have limited contact with	Name/E-mail address Basic contact information
Team	Members of your team or workgroup	Name/E-mail address Basic contact information Detailed contact information Additional numbers Location Meeting details
Company	Employees	Name/E-mail address Basic contact information Detailed contact information

For example, if a fictitious user named Tim is watching the presence of Joe, Joe can control what presence information Tim sees. If he places Tim in his Public container, Tim can see only Joe's name, e-mail address, and basic contact information. If Joe places Tim in his Personal container, Tim can see additional categories, such as detailed contact information, additional numbers, and location.

Office Communications Server 2007 notifies watchers of presence changes, depending on the containers for which each watcher has permission. For example, as a sales representative moves from one part of town to another, his supervisor and wife might be notified of his movements, whereas individuals without the necessary permission for that container are not notified. Office Communications Server 2007 supports this functionality through the use of rich access control lists (ACLs) that are based on containers and categories. ACLs contain the following:

- URI List (per user)
- Domain List
- Same Enterprise
- Federated Users
- Public Cloud Users

Administrators can also define custom states for a user or group, and Office Communicator retrieves these custom states with custom activities from a Web site. For example, an administrator might want to provide a way for a recruiter in the recruiting department to remain uninterrupted while conducting an interview. In this case, the administrator can create a custom state consisting of the Do Not Disturb icon and associate it with a string "interviewing" to define this activity. Office Communications Server also allows you to customize your presence states. There are a total of four possible custom states, which are policy driven and can be deployed company-wide.

Additional customizations allow application developers to create custom clients for publishing and subscribing to other publications from different clients.

How Enhanced Presence Works

Presence in Office Communications Server 2007 has the following characteristics:

- Presence information from multiple sensors
    1. Machine state
    2. User state
    3. Phone state
    4. Calendar state
- Server-side aggregation
- Extensible activities
- MPOP support

Figure 18-6 shows an overview of how enhanced presence works. The following sections describe this model in more detail.

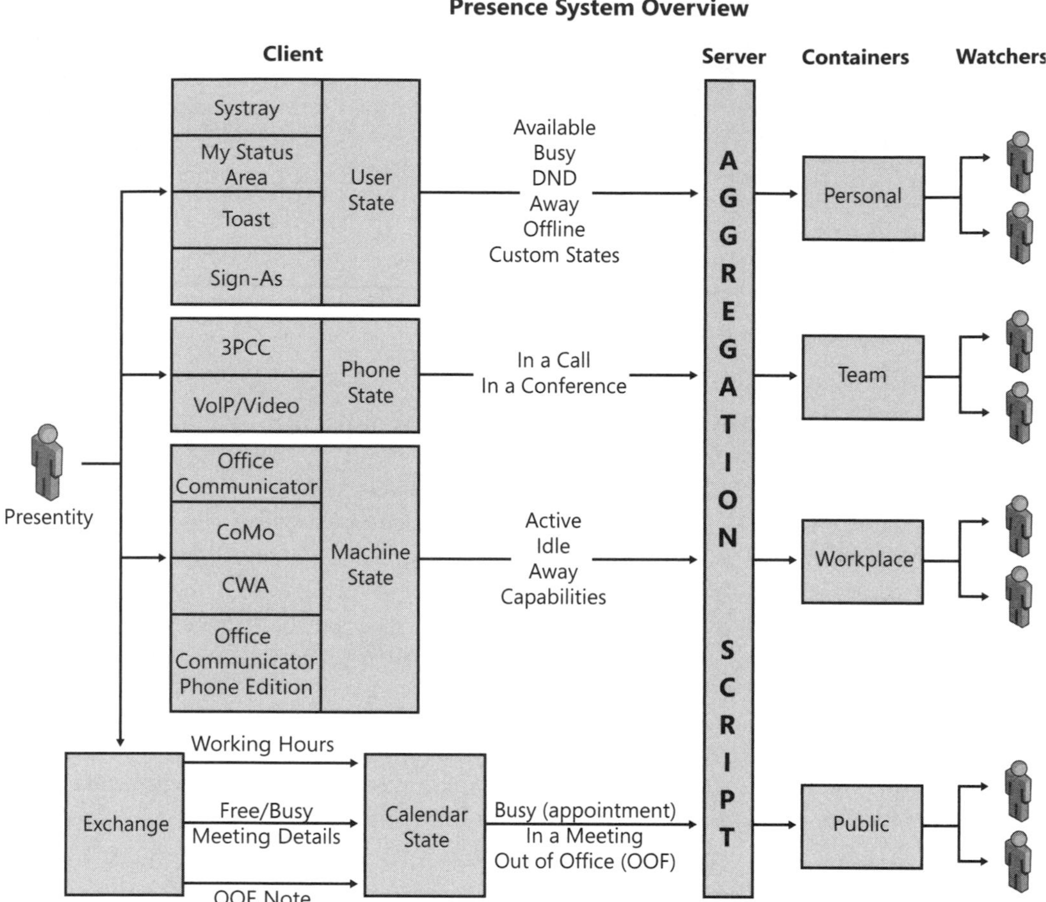

Figure 18-6 Presence system overview

Understanding Categories of Presence Information

Office Communications Server 2007 uses a publish/subscribe model to publish and subscribe to more granular pieces of data that are assigned to different categories for each presence entity. Categories identify the types of data being published, such as presence note, presence state, and devices. Each category describes how to interpret the data. For example, a presence note category might have the data "I'm currently out of office" stored with it. Having a category abstraction allows more extensibility for third-party clients–because clients can access new types of data and users can subscribe to more granular data. For example, if Joe wants to subscribe only to Tim's presence note, Joe can do so without having to receive all other types of data about Tim, such as all of his devices and calendar information.

An application can publish multiple instances of a category. The subscriber receives all instances of this category. Multiple instances are usually published by different endpoints of a given application, one instance for each endpoint. This is also known as *Multiple Points of Presence (MPOP)*.

Each publication, which is an instance of a category in a specific container, has a version associated with it. Each version starts with 1, and each time the data is changed the version increases by 1. If there is no version number specified by the client or the version number does not match the version maintained by the server, the data is rejected by the server. This is done so that data is kept in sync across multiple devices. For example, if Joe is logged in to multiple devices–such as a laptop and a desktop–each device will have the most up-to-date information.

Publications can also be time bound. For example, a publication can live forever, expire after some amount of time (such as calendar information), expire after a particular registered endpoint expires (such as logging off of your desktop computer), or expire after all the registered endpoints expire (such as when a user logs off or is disconnected on all devices). In the case that the publication expires, the subscriber gets put back into the default container. For example, joe@contoso.com is a subscriber of Cindy's presence, and he fits into container 400. If Cindy disconnects from all of her devices, joe@contoso.com now sees only the presence information published to everyone else until Cindy logs back in. When Cindy logs back in, joe@consoto.com gets re-evaluated and put back into the correct container, as it pertains to Cindy. A subscriber can also get re-evaluated at any time if any memberships, containers, or categories change.

Understanding Containers of Presence Information

Containers are identified by a number. A number is used, as opposed to a general string name, because the concept of ordering is applied to containers. Also, Office Communications Server 2007 knows only of a container number, and it is up to the client to assign the container number to a name. Container 0 is also assigned special status as a "default" container, and by default everyone is placed in this container. Subscribers are unaware of the containers that they are receiving information from.

Subscribers can fall into multiple containers. For example, joe@fabrikam.com might fall into my *same domain container* as well as my *personal container*. If Tim has different presence notes for each container, the server needs to figure out which presence note Joe will see because a subscriber gets a category subscription satisfied only from one container. If a subscriber is placed into multiple containers, there are a set of rules followed to determine which information should be given to the subscriber. First, the server looks at the category the user wants to subscribe to. If Joe wants to subscribe only to Tim's presence note, the server first looks only at the containers that contain presence notes.

After the server determines which containers to look at, the server looks at the membership in each container. As mentioned previously, there are five types of membership characteristics for ACLs. These characteristics are numbered for a reason. The server starts with the first characteristic, SIP URI, and then works its way down to the last characteristic, public cloud users. As soon as the server finds a match for the subscriber, it stops searching, and this is the container the subscriber will be placed into. For example, we see that joe@microsoft.com has been put in the personal container, which is higher ranked than the same domain membership characteristic, so the server gives the presence note for the personal container to joe@fabrikam.com instead of the presence note given to other people with the same domain. Let's say that joe@fabrikam.com still fits into two containers and the server did not know which presence note to publish. In this case, the server then looks at the container number. The highest container number wins.

As mentioned previously, a container holds a set of published items and a membership list describing who can see those items. An example of containers is shown in Figure 18-7.

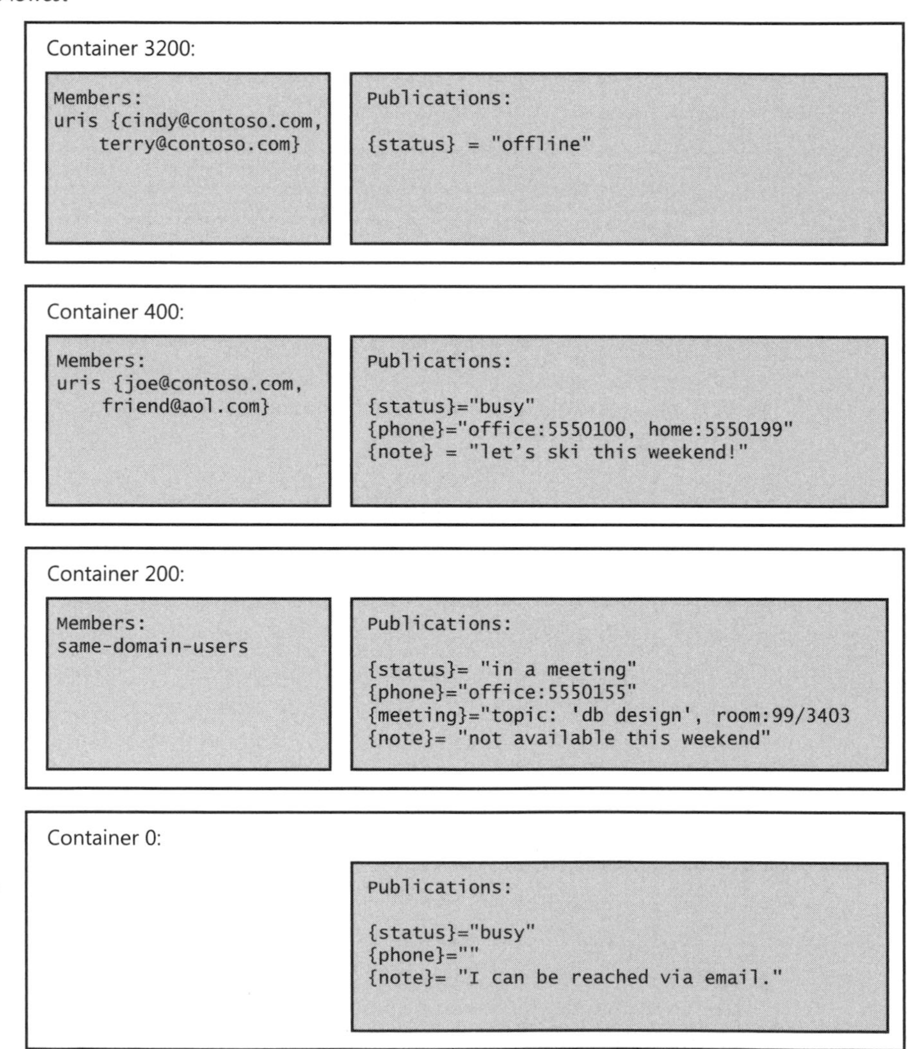

Figure 18-7 Container example

Container 0 shows default publications given to anyone who does not fall into the membership of higher containers. For example, public cloud and federated users are not specified anywhere else, so those users (except for friend@aol.com) get data from this default container.

Container 200 is the set of categories published to people in the same enterprise as the publisher, unless those people are satisfied by a higher container or a lower container with a more restrictive membership (such as being on a URI or domain list). For example, Joe is also in container 400, so he receives the published information for status, phone, and note, which are published to everyone in container 400. He also receives the meeting information published to everyone else in the enterprise.

Container 400 shows a more detailed view of phone and note information for the specific URIs that fall into the personal container. Friend@aol.com receives presence information published in this container instead of the default container.

Container 3200 has been set up to give two people a blocked view of status. The presence status these users see is an offline status. They can still, however, receive categories from other containers. Office Communicator publishes all categories with empty data to the block container to make sure blocked users do not receive any data from other containers.

Examples of Enhanced Presence

The following is an example of the presence state set to online:

```
<categories xmlns="http://schemas.microsoft.com/2006/09/sip
   /categories" uri="sip:joe@contoso.com">
<category name="state" instance="1" publishTime=
   "2007-08-14T06:05:43.783">
<state xsi:type="aggregateState" xmlns:xsi=
   "http://www.w3.org/2001/XMLSchema-instance" xmlns="http://schemas.microsoft.com/2006/09/
sip/state">
   <availability>3500</availability></state>
</category>
</categories>
```

The following is an example of the presence state set to Do Not Disturb and published to the team watchers:

```
<categories xmlns="http://schemas.microsoft.com/2006/09/sip
   /categories" uri="sip:joe@contoso.com">
  <category xmlns="http://schemas.microsoft.com/2006/09/sip
      /categories" name="state" instance="1" publishTime="2007-08-14T21:37:33.723">
    <state xsi:type="aggregateState" xmlns:xsi="http://www.w3.org/2001/XMLSchema-instance"
xmlns="http://schemas.microsoft.com/2006/09/sip/state">
      <availability>6900</availability>
      <activity token="urgent-interruptions-only" />
      <meetingSubject>Test Status</meetingSubject>
      <meetingLocation>TBD</meetingLocation>
    </state>
  </category>
</categories>
```

Understanding Authentication in Office Communications Server 2007

Authentication is the process of determining if someone is in fact who he says he is. There are several different types of authentication technologies. For example, in computer networks, typically authentication is done by the use of logon passwords. However, passwords can be stolen or accidentally revealed. For this reason, there is a more stringent authentication process. For example, digital certificates issued and verified by a certificate authority (CA) as part of a public key infrastructure (PKI) provides stronger authentication on the Internet.

The following sections discuss in more detail authentication technologies–such as Transport Layer Security (TLS), certificates, NTLM and Kerberos–that are used by Office Communications Server.

Using TLS and Certificates

You can configure TLS and certificates within your Office Communications Server 2007 deployment. Using TLS and certificates has the following benefits:

- **Confidentiality** Data that is transferred between clients and servers needs to be encrypted to prevent its exposure over public Internet links.
- **Mutual Server authentication** Servers need a way to verify the identity of each other during communication.

Office Communications Server 2007 uses certificates for the following purposes:

- TLS connections between client and server
- Mutual transport layer security (MTLS) connections between servers
- Federation between partners
- Remote access

> **Note** Certificates are discussed in more detail in Chapter 3, "Infrastructure and Security Considerations."

Overview of TLS

Transport Layer Security (TLS) is a protocol that ensures privacy between communicating applications and their users on the Internet. TLS ensures that no third party can eavesdrop or tamper with any message between the client and the server.

As described in RFC 2246, TLS is composed of two layers: the TLS Record Protocol and the TLS Handshake Protocol. The TLS Record Protocol provides connection security with some encryption method, such as the Data Encryption Standard (DES). The TLS Record Protocol can also be used without encryption. The TLS Handshake Protocol allows the server and client to authenticate each other and to negotiate an encryption algorithm and cryptographic keys before data is exchanged.

Example of a TLS Handshake over the Network

Figure 18-8 is an example of the call flow of a TLS handshake over the network as described in RFC 2246.

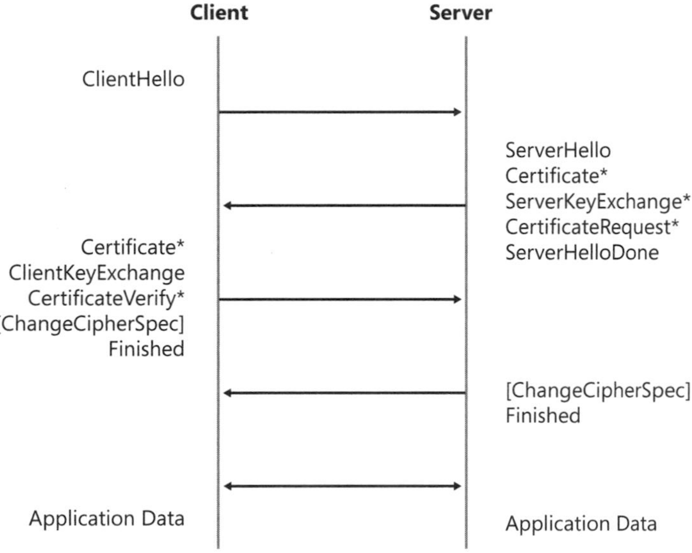

Figure 18-8 Example of a TLS handshake

Note In Figure 18-8 an asterisk (*) indicates optional or situation-dependent messages that are not always sent.

The TLS Handshake Protocol as described in RFC 2246 involves the following steps:

1. Exchange hello messages to agree on algorithms, exchange random values, and check for session resumption.
2. Exchange the necessary cryptographic parameters to allow the client and server to agree on a premaster secret.
3. Exchange certificates and cryptographic information to allow the client and server to authenticate themselves.
4. Generate a master secret from the premaster secret and exchanged random values.
5. Provide security parameters to the record layer.
6. Allow the client and server to verify that their peer has calculated the same security parameters and that the handshake occurred without tampering by an attacker.

The client sends a client hello message to which the server responds with a server hello message. The client hello and server hello are used to establish security enhancement capabilities between client and server. The client hello and server hello establish the following attributes: Protocol Version, Session ID, Cipher Suite, and Compression Method. Additionally, two random values are generated and exchanged: ClientHello.random and ServerHello.random.

The actual key exchange uses up to four messages: the server certificate, server key exchange, client certificate, and client key exchange. New key exchange methods can be created by specifying a format for these messages and defining the use of the messages to allow the client and server to agree upon a shared secret. This secret should be long. Currently defined key exchange methods exchange secrets that range from 48 to 128 bytes in length.

Following the hello messages, the server sends its certificate if it needs to be authenticated. Additionally, a server key exchange message might be sent if it is required. If the server is authenticated, it might request a certificate from the client, depending on the cipher suite selected. The server then sends the server hello done message, which indicates that the hello-message phase of the handshake is complete. The server then waits for a client response. If the server has sent a certificate request message, the client must send the certificate message. The client key exchange message is now sent, and the content of that message depends on the public key algorithm selected between the client hello and the server hello. If the client has sent a certificate with signing ability, a digitally-signed certificate verify message is sent to explicitly verify the certificate.

At this point, a change cipher spec message is sent by the client, and the client copies the pending Cipher Spec into the current Cipher Spec. The client then immediately sends the finished message under the new algorithms, keys, and secrets. In response, the server sends its own change cipher spec message, transfers the pending Cipher Spec to the current Cipher Spec, and sends its finished message under the new Cipher Spec. At this point, the handshake is complete and the client and server can begin to exchange application layer data.

TLS connections are recycled every 24 hours between servers. Similarly, idle TLS connections are recycled every 15 minutes.

Note For more information on how to adjust the cipher suites and the key exchange algorithms, see *http://support.microsoft.com/kb/216482* and *http://support.microsoft.com/kb/245030*.

Overview of NTLM and Kerberos

There are two enterprise user authentication mechanisms supported in Office Communications Server: NTLM and Kerberos. Anonymous conference participants are authenticated using Digest authentication.

NT Lan Manager (NTLM) is a Microsoft authentication protocol that is the successor of Microsoft Lan Manager (LANMAN). NTLM is a challenge/response authentication protocol. NTLM was followed by NTLM v2, the strongest authentication protocol of these three. NTLM v2 is a cryptographically strengthened replacement for NTLM v1.

Kerberos is a considerably more secure authentication protocol than NTLM v2. Kerberos provides mutual authentication as opposed to only client authentication. With NTLM, the client is challenged to provide credentials, but the client could be providing credentials to a bogus server. Kerberos, on the other hand, provides server authentication in addition to the client authentication. Unlike NTLM, Kerberos makes use of a trusted third party, called a Key Distribution Center (KDC), which maintains a database of secret keys. These secret keys are known only by the KDC, as well as by the client and the server. Knowledge of these keys prove the client or server identity.

Where possible, the client should always try to use the most secure authentication mechanism. However, when the client is accessing the server via an external network, the server will offer only NTLM v2 authentication because the client will be unable to assess the internal KDC or Active Directory.

The "Direct from the Source: How NTLM and Kerberos Work in SIP" sidebar describes in more detail the process of authentication using NTLM and Kerberos.

Direct from the Source: How NTLM and Kerberos Work in SIP

At the time a client issues its first request, there are no security associations (SA) between the client and any entities in the network. An SA is an establishment of shared security information between two endpoints to enable them to communicate securely. Typically, the first request a client issues is a REGISTER request as it registers its presence in the network. This registration process requires the establishment of SAs between the client and any proxies in the path that have proxy-level authentication enabled. In addition, the registrar might require authentication as well, establishing an SA between the client and the registrar.

The establishment of an SA is based on authentication using NTLM or Kerberos. Once an SA has been established, subsequent messages are signed using this SA. Multiple SAs might be established at this time, potentially one for each proxy along the signaling path and one for the registrar itself. Each of these SAs falls under the same security domain or realm.

For more information on NTLM and Kerberos requirements, see *http://www.microsoft.com/technet/prodtechnol/WindowsServer2003/Library/IIS/523ae943-5e6a-4200-9103-9808baa00157.mspx?mfr=true.*

Refreshing a Security Association

To avoid resource denial because of an abundance of inactive SAs, SAs that are inactive are dropped by Office Communications Server. *Inactive* means no properly signed message has been received or sent within the time-to-live (TTL) interval. The TTL interval is determined based on the registration refresh interval or any other session timers in the dialogs that traverse the server. A client can avoid resource denial by issuing another request in the defined time period and signing with the SA. Any properly signed request refreshes the SA. The server resets the time-to-live interval of the SA every time it authenticates a request with that SA. An SA lives a maximum of eight hours on the server, after which time a new SA must be established by the client. The SA is valid for the maximum of either the lifetime of the Kerberos ticket (if Kerberos is used to establish the SA) or 8 hours.

Pre-Authentication of a Message

Once an SA has been established between a client and server, the client might want to *pre-authenticate* future requests by inserting a *Proxy-Authorization:* header with credentials matching the SAs for proxies that are likely to be on the signaling path for that request. Pre-authenticating requests avoids one round trip from having the client's first hop server challenge a request, which it would do for a request without any *Proxy-Authorization:* header.

Within a SIP dialog established by an INVITE, SUBSCRIBE, or REGISTER request, the client pre-authenticates the request by inserting the same set of *Proxy-Authorization:* headers for all requests based on the proxies that challenged the first request of that session.

Additionally, the client keeps track of the SA that it established with the first authenticating proxy for REGISTER requests the client sends for registration. When the client receives a "401/407" challenge to a REGISTER request that is not signed by any other proxy (that is, there are no *Proxy-Authentication-Info* headers), the client remembers the SA established with this proxy. In all subsequent requests, the client pre-authenticates those requests by inserting a signature for the request using the SA established at registration time.

Note that in the case where a re-registration traverses a different path (and therefore has a different authenticating proxy), the new SA established with the new authenticating proxy replaces the old SA, and the client from that point on pre-authenticates with the new SA.

Example of NTLM in SIP

During an NTLM SA establishment phase, a three-way handshake occurs between the client and the server, as detailed in the following steps:

1. The client sends a request with no credentials or authentication information. The server responds to that request with a "401" or "407" response, indicating that it supports NTLM and Kerberos and requires authentication.

2. The client re-issues the request, indicating its preference for NTLM authentication. The server responds with an appropriate challenge in a "401" or "407" response.
3. The client re-issues the request with a response to the server's challenge. The server processes the request and responds, including its signature in the response.
4. The SA is now established on both the client and server, and subsequent messages between the client and server are signed.

The call flow shown in Figure 18-9 on the next page outlines how the NTLM authentication mechanism works for a local area network (LAN) user. At this point in time, the client discovers its outbound proxy and initializes a security context with it.

The process is detailed in the following steps:

1. Ned's client selects a home server at random from a list of servers attained from a DNS SRV query.
2. Ned's client sends a REGISTER request with no credentials (that is, no *Proxy-Authorization:* header) to the outbound server it selected.

```
REGISTER sip:registrar.northwind.com SIP/2.0
Via: SIP/2.0/TLS ned1.northwind.com;branch=z9hG4bK7
From: "Ned" <sip:ned@northwind.com>;tag=354354535;epid=6534555
To: "Ned" <sip:ned@northwind.com>
Call-ID: 123213@ned1.northwind.com
CSeq: 12345 REGISTER
Max-Forwards: 70
User-Agent: Windows RTC/1.1.2600
Contact: "Ned" <sip:ned@ned1.northwind.com>
Content-Length: 0
```

   The *epid* parameter on the *From:* header uniquely identifies this particular endpoint for the user. The server uses this value in subsequent messages to determine the SA with which to sign the message.

3. Authentication is enabled at the outbound server, and it challenges Ned's client. The server indicates support for NTLM and Kerberos in the challenge.

```
SIP/2.0 407 Proxy Authentication Required
Via: SIP/2.0/TLS ned1.northwind.com;branch=z9hG4bK7
From: "Ned" <sip:ned@northwind.com>;tag=354354535;epid=6534555
To: "Ned" <sip:ned@northwind.com>;tag=5564566
Call-ID: 123213@ned1.northwind.com
CSeq: 12345 REGISTER
Date: Sat, 13 Nov 2010 23:29:00 GMT
Proxy-Authenticate: Kerberos realm="SIP Communications Service",
   targetname="sip/hs1.northwind.com", qop="auth"
Proxy-Authenticate: NTLM realm="SIP Communications Service",
targetname="hs1.northwind.com", qop="auth"
Content-Length: 0
```

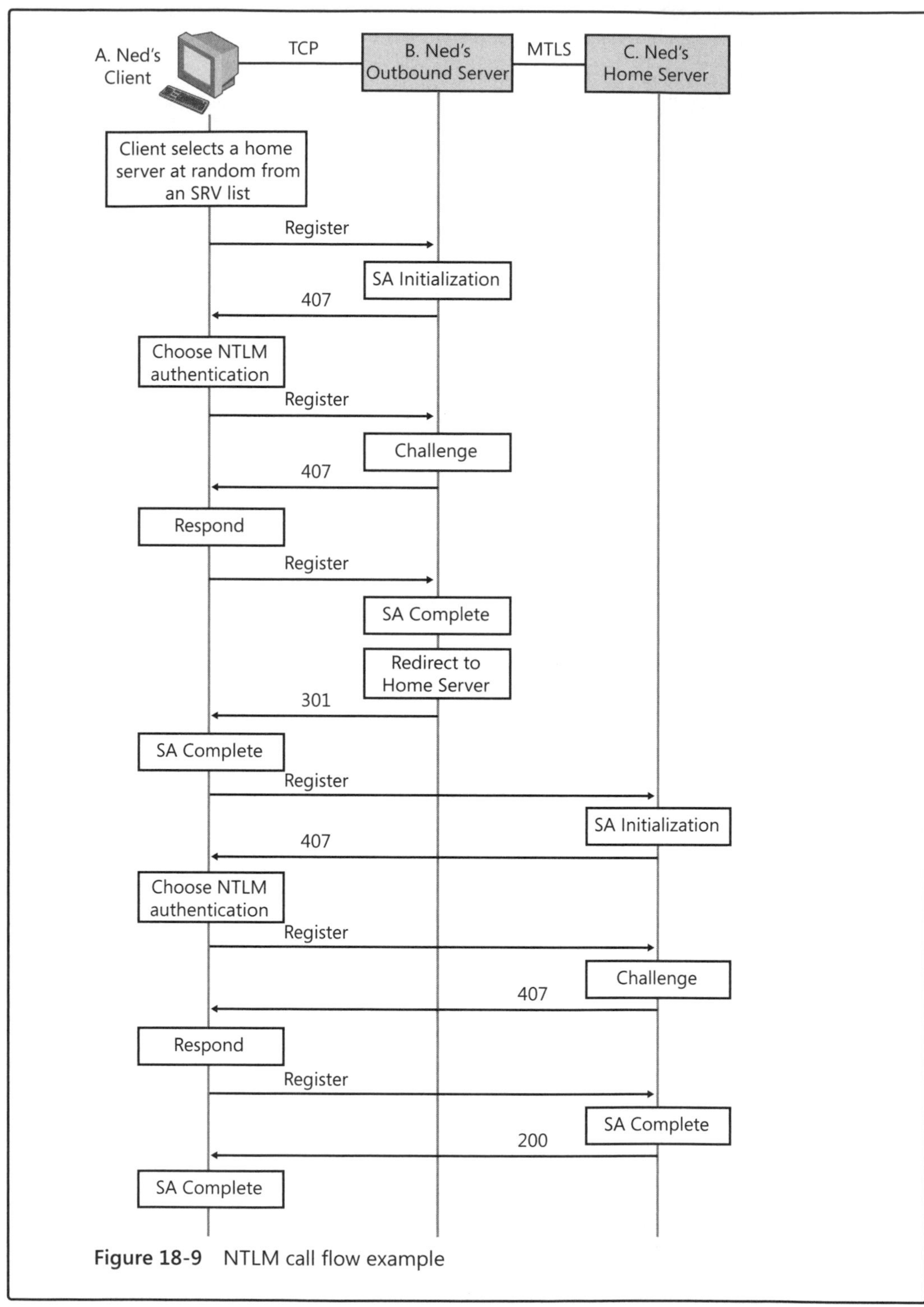

Figure 18-9 NTLM call flow example

The *targetname* parameter carries the FQDN for this proxy for NTLM and the service principal name (SPN) of the proxy for Kerberos. The actual contents of this parameter must be meaningful for this proxy, but they are opaque to other proxies and the client. It is merely a unique string for correlation of the message header to an SA. Three *Proxy-Authenticate:* headers are present, indicating the server's ability to do either Kerberos or NTLM authentication.

The proxy inserts a *Date:* header in the "407" challenge to allow the client to detect clock skew between the client and server. Both NTLMv2 and Kerberos V5 require synchronization of the client and server clocks. Clock skew can cause authentication to fail even with valid credentials. The presence of the *Date:* header allows the client to log this condition and the administrator to correct the deviation.

4. The client re-issues the REGISTER request, indicating support for NTLM authentication.

```
REGISTER sip:registrar.northwind.com SIP/2.0
Via: SIP/2.0/TLS ned1.northwind.com;branch=z9hG4bK8
From: "Ned" <sip:ned@northwind.com>;tag=354354535;epid=6534555
To: "Ned" <sip:ned@northwind.com>
Call-ID: 123213@ned1.northwind.com
CSeq: 12346 REGISTER
Max-Forwards: 70
User-Agent: Windows RTC/1.1.2600
Proxy-Authorization: NTLM realm="SIP Communications Service",
   targetname="hs1.northwind.com",qop="auth",gssapi-data=""
Contact: "Ned" <sip:ned@ned1.northwind.com>
Content-Length: 0
```

The *Cseq* number has been incremented. The *Call-ID* and *epid* remain the same.

The *targetname* parameter echoes the value of the *targetname* parameter in the previous *Proxy-Authenticate:* header. The empty *gssapi-data* parameter indicates that no credentials (password) are being sent in this header. The choice of NTLM authentication is indicated by the scheme (*NTLM*) shown as the first token in the header.

5. The outbound server responds with a "407" response containing a *Proxy-Authenticate:* header, which includes the NTLM challenge.

```
SIP/2.0 407 Proxy Authentication Required
Via: SIP/2.0/TLS ned1.northwind.com;branch=z9hG4bK8
From: "Ned" <sip:ned@northwind.com>;tag=354354535;epid=6534555
To: "Ned" <sip:ned@northwind.com>;tag=5564566
Call-ID: 123213@ned1.northwind.com
CSeq: 12346 REGISTER
Date: Sat, 13 Nov 2010 23:29:00 GMT
Proxy-Authenticate: NTLM realm="SIP Communications Service",
   targetname="hs1.northwind.com", qop="auth", gssapi-data
="345435acdecbba",opaque="ACDC123"
Content-Length: 0
```

The *gssapi-data* parameter carries the challenge. The *opaque* parameter serves as an index to the (incomplete) SA state on the proxy.

6. Ned's client re-issues the REGISTER request with a response to the outbound server's challenge.

```
REGISTER sip:registrar.northwind.com SIP/2.0
Via: SIP/2.0/TLS ned1.northwind.com;branch=z9hG4bK9
From: "Ned" <sip:ned@northwind.com>;tag=354354535;epid=6534555
To: "Ned" <sip:ned@northwind.com>
Call-ID: 123213@ned1.northwind.com
CSeq: 12347 REGISTER
Max-Forwards: 70
User-Agent: Windows RTC/1.1.2600
Proxy-Authorization: NTLM realm="SIP Communications Service",
   targetname="hs1.northwind.com",qop="auth",
gssapi-data="34fcdf9345345",opaque="ACDC123"
Contact: "Ned" <sip:ned@ned1.northwind.com>
Content-Length: 0
```

The *Cseq* number has been incremented. The *Call-ID* and *epid* remain the same. The *gssapi-data* parameter carries the client's response to the challenge. The *opaque* parameter is echoed from the previous challenge.

7. Upon receipt of the REGISTER request, the outbound server authenticates the user with the information in the *Proxy-Authorization:* header. Authentication succeeds, and a security association is created in the outbound server for Ned's client.

   The outbound server then redirects the REGISTER request to point the client at the appropriate home server for this user. The redirect response is signed using the newly established SA between the client and this proxy.

```
SIP/2.0 301 Moved Permanently
Via: SIP/2.0/TLS ned1.northwind.com;branch=z9hG4bK9
From: "Ned" <sip:ned@northwind.com>;tag=354354535;epid=6534555
To: "Ned" <sip:ned@northwind.com>
Call-ID: 123213@ned1.northwind.com
CSeq: 12347 REGISTER
Proxy-Authenticate-Info: NTLM realm="SIP Communications Service",
   targetname="hs1.northwind.com", qop="auth", opaque="ACDC123",
srand="3453453", snum=1, rspauth="23423acfdee2"
Contact: <sip:hs2.northwind.com>
Content-Length: 0
```

The *Proxy-Authenticate-Info:* header carries the signature for this SIP message. The *snum* is set to 1, as this is the first message signed with the newly established SA. The *srand* parameter contains the (random) SALT value used by the server to generate the signature.

8. The client receives the redirect response, verifies the signature by using the now complete SA for the outbound proxy, and it re-issues the REGISTER request to its proper home server.

```
REGISTER sip:hs2.northwind.com SIP/2.0
Via: SIP/2.0/TLS ned1.northwind.com;branch=z9hG4bKa
From: "Ned" <sip:ned@northwind.com>;tag=354354535;epid=6534555
To: "Ned" <sip:ned@northwind.com>
Call-ID: 123213@ned1.northwind.com
CSeq: 12348 REGISTER
Max-Forwards: 70
User-Agent: Windows RTC/1.1.2600
Contact: "Ned" <sip:ned@ned1.northwind.com>
Content-Length: 0
```

The client replaces its current outbound proxy with the proxy indicated in the *Contact:* header of the "301" response. The REGISTER request is sent to this new outbound proxy (the user's true home server). Because no SA exists yet with this new outbound proxy, no *Proxy-Authenticate:* header is present in the request.

9. Ned's home server receives the REGISTER request and issues a challenge indicating support for NTLM and Kerberos authentication.

```
SIP/2.0 407 Proxy Authentication Required
Via: SIP/2.0/TLS ned1.northwind.com;branch=z9hG4bKa
From: "Ned" <sip:ned@northwind.com>;tag=354354535;epid=6534555
To: "Ned" <sip:ned@northwind.com>;tag=8823488
Call-ID: 123213@ned1.northwind.com
CSeq: 12348 REGISTER
Date: Sat, 13 Nov 2010 23:29:00 GMT
Proxy-Authenticate: Kerberos realm="Northwind RTC Service
   Provider", targetname="hs2.northwind.com", qop="auth"
Proxy-Authenticate: NTLM realm="SIP Communications Service",
   targetname="hs2.northwind.com", qop="auth"
Content-Length: 0
```

The *targetname* parameter contains the FQDN for Ned's home server. The two *Proxy-Authenticate:* headers indicate support for Kerberos and NTLM, respectively. The *Realm* is the same as for HS1 because they fall under the same protection space. This means the client will use the same credentials in responding to HS2's challenge.

10. Ned's client receives the challenge, selects NTLM authentication, and re-issues the REGISTER request to his home server.

```
REGISTER sip:hs2.northwind.com SIP/2.0
Via: SIP/2.0/TLS ned1.northwind.com;branch=z9hG4bKb
From: "Ned" <sip:ned@northwind.com>;tag=354354535;epid=6534555
To: "Ned" <sip:ned@northwind.com>
Call-ID: 123213@ned1.northwind.com
CSeq: 12349 REGISTER
Max-Forwards: 70
User-Agent: Windows RTC/1.1.2600
Proxy-Authorization: NTLM realm="SIP Communications Service",
   targetname="hs2.northwind.com",qop="auth",gssapi-data=""
Contact: "Ned" <sip:ned@ned1.northwind.com>
Content-Length: 0
```

The *Cseq:* number is incremented. The *Call-ID* and *epid* remain the same. The *Proxy-Authorization:* header indicates support for NTLM authentication.

11. Ned's home server receives the REGISTER request and issues an appropriate NTLM challenge.

```
SIP/2.0 407 Proxy Authentication Required
Via: SIP/2.0/TLS ned1.northwind.com;branch=z9hG4bKb
From: "Ned" <sip:ned@northwind.com>;tag=354354535;epid=6534555
To: "Ned" <sip:ned@northwind.com>;tag=8823488
Call-ID: 123213@ned1.northwind.com
CSeq: 12349 REGISTER
Date: Sat, 13 Nov 2010 23:29:00 GMT
Proxy-Authenticate: NTLM realm="SIP Communications Service",
   targetname="hs2.northwind.com", qop="auth", opaque="CDEF1245",
gssapi-data="dfd345435d"
Content-Length: 0
```

The *gssapi-data* parameter contains the NTLM challenge. The *opaque* parameter identifies the (incomplete) SA on Ned's home server.

12. Ned's client responds to the challenge from Ned's home server by re-issuing the REGISTER request.

```
REGISTER sip:hs2.northwind.com SIP/2.0
Via: SIP/2.0/TLS ned1.northwind.com;branch=z9hG4bKc
From: "Ned" <sip:ned@northwind.com>;tag=354354535;epid=6534555
To: "Ned" <sip:ned@northwind.com>
Call-ID: 123213@ned1.northwind.com
CSeq: 12350 REGISTER
Max-Forwards: 70
User-Agent: Windows RTC/1.1.2600
Proxy-Authorization: NTLM realm="SIP Communications Service",
   targetname="hs2.northwind.com",qop="auth",
gssapi-data="8234934234", opaque="CDEF1245"
Contact: "Ned" <sip:ned@ned1.northwind.com>
Content-Length: 0
```

The *CSeq* number is incremented. The *Call-ID* remains the same. The *opaque* parameter is echoed from the server's challenge. The *gssapi-data* parameter carries the response to the server's challenge.

13. Ned's home server receives the REGISTER request, verifies the response to its challenge, and processes the REGISTER request. The SA between Ned's home server and Ned's client is now complete. The server responds to the REGISTER request and signs the response using the newly completed SA. The *epid* parameter from the *From:* header is saved as part of the registration information for Ned. This value will be inserted in the *To:* header of subsequent requests that are forwarded to Ned via his home server (registrar).

```
SIP/2.0 200 OK
Via: SIP/2.0/TLS ned1.northwind.com;branch=z9hG4bKc
From: "Ned" <sip:ned@northwind.com>;tag=354354535;epid=6534555
To: "Ned" <sip:ned@northwind.com>;tag=8823488
Call-ID: 123213@ned1.northwind.com
CSeq: 12350 REGISTER
Expires: 3600
Proxy-Authentication-Info: NTLM realm="SIP Communications Service",
   targetname="hs2.northwind.com", qop="auth", opaque="CDEF1245",
   rspauth="fefeacdd", srand=98984345, snum=1
Contact: "Ned" <sip:ned@ned1.northwind.com>
Content-Length: 0
```

The *epid* parameter on the *From:* header is used by the server to determine how to sign this response (find the SA). The signature for this response is carried in the *rspauth* parameter of the *Proxy-Authentication-Info:* header.

Example of Kerberos in SIP

During a Kerberos SA establishment phase, a two-way handshake occurs between the client and the server, as detailed in the following steps:

1. The client sends a request with no credential or authentication information. The server responds to that request with a "401" or "407" response, indicating that it supports NTLM and Kerberos and requires authentication.
2. The client requests a Kerberos ticket for the server and reissues the request with this encoded Kerberos ticket information.
3. The server processes the request and responds, including its signature in the response.
4. The SA is now established on both the client and server, and subsequent messages between the client and server are signed.

The fundamental difference between NTLM and Kerberos is the way in which the client answers a challenge from the server. With Kerberos, the client first acquires a Kerberos ticket from the KDC (on an Active Directory domain controller) for the specific server that is issuing the challenge. The server is identified by a SPN containing a fully qualified domain name (FQDN).

If the client is configured to talk to its local outbound proxy via TLS, the client allows any SPN for the very first challenge it receives. Otherwise, the client requires that the SPN for the very first challenge it receives match *sip/<FQDN of local outbound proxy>*. The intention is to require either TLS connectivity to the service provider or that the local outbound proxy authenticates the client. The SPN for a challenge is carried in the *targetname* parameter in the *Proxy-Authenticate:* header of the challenge.

In the event the client receives a challenge with an SPN of any other form, particularly one that has a service other than "sip", the client ignores the challenge (response) and, as necessary, fails the request if no other final response is received. This action is taken to prevent an attacker from obtaining Kerberos tickets from the client for any other service besides Office Communications Server.

The SPN of the server is associated with the service account under which the Office Communications Server runs. This association is managed in Active Directory and initialized at the time of installation of the server. Any changes in either the FQDN or the service account of the server requires the administrator to re-establish this association of SPN to server. Re-establishing the association is a manual process that the administrator must perform after installation.

Note The lifetime of the SA established using Kerberos is set to 8 hours (the same as for NTLM) regardless of the lifetime of the Kerberos ticket. If the Kerberos ticket expires before 8 hours, the underlying Security Support Provider Interface (SSPI) calls to verify or create a signature for a message will fail and, if possible, the server will challenge the request to establish a new SA.

The call flow shown in Figure 18-10 outlines how the Kerberos authentication mechanism works.

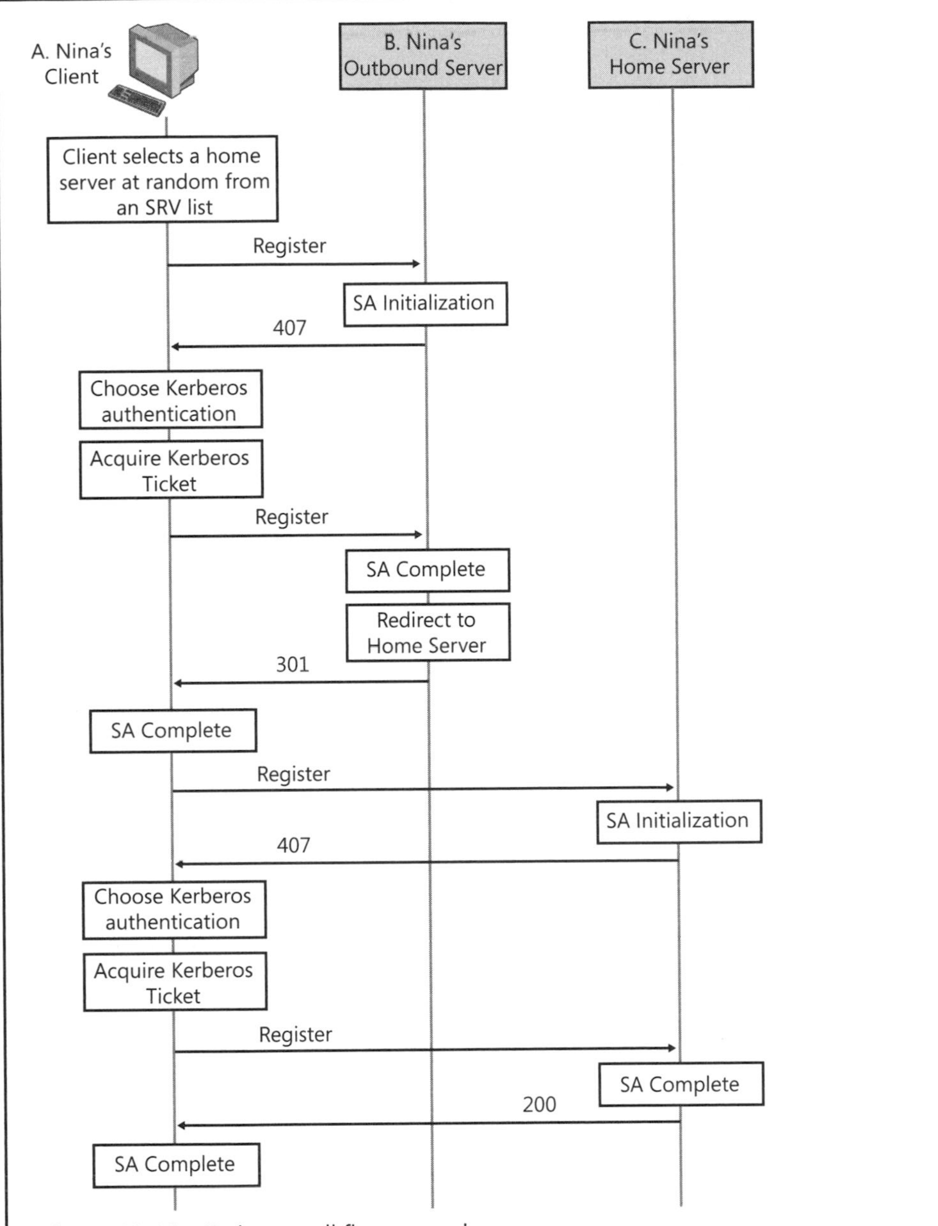

Figure 18-10 Kerberos call flow example

The process is detailed in the following steps:

1. Nina's client selects a home server at random from a list of servers attained from a DNS SRV query.
2. Nina's client sends a REGISTER request with no credentials (that is, no *Proxy-Authorization:* header) to the outbound server it selected.

```
REGISTER sip:registrar.northwind.com SIP/2.0
Via: SIP/2.0/TLS ned1.northwind.com;branch=z9hG4bK7
From: "Nina" <sip:nina@northwind.com>;tag=354354535;epid=6534555
To: "Nina" <sip:nina@northwind.com>
Call-ID: 123213@nina1.northwind.com
CSeq: 12345 REGISTER
Max-Forwards: 70
User-Agent: Windows RTC/1.1.2600
Contact: "Nina" <sip:nina@nina1.northwind.com>
Content-Length: 0
```

The *epid* parameter on the *From:* header uniquely identifies this particular endpoint for the user. The server uses this value in subsequent messages to determine the SA with which to sign the message.

3. Authentication is enabled at the outbound server, and it challenges Nina's client. The server indicates support for NTLM and Kerberos in the challenge.

```
SIP/2.0 407 Proxy Authentication Required
Via: SIP/2.0/TLS nina1.northwind.com;branch=z9hG4bK7
From: "Nina" <sip:nina@northwind.com>;tag=354354535;epid=6534555
To: "Nina" <sip:nina@northwind.com>;tag=5564566
Call-ID: 123213@nina1.northwind.com
CSeq: 12345 REGISTER
Date: Sat, 13 Nov 2010 23:29:00 GMT
Proxy-Authenticate: Kerberos realm="SIP Communications Service",
   targetname="sip/hs1.northwind.com", qop="auth"
Proxy-Authenticate: NTLM realm="Northwind RTC Service Provider",
   targetname="hs1.northwind.com", qop="auth"
Content-Length: 0
```

The *targetname* parameter carries the SPN for this proxy for Kerberos and the FQDN of the proxy for NTLM. The actual contents of this parameter must be meaningful for this proxy, but they are opaque to other proxies and the client. It is merely a unique string for correlation of the message header to an SA. Two *Proxy-Authenticate:* headers are present, indicating the server's ability to do either Kerberos or NTLM authentication.

The proxy inserts a *Date:* header in the "407" challenge to allow the client to detect clock skew between the client and server. Both NTLMv2 and Kerberos V5 require synchronization of the client and server clocks. Clock skew can cause authentication to fail even with valid credentials. The presence of the *Date:* header allows the client to log this condition and the administrator to correct the deviation.

4. The client acquires a Kerberos ticket for the server indicated in the *targetname* of the Kerberos *Proxy-Authenticate:* header. The client re-issues the request with a *Proxy-Authorization:* header containing the encoded Kerberos ticket.

```
REGISTER sip:registrar.northwind.com SIP/2.0
Via: SIP/2.0/TLS nina1.northwind.com;branch=z9hG4bK9
From: "Nina" <sip:nina@northwind.com>;tag=354354535;epid=6534555
To: "Nina" <sip:nina@northwind.com>
Call-ID: 123213@nina1.northwind.com
CSeq: 12346 REGISTER
Max-Forwards: 70
User-Agent: Windows RTC/1.1.2600
Proxy-Authorization: Kerberos realm="SIP Communications Service",
   targetname="sip/hs1.northwind.com",qop="auth",
gssapi-data="34fcdf9345345"
Contact: "Ned" <sip:ned@ned1.northwind.com>
Content-Length: 0
```

The *Cseq* number has been incremented. The *Call-ID* and *epid* remain the same.

The *targetname* parameter echoes the value of the *targetname* parameter in the previous *Proxy-Authenticate:* header. The *gssapi-data* parameter contains the Kerberos ticket information. The choice of Kerberos authentication is indicated by the scheme (*Kerberos*) as the first token in the header.

5. Upon reception of the REGISTER request, the outbound server authenticates the user with the information in the *Proxy-Authorization:* header. Authentication succeeds, and a security association is created in the outbound server for Nina's client.

   The outbound server then redirects the REGISTER request to point the client at the appropriate home server for this user. The redirect response is signed using the newly established SA between the client and this proxy.

```
SIP/2.0 301 Moved Permanently
Via: SIP/2.0/TLS nina1.northwind.com;branch=z9hG4bK9
From: "Nina" <sip:nina@northwind.com>;tag=354354535;epid=6534555
To: "Nina" <sip:nina@northwind.com>
Call-ID: 123213@nina1.northwind.com
CSeq: 12346 REGISTER
Proxy-Authenticate-Info: Kerberos realm="SIP Communications Service",
   targetname="sip/hs1.northwind.com", qop="auth", opaque="ACDC123",
   srand="3453453", snum=1, rspauth="23423acfdee2"
Contact: <sip:hs2.northwind.com>
Content-Length: 0
```

   The *Proxy-Authenticate-Info:* header carries the signature for this SIP message. The *snum* is set to 1, as this is the first message signed with the newly established SA. The *srand* parameter contains the (random) SALT value used by the server to generate the signature. The *opaque* parameter contains a unique token for this newly established SA.

6. The client receives the redirect response, verifies the signature using the now complete SA for the outbound proxy, and re-issues the REGISTER request to its proper home server.

```
REGISTER sip:hs2.northwind.com SIP/2.0
Via: SIP/2.0/TLS nina1.northwind.com;branch=z9hG4bKa
From: "Nina" <sip:nina@northwind.com>;tag=354354535;epid=6534555
To: "Nina" <sip:nina@northwind.com>
Call-ID: 123213@nina1.northwind.com
CSeq: 12347 REGISTER
Max-Forwards: 70
User-Agent: Windows RTC/1.1.2600
Contact: "Nina" <sip:nina@nina1.northwind.com>
Content-Length: 0
```

The client replaces its current outbound proxy with the proxy indicated in the *Contact:* header of the "301" response. The REGISTER request is sent to this new outbound proxy (the user's true home server). Because no SA exists yet with this new outbound proxy, no *Proxy-Authorization:* header is present in the request.

7. Nina's home server receives the REGISTER request and issues a challenge indicating support for NTLM and Kerberos.

```
SIP/2.0 407 Proxy Authentication Required
Via: SIP/2.0/TLS nina1.northwind.com;branch=z9hG4bKa
From: "Nina" <sip:nina@northwind.com>;tag=354354535;epid=6534555
To: "Nina" <sip:nina@northwind.com>;tag=8823488
Call-ID: 123213@nina1.northwind.com
CSeq: 12347 REGISTER
Date: Sat, 13 Nov 2010 23:29:00 GMT
Proxy-Authenticate: Kerberos realm="SIP Communications Service",
   targetname="sip/hs2.northwind.com", qop="auth"
Proxy-Authenticate: NTLM realm="Northwind RTC Service Provider",
   targetname="hs2.northwind.com", qop="auth"
Content-Length: 0
```

The *targetname* parameter for Kerberos contains the SPN for Nina's home server. The two *Proxy-Authenticate:* headers indicate support for Kerberos and NTLM, respectively. The *Realm* is the same as for HS1 because they fall under the same protection space. This means the client will use the same credentials in responding to HS2's challenge.

8. Nina's client receives the challenge, selects Kerberos authentication, and re-issues the REGISTER request to her home server. The client acquires a Kerberos ticket for HS2 and includes this information in the *gssapi-data* parameter of the *Proxy-Authorization:* header.

```
REGISTER sip:hs2.northwind.com SIP/2.0
Via: SIP/2.0/TLS nina1.northwind.com;branch=z9hG4bKc
From: "Nina" <sip:nina@northwind.com>;tag=354354535;epid=6534555
To: "Nina" <sip:nina@northwind.com>
Call-ID: 123213@nina1.northwind.com
CSeq: 12348 REGISTER
Max-Forwards: 70
User-Agent: Windows RTC/1.1.2600
Proxy-Authorization: Kerberos realm="SIP Communications Service",
   targetname="sip/hs2.northwind.com",qop="auth",
gssapi-data="8234934234", opaque="CDEF1245"
Contact: "Ned" <sip:ned@ned1.northwind.com>
Content-Length: 0
```

The *Cseq:* number is incremented. The *Call-ID* and *epid* remain the same. The *Proxy-Authorization:* header indicates support for Kerberos authentication.

9. Nina's home server receives the REGISTER request, verifies the Kerberos ticket, and processes the REGISTER request. The SA between Nina's home server and Nina's client is now complete. The server responds to the REGISTER request and signs the response using the newly completed SA. The *epid* parameter from the *From:* header is saved as part of the registration information for Nina. This value will be inserted in the *To:* header of subsequent requests that are forwarded to Nina via her home server (registrar).

```
SIP/2.0 200 OK
Via: SIP/2.0/TLS nina1.northwind.com;branch=z9hG4bKc
From: "Nina" <sip:nina@northwind.com>;tag=354354535;epid=6534555
To: "Nina" <sip:nina@northwind.com>;tag=8823488
Call-ID: 123213@nina1.northwind.com
CSeq: 12348 REGISTER
Expires: 3600
Proxy-Authentication-Info: Kerberos realm="SIP Communications
   Service", targetname="sip/hs2.northwind.com", qop="auth",
opaque="CDEF1245", rspauth="fefeacdd", srand=98984345, snum=1
Contact: "Nina" <sip:nina@nina1.northwind.com>
Content-Length: 0
```

The *epid* parameter on the *From:* header is used by the server to determine how to sign this response (that is, to find the SA). The signature for this response is carried in the *rspauth* parameter of the *Proxy-Authentication-Info:* header. The *opaque* parameter indicates the newly established SA. Because this is the first signed message from HS2 to the client, the *snum* parameter is set to 1.

The server generally challenges with a "407 Proxy Authentication Required" response. The headers associated with proxy authentication are *Proxy-Authenticate*, *Proxy-Authentication-Info*, and *Proxy-Authorization*. The format and content of these headers correspond to the *WWW-Authenticate*, *Authentication-Info*, and *Authorization* headers, respectively, which are used in conjunction with a "401 Unauthorized" response. Either a "401" or "407" response achieves the goals of this document.

The server inserts a *Date:* header into all "407" responses to the client so that the client can detect clock skew, which can cause NTLMv2 and Kerberos V5 authentication to fail.

The *Proxy-Authenticate:* header is used to signal that a proxy requires authentication and to carry a challenge (from a proxy) during the SA initialization phase. The server initially inserts one *Proxy-Authenticate:* header for every authentication method it supports (for example, NTLM, Kerberos, and so on). In the event the request has been forked, it is also possible to receive a "407" response containing a list of *Proxy-Authenticate:* headers–one for each proxy that requested authentication.

The *Proxy-Authorization:* header is used to carry the client's response to a challenge from an Office Communications Server (proxy). It is also used by a client in signing a request or response. There might be more than one *Proxy-Authorization:* header in a given request/response–one for each proxy with which the client has an SA established on this signaling path.

The *Proxy-Authentication-Info* header is used to carry the signature created by the Office Communications Server for a request or response once an SA has been established with the client.

The protocol information used during the SA establishment phase differs from the information used once an SA has been established. During the establishment phase, the *gssapi-data* parameter carries the bulk of the credentials information. The *realm* parameter provides additional context information. Once an SA has been established, the *srand*, *crand*, *cnum*, *snum*, and *opaque* parameters are used in the signing of requests and responses. Those signatures are carried in the *response* and *rspauth* parameters.

–Sean Olson
Principal Group Program Manager, OCS Server

Troubleshooting Sign-in Problems

In the event that problems occur while signing into Office Communications Server 2007, a "401" response might be sent back even though users have provided valid sign-in credentials. This can occur if you have configured Office Communications Server 2007 to use Kerberos authentication and one of the following is true:

- NetBIOS is disabled on the computer.
- The computer is running Microsoft Windows XP Home Edition.

- The computer is configured to run behind an Internet Connection Sharing device or behind another Universal Plug and Play (UPnP) Network Address Translation (NAT) device.
- The computer is not joined to the same domain as the Office Communications Server computer.
- The account is disabled, or time-based restrictions apply to the account login.

In certain Office Communications Server topologies, you cannot successfully sign in by entering your credentials in the user principal name (UPN) format (username@example.com). Additionally, you might have to specify the FQDN together with your user name when you enter it in Universal Naming Convention (UNC) format to successfully sign in. For example, when you type your user name information into a dialog box, you might have to use the following format to successfully sign in:

```
domain.example.com\username
```

In this format, *domain.example.com* is the FQDN of your domain, and *username* is your user name. If entering the FQDN of your domain does not work, try enabling NTLM instead of Kerberos.

Enabling NTLM v2

NTLM version 1 was used in legacy operating systems such as Windows NT and Windows 98. Recent improvements in computer hardware and software algorithms have made these protocols vulnerable to widely published attacks for obtaining user passwords. In its ongoing efforts to deliver more secure products to its customers, Microsoft has developed an enhancement, called NTLM version 2, that significantly improves both the authentication and session security mechanisms. You can enable NTLM version 2 on these legacy operating systems, thereby preventing the weaker NTLM version 1 from being used. For more information on how to enable NTLM version 2, see *http://support.microsoft.com/kb/239869*.

Security Features of Office Communications Server 2007

As with any network, Office Communications Server should be secured against unauthorized access or use from within and from outside the infrastructure. Intruders use a number of methods to compromise a system, including the following ones:

- **Trojan horses** Sending harmful programs or files into a network, where they are launched
- **SPIM** Unsolicited, commercial instant messaging, or spam over IM
- **Sniffing/Snooping** Unauthorized interception of communications or data
- **Spoofing** Hijacking an IP address from outside the network

- **Man-in-the-middle (MITM) attack** All communications intercepted by an attacker before they arrive at the intended recipient; attacker then forwards fake communications.
- **Viruses and worms**

The following sections discuss in more detail some of the security features that are used to help make the Office Communications Server deployment more secure.

Federation Domain Validation

Office Communications Server uses DNS-SRV resolution to locate the Access Edge Server of another federated partner for IM conversations. For a secure connection to take place, the name of the DNS-SRV domain must match the server name on the certificate issued by a public certification authority (located in the trusted root store in Windows Server 2003). This organization-to-organization federation using DNS-SRV resolution to identify the Access Edge Server for each partner is called *enhanced federation*. Network administrators can limit enhanced federation to specified external domains or extend it to any and all domains.

For additional security, you can establish a policy to disable federation for all users who do not require it.

Remote User Access

Remote user access allows users to securely access corporate resources by establishing an encrypted tunnel across the Internet. However, remote-access connectivity is a common point of entry for such threats as worms, viruses, spyware, hacking, data theft, and application abuse. As a result, remote access can lead to the following network threats:

- Allows remote users to bring malware into the main office network, causing virus outbreaks that infect other users and network servers.
- Enables theft of sensitive information, such as downloaded customer data.
- Enables hackers to hijack remote-access sessions, providing hackers access to the network as if they were legitimate users.

The best way possible to avoid such threats is to establish a policy to disable remote user access to all users who do not require it.

Managing Access Rights

Access control lists (ACLs) contain access control entries (ACEs) that grant individual (or group) access rights to such things as programs, processes, files, and contact data. In Office Communications Server, you can use Active Directory to change the ACLs on each domain rather than having to weed through dozens of lists spread across multiple domains. Thus, tracking and auditing is simplified because you can roll back an action by group membership, delete a group or certain members of the group, or perform a simple query for auditing purposes.

Privacy settings help ensure that public cloud watchers from MSN, AOL, and Yahoo! cannot see secure information about an Office Communications Server user, unless he or she elects to grant access to them. Items such as text notes, calendar free/busy information, or mobile phone numbers can now be displayed to users outside the enterprise. For standard federation (with other enterprises), basic status information is available by default. Enhanced presence attributes, such as phone numbers and calendar information, are not available by default.

However, because each user has the ability to make administrative decisions about user information, anything or anyone that has the user's credentials can modify the user's settings. So exercise caution over what personal information is shared. Office Communications Server 2007 uses containers and categories to manage this information, which in turn is controlled by ACLs.

Allowing URLs and File Transfers

Similar to SPAM for e-mail, Spam over Instant Messaging (SPIM) is an attack on instant messaging. With SPIM, the user is vulnerable to IM worms and unsolicited IM advertisements. In addition, a URL can be linked to a phishing Web site. A phishing Web site is typically hosted to lure a user into typing in information (such as credit card information), with the information going to a malicious user instead of a valid Web site.

In addition, users can potentially transfer dangerous file types, such as executables, that when run on one's system can cause irreparable damage.

Office Communications Server ships with Intelligent Instant Message Filter (IM Filter) and installs it by default. IM Filter helps prevent such things as Trojan horses and SPIM because it blocks messages that contain spurious URLs or attempts by intruders to initiate file transfers.

TLS and MTLS for Client and Server Message Integrity

Office Communicator and Office Communicator Servers use certificates to establish TLS and MTLS, as previously described. The use of M/TLS is very important to the integrity and confidentiality of the messages sent between clients and servers. Use of M/TLS greatly reduces the potential that an attacker will be able to intercept messages or establish a man in the middle attack by inserting himself between server and server or server and client.

By inserting in the middle of the authenticated channel established by M/TLS, the integrity of the message is broken because the certificates used to establish the M/TLS communication cannot be spoofed or faked. In addition, if the mutual authentication has taken place, a re-authentication will need to happen, causing an immediate failure as the attacker tries to use a false, stolen, or duplicate certificate that cannot be verified by the server or client.

Spoofing is mitigated by use of certificates to create M/TLS authentication. Because the certificates must be created and verified by trusted Certificate Authorities and bound to fully qualified domain names that are managed in DNS, spoofing a server or client is very difficult if not impossible.

Summary

This chapter provided a technical overview of six major areas of Office Communications Server 2007 technology: SIP, SIP routing, GRUU, enhanced presence, authentication, and security. These fundamental areas are necessary for establishing secure communications in your deployment. Now that you have read this chapter, you should have a better understanding of the main SIP verbs that are used to establish communication sessions. You should also now know what these call flows looks like, and you should be familiar with authentication technologies used when signing into Office Communications Server 2007, the different call flows for these technologies, and the routing logic used by Office Communications Server 2007 to route these main SIP requests inside and outside the enterprise. Finally, the chapter introduced you to some security concepts and some actions you can take to protect your environment. There are additional resources you can leverage to gain a deeper understanding of each of these areas, and this information is provided in the next section.

Additional Resources

For product documentation, community tools, frequently asked questions (FAQs), discussion groups, and pointers to up-to-date information on product and community events, see the Office Communications Server Home Page at *http://www.microsoft.com/livecomm/*. The following resources contain additional information and tools related to this chapter:

- For more information on NTLM and Kerberos requirements, see *http://www.microsoft.com/technet/prodtechnol/WindowsServer2003/Library/IIS/523ae943-5e6a-4200-9103-9808baa00157.mspx?mfr=true.*
- For information on TLS, see *http://technet2.microsoft.com/windowsserver/en/library/9d47b6a2-3216-45fc-9bb8-41a7d89e42d11033.mspx?mfr=true.*
- For information about SIP, see "Session Initiation Protocol [RFC 3261]" at *http://www.ietf.org/rfc/rfc3261.txt?number=3261.*
- For information about event notifications, see "Session Initiation Protocol (SIP) Specific Event Notification [RFC 3265]" at *http://www.ietf.org/rfc/rfc3265.txt.*
- For information about TLS, see "The TLS Protocol [RFC 2246]" at *http://www.ietf.org/rfc/rfc2246.txt.*
- For information about NTLM, Kerberos, and TLS/SSL, see the Windows Security Collection of the Windows 2003 Technical Reference at *http://technet2.microsoft.com/windowsserver/en/library/7cb7e9f7-2090-4c88-8d14-270c749fddb51033.mspx?mfr=true.*

- Additional customizations allow application developers to create custom clients for publishing and subscribing to other publications from different clients. For more information on creating custom clients for publishing and subscribing to other publications from different clients, see the Unified Communications Managed API documentation.

Related Information

- Knowledge Base article on NTLM and Kerberos (regarding problems signing in to Live Communications Server), found at *http://support.microsoft.com/kb/830539/en-us*
- Knowledge Base article on NTLM and Kerberos (regarding enabling diagnostic logging for Office Communicator and Windows Messenger), found at *http://support.microsoft.com/kb/871023/en-us*
- Knowledge Base article on NTLM and Kerberos (regarding enabling NTLM 2 authentication), found at *http://support.microsoft.com/kb/239869*
- Blog found at *https://ucforums.microsoft.com/ShowPost.aspx?PostID=24134* (this blog is with IIS and the Web Components in Office Communications Server 2007)
- Blog found at *https://ucforums.microsoft.com/ShowPost.aspx?PostID=24503* (regarding lack of support for HTTP proxy authentication in console)
- Blog found at *https://ucforums.microsoft.com/ShowPost.aspx?PostID=24503* (regarding authentication of Communicator tabs)

On the Companion CD

- There is no companion CD content for this chapter

Chapter 19

Microsoft Office Communications Server 2007 Internals

In this chapter:

Office Communications Server 2007 differs most significantly from earlier versions in the change from a monolithic server architecture to one with distributed server components. In addition, Office Communications Server 2007 introduces two new scenarios—conferencing and VoIP—and, as a result, new server roles. This chapter provides an architecture overview as well as an overview of the internal components that make up Office Communications Server.

Understanding the Office Communications Server 2007 Architecture

Office Communications Server 2007 extends the architecture of Live Communications Server 2005 to include components that support VoIP and conferencing. This section discusses the following architectural features:

- Pool configurations
- Front-end servers
- Conferencing components
- VoIP components
- Perimeter network configuration and components
- Conference protocols
- Conference call flow

Figure 19-1 illustrates a generic Office Communications Server topology, including the new Voice over Internet Protocol (VoIP) and conferencing components.

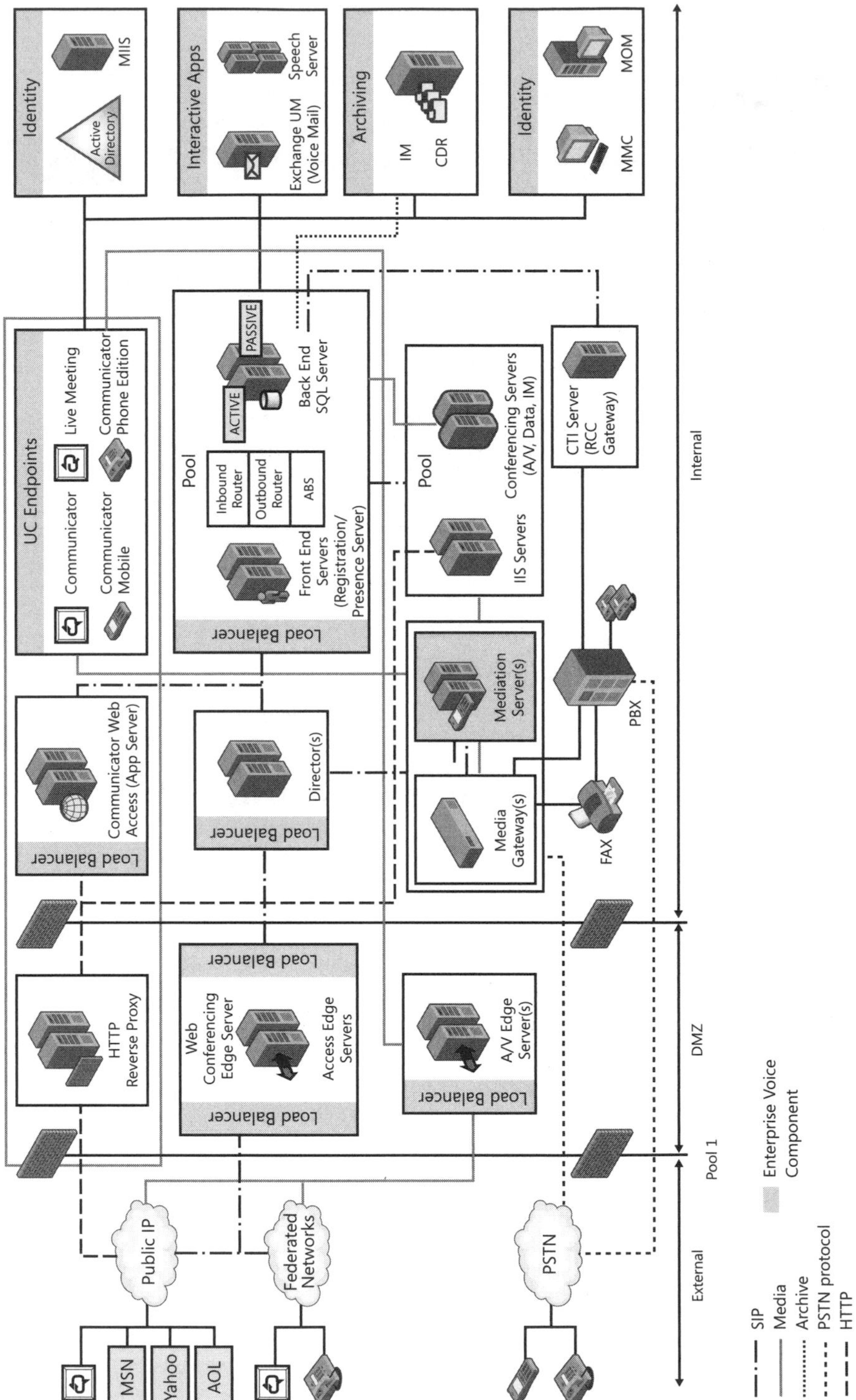

Figure 19-1 Office Communications Server 2007 reference architecture

The remainder of this section discusses the various servers in this topology and the functionality that each provides.

Understanding Pool Configurations

An Office Communications Server 2007 pool consists of one or more front-end servers that provide instant messaging (IM), presence, and conferencing services and are connected to a SQL Server database for storing user information, such as a user's configuration data, presence status, and conferencing details. Depending on the pool configuration, the database might reside on the same physical machine. In addition, certain conferencing components might be deployed on the same physical computer, depending on the chosen pool configuration.

Office Communications Server 2007 offers three pool configurations: one Standard Edition configuration, and the consolidated and expanded Enterprise Edition configurations. Both Enterprise Edition configurations consist of identical front-end servers that are connected to a separate dedicated Microsoft SQL Server 2005 back-end database. (In an Enterprise pool, the back-end database must be on a dedicated computer, separate from all Enterprise Edition servers.)

Examining the Standard Edition Configuration

As shown in Figure 19-2, a Standard Edition server hosts all necessary services on a single front-end server. Because it requires a minimal hardware investment and minimal management overhead, the Standard Edition configuration is ideal for small and medium-sized businesses and for branch offices. It is intended for deployments with fewer than 5000 users either in total or at a particular location where high availability is not a requirement.

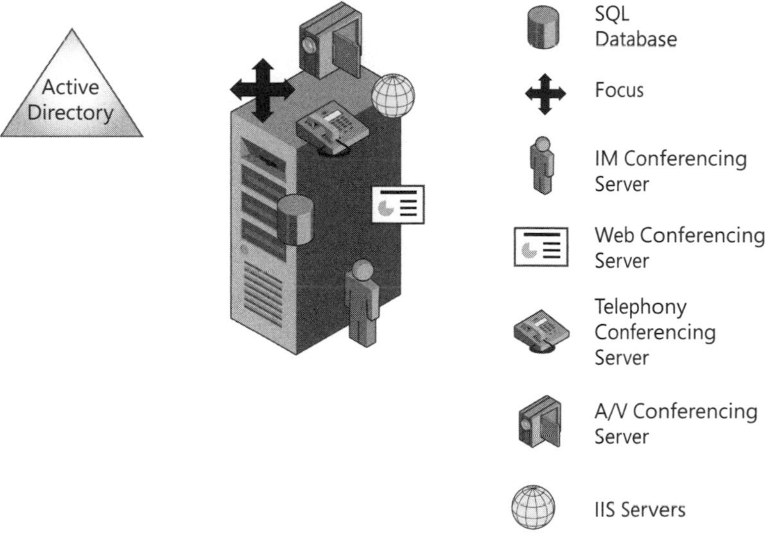

Figure 19-2 Standard Edition configuration

Examining the Enterprise Edition: Consolidated Configuration

As shown in Figure 19-3, the Enterprise Edition consolidated configuration is a pool configuration in which all server components are collocated on the pool's front-end servers (with the exception of the back-end database, which must reside on a separate dedicated computer). The consolidated configuration provides scalability and high availability and yet is easy to plan, deploy, and manage.

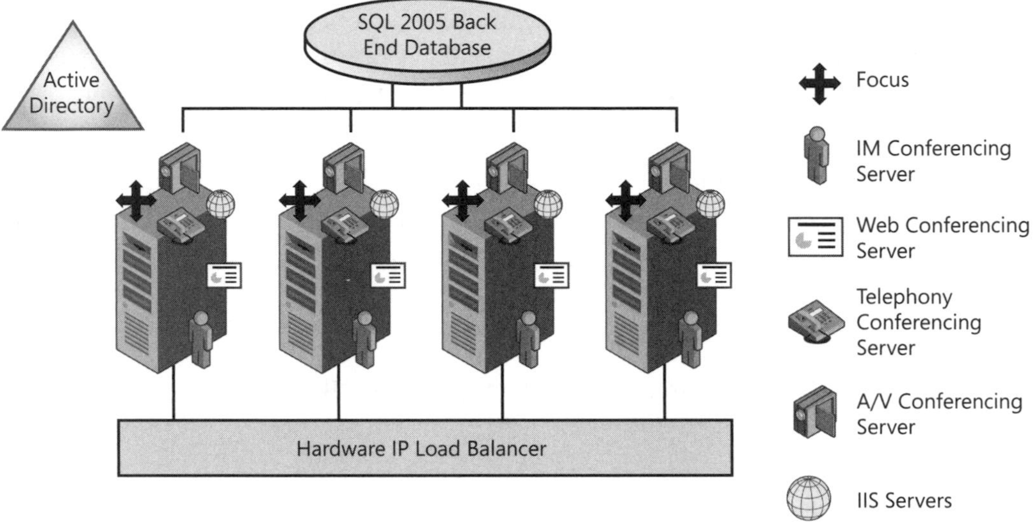

Figure 19-3 Enterprise Edition: consolidated configuration

Examining the Enterprise Edition: Expanded Configuration

The Enterprise Edition expanded configuration offers maximum capacity, performance, and availability for large organizations. As shown in Figure 19-4, Expanded Configuration, Internet Information Services (IIS), the Web Conferencing Server, and the Audio/Video Conferencing Server are installed on dedicated computers separate from the pool's front-end servers. Expanded configuration enables organizations to scale up audio/video or Web conferencing requirements independently from other Enterprise Edition server components. For example, if an organization's audio/video traffic increases more rapidly than other traffic, the organization can meet this increase by deploying only additional Audio/Video Conferencing Servers rather than entire front-end servers.

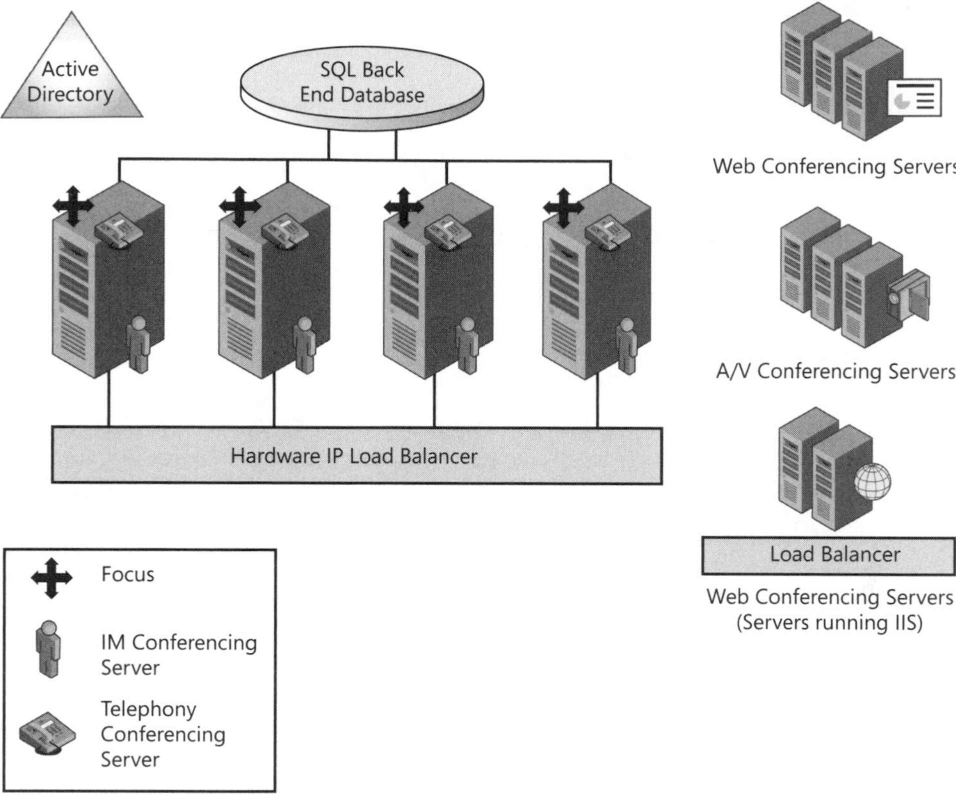

Figure 19-4 Enterprise Edition: expanded configuration

As Figure 19-4 shows, the IM Conferencing Server and Telephony Conferencing Server are located on the front-end server, even in the expanded configuration, whereas the Web Conferencing Server, A/V Conferencing Server, and IIS are installed on separate, dedicated computers. In the figure, the front-end servers are connected to one hardware load balancer and the servers running IIS (Web Components Servers) are connected to a separate load balancer. You can, however, also use the same hardware load balancer for both the Web Components Servers and the front-end servers.

The Office Communications Server 2007, Standard Edition or Enterprise Edition, front-end server is responsible for the following tasks:

- Handling signaling among servers and between servers and clients
- Authenticating users and maintaining user data, including all user endpoints
- Routing VoIP calls within the enterprise and to the Public Switched Telephone Network (PSTN)
- Initiating on-premise conferences and managing conference state
- Providing enhanced presence information to clients

- Routing IM and conferencing traffic
- Managing conferencing media
- Hosting applications
- Filtering SPIM (unsolicited commercial IM traffic)

Note For more information on the different server roles, see Chapter 2, "Server Roles." For more information on conferencing, see Chapter 5, "Conferencing Scenarios."

Understanding Enterprise Pools

Conceptually, a pool consists of one or more front-end servers and one or more databases on the back-end database server with a single SQL Server. All persistent state is stored in the database on the back-end database server so that, when a front-end server component fails, failover can be quick.

The Focus stores all conference state in the back-end database server to ensure it is accessible to all front-end servers. With this model, if a client loses connectivity to the conferencing server, the client can reconnect and its request can be handled by any of the front-end servers. This provides a natural failover model for front-end failures as well as for temporary loss of network connectivity from client to server. Similarly, information about conferencing server load also persists on the back-end database server so that it is available to a Conferencing Server Factory instance on any front-end server. This data can be written by a Conferencing Server Factory to the database, but any conferencing server for a particular media type under the control of the Conferencing Server Factory can read the database.

Figure 19-5 shows a sample pool with two front-end servers and one back-end database server. There is an IP load balancer for the front-end servers. All conferencing elements–Focus, Focus Factory, Conferencing Server Factory, A/V Conferencing Server, and Web Conferencing Server–are installed on all the front-end servers.

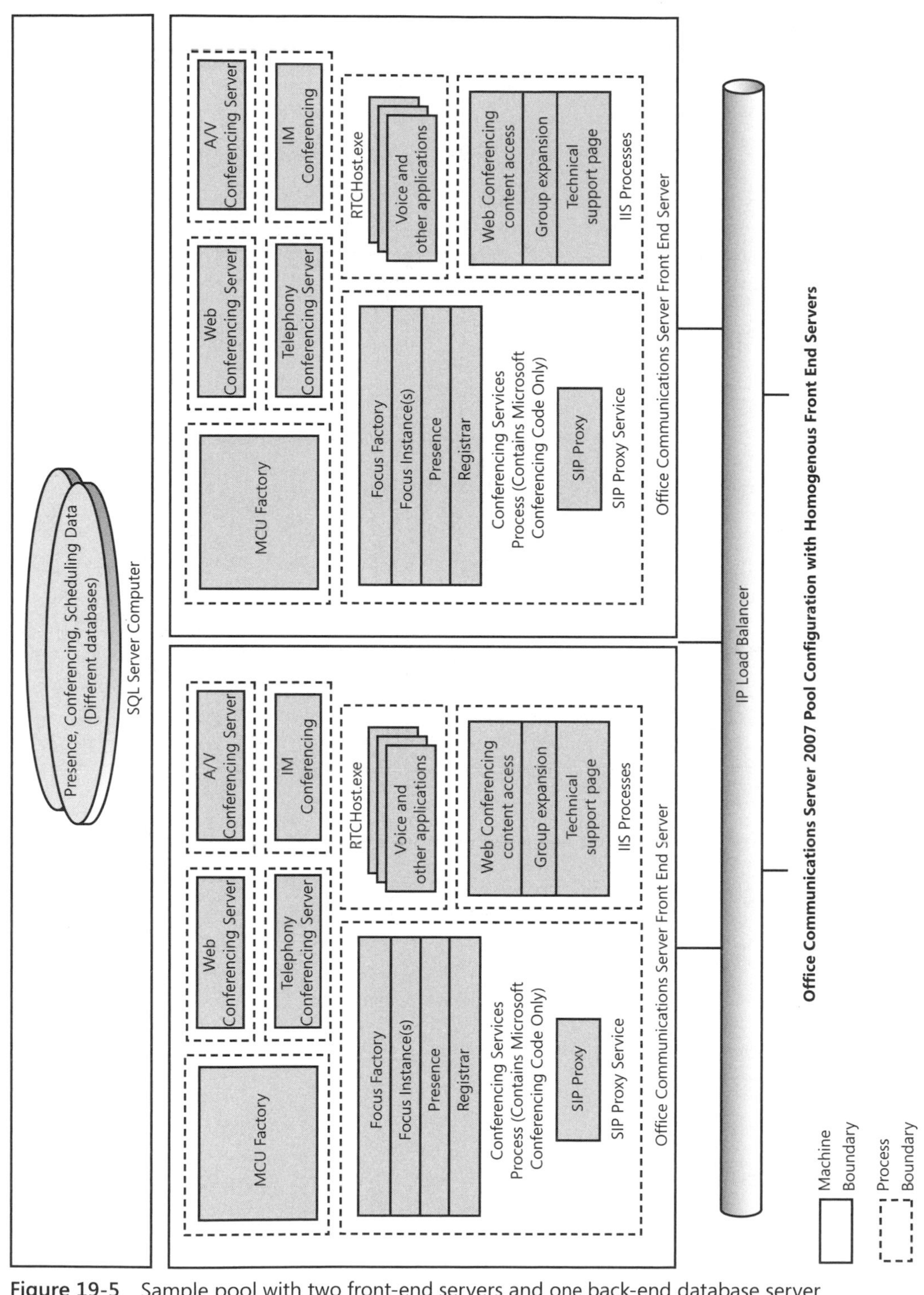

Figure 19-5 Sample pool with two front-end servers and one back-end database server

> **Note** More details on conferencing can be found in Chapter 5.

The remainder of this chapter focuses on the components that make up Office Communications Server, such as the sip stack, User Services module, Session Initiation Protocol (SIP) application programming interface (API), and archiving.

Understanding Office Communications Server 2007 Internal Components

Figure 19-6 illustrates the internal component architecture of Office Communications Server 2007.

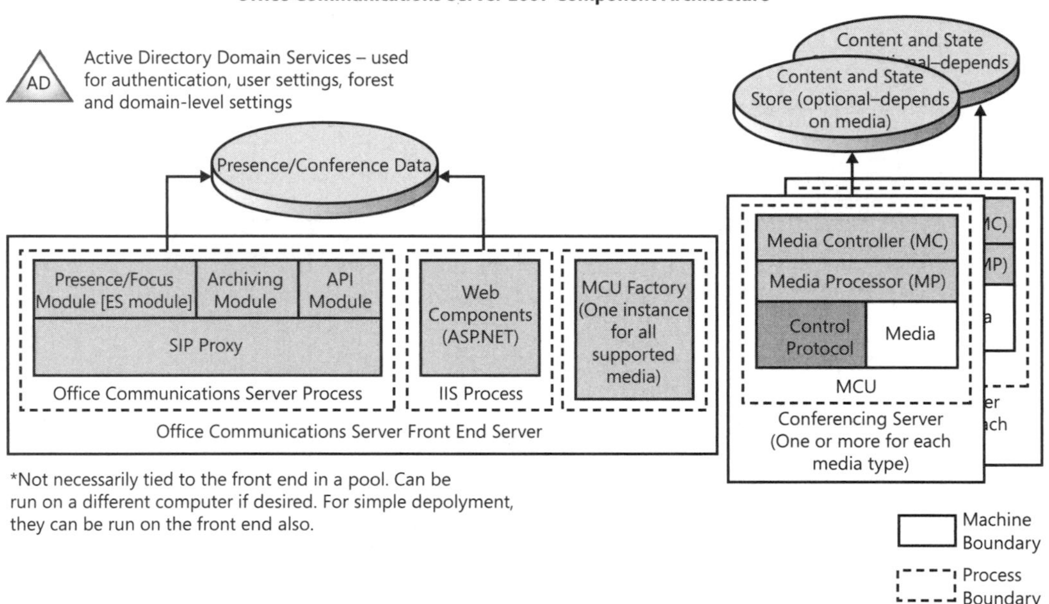

Figure 19-6 Office Communications Server component architecture

The Office Communications Server process of the front-end server contains the following components:

- Core components
- Presence components
- Conferencing components
- Voice components

The following sections will describe each of these components in more detail.

Examining Core Components

The two core components that make up Office Communications Server are RTCsrv.exe and RTChost.exe. RTCsrv.exe is the core process of the Office Communications Server, and RTChost.exe hosts several different applications that sit on top of the Server API module. Both RTCsrv.exe and RTChost.exe are explained in more detail in the following sections.

Examining the RTCsrv.exe Process

The rtcsrv.exe component is the core process of Office Communications Server. (See Figure 19-7.) This process includes the User Services (ES) module, server API module, archiving module, and the SIP Proxy. As shown in Figure 19-7, all these modules sit on top of the SIP Proxy, and a message dispatcher is used to send messages back and forth between the modules and the SIP Proxy.

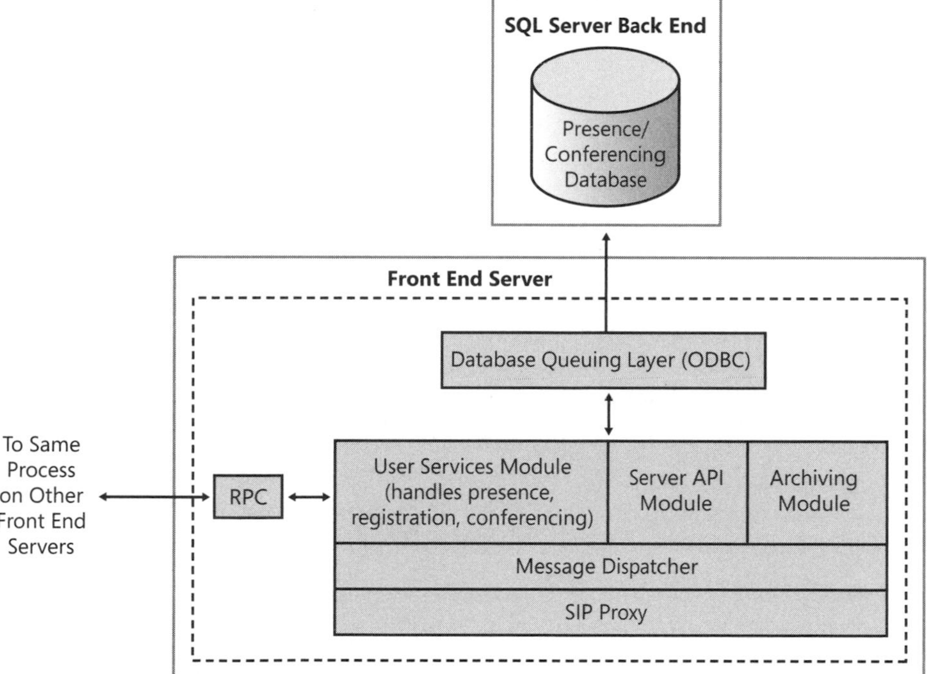

Figure 19-7 Office Communications Server process (Rtcsrvc.exe)

Understanding the SIP Proxy The SIP Proxy (also known as the protocol stack or SIP stack) is the core protocol platform on which all other services are built. It provides the basic structure for networking and security, and it performs connection management, message header parsing, routing, authentication, and state management.

Understanding User Services Module The User Services module provides closely integrated IM, presence, and conferencing features built on top of the SIP Proxy. It also includes the Focus and Focus Factory, which are explained in more detail in the "Examining Conferencing Components" section later in the chapter.

As shown in Figure 19-7, all the presence and conferencing data is stored in a SQL Server back end. The data passed from the User Services module is passed through the Database Queuing Layer (ODBC). Open Database Connectivity (ODBC) provides a standard API that is used to run SQL queries against the SQL Server back end.

The user replicator, shown as *UR* in Figure 19-10, is used to update the user database to be synchronized with Active Directory. The Address Book Server uses information provided by the user replicator to update information from the global address list.

Also, as shown in Figure 19-7, the User Services module on each front-end server communicates with other front-end servers using remote procedure calls (RPCs) to the same process.

Understanding the Archiving Module The archiving module is an agent that connects to the Archiving Server using MSMQ. The Archiving Server either has its own database or connects to a database on a different computer that stores all the archived data. Figure 19-8 illustrates the archiving architecture in Office Communications Server 2007.

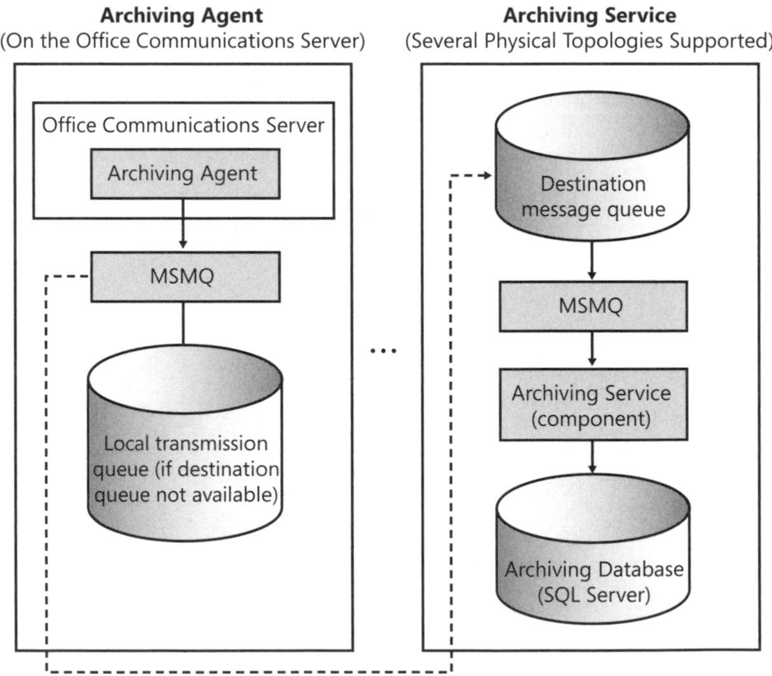

Figure 19-8 Archiving logical components diagram

The Enterprise Pool, Standard Edition server (or the Proxy Server if configured for archiving) activates the archiving agent. The archiving agent then checks all outgoing SIP messages on the Office Communications Server to determine whether it should be archived and in what form. This requires the archiving agent to look up the archiving settings for the sender and receiver of the message (set per user). Based on these archiving settings, the archiving agent takes one of the following actions:

- Do not archive.
- Send message for archiving.

When messages are sent for archiving, the archiving agent queues the message to the configured MSMQ. The archiving service is listening to the destination message of the MSMQ and on receiving this message, it writes it to the designated SQL server.

Understanding the API Module The server API module provides basic scripting capability for creating custom message filters and routing applications. The scripts can either run in process or, where required, can be dispatched to a managed code application that is running in a separate process. Figure 19-9 shows what the managed server API architecture looks like.

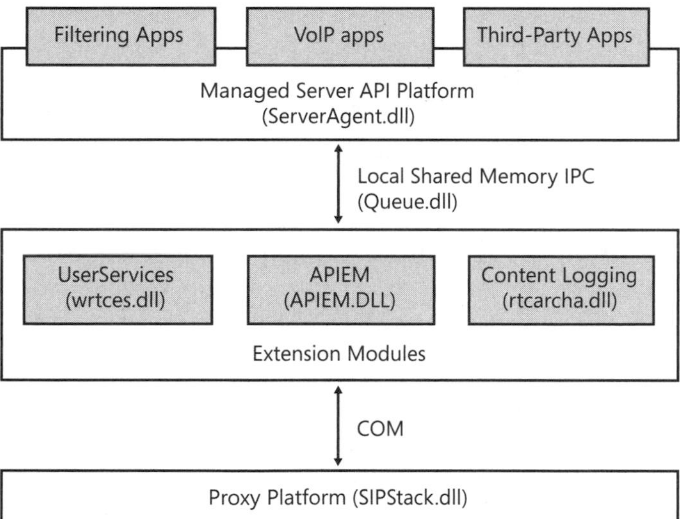

Figure 19-9 Office Communications Server API architecture

The core Proxy Platform performs various core SIP-message processing tasks such as parsing, transports, compression, authentication, and transaction state management. The message-processing duties are further extended using three native extension modules: User Services (responsible for Message Authorization, Registration and Presence services, and Conferencing services), the API Extension Module (responsible for hosting and managing managed server applications and shown as *APIEM* in Figure 19-8), and Content Logging (archiving service). These extension modules run in-process inside RTCSRV.exe, and they use a proprietary internal COM API to communicate with the Proxy Platform.

There are managed applications written using the managed API that run out of process to Office Communications Server. These are full-fledged SIP-aware applications that use the Server API to perform various message-processing tasks. The Managed Server API is exposed via the *Microsoft.Rtc.Sip* namespace and is implemented in the ServerAgent.dll assembly. Each managed application loads the ServerAgent.dll and executes in its own process space. Applications are isolated from each other in the sense that a faulty application is guaranteed not to affect other applications. The ServerAgent.dll uses a proprietary shared-memory message passing, Inter-Process Communication (IPC), to communicate with the APIEM, and this is completely abstracted from the application developer.

The two major components of the Server API are the application manifest and the *Microsoft.Rtc.Sip* class library. The application manifest is a script written using Microsoft SIP Processing Language (MSSPL), and it describes an application to the server. It is presented to the server when the application registers itself with the server via the *ServerAgent* class. It fulfills multiple roles, which include providing details about the type of application and the state it needs the server to maintain. This allows the server to optimize its efforts for that application. The application manifest contains a message filter script that allows an application to specify, to a fine grain, which messages (requests and/or responses) it is interested in seeing. For messages that the application decides it cares about, it has a set of built-in actions it can invoke. For applications in which the built-in actions are not sufficient for all their needs, there is the ability to call out to managed code in a separate application process, passing all or parts of the relevant message to the code in the application process. The intent is to avoid cross-process calls to do simple if/then/else processing that will decide to not handle the message. The application manifest provides the application writer the ability to specify a fair amount of logic that is executed by an interpreter inside the APIEM. Only when the functionality of the interpreter is insufficient does a cross-process call occur, and then it occurs once and contains only the portions of the message the application cared about. The application manifest contains an Application URI that uniquely identifies this application to Office Communications Server. This URI is expected to be an HTTP URL, but the resource referred by the HTTP URL is not validated.

The *Microsoft.Rtc.Sip* class library contains various classes to help with SIP message and transaction processing. In addition, the class library contains the *ServerAgent* class that implements the bulk of the logic needed to manage sessions with the server. The *ServerAgent* class is the entry point for the managed Server API. Each application instantiates an instance of *ServerAgent* and supplies an *ApplicationManifest* instance to it. The *ServerAgent* is responsible for managing the application's session with the server. It compiles the *ApplicationManifest* and registers itself with the Office Communications Server 2007 server. If the registration succeeds, it sets up the environment necessary to receive and process SIP messages from the server. Application-specified event handlers are invoked by the *ServerAgent* for various events such as message events and transaction events. When the application decides to exit, it disposes of the *ServerAgent* object, which in turn closes the session with the server. At any point in the lifetime of the application, there is exactly one *ServerAgent* object that is managing the application's session with the Office Communications Server 2007 server.

Understanding WMI Consumers Windows Management Instrumentation (WMI) consumers are the final layer in the WMI infrastructure. A consumer can be a script, an enterprise management application, a Web-based application, or some other administrative tool such as the MMC that accesses and controls management information available through the WMI infrastructure. When you administer your Office Communications Server deployment, these settings get pushed through WMI, then get sent to the Message Dispatcher for message processing.

Examining the RTChost.exe Process

RTChost.exe hosts sit on top of the Server API module and host several applications that run inside it. These applications fall under five categories: the Intelligent IM Filter, Client Version, VoIP Applications, the Conferencing Server Factory, and the RTC Aggregate Application.

Understanding the Intelligent IM Filter The Intelligent IM Filter filters incoming IM traffic by using administrator-specified criteria. It is used to block unsolicited or potentially harmful IM items from unknown endpoints outside the corporate firewall.

Understanding the Client Version The client version application is responsible for checking the version in the header information. It checks version information to decide which client applications are allowed to talk to the server. It can be configured using the user interface available as part of the management snap-in.

Understanding the RTC Aggregate Application The RTC aggregate application handles the aggregation of presence information across multiple endpoints. When a user is logged on to multiple devices, each device publishes presence information for its device. The RTC aggregate application ensures that it takes all presence information and aggregates it to produce one presence status that represents all devices. More information on presence and aggregation can be found in the "Examining Presence Components" section.

Understanding the Conferencing Server Factory All conferencing servers register themselves with the Conferencing Server Factory. When the focus requests a particular conferencing server for a meeting, the Focus sends the request to the Conferencing Server Factory, which determines which conferencing server is available to service the request and returns its URL to the Focus. More details on the Conferencing Server Factory can be found in the "Examining Conferencing Components" section.

Understanding the VoIP Applications The VoIP applications can be divided into the following three types of applications: inbound routing, translation services, and outbound routing. Each of these applications is discussed in the "Examining VoIP Components" section.

Examining Presence Components

In the "Examining Core Components" section, we discussed the User Services module. One of the responsibilities of the User Services module is to process registration requests as well as presence information. The User Services module comprises the registration and presence components. See Figure 19-10.

Every time a user sends a REGISTER request, the REGISTER subcomponent caches the endpoint route information so that we can avoid a database lookup while routing requests. The SERVICE subcomponent processes all SERVICE requests. The SUBSCRIBE subcomponent processes all SUBSCRIBE requests, and the NOTIFY subcomponent generates and sends NOTIFYs from the User Services module. Each of these subcomponents goes through the ODBC to store the registration and presence data in a SQL Server back-end database.

When a user is logged on to multiple devices, each device publishes presence information for its device. The RTC aggregate application, a managed, server application that runs on top of the Server API module, ensures that it takes all presence information from all endpoints, aggregates it, and produces one presence status that represents all devices. The SPL Access Layer provides the RTC aggregation application access to the database for user information that is exposed by this SPL script.

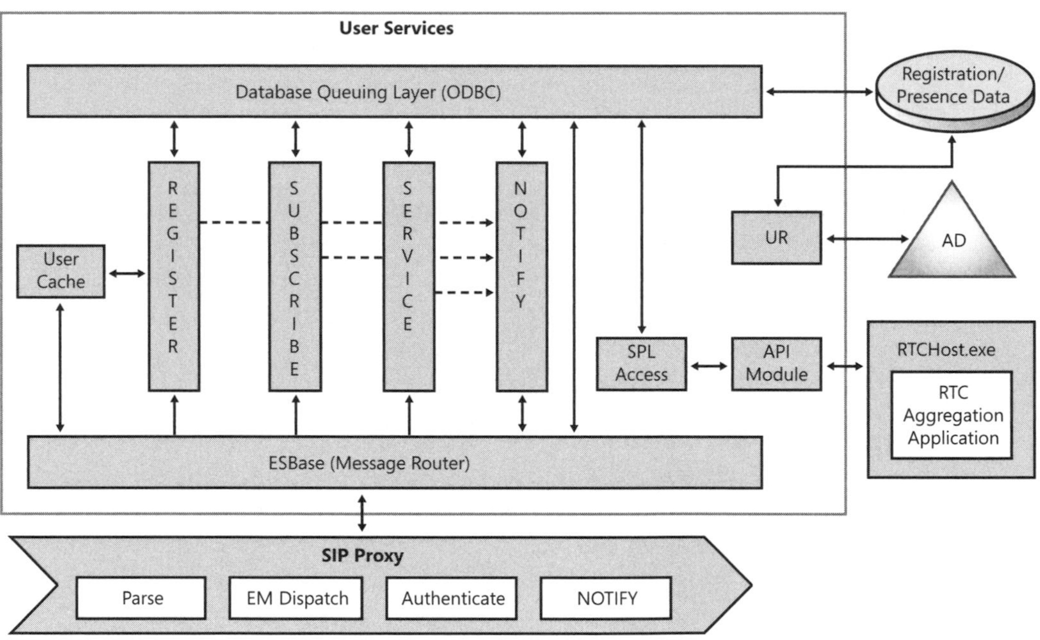

Figure 19-10 Presence components

Examining Conferencing Components

This section describes the conferencing components and the relationship between these components. It will also show the proposed process boundaries for the various components.

The main conferencing components of Office Communications Server are the Focus instances, Focus Factory, Conferencing Server Factory, and conferencing servers (also known as MCUs) for each media type. SQL Server databases are used for storing the persistent state. (See Figure 19-11.)

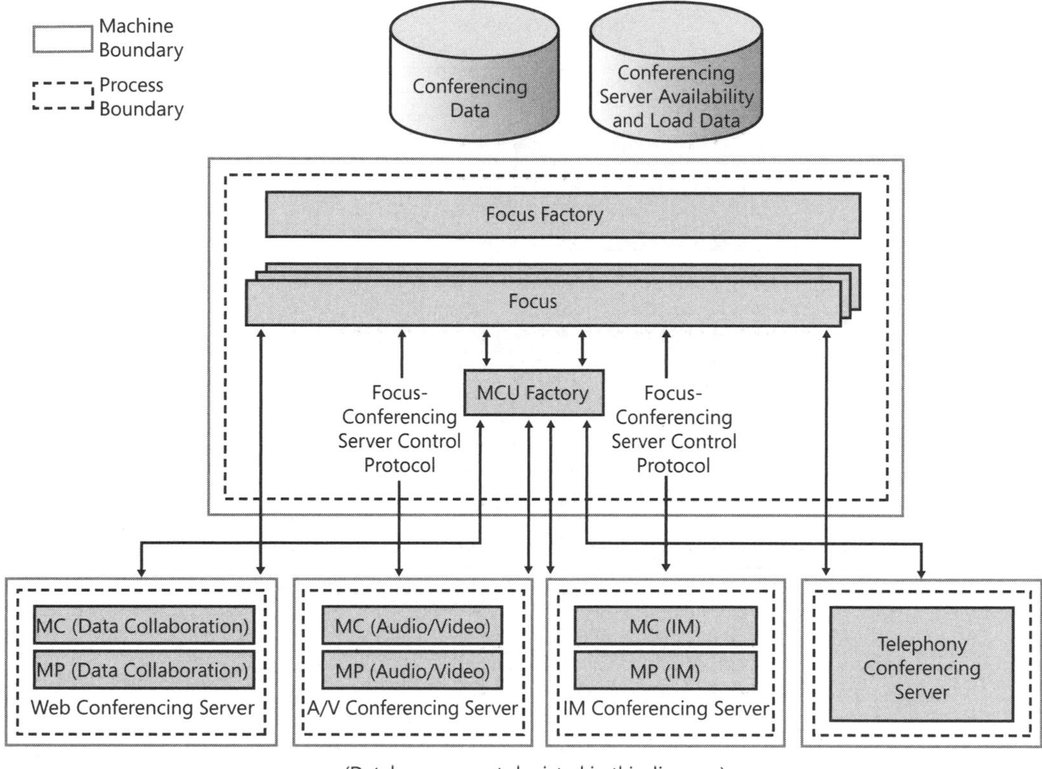

Figure 19-11 Office Communications Server 2007 conferencing component interrelationships

The Focus Factory and Focus components run in the main conferencing process, which is also the SIP proxy process. The Conferencing Server Factory is a fairly lightweight component that is accessed by the Focus once for each media type when that media type needs to be activated for the conference. The Conferencing Server Factory is an application running on each front-end server and uses an HTTP interface. Communication between the Focus and conferencing servers and between the Conferencing Server Factory and conferencing servers is HTTP based.

Understanding the Focus

The Focus is the central policy and state manager for a conference and acts as the coordinator for all aspects of the conference. A Focus is responsible for enforcing the conference control policy, managing the overall security for a conference, managing conference participant roles and privileges, sending conference state notifications to the clients, and providing a conduit for control commands to flow between clients and the conferencing servers. Figure 19-12 shows what the internal components of the Focus look like inside the User Services module.

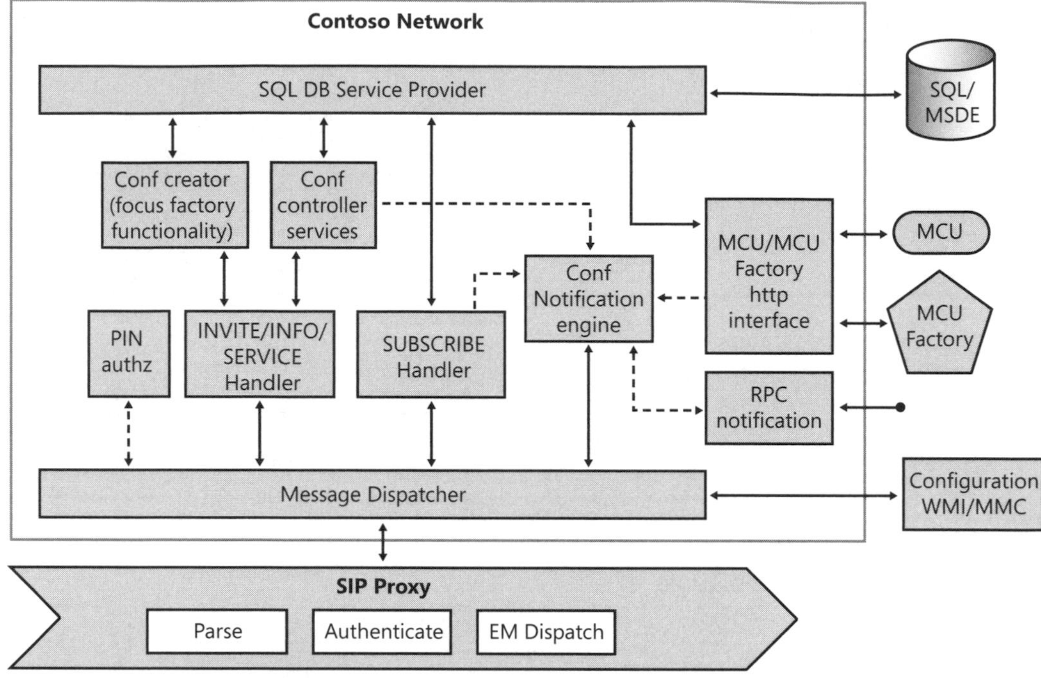

Figure 19-12 Focus architecture

When a new media type needs to be activated for a conference, the Focus also instantiates the conference on the appropriate conferencing server, communicates with the conferencing server about adding a new user, fetches the authorization credentials so that the client can connect to that conference, and then sends the media information to the client. The same sequence is repeated for all clients who want to add this media. When a new media type is added to the conference, the sequence is repeated with the new conferencing server for that media type. By centralizing the security enforcement and roster management, the Focus relieves each of the conferencing servers of this duty.

Understanding the Focus Factory

The Focus Factory is a SIP entity that creates, deletes, and modifies meetings in the conferencing database. The Focus Factory manipulates meetings in the conferencing database according to C3P commands issued by clients.

Understanding the Conferencing Server Factory

The Conferencing Server Factory is responsible for provisioning a conference for a particular media type on a conferencing server. The Conferencing Server Factory can also take into account the current load on the conferencing servers before assigning a conferencing server to a conference. There is one Conferencing Server Factory instance on each front-end server that handles all media types.

Understanding the Conferencing Database

A Focus holds important information for the entire conference, including all conference participants. If a Focus instance fails, it must be possible to restart the conference. To support this, any state information needed to resume the conference persists in a conferencing database, which runs on the SQL Server back end. In Office Communications Server, presence/registrar information and conferencing information are stored in different tables of the same physical database.

The important metadata associated with a conference in the conferencing database includes the following:

- Conference ID
- Expiration date and time of the conference
- A list of meeting participant roles and the privileges associated with those roles
- Conference key for participants without an identity in Active Directory
- Supported media types
- Authorization types, such as closed, open, and anonymous

As mentioned in the "Understanding the Focus" section, a conferencing database contains the metadata for a conference but does not contain calendar information. Supporting a meeting start time and end time, recurrence schedule, and exceptions to recurrence are all important for a prescheduled conference, but that information is maintained outside of the conferencing database. Instead, conference calendar information is maintained by scheduling clients, as appropriate, typically as a Microsoft Exchange Server calendar item.

Examining VoIP Components

The principal VoIP components on the front-end server are as follows:

- Translation Service
- Inbound Routing
- Outbound Routing

Each of these components runs inside the rtchost.exe, which resides on top of the server API module. Each of these components is an application that helps with the routing of VoIP calls. Each of these components is discussed in more detail in the following sections. The architecture diagram in Figure 19-13 shows the translation service, inbound routing, and outbound routing components.

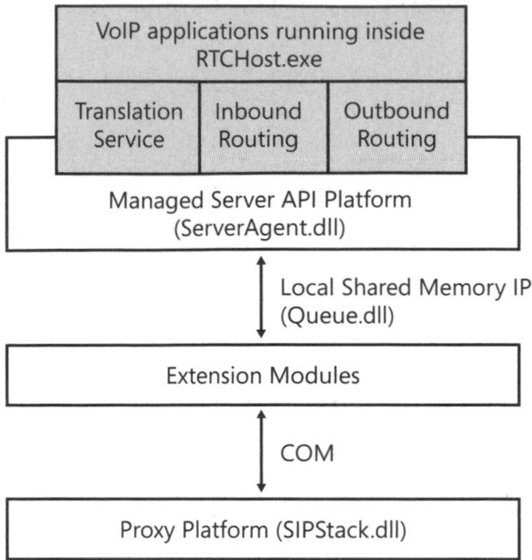

Figure 19-13 VoIP components architecture

Understanding the Translation Service

The Translation Service is the server component that is responsible for translating a dialed number into E.164 format according to the normalization rules that are defined by the administrator.

Phone number normalization is the process of translating number strings that are entered in various formats into a single standard format. Enterprise Voice requires normalized phone numbers to do the following:

- Provide a consistent reference for reverse number lookup. Reverse number lookup is the process of mapping a user's number to a corresponding SIP-URI for the purpose of routing calls over the IP network to multiple user endpoints, including Office Communicator, the Office Communicator Telephone Experience, and call-handling options such as call forwarding and call answering.
- Identify and apply phone usage authorization (comparable to traditional "class of service" options) for the calling party.
- Route calls to the appropriate media gateway.

Communications Server 2007 normalizes numbers prior to performing reverse number lookup. If the normalized number matches the designated primary work number of a user with an Active Directory identity, the call is forked to the endpoints associated with that user's SIP-URI. If the server does not find a match, which means the target number is probably outside the enterprise, the Outbound Routing component checks the caller's phone usage to determine if a call to that number is authorized, and then either directs the call to the appropriate media gateway or notifies the caller that the call is not allowed.

Understanding the Inbound Routing Component

The Inbound Routing component handles incoming calls largely according to preferences that are specified by users on their Enterprise Voice clients. For example, users specify whether unanswered calls are forwarded or simply logged for notification. If call forwarding is enabled, users can specify whether unanswered calls should be forwarded to another number or to an Exchange 2007 Unified Messaging server that has been configured to provide call answering. The Inbound Routing component is installed by default on all Standard Edition servers and Enterprise Edition front-end servers.

Understanding the Outbound Routing Component

The Outbound Routing component routes calls to PBX or PSTN destinations. It applies call authorization rules to callers and determines the optimal media gateway for routing each call. The Outbound Routing component is installed by default on all Standard Edition and Enterprise Edition servers and on Enterprise Edition front-end servers.

The routing logic that is used by the Outbound Routing Component is in large measure configured by network or telephony administrators according to the requirements of their organizations.

Summary

Understanding the internal components of Office Communications Server 2007 is essential for proper implementation planning and troubleshooting, and this chapter has provided an overview of the architecture and components of Microsoft Office Communications Server 2007. The Office Communications Server architecture was first described, including a description of pool configurations, component architecture, and enterprise pools. This was followed by a discussion of the internal components of Office Communications Server, including the core, presence, conferencing, and VoIP components of the platform.

Additional Resources

- For more information on deploying Voice in your Office Communications Server 2007 deployment, see the "Office Communications Server 2007 Document: Enterprise Voice Planning and Deployment Guide," found at *http://www.microsoft.com/downloads/details.aspx?FamilyID=24e72dac-2b26-4f43-bba2-60488f2aca8d&displaylang=en*.
- For more information on other server roles, see the "Office Communications Server 2007 Document: Planning Guide," available at *http://www.microsoft.com/downloads/details.aspx?familyid=723347c6-fa1f-44d8-a7fa-8974c3b596f4&displaylang=en*.

On the Companion CD

There are no companion CD components for this chapter.

About the Authors

Jeremy Buch was a Senior Development Lead for the Microsoft Office Communications Server SIP protocol stack and had been developing conferencing, network protocols, and secure federation technology for more than eight years. He was a presenter for several internal and external training sessions on the protocol, topology, and federation technologies in use by the Office Communications Server. He has also been part of the development team for preceding technology in products such as Live Communications Server, Exchange Instant Messaging Server, and Exchange Conferencing Server. Jeremy changed roles in 2006 and is currently working for Microsoft Virtual Earth in Boulder, Colorado, as a Senior Development Lead for 3D Urban Modeling.

Rui Maximo is a lead program manager in the Unified Communications Group. He's worked on various aspects of Live Communications Server 2003, 2005, and SP1 and Office Communications Server 2007 from migration, topologies, Active Directory schema extensions, and management to VoIP and Communicator Web Access. With 11 years of experience at Microsoft, Rui has been fortunate to work in diverse roles and various products (including Windows NT 4.0 Option Pack, Windows 2000, Windows XP, Smartphone 2002, Pocket PC 2002, and Microsoft Information Server 2002). Prior to joining Microsoft and during his graduate studies learning about abstract algebra, Rui was a Unix systems administrator, which explains his tendency to break into a command window shell and use VIM as his favorite editor. During his undergraduate studies, Rui was hired at IBM EduQuest, where he was introduced to the idea of making a living out of programming computers. Before then, the closest thing to a computer he had known was the Canon X-07, which unfortunately broke down prematurely due to the hot temperatures in Africa where he grew up.

Jochen Kunert is a Senior Program Manager at Microsoft Corporation in Redmond, Washington, and a voice expert. As a member of the Technology Adoption Group for Microsoft's Unified Communications (UC) solution, he is helping customers to deploy new and yet unreleased versions of UC software and devices to assure market readiness and quality at release time. He joined Microsoft as part of the acquisition of the company media-streams.com in Switzerland, where he was working as General Manager and Business Development Manager for the German subsidiary of media-streams.com. Prior to that, Jochen worked for Siemens Switzerland with delegation to Siemens Corporation Headquarters in Munich, Germany as a product manager for VoIP products. Jochen has a Masters Degree in Industrial Engineering - Business Administration, Law and Economics, and Electrical Engineering from the University of Technology in Darmstadt, Germany. He is married to his wife Anikó and they currently have one son, Quentin.

Byron Spurlock works in the services division at Microsoft Consulting Services. He has been with Microsoft for three years and has a background in messaging and collaboration. Byron's experience with messaging dates back to Exchange 5.5, and he has been involved with Office Communications Server since 2003. In his spare time he enjoys coaching his son Nicholas's t-ball team, playing with his daughter Jada, and spending time with his lovely wife of eight years, Maggie.

Hao Yan joined Microsoft in July 2005 as a Program Manager. He has worked on conferencing features in Microsoft Office Communications Server since then. Before Microsoft, Hao worked at Oracle Corporation as a Senior Member of Technical Staff and at Palo Alto Research Center as a Senior Member of Research Staff. Hao holds a Master's Degree in Media Arts and Sciences from Massachusetts Institute of Technology.

James O'Neill was born in 1965 and started using Microsoft products in 1979. Being something of a slow developer, it took him until 2000 to join Microsoft. His career has been spent working on operating system and messaging technologies, and passing on his knowledge of them to others, first in support, then as a trainer. He became an IT Pro Evangelist in March 2006 after six years working for Microsoft Consulting Services on a variety of projects for several well known, large organizations. He has been a Microsoft Certified Professional since 1993, holding MCSE from NT 3.1 to Windows 2003. Outside of work, his free time is divided among his two small children, photography, and scuba diving. He irritates people with a vast knowledge of trivia and by writing about himself in the third person.

John Clarkson was most recently a programming writer with the Speech Server team. He has also written for the Visual Basic team and the OfficeDev Web site team.

Kintan Brahmbhatt is a Program Manager in the Unified Communications Group at Microsoft. His areas of expertise include communication and collaboration technologies, manageability, compliance, and security. He drove and designed several areas for Office Communications Server 2007, including monitoring, backup and restore, disaster recovery, compliance, and security. Prior to joining Microsoft, Kintan was the founder of Securamed Corporation, a healthcare communication company. He frequently writes about technology and design on his blog, *www.kintya.com*.

Mitch Tulloch is an expert on Windows administration, networking, and security. He has written over a dozen books, including *Introducing Windows Server 2008*. Mitch was also lead author for the popular *Windows Vista Resource Kit* from Microsoft Press. Mitch is President of MTIT Enterprises, an Information Technology content-development business based in Winnipeg, Canada. Before starting his own business in 1998, Mitch worked as a Microsoft Certified Trainer (MCT) for Productivity Point. For more information about Mitch, see his Web site at *http://www.mtit.com*. You can contact Mitch at info@mtit.com.

Robert Heuer has been a freelance technical writer, marketing writer, and business analysis consultant since 1993. He is based in Seattle, Washington and New York City. For more information about his projects, visit *www.studio1312.com*.

Stephanie Lindsey was a Program Manager in the Unified Communications Group for five years and worked on various aspects of the products including the MMC, Windows Messenger, Real-time Collaboration APIs 1.3, as well as integrating presence and real-time collaboration into Office 2003 SP2 and Office 2007. Stephanie is now a Senior Technical Writer for Microsoft Office Communications Server.

Index

B

C

F

Q

R

S

System Requirements

As described in the sections below, these are the specific requirements necessary to view and use the tools and documents that are included on the companion CD.

System Requirements for OCS-All.ps1 PowerShell Script

- Supported operating systems: Windows Server 2003 SP1, Windows XP SP2, Windows Vista, and Windows Server 2008
- Supported processor architecture: x86, x64, IA64
- Installation of .Net Framework 2.0 or greater
    - For x86: *http://www.microsoft.com/downloads/details.aspx?FamilyID=0856eacb-4362-4b0d-8edd-aab15c5e04f5&displaylang=en*
    - For x64: *http://www.microsoft.com/downloads/details.aspx?familyid=B44A0000-ACF8-4FA1-AFFB-40E78D788B00&displaylang=en*
    - For IA64: *http://www.microsoft.com/downloads/details.aspx?familyid=53C2548B-BEC7-4AB4-8CBE-33E07CFC83A7&displaylang=en*
- Installation of PowerShell 1.0
    - All versions of PowerShell are available at *http://www.microsoft.com/windowsserver2003/technologies/management/powershell/download.mspx*
- After installation of .Net Framework 2.0 and PowerShell, refer to Appendix A, in the /Appendixes,Scripts,Resources folder on the companion CD, for detailed information about how to configure the environment and PowerShell to properly run the sample Windows PowerShell functions contained in the OCS-All.ps1 script. Failure to follow the directions in Appendix A might result in unexpected behavior of the script, up to and including loss of data.

System Requirements for Resource Kit Tools and Reference Material

- Supported operating systems for Resource Kit: Windows Server 2003 with Office Communications Server 2007

Resource Kit tools are generally meant to extend the maintenance and management of the Office Communications Server. Because of this, it is generally expected that the user will be an Administrator-level security principal on the system on which the tool is being run. Many tools will not function properly, if at all, if the user is not an Administrator or a member of the Administrators group.

These tools are specifically for the aforementioned operating system and server system. Support on previous versions is not intended nor supported.

Documents provided on the companion CD can be viewed with Microsoft Office Word and Excel, as delivered in Microsoft Office 2000 and later. Or, viewers are available at the following locations from the Microsoft Download Center:

- Word viewer: *http://www.microsoft.com/downloads/details.aspx?FamilyID=3657ce88-7cfa-457a-9aec-f4f827f20cac&DisplayLang=en*
- Excel viewer: *http://www.microsoft.com/downloads/details.aspx?FamilyID=c8378bf4-996c-4569-b547-75edbd03aaf0&DisplayLang=en*

What do you think of this book?

We want to hear from you!

Do you have a few minutes to participate in a brief online survey?

Microsoft is interested in hearing your feedback so we can continually improve our books and learning resources for you.

To participate in our survey, please visit:

www.microsoft.com/learning/booksurvey/

...and enter this book's ISBN-10 or ISBN-13 number (located above barcode on back cover*). As a thank-you to survey participants in the United States and Canada, each month we'll randomly select five respondents to win one of five $100 gift certificates from a leading online merchant. At the conclusion of the survey, you can enter the drawing by providing your e-mail address, which will be used for prize notification only.

Thanks in advance for your input. Your opinion counts!

* Where to find the ISBN on back cover

Example only. Each book has unique ISBN.

No purchase necessary. Void where prohibited. Open only to residents of the 50 United States (includes District of Columbia) and Canada (void in Quebec). For official rules and entry dates see:

www.microsoft.com/learning/booksurvey/